What Is a Thesaurus?

"A *Thesaurus* is the opposite of a dictionary. You turn to it when you have the meaning already but don't yet have the word. It may be on the tip of your tongue, but what it is you don't yet know. It is like the missing piece of a puzzle. You know well enough that the other words you try out won't do. They say too much or too little. They haven't the punch or have too much. They are too flat or too showy, too kind or too cruel. But the word which just fills the bill won't come, so you reach for the *Thesaurus*."

—*From the Introduction by* I. A. RICHARDS

ROGET'S

Pocket Thesaurus

BASED ON

ROGET'S International Thesaurus
of English Words and Phrases

Edited by
C. O. SYLVESTER MAWSON

Assisted by
KATHARINE ALDRICH WHITING

A KANGAROO BOOK
PUBLISHED BY POCKET BOOKS NEW YORK

POCKET BOOKS, a Simon & Schuster division of
GULF & WESTERN CORPORATION
1230 Avenue of the Americas, New York, N.Y. 10020

ISBN: 0-671-80001-9

First Pocket Books printing September, 1946

112th printing

Trademarks registered in the United States and other countries.

Printed in the U.S.A.

INTRODUCTION

A *Thesaurus*, says the dictionary, is "a treasury or storehouse; hence a repository, especially of words, as a dictionary." But, in a sense, this book is the opposite of a dictionary. You turn to a dictionary when you have a word but are not sure enough what it means—how it has been used and what it may be expected to do. You turn to the *Thesaurus* when you have your meaning already but don't yet have the word. It may be on the tip of your tongue, or in the back of your mind or the hollow of your thought, but what it is you don't yet know. It is like the missing piece of a puzzle. You know well enough that the other words you try out won't do. They are not the right shape. They say too much or too little. They haven't the punch or have too much. They are too flat or too showy, too kind or too cruel. But the word which just fills the bill won't come, so you reach for the *Thesaurus*.

Like the dictionary, it is a dangerous book in all sorts of ways. Sometimes you wake up—after half an hour—and realize that the problem of the missing word is still where it was. You have just been wandering happily about in the treasure house looking its riches over, forgetting what you came in for. It has worse dangers. Sometimes the words you find start new streams of thought which wash everything out.

Then not the word only but the idea too will be missing. In this "Lost Chord" situation, the best thing to conclude is that so evanescent an idea was hardly worth keeping. Sometimes, worse still, Temptation assails you. Instead of the right word—the word your thought was yearning for as its mysterious predestined mate—some

brazen hussy or wastrel of a vocable, never met and
never thought of before, seizes your regard.

> *O these encounterers*
> *That give a coasting welcome ere it comes*

Beware! As Confucius' pupil said, "For one word a man
is often deemed to be wise and for one word he is often
deemed to be foolish. We ought to be careful indeed
what we say."

A big vocabulary is a grand thing when well understood and resourcefully used. But all grandeurs have
their penalties. It is the business of a *Thesaurus* to take
us into all verbal company—to introduce us to every sort
and condition of word, with no guarantee, expressed or
implied, as to what they may not do to us if we trust
them without proper inquiry.

> *Who hath given man speech*
> *Or who hath set therein*
> *A thorn for peril and a snare for sin*

cries the Chorus in *Atalanta in Calydon.*

The great Railway strike in England turned upon the
phrase "definitive terms." One side took it to mean "unchangeable"; the other explained too late that they only
meant "full and detailed." Well does Peter Mark Roget
observe, "A misapplied or misapprehended term is sufficient to give rise to fierce and interminable disputes; a
misnomer has turned the tide of popular opinion; a verbal
sophism has decided a party question; an artful watch
word, thrown among combustible materials has kindled
the flame of deadly warfare and changed the destiny of
an empire."

That is the tragic side. The comic possibilities more
concern us here. People who swagger about in borrowed
words may, like Porthos in *The Three Musketeers*, im-

press the inexperienced. They bring the wrong sorts of smiles to the lips of the discerning.

To know the words without the things is perilous indeed. "How often," said the lecturer, "have I dallied by the shores of Lac Leman or strolled on the delightful slopes overlooking Lake Geneva." "Pardon me," said a member of the audience, "but are they not synonymous?" "You may think so, Sir," replied the speaker, "but for my part I consider Lac Leman by far the more synonymous of the two." Awful warnings of this sort abound. "I always tell my children to look it up in the dictionary or the encyclopedia," said the Sea Captain. "That is what they are there for. Always be exact . . . No, I don't wear my ribbons in public places. Seems to me they are a bit promiscuous."

But when is a word our own? What is a mastery of language? How in fact do we acquire a vocabulary worthy of the name?

The answer of course is: By experience with words, by living with great books and good talkers, by watching their words at work and at play—in brief, by becoming *familiar* with words. Mere acquaintanceship with them is not profitable here. An acquaintance is one whose name and face you know, without more than a rough idea of his being and business. A familiar is one about whom you know as much as possible. Words are astonishingly like people. They have characters, they almost have personalities—are honest, useful, obliging . . . or treacherous, vain, stubborn . . . They shift, as people do, their conduct with their company. They are an endless study in which we are studying nature and ourselves at that meeting point where our minds are trying to give form to or take it from the world.

Peter Mark Roget a century ago had high hopes of the help his arrangement of words might be to thought and to the construction of a common second language such

as Basic English may become. There is nothing fantastic
about such hopes. In drawing up his scheme of divisions
his model was biological classification. He was a physician
and Secretary of the Royal Society. But we need not take
Roget's actual categories too seriously. To criticize them
would be to bring up all the hardest problems there are.
They serve their purpose—which is to remind us systematically of all that we know about words. "It is not suf-
ficiently considered," said Dr. Johnson, "that men require more often to be reminded than to be informed."
For information about words we go to the dictionary—
the bigger it is the better. We go to the *Thesaurus* in the
hope that something we really know already will come
back to us in our need. How vast is the realm of our current oblivion. "I know," said Benjamin Paul Blood, "as
having known, the secret of existence." Nothing will better make us realize how nearly true this is than an hour
spent in the treasury. How incredibly much we understand if only we can mobilize our understanding. Roget's
Thesaurus is one of the greatest of all *memoria technica*.
It is an astonishing thought that we can carry it in the
pocket.

I. A. RICHARDS

CONTENTS

POCKET THESAURUS AND WORD FINDER

CLASS I
WORDS EXPRESSING ABSTRACT RELATIONS

CLASS II
WORDS RELATING TO SPACE

CLASS III
WORDS RELATING TO MATTER

CLASS IV
WORDS RELATING TO THE INTELLECTUAL FACULTIES

CLASS V
WORDS RELATING TO THE VOLUNTARY POWERS

CLASS VI
WORDS RELATING TO THE SENTIENT & MORAL POWERS

ABBREVIATIONS USED IN THIS BOOK

abbr. abbreviated, abbreviation
adj. adjective, adjectival expression
adv. adverb, adverbial expression
Am. *or* Amer. America, American
Am. hist. American history
Am. Ind. American Indian
anat. anatomy
anon. anonymous
Ar. Arabic
arch. architecture
archæol. archæology
arith. arithmetic
astrol. astrology
astron. astronomy
Bib. Biblical
biol. biology
bot. botany
Brit. British
Can. Canada, Canadian
chem. chemistry
Chin. Chinese
class. classical
colloq. colloquial
com. commerce, commercial
conj. conjunction
Du. Dutch
Dan. Danish
dial. dialect, dialectal
dim. diminutive
E. East
eccl. ecclesiastical
Eng. English, England
erron. erroneous, -ly
esp. especially
exc. except
F. French
fem. feminine
fig. figurative, -ly
G. *or* Ger. German
Gr. Greek
Gr. Brit. Great Britain
her. heraldry
Hind. Hindustani
hist. history, historical
Icel. Icelandic
Ind. Indian
Ir. Irish, Ireland
int. interjection
It. Italian

Jap. Japanese
joc. jocular
L. Latin
l.c. lower case
masc. masculine
math. mathematics
mil. military
Moham. Mohammedan
myth. mythology
n. noun
naut. nautical
neut. neuter
Norw. Norwegian
obs. obsolete
opp. opposed
orig. original, -ly
parl. parliamentary
path. pathology
Pg. Portuguese
pharm. pharmacy
philos. philosophy
physiol. physiology
pl. plural
pol. *or* polit. political
pop. popular, -ly
prep. preposition
prov. proverb, provincial
psychol. psychology
R. C. Ch. Roman Catholic Church
relig. religion
rhet. rhetoric, rhetorical
Russ. Russian
S. Am. South American
Scand. Scandinavian
Scot. Scottish, Scotland
sing. singular
Skr. Sanskrit
Sp. Spanish
surg. surgery
Sw. Swedish
tech. technical
theat. theatrical
theol. theology
typog. typography
Univ. University
U. S. United States
v. verb
zool. zoology

x

HOW TO USE THE BOOK

I. To find a synonym or antonym for any given WORD:

Turn to the Index* and find the particular word or any term of
kindred meaning; then refer to the category indicated (the numbers printed in bold face at the top outer corner of each page).
There in its proper grouping, the indexed word will be found, together with a wide selection of related terms. Synonyms and
antonyms are placed in adjoining positions. For example, suppose a
synonym is wanted for the word "cold" in the sense of "indifferent."
Turn to the Index, where the following references will be found:

> cold, *adj.*
> *frigid* **383**
> *insensible* **823**
> *indifferent* **866**

The italicized words give the general sense of the synonyms in the
respective categories. The bold-faced figures denote that the indexed word is itself the heading or keyword of a distinct group.
Thus, in this example, under **383** we find a list of adjectives
grouped under the word "cold" in the literal sense of the term.

Turning to No. **866** (the sense required), we read through the varied list of
synonyms ("indifferent, frigid, lukewarm," etc.) and select the most appropriate
expression. To widen the selection, suggested references are given to allied lists;
while in the adjoining category (No. **865**) are grouped the corresponding antonyms
("eager, keen, burning, ardent," etc.). The groups are arranged, not merely to
supply synonyms for some special word, but also to suggest new lines of thought
and to stimulate the imagination.

II. To find suitable words to express a given IDEA:

Find in the Index some word relating to the idea, and the categories referred to will supply the need.

For example, suppose a writer wishes to convey the idea of "rest." Turning to
No. **265**, he will find *nouns* giving such associated senses as "quiet," "pause,"
"resting place," or *verbs* with the sense of "be still," "remain," "quell," or *adjectives* such as "quiescent," "still," "silent," and the like. The mere reading of the
entire list will help to crystallize the idea and give it utterance.

III. To find appropriate words or new ideas on any given SUB-
JECT:

Turn up the subject or any branch of it. The Index itself will
frequently suggest various lines of thought, while reference to the
indicated groups will provide many words and phrases that
should prove helpful.

Thus, suppose "poetry" is the theme, No. **597** will be found most suggestive.
Or again, the subject may be "the drama" (**599**), "music" (**415**), "the vegetable
kingdom" (**367**), "national legislatures" (**696**), "psychical research" (**992a**), or

*(page 311)

"mythology" (979). The writer may perhaps be hazy about the titles of the ruling chiefs of India. Reference to 875 will prevent his applying a Hindu title to a Mohammedan prince. He may wish to know the term for a "plain" in different parts of the world; No. 344 will tell him exactly. The subject may be such an everyday one as "food" (298), "automobiles" (272), "aviation" (267 and 269a), or various kinds of "amusements" (840); whatever it is, the search will not prove altogether unprofitable.

N.B.—To grasp the underlying principle of the classification, study the *Tabular Synopsis of Categories* (pp. xiv-xxviii).

The guide numbers always refer to the *section* numbers in the text, and *not* to pages.

PLAN OF CLASSIFICATION

TABULAR SYNOPSIS OF CATEGORIES

Class III. MATTER

I. MATTER IN GENERAL

II. INORGANIC MATTER

(1) Solids

(2) Fluids

CLASS IV. INTELLECT

I. FORMATION OF IDEAS

469. Qualification

470. Possibility
472. Probability
474. Certainty
476. Reasoning
478. Demonstration
480. Judgment
480a. Discovery
482. Overestimation
484. Belief
486. Credulity
488. Assent
490. Knowledge
492. Scholar
494. Truth
496. Maxim
498. Intelligence. Wisdom
500. Sage
502. Sanity

505. Memory
507. Expectation

471. Impossibility
473. Improbability
475. Uncertainty
477. Intuition. Sophistry
479. Confutation
481. Misjudgment

483. Underestimation
485. Unbelief. Doubt
487. Incredulity
489. Dissent
491. Ignorance
493. Ignoramus
495. Error
497. Absurdity
499. Imbecility. Folly
501. Fool
503. Insanity
504. Madman
506. Oblivion
508. Nonexpectation
509. Disappointment

510. Foresight
511. Prediction
512. Omen
513. Oracle
514. Supposition
515. Imagination

II. COMMUNICATION OF IDEAS

516. Meaning
518. Intelligibility

517. Unmeaningness
519. Unintelligibility

520. Equivocalness

521. Figure of Speech
522. Interpretation
524. Interpreter
525. Manifestation
527. Information
529. Disclosure
531. Publication
532. News
534. Messenger
535. Affirmation
537. Teaching

540. Teacher

523. Misinterpretation

526. Latency
528. Concealment
530. Ambush

533. Secret

536. Negation
538. Misteaching
539. Learning
541. Learner

542. School

543. Veracity

544. Falsehood

Class V. VOLITION

I. INDIVIDUAL VOLITION

742. Disobedience
744. Compulsion
745. Master
747. Scepter
748. Freedom
750. Liberation

753. Keeper
755. Commission

758. Consignee
759. Deputy
760. Permission
762. Consent
763. Offer
765. Request
767. Petitioner
768. Promise
769. Compact
770. Conditions
771. Security
772. Observance

743. Obedience

746. Servant

749. Subjection
751. Restraint
752. Prison
754. Prisoner
756. Annulment
757. Resignation

761. Prohibition

764. Refusal
766. Deprecation

773. Nonobservance
774. Compromise

PERSONAL RELATIONS

(1) *Property*

775. Acquisition
777. Possession
778. Participation
779. Possessor
780. Property
781. Retention
783. Transfer
784. Giving
786. Apportionment
787. Lending
789. Taking
791. Stealing
792. Thief
793. Booty
794. Barter
795. Purchase
797. Merchant
798. Merchandise
799. Mart

776. Loss
777a. Exemption

782. Riddance

785. Receiving

788. Borrowing
790. Restitution

796. Sale

(2) *Money*

800. Money
801. Treasurer

935. Flatterer
937. Vindication
939. Probity

942. Disinterestedness
944. Virtue
946. Innocence
948. Good Man. Good Woman
950. Penitence
952. Atonement
953. Temperance

955. Asceticism
956. Fasting
958. Sobriety
960. Purity

963. Legality
965. Jurisprudence
966. Tribunal
967. Judge
968. Lawyer
969. Lawsuit
970. Acquittal
973. Reward

936. Detractor
938. Accusation
940. Improbity
941. Knave
943. Selfishness
945. Vice
947. Guilt
949. Bad Man. Bad Woman
951. Impenitence

954. Intemperance
954a. Sensualist

957. Gluttony
959. Drunkenness
961. Impurity
962. Libertine
964. Illegality

971. Condemnation
972. Punishment
974. Penalty
975. Scourge

V. RELIGIOUS AFFECTIONS

976. Deity
977. Angel
979. Mythic and Pagan Deities
980a. Specter
981. Heaven
983. Theology
983a. Orthodoxy
985. Revelation (Biblical)

987. Piety

990. Worship

995. Churchdom
996. Clergy
998. Rite
999. Canonicals
1000. Temple

978. Satan
980. Evil Spirits

982. Hell

984. Heterodoxy
986. Sacred Writings (Non-Biblical)
988. Impiety
989. Irreligion
991. Idolatry
992. Sorcery
992a. Psychical Research
993. Spell
994. Sorcerer

997. Laity

ROGET'S POCKET THESAURUS AND WORD FINDER

CLASS I

Words Expressing ABSTRACT RELATIONS

I. EXISTENCE

1. EXISTENCE. — *N.* **existence,** being, entity, subsistence, presence, omnipresence, ubiquity.

reality, actuality, fact, matter of fact, truth, verity.

essence, inner reality, vital principle.

Science of existence: ontology.

V. **exist,** be, subsist, live, breathe; vegetate; happen, take place; occur, prevail.

consist in, lie in; be comprised in.

abide, continue, endure, last, remain.

Adj. **existent,** subsistent, extant; afloat, on foot, current, prevalent.

real, actual, positive, absolute; veritable, true; substantial, essential.

well founded, well grounded, authentic.

Adv. **actually,** in fact, in reality; indeed.

2. NONEXISTENCE. — *N.* **nonexistence,** inexistence; nonentity; nullity; nihilism; blank; absence, emptiness, void, vacuum; nothingness.

annihilation, extinction, destruction, abolition, extirpation, nirvana, obliteration.

V. **not exist,** be null and void; cease to exist; pass away, perish, be *or* become extinct; die out; disappear, vanish, fade, melt away, dissolve, be no more; die, etc., 360.

annihilate, nullify; abrogate, etc., 756; destroy, etc., 162; remove, displace, vacate; obliterate, extirpate.

Adj. **inexistent,** nonexistent; negative, blank; null, missing, absent, etc., 187.

unreal, baseless, unsubstantial, shadowy, spectral, visionary.

unborn, uncreated, unbegotten.

extinct, gone, lost, departed; defunct, etc. (*dead*), 360.

fabulous, ideal, etc. (*imaginary*), 515.

3. SUBSTANTIALITY.—*N.* substantiality; person, thing, object, article; something, a being, creature, body, substance, matter, etc., 316; groundwork, materiality.

Adj. substantial, essential; personal, bodily, corporeal, tangible, etc. (*material*), 316.

4. UNSUBSTANTIALITY.—*N.* unsubstantiality, nothingness, nihility; bubble, etc., 353.

nothing, naught, *nil* [L.], nullity, zero, cipher; blank, void, hollowness.

thing of naught, man of straw, lay figure; nonentity.

phantom, apparition, specter, shadow, dream, vision, will-o'-the-wisp, *ignis fatuus* [L.].

V. **vanish,** evaporate, fade, sink, fly, dissolve, melt away; die away, die out; disappear, etc., 449.

Adj. **unsubstantial;** baseless, groundless; ungrounded; without foundation.

visionary, imaginary, immaterial, spectral, etc., 980a; dreamy; shadowy; ethereal, airy, gaseous, imponderable, tenuous, vague, vaporous, dreamlike, illusory, unreal.

vacant, vacuous; empty, void, blank, hollow.

5. SUBJECTIVENESS.—*N.* subjectiveness, intrinsicality, inherence, immanence, indwelling; ego; essence, quintessence, elixir; gist, pith, core, kernel, marrow, backbone, heart, soul, life, substance.

principle, nature, constitution.

temper, temperament; spirit, humor, quality, disposition.

aspect, mood, feature, peculiarity, idiosyncrasy.

Adj. **intrinsic,** subjective; fundamental, implanted, inherent, essential, natural; innate, inborn, inbred, ingrained, indwelling, immanent, inwrought; radical, incarnate, hereditary, inherited, congenital, indigenous, native; in the grain, bred in the bone, instinctive; characteristic, ineradicable, fixed.

Adv. **practically,** virtually, substantially, in effect.

6. OBJECTIVENESS.—*N.* objectiveness, extraneousness, extrinsicality.

Adj. **extrinsic,** objective; extraneous, external, incidental, accidental, nonessential, unessential, accessory; contingent, fortuitous, casual.

implanted, ingrafted; inculcated, infused.

7. STATE.—*N.* state, condition, category; estate, lot, mood, temper.

dilemma, pass, predicament, quandary, corner, fix [*colloq.*], plight.

frame, fabric, stamp, mold; constitution.

form, shape; tone, tenor, trim, guise, fashion, mode, style, character.

8. CIRCUMSTANCE.—*N.* circumstance, situation, phase, position; footing, standing, status.

occasion, juncture, contingency.

predicament, emergency; exigency, crisis, pinch, pass, plight.

Adj. circumstantial, conditional, provisional; contingent, incidental; adventitious.

Adv. thus, in such wise; in *or* under the circumstances (*or* conditions).

accordingly, that being the case; since, seeing that.

conditionally, provided, if, in case; if so, unless, in the event of; provisionally.

II. RELATION

9. RELATION.—*N.* relation, bearing, relativity, reference, connection, concern; analogy; similarity; homogeneity, affinity, alliance, nearness, association; consanguinity, etc., 11; relationship, relevancy.

ratio, proportion; comparison.

link, tie, bond.

V. relate to, refer to; bear upon, regard, concern, touch, affect, pertain to, belong to; correlate.

associate, connect; link, bind.

Adj. relative, relating to, referable to; belonging to.

related, connected, associated, affiliated; allied, collateral, cognate, affinitive.

relevant, applicable, in the same category.

Adv. as regards, concerning, with relation to, with regard to; by the way, in the matter of.

10. [Want or absence of relation] IRRELATION.—*N.* irrelation, dissociation; inapplicability; disconnection, disjunction; inconsequence, disagreement, heterogeneity; irrelevancy.

V. have no relation to, have no bearing upon, have nothing to do with.

Adj. unrelated, irrespective, unallied, disconnected, unconnected, heterogeneous; isolated.

extraneous, strange, alien, foreign, outlandish, exotic.

irrelevant, inapplicable, not pertinent, unessential, inapposite, beside the mark.

remote, farfetched, out-of-the-way, forced, detached, apart.
incidental, parenthetical, episodic.

Adv. **parenthetically,** by the way, by the by; incidentally, without regard to.

11. [Relations of kindred] CONSANGUINITY.—*N.* **consanguinity,** relationship, kindred, blood; parentage, paternity; lineage, connection, alliance; people [as, *my people*], family, ties of blood, blood relation.

kinsman, kinsfolk; kith and kin; relative, relation; connection; next of kin; near relation, distant relation.

family, fraternity; brotherhood, sisterhood.

race, stock, generation; clan, tribe; strain, breed.

V. **be related to,** claim kinship with.

Adj. **related,** akin, consanguineous, allied, affiliated; kindred.

12. [Double or reciprocal relation] CORRELATION.—*N.* **correlation,** interdependence, reciprocity, mutuality, correspondence, interchange, exchange, barter.

alternation, seesaw, to-and-fro.

V. **reciprocate,** alternate, interact; interchange, exchange; correlate.

Adj. **reciprocal,** mutual, correlative; correspondent, corresponding; alternate; interchangeable; equivalent, complementary.

13. IDENTITY.—*N.* **identity,** sameness, unity, convertibility; equality, etc., 27; homogeneity; self, oneself.

monotony, repetition, etc., 104.

facsimile, etc. *(copy),* 21; similarity, etc., 17; exactness, fidelity; same, selfsame, counterpart.

V. **coincide,** coalesce.

treat as identical *(or* the same), render identical; identify.

Adj. **identical,** self, selfsame, ditto.

coincident, coinciding, coalescent, indistinguishable; one; equivalent, convertible, equal.

14. CONTRARIETY.—*N.* **contrariety,** contrast, foil, antithesis, counterpart, complement; oppositeness; antagonism, opposition, clashing, repugnance, antipathy.

inversion, subversion, reversal, the opposite, the reverse, the inverse, the converse, antipodes.

V. **be contrary,** contrast with, oppose, differ from.

invert, reverse, turn topsy-turvy, turn upside down, transpose.

contradict, contravene; antagonize, etc., 708.

Adj. **contrary,** opposite, counter, adverse, averse, converse, reverse; opposed, antithetical, contrasted, antipodean, diametrically opposite; antagonistic, conflicting, inconsistent, contradictory; hostile, inimical.

15. DIFFERENCE.—*N.* difference, dissimilarity, variance, variation, variety; diversity, divergence, heterogeneity, contrast, antithesis; disagreement, disparity, inequality, distinction, contradiction, contrariety.

nice (*or* fine, subtle) distinction, discrimination; modification.

V. differ, vary; mismatch, contrast; diverge from, depart from, deviate from; modify, change, alter.

discriminate, distinguish, etc., 465.

Adj. different, diverse, heterogeneous; varied, variant, divergent, incongruous, modified; diversified, various.

other, another, not the same; unequal, etc., 28; unmatched, widely apart.

distinctive, characteristic, discriminative, distinguishing; diagnostic.

16. UNIFORMITY.—*N.* uniformity; homogeneity, stability, continuity, permanence, consistency, accordance, conformity; agreement, etc., 23; consonance.

regularity, constancy, evenness, sameness, unity, even tenor, routine.

V. accord with, etc., 23; conform to; assimilate; level, smooth.

Adj. uniform, homogeneous, of a piece, consistent; even, equable, constant, level; invariable, regular, unvaried, undiversified, unvarying, singsong, dreary, monotonous.

Adv. always, ever, evermore, perpetually, forever, everlastingly, invariably.

16a. WANT OF UNIFORMITY.—*N.* diversity, irregularity, unevenness; uncomformity, dissimilarity, dissimilitude, divergence, heterogeneity.

Adj. diversified, varied, irregular, checkered, uneven; multifarious, of various kinds.

17. SIMILARITY.—*N.* similarity, resemblance, likeness, semblance, affinity, approximation, parallelism; agreement, etc., 23; analogy, correspondence; brotherhood, family likeness.

repetition, etc., 104; sameness, etc. (*identity*), 13; uniformity, etc., 16.

the like; match, fellow, companion, pair, mate, twin, double, counterpart, brother, sister; one's second self, *alter ego* [L.]; chip of the old block, birds of a feather.

simile, parallel, type, image, etc. (*representation*), 554.

V. resemble, look like, favor [*colloq.*], follow, echo, reproduce, bear resemblance; savor of, smack of; approximate; parallel, match, rhyme with; take after; imitate, etc., 19.

Adj. similar, resembling, like, alike; twin.

analogous, parallel, of a piece; such as.

akin to, etc. (*consanguineous*), 11; correlative, corresponding, cognate, allied to.

approximate, near, close, something like, near [as, *near* silk, *colloq.*], mock, pseudo, simulating, representing.

exact, etc. (*true*), 494; lifelike, faithful, true to life; the very image of, cast in the same mold.

Adv. as if, so to speak; as it were, as if it were; *quasi* [L.], just as.

18. DISSIMILARITY.—*N.* dissimilarity, dissimilitude; unlikeness, diversity, disparity, divergence, variation; difference, etc., 15; novelty, originality.

V. vary, etc. (*differ*), 15; differ from; diversify.

Adj. dissimilar, unlike, disparate; divergent, nonidentical, unique, new, novel, unprecedented, original; diversified, etc., 16*a*.

Adv. otherwise, alias.

19. IMITATION.—*N.* imitation, copying; repetition, duplication; quotation; reproduction.

mockery, aping, mimicry.

simulation, impersonation; parrotism, parrotry; representation, etc., 554; semblance, pretense; copy, etc., 21.

paraphrase; parody, etc., 21.

plagiarism; forgery, etc., 544.

imitator, echo, cuckoo, parrot, ape, monkey, mimic; copyist.

V. imitate, copy, mirror, reflect, reproduce, repeat; do like, echo, re-echo, catch; match, parallel; forge, counterfeit.

mimic, ape, simulate, impersonate, act, etc. (*drama*), 599; represent, etc., 554; parody, travesty, caricature, burlesque, take off, mock; borrow.

follow in the steps (*or* wake) of, take pattern by, follow suit [*colloq.*], follow the example of, walk in the shoes of, take after, model after; emulate.

Adj. imitative, modeled after; molded on, borrowed, counterfeit, imitation, false, pseudo, near [as, *near* silk, *colloq.*]; mock, mimic.

Adv. literally, verbatim, word for word, exactly, precisely.

20. NONIMITATION.—*N.* nonimitation, originality, creativeness.

Adj. unimitated, uncopied; unmatched, unparalleled; inimitable, etc., 33; unique, original, primordial, creative; exceptional, rare, uncommon, unexampled, out-of-the-way, unwonted.

20a. VARIATION.—*N.* variation, alteration, change, imitation; modification; discrepancy.

divergency, deviation, deflection; aberration; innovation.

V. vary, etc. (*change*), 140; deviate, etc., 279; diverge; alternate.

Adj. **varied,** modified; diversified, etc., 16*a*; dissimilar, etc., 18.

21. [Result of imitation] COPY.—*N.* copy, facsimile, counterpart, effigy, form, likeness, similitude, semblance, cast, tracing; imitation, etc., 19; model, representation, study; portrait, etc., 554; duplicate, transcript, transcription; reflection, shadow, echo; reprint, replica, transfer, reproduction, repetition.

servile copy, counterfeit, forgery.

parody, caricature, burlesque, travesty, paraphrase; cartoon.

Adj. **faithful,** lifelike, similar, close, exact.

22. [Thing copied] PROTOTYPE.—*N.* prototype, original, model, pattern, precedent, standard; type; archetype, exemplar, example.

copy, text, design; keynote.

die, mold; matrix, last, mint, seal, punch, stamp, intaglio, negative.

V. be an example, set an example.

23. AGREEMENT.—*N.* agreement, accord, accordance, unison, harmony, concord, union, unity, unanimity; understanding, *entente cordiale* [F.], concert [as, the *concert* of Europe].

conformity, uniformity, consistency; correspondence, parallelism, apposition.

fitness, aptness, relevancy; pertinence, aptitude, propriety, applicability, admissibility, compatibility.

adaptation, adjustment, accommodation; assimilation.

consent, etc. (*assent*), 488; concurrence, consensus; co-operation.

V. **agree,** accord, harmonize; correspond, tally, consent, etc. (*assent*), 488; suit, fit, befit; square with, dovetail, match, resemble, parallel.

adapt, accommodate, graduate; adjust, etc. (*render equal*), 27; regulate, reconcile.

Adj. **agreeing,** accordant, correspondent, congenial; coherent; harmonious, reconcilable, conformable; consistent, compatible; in accordance with, in harmony with, in keeping with.

apt, apposite, pertinent, pat; to the point; happy, felicitous, germane, applicable, relevant, admissible.

fit, adapted, appropriate, suitable; meet, etc. (*expedient*), 646.

24. DISAGREEMENT.—*N.* disagreement, discord, dissonance, disunion, discrepancy, unconformity, incongruity, dissension, conflict, opposition, antagonism, difference, misunderstanding.

disparity, disproportion; inequality, variance, divergence.

unfitness, inaptitude, impropriety, inapplicability, irrelevancy.

V. **disagree,** clash, conflict, dispute, quarrel, jar, interfere.

Adj. **disagreeing,** discordant, inharmonious; hostile, antagonistic, repugnant, clashing, jarring, factious, dissentient, incompatible, irreconcilable, inconsistent with; incongruous; repugnant to.

inapt, inept, inappropriate, improper, unsuited, unsuitable, inapplicable; unfit, unbefitting, unbecoming; ill-timed, unseasonable, ill-adapted, infelicitous, irrelevant.

uncongenial, unsympathetic, ill-assorted, mismatched.

Adv. in defiance of, in contempt of, in spite of.

III. QUANTITY

25. [Absolute quantity] **QUANTITY.**—*N.* quantity, magnitude; size, bulk, volume, mass, amount, measure, measurement, substance, strength.

[Science of quantity] mathematics.

[Definite quantity] armful, handful, mouthful, spoonful, stock, batch, lot, dose; quota, pittance, driblet.

Adj. quantitative, some, any, more or less.

26. [Relative quantity] **DEGREE.**—*N.* degree, grade, step, extent, measure, amount, ratio, standard, height, pitch; reach, mark, stage, rate, range, scope, caliber; gradation, shade; tenor, compass; sphere, station, rank, standing; interval, space [*music*]; intensity, strength.

V. graduate, calibrate, measure.

Adj. comparative, gradual, shading off.

Adv. by degrees, gradually, step by step, little by little, inch by inch, drop by drop; to some extent.

27. [Sameness of quantity or degree] **EQUALITY.**—*N.* equality, parity, symmetry, balance, poise; evenness, monotony, level; equivalence, equipoise, equilibrium; par, quits; distinction without a difference, identity, similarity.

tie, dead heat; drawn game, drawn battle; neck-and-neck race.

match, peer, compeer, equal, mate, fellow, brother; equivalent.

V. equal, match, keep pace with, run abreast; come up to; balance.

equalize, level, dress [*mil.*], balance, handicap, trim, adjust, poise; strike a balance; restore equilibrium.

Adj. equal, even, level, monotonous, symmetrical, co-ordinate; on a par with, on a level with, up to the mark.

equivalent, tantamount; quits; synonymous; convertible; all one, all the same; drawn [as, *a game*].

Adv. equally, to all intents and purposes.

28. [Difference of quantity or degree] **INEQUALITY.**—*N.* inequality, disparity, odds; difference, etc., 15; unevenness, shortcoming; superiority, etc., 33; inferiority, deficiency, inadequacy.

V. **be unequal,** have the advantage, turn the scale; overmatch, etc., 33; fall short of.

Adj. **unequal,** uneven, partial, inadequate, deficient; overbalanced, unbalanced, top-heavy, lopsided.

unequaled, unparalleled, unrivaled, unique, matchless, inimitable, peerless.

29. MEAN.—*N.* **mean,** medium, average, balance, rule, run, golden mean, middle; compromise, neutrality.

V. **average,** split the difference, strike a balance, pair off.

Adj. **mean,** intermediate; middle, etc., 68; average, normal, standard; neutral.

mediocre, middle class, bourgeois, commonplace.

Adv. **on an average,** in the long run; in round numbers.

30. COMPENSATION.—*N.* **compensation,** equation; indemnification; compromise, measure for measure, retaliation, equalization.

setoff, offset; makeweight, counterpoise, ballast; indemnity, equivalent, *quid pro quo* [L.]; amends, counterbalance, counterclaim.

pay, payment, reward, etc., 973.

V. **compensate,** indemnify; counterpoise, balance, counterbalance, offset, set off; square, make up for, equalize, etc., 27; recoup, redeem; pay, reward, etc., 973.

Adj. **compensating,** compensatory, equivalent, equal.

Adv. **notwithstanding,** but, however, yet, still, nevertheless, although, though; howbeit, albeit; at all events, in spite of, despite, on the other hand, at the same time.

31. GREATNESS.—*N.* **greatness,** vastness, magnitude; size, etc., 192; multitude; immensity, enormity, might, strength, intensity, fullness.

great quantity, quantity, deal [*colloq.*], volume, bulk, mass, heap; stock, store, load, shipload; abundance, sufficiency.

fame, distinction, grandeur, dignity; importance, etc., 642.

V. **be great,** soar, tower, loom, rise above, transcend; bulk, bulk large.

enlarge, etc. (*increase*), 35; wax, magnify, grow, expand, swell, dilate.

Adj. **great,** large, considerable, big, bulky, huge, etc., 192; titanic; voluminous, ample, abundant; many, etc., 102; full, intense; signal.

goodly, noble, precious, mighty; extraordinary; important, etc., 642; supreme, etc., 33; complete, etc., 52; arrant, downright; uttermost; profound, intense, consummate; rank, unmitigated, glaring, flagrant.

world-wide, widespread, far-famed, extensive.

august, grand, dignified, sublime, majestic.

vast, immense, enormous, extreme; inordinate, excessive, extravagant, monstrous, crass, gross; towering, stupendous, prodigious.

unlimited, etc. (*infinite*), 105; unutterable, indescribable, ineffable, unspeakable, inexpressible, fabulous.

absolute, positive, stark, decided, unequivocal, essential, perfect.

remarkable, notable, noticeable, noteworthy, renowned.

Adv. in a great or high degree: greatly, much, indeed, very, very much, most; pretty, enough, in a great measure, passing, richly; on a large scale; by wholesale; mightily, powerfully; extremely, exceedingly, intensely, indefinitely, immeasurably, incalculably, infinitely.

in a positive degree: truly, etc. (*truth*), 494; decidedly, unequivocally, absolutely, essentially, fundamentally, radically, downright, in all conscience.

in a complete degree: entirely, completely, wholly; abundantly, amply, fully, widely.

in a supreme degree: pre-eminently, superlatively, supremely, incomparably.

in a too great degree: immoderately, monstrously, preposterously, exorbitantly, excessively, enormously, out of all proportion.

in a marked degree: particularly, remarkably, singularly, curiously, uncommonly, unusually, peculiarly, notably, signally, strikingly, pointedly, chiefly; famously, egregiously, prominently, glaringly, emphatically, incredibly.

in a violent degree: furiously, violently, severely, desperately, tremendously, extravagantly.

in a painful degree: painfully, sadly, sorely, bitterly, piteously, grievously, miserably, cruelly, woefully, lamentably, shockingly, frightfully, dreadfully, fearfully, terribly, horribly, distressingly, balefully.

32. SMALLNESS.—*N.* smallness, littleness, paucity; fewness, sparseness, scarcity, insignificance, unimportance.

small quantity, modicum, minimum; atom, particle, trifle, electron, molecule, corpuscle, point, speck, dot, mote, jot, iota; minutiæ, details; tittle, spark; grain, scruple, minim; drop, sprinkling, dab, dash, tinge, dole, mite, bit, morsel, crumb, scrap, shred, tag, splinter, rag; snip, sliver, paring, shaving, hair; thimbleful, handful, capful, mouthful; fragment, fraction.

V. be small, lie in a nutshell.

diminish, etc. (*decrease*), 36; contract, shrink, dwindle, wane.

Adj. small, little, stunted; diminutive, etc. (*small in size*), 193; minute, miniature, inconsiderable, paltry, etc. (*unimportant*), 643; scanty, scant, limited, meager, sparing; few, etc., 103; moderate, modest.

inappreciable, infinitesimal, atomic, microscopic, molecular.

mere, simple, sheer, stark, bare.

Adv. **in a small degree:** to a small extent, on a small scale; a little, slightly, imperceptibly; miserably, wretchedly; insufficiently, imperfectly, faintly, feebly, passably.

in a certain or limited degree: partially, in part, in a certain degree, to a certain degree *or* extent; comparatively, rather, in some degree *or* measure; somewhat; simply, only, purely, merely; at least, at most, ever so little, thus far, after a fashion.

almost, nearly, well-nigh, not quite, all but, near upon, close upon, near the mark; within an ace (*or* inch) of, on the brink of; scarcely, hardly, barely, only just, no more than.

in an uncertain degree: about, thereabouts, somewhere about, nearly.

in no degree: noway, nowise, not at all, not in the least, not a bit, not a jot, in no wise, in no respect, by no means, on no account.

33. SUPERIORITY.—*N.* superiority, majority, plurality; advantage; preponderance, prevalence.

nobility, etc. (*rank*), 875; superman, overman.

supremacy, supremeness, primacy, pre-eminence, lead; maximum, record; crest, climax, culmination, summit, peak, transcendence; lion's share, excess, surplus, overweight, redundance.

V. **exceed,** excel, transcend, outdo, outbalance, overbalance, outweigh, outrank, outrival, out-Herod Herod; pass, surpass, overtop, overmatch; cap, culminate, beat, cut out [*colloq.*]; beat hollow [*colloq.*], outstrip, eclipse, throw into the shade; predominate, prevail; precede, take precedence, come first, bear the palm, break the record.

Adj. **superior,** greater, major, higher, exceeding; distinguished, ultra.

supreme, greatest, maximum, utmost, paramount, pre-eminent, foremost, crowning, excellent, peerless, matchless; unrivaled, unparalleled, unequaled, unapproached, unsurpassed; superlative, incomparable, transcendent.

Adv. **beyond,** more, over; over and above; at its height.

in a superior or supreme degree: eminently, pre-eminently, surpassing, superlatively, supremely, principally, especially, particularly, peculiarly.

34. INFERIORITY.—*N.* inferiority, shortcoming, deficiency; minimum; imperfection; meanness, poorness, baseness, shabbiness.

Personal inferiority: the people, etc., 876; subordination.

V. **be inferior,** fall short of, come short of, not come up to; become smaller, decrease, yield the palm, play second fiddle.

Adj. **inferior,** smaller; less, lesser, deficient, reduced, lower, subordinate, secondary, junior, minor, humble; second rate; unimportant, etc., 643.

Adv. **less,** short of, under.

35. INCREASE.—*N.* **increase,** augmentation, addition, enlargement, extension, expansion, growth, increment, accretion, development, accumulation, inflation, enhancement, aggravation, exaggeration.

gain, produce, product, profit, advantage, booty, plunder.

V. **increase,** augment, add to, enlarge, etc., 31; advance, rise, mount, ascend.

aggrandize, raise, exalt; deepen, heighten, lengthen, thicken; inflate, intensify, enhance, magnify, redouble, double; aggravate, exaggerate.

Adj. **increasing,** growing, crescent, multiplying, intensifying, intensive.

Adv. **crescendo,** increasingly.

36. DECREASE.—*N.* **decrease,** diminution, lessening, subtraction, reduction, abatement, declension; shrinkage, contraction, curtailment, abridgment.

subsidence, wane, ebb, decline; ebb tide, neap tide, ebbing.

V. **decrease,** diminish, lessen; abridge, shorten, shrink, contract; dwindle, fall away, waste, wear; wane, ebb, decline, subside, languish, decay, crumble.

discount, belittle, minimize, depreciate, extenuate, lower, weaken, attenuate; dwarf, reduce, shorten, subtract; mitigate, ease, moderate.

Adv. **decrescendo,** decreasingly.

37. ADDITION.—*N.* **addition,** annexation, accession, re-enforcement; increase, etc., 35; increment.

affix, codicil, tag, appendage, postscript, adjunct, supplement; accompaniment, insertion.

V. **add,** annex, affix, subjoin, tack to, append, tag, attach; interpose, introduce, insert.

compute, total, cast (*or* sum, count) up.

re-enforce, strengthen, augment.

Adj. **additional,** supplemental, supplementary; extra, spare, further, fresh, more, other, auxiliary, contributory, accessory.

Adv. **in addition,** more; and, also, likewise, too, furthermore, further; besides, to boot; over and above, moreover; as well as, together with, along with, in conjunction with.

38. DEDUCTION.—*N.* **deduction,** subtraction, retrenchment; abstraction, mutilation, amputation, curtailment, abbreviation.

rebate, etc. (*decrement*), 40*a*; minuend, subtrahend; decrease, etc., 36.

V. deduct, subtract, retrench; withdraw; take from, take away; detract, reduce, eliminate, diminish, curtail, shorten; deprive of, etc. (*take*), 789; weaken.

mutilate, amputate, cut off, cut away, excise.

pare, thin, prune, scrape, file.

Adv. less; short of; minus, without, except, excepting, with the exception of, save, exclusive of.

39. [Thing added] ADJUNCT.—*N.* adjunct, addition, affix, suffix, appendage, annex, augmentation, increment, re-enforcement, accessory, accompaniment, etc., 88; addendum (*pl.* addenda); complement, supplement, sequel.

rider, offshoot, episode, side issue, corollary, codicil, etc. (*addition*), 37.

V. add, annex, etc., 37.

Adj. additional, etc., 37.

40. [Thing remaining] REMAINDER.—*N.* remainder, residue, remains, remnant, rest, relic; leavings, odds and ends, residuum, dregs, refuse, stubble, ruins, wreck, skeleton, fossil, stump, rump.

surplus, excess; balance [*commercial slang*], result; superfluity, redundance; survival.

V. remain, survive, be left; exceed.

Adj. remaining, left, residual, residuary; over, odd; surviving; net; superfluous, etc. (*redundant*), 641.

40a. [Thing deducted] DECREMENT.—*N.* decrement, discount, rebate, defect, loss, deduction; waste.

41. MIXTURE.—*N.* mixture, admixture, junction, etc., 43; amalgamation, combination, etc., 48; infusion, transfusion; infiltration; interlarding, interpolation, etc., 228; adulteration.

Thing mixed: tinge, tincture, touch, dash, smack, spice, seasoning, infusion.

Compounds: alloy, amalgam; brass, pewter; miscellany, medley, mess, hash, hodgepodge, patchwork, jumble; potpourri, mosaic.

half-blood, half-breed, half-caste, crossbreed; mulatto, quadroon, octoroon, Eurasian; mule, cross, hybrid, mongrel.

V. mix, join, etc., 43; combine, etc., 48; mingle, commingle, intermingle, interlard, interpolate, intertwine, interweave; associate with.

imbue, infuse, diffuse, suffuse, transfuse, instill, infiltrate, dash, tinge, tincture, season, blend, cross; alloy, amalgamate, compound, adulterate.

Adj. **mixed,** composite, half-and-half, hybrid, mongrel, heterogeneous; motley, variegated, miscellaneous, promiscuous, indiscriminate.

Adv. **among,** amid, with; in the midst of.

42. [Freedom from mixture] SIMPLENESS.—*N.* simpleness, purity, homogeneity.

elimination, sifting, purification, etc. (*cleanness*), 652.

V. **render simple,** simplify.

sift, winnow, bolt, eliminate; exclude, get rid of; clear, purify, etc. (*clean*), 652.

Adj. **simple,** uniform, homogeneous, single, pure, clear; elemental, elementary.

43. JUNCTION.—*N.* junction, joining, union; connection, conjunction, annexation, attachment; marriage, wedlock; confluence, communication, meeting, reunion; assemblage, etc., 72; coherence, etc., 46; combination, etc., 48.

joint, joining, juncture, pivot, hinge, articulation; seam, gore, gusset, link, bond.

contingency, emergency, predicament, crisis, concurrence.

V. **join,** unite, connect; associate; put together, piece together, embody.

attach, fix, fasten, bind, secure, tighten, clinch, tie, strap, sew, lace, stitch, knit, button, buckle, hitch, lash, splice, gird, tether, moor, picket, chain; fetter, hook, link, yoke, bracket; marry; bridge over, span.

pin, nail, screw, bolt, hasp, clasp, clamp, rivet; solder, cement, etc., 46.

entwine, interlace, intertwine, interweave; entangle.

Adj. **joined,** joint; corporate, compact.

firm, fast, close, tight, taut, secure, inseparable, indissoluble.

Adv. **jointly,** in conjunction with, etc. (*in addition to*), 37; fast, firmly.

44. DISJUNCTION.—*N.* disjunction, disconnection, disunion, disengagement, dissociation, discontinuity, etc., 70; isolation, insularity, insulation, separateness; dispersion.

separation, parting; detachment, segregation; divorce; cæsura, division, subdivision, break, fracture, rupture; dismemberment, dissection, disintegration, severance, disruption, cleavage.

fissure, breach, rent, rift, crack, slit, cut, incision.

V. **disjoin,** disconnect, disengage, disunite, dissociate, divorce, part, detach, unfasten, separate, disentangle, cut off, segregate; set apart, keep apart; insulate, isolate; cut adrift, loose, set free, liberate.

divide, sunder, subdivide, sever, dissever, cut, chop, saw, snip, nip, cleave, rive, rend, slit, rip, split, splinter, chip, crack, snap, break, tear, burst; wrench, rupture, hack, hew, slash, slice, carve, quarter, dissect, anatomize; partition, parcel.

disintegrate, dismember, disband; disperse, etc., 73; dislocate, break up.

part, part company; separate, leave; alienate, estrange.

Adj. disjoined, discontinuous, disjunctive; isolated, insular; separate, apart, asunder, loose, free, adrift.

Adv. separately, one by one, severally, apart, asunder.

45. [Connecting medium] VINCULUM.—*N.* vinculum, link; connective, connection; junction, etc., 43; hyphen; bracket; bridge, steppingstone; bond, cord; rope, line, cable, hawser, painter; chain; string, etc. (*filament*), 205.

fastening, tie; ligament, ligature; strap; tackle, rigging; yoke, band, headband, fillet, snood, brace, thong, girdle, noose, lariat, lasso, knot, girth, cinch.

cement, glue, gum, paste, size, solder, mortar, plaster, putty.
shackle, rein, etc. (*means of restraint*), 752.

V. bridge over, span; connect, etc., 43.

46. COHERENCE.—*N.* coherence, cohesion, cohesiveness, adherence, adhesion, adhesiveness; conglomeration, aggregation, consolidation, soldering, connection; relativity.

tenacity, toughness; stickiness; inseparability.
conglomerate, concrete, etc., 321.

V. cohere, adhere, coagulate, stick, cling, cleave, hold, close with, clasp, hug.

glue, agglutinate, cement, paste, gum; solder, weld; cake, consolidate, solidify, agglomerate.

Adj. adhesive, cohesive, adhering, tenacious, tough; sticky, etc., 352.

47. INCOHERENCE.—*N.* incoherence, nonadhesion; looseness, laxity, relaxation; loosening, disjunction, etc., 44.

V. loosen, make loose, slacken, relax; unglue, etc., 46; detach, etc., 44.

Adj. nonadhesive, noncohesive, incoherent, detached, loose, baggy, slack, lax, relaxed, segregated, unconsolidated; uncombined, etc., 48.

48. COMBINATION.—*N.* combination, mixture, etc., 41; junction, etc., 43; union, unification, synthesis, incorporation, amalgamation, coalescence, fusion, brew, blend, blending; centralization.

alloy, compound, amalgam, composition, resultant.

V. **combine,** unite, incorporate, alloy, intermix, interfuse, interlard, amalgamate, embody, absorb, blend, merge, fuse, consolidate, coalesce, solidify, impregnate, centralize.

league, federate, confederate, fraternize, club, associate, amalgamate, couple, pair, ally.

Adj. **combined,** conjoint; ingrained, imbued.

allied, amalgamated, federate, confederate, corporate, leagued.

49. DECOMPOSITION.—*N.* **decomposition,** analysis, dissection, dissolution, breakup; disjunction, etc., 44; disintegration.

decay, rot, putrefaction, putrescence, putridity, caries, corruption.

V. **decompose,** analyze, dissolve; resolve into its elements, dissect, disintegrate, disperse; crumble into dust.

rot, decay, consume, putrefy.

50. [Principal part] WHOLE.—*N.* **whole,** totality, integrity, entirety, completeness; integer, integral.

all, the whole, total, aggregate, sum, sum total.

bulk, mass, lump, tissue, staple, body, greater part, main part; lion's share.

V. **form a whole,** embody, amass; aggregate, assemble; amount to.

Adj. **whole,** total, gross, entire; complete, etc., 52; wholesale, sweeping; comprehensive.

indivisible, indissoluble, indissolvable.

Adv. **wholly,** altogether; as a whole, totally, completely, entirely, all, all in all, wholesale, in a body, collectively, in the aggregate, in the main, on the whole, bodily, substantially.

51. PART.—*N.* **part,** portion; item, particular; aught, any; division; sector, segment; fraction, fragment; detachment, subdivision.

section, chapter, verse; article, clause.

piece, lump, bit, cut, cutting; chip, chunk, slice, scrap, crumb, morsel, moiety, particle; installment, dividend; share.

member, limb, arm, wing, scion, branch, bough, joint, link, offshoot, ramification, twig, spray, spring; runner, tendril; leaf, leaflet; stump.

V. **part,** divide, disjoin, etc., 44; partition, etc. (*apportion*), 786.

Adj. **fractional,** fragmentary, sectional; incomplete, partial.

divided, broken, cut, cropped, shorn.

divisible, dissoluble, dissolvable.

Adv. **partly,** in part, partially; piecemeal, by installments, in detail.

52. COMPLETENESS.—*N.* **completeness,** intactness, completion, etc., 729; fill, saturation, entirety; totality, integrity; perfection, etc., 650; solidarity, unity, all, high tide, flood tide, spring tide.

V. complete, etc. (*accomplish*), 729; fill, charge, load, replenish; make up, eke out, supply deficiencies; fill up, fill in, satiate; saturate.

Adj. complete, entire, whole, intact, perfect, full, absolute, thorough; solid, undivided.

brimful, brimming, chock-full; saturated, crammed; replete, etc. (*redundant*), 641; fraught, laden.

exhaustive, radical, sweeping, thoroughgoing.

regular, unmitigated, sheer, unqualified, unconditional, free, abundant, etc. (*sufficient*), 639.

completing, supplemental, supplementary.

Adv. completely, altogether, outright, wholly, totally, utterly, quite; effectually, fully, in all respects, in every respect; out and out; throughout, from first to last, from head to foot, from top to toe, every whit, every inch.

53. INCOMPLETENESS.—*N.* incompleteness, deficiency, shortcoming, want, lack, insufficiency, imperfection, etc., 651; immaturity.

Part wanting: defect, deficit, omission; shortage; break, etc. (*discontinuity*), 70; missing link.

V. be incomplete, fall short of, lack, etc. (*be insufficient*), 640.

Adj. incomplete, uncompleted, imperfect, unfinished; defective, deficient, wanting, failing, in arrear, short, short of; perfunctory, sketchy, crude, immature.

mutilated, garbled, hashed, mangled, butchered, docked, truncated.

in progress, in hand; going on, proceeding.

54. COMPOSITION.—*N.* composition, constitution; make-up; combination, etc., 48; embodiment; formation.

authorship, compilation, composition, production, invention; writing.

painting, etching, design, etc. (*painting*), 556; relief, etc. (*sculpture*), 557.

typesetting, typography, etc., 591.

V. be composed of, consist of.

include, etc., 76; contain, hold, comprehend, admit, embrace, embody.

compose, constitute, form, make; fabricate, weave, construct; compile, scribble, draw, write.

55. EXCLUSION.—*N.* exclusion, omission, exception, rejection, repudiation; exile, seclusion, lockout, ostracism, prohibition.

separation, segregation, elimination, expulsion.

V. **exclude,** bar; leave out, shut out; reject, repudiate, black-ball, ostracize; lay aside, put aside, set apart; relegate, segregate; strike off, strike out; neglect, banish, etc. (*seclude*), 893; separate, etc. (*disjoin*), 44.

pass over, omit; eliminate, weed out.

Adj. **exclusive,** inadmissible, preclusive, preventive, prohibitive.

Adv. **except,** exclusive of, save.

56. COMPONENT.—*N.* **component,** integral part, element, constituent, ingredient, contents; feature; member, etc. (*part*), 51; personnel.

V. **enter into,** be *or* form part of, etc., 51; merge in, share in, participate; belong to, appertain to; combine, unite.

form, make, constitute, compose, fabricate, etc., 54.

Adj. **inherent,** intrinsic, essential.

inclusive, all-embracing, comprehensive.

57. EXTRANEOUSNESS.—*N.* **extraneousness,** extrinsicality; exclusion; alienism.

foreign body (substance *or* element).

alien, stranger, intruder, interloper, foreigner, newcomer; immigrant, emigrant; outsider, barbarian, tenderfoot [*slang*].

Adj. **extraneous,** foreign, alien, exterior, external; outlandish, barbaric, barbarian.

excluded, inadmissible; exceptional.

Adv. **abroad,** in foreign parts, in foreign lands; oversea, overseas.

IV. ORDER

58. ORDER.—*N.* **order,** regularity, uniformity, symmetry, harmony; course, routine; method, disposition, arrangement, array, system, economy, discipline, orderliness, subordination.

gradation, progression; series, etc. (*continuity*), 69.

rank, place, etc. (*term*), 71.

V. **adjust,** regulate, systematize, standardize; time.

Adj. **orderly,** regular; in order, in trim, neat, tidy, methodical, uniform, symmetrical, shipshape, businesslike, systematic, normal, habitual.

Adv. **in order,** methodically, in turn, in its turn; step by step; systematically, by clockwork.

59. DISORDER.—*N.* **disorder,** derangement; irregularity; untidiness; anomaly, etc. (*unconformity*), 83; anarchy, anarchism; disunion; discord.

confusion, disarray, jumble, botch, litter, farrago, mess, muddle, hodgepodge, imbroglio, chaos, clutter, medley.

complexity, complication, entanglement, intricacy; perplexity; network, maze, labyrinth; wilderness, jungle; tangled skein.

turmoil, ferment, etc. (*agitation*), 315; trouble, disturbance, convulsion, tumult, uproar, riot, rumpus [*colloq.*], fracas, pandemonium, Babel, saturnalia.

V. **disorder,** botch, disturb, derange, etc., 61; entangle, ravel, ruffle, rumple.

Adj. **disorderly,** out of order, out of place, irregular, desultory; anomalous, etc. (*unconformable*), 83; disorganized; straggling; unmethodical, unsystematic; untidy, slovenly, messy [*colloq.*], indiscriminate, chaotic, confused; deranged, etc., 61; topsy-turvy, disjointed, out of joint.

complex, intricate, complicated, perplexed, involved, entangled, knotted, tangled, inextricable.

troublous, tumultuous, turbulent; riotous, etc. (*violent*), 173.

60. [Reduction to Order] ARRANGEMENT.—*N.* **arrangement,** plan, etc., 626; preparation, provision; disposal, disposition; distribution, sorting, assortment, allotment, apportionment, graduation, organization, groupings; analysis, classification, division, systematization, codification.

Result of arrangement: orderliness, form, array, digest; synopsis, etc. (*compendium*), 596; table; register, etc. (*record*), 551; organism; stipulation, settlement.

V. **arrange,** dispose, fix, place; form; set in order, set out; compose, space, range, graduate, marshal, array, rank, group, parcel out, allot, apportion, distribute, assign the parts; dispose of, assort, sort; tidy [*colloq.*].

classify, class, file, list; register, etc. (*record*), 551; catalogue, tabulate, index, alphabetize, grade, codify.

methodize, regulate, systematize, co-ordinate, organize; unravel, disentangle.

Adj. **arranged,** embattled, in battle array; cut and dried; methodical, orderly, regular, systematic, on file; tabular.

61. [Bringing into disorder] DERANGEMENT.—*N.* **derangement,** muss [*colloq.* U. S.], mess; disorder, etc., 59; discomposure, disturbance; disorganization, dislocation; inversion, etc., 218; insanity, etc., 503.

V. **derange,** disarrange, discompose, displace, misplace; mislay, disorder; disorganize; embroil, convulse, unsettle, disturb, confuse, trouble, perturb, disconcert, jumble; muddle; unhinge, dislocate, put out of joint, throw out of gear.

turn topsy-turvy, etc. (*invert*), 218; bedevil; complicate, involve, perplex, confound; tangle, entangle; tousle [*colloq.*], dishevel, ruffle; rumple, etc. (*fold*), 258; become insane, etc., 503.

litter, scatter; mix, etc., 41.

62. [Consecutive Order] PRECEDENCE.—*N.* precedence, the lead, superiority, etc., 33; importance, consequence; premise; antecedence, precursor, etc., 64; priority, preference.

prefix, affix; preamble; prelude, overture, voluntary.

V. **precede,** forerun, come before, come first; head, lead, lead the way; introduce, usher in; rank, outrank; take precedence.

prefix; premise, prelude, preface; affix.

Adj. **preceding,** precedent, antecedent; anterior; prior, etc., 116; before; former, foregoing, aforesaid, said; introductory, etc., 64.

Adv. **before;** in advance, etc. (*precession*), 280.

63. SEQUENCE.—*N.* sequence, train; following, succession; afterclap, afterglow, aftermath, afterpiece, aftertaste.

continuation, prolongation; order of succession.

V. **succeed,** come after, ensue, come next.

follow, tag [*colloq.*], heel, dog, shadow, hound, hunt; trace, retrace.

append, place after, subjoin.

Adj. **succeeding,** sequent; subsequent; proximate, next; consecutive, etc. (*continuity*), 69.

latter, posterior, etc., 117.

Adv. **after,** subsequently; behind, etc. (*rear*), 235.

64. PRECURSOR.—*N.* precursor, antecedent, precedent, predecessor; forerunner, pioneer; outrider; leader, bellwether; herald, harbinger.

prelude, preamble, preface, prologue, foreword, proem, exordium, introduction; heading, frontispiece, groundwork; preparation, etc., 673; overture, voluntary; premises.

prefigurement, etc., 511; omen, etc., 512.

Adj. **introductory,** preludial, prefatory, precursory, inaugural, preliminary.

65. SEQUEL.—*N.* sequel, suffix, tail, queue, train, wake, trail, rear; retinue, suite; appendix, postscript, postlude, conclusion, epilogue; peroration; codicil; continuation; appendage, tag, aftergrowth, afterpiece, afterthought, second thoughts; outgrowth.

follower, successor, pursuer, adherent, partisan, disciple, client; sycophant, parasite.

66. BEGINNING.—*N.* beginning, commencement, opening, outset, incipience, inception; introduction, etc. (*prelude*), 64; initial; inauguration, embarkation, rising of the curtain; curtain raiser, maiden speech; exordium; outbreak, onset, brunt; initiative, first move; start, starting point; dawn, etc. (*morning*), 125.

origin, etc. (*cause*), 153; source, rise; bud, germ, egg, embryo, rudiment; genesis, birth, nativity, cradle, infancy.

head, heading; title page; van, etc. (*front*), 234.

entrance, entry; inlet, orifice, mouth, porch, portal, portico, door; gate, gateway; postern, wicket, threshold, vestibule; border, frontier.

rudiments, elements, outlines, grammar, alphabet, ABC.

V. begin, commence; rise, arise; originate, initiate, open, start; dawn, set in, take its rise, enter upon; set out, etc. (*depart*), 293; embark in; make one's debut; institute; set about, set to work; make a start; break ground, cross the Rubicon; undertake, etc., 676.

usher in, lead the way, take the lead *or* initiative; inaugurate, head; lay the foundations, etc. (*prepare*), 673; found, etc. (*cause*), 153; set up, set on foot, launch, broach; open up, open the door to.

come into existence, take birth; burst forth, break out; spring up, crop up.

recommence; begin at the beginning, begin again, start afresh.

Adj. initial, prime, introductory, incipient; inaugural; embryonic, rudimentary; primal, primary, primeval, etc. (*old*), 124; aboriginal; natal.

first, maiden, foremost, front, head, leading.

Adv. first, in the first place, in the bud, in embryo, from the beginning, formerly.

67. END.—*N.* end, close, termination, conclusion, finish, completion, finis, finale, period, term, terminus, last, extreme, extremity; fag end, tip, nib, point, tail, tag, peroration, appendix, epilogue; consummation, denouement, fall of the curtain; goal, destination, terminal, limit, stoppage; expiration; dissolution, death, etc., 360; doomsday.

last stage, evening (*of life*); *coup de grâce* [F.], deathblow; knockout.

V. end, close, finish, terminate, conclude; expire, die, etc., 360; come to a close, perorate; run out, pass away.

bring to an end, put an end to, make an end of; achieve, etc. (*complete*), 729; stop, etc., 142.

Adj. final, terminal; conclusive; crowning, etc. (*completing*), 729; last, ultimate; hindermost; rear, etc., 235.

ended, settled, decided, over.

Adv. finally, in fine; at the last; once for all.

68. MIDDLE.—*N.* middle, midst, thick, midmost; mean, etc., 29; medium, middle term; center, core, kernel, nucleus, hub, heart, bull's-eye; mid-course, neutrality, compromise.

equidistance, bisection; equator, diaphragm, midriff.

Adj. **middle,** medial, mid, midmost; intermediate, equidistant, central, pivotal, mediterranean, equatorial.

Adv. **midway,** halfway, in the middle; amidships.

69. [Uninterrupted sequence] CONTINUITY.—continuity, continuousness, succession, round, suite, progression, series, train, chain; scale; gradation, course; perpetuity.

procession, cavalcade, parade; column; retinue, cortege, funeral, ovation.

pedigree, genealogy, lineage, history, family tree, race; ancestry, descent, family, house; line, line of ancestors; strain.

rank, file, line, row, range, tier.

V. **arrange in a series,** string together, file, list, thread, tabulate.

Adj. **continuous,** continued; consecutive, progressive, gradual, serial, successive; uninterrupted, unbroken, entire; linear; perennial, constant.

Adv. **continuously,** in a line, in succession, in turn; running, gradually, in file, in single file, in Indian file.

70. [Interrupted sequence] DISCONTINUITY.—*N.* discontinuity, disconnectedness; disconnection, etc., 44; interruption, break, fracture, flaw, fault, crack, cut; gap, etc. (*interval*), 198; intermission, alternation.

V. **alternate,** interchange, intermit.

discontinue, pause, interrupt, intervene; break, break off; interpose, etc., 228; disconnect, etc. (*disjoin*), 44; dissever.

Adj. **discontinuous,** disconnected, broken, interrupted, fitful, irregular, spasmodic, desultory; intermittent, alternate, recurrent, periodic.

Adv. **at intervals,** by snatches, by jerks, by fits and starts.

71. TERM.—*N.* term, rank, station, stage, step; degree, etc., 26; scale, grade, status, state, position, standing, footing, place, mark, period, range.

72. [Collective Order] ASSEMBLAGE.—*N.* assemblage, collection, levy, gathering, ingathering, mobilization, meet, forgathering, muster, team; concourse, conflux, congregation.

meeting, levee, reunion, drawing room, at home; social gathering, 892; assembly, congress, house, senate, legislature, etc., 696; convocation, caucus, convention.

company, platoon, faction, caravan, posse, watch, squad, corps, troop, troupe; army, regiment.

miscellany, miscellanea, compilation; symposium; library, etc. (*store*), 636.

crowd, throng; flood, rush, deluge; rabble, mob, host, etc. (*multitude*), 102; rout, press, crush, horde, body, tribe; crew, gang, knot, squad, force, band, party; bunch, drive, roundup.

clan, brotherhood, association, etc. (*party*), 712.

group, cluster, clump, set, batch, lot, pack; budget, assortment, bunch; parcel, packet, bundle, package, bale, fagot, wisp, truss, tuft, shock, clump; grove, thicket; rick, stack, sheaf, swath; volley, shower, storm, cloud.

accumulation, etc. (*store*), 636; heap, lump, pile, mass, pyramid; drift, snowball, snowdrift; amassment; conglomeration, aggregation, concentration, convergence, congestion, quantity, etc. (*greatness*), 31.

V. **be** *or* **come together,** assemble, collect, muster; meet, unite, join, rejoin; cluster, flock, swarm, surge, stream, herd, crowd, huddle, throng, associate; congregate, concentrate, resort, forgather.

bring together, assemble, muster, collect, gather; hold a meeting, convene, convoke; rake up, dredge, heap, mass, pile; pack, cram, lump together; compile, group, concentrate, unite, amass, accumulate, hoard, store.

Adj. **dense,** serried, teeming, swarming, populous.

73. DISPERSION.—*N.* dispersion, disjunct on, etc., 44; divergence, radiation, broadcast, spread, dissemination, diffusion, dissipation, distribution; apportionment, allotment.

V. **disperse,** scatter, sow, disseminate, sow broadcast, diffuse, radiate, broadcast, shed, spread, bestrew, dispense, disband, dismember, distribute; apportion, etc., 786; dispel, cast forth, draft off; strew, cast, sprinkle; issue, deal out, retail, utter.

Adj. **scattered,** disseminated, strown, strewn, dispersed, diffuse, diffusive, sparse, broadcast, sporadic, widespread; epidemic, etc. (*general*), 78; adrift, stray; disheveled.

74. [Place of meeting] FOCUS.—*N.* focus, center, gathering place, rendezvous, rallying point, headquarters, resort, haunt, retreat, club; tryst, trysting place, place of meeting.

V. **focus,** bring to a point, bring to a focus; rally, meet.

75. [Distributive Order] CLASS.—*N.* class, division, subdivision, category, head, order, section; department, province, domain, sphere.

kind, sort, type, estate, genus, species, variety, family, race, tribe, caste, clan, breed, kin; clique, coterie, set; sect, gender, sex.

description, denomination, persuasion, connection, designation, character, stamp; selection, specification.

76. INCLUSION.—*N.* inclusion, admission, incorporation, comprisal, reception.

composition, embodiment, formation.

V. **include,** comprise, comprehend, contain, admit, embrace, receive, inclose, etc. (*circumscribe*), 229; incorporate, cover, embody, encircle; reckon among, number among; refer to; place under, arrange under, take into account.

Adj. inclusive, included, including; comprehensive, sweeping, all-embracing.

77. EXCLUSION [from a class].—*N.* exclusion, rejection; *see* exclusion (*from a compound*), 55.

78. GENERALITY.—*N.* generality, universality, catholicity, miscellany, miscellaneousness; common run, prevalence, rifeness.

everyone, everybody, all hands [*colloq.*], all the world and his wife [*humorous*], anybody.

V. be general, prevail.

render general, spread, broaden, universalize, generalize.

Adj. general, generic, collective; current, wide, broad, comprehensive, sweeping; encyclopedic, panoramic; widespread, etc. (*dispersed*), 73; common, prevalent, prevailing, rife, epidemic.

universal, catholic, world-wide.

every, all, unspecified, miscellaneous, indefinite.

Adv. generally, always, in general, generally speaking; for the most part.

79. SPECIALTY.—*N.* specialty, speciality, individuality, peculiarity; personality, characteristic, mannerism, idiosyncrasy, singularity, originality; trait, distinctive feature.

particulars, details, items, counts; minutiæ.

V. specify, particularize; individualize, specialize; designate, determine; denote, indicate, point out, select, differentiate; itemize, enter into detail.

Adj. special, especial, particular, individual, specific, proper, personal, original, private, respective, definite, minute, certain, peculiar, marked, appropriate, characteristic, exclusive, restricted; singular, exceptional; typical, representative.

Adv. each, apiece, one by one, severally, respectively, in detail.

namely, that is to say, viz.; to wit.

80. RULE.—*N.* regularity, uniformity, constancy, clockwork precision; punctuality, etc. (*exactness*), 494; even tenor, rut; system; routine, custom; formula; canon, convention, maxim, rule, regulation; standard, model, precedent; conformity, etc., 82.

law, order of things; normality, normalcy, normal state, ordinary condition, standing order; hard and fast rule.

Adj. regular, uniform, symmetrical, constant, steady; according to rule, etc., 82; normal, habitual, customary, etc., 613; methodical, orderly, systematic.

81. MULTIFORMITY.—*N.* multiformity, variety, diversity.

Adj. multiform, multifold, multifarious, multiplex; manifold, many-sided; protean, heterogeneous, motley, mosaic.

indiscriminate, irregular, diversified, diverse; of every description.

82. CONFORMITY.—_N._ **conformity,** observance; conventionality, etc. (_custom_), 613; agreement, accord.

example, instance, exemplification, illustration, specimen, sample.

conventionalist, formalist, bromide [_slang_], Philistine.

_V._ **conform to,** adapt oneself to.

be regular, travel in a rut; obey rules; agree with, comply with, fall in with; be guided by, harmonize, conventionalize, follow the fashion; do at Rome as the Romans do; swim with the stream.

exemplify, illustrate, cite, quote.

Adj. **conformable to rule,** adaptable, consistent, agreeable, compliant; regular, etc., 80; according to rule, well regulated, orderly, uniform, symmetric.

conventional, etc. (_customary_), 613; ordinary, common, habitual, usual; strict, rigid, uncompromising.

typical, normal, formal; canonical, orthodox, exemplary, illustrative, in point.

Adv. **conformably,** by rule; in accordance with, in keeping with; according to; as usual, as a matter of course.

invariably, etc. (_uniformly_), 16.

83. UNCONFORMITY.—_N._ **nonconformity,** unconformity, nonobservance, unconventionality, informality; anomaly, anomalousness, exception, peculiarity; breach _or_ violation of custom; eccentricity, oddity, rarity.

individuality, singularity, originality, idiosyncrasy, mannerism.

aberration, irregularity; singularity; exemption; qualification, proviso.

nonconformist, Bohemian, nondescript character, original, freak, prodigy, wonder, miracle, curiosity.

mongrel, half-caste, etc., 41.

outcast, outlaw, Ishmael, pariah.

_V._ **be uncomformable,** leave the beaten path; break (_or_ violate) a law _or_ custom; stretch a point.

Adj. **uncomformable,** exceptional, eccentric; abnormal, unnatural, anomalous, misplaced, out of order, irregular, arbitrary, lawless; informal, stray, eccentric, peculiar, exclusive, egregious.

unusual, unaccustomed, unwonted, uncommon; rare, singular, unique, curious, odd, extraordinary, strange, monstrous; wonderful, etc., 870; remarkable, noteworthy, queer, quaint, nondescript, original, unorthodox, unconventional, Bohemian, unprecedented, unparalleled, unexampled, unheard of; fantastic, newfangled, eccentric, grotesque, bizarre; unfamiliar, outlandish.

heterogeneous, amorphous, mongrel, hybrid; unsymmetric, etc., 243.

Adv. unconformably; except, unless, save.

V. NUMBER

84. NUMBER.—*N.* number, symbol, numeral, figure, cipher, digit, integer, round number: series.

sum, product, total, aggregate, difference.

ratio, proportion, percentage; progression; arithmetical progression.

power, root, exponent, index, logarithm.

85. NUMERATION.—*N.* numeration, numbering; tale, tally, enumeration, reckoning, computation, calculation, calculus; measurement, etc., 466; statistics.

arithmetic, algebra, differential calculus, calculus of differences.

muster, poll, census, roll call; account, etc. (*list*), 86.

Instruments: abacus, calculating machine, adding machine, cash register.

arithmetician, calculator, algebraist, geometrician, trigonometrician, mathematician, actuary, statistician.

V. number, count, enumerate; call over, run over; take an account of, call the roll, muster, poll; sum up, cast up; tell off, cipher, reckon, reckon up, estimate, compute, calculate.

check, prove, demonstrate, balance, audit, overhaul, take stock.

total, amount to, come to.

Adj. numeral, numerical; arithmetical, analytic, algebraic, statistical, computable, calculable, commensurable, commensurate.

86. LIST.—*N.* list, catalogue, card index; inventory, schedule; register, etc. (*record*), 551; account; bill, bill of costs; tally, file, index, table, contents; book, ledger; synopsis, syllabus; scroll, screed, invoice, manifest, bill of lading; prospectus, program; bill of fare, menu; score, bulletin, census, statistics, returns; directory, atlas, gazetteer; calendar, almanac.

dictionary, lexicon, glossary, vocabulary, wordbook, thesaurus.

roll; muster roll; roll of honor; roster, slate, poll, panel.

V. list, enroll, schedule, inventory, register, catalogue, invoice, bill, book, slate, post, docket; empanel, tally, file, index, tabulate, enter, census.

87. UNITY.—*N.* unity, oneness; individuality; unification, etc., 48; completeness, completion.

one, unit; individual.

V. isolate, insulate.

render one; unite, etc. (*join*), 43, (*combine*), 48.

Adj. **one**, sole, lone, single, solitary; individual, apart, alone; unaccompanied, unattended, singlehanded; singular, odd, unique, isolated; insular.

88. ACCOMPANIMENT.—*N.* accompaniment, adjunct, accessory; context; appendage, appurtenance; attribute.

company, association, partnership; companionship.

attendant, companion, associate, colleague, partner; consort, spouse; satellite, hanger-on, shadow; escort, suite, train, retinue, convoy, follower, etc., 65.

V. **accompany**, attend, convoy, chaperon; associate with, couple with.

Adj. **accompanying**, fellow, twin, joint; associated with, coupled with; accessory, attendant.

Adv. **with**, withal; together with, along with, in company with; therewith, herewith; and, etc. (*addition*), 37.

together, in a body, collectively, in conjunction.

89. DUALITY.—*N.* duality, dualism; duplicity; polarity.

two, deuce, couple, couplet, both, twain, brace, pair, twins, Castor and Pollux, gemini, fellows; yoke, span; distich.

V. **pair**, mate, couple, bracket, yoke.

Adj. **two**, twain, both; dual, twin; duplex, etc., 90; tête-à-tête.

90. DUPLICATION.—*N.* duplication, doubling, reduplication, iteration, etc. (*repetition*), 104; renewal.

duplicate, facsimile, copy, replica, counterpart, etc. (*copy*), 21.

V. **double**; redouble, reduplicate; repeat, etc., 104; renew, renovate.

Adj. **double**; doubled; twofold, two-sided, duplex; double-faced, double-headed; twin, duplicate, second; dual.

Adv. **twice**, once more; over again, etc. (*repeatedly*), 104.

91. [Division into two parts] BISECTION.—*N.* bisection, halving, bifurcation, forking, branching, ramification, dichotomy.

half, moiety.

V. **bisect**, halve, divide, separate, split, cut in two, cleave.

fork, bifurcate, branch off *or* out, ramify.

Adj. **bisected**, cloven, cleft; bifurcated; semi-, demi-, hemi-.

92. TRIALITY.—*N.* triality [*rare*], trinity,[1] triunity.

three, triad, triplet, trio; triangle, trident, tripod, trireme, triumvirate.

third power, cube.

Adj. **three**; triform, tertiary.

93. TRIPLICATION.—*N.* triplication, triplicity; trilogy.

V. **treble**, triple; cube.

Adj. **treble**, triple; threefold; third.

[1]*Trinity* is hardly ever used except in a theological sense; *see* Deity, 976.

Adv. **three times,** thrice; in the third place, thirdly; threefold, triply, trebly.

94. [**Division into three parts**] **TRISECTION.**—*N.* trisection, tripartition, third, third part.

V. **trisect,** divide into three parts, third.

95. **QUATERNITY.**—*N.* quaternity [*rare*], four, quartet, quadruplet; square, quadrilateral; quadrangle.

V. **square,** biquadrate, reduce to a square.

Adj. **four;** quadratic; quadrangular, quadrilateral.

96. **QUADRUPLICATION.**—*N.* quadruplication.

V. **quadruplicate,** multiply by four.

Adj. **fourfold,** quadruple; fourth.

Adv. **four times,** in the fourth place, fourthly.

97. [**Division into four parts**] **QUADRISECTION.**—*N.* quadrisection, quadripartition; quartering; fourth; quart, quarter; farthing; quarto.

V. **quarter,** divide into four parts, quadrisect.

98. **FIVE, ETC.**—*N.* **five,** quintet, pentagon, pentameter.

six, half a dozen; hexagon, hexameter, sextet.

seven, heptagon, heptameter, heptarchy.

eight, octave, octagon, octameter, octavo, octet.

nine, nonagon.

ten, decade, decagon, decasyllable, decemvir, decemvirate, decennium.

twelve, dozen; **thirteen,** long dozen, baker's dozen; **twenty,** score; **fifty,** half a hundred; **sixty,** threescore; **seventy,** threescore and ten; **eighty,** fourscore; **ninety,** fourscore and ten.

hundred, centenary, century; bicentenary, tercentenary.

thousand, millennium; myriad.

V. **quintuplicate,** sextuple; centuplicate.

Adj. **five,** fifth, quintuple; pentangular, pentagonal. **sixth,** sextuple, hexagonal, hexangular. **seventh,** septuple, heptagonal, heptangular. **eight,** octuple, octagonal, octangular. **tenth,** tenfold, decimal, decagonal, decasyllabic. **eleventh,** undecennial, undecennary. **twelfth,** duodenary, duodenal. **sixtieth,** sexagesimal. **seventieth,** septuagesimal.

centuple, centuplicate, centennial, centenary; hundredth; thousandth, millenary, millennial, etc.

99. **QUINQUESECTION, ETC.**—*N.* **quinquesection,** division by five, etc., 98; decimation; tithe; fifth, etc.

Adj. **decimal,** tenth; duodecimal, twelfth; sexagesimal, sexagenary; hundredth, centesimal; millesimal, etc.

100. [**More than one**] **PLURALITY.**—*N.* **plurality,** one or two, two or three, etc.; a few, several; multitude, etc., 102; majority.

Adj. **plural,** more than one, upwards of, some, certain.

100a. [**Less than one**] **FRACTION.**—*N.* **fraction,** fractional part; part, portion, fragment, etc., 51.

Adj. **fractional,** fragmentary, inconsiderable, partial.

101. ZERO.—*N.* **zero,** nothing; naught, nought; cipher; none, nobody.

102. MULTITUDE.—*N.* **multitude,** multitudinousness, multiplicity; profusion, etc. (*plenty*), 639; legion, host, array, army, galaxy; numbers, scores; heap, power, sight, lot, lots [*all five colloq.*], swarm, bevy, cloud, flock, herd, drove, shoal, school, flight, covey, hive, brood, litter, farrow, fry, nest; mob, crowd, etc. (*assemblage*), 72.

V. **be numerous,** swarm with, teem with, be alive with, crowd, swarm, outnumber, multiply; people.

Adj. **many,** several, sundry, various, alive with; numerous; profuse, manifold, multitudinous, teeming, populous, outnumbering, crowded, thick, galore [*colloq.*]; thick-coming, endless, etc. (*infinite*), 105.

103. FEWNESS.—*N.* **fewness,** paucity, scarcity, sparseness, sparsity; handful; small quantity, etc., 32; rarity, infrequency; minority.

Diminution of number: reduction, weeding, elimination; decimation; eradication.

V. **render few,** reduce, diminish, weed out, eliminate, thin, decimate.

Adj. **few,** scant, scanty; thin, rare, scarce, sparse, few and far between; exiguous; infrequent.

104. REPETITION.—*N.* **repetition,** iteration, recapitulation, reiteration; monotone; duplication, reduplication, monotony, harping, recurrence; reappearance, reproduction; periodicity, etc., 138; succession, run; alliteration; rhythm, tautology; diffuseness, redundancy.

echo, encore, burden of a song, refrain, undersong.

cuckoo, etc. (*imitation*), 19; reverberation, vibration, resonance; drumming, etc. (*roll*), 407; renewal, etc. (*restoration*), 660.

V. **repeat,** iterate, reiterate, redouble, reproduce, echo, re-echo, drum, harp upon, hammer; rehearse; resume, return to, recapitulate.

recur, revert, return, reappear; renew, etc. (*restore*), 660.
duplicate, reduplicate.

Adj. **repeated,** repetitious, recurrent, recurring; frequent, incessant; redundant, tautological; another.

monotonous, harping, iterative, unvaried; habitual, etc., 613.
aforesaid, aforenamed; said.

Adv. **repeatedly,** often, again, anew, afresh, once more; ditto, encore, again and again; over and over, frequently, etc., 136.

105. INFINITY.—*N.* infinity, infinitude, infiniteness; perpetuity, immortality; inexhaustibility, immensity, boundlessness.

V. **be infinite,** have no limits (*or* bounds), go on forever.

Adj. **infinite,** immense; numberless, countless, measureless, innumerable, immeasurable, incalculable, illimitable, interminable, unfathomable; without limit, without end, limitless, endless, boundless; untold, unnumbered, unmeasured, unbounded, unlimited; perpetual, etc., 112.

VI. TIME

106. TIME.—*N.* time, duration; period, term, stage, space, span, spell, snap, season; course.

intermediate time, while, interim, interval; intermission, interregnum, interlude; respite.

era, epoch, eon, cycle, age, reign, dynasty, administration.

V. **continue,** last, endure, stay, go on, remain, persist, abide, stand, stick [*colloq.*], hold out; intervene; elapse, etc., 109.

pass time, spend *or* while away time, tide over; employ time; seize an opportunity; linger on, drag on; tarry, etc., 110; waste time, etc. (*be inactive*), 683; procrastinate, etc., 133.

Adj. **permanent,** etc. (*durable*), 110; timely, opportune, seasonable.

Adv. **while,** whilst, during; in the course of; in the time of; when; meantime, meanwhile, in the meantime, in the interim; from day to day; for a time, for a season; till, until, up to, yet; the whole time, all the time; throughout; for good, permanently, always.

then, hereupon, thereupon, whereupon.

107. Absence of time.—*N.* no time.

Adv. **never,** ne'er; at no time, at no period; on no occasion, nevermore.

108. [Definite duration or portion of time] PERIOD.—*N.* period; octave, semester, quarter, moon, year, decennial, decennium; decade, lifetime, generation; epoch, era, century, age, millennium.

109. [Indefinite duration] COURSE.—*N.* corridors (*or* sweep, vista, halls, progress, process, lapse, flow, tide, march, flight) of time; duration, etc., 106.

Indefinite time: eon, age.

V. **elapse,** lapse, flow, run, proceed, advance, pass; fly, slip, slide, glide; crawl, drag; expire, go by, pass by, be past.

Adv. **in time,** in due time (*or* season, course); in course of time, in the fullness of time.

110. [Long duration] DURABILITY.—*N.* durability, durableness, permanence, continuance, persistence, lastingness, standing; immutability, stability; survival; longevity, etc. (*age*), 128; delay, etc. (*lateness*), 133; slowness.

an age, a long time, eon, century, an eternity; perpetuity, etc., 112.

V. **last,** endure, stand, remain, abide, continue, etc., 106.

tarry, etc., 133; drag on, protract, prolong; spin out, eke out, draw out; temporize, gain time.

outlast, outlive, survive.

Adj. **permanent,** durable, lasting; chronic, long-standing; persistent; lifelong, livelong; endless, fixed, long-lived, perennial; perpetual, etc., 112.

prolonged, protracted, spun out; lingering, long-winded; slow, etc., 275.

Adv. **long,** for a long time; long ago, etc. (*in a past time*), 122; all the day long, the livelong day; all the year round; permanently.

111. [Short duration] TRANSIENCE.—*N.* transience, transiency, evanescence, impermanence; changeableness, etc., 149; mortality; span; nine days' wonder, bubble; interregnum, interim.

velocity, etc., 274; suddenness, abruptness.

V. **be transient,** flit, pass away, fly, gallop, vanish, sink, melt, fade, evaporate.

Adj. **transient,** transitory, passing, evanescent, fleeting, fugitive; temporal, temporary, provisional, provisory; cursory; short-lived, ephemeral; deciduous; perishable, mortal; precarious; impermanent.

brief, quick, brisk, fleet; meteoric, volatile, summary; pressed for time, etc. (*haste*), 684; sudden, momentary, spasmodic, instantaneous.

Adv. **temporarily,** for the moment, for a time; awhile, soon, etc. (*early*), 132; briefly.

112. [Endless duration] PERPETUITY.—*N.* perpetuity, eternity, aye; immortality, perpetuation.

V. **eternalize,** immortalize, eternize, perpetuate.

Adj. **perpetual,** eternal, everlasting, continual, endless, unending; ceaseless, incessant, uninterrupted, unceasing; interminable; unfading, never-ending, deathless, immortal, undying, imperishable.

Adv. **perpetually,** always, ever, evermore, aye; forever, in all ages, without end, to the end of time; till doomsday; constantly, etc. (*very frequently*), 136.

113. [Point of time] **INSTANTANEITY.**—*N.* instantaneity, instantaneousness; suddenness, abruptness.

moment, instant, second, twinkling, flash, breath.

V. be instantaneous; flash.

Adj. instantaneous, momentary, extempore, sudden, abrupt.

Adv. instantaneously, in no time; presto, instanter, in a trice, in a jiffy [*colloq.*], suddenly, in the same breath; at once, plump; immediately, etc. (*early*), 132; extempore, on the spur of the moment; slapdash, etc. (*haste*), 684.

114. [Estimation, measurement, and record of time] **CHRONOMETRY.**—*N.* chronometry, chronology, horology.

almanac, calendar; register, registry; chronicle, annals, journal, diary.

timekeeper, clock, watch, repeater; chronometer, timepiece; dial, sundial, hourglass.

V. register, date, chronicle; measure time, beat time, mark time.

Adj. chronologic *or* chronological, temporal.

115. [False estimate of time] **ANACHRONISM.**—*N.* anachronism, error in time, error in chronology, misdate; anticipation; disregard (*or* neglect, oblivion) of time.

V. misdate; antedate, postdate, anticipate; take no note of time.

Adj. misdated; undated; overdue; out of date, anachronistic, behind time, ahead of time.

116. PRIORITY.—*N.* priority, predecessor, precedence, preexistence; precursor, antecedent, forerunner; the past, etc., 122.

V. precede, come before; pre-exist, forerun; go before, lead, head; presage, herald, usher in, introduce, announce.

be beforehand, etc. (*be early*), 132; anticipate, forestall.

Adj. prior, previous, preceding, anterior, antecedent; preexistent; former, aforementioned, foregoing, before-mentioned, aforesaid, said; introductory, etc. (*precursory*), 64.

Adv. before, prior to; earlier; previously, ere, already, yet, beforehand; on the eve of.

117. POSTERIORITY.—*N.* posteriority; succession, sequence; following, continuance, prolongation; futurity, future; successor; sequel, etc., 65; remainder.

V. follow after, pursue, come after, go after; succeed, supervene; ensue, result.

Adj. subsequent, posterior, following, after, later, succeeding, successive, ensuing, posthumous; future, etc., 121; after-dinner.

Adv. subsequently, after, afterward, since, later; next, close upon, thereafter, thereupon.

118. PRESENT TIME.—*N.* the present time, the present juncture *or* occasion; the times, time being; twentieth century.

Adj. present, actual, instant, current, latest, existing.

Adv. at this time, at this moment, etc., 113; now, at present; today, nowadays; already; even now, but now, just now; for the time being.

119. DIFFERENT TIME.—*N.* different time, other time.

Adv. then, at that time (*or* moment, instant); on that occasion. when; whenever, whensoever; whereupon, upon which; at various times.

once, formerly, once upon a time.

120. SIMULTANEOUSNESS.—*N.* simultaneousness, synchronism, coexistence, coincidence, concurrence.

contemporary, coeval.

V. coexist, concur, accompany, keep pace with; synchronize.

Adj. simultaneous, coexisting, coincident, synchronous, concomitant, concurrent; coeval; contemporary, contemporaneous.

Adv. simultaneously, together, in concert; in the same breath.

121. THE FUTURE.—*N.* future, futurity, hereafter, time to come; morrow, tomorrow, by and by, doomsday, day of judgment, crack of doom.

approach of time, advent; destiny, etc., 152.

heritage, heirs, posterity, descendants.

prospect, anticipation, expectation; foresight, etc., 510.

V. anticipate, expect, await, foresee; forestall, etc. (*be early*), 132.

approach, await, threaten; impend, etc. (*be destined*), 152; come on, draw near.

Adj. future, to come; coming, impending, overhanging, imminent; next, near, close at hand; eventual, ulterior; prospective, in prospect.

Adv. prospectively, hereafter, in future; in course of time, eventually, ultimately, sooner or later.

soon, early; on the eve of, on the point of, about to.

122. THE PAST.—*N.* the past, past time, days of yore, days of old, times past, former times, yesterday, the olden time; retrospection, memory, priority.

antiquity, antiqueness, time immemorial, history, remote time; remote past; paleontology, archeology, antiquarianism.

antiquary, antiquarian, archeologist.

ancestry, lineage, forefathers.

V. pass, lapse, blow over.

Adj. past, gone, gone by, over, passed away, bygone, elapsed,

lapsed, expired, extinct, exploded, forgotten, irrecoverable; obsolete, antiquated, outworn.

former, pristine, quondam, late; ancestral.

foregoing, last, latter; recent.

looking back, retrospective, retroactive; archeological.

Adv. formerly, of old, of yore, time was, ago; anciently, long ago; lately, latterly, of late; ere now, before now, hitherto, heretofore; already, yet, up to this time.

123. NEWNESS.—*N.* newness, novelty; youth, juvenility, immaturity.

innovation; renovation, restoration.

upstart, *nouveau riche* [F.], parvenu.

modernism, modernness, modernity; modernization; latest fashion.

V. renew, renovate; rejuvenate; modernize.

Adj. new, novel, recent, fresh, green; young, etc., 127; raw, immature; virgin, untried; modern, late; newborn, new-fashioned, newfangled, newfledged; just out [*colloq.*], unhandled; brand-new, up-to-date [*colloq.*], renovated, spick-and-span.

Adv. newly, afresh, anew, lately, just now, latterly, of late.

124. OLDNESS.—*N.* oldness, age, antiquity.

maturity, matureness, ripeness.

decline, decay; senility, superannuation, dotage.

archaism, antiquarianism; thing of the past, relic of the past.

tradition, custom, immemorial usage, common law; folklore.

V. be old, have had its day, have seen its day.

become old, age, fade.

Adj. old, ancient, antique; time-honored, venerable, hoary; elder, eldest; firstborn; senile, etc., 128.

primitive, prime, primeval, aboriginal; antediluvian, prehistoric, dateless, patriarchal, archaic, classic, medieval; ancestral.

immemorial, traditional, unwritten, inveterate, rooted.

antiquated, of other times, of the old school, old world; obsolete, out-of-date, out-of-fashion, gone by, stale, old-fashioned, exploded, extinct, timeworn, crumbling, secondhand.

125. MORNING. [Noon]—*N.* morning, morn, forenoon, antemeridian, A.M., prime, dawn, daybreak; dayspring, peep of day, break of day, aurora, sunrise, daylight, cockcrow.

noon, midday, noonday, noontide, meridian, prime; nooning, noontime.

spring, springtide, springtime, seedtime; vernal equinox.

summer, summertide, summertime, midsummer.

Adj. matin, matutinal.

noon, noonday, midday.

spring, vernal.
summer, estival.
126. EVENING. [Midnight]—*N.* evening, eve, decline of day,
close of day, eventide, vespers, nightfall, curfew, dusk, gloaming,
twilight, sunset, sundown, bedtime.
afternoon, post meridiem [L.], P.M.
midnight; dead of night, witching time.
autumn, fall; harvesttime; autumnal equinox; Indian summer.
winter.
Adj. vesper, nightly, nocturnal; autumnal.
wintry, winterly.
127. YOUTH.—*N.* youth; juvenility; infancy, babyhood; childhood; boyhood, girlhood; rising generation; minority, immaturity, teens, tender age, bloom.
cradle, nursery.
flower of life, springtide of life, seedtime of life, golden season of
life; heyday of youth, school days.
Adj. young, youthful, juvenile, green, callow, sappy, beardless,
underage, in one's teens; younger, junior; newfledged, unfledged,
unripe.
128. AGE.—*N.* age; oldness, old age, advanced age, senility,
years, gray hairs, declining years, decrepitude, superannuation,
second childhood, dotage; vale of years, decline of life; green old
age, ripe age; longevity.
seniority, eldership, primogeniture; elders, etc. (*veteran*), 130;
dean, father.
V. age, grow old, decline, wane.
Adj. aged; old, etc., 124; elderly, senile; ripe, mellow, declining,
waning, past one's prime; gray, gray-headed, hoar, hoary, venerable, patriarchal, timeworn, antiquated, effete, decrepit, superannuated; advanced in life (*or* years); stricken in years; doting,
etc. (*imbecile*), 499.
older, elder, oldest, eldest; senior; firstborn.
129. INFANT.—*N.* infant, babe, baby; nursling, suckling.
child, tot, mite, chick, kid [*slang*], little one, brat, pickaninny
[*colored child*], urchin, elf.
youth, boy, lad, laddie, slip, sprig, stripling, youngster, cub,
whippersnapper [*colloq.*], schoolboy, hobbledehoy, young hopeful,
cadet, minor.
girl, lass, lassie, wench, damsel; maid, maiden, virgin; nymph,
colleen, flapper, minx, schoolgirl; hoyden, tomboy, romp.
Adj. infantile, infantine, puerile, boyish, girlish, childish,
babyish, kittenish; boylike, girllike, newborn; young, etc., 127.
130. VETERAN.—*N.* veteran, old man, patriarch, graybeard;

grandfather, sexagenarian, octogenarian, nonagenarian, centenarian; Methuselah; elders, forefathers; dotard, etc., 501.

granny, crone, hag, beldam.

Adj. veteran; aged, etc., 128.

131. ADOLESCENCE.—*N.* adolescence, majority, adulthood, womanhood, manhood, virility; flower of age; full bloom; spring of life.

man, etc., 373; woman, etc., 374; adult.

middle age, maturity, full age, prime of life, meridian of life.

V. come of age, come to man's estate, come to years of discretion; attain majority; come out [*colloq.*].

Adj. adolescent, pubescent, of age, of full age, of ripe age; out of one's teens, grown up, full-grown, manly, manlike, virile, adult; womanly; marriageable.

middle-aged, mature, in one's prime; matronly.

132. EARLINESS.—*N.* earliness, punctuality, promptitude, readiness, expedition, quickness, haste, etc. (*velocity*), 274; suddenness.

prematurity, precocity, precipitation, anticipation.

V. be early, be beforehand.

anticipate, forestall, take time by the forelock, steal a march upon; bespeak, secure, engage, pre-engage.

accelerate, expedite, etc. (*quicken*), 274; make haste, etc. (*hurry*), 684.

Adj. early, timely, seasonable, punctual, forward; prompt, etc. (*active*), 682.

premature, precipitate, precocious, anticipatory.

sudden, instantaneous, immediate; unexpected, etc., 508.

imminent, impending, near.

Adv. early, soon, anon, betimes, ere long, before long; punctually, in time; on time, on the dot [*slang*].

beforehand; prematurely, too soon; precipitately, hastily; in anticipation; unexpectedly, unawares.

suddenly, etc. (*instantaneously*), 113; at short notice, extempore; on the spur of the moment, at once; on the spot, on the instant, at sight, offhand, straight, straightway; forthwith, immediately, quickly, speedily, apace; presently, by and by, directly.

133. LATENESS.—*N.* lateness; tardiness, etc. (*slowness*), 275.

delay, procrastination, postponement, adjournment, prorogation, retardation; protraction, prolongation; moratorium; aftertime; respite, truce, reprieve, stop, stay, suspension, remand.

V. be late, tarry, wait, stay, bide, take time; dawdle, etc. (*be inactive*), 683; linger, loiter, gain time; hang fire; stand over, lie over; hang.

put off, defer, delay, lay over, suspend; stave off; retard, postpone, adjourn, prorogue, procrastinate; dally, prolong, protract, spin out, draw out, table, lay on the table, shelve; reserve, temporize, filibuster, stall [*slang*].

be kept waiting, dance attendance; cool one's heels [*colloq.*]; await, expect, wait for.

Adj. late, tardy, dilatory; slow, leisurely, behindhand, backward, unpunctual; overdue, belated, delayed; posthumous.

Adv. late; backward, at the eleventh hour, at length, at last; ultimately; behind time; too late.

slowly, deliberately, at one's leisure.

134. TIMELINESS.—*N.* timeliness, opportunity, opening, occasion, show [*colloq.*]; suitable time *or* season, high time; nick of time; golden opportunity, clear stage, fair field; spare time, leisure.

crisis, turn, emergency, juncture, conjuncture; turning point.

V. improve the occasion; seize an opportunity; use (*or* profit by) an opportunity; give (*or* grant) an opportunity; suit the occasion, etc. (*be expedient*), 646; strike the iron while it is hot, make hay while the sun shines.

Adj. timely, well timed, opportune, seasonable; appropriate, suitable.

lucky, providential, fortunate, happy, favorable, propitious, auspicious.

occasional, accidental, extemporaneous, extemporary; contingent, provisional.

Adv. opportunity, in due time; for the nonce; in the nick of time, just in time; at the eleventh hour, now or never.

by the way, by the by; while on this subject, speaking of; extempore; on the spur of the moment.

135. UNTIMELINESS.—*N.* untimeliness, unseasonableness, unsuitable time, improper time; evil hour; intrusion; anachronism.

V. be ill-timed, mistime, intrude, come amiss, break in upon; be busy, be occupied, be engaged.

lose an opportunity; neglect an opportunity; allow *or* suffer the opportunity to pass (*or* slip, go by, escape); waste time; let slip through the fingers.

Adj. ill-timed, mistimed, ill-fated, ill-omened, ill-starred; untimely, unseasonable, out of season; inopportune, inconvenient, untoward, unlucky, inauspicious, unpropitious, unfortunate, unfavorable, unsuited; inexpedient.

unpunctual, etc. (*late*), 133; premature, etc. (*early*), 132.

136. FREQUENCY.—*N.* frequency, repetition, iteration, reiteration.

V. **keep on**; reiterate, repeat, recur, etc., 104; do nothing but.

Adj. **frequent**, not rare, thick-coming, incessant, perpetual, continual, constant, habitual, etc., 613.

Adv. **often**, oft, ofttimes, frequently; repeatedly, in quick succession; daily, every day; habitually, commonly.

perpetually, continually, constantly, incessantly, at all times.

sometimes, occasionally, at times, now and then, again and again.

137. INFREQUENCY.—*N.* **infrequency**, infrequence, rarity; uncommonness.

Adj. **infrequent**, uncommon, sporadic; rare, few, scant, scarce; unprecedented.

Adv. **seldom**, rarely, scarcely, hardly; not often, infrequently, uncommonly, sparsely, scarcely ever, hardly ever.

138. REGULARITY [of recurrence].—*N.* **periodicity**, intermittence; oscillation, vibration; beat, pulse, pulsation; rhythm, alternation; round, revolution, rotation, regularity, bout, turn; routine; cycle.

anniversary, biennial, triennial, quadrennial, quinquennial, sextennial, septennial, octennial, decennial; tricennial, jubilee, centennial, centenary, bicentennial, bicentenary, tercentenary; birthday, natal day, fete day, saint's day, feast, festival, fast, holiday.

Christmas, Yuletide, New Year's Day, Ash Wednesday, Maundy Thursday, Good Friday, Easter; Halloween, All Saints' Day; All Souls' Day; Candlemas; Memorial *or* Decoration Day, Independence Day, Labor Day, Thanksgiving, ground-hog day, woodchuck day, leap year, St. Swithin's Day, Midsummer Day; May Day.

V. **return**, revolve, recur, come round again; beat, pulsate; alternate; intermit.

Adj. **periodic**, periodical; serial, recurrent, cyclic, cyclical, rhythmic, recurring, intermittent; alternate, every other; every.

regular, steady, constant, methodical, punctual.

Adv. **by turns**, in turn, in rotation, alternately, off and on, round and round.

139. IRREGULARITY [of recurrence].—*N.* **irregularity**, uncertainty, unpunctuality; fitfulness, capriciousness.

Adj. **irregular**, uncertain, unpunctual, capricious, erratic, desultory, fitful, flickering; rambling, spasmodic; unmethodical, unsystematic, unequal, uneven, variable.

Adv. **by fits and starts**.

VII. CHANGE

140. CHANGE.—*N.* **change**, alteration, mutation, permutation, variation, modification, modulation, inflection, mood, qualification, innovation, deviation, shift, turn; diversion, variety, break.

conversion, etc. (*gradual change*), 144; revolution, etc., 146; inversion, reversal; displacement, transposition, removal, transference.

transformation, metamorphosis, transfiguration, transmutation; transubstantiation; transmigration, metempsychosis; avatar.

changeableness, etc., 149.

V. change, alter, vary, modulate, diversify, qualify, tamper with; turn, shift, veer, jibe, jib, tack, chop, warp, swerve, deviate, dodge; turn aside; take a turn, turn the corner.

modify, work a change, patch, piece, transform, transfigure, transmute, convert, revolutionize; metamorphose, ring the changes; innovate, introduce new blood, shuffle the cards; shift the scene, turn over a new leaf.

recast, remodel; reverse, etc., 218; convert into, etc., 144.

Adj. changed, newfangled; changeable, changeful, variable, devious, transitional.

141. PERMANENCE.—*N.* permanence, fixity, persistence, endurance; durability; standing, *status quo* [L.]; maintenance, preservation, conservation; conservatism; stability, constancy; quiescence, etc., 265; obstinacy, inflexibility.

V. endure, persist, remain, stay, tarry, rest, hold, last, bide, abide, dwell, maintain, keep; stand fast, subsist, live, outlive, survive; hold one's ground (*or* footing).

Adj. permanent, stable, fixed, settled, established, irremovable, durable; unchanged, intact, inviolate; persistent; conservative; unfailing, unfading.

Adv. for good, at a stand, at a standstill, as you were!

142. CESSATION.—*N.* cessation, discontinuance; intermission, remission; suspense, suspension; interruption; stop; hitch [*colloq.*]; stoppage, halt.

pause, rest, lull, respite, truce, armistice, stay; interregnum. In debate: closure, cloture.

deadlock, checkmate, dead center, dead stand, dead stop; end. punctuation: comma, semicolon, colon, period, full stop; cæsura

V. cease, discontinue, desist, stay; break off, leave off; hold, stop, pull up, stop short; check, stick, hang fire; halt, pause, rest, come to a stand; arrive, etc., 292; go out, die away, wear away, pass away, lapse; be at an end.

have done with, give over; give up, etc. (*relinquish*), 624.

interrupt, suspend, intermit, remit; put an end to, bring to a stand (*or* standstill), stop, cut short, arrest.

143. CONTINUANCE [in action].—*N.* continuance, continuation; pursuance, maintenance, extension, perpetuation, prolongation; persistence, perseverance; repetition.

V. **continue,** persist, go on, keep on, hold on; abide, pursue; stick to; maintain its course; keep up, drag on, stick [*colloq.*], persevere, endure, carry on; keep the field, keep the ball rolling.

sustain, uphold, hold up, follow up, perpetuate, prolong, maintain; preserve.

Adj. **continuing,** uninterrupted, unvarying, persistent, unceasing, unvaried, sustained, chronic; undying, immortal, perpetual.

144. [Gradual change to something different] CONVERSION. —*N.* **conversion,** reduction, transmutation, assimilation; chemistry, alchemy; growth, progress; naturalization; transportation.

passage, transit, transition, transmigration; shifting, flux; phase.

convert, neophyte, proselyte; pervert, renegade, apostate, turncoat.

V. **be converted into;** become, turn to *or* into; turn out, lapse, shift; pass into, grow into, merge into; melt, grow, wax, mature, mellow.

convert into, resolve into; make, render; mold, form, remodel, reform, reorganize; bring to, reduce to.

145. REVERSION.—*N.* **reversion,** return; revulsion; turning point, turn of the tide; alternation, rotation; inversion, etc., 218; recoil, reaction; retrospection, retrogression; restoration, relapse, atavism, throwback.

V. **revert,** reverse, return, turn back; relapse; invert; recoil; retreat; restore; undo, unmake; turn the scale.

146. [Sudden or violent change] REVOLUTION.—*N.* **revolution,** revolt; breakup; destruction, etc., 162; clean sweep, debacle, overturn, overthrow, rebellion, rising, uprising, mutiny, counter-revolution, bolshevism.

spasm, convulsion, throe, revulsion; earthquake, eruption, upheaval, cataclysm, explosion.

V. **revolutionize,** revolt, rebel, rise; remodel, recast.

Adj. **revolutionary,** catastrophic, cataclysmic, cataclysmal, insurgent, Red, insurrectionary, mutinous, rebellious; bolshevistic *or* bolshevik.

147. [Change of one thing for another] SUBSTITUTION.—*N.* **substitution,** commutation, supplanting.

substitute, scapegoat; alternative; makeshift, temporary expedient, shift, apology, stopgap; alternate; dummy, double; changeling; representative, deputy.

price, purchase money, consideration, equivalent.

V. **substitute,** put in the place of, change for, give place to; take the place of, supplant, supersede, replace, cut out [*colloq.*]; commute, redeem, compound for.

Adj. substituted, vicarious.

Adv. instead; by proxy; in place of, in lieu of.

148. [Double or mutual change] INTERCHANGE.—*N.* interchange, exchange; commutation, permutation; transposition, shuffle; alternation, reciprocity; swap [*colloq.*], barter, exchange; retaliation, reprisal; retort, requital, cross fire.

V. interchange, exchange, bandy, barter, transpose, swap [*colloq.*], reciprocate, commute; give and take, retaliate; retort; requite.

Adj. reciprocal, mutual; interchangeable.

international, interstate, interurban, interdenominational; interscholastic, intercollegiate.

Adv. in exchange, vice versa, conversely, by turns, turn about.

149. CHANGEABLENESS.—*N.* changeableness, mutability, inconstancy; versatility, mobility; instability, vacillation, irresolution, indecision; fluctuation, vicissitude; alternation, oscillation.

Comparisons: moon, kaleidoscope, chameleon, quicksilver, shifting sands, weathercock, vane, weathervane, harlequin, turncoat; wheel of fortune.

restlessness, fidgets, disquiet; disquietude, unrest; agitation, etc., 315.

V. fluctuate, vary, waver, flicker, flutter, shift, shuffle, shake, totter, tremble, vacillate, shift to and fro; oscillate, pulsate, vibrate; alternate.

Adj. changeable, changeful; changing, mutable, variable, kaleidoscopic; protean, versatile, mobile.

inconstant, unsteady, unstable, unfixed, unsettled; fluctuating, wavering, vibratory, restless, tremulous; erratic, fickle; mercurial, irresolute, indecisive; capricious, fitful, spasmodic; vagrant, wayward; desultory, transient, etc., 111.

150. STABILITY.—*N.* stability, immutability, unchangeableness, constancy; immobility; soundness, vitality, stabilization; stiffness, solidity; permanence, etc., 141; obstinacy, obduracy.

fixture, establishment; leopard's spots.

standpatter [*politics*].

V. be firm, stick fast; stand firm, remain firm; stand pat [*colloq.*].

establish, settle, fix, set, stabilize; retain, keep hold; make good, make sure; fasten, etc. (*join*), 43; perpetuate.

settle down; strike root, take root.

Adj. unchangeable, immutable; unaltered, unalterable, constant; permanent, persistent, invariable, undeviating; stable, durable, perennial; irretrievable, irrevocable, indissoluble, indestructible, imperishable, indelible.

fixed, steadfast, firm, solid; deep-rooted, ineradicable; fast, steady, confirmed, inveterate; immovable, rooted; settled, stereotyped, established, vested; obstinate, etc., 606; incontrovertible, valid.

stuck fast, transfixed, aground, stranded.

151. PRESENT EVENTS.—*N.* **eventuality,** event, occurrence, incident, affair, transaction, proceeding, fact; phenomenon.

circumstance, particular; happening, adventure; crisis, pass, emergency, contingency; concern, business.

consequence, issue, result, termination, conclusion.

affairs, matters; the world, life, things, doings; the times.

V. **happen,** occur; take place, come to pass, take effect; present itself; fall out, turn out, befall, betide; turn up, crop up, arrive; ensue, result; arise, start; take its course, pass off.

experience; meet with; fall to the lot of; be one's lot; find, encounter; undergo, pass through, go through, endure, bear, suffer, abide, stand, brook.

Adj. **eventful,** stirring, full of incident; memorable, momentous, signal; current, on foot, at issue, in question; incidental.

Adv. **eventually,** ultimately, finally; in the event of, in case.

152. FUTURE EVENTS.—*N.* **destiny,** fatality, fate, lot, doom, fortune; future, future state; future existence, hereafter‧ next world, world to come; life to come; prospect.

V. **impend,** hang over, threaten, loom, await, approach; foreordain, preordain; destine, predestine, doom.

Adj. **impending,** destined; coming, in store, to come, instant, at hand, near, imminent; in the wind, in prospect.

Adv. **in time,** in the long run; all in good time; eventually.

VIII. CAUSATION

153. CAUSE.—*N.* **cause,** origin, source, principle, element; prime mover, ultimate cause; author, producer, creator, determinant; mainspring, agent; leaven; groundwork, foundation, support.

causality, causation; origination; production, etc., 161.

spring, fountain, well; fountainhead, reservoir, wellspring; genesis; derivation; remote cause; influence.

pivot, hinge, turning point; heart, hub, focus.

reason, reason why; ground, occasion; final cause; undercurrents.

rudiment, egg, germ, nucleus, seed.

nest, cradle, nursery, birthplace, hotbed.

V. **cause,** originate, give rise to, occasion, sow the seeds of; bring to pass, bring about; produce; create, develop; set on foot, entail; found, institute.

procure, induce, draw down, superinduce, evoke, elicit, provoke.

contribute, conduce to, have a hand in, influence; determine, decide, turn the scale.

Adj. **causal,** original; primary, originative, generative, productive, creative; formative; radical; in embryo, embryonic.

Adv. **from the beginning,** in the first place; because, etc., 155.

154. EFFECT.—*N.* **effect,** consequence; aftergrowth, afterclap, aftermath; derivative; derivation; result; resultant; upshot, issue, outcome, conclusion; catastrophe, end; development, outgrowth; fruit, crop, harvest, product.

production, work, handiwork, fabric, performance; creature, creation; offspring, offshoot; first fruits.

V. **be the effect of,** be due to, be owing to; originate in *or* from; rise from, spring from, emanate from, come from, issue from, flow from, result from; depend upon, hang upon, hinge upon, turn upon.

Adj. **owing to;** resulting from; due to; caused by; derived from, evolved from; derivative; hereditary.

Adv. **consequently,** it follows that, as a consequence, in consequence; necessarily, eventually.

155. [Assignment of cause] ATTRIBUTION —*N.* **attribution,** theory, assignment, reference to, accounting for; imputation; derivation.

explanation, interpretation, reason why.

V. **attribute to,** ascribe to, impute to, refer to, lay to, trace to; blame; saddle; account for, derive from; theorize.

Adj. **attributed;** attributable, referable; due to; owing to.

Adv. **hence,** thence, therefore, for, since, on account of, because, owing to; forasmuch as; whence.

why? wherefore? whence? how comes it? how is it? how so?

156. [Absence of assignable cause] CHANCE[1].—*N.* **chance,** accident, fortune, hazard, luck, fluke [*cant*], casualty, hit; fate, lottery, tossup [*colloq.*]; throw of the dice; heads or tails, wheel of fortune.

probability, possibility, contingency, odds, run of luck; main chance.

gamble, speculation, gaming, game of chance.

V. **chance,** turn up; fall to one's lot; be one's fate; stumble on, light upon; blunder upon, hit, hit upon.

Adj. **casual,** fortuitous, accidental, chance, haphazard, random, incidental, unintentional, unpremeditated.

---

[1]The word *chance* has two distinct meanings: the first, the absence of assignable *cause*, as above; and the second, the absence of *design*—for the latter see 621.

Adv. **by chance,** by accident; at random, casually; perchance, etc. (*possibly*), 470.

157. POWER.—*N.* **power;** potency, efficacy, puissance, might, energy, vigor, force; ascendancy, sway, almightiness, omnipotence; authority, weight, control; influence, predominance.

ability, competence, efficiency, efficacy; validity, cogency; vantage ground.

capability, capacity: faculty, quality, attribute, endowment, virtue, gift, property, qualification.

V. **empower;** give *or* confer power; invest, endue; endow, arm; strengthen, etc., 159.

electrify, magnetize, energize, galvanize.

Adj. **powerful,** puissant, potent, capable, able; cogent, valid, effective, effectual, efficient, efficacious, adequate, competent; predominant; mighty, omnipotent, almighty.

forcible, energetic; influential; productive.

electric, magnetic, galvanic, dynamic, potential.

Adv. **by virtue of,** by dint of.

158. IMPOTENCE.—*N.* **impotence;** inability, disability. incapacity, incapability; ineptitude; inefficiency, incompetence, disqualification; inefficacy, etc. (*inutility*), 645; failure, etc., 732.

helplessness, prostration, paralysis, collapse, exhaustion, senility, superannuation, decrepitude, imbecility, inanition.

mollycoddle, old woman, milksop, sissy [*colloq.*], mother's darling.

collapse, faint, swoon, drop; go by the board; end in smoke, etc. (*fail*), 732.

render powerless, disable, disarm, incapacitate, disqualify, unfit, invalidate, undermine, deaden, cramp, tie the hands; prostrate, paralyze, muzzle, cripple, maim, lame, throttle, strangle, silence, spike the guns; unhinge, unfit; put out of gear.

unman, unnerve, devitalize, attenuate, enervate.

shatter, exhaust; weaken, enfeeble.

Adj. **powerless,** impotent, helpless; incapable, incompetent, inefficient, ineffective, unfit, unfitted, unqualified, disqualified; crippled, disabled; senile, decrepit, superannuated; paralytic, paralyzed, nerveless, out of joint, out of gear; unnerved, unhinged; done up [*colloq.*], done for [*colloq.*], dead-beat [*colloq.*], exhausted, shattered, prostrate, demoralized, harmless; unarmed, weaponless, defenseless.

nugatory, null and void, inoperative, good for nothing, ineffectual, inadequate, inefficacious, etc. (*useless*), 645.

159. STRENGTH.—*N.* **strength;** power, etc., 157; energy, vigor, force; main (*or* physical, brute) force; spring, elasticity.

vitality, virility, lustihood, stamina, nerve, muscle, sinews, physique; grit.

athletics, athleticism; gymnastics, calisthenics.

athlete, gymnast, acrobat; Atlas, Hercules.

strengthening, invigoration, refreshment.

Science of forces: dynamics, statics.

V. **strengthen**, invigorate, brace, nerve, fortify, buttress, sustain, harden, steel; gird, set up, gird up one's loins; recruit, set on one's legs [*colloq.*]; vivify; refresh, reinforce, restore.

Adj. **strong**, mighty, vigorous, forcible; hard, stout, robust, sound, sturdy, husky [*colloq.*], hardy, powerful, potent, puissant.

resistless, irresistible, invincible, impregnable, unconquerable, indomitable, incontestable, valid; overpowering, overwhelming, all-powerful.

able-bodied; athletic, Herculean, muscular, brawny, wiry, well knit, sinewy, strapping, stalwart, lusty.

manly, manful; masculine, male, virile, in the prime of manhood.

Adv. **strongly**, by force, by main force.

160. WEAKNESS.—*N.* **weakness**, debility, relaxation, languor, enervation; impotence, etc., 158; infirmity, effeminacy; fragility; inactivity, etc., 683.

anemia, bloodlessness, deficiency of blood, poverty of blood.

loss of strength, delicacy; decrepitude; invalidism.

V. **be weak**; drop, crumble, give way; totter, dodder; tremble, shake; halt, limp; fade, languish, decline, flag, fail.

weaken, enfeeble, debilitate, shake, relax, sap, enervate, unnerve; cripple, unman; cramp, reduce, sprain, strain, dilute, impoverish.

Adj. **weak**, faint, feeble, infirm; impotent; relaxed, unnerved, unstrung, limp, strengthless, powerless; weakly, sickly, flaccid.

soft, effeminate, womanish.

frail, fragile; flimsy, sleazy, papery, unsubstantial, gimcrack, rickety, jerry-built; broken, decrepit, lame, shattered, shaken, crazy, shaky, tumbledown.

unsound, spent, effete; decayed, rotten, worn, seedy, languishing, wasted, laid low, the worse for wear; on its last legs.

161. [Power in operation] PRODUCTION.—*N.* **production**, creation, construction, formation, fabrication, manufacture; building, architecture, erection; organization; establishment; workmanship, performance; achievement; flowering, efflorescence, fruition; genesis, birth; evolution, development, growth; breeding; propagation.

publication; works, opus (*pl.* opera) [L.]; authorship.

structure, building, edifice, fabric, erection, pile.

V. **produce,** perform, operate, do, make, form, construct, fabricate, frame, contrive, manufacture; build, raise, rear, erect; establish, constitute, compose, evolve, coin, organize, institute; achieve, accomplish.

flower, blossom, bear fruit, bear, bring forth, give birth to, usher into the world; generate, propagate, engender, create; breed, develop, bring up.

induce, superinduce; cause, etc., 153.

Adj. **productive;** prolific, etc., 168; creative, formative, constructive; generative; teeming.

162. [Nonproduction] **DESTRUCTION.**—*N.* destruction; waste, dissolution, breaking up, disruption; disorganization; demolition, overthrow, subversion, suppression; abolition, etc., 756; sacrifice; ravage, devastation, incendiarism; revolution, etc., 146; road to ruin; sabotage.

fall, downfall, ruin, perdition; breakdown, breakup; cave-in [*colloq.*]; wreck, shipwreck, cataclysm.

extinction, extermination, annihilation; doom, crack of doom.

V. **perish,** fall, fall to the ground, tumble, topple; fall to pieces, break up, crumble, go to wrack and ruin; go by the board, be all over with, go to pieces, totter to its fall.

destroy, do (*or* make) away with, waste; nullify, annul, sacrifice, demolish, overturn, overthrow, overwhelm; upset, subvert, put an end to; do for [*colloq.*], undo, break down, cut down, pull down, dismantle, mow down, blow down; suppress, quash, put down, crush, blot out, efface, obliterate, cancel, erase, strike out, expunge, delete; dispel, dissipate, dissolve; consume.

smash, crash, quell, squash [*colloq.*], shatter, shiver, batter; tear (*or* pull, crush) to pieces; ruin, fell; sink, swamp, scuttle, wreck, shipwreck, engulf, submerged; lay in ruins, raze, level; deal destruction, lay waste, ravage, gut; devour, desolate, devastate, blast, exterminate, eradicate, annihilate.

Adj. **destructive,** subversive, cataclysmic, ruinous, incendiary, suicidal, deadly, all-destroying, all-devouring.

163. REPRODUCTION.—*N.* reproduction, renovation; restoration, etc., 660; renewal, revival, regeneration, revivification; apotheosis; resuscitation, reanimation, resurrection, reappearance.

V. **reproduce,** restore, etc., 660; revive, renovate, renew, repeat, regenerate, revivify, resuscitate, reanimate, refashion, multiply.

Adj. **reproductive,** resurgent, reappearing; renascent; Hydra-headed.

164. PRODUCER.—*N.* producer, originator, inventor, author, founder, generator, mover, architect, grower, raiser, introducer, creator; maker, etc. (*agent*), 690; prime mover.

165. DESTROYER.—*N.* destroyer, wrecker, annihilator; cankerworm, etc. (*bane*), 663; assassin, etc. (*killer*), 361; executioner, etc. (*punish*), 975; iconoclast, vandal, nihilist.

166. PATERNITY.—*N.* paternity, fathership, fatherhood; parentage.

parent, father, sire, dad [*colloq.*], papa, pater [*colloq.*], daddy [*colloq.*], paterfamilias; ancestor.

motherhood, maternity, mother, dam, mamma, mammy, mam [*colloq.*], matriarch, materfamilias.

stem, trunk, tree, stock, pedigree, house, lineage, line, family, race, tribe, clan; genealogy, family tree, descent, extraction, birth, ancestry; forefathers, forebears.

Adj. parental; paternal; maternal; ancestral, linear, patriarchal; racial.

167. POSTERITY.—*N.* posterity, progeny, breed, issue, offspring, brood, family, children, heirs; rising generation.

descendant, scion, offshoot, chip of the old block, heir, heiress, heir apparent, heir presumptive.

child, son, daughter, baby, kid [*colloq.*], imp, brat, cherub, tot, innocent, urchin, chit [*colloq.*]; infant, etc., 129.

lineage, line, straight descent, heredity, sonship, primogeniture.

Adj. hereditary, lineal.

filial, sonlike, daughterly, dutiful.

168. PRODUCTIVENESS.—*N.* productiveness, fecundity, fertility, luxuriance; multiplication, propagation, fructification.

V. fructify; generate, impregnate; teem, spawn, multiply; produce, etc., 161; conceive.

Adj. productive, prolific, copious; teeming, fertile, fruitful, plenteous, luxuriant; generative, life-giving; originative.

169. UNPRODUCTIVENESS.—*N.* unproductiveness, infertility, sterility, barrenness, unfruitfulness; unprofitableness, etc. (*inutility*), 645.

waste, desert, Sahara, wild, wilderness.

V. be unproductive; hang fire, flash in the pan, come to nothing.

Adj. unproductive, barren, unfertile, arid, sterile, unfruitful, fruitless, useless, fallow; unprofitable, etc. (*useless*), 645.

170. AGENCY.—*N.* agency, operation, force, function, office, maintenance, exercise, work, swing, play.

causation, impelling force; mediation, intervention, instrumentality; influence, etc., 175; action, etc. (*voluntary*), 680; method, procedure.

V. **operate,** work; act, perform, play, support, sustain, maintain, take effect, quicken, strike; have play, have free play; bring to bear upon.

Adj. **operative,** efficient, efficacious, practical, effectual; at work, on foot; acting, in operation, in force, in action.

171. ENERGY.—*N.* **energy,** force; intensity, vigor, strength, backbone [*colloq.*], vim [*colloq.*], mettle, pep [*slang*], fire, go [*colloq.*], high pressure; human dynamo.

activity, agitation, effervescence, ferment, fermentation, ebullition, stir, bustle; voluntary, energy, etc., 682; mental energy, etc., 604; resolution, stimulation; exertion, etc. (*effort*), 686.

V. **give energy,** energize, stimulate, strengthen, invigorate, kindle, excite, inflame, exert; sharpen, intensify.

Adj. **energetic,** strong, forcible, active, strenuous, brisk, forceful, mettlesome, enterprising, go-ahead [*colloq.*]; potent, etc. (*powerful*), 157; intense, keen, sharp, acute, incisive, trenchant.

poignant, virulent, caustic, corrosive, mordant; harsh, stringent, drastic.

172. INERTNESS.—*N.* **inertness,** inertia, inactivity, torpor, languor, quiescence, inaction, passivity, stagnation.

mental inertness; sloth; inexcitability, etc., 826; irresolution, indecision, vacillation; obstinacy, etc., 606.

V. **be inert,** hang fire, be inactive; smolder.

Adj. **inert,** inactive, passive; torpid, etc., 683; sluggish, logy, stagnant, dull, heavy, slack, tame, slow, lifeless, dead.

latent, dormant, smoldering, unexerted.

Adv. in suspense, in abeyance.

173. VIOLENCE.—*N.* **violence,** vehemence, might, impetuosity, boisterousness, disorder, effervescence, ebullition; turbulence, bluster; uproar, riot, row [*colloq.*], rumpus [*colloq.*].

ferocity, rage, fury, exasperation; malignity; severity, etc., 739; force, brute force; outrage.

fit, paroxysm, spasm, convulsion, throe; hysterics, passion, etc., 825.

outbreak, outburst, discharge, volley, explosion, blast, detonation, eruption, volcano, earthquake, thunderstorm.

fury, berserk, dragon, demon, tiger, wild beast; fire-eater [*colloq.*], etc. (*blusterer*), 887.

V. **be violent;** ferment, effervesce; rampage; run wild, run amuck, rage, roar, riot, storm; boil, boil over; fume, foam, ride roughshod, out-Herod Herod.

explode, go off, detonate, fulminate, let off, let fly, discharge, thunder, blow up, flash, flare, burst.

render violent; stir up, quicken, excite, incite, urge, lash, stimulate; irritate, inflame, kindle, foment, exasperate, convulse, infuriate, madden, lash into fury.

Adj. **violent,** vehement, acute, sharp; rough, tough [*colloq.*], rude, bluff, brusque, abrupt, boisterous, wild, impetuous, rampant; savage, fierce, ferocious.

turbulent, tumultuous; disorderly, raging, troublous, riotous, obstreperous, uproarious; frenzied, mad, insane; desperate, rash; infuriate, furious, frantic, outrageous; stormy, etc. (*wind*), 349.

fiery, flaming, scorching, hot, red-hot.

unbridled, unruly; headstrong, ungovernable, uncontrollable, irrepressible.

spasmodic, convulsive, explosive; detonating; volcanic, meteoric.

Adv. **violently,** amain; by storm, by force, by main force, with might and main, at one fell swoop; in desperation, with a vengeance.

174. MODERATION.—*N.* **moderation;** lenity, etc., 740; temperateness, temperance, gentleness, mildness, quiet, sobriety; mental calmness, composure, etc. (*inexcitability*), 826.

alleviation, assuagement, mitigation, relaxation, tranquilization, pacification.

moderator; sedative, lenitive, palliative; opiate, balm.

V. **moderate,** slacken, soften, mitigate, palliate, alleviate, allay, assuage, appease, temper, mollify, lull, soothe, compose, still, calm, cool, quiet, tranquilize, hush, quell, sober, pacify, smooth, deaden, smother; blunt, subdue, chasten; weaken, etc., 160; lessen, decrease; check, tame, curb, restrain.

Adj. **moderate,** gentle, mild; cool, sober, temperate, reasonable, lenient, measured; calm, unruffled, quiet, tranquil, still, halcyon; peaceful, peaceable, pacific.

Adv. in moderation, within bounds.

175. [Indirect Power] INFLUENCE.—*N.* **influence;** importance, etc., 642; weight, pressure, pull [*colloq. or slang*]; interest; preponderance, prevalence, sway; predominance, upper hand, ascendancy; dominance, reign; control, domination, hold; authority, power, potency, capability, spell, magic, magnetism.

footing; purchase, support; play, leverage, vantage ground, advantage.

patronage, protection, auspices; patron, etc. (*auxiliary*), 711; tower of strength.

V. **be influential,** carry weight, sway, bias, actuate, weight, tell; magnetize, work upon; take root, take hold; pervade, run through; be rife.

dominate, subject; predominate, outweigh; override, overbear; have *or* gain the upper hand, prevail.

lead, control, rule, manage, master, get control of, make one's influence felt; take the lead, pull the strings; turn the scale; set the fashion.

Adj. influential, effective, potent; important, etc., 642; weighty; prevalent, rife, rampant; dominant, predominant, authoritative, recognized.

Adv. with telling effect, with authority.

176. TENDENCY.—*N.* tendency, aptness, aptitude, proneness, proclivity, bent, turn, tone, bias, set, warp, leaning (*with* to *or* toward), predisposition, inclination, liability, propensity, susceptibility; quality, nature, temperament; idiosyncrasy; cast, vein, grain, humor, mood, trend, drift.

V. tend, contribute, conduce, lead, influence, dispose, incline, verge, bend to, warp, turn, work toward, gravitate toward, trend; affect; carry, redound to, bid fair to; promote, etc. (*aid*), 707.

Adj. tending; conducive, working toward, in a fair way to, likely to, calculated to; liable, etc., 177; subservient, instrumental, useful; subsidiary, accessory.

177. LIABILITY.—*N.* liability, susceptibility; possibility, contingency.

V. be liable, incur, lay oneself open to, be subjected to, run the chance, stand a chance; lie under, expose oneself to, open a door to.

Adj. liable, subject, in danger, open to, exposed to; answerable, responsible, accountable, amenable; apt to; dependent on.

contingent, incidental, possible, on the cards, within range of, at the mercy of.

178. CONCURRENCE.—*N.* concurrence, co-operation, collaboration; conformity, agreement, accord; alliance; complicity, collusion, partnership, union.

V. concur, conduce, conspire, contribute; agree, unite, harmonize, combine; hang *or* pull together, co-operate; keep pace with, run parallel.

Adj. concurrent, conformable, joint, co-operative, concordant, harmonious, in alliance with, of one mind, at one with.

179. COUNTERACTION.—*N.* counteraction, opposition; contrariety, contradiction; antagonism, polarity; clashing, collision, interference, resistance, friction; reaction, recoil; counterblast, neutralization, check, hindrance; repression, restraint.

V. counteract, clash, cross, interfere with, conflict with; contravene; jostle; militate against, stultify, antagonize, frustrate, oppose, overcome, overpower, withstand, resist, impede, hinder, repress, restrain; recoil, react.

neutralize, offset, undo, cancel; counterpoise, counterbalance.
Adj. antagonistic, conflicting, reactionary; contrary, etc., 14.
Adv. although, notwithstanding; in spite of; against.

CLASS II

Words Relating To SPACE

I. SPACE IN GENERAL

180. [Indefinite space] SPACE.—*N.* space, extension, extent, proportions, expanse, stretch; room, accommodation, capacity; scope, compass, range, latitude, field; sweep, play, swing; spread, expansion.

elbowroom, leeway, seaway, headway; margin; sphere, arena.

open space, free space, void, waste, desert, wild, wilderness; moor, down, downs, upland, moorland; prairie, steppe, llano, campagna.

unlimited space; heavens, ether, infinity; world, wide world.

Adj. spacious, roomy, extensive, extended, expansive, capacious, ample; widespread, vast, world-wide, wide, far-flung, boundless, limitless, endless, infinite; shoreless, trackless, pathless.

Adv. extensively; by and large; everywhere, far and near (*or* wide), here, there, and everywhere; from pole to pole, from the four corners of the earth, from all points of the compass; to the four winds, to the uttermost parts of the earth.

181. [Definite space] REGION.—*N.* region, sphere, ground, soil, area, realm, hemisphere, quarter, orb, circuit, circle; pale, etc. (*limit*), 233; tract, clearing; domain.

county, shire, canton, province, department, parish, diocese, township, commune, ward, bailiwick; principality, duchy, palatinate, archduchy, dukedom, dominion, colony, commonwealth, territory, country; fatherland, motherland; kingdom, empire.

precinct, arena, district, beat; patch, plot, inclosure, close, enclave, field, paddock, etc. (*inclosure*), 232; street.

clime, climate, zone, meridian, latitude.

Adj. territorial, provincial, regional, insular; local, parochial.

182. [Limited space] PLACE.—*N.* place, spot, whereabouts, point; niche, nook, corner, hole, pigeonhole, etc. (*receptacle*), 191; compartment; premises, courtyard, square, place, piazza, plaza, forum; hamlet, village, etc. (*abode*), 189; pen, etc. (*inclosure*), 232; location, site, locality, situation.

Adv. somewhere, in some place, here and there, in various places.

183. SITUATION.—*N.* situation, position, locality, latitude and longitude; footing, status, standing; standpoint; stage; aspect, attitude, posture, pose.

place, site; station, post, seat, whereabouts; environment, ground; bearings, direction, spot, etc. (*limited space*), 182.

topography, geography; map, plan, chart.

V. **be situated,** be situate, be located; lie; have its seat in.

Adj. **situate,** situated; local, topical, topographical.

Adv. hereabouts, thereabouts, whereabouts; in place, here, there.

184. LOCATION.—*N.* **location,** situation, lodgment; stowage; packing, lading; establishment, settlement, installation; insertion, etc., 300.

anchorage, roadstead, mooring.

settlement, plantation, colony; habitation, etc. (*abode*), 189. **domestication;** colonization; naturalization.

V. **place,** situate, locate, localize, put, lay, set, seat; station, park (as, *an automobile*), lodge, quarter, post, install; house, stow, pack; load, lade; establish, fix, root; graft; plant, etc. (*insert*), 300; deposit, store, store away.

billet on, quarter upon, saddle with.

settle, domesticate, colonize, found, people; take root, strike root, anchor, cast anchor, moor, tether, picket· settle down; take up one's abode, establish *or* locate oneself; keep house; squat, burrow, get a footing; bivouac, encamp, pitch one's tent; inhabit, etc., 186.

Adj. **placed;** situate, ensconced, imbedded, rooted; moored, at anchor.

185. DISPLACEMENT.—*N.* **displacement,** misplacement, dislocation, derangement, transposition.

ejection, expulsion, eviction; exile, banishment, ostracism.

removal, etc. (*transference*), 270; transshipment, moving, shift.

V. **displace,** dislodge, disestablish; misplace, unseat, disturb; set aside, remove, take away, cart away, draft off; exile, etc. (*seclude*), 893.

unload, empty, etc. (*eject*), 297; transfer, etc., 270; dispel.

vacate, depart, evacuate.

Adj. **displaced;** unplaced, unhoused, unsettled; houseless, homeless, out of place; out of a situation.

186. PRESENCE.—*N.* **presence,** attendance; occupancy, occupation; ubiquity, omnipresence.

permeation, pervasion; diffusion.

bystander, etc. (*spectator*), 444.

V. **be present,** make one of; look on, attend, remain; find *or* present oneself; lie, stand.

inhabit, occupy, dwell, reside; stay, sojourn; live, abide; lodge, tenant; people.

frequent, resort to, haunt; revisit.

pervade, permeate; overspread; fill, run through.

Adj. present; situate; moored, at anchor; resident, domiciled; ubiquitous, omnipresent.

peopled, inhabited, populous.

Adv. here, there, everywhere; aboard, on board, at home, afield; on the spot; in presence of, before.

187. ABSENCE.—*N.* absence, nonresidence, absenteeism; nonattendance, cut [*colloq.*]; alibi.

emptiness; void, vacuum, vacancy.

interval, hiatus, interruption; interregnum.

truant, absentee.

V. be absent; keep away, play truant, absent oneself, stay away, hold aloof.

withdraw, retreat, retire; go away.

Adj. absent, not present, away, nonresident, gone, from home; missing; lost; wanting; omitted.

empty. void; vacant, vacuous, blank; untenanted, unoccupied, uninhabited, tenantless; desert, deserted, uninhabitable.

Adv. without, minus, nowhere; elsewhere; in default of; sans.

188. INHABITANT.—*N.* inhabitant; resident, dweller, indweller, addressee, occupier, occupant, householder; inmate; tenant, incumbent; settler, squatter, backwoodsman, planter, habitant, colonist; islander; denizen, citizen; burgher, townsman, burgess; villager; cottager, cotter; boarder, lodger.

native, aborigine, aboriginal.

people, etc. (*mankind*), 372; population; colony, settlement; household.

V. inhabit, dwell, etc., 186.

Adj. indigenous, native, domestic; domiciled; naturalized; vernacular.

189. HABITATION.—*N.* habitation, abode, dwelling, lodging, domicile, residence, address, berth, housing. quarters, headquarters.

home, fatherland, motherland, country; homestead, hearth, chimney corner; roof, household, housing, native soil, native land.

county, parish, etc. (*region*), 181.

retreat, haunt, habitat, resort; nest, arbor, bower, grotto; lair, den, cave, hole, hiding place, cell, sanctum sanctorum, eyrie, rookery, hive; covert, perch, roost.

anchorage, roadstead, roads; dock, basin, wharf, quay, port, harbor.

camp, bivouac, encampment, cantonment, barracks, quarters; tent, wigwam, tepee; igloo.

farm, farmhouse, grange.

cot, cabin, hut, hovel; shanty, dugout, chalet, log cabin, log house; shack [*colloq*], shed, booth, stall, pen, fold; stable, barn; kennel, sty, cote, dovecote, coop, hutch; cowhouse, cowshed.

house, mansion, place, villa, cottage, lodge, hermitage, rotunda, tower, château, castle, pavilion, hotel, court, manor house, hall, palace; kiosk, bungalow, country seat; apartment (*or* brownstone, duplex, frame, shingle, flat, tenement) house; three-decker; building, buildings.

hamlet, village, dorp [Dutch], rancho [Sp. Amer.].

town, borough, city, capital, metropolis; suburb; province, country; county town, county seat.

street, place, terrace, parade, esplanade, boardwalk, embankment, road, row, lane, alley, court, quadrangle, close, yard, passage.

square, polygon, circus, crescent, block, arcade, colonnade, cloister; market place.

assembly room, auditorium, concert hall, armory, gymnasium; cathedral, church, chapel, meetinghouse, etc. (*temple*), 1000; parliament, etc. (*council*), 696.

inn, hotel, tavern, caravansary, alehouse, saloon, club, clubhouse; grill room, chophouse, coffeehouse, eating house; canteen, restaurant, buffet, café, cabaret.

sanatorium, health resort, sanitarium; spa, watering place.

V. inhabit, etc., 186; take up one's abode, etc. (*locate oneself*), 184.

Adj. urban, metropolitan; cosmopolitan; suburban.

provincial, rural, rustic, country, countrified.

190. [Things contained] CONTENTS.—*N.* contents; cargo, lading, freight, shipment, load, bale, burden; cartload, shipload; stuffing.

V. load, lade, ship, pile, fill, stuff.

191. RECEPTACLE.—*N.* receptacle, container; inclosure; etc., 232; recipient, receiver; compartment, cell; hole, corner, niche, recess, nook, crypt; stall; pigeonhole; mouth.

stomach, paunch, belly, crop, craw, maw.

bag, sack, wallet, pocket, pouch; purse; knapsack, haversack, satchel, reticule; saddlebags; portfolio; valise, grip [*colloq.*], suitcase, handbag, schoolbag, brief case, traveling bag, Gladstone bag.

case, chest, box, coffer, caddy, casket; reliquary, shrine; caisson; desk, bureau; trunk, portmanteau, bandbox.

vessel, utensil; vase, canister, jar; basket, pannier, hamper; crate; creel; cradle, bassinet.

For liquids: cistern, reservoir; vat, caldron, barrel, cask, keg, tun, butt, firkin; tub; bottle, jar, decanter, ewer, carafe, canteen, flagon; demijohn; flask, vial, phial; cruet, caster; urn, percolator, coffeepot, teapot, samovar; bucket, pail; pot, tankard, jug, pitcher, mug, porringer; receiver, retort, alembic, crucible; can, kettle; bowl, basin; punch bowl, cup, goblet, beaker, chalice, tumbler, glass.

plate, platter, dish, tray, waiter, salver.

ladle, dipper; shovel, trowel, spatula.

cupboard, closet; locker, bin; buffet, sideboard; drawer, chest of drawers, chiffonier; till, safe; bookcase, cabinet.

chamber, apartment, room, cabin; office, court, hall, suite of rooms, apartment, flat, tenement; parlor, living (*or* sitting, drawing, reception) room; best room [*colloq.*]; boudoir; sanctum; bedroom, dormitory; refectory, dining room; nursery, schoolroom; library, study; studio; smoking room, den.

attic, loft, garret; cellar, vault, hold, cockpit; cubbyhole; basement, kitchen, pantry, scullery; storeroom, lumber room; dairy, laundry; garage; hangar; outhouse, penthouse; lean-to, shed.

portico, porch, stoop, veranda, piazza.

bower, arbor, summerhouse; grotto; conservatory, greenhouse.

II. DIMENSIONS

192. SIZE.—*N.* **size,** dimensions, proportions; magnitude, bulk, volume; largeness, greatness; expanse, amplitude, mass; capacity; tonnage; cordage; caliber.

lump, block, mass; clod, mountain, mound; heap, etc. (*assemblage*), 72.

corpulence, obesity, plumpness.

immensity, hugeness, monstrosity, enormity.

giant, Titan, Hercules, Gargantua; monster, mammoth, whale, behemoth, leviathan, elephant, jumbo [*colloq.*]; colossus.

V. **be large,** become large, etc. (*expand*), 194.

Adj. **large,** big, great, considerable, bulky, voluminous, ample, massive; capacious, comprehensive, spacious; mighty, towering.

stout, corpulent, fat, plump, chubby; portly, burly, brawny, fleshy.

unwieldy, hulky, hulking, lumpish, overgrown; puffy, swollen, bloated.

huge, immense, enormous, titanic, mighty; vast; stupendous; monster, monstrous; gigantic; elephantine, mammoth; giant, colossal, cyclopean, Gargantuan.

193. LITTLENESS.—*N.* **littleness,** smallness; epitome; microcosm; vanishing point.

dwarf, pygmy, midget; Lilliputian, elf; doll, puppet, manikin; Tom Thumb.

mite, insect, arthropod, ephemerid, ephemera, bug [*pop.*], larva.
atom, monad, animalcule, animalculum (*pl.* animalcula), molecule, microbe, germ, micro-organism, bacterium (*pl.* bacteria), amoeba.

particle, speck, dot, mote; scrap; spark; scintilla; fragment, fraction; grain, powder, dust; minutiæ, etc. (*unimportance*), 643.

V. **belittle,** lie in a nutshell; become small, decrease; contract, etc., 195.

Adj. **little,** small, minute, diminutive, microscopic; inconsiderable, petty; limited, cramped; puny, runty, tiny, wee [*colloq.*], elfin, miniature, pocket; undersized, stunted, dwarf, dwarfed, dwarfish, pygmy; Lilliputian; invisible, infinitesimal, homeopathic.

Adv. in a small compass, in a nutshell; on a small scale.

194. EXPANSION.—*N.* **expansion,** dilation; growth, increase, enlargement, amplification; extension, augmentation, aggrandizement; spread, increment, development, swell, dilatation; obesity, corpulence; dropsy, swelling, distension, puffiness, inflation.

V. **enlarge,** expand, widen, extend, grow, increase, swell, fill out; dilate, stretch, spread; wax; bud, shoot, sprout, germinate, put forth, open, burst forth; outgrow; overrun.

spread, augment, aggrandize; distend, develop, amplify, spread out, widen, magnify; inflate, blow up; stuff, fatten, pad, cram, bloat; exaggerate.

Adj. **expanded,** larger; swollen, expansive, widespread, over-grown, exaggerated, bloated, fat, tumid, dropsical; corpulent, obese; puffy, distend, bulbous; full-blown, full-grown; big, etc., 192.

195. CONTRACTION.—*N.* **contraction,** reduction, diminution; decrease, etc., 36; lessening, shrinking; atrophy; emaciation, attenuation.

compression, condensation, constraint, compactness; compendium, abstract, epitome; strangulation; astringency.

V. **decrease,** lessen, grow less, dwindle, shrink, contract, narrow, shrivel, collapse, wither, fall away, waste, wane, ebb.

diminish, boil down; deflate, exhaust, empty; constrict, condense, compress, squeeze, crush; pinch, tighten, strangle; cramp; dwarf; shorten, etc., 201; circumscribe, limit, bound, confine.

pare, reduce; attenuate; rub down, scrape, file, grind, chip, shave, shear.

Adj. **contracting,** astringent; shrunk, shrunken, contracted; strangulated; wizened; stunted; waning; compact.

196. DISTANCE.—*N.* **distance,** remoteness; space, etc., 180; far cry to; elongation; drift, offing, background; remote region; reach, span.

outpost, outskirt; horizon, skyline; foreign parts, antipodes.

V. **be distant;** extend to, stretch to, reach to, spread to, stretch away to; range, outreach.

Adj. **distant,** far, far off, far away, remote; telescopic; yon, yonder; ulterior; transatlantic, transalpine; ultramundane, antipodean; inaccessible, out-of-the-way; unapproachable.

Adv. **far off,** far away, afar, afar off; away; beyond range, aloof; wide of, clear of; abroad, yonder, farther, further, beyond; far and wide, from pole to pole; out of range, out of hearing.

apart, asunder; at arm's length.

197. NEARNESS.—*N.* **nearness,** proximity, propinquity; vicinity, vicinage, neighborhood, contiguity, etc., 199.

short distance, short cut; earshot, close quarters, range, stone's throw; gunshot, hair's breadth, span.

purlieus, neighborhood, vicinage, environs, suburbs, confines.

bystander, spectator; neighbor.

approach, approximation, access; convergence, meeting.

V. **be near,** adjoin, abut, neighbor, trench on; border upon, verge upon; approximate; stand by, hang about; cling to, clasp, hug; huddle; hover over.

bring or draw near; converge, etc., 290; crowd, pack, huddle.

Adj. **near**, nigh, close (*or* near) at hand, close, neighboring, bordering upon, contiguous, adjacent, adjoining; proximate, approximate; at hand, handy; intimate.

Adv. **near**, nigh, hard by, close to, close upon; hard upon; at the point of; next door to; within reach (*or* call, hearing, earshot, range); on the verge of; in sight of; at close quarters; beside, alongside, side by side, in juxtaposition; at the heels of.

about; thereabouts; roughly, in round numbers; approximately, as good as, well-nigh.

198. INTERVAL.—*N.* **interval**, space; separation, division; hiatus, cæsura; interruption; interregnum; interstice.

parenthesis; void, vacuum; incompleteness, deficiency.

cleft, break, gap, opening; hole, puncture; chasm, mesh, crevice, chink, cranny, crack, slit, fissure, rift, fault, flaw, breach, fracture, rent, gash, cut.

gorge, defile, pass, ravine, canyon, crevasse; abyss, abysm; gulf; inlet, strait; furrow, etc., 259; gully, gulch, notch.

V. **gape**, yawn; separate, etc., 44.

199. CONTACT.—*N.* **contact**, contiguity, contiguousness, proximity, apposition, abuttal, abutment, juxtaposition, touching, meeting; conjunction, adhesion, etc., 46.

borderland; frontier, etc. (*limit*), 233.

V. **adjoin**, join, abut on, neighbor, border, march with; graze, touch, meet; coincide; coexist; adhere, etc., 46.

Adj. **contiguous**, touching, in contact, conterminous, end to end; close, etc. (*near*), 197.

200. [Linear Dimensions] LENGTH.—*N.* **length**, longitude, extent, span; mileage.

line, bar, rule, stripe, streak.

lengthening, prolongation, production, protraction; tension, extension.

Measures of length: line, nail, inch, hand, palm, foot, cubit, yard, ell, fathom, rood, pole, furlong, mile, knot, league; chain; meter, kilometer, centimeter, etc. pedometer, odometer, odograph, viameter, log [*naut.*], speedometer, telemeter, scale.

V. **be long**, stretch out, sprawl; extend to, reach to, stretch to.

lengthen, let out, extend, elongate; stretch; prolong, protract; draw out, spin out.

Adj. **long**, elongate, lengthy, outstretched, extended; lengthened, interminable.

linear, lineal; longitudinal.

lanky, lank, slab-sided [*slang*], rangy; tall; long-limbed.

Adv. **lengthwise**, at length, longitudinally, along; tandem; in a line; from end to end, from stem to stern, from head to foot, from top to toe; fore and aft; over all.

201. SHORTNESS.—*N.* **shortness,** brevity, littleness, etc., 193; a span.

abridgment, shortening, abbreviation, retrenchment, curtailment, epitomization, condensation; reduction, etc. (*contraction*), 195; epitome, etc. (*compendium*), 596.

elision, ellipsis; conciseness, brevity.

V. **shorten,** curtail, retrench, abridge, abbreviate; take in, reduce; compress, contract; epitomize, abstract, summarize, condense; cut, pare down, clip, dock, lop, prune, shear, shave, mow, crop, stunt; nip, check the growth of, foreshorten [*drawing*].

Adj. **short,** brief, curt; compendious, compact; stubby, pudgy, squatty; stumpy [*colloq.*], thickset, chunky, scrub, stocky, squat, dumpy; pug, turned up; little, etc., 193; concise, etc., 572; summary.

202. BREADTH, THICKNESS.—*N.* **breadth,** width, latitude, amplitude.

diameter, bore, caliber; radius.

thickness; corpulence, etc. (*size*), 192; expansion, dilatation.
V. **expand,** etc., 194; thicken, widen.

Adj. **broad,** wide, ample, extended, outspread, outstretched.
thick, dumpy, squat, thickset, stubby, etc., 201.

203. NARROWNESS, THINNESS.—*N.* **narrowness,** slenderness; closeness.

line; hair's breadth.

thinness, tenuity; leanness, lankiness, emaciation.

shaving; strip, etc. (*filament*), 205; thread, skeleton, shadow, scrag, mere skin and bone.

narrowing, tapering; contraction, etc., 195.

V. **narrow,** taper; contract, etc., 195.

Adj. **narrow,** close; slender, thin, fine, delicate, threadlike, finespun, taper, slim; scant, scanty, spare; contracted.

lean, emaciated, skinny, scrawny, meager, gaunt, rawboned, lank, lanky, weedy [*colloq.*]; starved, starveling; attenuated, shriveled, pinched, spindle-legged, spindle-shanked, spindling; worn to a shadow; hatchet-faced; lantern-jawed.

204. LAYER.—*N.* **layer,** stratum, course, bed, coping, substratum, floor, stage, story, tier.

leaf, sheet, flake, scale, coat, peel, membrane, film, slice, shaving, wafer.

stratification, lamination, foliation; scaliness.

V. **slice,** shave, pare, peel.

plate, coat, veneer; cover, etc., 223.

Adj. scaly, filmy, membranous, flaky, foliated, stratified.

205. FILAMENT.—*N.* filament, line; fiber, vein, hair, cobweb, capillary, strand, tendril, gossamer.

thread, yarn, packthread, cotton.

string, twine, twist, cord, rope, tape, ribbon, wire.

strip, shred, slip, band, fillet, lath, splinter.

Adj. fibrous, threadlike, wiry, stringy, ropy; capillary, wire-drawn; hairy, etc. (*rough*), 256.

206. HEIGHT.—*N.* height, altitude, elevation, eminence, pitch; loftiness, sublimity.

tallness, stature; prominence, etc., 250; apex, zenith, culmination.

colossus, etc. (*size*), 192; giant.

height, mount, mountain, hill; headland, foreland, promontory; ridge, dune, rising ground, down, uplands, highlands; knoll, hummock, hillock, mound; bluff, cliff, peak.

tower, pillar, column, obelisk, monument, belfry, steeple, spire, minaret, campanile, turret, dome, cupola; pyramid, pagoda.

pole, pikestaff, Maypole, flagstaff; mast, mainmast, topmast.

high water; high (*or* flood, spring) tide.

V. tower, soar, hover; cap, culminate; overhang, surmount, rise above, command, overtop, rise, ascend.

heighten, uprear, uplift, upraise, elevate.

Adj. high, elevated, eminent, exalted, lofty, sublime; tall, gigantic, big, colossal; towering, beetling, soaring, elevated; higher, superior, upper, supernal; highest, etc. (*topmost*), 210.

lanky, etc. (*thin*), 203.

upland, hilly, mountainous, alpine, heaven-kissing, cloud-capped.

overhanging, impending, incumbent, overlying; superimposed.

Adv. on high, high up, aloft, up, above, overhead; in the clouds.

207. LOWNESS.—*N.* lowness, levelness, flatness; debasement, prostration; depression, hollow; lowlands.

basement, cellar, vault, crypt, cavern; hold; base, etc., 211.

low water, low (*or* ebb, neap) tide.

V. be low, lie low, underlie; crouch, wallow, grovel; lower, etc. (*depress*), 308.

Adj. low, low-lying, level; flat; crouched, squat, prostrate, depressed, debased.

lower, inferior, under, nether.

lowest, nethermost, lowermost.

Adv. under, beneath, underneath, below, down, downward; underfoot, underground; downstairs, belowstairs; at a low ebb; below par.

208. DEPTH.—*N.* depth, profundity, depression, hollow.

pit, shaft, well, crater, chasm, crevasse, deep, abyss, bowels of the earth, bottomless pit.

soundings, draft, submersion, plunge, dive; plummet, lead.

V. deepen, sink, excavate, mine, sap, dig, burrow.

sound, heave the lead, take soundings.

Adj. deep, deep-seated, profound, buried; sunk, submerged, subaqueous, submarine, subterranean, underground.

bottomless, fathomless, unfathomed, unfathomable, abysmal, down-reaching, yawning.

Adv. out of one's depth, beyond one's depth; over head and ears.

209. SHALLOWNESS.—*N.* shallowness, superficiality; shoals.

Adj. shallow, slight, superficial; skin-deep, ankle-deep, knee-deep, shoal.

210. SUMMIT.—*N.* summit, top, vertex, apex, zenith, pinnacle, acme, crown; height, pitch, maximum; goal, consummation; climax, turning point; culmination; turn of the tide, fountainhead.

tip, tiptop; crest, crow's-nest, cap, peak; brow, head.

architrave, frieze, cornice, coping, coping stone, capital, headpiece, capstone, pediment, entablature; attic, loft, garret, housetop, upper story, roof (*covering*), 223.

V. crown, top, cap, crest, surmount, overtop; culminate.

Adj. highest (high, etc., 206), top, topmost, overmost, uppermost, tiptop; capital, head, polar; supreme, supernal.

211. Base.—*N.* base, basement; plinth, dado, wainscot; baseboard, mopboard; bedrock, hardpan; foundation, substructure, substratum, ground, earth, pavement, floor, paving; footing, groundwork, basis.

bottom, nadir, foot, sole, toe, hoof, root; keel.

Adj. bottom, undermost, nethermost; fundamental; founded on, based on.

212. VERTICALITY.—*N.* verticality, perpendicularity, erectness.

cliff, steep, crag, bluff, palisades; wall, precipice.

V. be vertical, stand erect *or* upright, stick up, cock up.

render vertical, set up, raise up, erect, rear, raise, pitch.

Adj. vertical; upright, erect, perpendicular, plumb, bolt upright.

Adv. on end; endwise; at right angles.

213. HORIZONTALITY.—*N.* horizontality; flatness; level, plane, stratum.

recumbency; lying down, reclination, proneness, supination, prostration.

V. be horizontal, lie, recline, lie flat; sprawl, loll.

render horizontal, lay, level, flatten, even, raze, smooth, align.

prostrate, knock down, floor, fell, ground, cut (*or* hew) down, mow down.

Adj. **horizontal,** level, even, plane, flush; flat, smooth.

recumbent, prone, supine, prostrate.

Adv. on one's back; on all fours; on its beam ends.

214. PENDENCY.—*N.* **pendency,** dependency; suspension, hanging.

pendant, drop, eardrop, tassel, lobe; tail, train, queue, pigtail; pendulum.

chandelier, gaselier.

V. **be pendent;** hang, depend, swing, dangle, lower, droop; flap, trail, beetle, jut, overhang.

suspend, hang, sling, hook up, hitch, fasten to, append.

Adj. **pendent,** pendulous, hanging; dependent; beetling, jutting over, overhanging; lowering; suspended.

215. SUPPORT.—*N.* **support,** ground, foundation, base, basis, fulcrum, purchase, footing, hold; stage, platform; rest, resting place; groundwork, substratum; floor.

supporter; aid, etc., 707; prop, truss, stand, stalk; bracket; ledge, shelf, table, trestle; rung, round; staff, stick, crook, crutch.

post, pillar, column, pediment, pedestal; caryatid; buttress, jamb, mullion, stile, abutment.

frame, framework; scaffold, skeleton, beam, rafter, girder, lintel, joist; keystone; arch; mainstay.

seat, throne, dais; divan, ottoman, sofa, davenport, couch, daybed; stall; chair, wing chair, armchair, easy chair, elbowchair, rocking chair, Morris chair; settee, form, bench; saddle, sidesaddle, pillion; packsaddle; pommel, horn.

stool, hassock, footstool.

bed, bedstead, four-poster; pallet; cot; hammock, shakedown; crib, trundle bed, cradle; litter, stretcher; bunk, berth; mat, rug, cushion; lap.

V. **support,** bear, carry, hold, sustain, shoulder; hold up, back up, bolster up, shore up, uphold, brace, truss, stay, prop; maintain; aid, etc., 707.

Adj. **supporting,** supported; fundamental.

216. PARALLELISM.—*N.* **parallelism,** equidistance, concentricity.

V. **be parallel,** parallel, equal.

Adj. **parallel,** coextensive, equidistant; collateral, concentric, concurrent; abreast, equal, even, alongside.

Adv. alongside, abreast, broadside on.

217. OBLIQUITY.—*N.* **obliquity,** inclination, incline, slope, slant; leaning, tilt; bias, diagonal, zigzag, list, twist, sag, cant, lurch; distortion, etc., 243; bend, curve.

acclivity, steepness; rise, ascent, pitch, grade, rising ground, hill, bank; cliff, precipice, etc. (*vertical*), 212; shelving beach; declivity, dip, fall.

V. **be oblique;** slope, slant, lean, cant, incline, shelve, decline, descend, bend; heel over, careen; sag, slouch, sidle, skid.

render oblique; sway, bias; slope, slant, tilt; incline, bend, crook; distort, etc., 243; zigzag, stagger [mech.].

Adj. oblique, inclined; sloping, tilted; askew, asquint, bias, aslant, diagonal, transverse, athwart; indirect, wry, awry, crooked; sinuous, zigzag; knock-kneed, etc. (*distorted*), 243.

uphill, rising, ascending; steep, abrupt, precipitous.

downhill, falling, descending; declining, shelving, declivitous.

Adv. obliquely; on one side, askew, askance, awry, edgewise, at an angle; sidelong, sidewise, slantwise.

218. INVERSION.—*N.* inversion, subversion, reversion; opposition, polarity; contrariety, contradiction, reversal, transposition, transposal; turn of the tide; overturn, revolution; somersault; revulsion.

V. be inverted, turn (*or* go, wheel) about, turn (*or* tilt, topple) over; capsize, turn turtle.

invert, subvert; reverse; upturn, overturn, upset, overset, turn topsy-turvy; transpose.

Adj. inverted, wrong side out (*or* up); inside out, upside down; on one's head, topsy-turvy.

inverse; reverse, etc. (*contrary*), 14; opposite.

Adv. inversely, conversely; heels over head, head over heels.

219. CROSSING.—*N.* crossing; intersection, grade crossing.

network, reticulation; net, web, mesh, netting, lace, plait; sieve, screen; wicker; mat, matting; trellis, lattice, grating, grille, gridiron, tracery, fretwork, filigree; entanglement.

crucifix, cross, rood, crisscross.

V. cross, intersect, interlace, intertwine, intertwist, interweave, interlink, crisscross; twine, entwine, weave, twist, wreathe; dovetail, mortise, splice, link.

plait, pleat, plat, braid; entangle, ravel; net, knot.

Adj. crossed, matted, transverse, intersected, cross; cross-shaped, cruciform; netlike, retiform, latticed, grated, barred, streaked.

Adv. cross, athwart, thwart, transversely; at grade; crosswise, across.

220. EXTERIORITY.—*N.* exteriority; outside, exterior; surface, superficies; skin, covering; face, facet.

V. be exterior, lie around, environ, encircle.

externalize, objectify, visualize, envisage, actualize.

Adj. exterior, external, extraneous; outer, outermost; outward, outlying, outside, outdoor.

outstanding; extrinsic, incidental; superficial, skin-deep.

Adv. externally, out, without, over, outwards, out of doors, in the open air.

221. INTERIORITY.—*N.* interiority; inside, interior; interspace, subsoil.

contents, etc., 190; substance, pith, marrow; heart, bosom, breast; recesses, innermost recesses; cave, etc. (*concavity*), 252.

inmate, intern, inhabitant, etc., 188.

V. **inclose,** etc. (*circumscribe*), 229; intern; embed, etc. (*insert*), 300; place within, keep within.

Adj. **interior,** internal; inner, intimate, inside, inward, inmost, innermost; deep-seated, inherent, ingrained, innate, inborn, inbred, intrinsic.

home, inland, domestic, family, indoor.

Adv. **internally;** inwards, within, indoors, withindoors; at home.

222. CENTRALITY.—*N.* centrality; centralization, concentration; center; middle, midst; focus; center of gravity.

core, kernel, nucleus; heart, pole, axis, bull's-eye, nave, hub; marrow, pith; metropolis.

V. **centralize,** concentrate; bring to a focus; converge, etc., 290.

Adj. **central;** middle, axial, pivotal, nuclear, focal, concentric; middlemost; metropolitan.

223. COVERING.—*N.* covering, cover; canopy, awning, tent, marquee, wigwam, tepee; umbrella, parasol, sunshade; veil; shield, etc. (*defense*), 717.

roof, ceiling, thatch, tiles, slates, leads, shingles; dome, cupola.

coverlet, counterpane, sheet, quilt, blanket, rug; eiderdown quilt, comforter; pillowcase, pillowslip; linoleum, oilcloth; tarpaulin.

integument: skin, pellicle, fleece, fur, leather, lambskin, sable, beaver, ermine, hide, coat, buff, pelt, peltry [*collective noun*]; cuticle, cutis, epidermis; clothing, etc., 225.

peel, rind, crust, bark, husk, shell.

sheath, sheathing, capsule, pod, casing, case, wrapping, wrapper; envelope; cornhusk, corn shuck.

veneer, facing; scale, layer; incrustation, coating, paint, stain, varnish, enamel, whitewash, plaster, stucco.

V. **cover,** superimpose, overlay, overspread; wrap, incase, face, case, veneer, paper; clapboard, shingle; conceal, etc., 528.

coat, paint, stain, varnish, incrust, crust, cement, stucco, plaster; smear, daub, besmear, bedaub; gild, plate, japan, lacquer, enamel, whitewash.

Adj. **covered,** hooded, cowled, armored, armor-plated; ironclad; scaly.

224. LINING.—*N.* lining, coating, inner coating; filling, stuffing, wadding, padding; facing, bushing; sheathing.

V. **line,** stuff, incrust, wad, pad, fill, face, ceil, bush, wainscot, sheathe.

225. CLOTHING.—*N.* clothing, dress; covering, etc., 223; raiment, costume, attire, toilet, habiliment; vesture, vestment;

garment, garb, wardrobe, apparel, wearing apparel, clothes, finery, etc. (*ornament*), 847.

outfit, equipment, trousseau; uniform, khaki; livery, gear, harness, turnout, accouterment, caparison, suit, trappings.

dishabille, undress, tea gown, wrapper, negligee, dressing gown, kimono; rags, tatters, old clothes.

robe, habit, gown, dress, frock; blouse, middy blouse, waist, shirtwaist; suit; coat; toga, tunic, smock

dress suit, dress clothes, evening dress, dinner coat, dinner jacket; Tuxedo [*colloq.*]; glad rags [*slang*]

cloak, mantle, shawl, veil; cape, plaid [Scot.], muffler, overcoat, greatcoat; oilskins, slicker, mackintosh, waterproof, ulster; poncho; pea-jacket; sweater, blazer, cardigan, jersey; Mackinaw coat.

jacket, vest, waistcoat; gaberdine.

skirt, petticoat, kilt; bloomers.

trousers, breeches, pants [*colloq.*]; overalls; shorts; tights; drawers; knickers [*colloq.*].

headdress, headgear, coiffure [F.], crush hat, opera hat; tam-o'-shanter, topee [India], sombrero; cap, hat, bonnet, panama, leghorn; derby; nightcap, skullcap; hood coif; wimple: snood; crown, etc., 247; wig, front, peruke, periwig; turban, fez, tarboosh, shako, busby, bearskin; kepi, helmet; mask, domino.

body clothes, underclothing, linen; shirt, undervest, undershirt; smock, shift, chemise; nightgown, nightshirt, pajamas; bedgown.

tie, neckerchief, neckcloth; ruff, collar, cravat, stock, handkerchief, scarf; bib, tucker; boa; girdle, cummerbund [India].

shoe, Oxford shoe, Oxford tie, pump, sneakers, boot, slipper, moccasin, sandal, galosh, arctic, overshoe, rubber; patten, clog; snowshoes, ski.

stocking, hose, sock; hosiery.

glove, gauntlet; mitten, mitt.

V. **clothe,** array, dress, accouter, rig, fit out, deck, drape, robe, enrobe, gown, attire, apparel, equip; harness, caparison; cover, wrap, shroud, swathe, swaddle.

wear; don; put on, slip on; mantle.

Adj. **clothed,** clad, invested, habited.

226. DIVESTMENT.—*N.* divestment; nudity, bareness, nakedness; dishabille, etc., 225.

baldness, hairlessness.

V. **divest,** uncover, expose, lay open, lay bare, denude, bare, strip; undress, disrobe, dismantle; put off, take off, doff.

peel, bare, slough, excoriate, skin, scalp, flay, bark, husk.

Adj. **naked,** nude, bare, stark-naked, exposed; undressed, undraped, unclad, ungarmented, unclothed.

bald, hairless, beardless; shaven, clean-shaven.

227. ENVIRONMENT.—*N.* environment, encompassment; surroundings, outskirts, suburbs, purlieus, precincts, environs, entourage, neighborhood, vicinage, vicinity.

V. **environ,** surround, beset, compass, encompass, inclose, encircle, circle, girdle, hedge, embrace, gird, belt, engird; skirt, hem in; circumscribe, etc., 229; beleaguer, invest, besiege, beset, blockade.

Adj. **surrounding,** begirt; suburban.

Adv. **around,** about: without; on every side, on all sides.

228. INTERLOCATION.—*N.* **interlocation,** interjacence, interpenetration; interjection, interpolation, interlineation, interspersion, intercalation.

intervention, interference, interposition, intrusion; insinuation; insertion.

intermediary, go-between, interagent, middleman, medium.

partition, diaphragm, midriff; wall, party wall; panel, bulkhead.

V. **intervene,** come between, get between, interpenetrate.

introduce, import; throw in, edge in, run in, work in; interpose, insinuate, interject, interpolate, insert, intersperse, interlard, dovetail, splice, mortise.

interfere, intrude, obtrude; thrust in, etc. (*insert*), 300.

Adj. **intervening,** parenthetical, episodic; intrusive; embosomed.

Adv. **between,** among; amid, amidst; in the thick of; betwixt and between [*colloq.*]; parenthetically.

229. CIRCUMSCRIPTION.—*N.* **circumscription,** limitation, inclosure; confinement, etc. (*restraint*), 751; envelope, case.

V. **circumscribe,** limit, bound, confine, inclose; surround, etc., 227; hedge in, rail in, fence round, hedge round; picket; corral; imprison, restrain.

enfold, bury, incase, enshrine, enclasp; clothe, 225; embosom.

Adj. **circumscribed,** begirt, girt; lapped; buried in, immersed in; embosomed, imbedded, mewed up; imprisoned, etc., 751; landlocked.

230. OUTLINE.—*N.* **outline,** circumference; perimeter, periphery; circuit, lines, contour, profile, silhouette, lineaments, relief, bounds; coast line, horizon.

zone, belt, girdle; girth; band; baldric, zodiac; tire, pale, etc. (*inclosure*), 232; circlet, etc., 247.

V. **outline,** delineate, silhouette, block, sketch, circumscribe, etc., 229.

231. EDGE.—*N.* **edge,** verge, brink, brow, brim, margin, border, confine, skirt, rim, side; lip.

threshold, door, porch; portal, etc. (*opening*), 260.

shore, coast, strand, bank; quay, wharf, dock, mole, landing.

fringe, flounce, frill, furbelow; valance; trimming, edging, skirting, hem, selvage, welt; frame.

V. **edge,** coast, border, skirt; fringe, flounce, hem.

232. INCLOSURE.—*N.* **inclosure,** envelope; case, etc. (*receptacle*), 191; wrapper; girdle, etc., 230.

pen, fold; sty, paddock, pasture; pound; corral, yard; net, seine.

fence, pale, paling, balustrade, rail, railing, wall; hedge, hedgerow.

barrier, barricade, cordon, stockade; gate, gateway; weir; door, hatch, prison, etc., 752.

dike, ditch, trench, drain, moat.

V. **inclose,** circumscribe, etc., 229.

233. LIMIT.—*N.* limit, boundary, bounds, pale, confine, term, bourn, verge; termination, terminus, terminal; stint; frontier, border, marches.

boundary line, landmark; turning point.

V. **limit,** bound, compass, confine, define, circumscribe.

Adj. **definite;** terminal; frontier, bordering, border, boundary.

Adv. **thus far,** thus far and no further.

234. FRONT.—*N.* front, foreground, forefront; face, frontage, façade, proscenium, frontispiece; priority; obverse (*of a medal*).

van, vanguard, advanced guard; front rank; outpost; first line; scout.

brow, forehead; visage, physiognomy, features, countenance; bow, stem, prow; jib; bowsprit.

pioneer, etc. (*precursor*), 64.

V. **front,** face, confront, brave, dare, defy, oppose; breast; come to the front *or* fore.

Adj. **fore,** foremost, headmost; forward, anterior, front, frontal.

Adv. **before,** in front, in the van, in advance; ahead; in the foreground.

235. REAR.—*N.* rear, back; rear rank, rearguard; background, hinterland.

tail, scut (*as of a hare*), brush (*of a fox*).

afterpart; stern, poop; postern door; tailpiece, crupper.

wake; train, retinue, suite, cortege.

reverse; other side of the shield.

V. **be behind;** fall astern; bring up the rear; heel, tag, shadow, follow, pursue.

Adj. **back,** rear, hindmost; posterior; after.

Adv. **behind,** in the rear *or* background; at the heels of; after, aft, abaft, astern, rearward, backward.

236. SIDE.—*N.* side, flank, quarter, lee; wing; profile; gable, gable end; broadside.

points of the compass; East, sunrise, Orient, Levant; West, Occident, sunset.

V. **flank,** skirt, outflank; sidle; border; be on one side.

Adj. **lateral,** sidelong; collateral; flanking, skirting.

eastern, eastward, east, Orient, Oriental, auroral, Levantine.

western, west, westerly, westward, Occidental.

Adv. **sidewise,** sidelong, sideling, broadside on; abreast, alongside, beside; aside; by, by the side of; side by side; to windward, to leeward; laterally; right and left.

237. OPPOSITE.—*N.* opposite, opposite side, reverse, inverse; counterpart, antithesis; opposition, polarity; inversion, etc., 218.

antipodes, opposite poles; North and South.

Adj. opposite, reverse, converse; antipodal, diametrical, antithetic, counter; fronting, facing.

northern, north, northerly, northward, hyperborean, boreal, polar, arctic.

southern, south, southerly, southward, austral, antarctic.

Adv. over, over the way, over against; against; face to face, vis-à-vis [F.].

238. RIGHT.—*N.* right, right hand; offside, starboard.

Adj. dextral, dexterous, right-handed, dexter.

ambidexter, ambidextrous.

239. LEFT.—*N.* left, left hand, south paw [*slang*]; near side; larboard, port.

Adj. left-handed, sinistral.

III. FORM

240. FORM.—*N.* form, figure, shape, make, formation, frame, construction, cut, build, contour, outline, stamp, type, cast, mold, fashion; structure, etc., 329; sculpture, architecture.

feature, lineament, turn; phase, etc. (*aspect*), 448; posture, attitude, pose.

V. form, shape, figure, fashion, carve, cut, chisel, hew, cast; roughhew, sketch, block out; trim, model, knead, mold, sculpture; cast, stamp; build, etc. (*construct*), 161.

Adj. structural; plastic, formative, impressible; creative.

shapely, well proportioned, symmetrical, well made, well formed, trim, neat.

241. ABSENCE OF FORM.—*N.* formlessness, shapelessness, misproportion, uncouthness; rough diamond; disorder, etc., 59; deformity, etc., 243; disfigurement, defacement; mutilation.

V. deface, disfigure, deform, mutilate, derange, etc., 61; blemish, mar.

Adj. formless, shapeless, amorphous, unshapely, misshapen, unsymmetrical, malformed, unformed; anomalous.

rough, rude, barbarous, rugged, scraggy; in the rough.

242. [Regularity of form] SYMMETRY.—*N.* symmetry, shapeliness, finish; beauty, etc., 845; proportion, eurythmics, uniformity, parallelism; centrality; radiation; branching, ramification; regularity, evenness.

Adj. **symmetrical,** shapely, well set, finished; beautiful, etc., 845; classic, chaste, severe.

regular, uniform, balanced; equal, even, parallel.

243. [Irregularity of form] DISTORTION.—*N.* distortion, contortion; knot, warp, buckle, screw, twist; crookedness, obliquity; grimace, deformity; malformation; monstrosity, misproportion, ugliness, disfigurement.

V. **distort,** contort, twist, warp, buckle, screw, wrench, wrest, writhe, deform, misshape.

Adj. **distorted,** out of shape, irregular, unsymmetric, awry, wry, askew, crooked, gnarled; not true, not straight; deformed; misshapen, misproportioned, ill-proportioned; ill-made; humpbacked, hunchbacked; bandy-legged, bow-legged; knock-kneed.

244. ANGULARITY.—*N.* angularity, bifurcation; fold, etc., 258; notch, etc., 257; fork, crotch, angle, bend, elbow, knee, knuckle; zigzag; right angle, acute angle, obtuse angle; obliquity, etc., 217.

corner, nook, recess, niche.

triangle; rectangle, square; lozenge, diamond; rhomb, rhombus, rhomboid; quadrangle, quadrilateral; parallelogram; polygon, pentagon, hexagon, heptagon, octagon, oxygon, decagon; cube, prism, pyramid.

V. **fork,** branch, ramify, bifurcate, bend hook.

Adj. **angular,** bent, crooked, aquiline, jagged, serrated; forked, bifurcate, crotched, zigzag, hooked; akimbo; oblique, etc., 217.

245. CURVATURE.—*N.* curvature, curvedness, incurvature, bend; flexure, crook, hook, bending; deflection, turn; deviation, detour; sweep; curl; sinuosity, etc., 248.

curve, arc, arch, arcade, vault, bow, cresent, half-moon, horseshoe, loop, festoon; parabola, hyperbola; tracery.

V. **be curved,** sweep, sag; deviate, etc., 279; turn; re-enter.

render curved, bend, curve, deflect, inflect; crook; turn, round, arch, arch over, bow, coil, curl, recurve.

Adj. **curved,** curvate, devious; recurved, arched, vaulted; oblique, etc., 217; circular, etc., 247; bell-shaped; bow-shaped, embowed; crescent, crescent-shaped, horned; heart-shaped, cordate; hook-shaped, hooked, hooklike; moon-shaped, lunar, sickle-shaped.

246. STRAIGHTNESS.—*N.* straightness, directness; inflexibility; straight (*or* bee, right, direct) line; short cut.

V. **be straight,** have no turning, go straight, steer for.

render straight, straighten, rectify; set *or* put straight; unbend, unfold, uncurl, uncoil, unravel.

Adj. **straight,** rectilinear; direct, even, right, true, in a line; undeviating, unswerving, straight as an arrow; inflexible.

perpendicular, plumb, vertical, upright, erect.

247. [Simple circularity] **CIRCULARITY.**—*N.* circularity, roundness; rotundity, etc., 249.

circle, circlet, ring, hoop; bracelet, armlet; loop, wheel, cycle, orb, orbit, disk, circuit, zone, belt, cordon, band; hub, nave; sash, girdle, cestus, cincture, baldric, wreath, garland; crown, coronet, chaplet, snood, fillet; necklace, collar; noose, lasso.

ellipse, oval; ellipsoid, cycloid.

V. **round**; ring, encircle, etc., 227.

Adj. **round,** rounded, circular, oval, elliptic, elliptical, egg-shaped.

248. [Complex circularity] **CONVOLUTION.**—*N.* convolution, involution, winding, wave, undulation, sinuosity, sinuousness, meandering, twist, twirl; contortion.

coil, roll, curl, spiral, corkscrew, worm, tendril, scallop, kink; serpent, snake, eel; maze, labyrinth.

V. **wind,** twine, twirl, wreathe, entwine; wave, undulate, meander; twist, coil, roll; wrinkle; curl, friz, indent, scallop; wring, contort.

Adj. **winding,** twisted, convoluted; circling, snaky, serpentine, sinuous, undulating, undulated, wavy.

involved, intricate, mazy, tortuous, labyrinthine; circuitous, kinky, curly.

spiral, coiled, screw-shaped.

Adv. in and out, round and round.

249. ROTUNDITY.—*N.* rotundity, roundness, sphericity, globularity.

cylinder, barrel, drum; roll, roller, rolling pin, column.

sphere, globe, ball, spheroid, globule; bulb, bullet, pellet, pill, marble, pea, knob.

V. **sphere,** form into a sphere, roll into a ball, give rotundity, round.

Adj. **rotund**; round, etc. (*circular*), 247; cylindrical, conical, spherical, globular, bulbous; egg-shaped, ovoid, ovate; bell-shaped, etc., 245.

250. CONVEXITY.—*N.* **convexity,** prominence, projection, swelling, swell, bulge, protuberance, protrusion, excrescency.

excrescence, hump; bow; clump, bunch; bulb, bump, knob; knot; boss; tooth, peg; ridge, rib, snag; peak, etc. (*sharpness*), 253; growth, tumor; pimple, wart, wen; fungus, blister; nipple, teat, dug, breast.

proboscis, nose, beak, snout, nozzle.

belly, paunch; abdomen.

arch, cupola, dome, vault.

relief, cameo; low relief, bas-relief, high relief.

point of land, hill, mount, mountain; cape, promontory; fore-land, headland; hummock, ledge, spur.

V. **project,** bulge, protrude; bag, belly, pout, bunch; jut out, stand out, stick out, stick up; hang over, beetle.

raise, etc., 307; emboss.

Adj. **prominent,** protuberant, projecting; bossed, bossy, con-vex, bunchy, hummocky, bulbous; bloated, swollen, distended; bowed, arched; bold; bellied; gibbous; club-shaped, knobby, gnarled; salient, in relief, raised.

251. FLATNESS.—*N.* **flatness;** smoothness.

plane; level, plain, tableland, plateau; stratum; plate, table, tablet, slab.

V. **flatten;** level, etc., 213; fell.

Adj. **flat,** plane, even, smooth; flush; level, horizontal; recum-bent, supine, prostrate.

Adv. **flat,** flatwise, lengthwise, horizontally.

252. CONCAVITY.—*N.* **concavity,** depression, dip; hollow, hollowness; indentation, intaglio, cavity, dent, dint, dimple; honeycomb.

excavation, pit, sap, mine, shaft; caisson; trough, etc. (*furrow*), 259; bay, etc. (*of the sea*), 343.

cup, basin, crater; punch bowl; cell, etc.(*receptacle*), 191; socket.
valley, vale, dale, dell, dingle, glen.

cave, cavern, cove; grot, grotto; hole, burrow, kennel, tunnel; gully, etc., 198.

excavator, sapper, miner.

V. **render concave;** depress, hollow, gouge; stave in; scoop, scoop out; dig, delve, excavate, dent, dint, perforate; mine, sap, undermine, burrow, tunnel.

Adj. **concave,** hollow; funnel-shaped; retreating; cavernous; porous, perforated; honeycombed.

253. SHARPNESS.—*N.* **sharpness,** acuteness; saliency.

point, spike, spine, spit, needle, pin; prick, barb; spur; horn, antler; snag; tag; thorn, bristle; tooth, tusk; tine.

beard, porcupine, hedgehog, brier, bramble, thistle, bur; curry-comb, comb.

peak, crag, crest, cone, sugar loaf; spire, pyramid, steeple.

cutting edge, knife edge, blade, edge tool, cutlery, knife, pen-knife, razor; scalpel, lancet; plowshare, colter; hatchet, ax, pick, cleaver, scythe, sickle, scissors, shears; sword, etc. (*arms*), 727; bodkin, etc. (*perforator*), 262.

sharpener; hone, strop; grindstone, whetstone, steel, emery, carborundum.

V. **be sharp;** taper to a point; bristle with; cut, etc., 44.

sharpen, whet, point, barb, set, strop, grind.

Adj. **sharp,** keen; acute, pointed; tapering; spiked, spiky, studded, peaked, salient; prickly, spiny, thorny, bristling, barbed, spurred, bearded, thistly, briery; craggy, jagged, snaggy; cone-shaped, conical.

keen-edged, cutting; sharp-edged, knife-edged; sharpened.

254. BLUNTNESS.—*N.* **bluntness,** dullness.

V. **be** *or* **render blunt,** dull; take off the point *or* edge; blunt, turn.

Adj. **blunt,** dull, dullish, obtuse, pointless, unpointed; unsharpened.

255. SMOOTHNESS.—*N.* **smoothness;** polish, gloss; lubrication.

smoother; roller, steam roller; sandpaper, emery paper; flatiron, sadiron; burnisher.

V. **smooth;** plane; file; mow, shave; level, roll; macadamize; polish, burnish, sleek, iron, press, mangle; lubricate, oil, grease, wax, anoint.

Adj. **smooth;** polished; even; sleek, glossy, silken, silky; velvety; slippery, glassy, oily.

256. ROUGHNESS.—*N.* **roughness,** asperity; corrugation.

hair, mat, thatch, mop; scalp lock; tress, lock, curl, ringlet; shag; mane; eyelashes, lashes; beard, whiskers; mustache; imperial, goatee; fringe; hair shirt.

plumage; plume, crest; feather, tuft.

nap, pile, grain, texture.

V. **roughen,** rough, rough up, crinkle, ruffle, crumple, rumple; corrugate; stroke the wrong way, rub the fur the wrong way.

Adj. **rough,** uneven; rugged, jagged; cross-grained, gnarled, gnarly, knotted, scraggly, scraggy; craggy, cragged; unkempt, unpolished, roughhewn; prickly, etc. (*sharp*), 253.

hairy, bristly, hirsute, tufted, bushy; nappy, bearded, shaggy.

Adv. **against the grain;** in the rough; on edge.

257. NOTCH.—*N.* **notch,** dent, nick, cut, indent, indentation; embrasure, battlement.

saw, tooth, scallop; jag.

V. **notch,** nick, mill, score, cut, dent, indent, jag, scarify, scallop.

Adj. **notched,** dentate, toothed, serrate *or* serrated.

258. FOLD.—*N.* **fold,** crease, flexure, pleat, plait, tuck, gather; joint, elbow, double; wrinkle, pucker, crow's-feet; crinkle, crumple; dog's-ear; ruffle, flounce; corrugation.

V. **fold,** double, pleat, plait, crease, wrinkle, cocker, crinkle, curl, shrivel, rumple, corrugate, ruffle, crumple, pucker; dog's-ear, tuck, ruck, hem, gather.

259. FURROW.—*N.* furrow, groove, rut, scratch, streak, crack, score, incision, slit.

trench, ditch, dike, moat, trough, channel, gutter, ravine, etc., 198; depression.

V. furrow, flute, groove, carve, corrugate, cut, chisel, plow; incise, engrave, etch, grave.

Adj. furrowed, ribbed, striated, fluted, corduroy.

260. OPENING.—*N.* opening, aperture, yawning; chasm, etc., 198.

outlet, inlet; pore; vent, venthole, blowhole, airhole; orifice, mouth, sucker, muzzle, throat, gullet, nozzle.

window, casement, lattice; embrasure; light; skylight, fanlight; bay window, bow window, oriel, dormer.

portal, porch, gate, postern, wicket, trapdoor, hatch, door; cellarway, driveway, gateway, doorway, hatchway, gangway.

way, path, etc., 627; thoroughfare; channel, gully; passage, passageway.

alley, lane, mall, aisle, glade, vista.

tube, pipe, main; water pipe, etc., 350; air pipe, etc., 351; vessel, canal, gut, fistula; smokestack, chimney, flue; bore, caliber.

tunnel, mine, pit, shaft; gallery.

hole, puncture, perforation; pinhole, loophole, peephole, eye, eyelet; slot.

sieve, strainer, colander, riddle, screen.

opener, key, master key; open-sesame.

V. open, gape, yawn, fly open.

perforate, pierce, tap, bore, drill; transpierce, transfix; enfilade, impale, spike, spear, gore, spit, stab, pink, puncture, lance; stick, prick, riddle.

uncover, unclose; punch, stave in; mine, etc. (*scoop out*), 252.

Adj. open; perforated, wide-open, agape, ajar, unclosed; gaping, yawning; patent.

tubular; pervious, permeable; porous, honeycombed.

261. CLOSURE.—*N.* closure, blockade, shutting up, sealing, obstruction; contraction, constipation; impermeability; blind alley; cul-de-sac [F.].

V. close, plug, block up, stop up, fill up, cork up, button up, stuff up, dam up; blockade; obstruct, bar, bolt, stop, seal; choke, throttle; ram down, dam, cram; clinch; shut, slam, snap.

Adj. closed, shut, unopened; unpierced, impervious, impermeable; impenetrable; impassable, pathless, wayless; untrodden.

tight, unventilated, airtight, watertight, hermetically sealed; snug.

262. PERFORATOR.—*N.* perforator, piercer, borer, auger, chisel, gimlet, drill, awl, scoop, corkscrew, dibble, trepan, lancet, probe, bodkin, needle, stiletto; punch, gouge; spear, etc. (*weapon*), 727; puncher; punching machine, punching press.

263. STOPPER.—*N.* stopper, stopple; plug, cork, bung, spike, spill, stopcock, tap, faucet; valve, spigot; rammer; ram, ramrod; piston; stopgap; wadding, stuffing, padding, sponge [*surg.*], tourniquet.

doorkeeper, gatekeeper, janitor, concierge [F.], porter, warder, beadle, usher, guard, sentinel; watchdog.

IV. MOTION

264. MOTION.—*N.* motion, movement; move; mobility, movableness, motive power; mobilization.

stream, flow, flux, run, course, stir.

rate, pace, tread, footfall, step, stride, gait; velocity, clip [*colloq.*]; progress, locomotion.

journey, etc., 266; voyage, sail, cruise, passage; transit, etc., 270.

unrest, restlessness, etc., 149.

V. move, go, hie, budge, stir, pass, flit; hover around *or* about; shift, slide, glide, roll, flow, stream, run, drift, sweep along; wander, etc. (*deviate*), 279; walk, etc., 266.

put in motion, set in motion; impel, etc., 276; propel, etc., 284; mobilize.

Adj. moving, in motion, traveling; transitional, shifting, movable, mobile, motive, motor; mercurial; restless, etc. (*changeable*), 149; nomadic, etc., 266; erratic, etc., 279; evolutionary.

Adv. under way; on the move (*or* wing, fly, tramp, march).

265. REST.—*N.* rest; stillness, quiescence; stagnation, stagnancy, fixity, immobility, catalepsy; quietism.

quiet, tranquility, calm; repose, relaxation; dead calm; silence, peace, hush; sleep, etc. (*inactivity*), 683.

pause, lull, etc. (*cessation*), 142; stand, standstill; deadlock, dead stand; full stop; embargo.

resting place; bivouac; home, abode; bed, etc. (*support*), 215; haven, etc (*refuge*), 666; goal, destination, bourn.

V. be still, stand still, stand fast, stand firm, lie still, keep quiet, repose, rest; vegetate, stagnate.

remain, stay; stand, tarry, mark time; pull up, draw up; hold, halt, stop, discontinue, stop short, pause; bring to, heave to, lay to; anchor, cast anchor, come to anchor, ride at anchor, lie to; rest on one's laurels, take breath.

dwell, etc., 186; settle, settle down; alight, dismount, arrive.

quell, becalm, hush, calm, still, tranquilize, stay, lull to sleep, lay an embargo on.

Adj. quiescent, still; silent, hushed, quiet; motionless, moveless; fixed; stationary; at rest, at a stand, at a standstill, at anchor; stock-still; sedentary, untraveled, stay-at-home; becalmed, stagnant, quiet; unmoved, calm, restful; immovable, stable; sleeping, etc. (*inactive*), 683.

266. [Locomotion by land] JOURNEY.—*N.* travel, traveling, wayfaring; campaigning.

excursion, journey, expedition, tour, trip, circuit, pilgrimage, march, walk, promenade, constitutional [*colloq.*], stroll, saunter, ramble, hike [*colloq.*], tramp, turn, stalk, perambulation; outing, ride, drive, airing, jaunt.

riding, equitation, horsemanship.

roving, vagrancy, nomadism; vagabondism, hoboism; migration; emigration, immigration. *Wanderlust*, [Ger.].

itinerary, route, guide; handbook; roadbook; Baedeker.

procession, parade, cavalcade, caravan, file, cortege, column.

vehicle, etc., 272.

traveler, etc., 268.

station, stop, stopping place, terminal, terminus, depot, railway station.

V. travel, journey, flit, take wing; migrate, emigrate, immigrate; trek; tour, peregrinate.

motor, bicycle, cycle [*colloq.*], spin, speed; trolley [*colloq.*]. motorize, electrify.

wander, roam, range, prowl, rove, jaunt, ramble, stroll, saunter, perambulate, meander, straggle; gad, gad about.

take horse, ride, drive, trot, amble, canter, gallop, prance, frisk, caracole.

walk, march, step, tread, pace; plod, trudge, wend; promenade; track; hike [*colloq.*], tramp; stalk, stride; strut, bowl along, toddle; paddle; peg on, jog on, shuffle on.

glide, slide, coast, skim, skate.

file off, march in procession, defile.

go to, repair to, resort to, hie to, betake oneself to.

Adj. traveling, journeying; itinerant, peripatetic, roving, rambling, vagrant, migratory, nomadic.

self-moving, automobile, automotive, locomotive.

wayfaring, wayworn; travel-stained.

267. [Locomotion by water or air] NAVIGATION.—*N.* voyage, cruise, sail, passage, aquatics; boating, yachting, cruising; ship, etc., 273.

headway, sternway, leeway; fairway.

oar, scull, sweep, pole; paddle, screw, propeller, turbine; sail, canvas.

aeronautics, aerial navigation, balloonery; balloon, etc., 273; ballooning; aviation, airmanship; flying, flight, volplaning, planing [*colloq.*], hydroplaning, volplane, glide, dive, nose-dive, spin, looping the loop; wing; pinion, aileron.

mariner, etc., 269; aviator, etc., 269*a*.

V. **sail**; embark, etc., 293; spread sail, gather way, make sail, carry sail; ride the waves, ride out the storm.

navigate, scud, boom, drift, course, cruise, steam; coast, hug the shore.

row, paddle, pull, scull, punt.

float, swim, skim, dive, wade.

Aeronautics: fly, soar, drift, hover, aviate; volplane, plane [*colloq.*], glide, dive, fly over, nose-dive, spin, loop the loop, land; take wing, take a flight.

Adj. **nautical**, maritime, naval; seafaring, seagoing; coasting; afloat; navigable.

aeronautic, aeronautical, aerial.

aquatic, natatory, natatorial.

Adv. **under way** (*or* sail, canvas, steam), in motion, in progress, on the wing; afloat.

268. TRAVELER.—*N.* traveler, wayfarer, voyager, passenger; commuter, straphanger [*colloq.*].

tourist, excursionist, globe-trotter [*colloq.*]; explorer, adventurer, mountaineer; wanderer, rover, straggler, rambler; landsman, landlubber, vagrant, loafer, tramp, hobo, vagabond, Bohemian, gypsy, nomad, Arab; pilgrim, palmer; immigrant; emigrant.

fugitive, refugee; runaway; renegade.

courier, messenger, runner; Mercury.

pedestrian, walker, foot passenger, hiker [*colloq.*], tramper.

rider, horseman, equestrian, cavalier; jockey, trainer, breaker, roughrider; huntsman, whip; postilion, postboy.

driver, coachman, charioteer, carter, wagoner, drayman, truckman; cabman, cab driver.

Railroad: engineer; fireman, stoker; conductor, motorman.

Automobile: driver, chauffeur, automobilist, motorist.

269. MARINER.—*N.* mariner, navigator; sailor, seaman, seafarer, seafaring man, sea dog [*colloq.*]; tar, bluejacket, gob [*slang*]; marine; midshipman, middy [*colloq.*]; able seaman, hand; crew; captain, commander, master mariner, skipper; mate, boatswain; boatman, ferryman, waterman, lighterman, longshoreman; gondolier; oar, oarsman, rower.

steersman, coxswain, cox [*colloq.*], helmsman, pilot.

269a. AERONAUT.—*N.* aeronaut, aviator, airman, flier, aviatress *or* aviatrix, pilot, observer, spotter [*mil. cant*], scout, bomber, ace; balloonist.

270. TRANSFERENCE.—*N.* transfer, transference; removal; deportation, extradition; conveyance, carriage; contagion, infection; transfusion; transfer, etc. (*of property*), 783.

transit, transition; passage, ferry; portage, carry; carting, cartage; shipment, freight; transmission, transport, transportation; translation; transposition, transposal.

deposit, moraine, drift, alluvium.

gift, bequest, legacy, deed, lease; quitclaim.

freight, cargo, mail, baggage, luggage, goods.

V. transfer, transmit, transport, transplant, transfuse; convey, carry, bear; hand, pass, forward; shift; bring, fetch, reach; conduct, convoy.

send, delegate, consign, relegate, deliver; ship, freight, embark; transpose; drag, etc., 285; mail, post.

Adj. transferable, assignable, negotiable, transmissible, movable, portable; contagious, infectious.

271. CARRIER.—*N.* carrier, porter, redcap, bearer, freighter, expressman; stevedore; coolie; conductor, chauffeur, truck driver; letter carrier, postman; pigeon post, carrier pigeon.

beast of burden, beast, cattle, horse, steed; charger, war horse; hunter; race horse, racer, courser, Arab, barb; blood horse, thoroughbred; palfrey, cob; nag, jade, hack; pack (*or* draft, cart, dray) horse; mare, filly, colt, foal.
pony, Shetland; broncho, cow pony, mustang.
ass, donkey, jackass, burro; mule.
reindeer; camel, dromedary, llama, elephant.

vehicle, etc., 272; ship, etc., 273.
Adj. equine, asinine; electric, motor, express.

272. VEHICLE.—*N.* vehicle, conveyance, carriage, caravan, car, van.

wagon, dray, cart, lorry, truck.

tumbrel, barrow, wheelbarrow, handbarrow; dump cart; baby carriage, gocart, perambulator; wheel chair; police van, patrol wagon, Black Maria [*colloq.*]; Conestoga wagon, prairie schooner; jinrikisha, ricksha [*colloq.*].
equipage, coach, chariot, phaeton, wagonette, break, drag, landau, barouche, victoria, brougham; sulky, runabout.
post chaise, mail stage, diligence, stage, stagecoach; horsecar, omnibus, bus [*colloq.*]; cab, hansom, four-wheeler, hack; dogcart, trap [*colloq.*], buggy, chaise.
team, pair, span, tandem, four-in-hand.
litter, palanquin, sedan; stretcher, hurdle; ambulance.
sled, bob, bobsled; toboggan; sledge, sleigh; ski, snowshoes, skates, roller skates.

cycle, bicycle, tricycle, tandem; machine [*colloq.*], wheel [*colloq.*], motorcycle; velocipede, hobbyhorse.

automobile, motorcar, limousine, sedan, touring car, roadster, coupé, motor [*colloq.*], machine [*colloq.*], car, auto [*colloq.*], autocar, runabout; truck, tractor; taxicab, taxi [*colloq.*], motorbus; flivver [*slang*], jitney [*colloq.*].

Allied automobile terms: tonneau, chassis, hood, top, ignition, spark plug, generator, distributor, magneto, self-starter, gear, gear box, differential, cylinder, manifold, intake, exhaust, carburetor, ammeter, speedometer, oil gauge, primer, clutch, universal joint, crank shaft, transmission, tire, rim; gasoline; trailer; garage; chauffeur, etc., 268.

train; express, mail; car, coach; baggage car; rolling stock; trolley, electric car, electric [*colloq.*].

Adj. vehicular; traveling, etc., 266.

273. SHIP.—*N.* ship, vessel, boat, sail; craft, bottom.

navy, marine, fleet, flotilla.

shipping, man-of-war, etc., 726; merchant ship, merchantman; packet, liner; whaler; slaver; collier; coaster, freight steamer, freighter, lighter; trawler, fishing boat; pilot boat; yacht.

ship, sailing vessel, clipper ship, windjammer [*colloq.*], bark; brig, brigantine, schooner; fore-and-after [*colloq.*]; sloop, cutter, revenue cutter, yawl, ketch, smack, lugger, barge, scow, cat, catboat.
steamer, steamboat, steamship; tug.
boat, rowboat; shallop, skiff, pinnace; launch; lifeboat, longboat, jolly boat, gig, cockboat, tender, cockleshell, dory, canoe, dugout, dinghy, punt, outrigger; float, raft, iceboat.
coracle, gondola, galley, argosy, galleon; junk, sampan [both Chinese]; dhow [Arab.]; trireme; derelict.

Aeronautics: aircraft; balloon, airship, dirigible, zeppelin, airplane, monoplane, biplane, triplane; air cruiser, flying boat, hydroplane; kite, parachute.

Allied aeronautical terms: fuselage, gondola, wings, controls, aileron, lifting power, rudder; tail, hangar.

Adj. marine, maritime, naval, nautical, seafaring, ocean-going; seaworthy.

aeronautic, aerial; airworthy.

Adv. afloat, aboard; on board, on shipboard.

274. VELOCITY.—*N.* velocity, speed, celerity, swiftness, rapidity; expedition, etc. (*activity*), 682; acceleration; haste, etc., 684.

spurt, sprint, rush, dash, race, steeplechase; round pace; flight.

pace, gallop, canter, trot, round trot, run, hand gallop.

V. speed, hie, hasten, spurt, sprint, scamper, scuttle, trip, post; scud, scurry, whiz; run, dart, swoop, fly, race, shoot, tear, whisk, sweep, skim, scorch [*colloq.*], rush, dash; bolt, run away; ride hard; hurry, hasten, haste; accelerate, quicken; carry sail, crowd sail.

Adj. fast, speedy, swift, rapid, quick, fleet; nimble, agile, expeditious; express; active, brisk, light-footed, nimble-footed; winged.

Adv. apace; at full speed, full gallop; posthaste; in double-quick time; whip and spur; by leaps and bounds; in high (gear *or* speed) [*automobiling*].

275. SLOWNESS.—*N.* slowness, tardiness; languor, etc. (*inactivity*), 683; drawl.

jog trot, dogtrot; amble, rack, pace, single-foot, walk; mincing steps; dead march, slow march.

retardation; slackening; delay, etc. (*lateness*), 133.

slow goer, slowpoke [*colloq.*]; loiterer, sluggard, dawdler; tortoise, snail.

V. move slowly; creep, crawl, lag, walk, linger, loiter, saunter; plod, trudge, lumber; trail, drag; dawdle, etc., 683; worm one's way, inch, inch along, jog on, toddle, waddle, slouch, shuffle, halt, hobble, limp, shamble; flag, falter, totter, stagger; mince, take one's time.

retard, relax, slacken, check, moderate, rein in, curb; reef, shorten *or* take in sail; brake, slacken speed, backwater, back pedal.

Adj. slow, slack; tardy; dilatory, etc. (*inactive*), 683; leisurely; deliberate, gradual; languid, sluggish, apathetic, phlegmatic, lymphatic; moderate.

dull, slow [*colloq.*], prosaic, boring, wearisome, uninteresting, humdrum.

Adv. at half speed, in slow time; with clipped wings; in low (gear *or* speed) [*automobiling*].

gradually, by degrees, step by step, bit by bit.

276. [Motion conjoined with force] IMPULSE.—*N.* impulse, impetus; momentum; push, thrust, shove, boom, boost, explosion, etc. (*violence*), 173; propulsion, etc., 284.

clash, collision, encounter, shock, brunt, crash, bump; impact; charge, onset; percussion, concussion.

blow, stroke, knock, tap, rap, slap, smack, pat, dab; fillip; bang; hit, whack, thwack, cuff, buffet, punch, thump, kick, cut, thrust, lunge; carom, cannon; jab.

Science of mechanical forces: mechanics, dynamics.

V. impel, push; start, set going; drive, urge; boom, boost; thrust, prod; elbow, shoulder, jostle, hurtle, shove, butt, jog, jolt; throw, etc. (*propel*), 284.

strike, knock, thump, beat, bang, slam, dash, punch, thwack, whack; batter, tamp, buffet, cudgel, belabor; lunge, jab, kick; hit, tap, rap, slap, pat.

collide, foul; telescope; bump, butt.

Adj. impulsive, propulsive, dynamic.

277. RECOIL.—*N.* recoil, rebound, ricochet, backlash, boom-

erang: kick; elasticity, etc., 325; reflex, reflux; reverberation, resonance, repulse; reaction, revulsion.

reactionary, recalcitrant.

V. recoil, react; balk, jib; rebound, reverberate, echo; ricochet.

Adj. refluent, recalcitrant, reactionary.

278. DIRECTION.—*N.* direction, bearing, course, set, trend, run, drift, tenor; tendency, etc., 176; dip, tack, aim.

points of the compass, cardinal points.

line, path, road, range, line of march, alignment; airline, beeline.

V. tend toward, conduct to, go to; point to, bend, verge, incline; dip; steer for, make for, aim at, level at; take aim; hold a course; be bound for; make a beeline for.

Adj. bound for; direct, straight; undeviating, unswerving.

directable, steerable, dirigible, guidable.

Adv. toward, on the road to; hither, thither, whither; directly; straight, point-blank; in a bee (*or* direct, straight) line to, as the crow flies; windward, in the wind's eye.

through, via, by way of.

279. DEVIATION.—*N.* deviation; warp, refraction; sweep; deflection, zigzag.

diversion, digression, aberration, drift, sheer, divergence, ramification, forking; detour.

Oblique motion: tack, yaw [*both naut.*]; echelon [*mil.*]; knight's move [*chess*].

V. deviate, alter one's course, turn, bend, curve, swerve, heel, bear off; jibe, yaw, wear, sheer, tack [*all naut.*]; sidle, edge, veer, diverge; wind, twist; turn aside, wheel, steer clear of; dodge, step aside, shy, jib; glance off.

deflect; divert, shift, switch, shunt; sidetrack.

stray, straggle; digress, wander, meander; go astray, ramble, rove, drift.

Adj. deviating, errant; excursive, discursive; devious, desultory, rambling; stray, vagrant, circuitous, roundabout, sidelong, indirect, crooked, zigzag; oblique.

280. PRECEDING.—*N.* preceding, leading, heading, precedence, priority, the lead, van, front; precursor, etc., 64.

V. precede, go before, forerun; introduce, herald; head, take the lead; lead, steal a march, get ahead, outstrip; take precedence.

Adv. in advance, before, ahead, in the van, in front.

281. FOLLOWING.—*N.* following, attendance; pursuant; sequence, sequel.

follower, attendant, satellite, pursuer, shadow, dangler, train.

V. follow; pursue, etc., 622; go after; attend, dance attendance on, dog; shadow; hang on the skirts of; camp on the trail.

lag, loiter, linger, fall behind.

Adv. **behind**; in the rear; after, etc. (*order*), 63 (*time*), 117.

282. [Motion forward] PROGRESSION.—*N.* progression, progress, progressiveness; advance, advancement, headway; march, etc., 266; rise, improvement, etc., 658.

V. **advance**; proceed, go, go on, progress, get on, gain ground, forge ahead, press onward, step forward, make progress (*or* head, headway); go ahead, shoot ahead; distance.

Adj. **progressive**, advanced, up-to-date; enterprising, go-ahead [*colloq.*].

Adv. **forward**, onward; forth, on, ahead, under way.

283. [Motion backward] REGRESSION.—*N.* regression, retrogression, retreat, retirement, recession, withdrawal.

reflux, refluence, backwater, ebb, return; reflexion, recoil.

countermotion, countermovement, countermarch; tergiversation, backsliding, fall; deterioration, relapse, reversion.

V. **recede**, return, revert, retreat, retire; retrograde, back, back out [*colloq.*], back down [*colloq.*], balk; withdraw; recoil, rebound; turn back, fall back, put back; lose ground; drop astern; backwater, put about [*naut.*], veer, shy, double, wheel, countermarch; ebb, regurgitate.

Adj. **retrograde**, retrogressive; regressive, refluent, reflex, contraclockwise, counterclockwise; balky, perverse, reactionary.

284. PROPULSION.—*N.* propulsion, projection; push, etc. (*impulse*), 276; ejection; throw, fling, toss, shot, discharge, shy.

Science of propulsion: gunnery, ballistics.

missile, projectile; gun, etc. (*arms*), 727.

marksman, rifleman, good shot, dead shot, crack shot; sharpshooter, etc. (*combatant*), 726; gunner; archer, bowman.

V. **propel**, project, throw, fling, cast, pitch, toss, jerk, heave, shy, hurl.

dart, lance, tilt; drive, sling, pelt, pitchfork.

send; let off, fire off, discharge, shoot; launch, send forth, let fly; dash.

start, put *or* set in motion, set going, trundle, bundle off; impel, etc., 276; expel, eject.

Adj. **propulsive**, projectile, ballistic.

285. TRACTION.—*N.* traction, draft, pull, haul.

V. **draw**, pull, haul, lug, rake, trawl, draggle, drag, tug, tow, trail, train; take in tow.

Adj. **tractile**, tractional, ductile.

286. [Motion toward] APPROACH.—*N.* approach, approximation; access; advent.

pursuit, chase, hunt.

V. **approach,** converge, near, get (*or* draw) near; move toward, drift; gain upon; pursue, etc., 622; make land.

Adj. **approximate,** convergent; impending, imminent.

287. [Motion from] **RECESSION.**—*N.* **recession,** retirement, withdrawal; retreat; regression, etc., 283; departure, etc., 293; flight.

V. **recede,** go, go back, move back, retire, withdraw, ebb; shrink; drift away; depart, etc., 293; retreat, retire, fall back; run away, fly, flee.

288. ATTRACTION.—*N.* **attraction,** attractiveness; pull, magnetism, gravity.

loadstone, lodestar, polestar, magnet.

lure, bait, charm, decoy.

V. **attract,** pull, drag, draw, magnetize, bait, trap, decoy, charm, lure, allure.

Adj. **attractive,** attracting, seductive.

289. REPULSION.—*N.* **repulsion;** antipathy; repulse, abduction.

V. **repel,** push *or* drive from, etc., 276; chase, dispel; abduct; send away; repulse; keep at arm's length, turn one's back upon.

Adj. **repellent,** repulsive.

290. [Motion nearer to] **CONVERGENCE.**—*N.* **convergence,** confluence, concourse, concurrence, concentration; meeting.

assemblage, etc., 72; resort, etc., 74.

V. **converge,** concur; come together, unite, meet, close in upon; center, concentrate.

Adj. **convergent,** confluent, concurrent; centripetal.

291. [Motion farther off] **DIVERGENCE.**—*N.* **divergence,** ramification, forking; separation, detachment, dispersion, deviation, etc., 279.

V. **diverge,** ramify, branch off, fly off; spread, scatter, disperse, etc., 73; part, sever, separate, sunder.

Adj. **divergent,** radial, centrifugal.

Adv. **broadcast.**

292. ARRIVAL.—*N.* **arrival,** advent; landing; debarkation, disembarkation.

destination, bourn, goal; harbor, haven, port; terminus, terminal; home, journey's end; anchorage, refuge.

meeting, joining, encounter, rejoining; return, re-entry.

V. **arrive,** get to, come to; come; reach, attain; overtake; make, fetch; join, rejoin; return; enter, appear, drop in, visit.

alight, light, dismount, detrain.

land, cast anchor, put in, debark, disembark.

meet, encounter, come across; come (*or* light) upon.

Adv. here, hither.

293. DEPARTURE.—*N.* departure, embarkation; outset, start; removal; exit, etc. (*egress*), 295; exodus, hegira, flight.

leave-taking, adieu, farewell, good-by, Godspeed; valediction, valedictory, valedictorian.

V. **depart;** go, go away, go off, set out, start, issue, march out, debouch, sally forth; sally, go forth; retire, withdraw, remove; cut [*colloq. or slang*], take flight, take wing; fly, flit; strike tents, decamp, break camp, take leave; disappear, etc., 449; entrain; saddle, bridle, harness up, hitch up [*colloq.*].

quit, vacate, evacuate, abandon.

embark, go abroad; set sail, put to sea, sail, take ship; get under way, weigh anchor.

Adv. hence, whence, thence.

294. [Motion into] INGRESS.—*N.* ingress; entrance, entry; influx, inroad, incursion, invasion, irruption; penetration, infiltration; insinuation, insertion, etc., 300.

immigration, incoming, foreign influx.

import [*used esp. in pl.*], importation.

immigrant, incomer, newcomer, colonist.

inlet; mouth, door, etc. (*opening*), 260; path, etc., 627; conduit, etc., 350.

V. **enter;** come in, pour in, flow in; set foot on; burst *or* break in upon, invade; penetrate, infiltrate.

Adj. **incoming,** inbound, inward.

295. [Motion out of] EGRESS.—*N.* egress, exit, issue; emergence; outbreak; outburst, eruption; emanation; evacuation; leakage, percolation, oozing, drain, drainage; gush, outpour, effluence, outflow, discharge.

export [*used esp. in pl.*], exportation; shipment.

emigration, exodus, departure.

emigrant, migrant, colonist.

outlet, vent, spout, faucet, tap, sluice, floodgate; mouth, opening, door; pathway; conduit.

V. **emerge,** emanate, issue; go (*or* come, pass, pour, flow) out of.

exude, discharge, leak; run through, percolate; strain, distill; perspire, sweat; drain, seep, ooze, filter, infiltrate, gush, spout, flow out; pour, trickle; find vent; escape, etc., 671.

Adj. **eruptive,** porous, pervious, leaky; outgoing, outbound, outward bound.

296. [Motion into, actively] RECEPTION.—*N.* reception; admission, admittance, entree; importation; initiation, introduction, absorption; suction, sucking; eating, drinking, etc. (*food*), 298; insertion, etc., 300.

V. **give entrance to,** introduce, usher, admit, initiate; receive, import, bring in; absorb, imbibe, instill, implant, induct, inhale; let in, take in.

swallow, gulp; eat, drink, etc., 298.

Adj. **introductory,** initiatory, preliminary.

297. [Motion out of, actively] EJECTION.—*N.* **ejection,** rejection, expulsion, eviction, dislodgment, banishment, exile, deportation, expedition; discharge, evacuation, eruption, eruptiveness; tapping, drainage; emetic; vomiting.

V. **eject,** reject; expel, discard; ostracize, boycott; banish, exile, fire [*slang*], throw away *or* aside, push out *or* off, send off *or* away; discharge, dismiss, turn *or* cast adrift; turn out, throw overboard.

evict, oust, dislodge; turn out of doors, deport, expatriate.

emit, send out, pour out, dispatch, shed, void, evacuate; give vent to; tap, draw off; pour forth; squirt, spurt, spill; breathe, blow, exhale.

empty; drain, sweep off; clear off, draw off; clean out, purge; tap, broach.

root out, root up, unearth, eradicate; weed out, get out; eliminate, get rid of, do away with, shake off.

vomit, spew; cast up, bring up; disgorge.

unpack, unlade, unload, unship; dump.

298. [Eating] FOOD. –*N.* **eating,** mastication, rumination; gastronomy, carnivorousness, vegetarianism, gluttony, etc., 957.

mouth, jaws, mandible [*esp. of birds*], chops.

drinking, potation, draft, libation; carousal, etc. (*amusement*), 840; drunkenness, etc., 959.

food, meat, nourishment, nutriment, sustenance, nurture, subsistence, provender, corn, feed, fodder, provision, ration, board; commissariat, etc. (*provisions*), 637; prey, forage, pasture, pasturage; fare, cheer; diet, dietary; regimen; staff of life, bread.

eatables, victuals, edibles, grub [*slang*], meat; bread, viands, delicacy, dainty, creature comforts, ambrosia; good cheer, good living.

table, cuisine [F.], bill of fare, menu, table d'hôte [F.], à la carte [F.].

meal, repast, feed [*colloq.*], spread [*colloq.*]; mess; refreshment, entertainment; refection, collation, picnic, feast, banquet, potluck.

mouthful, tidbit, morsel.

drink, beverage, liquor, potion, dram, draft.

restaurant, café, eating house.

V. **eat,** feed, fare, devour, swallow, take; gulp; bolt; fall to; dispatch; tuck in [*slang*], dine, banquet, gormandize, etc., 957; crunch, chew, masticate, nibble, gnaw, mumble.

live on; feed upon; browse, graze, crop; bite, champ, munch, ruminate.

drink, quaff, sip, sup; lap; tipple, guzzle, carouse.

cater, purvey, etc., 637.

Adj. eatable, edible, esculent; dietetic; culinary; nutritive, nutritious; succulent.

underdone, rare; well done; overdone; high [*of game*]; ripe [*of cheese*].

drinkable, potable; bibulous.

omnivorous, carnivorous, flesh-eating, herbivorous, graminivorous, piscivorous.

299. EXCRETION.—*N.* excretion, discharge, emanation, exhalation, secretion, effusion, perspiration, sweat.

hemorrhage, bleeding; outpouring, etc. (*egress*), 295; diarrhea.

saliva, spittle, sputum (*pl.* sputa), spit; catarrh; lava.

V. excrete, etc. (*eject*), 297; secrete; exhale, emanate, etc. (*come out*), 295.

300. [Forcible ingress] INSERTION.—*N.* insertion, implantation, introduction; interpolation, interlineation, insinuation, etc. (*intervention*), 228; injection, inoculation, infusion; ingress, etc., 294; immersion; submersion, dip, plunge.

V. insert, introduce, put in (*or* into), run into; inject; imbed, inlay, inweave; interject, etc., 228; infuse, instill, inoculate, impregnate, imbue.

graft, ingraft, bud, plant, implant.

obtrude; thrust in, stick in, ram in, stuff in, tuck in, press in, drive in; pierce, etc. (*make a hole*), 260.

immerse, merge; bathe, soak, etc. (*water*), 337; dip, plunge, etc., 310.

301. [Forcible egress] EXTRACTION.—*N.* extraction; removal, elimination, extrication, eradication, extirpation, extermination; ejection, etc., 297; export, etc. (*egress*), 295; wrench.

V. extract, draw; take out, draw out, pull out, tear out, pluck out, pick out, get out; wring from, wrench; extort; root up, weed out; eradicate, uproot, pull up, extirpate.

elicit, evolve, bring forth, draw forth; extricate.

eliminate, etc. (*eject*), 297; remove.

express, squeeze out, press out, distill.

302. [Motion through] PASSAGE.—*N.* passage, transmission; permeation, penetration; infiltration; ingress; egress, exit, issue; path, road, way; conduit, opening; journey, voyage, sail, cruise.

V. pass, pass through; perforate, penetrate, permeate, thread, cut across; ford, cross; make (*or* work, thread, worm, force) one's way; find a way (*or* vent); transmit, make way, traverse.

303. [Motion beyond] OVERRUNNING.—*N.* overrunning, overrun, inroad, advance, infraction, transgression, encroachment, infringement; transcendence; redundance, etc., 641.

V. **overrun**, pass, go beyond, go by, shoot ahead of; steal a march upon, gain upon.

outstrip, override, overshoot the mark; outrun, outride, outrival, outdo; beat; distance; throw into the shade; exceed, transcend, surmount; tower above, surpass.

encroach, overstep, transgress, trespass, infringe, intrude, invade.

Adv. ahead, beyond the mark.

304. [Motion short of] SHORTCOMING.—*N.* shortcoming, failure, falling short; default, defalcation; delinquency; fizzle [*colloq.*], slump [*colloq.*]; flash in the pan.

incompleteness, deficiency; defect, imperfection, fault; insufficiency, etc., 640; noncompletion, nonfulfillment; failure, etc., 732.

V. **fall short**, come short of, not reach; want; keep within bounds (*or* the mark, compass).

collapse, fail, break down, flat out [*colloq.*], come to nothing; fall down, slump, fizzle out [*all colloq.*]; fall through, fall to the ground; cave in [*colloq.*], end in smoke, miss the mark.

Adj. **deficient**; at fault; short, short of; out of depth; perfunctory, remiss.

305. [Motion upward] ASCENT.—*N.* ascent, ascension; rising, rise, upgrowth, upward flight; upgrade; leap, etc., 309; grade, ramp, acclivity, hill, etc., 217.

stairway, staircase, stairs; flight of steps *or* stairs; ladder, scaling ladder; companionway [*naut.*]; escalator, elevator.

V. **ascend**, rise, mount, arise, uprise; go up, get up, work one's way up, start up, spring up, shoot up; aspire, aim high.

climb, shin [*colloq.*], swarm [*colloq.*], clamber, scramble, escalade, surmount, wind upward, scale.

tower, soar, spire, go aloft, fly aloft; surge; leap, etc., 309.

Adj. **rising**; ascendant; upcast; buoyant.

Adv. **up**, upward, skyward, heavenward; upturned; uphill.

306. [Motion downward] DESCENT.—*N.* descent, inclination, declension, declination; drop; cadence; subsidence, lapse; downcome, comedown, setback, fall; slump [*colloq.*], downfall, tumble, stumble, slip, tilt, trip, lurch.

avalanche, landslide, slide, snowslide, glissade.

declivity, dip, decline, pitch, drop, downgrade.

V. **descend**, go (*or* drop, come) down, fall, gravitate, drop, slip, skid, slide, settle; decline, sink, subside, droop, slump [*colloq.*].

get down, dismount, alight, light; swoop; stoop, etc., 308; fall prostrate, precipitate oneself; let fall.

tumble, trip, stumble, lurch, pitch, topple; tilt, sprawl.

Adj. steep, sloping, declivitous; beetling, overhanging; bottomless, fathomless, abysmal.

descending; down, downcast, descendent; deciduous.

Adv. downward, downhill.

307. ELEVATION.—*N.* elevation; raising; erection, lift; upheaval; sublimation, exaltation; prominence, relief.

lever, crowbar, crane, derrick, windlass, capstan, winch; dredge, dredger.

elevator, dumbwaiter; escalator.

V. elevate, raise, heighten, lift, erect; set up, tilt up; rear, hoist, heave; uplift, upraise, uprear; buoy, mount, exalt; sublimate.

take up, drag up, fish up; dredge.

Adj. elevated, upturned, stilted, rampant.

308. DEPRESSION.—*N.* depression, lowering; dip, etc. (*concavity*), 252.

overthrow, overturn; upset; prostration, reduction, abasement, subversion.

bow, curtsy, dip [*colloq.*], bob, duck, genuflexion, kowtow, obeisance, salaam.

V. depress, lower, cast down, let drop, let fall; sink, debase, bring low, abase, reduce, precipitate.

overthrow, overturn, overset, upset, prostrate, level, fell; down [*colloq.*], cast (*or* throw, fling, dash, pull, knock, hew) down, raze.

sit, sit down, squat; recline, sprawl.

crouch, stoop, bend, cower.

bow, curtsy, genuflect, kowtow, duck, bob, dip, kneel; incline, make obeisance, salaam, prostrate oneself, bow down.

Adj. depressed; at a low ebb; prostrate, horizontal.

309. LEAP.—*N.* leap, jump, hop, spring. bound, vault.

caper, dance, gambol, frisk, prance, curvet, caracole, buck; hop, skip, and jump.

V. leap, jump, hop, spring, bound, vault, clear, ramp, skip.

prance, dance, caper; buck; curvet, caracole, bob, bounce, flounce; frisk, jump about, romp, frolic, gambol; cavort, cut capers [*colloq.*].

Adj. leaping, saltatorial; frisky, lively, frolicsome.

Adv. on the light fantastic toe.

310. PLUNGE.—*N.* plunge, dip, dive, nose-dive [*aviation*], header [*colloq.*], submergence, submersion, immersion.

diver; diving bird.

V. plunge, dip, souse, duck; dive, plump; take a header [*colloq.*]; make a plunge; bathe; pitch.

submerge, submerse; immerse; douse, sink, engulf, send to the bottom.

founder,welter,wallow; get out of one's depth; go to the bottom.

Adj. submergible, submersible.

311. CIRCULAR MOTION.—*N.* circulation, turn, excursion, circumnavigation, circumflexion; wheel, compass, lap, circuit; turning, evolution; coil, spiral.

V. **turn,** bend, wheel; go about, put about [*both naut.*]; go (*or* turn) round, round, turn a corner; double a point [*naut.*]; make a detour.

circle, encircle, circumscribe, circuit, describe a circle, circumnavigate; go the round.

wind, circulate, meander; whisk, twirl, twist, coil.

wallow, welter, roll.

Adj. circuitous, roundabout, devious.

312. ROTATION—*N.* rotation, revolution, gyration, circulation, roll; pirouette, convolution.

eddy, vortex, whirlpool, maelstrom; swirl, surge; whir, whirl; cyclone, tornado; vertiginousness, vertigo.

V. **rotate,** roll, revolve, spin, turn, turn round, encircle, circulate, swirl, gyrate,wheel,whirl, twirl; roll up, furl; box the compass.

Adj. rotating, rotary; vertiginous.

313. UNFOLDMENT.—*N.* **unfoldment,** unfolding, development; evolvement, evolution; inversion.

V. **evolve;** unfold, unroll, unwind, uncoil, untwist, unfurl, untwine, unravel; disentangle; develop.

Adj. evolutional, evolutionary.

314. [Motion to and fro] **OSCILLATION.**—*N.* oscillation, vibration, undulation, pulsation; pulse, beat, throb.

alternation; coming and going; ebb and flow, flux and reflux, systole and diastole; ups and downs.

fluctuation; vacillation, irresolution, indecision.

swing, wave, beat, shake, wag, seesaw, teeter.

V. **oscillate,** vibrate, undulate, wave; rock, teeter, sway, swing, dangle; pulsate, beat; wag, waggle; nod, bob, curtsy; wobble.

fluctuate, reel, quake; quiver, quaver, shake, flicker; wriggle; roll, toss, pitch; flounder, stagger, totter.

alternate, pass and repass, shuttle, ebb and flow, come and go; vacillate.

Adj. **oscillating;** undulatory, vibratory; pendulous.

Adv. **to and fro,** up and down, back and forth, in and out, seesaw, zigzag, from side to side, shuttlewise.

315. [Irregular motion] **AGITATION.**—*N.* **agitation,** stir, tremor, shuffling, shake, ripple, jog, jolt, jar, jerk, shock, trepidation, quiver, quaver, dance; tarantella; twitter, flicker, flutter.

disquiet, perturbation, commotion, turmoil, turbulence; tumult, hubbub, rout, bustle, fuss, racket.

twitching, chorea, St. Vitus' dance; staggers, blind staggers; epilepsy, fits.

spasm, throe, throb, palpitation, convulsion, paroxysm, seizure, grip, cramp.

disturbance, disorder; restlessness, changeableness, instability.

ferment, fermentation, ebullition, effervescence, hurly-burly; tempest, storm, whirlpool, vortex, etc., 312; whirlwind, tornado, cyclone, typhoon.

V. be agitated; shake, tremble, flutter, flicker; quiver, quaver, quake; shiver, writhe, toss; shuffle, tumble, stagger, bob, reel, sway; wag, waggle, wriggle; stumble, shamble, flounder, totter, flounce, flop, dance, curvet, prance, cavort; squirm; twitch; bustle.

throb, pulsate, beat, palpitate, go pitapat.

ferment, effervesce, foam, boil, boil over, bubble, bubble up; simmer.

agitate, shake, convulse, toss, tumble, wield, brandish, flap, flourish, whisk, jerk, jolt, jog, joggle, disturb, stir, shake up, churn.

Adj. agitated, shaking, tremulous; convulsive, jerky; effervescent, unquiet, restless.

Adv. by fits and starts; in convulsions, in fits, in a flutter.

CLASS III

Words Relating to MATTER

I. MATTER IN GENERAL

316. MATERIALITY.—N. materiality, corporality; substantiality, material existence; incarnation, flesh and blood.

matter, body, substance, brute matter, protoplasm, stuff, element, principle, material, substratum.

object, article, thing, something; still life; materials, etc., 635.
Science of matter: physics; natural philosophy; physical science.
materialist, physicist.

V. materialize, substantiate, incorporate, embody, incarnate.
Adj. material, bodily, corporeal, corporal, physical, incarnate, materialized, embodied; sensible, tangible, ponderable, palpable, substantial; unspiritual, materialistic.

objective, impersonal, nonsubjective.

317. IMMATERIALITY.—*N.* immateriality, insubstantiality, incorporality, unsubstantiality, spirituality; astral plane.

personality; I, myself, me.

ego, spirit, etc. (*soul*), 450; astral body, etheric double, subliminal self, subconscious self, higher self.

spiritualism, spiritism; animism.

spiritualist, spiritist; animist.

V. **dematerialize,** disembody, spiritualize.

Adj. **immaterial,** incorporeal, incorporate, unsubstantial; spiritistic, animistic; discarnate, bodiless, disembodied; extramundane, unearthly; spiritual, etc. (*psychical*), 450.

subjective, personál, nonobjective.

318. WORLD.—*N.* world, creation, nature, universe; earth, globe, sphere, wide world; cosmos, macrocosm.

heavens, sky, empyrean, starry cope (*or* host); firmament.

heavenly bodies, luminaries, stars, asteroids; galaxy, Milky Way; constellations, planets, satellites; comet, meteor, falling (*or* shooting) star; solar system.

sun, orb of day, daystar [*poetic*], Helios, Apollo, Phoebus, etc. (*sun god*), 423.

moon, Diana, Luna, Phoebe, Cynthia, Selene, silver-footed queen.

Adj. **cosmic,** mundane, terrestrial, earthly, sublunary.

celestial, empyreal, heavenly, solar; lunar; starry, stellar, sidereal, astral; nebular.

Adv. in all creation, on the face of the globe, here below, under the sun.

319. GRAVITY.—*N.* gravity, gravitation; weight, heft, heaviness, ponderousness, specific gravity, pressure, load, burden, ballast, counterpoise; mass.

Weighing instrument: balance, scales, steelyard, beam, weighbridge.

Science of gravity: statics.

V. **weigh,** load, press; counterweigh, poise; gravitate.

Adj. **weighty,** heavy, ponderous, ponderable; cumbersome, burdensome, cumbrous, unwieldy, massive; static.

320. LEVITY.—*N.* levity, lightness, imponderability, buoyancy, volatility.

ferment, leaven, yeast, pepsin.

V. **be light,** float, swim.

render light, lighten.

ferment, work, raise, leaven.

Adj. **light,** subtle, imponderous, imponderable, ethereal, airy, feathery, gossamery; volatile, vaporous, buoyant, floating, foamy, frothy; portable.

fermenting, fermentative, yeasty.

II. INORGANIC MATTER

(1) Solids

321. DENSITY.—*N.* **density,** solidity, solidness; impenetrability, impermeability; costiveness, constipation.

condensation; solidification, consolidation, concretion, coagulation; cohesion, etc., 46; petrifaction, etc. (*hardening*), 323; thickening, crystallization, precipitation.

solid body, mass, block, lump; concretion, concrete, conglomerate; stone, rock, cake; card.

sediment, lees, dregs, settlings.

V. **be dense,** compress, squeeze, ram down; solidify; cement, set, consolidate, condense, congeal, coagulate, curd, curdle; fix, clot, thicken, cake, candy, precipitate, deposit, cohere, crystallize; petrify, harden, stiffen.

compress, squeeze, ram down.

Adj. **dense,** solid, solidified; coherent, cohesive, compact; close, serried, thickset; substantial, massive, impenetrable, concrete, hard; crystalline, thick, stodgy.

undissolved, unmelted, unliquefied, unthawed.

indivisible; indissoluble, insoluble.

322. RARITY.—*N.* **rarity,** tenuity; subtlety.

rarefaction, attenuation, expansion, inflation; ether, etc. (*gas*), 334.

V. **rarefy,** expand, dilate, attenuate, thin.

Adj. **rare,** subtle, thin, fine, tenuous, compressible, flimsy, slight, light, porous; rarefied, unsubstantial.

323. HARDNESS.—*N.* **hardness,** firmness, rigidity, inflexibility, temper, callosity; induration, petrifaction, ossification; crystallization.

V. **harden,** render hard, temper, stiffen, cement, indurate, petrify, ossify.

Adj. **hard,** rigid, stubborn, stiff, firm; stark, unbending, unyielding, inflexible, tense.

adamantine, stony, granitic, rocky, horny, callous, bony, cartilaginous.

324. SOFTNESS.—*N.* **softness,** pliableness, flexibility, pliancy, pliability, malleability, ductility, tractility, plasticity, flaccidity, laxity, flabbiness, mollification, softening.

V. **soften,** render soft, mollify, mellow; mash; knead, massage.

bend, give, yield, relent, relax.

Adj. **soft,** tender; mollified; supple, pliant, pliable, flexible, lithe, lithesome, limber; plastic; ductile, malleable, tractable; yielding; flabby, flaccid, lax, limp, flimsy; mellow; spongy.

downy, woolly, fluffy, feathery.

325. ELASTICITY.—*N.* **elasticity,** springiness, spring, resilience *or* resiliency, buoyancy; recoil, rebound, reflex.

V. **be elastic;** spring back, recoil.

Adj. **elastic,** springy, resilient, buoyant.

326. INELASTICITY.—*N.* **inelasticity,** flaccidity, laxity; want of elasticity, etc., 325.

Adj. **inelastic,** flaccid, yielding; not elastic.

327. TENACITY.—*N.* **tenacity,** toughness, strength; cohesiveness, cohesion, adhesion; stubbornness, etc. (*obstinacy*), 606; gumminess, glutinousness, viscidity.

Adj. **tenacious,** cohesive, tough, strong, resisting; adhesive, stringy, viscid, gummy, glutinous, gristly, cartilaginous; stubborn, etc. (*obstinate*), 606.

328. BRITTLENESS.—*N.* **brittleness,** fragility; frailty; shortness.

V. **break,** crack, snap, split, shiver, splinter, crumble, crash, crush, burst, give way; fall to pieces; crumble to dust.

Adj. **brittle,** breakable, delicate, fragile, frail; splintery; crisp, short [*as of pastry*].

329. STRUCTURE.—*N.* **structure,** organization, constitution, organism, anatomy, frame, mold, fabric, construction; framework, architecture; stratification.

texture, contexture; tissue, grain, web, surface, nap; roughness; warp and woof (*or* weft); fineness (*or* coarseness) of grain.

Adj. **structural,** organic; anatomic *or* anatomical.

textile; fine-grained, coarse-grained, ingrained; ingrain; fine, delicate, subtile, subtle, gossamer, gossamery, filmy; coarse; homespun, linsey-woolsey.

330. POWDERINESS.—*N.* **powderiness,** grittiness, sandiness, friability.

powder, dust, sand, shingle; sawdust; grit; meal, bran, flour, rice, spore; crumb, seed, grain; particle.

Reduction to powder: pulverization, comminution, granulation, disintegration, abrasion, detrition; mill, grater, rasp, file, pestle and mortar, grindstone, quern, millstone.

V. **pulverize,** powder, comminute, granulate, reduce to powder; scrape, file, abrade, grind, grate, rasp, pound, bruise, beat, crush, craunch, crunch, crumble, disintegrate.

Adj. powdery, granular, mealy, floury, farinaceous, branny, dusty, sandy, gritty.

pulverable *or* pulverizable, friable, crumbly, shivery.

331. FRICTION.—*N.* friction, rubbing, abrasion, rub; massage; erasure; elbow grease [*colloq.*].

eraser, rubber, India rubber.

V. rub, abrade, scratch, scrape, scrub, fray, rasp, graze, curry, scour, polish, rub out, erase, file, grind, etc. (*pulverize*), 330; massage.

332. [Absence or prevention of friction] LUBRICATION.—*N.* lubrication, anointment, oiling.

smoothness, polish, gloss; unctuousness.

lubricant, lubricator; ointment, salve, balm, unguent.

V. lubricate, oil, grease; lather, soap; wax; anoint.

(2) Fluids

333. FLUIDITY.—*N.* fluidity, liquidity, liquidness; liquefaction; solubility; gaseity, etc., 334.

solution; fluid; liquid; juice, sap, lymph, serum.

Science of liquids at rest: hydrostatics, hydrodynamics, hydrokinetics.

V. be fluid; run; flow, etc. (*water in motion*), 348; liquefy, etc., 335.

Adj. liquid, fluid; juicy, succulent, sappy; rheumy; fluent, flowing; liquefied, uncongealed; soluble.

334. GASEITY.—*N.* gaseity, gaseousness, vaporousness; volatility; aeration; gasification; flatulence.

elastic fluid, gas, air, vapor, ether, steam, fume, effluvium; cloud, etc., 353.

Science of elastic fluids: pneumatics, aerostatics, aerodynamics, aerography, aeromechanics.

V. gasify, render gaseous; aerate; vaporize, etc., 336.

Adj. gaseous, ethereal, aery, aerial, airy, vaporous, volatile, flatulent.

335. LIQUEFACTION.—*N.* liquefaction, liquescence; deliquescence; melting, fusion; thaw; solubleness; solution.

mixture, decoction, infusion, solution.

V. dissolve, liquefy; run; melt, thaw, fuse; hold in solution; percolate.

Adj. liquefied; soluble, dissolvable; solvent, dissolvent.

336. VAPORIZATION.—*N.* vaporization, atomization; fumigation, steaming; distillation; gasification; evaporation.

vaporizer, atomizer, spray, evaporator, still, retort.

V. **vaporize,** gasify, atomize; spray; distill, sublimate, evaporate; exhale, emit vapor; fumigate; fume, smoke, reek, steam.

Adj. **volatile,** vapory, vaporous, gaseous; volatilized.

337. WATER.—*N.* **water,** lymph; aqua [L.], *eau* [F.]; fluid, etc., 333.

washing, bathing, bath, immersion; dilution; infiltration, irrigation, seepage.

deluge, etc. (*water in motion*), 348; high water, flood tide, spring-tide.

sprinkler, shower *or* shower bath; nozzle; atomizer, etc., 336.

water, dilute, add water; moisten, etc., 339; steep, soak, drench, wet, dip, immerse, submerge; duck; drown; wash, lave, bathe, sprinkle, dabble; inundate, deluge; irrigate; infiltrate, percolate, seep.

inject; gargle, syringe.

Adj. **watery,** aquatic, lymphatic; infiltrative, seepy; drenching; diluted, weak; wet, etc. (*moist*), 339.

338. AIR.—*N.* **air,** etc. (*gas*), 334; atmosphere; ventilation.

the open, open air; sky, blue sky.

weather, climate; rise and fall of the barometer (*or* mercury).

Science of air: aerology, aerometry, aerography; meteorology, climatology; pneumatics; aeronautics, etc., 267.

aeronaut, etc., 269*a*.

barometer, aneroid, weatherglass, weather gauge.

weather vane, weathercock, vane.

V. **air,** ventilate, fan, etc. (*wind*), 349.

fly, soar, drift, hover; aviate, etc. (*aeronautics*), 267.

Adj. **containing air,** flatulent, effervescent; windy, etc., 349.

atmospheric, airy; aerial, aeriform; aery, pneumatic.

meteorological, barometric, aerographic, weatherwise.

Adv. **in the open air,** in the open, under the stars, out of doors, outdoors; alfresco [It.].

339. MOISTURE.—*N.* **moisture;** moistness, humidity; dew; marsh, etc., 345.

V. **moisten,** wet, sponge, damp, bedew; infiltrate, saturate; soak, sodden, seethe, sop; drench, etc. (*water*), 337.

perspire, etc. (*exude*), 295.

Adj. **moist,** damp; watery, etc., 337; undried, humid, wet, dank, muggy; dewy; juicy.

sodden, soppy, soggy, dabbled; reeking, dripping, soaking, saturated, soft, sloppy, muddy; swampy, etc. (*marshy*), 345; irriguous.

340. DRYNESS.—*N.* **dryness,** aridness, aridity, drought.

desiccation, evaporation; drainage.

V. **dry,** dry up, soak up; sponge, swab, wipe, drain, parch, sear; desiccate, evaporate.

Adj. **dry,** rainless, fair, pleasant, fine; arid, sear, droughty, waterless, dried, desiccated; juiceless, sapless; corky; husky, parched; waterproof, watertight.

341. OCEAN—*N.* **ocean,** sea, main, high seas, deep, salt water; waters, waves, billows; tide, etc. (*water in motion*), 348; offing, watery waste, pond [*humorous for Atlantic*], the seven seas; ocean lane, steamer track.

Neptune, Poseidon, Oceanus, Thetis, Triton, naiad, Nereid; sea nymph, siren, mermaid, merman; trident, dolphin.

oceanography; oceanographer.

Adj. **oceanic,** marine, maritime; seaworthy, seagoing.

342. LAND.—*N.* **land,** earth, ground, soil, dry land, terra firma [L.].

continent; mainland, main; peninsula, chersonese; delta; neck of land, isthmus; oasis: promontory, etc. (*projection*), 250; highland, etc. (*height*), 206; plain, etc., 344.

realty, real estate, property, acres.

coast, shore, strand, beach; bank; seaboard, seaside, seacoast, seashore; reclamation, made land.

fatherland, home, country, native land; region, etc., 181.

soil, glebe, clay, loam, marl, gravel, mold, subsoil, clod.

rock, crag, cliff, boulder.

landsman, landlubber, tiller of the soil; agriculturist, etc., 371.

V. **land,** disembark, debark, come to land, come (*or* go) ashore.

Adj. **earthy;** continental, midland; earthly, terrestrial; littoral, alluvial; landed, territorial; geographic *or* geographical.

Adv. **ashore,** on shore, on land, on dry land, on terra firma.

343. GULF, LAKE.—*N.* **gulf,** bay, inlet, bight, estuary, bayou, fiord, frith *or* firth; mouth; lagoon, cove, creek; natural harbor; roads; sound, strait, narrows.

lake, loch [Scot.], mere, tarn, pond, pool; well, artesian well; ditch, dike, dam, race, millrace; tank, reservoir.

344. PLAIN.—*N.* **plain,** open country; basin, downs, waste, desert, wild, steppe [*Russia*], grassland; tundra [*Arctic*], pampas [*esp. in Argentina*], savanna [*as in Brazil; also, a treeless plain, as in Florida*], campo [*S. Amer.*], llano [*S. Amer.*], prairie, heath, common, moor, moorland; bush; plateau, tableland, mesa; uplands; reach, stretch, expanse; alkali flat.

meadow, mead, pasture, lea, pasturage, field.

lawn, green, plot, grassplot.

greensward, sward, turf, sod, grass; heather.

grounds; estate, park, common, campus.

345. MARSH.—*N.* marsh, swamp, morass, peat bog, fen, bog, quagmire, slough; mud, slush.

Adj. marsh, marshy, fenny, swampy, boggy, soft; muddy, squashy, spongy.

346. ISLAND.—*N.* island, isle, islet; reef, atoll; archipelago; islander.

V. insulate, island.

Adj. insular, seagirt; archipelagic.

347. [Fluid in motion] STREAM.—*N.* stream, etc. (*of water*), 348 (*of air*), 349.

V. flow, etc., 348; blow, etc., 349.

348. [Water in motion] RIVER.—*N.* running water, jet, squirt, spout, splash, rush, gush, sluice.

waterspout, waterfall; fall, cascade, Niagara; cataract, inundation, deluge; chute, washout.

rain, rainfall; drizzle, shower; downpour, cloudburst; rains, rainy season, monsoon.

stream, course, flux, flow, current, tide, race, millrace, tiderace.

spring, fount, fountain; rill, rivulet, streamlet, brooklet; branch; brook, river; reach; tributary.

body of water, torrent, rapids, flood; spring (*or* high, flood, full) tide; bore, eagre; ebb, reflux; undercurrent, undertow; eddy, vortex, whirlpool, maelstrom.

wave, billow, surge, swell, ripple; tidal wave; comber, rollers, ground swell, surf, breakers, white horses.

Science of fluids in motion: hydrodynamics; hydraulics, hydrostatics, hydrokinetics, hydromechanics.

V. flow, run; meander; gush, pour, spout, roll, jet, well, issue; drop, drip, dribble, plash, trickle, distill, percolate; stream, surge, swirl, overflow, inundate, deluge, flow over, splash, swash; murmur, babble, purl, gurgle, spurt, ooze, flow out, etc. (*egress*), 295.

flow into, fall into, open into, drain into; discharge itself, disembogue.

Cause a flow: pour; pour out, etc. (*emit*), 297; shower down; irrigate, drench, etc. (*wet*), 337; spill, splash.

Stop a flow: stanch; dam, plug, stop up, cork, dam up, obstruct, choke, cut off.

rain; pour; shower, sprinkle, drizzle; set in.

Adj. flowing, fluent, meandering, flexuous; choppy, rolling; tidal.

rainy, showery, drizzly, drizzling, wet.

349. [Air in motion] WIND.—*N.* wind, draft, air; breath, puff, whiff, zephyr, blow, stream, current.

gust, blast, breeze, squall, half a gale, gale.

trade wind, trades, monsoon.

storm, tempest, hurricane, whirlwind, tornado, cyclone, typhoon, simoom [*as in Asia Minor*], harmattan [*W. coast of Africa*], sirocco [*as in W. Africa, Texas, and Kansas*], khamsin [*Egypt*], mistral [*Mediterranean*]; blizzard, norther, northeaster, northeast gale.

wind gauge, anemometer, anemograph; weathercock, weather vane, vane.

breathing, respiration, inspiration, inhalation, expiration, exhalation; blowing, fanning, inflation; ventilation.

V. **blow,** waft; storm.

respire, breathe, inhale, exhale; inspire, expire; puff, gasp, wheeze: snuff, snuffle; sniff, sniffle; sneeze, cough, hiccup.

inflate, pump, blow up.

whistle, scream, roar, howl, sing, sing in the shrouds, growl.
Adj. **windy,** breezy, gusty, squally.

stormy, tempestuous, blustering, cyclonic, typhonic; boisterous, violent.

350. [Channel for the passage of water] CONDUIT.—*N.* conduit, channel, duct, watercourse, canyon, coulee, water gap, gorge, ravine, chasm; race; aqueduct, canal; flume, dike, main; arroyo, gully, gulch; moat, ditch; gutter, drain, sewer, culvert; scupper; funnel, trough, siphon, pump, hose; pipe, tube; artery; spout, gargoyle; weir, floodgate, water gate, sluice, lock, valve.

Anatomy: artery, vein, blood vessel, pore; aorta; intestines, bowels; esophagus, gullet; throat.

351. [Channel for the passage of air] AIR PIPE—*N.* air pipe, airhole, blowhole, breathing hole, touchhole, venthole, spilehole, bung, bunghole; shaft, air shaft, smoke shaft, flue, chimney, funnel, vent, ventilator.

nostril, nozzle, throat; windpipe, trachea.

352. SEMILIQUIDITY.—*N.* semiliquidity; stickiness, pastiness, adhesiveness; thickening, jellification.

mud, slush, slime, ooze; moisture, humidity; marsh, etc., 345.

V. **thicken,** coagulate, gelatinize; jellify, jelly, jell [*colloq.*]; emulsify; mash, squash [*colloq.*], churn, beat up.

Adj. **semifluid,** semiliquid; half-melted, half-frozen; milky, muddy, curdled; thick, gelatinous, mucilaginous, glutinous, sticky; ropy; clotted.

353. [Mixture of air and water] BUBBLE, CLOUD.—*N.* bubble; foam, froth, spray, surf; spume, scum; lather, suds, yeast.

effervescence, babbling, fermentation; evaporation.

cloud, vapor, fog, mist, haze, steam; scud, rack, cumulus; nebula, cirrus, curl cloud; thunderhead; stratus.

V. **bubble**, boil, foam, spume, froth; effervesce, ferment, fizz; aerate.

cloud, overcast, overcloud, befog, becloud, mist, fog, overshadow, shadow.

Adj. **bubbling**, frothy, effervescent, sparkling, fizzy, heady. cloudy, nebulous; vaporous; overcast.

354. PULPINESS.—*N.* **pulpiness**; fleshiness; pulp, paste, dough, sponge, batter, curd, pap, jam, poultice.

V. **pulp**, mash, squash [*colloq.*], macerate; coagulate, etc., 352.

Adj. **pulpy**; [*of fruit*] fleshy, succulent.

355. UNCTUOUSNESS.—*N.* **unctuousness**, oiliness; lubrication; unguent, salve, cerate; ointment, etc. (*oil*), 356; anointment; lubricant.

V. **oil**, anoint, lubricate, etc., 332; smear, salve, grease, lard.

Adj. **unctuous**, oily, oleaginous, fat, fatty, greasy; waxy, soapy, slippery.

356. OIL.—*N.* **oil**, fat, butter, cream, grease, tallow, suet, lard, dripping, blubber; glycerin; coconut butter; soap, soft soap; wax; paraffin, benzine, kerosene, naphtha, gasoline, petroleum; ointment, pomade, unguent, liniment.

356a. RESIN.—*N.* **resin**, rosin, gum; shellac, varnish, mastic, lacquer, sealing wax; amber, ambergris; bitumen, pitch, tar, asphalt.

V. **varnish**, etc. (*overlay*), 223; rosin, resin.

Adj. **resinous**, lacquered, tarred, tarry, pitched, pitchy, gummed, gummy, waxed; bituminous, asphaltic.

III. ORGANIC MATTER

(1) Vitality

357. ORGANIZATION.—*N.* **organization**, structure, organized nature, animated nature; living beings; organic remains; organism; animal and plant life, fauna and flora.

fossils; fossilization, petrifaction; paleontology; paleontologist.

Science of living beings: biology, natural history;[1] zoology, etc., 368, botany; physiology, anatomy, organic chemistry; evolution, Darwinism.

protoplasm, bioplasm; cell, proteid, protein, albumen, germinal matter, germ plasm, germ cell; amoeba, protozoan.

naturalist, biologist, zoologist, botanist, bacteriologist, embryologist.

---

[1]The term *natural history* is also used as relating to all the objects in nature whether organic or inorganic, and including, therefore, *mineralogy, geology, meteorology,* etc.

V. organize, systematize, form, arrange, construct.

fossilize, petrify, mummify.

Adj. organic, organized, structural; cellular, protoplasmic.

fossilized, petrified.

358. INORGANIZATION.—*N.* mineral kingdom, mineral world; unorganized (*or* inorganic) matter.

Science of the mineral kingdom: mineralogy, geology, metallurgy.

V. mineralize; pulverize, turn to dust.

Adj. inorganic, inanimate, unorganized, mineral.

359. LIFE.—*N.* life; vitality; existence, etc.; animation.

vital spark, vital flame, lifeblood; respiration, breath, breath of life.

vivification; oxygen; life force; vitalization; revival; revivification, etc., 163; life to come, etc. (*destiny*), 152.

Science of life: physiology, biology, embryology.

nourishment, nutriment, etc. (*food*), 298.

V. live, be alive, breathe, subsist, exist, walk the earth.

be born, see the light, come into the world; quicken; revive; come to life.

give birth to, etc. (*produce*), 161; bring to life, put life into, vitalize; vivify, reanimate, restore, resuscitate.

Adj. living, alive; in life, in the flesh, breathing, quick, animated; lively, etc. (*active*), 682; vital, vivifying.

360. DEATH.—*N.* death, decease, demise; mortality; dying, dissolution, departure, release, rest, eternal rest; loss, bereavement.

cessation (*or* loss, extinction) of life.

river of death; Jordan, Stygian shore; the great adventure.

angel of death, death's bright angel; death, doom, fate, destiny.

death song, dirge, requiem, elegy, threnody.

V. die, expire, perish; breathe one's last; lose *or* lay down one's life; die a violent death; give (*or* yield) up the ghost.

die for one's country, make the supreme sacrifice, go West [*First World War euphemism*].

Adj. dead, lifeless, inanimate; deceased, late; departed, defunct; gone, no more; bereft of life.

deadly, mortal, fatal.

dying, moribund, at the point of death, at death's door, at the last gasp.

361. [Destruction of life; violent death] KILLING.—*N.* killing; homicide, manslaughter; murder, assassination; effusion of blood; bloodshed, slaughter, carnage, butchery, massacre.

war, warfare, organized murder; battle; war to the death, etc. (*warfare*), 722; Armageddon; deadly weapon, etc. (*arms*), 727.

deathblow, finishing stroke, *coup de grace* [F.], quietus; execution, etc. (*capital punishment*), 972; martyrdom.

suffocation, strangulation, garrote; hanging, etc., *v.*

slayer, butcher, murderer, Cain, assassin, cutthroat, garroter, thug, gallows, executioner, etc. (*punishment*), 975; apache, gunman [*colloq.*], bandit.

regicide, parricide, fratricide [*these words refer to both doer and deed*].

suicide, self-murder, self-destruction, hara-kiri [Jap.], suttee; immolation, holocaust.

fatal accident, violent death, casualty, disaster, calamity.

Destruction of animals: slaughtering, sport; the chase, venery hunting, coursing, shooting, fishing; pigsticking.

sportsman, huntsman, hunter, Nimrod; fisherman, angler.

shambles, slaughterhouse.

V. **kill,** put to death, slay, shed blood; murder, assassinate butcher, slaughter, immolate; massacre, decimate; put an end to; dispatch, do to death, do for [*colloq.*]; hunt, shoot, saber, stab, bayonet, put to the sword.

strangle, garrote, hang, throttle, choke, stifle, suffocate; smother, asphyxiate, drown.

execute; behead, guillotine; hang; electrocute.

die a violent death; commit suicide; kill (*or* make away with, put an end to) oneself.

Adj. **murderous,** slaughterous, sanguinary, bloody-minded, bloodthirsty; homicidal; red-handed, bloody, bloodstained, gory.

mortal, fatal, deadly, lethal; mutually destructive, internecine; suicidal.

362. CORPSE.—*N.* corpse, carcass, skeleton, relics, remains, dust, ashes, earth, clay; mummy; carrion.

ghost, shade, phantom, specter, apparition, spirit, revenant, spook [*colloq.*].

363. INTERMENT.—*N.* interment, burial, sepulture, entombment; obsequies, funeral, funeral rite, wake; knell, passing bell, death bell, tolling; dirge, etc. (*lamentation*), 839; dead march, muffled drum; pall, bier, litter, hearse, catafalque.

cremation, burning; pyre, funeral pile.

undertaker, funeral director.

mourner, mute; pallbearer, bearer.

graveclothes, shroud, winding sheet; cerecloth, cerements.

coffin, casket; urn; sarcophagus.

burial place, grave, pit, sepulcher, tomb, vault, crypt, catacomb, mausoleum; cemetery, burial ground, graveyard, churchyard; God's acre; potter's field; barrow, tumulus; charnel house, dead-house; morgue, mortuary; burning ghat [India]; crematorium, crematory.

gravedigger, sexton.

monument; gravestone, headstone, tombstone; hatchment, stone, marker, cross; epitaph, inscription.

autopsy, post-mortem examination *or* post mortem [L.].

disinterment, exhumation.

V. **inter,** bury, entomb; inurn; cremate.

disinter, exhume, unearth.

Adj. **funereal,** funeral, mortuary, sepulchral, cinerary; burial; elegiac.

364. ANIMAL LIFE.—*N.* **animal life,** animalism.

human system; breath; flesh, flesh and blood; physique, strength, power, vigor, force; spring, elasticity, tone.

V. **incarnate,** incorporate.

Adj. **fleshly,** carnal, human, corporeal.

365. VEGETATION.—*N.* **vegetation,** vegetable life, growth, herbage, flowerage.

V. **vegetate,** germinate, sprout, grow, shoot up, luxuriate, grow rank, flourish, flower, blossom; cultivate.

Adj. **vegetative,** vegetal, vegetable; leguminous, etc., 367.

luxuriant, rank, dense, lush, wild.

366. ANIMAL.—*N.* **animal kingdom,** fauna, brute creation.

animal, creature, created being, living thing; dumb animal, dumb friend, dumb creature; brute, beast.

mammal, quadruped, bird, reptile, fish, crustacean, shellfish, mollusk, worm, insect, zoophyte; animalcule, etc., 193.

beasts of the field, fowls of the air; flocks and herds, livestock, domestic animals, wild animals, game.

Domestic animals: horse, etc. (*beast of burden*), 271; cattle, ox; bull, bullock; cow, milch cow, Jersey, calf, heifer, shorthorn, yearling, steer; sheep; lamb, ewe, ram; pig, swine, boar, hog, sow; yak, zebu, buffalo.

dog, hound, canine; pup, puppy; whelp, cur [*contemptuous*], mongrel.

cat, feline, puss, pussy, tabby; tomcat *or* tom; mouser; Angora, Persian, Maltese, tortoise-shell; kitten, kitty.

Wild animals: deer, buck, doe, fawn, stag, hart, hind, roe, roebuck, caribou, elk, moose, reindeer, wapiti *or* American elk, fallow deer, red deer.

antelope, gazelle, American antelope *or* pronghorn, chamois.

ape, monkey, gorilla, marmoset, chimpanzee, lemur, baboon, orangutan.

fox, reynard, vixen [*fem.*]; dingo, coyote; wildcat, lynx, bobcat; skunk.

lion, tiger, etc. (*wild beast*), 913.

rat, mouse.

lizard, saurian, iguana, newt, chameleon, Gila monster, dragon; crocodile, alligator.

whale, shark, porpoise, walrus, seal, octopus, devilfish; swordfish; pike; salmon, trout, etc.

Birds: feathered tribes, singing bird, warbler, dickybird [*colloq.*].

canary, vireo, linnet, finch, goldfinch, siskin, crossbill, chewink, peewee, titmouse *or* chickadee, nightingale, lark; magpie, cuckoo, mocking bird, catbird, starling; robin, sparrow, swallow, etc.

swan, cygnet, goose, gander, duck, drake, wild duck, mallard.

gull, sea gull, albatross, petrel, stormy petrel *or* Mother Carey's chicken; owl, bird of night; hawk, vulture, buzzard; eagle, bird of freedom.

game, ruffed grouse, grouse, blackcock, duck, plover, rail, snipe, pheasant.

poultry, fowl, cock, rooster, chanticleer, barndoor fowl, barnyard fowl, hen, chicken, chick; guinea fowl, guinea hen; peafowl, peacock, peahen.

Insects: bee, honeybee, queen bee, drone; ant, white ant, termite; wasp, locust, grasshopper, cicada, cicala, cricket; dragonfly; beetle; butterfly, moth; fly, mosquito; earwig; bug, buffalo bug, gypsy moth, weevil.

vermin, lice, cooties [*slang*], flies, fleas, cockroaches *or* roaches, water bugs, bugs, bedbugs, mosquitoes; rats, mice, weasels.

snake, serpent, viper; asp, adder, coral snake *or* harlequin snake, krait [India], cobra, cobra de capello, king cobra, rattlesnake *or* rattler, copperhead, constrictor, boa constrictor, boa, python.

Mythological: basilisk, cockatrice, salamander; griffin; chimera; Python, Hydra, Cerberus.

Adj. animal; zoological; equine; bovine; canine; feline; fishy, piscatorial; ophidian, reptilian, snakelike.

367. VEGETABLE.—*N.* vegetable, vegetable kingdom; flora.

organism, plant, tree, shrub, bush, creeper, vine; herb, seedling; exotic; annual, perennial; pulse, greens.

foliage, leafage, verdure; branch, bough, stem, trunk; leaf, spray, leaflet, frond, pad, flag, petal, needle, sepal; spray, runner, shoot, tendril.

flower, blossom, bud, floweret, flowering plant.

tree, sapling, seedling; oak, elm, beech, birch, timber tree, pine, palm, spruce, fir, hemlock, yew, larch, cedar, juniper, chestnut, maple, alder, ash, myrtle, magnolia, walnut, olive, poplar, willow, linden, lime; fruit tree; arboretum, etc., 371.

banyan, teak, acacia, deodar, fig tree, eucalyptus, gum tree.

woodlands, virgin forest, forest primeval, forest, wood, timberland, timber, wood lot; weald, park, greenwood, grove, copse, coppice, thicket, chaparral, jungle, bush.

undergrowth, underwood, brushwood, brake, scrub, heath, heather, fern, bracken, furze, gorse, broom, sedge, rush, bulrush, bamboo; weed, moss, lichen, turf, grass, herbage.

grassland, plain, etc., 344.

seaweed, alga (*pl.* algae), dulse, kelp, rockweed, sea lettuce, gulfweed, sargasso, sargassum; Sargasso Sea.

V. vegetate, grow, flourish, bloom, flower, blossom; bud, etc. (*expand*), 194; timber, retimber, plant, trim, graft, prune, cut.

Adj. vegetable, vegetative, vegetarian; leguminous, herbaceous, herbal, botanic *or* botanical; arboreous, arboreal, sylvan; grassy, verdant, verdurous; floral; ligneous, wooden, woody; bosky, copsy; mossy, turfy, deciduous, evergreen.

native, domestic, indigenous, native-grown, home-grown.

368. [Science of animals] ZOOLOGY.—*N.* zoology, zoography, morphology, anatomy, histology, embryology; comparative anatomy, animal physiology, comparative physiology, anthropology, ornithology, ichthyology, entomology, paleontology.

zoologist, zoographer, zoographist, anatomist, anthropologist, ornithologist, ichthyologist, entomologist, paleontologist.

Adj. **zoological,** zoologic; zoographical.

369. [Science of plants] BOTANY.—*N.* **botany,** phytology, phytobiology, vegetable chemistry; vegetable physiology, dendrology; flora; botanic garden, etc. (*garden*), 371.

botanist, phytologist, phytobiologist, dendrologist; horticulturist, etc., 371; herbalist, herbist, herbarian.

V. **botanize,** herborize.

Adj. **botanic** *or* botanical, dendroid, dendriform, herby, herbal; horticultural.

370. MANAGEMENT OF ANIMALS.—*N.* **domestication,** domesticity, manège, veterinary art; breeding, taming.

menagerie, zoological garden, zoo [*colloq.*]; bear pit; aviary; apiary, beehive, hive; aquarium, fishery, fish hatchery, fish pond; hennery, incubator.
Keeper: herder, cowherd, grazier, drover, cowkeeper; shepherd, shepherdess; gamekeeper; trainer, breeder; cowboy, cowpuncher; horse trainer, bronchobuster [*slang*]; beekeeper, apiarist, apiculturist.

veterinarian, veterinary surgeon, vet [*colloq.*], horse doctor, horseshoer.

inclosure, stable, barn; sheepfold, sty; cage, hencoop.

V. **tame,** domesticate; corral, round up; break in, gentle, break, bust [*slang*], break to harness, train; ride, drive; spur, prick, lash, goad, whip; yoke, harness, harness up [*colloq.*], hitch, hitch up [*colloq.*], cinch.

groom, tend, rub down, brush, currycomb; water, feed, fodder; bed down, litter.

tend stock, milk, shear; water, etc. (*groom*), *v.*; herd; raise, bring up.

hatch, incubate, sit, brood, cover.

Adj. **tame,** domestic, domesticated, housebroken, broken, gentle, docile.

371. MANAGEMENT OF PLANTS.—*N.* **agriculture,** cultivation, husbandry, farming; tillage, gardening, vintage; horticulture, arboriculture, forestry; floriculture; landscape gardening.

husbandman, horticulturist, gardener, florist; agriculturist, yeoman, farmer, granger, cultivator, tiller of the soil, plowman; logger, lumberman, lumberjack, forester, woodcutter, pioneer, backwoodsman.
garden; botanic (*or* flower, kitchen, market, truck) garden; nursery; greenhouse, hothouse, conservatory; grassplot, lawn; shrubbery, arboretum, orchard; vineyard, orangery.

field, meadow, mead, green, common.

V. **cultivate,** till, till the soil, farm, garden, sow, plant; reap, mow, cut; manure, dress the ground; dig, spade, delve, hoe, plow, harrow, rake, weed; force, seed, turf; transplant, thin out, bed, prune, graft.

Adj. arable, plowable, tillable.

rural, rustic, country, agrarian, pastoral, bucolic, Arcadian.

372. MANKIND.—*N.* mankind, man; human race (*or* species, kind, nature); humanity, mortality, generation.

Science of man: anthropology, ethnology, ethnography.

human being; person, personage; individual, creature, fellow creature, mortal, body, somebody, one, someone; soul, living soul; party [*slang or vulgar*].

people, persons, folk, public, society, world; community, general public; nation, state, realm, republic; commonweal, commonwealth; body politic; the masses, etc. (*commonalty*), 876; population; lords of creation; ourselves.

Adj. human, mortal, personal, individual; national, civic, public social.

373. MAN.—*N.* man, male; gentleman, sir, master; yeoman, chap [*colloq.*], swain, fellow, blade, beau; husband, etc. (*youth*), 129.

mister, Mr., *monsieur* (*abbr.* M., *pl.* Messrs.) [F.], *Herr* [Ger.], *signor* [It., *used before name*], *signore* [It.], *signorino* [It., *dim. of signore*], *señor* [Sp.], *senhor* [Pg.].

Male animal: cock, drake, gander, dog, boar, stag, hart, buck, horse, stallion, gelding; tom, tomcat; he-goat, billy goat [*colloq.*]; ram; bull, bullock; capon; ox, steer.

Adj. male, masculine, manly, virile; unwomanly, unfeminine.

374. WOMAN.—*N.* woman, female, petticoat.

womankind, womanhood; the sex, fair sex, softer sex.

dame [*archaic except as an elderly woman or as slang*], madam, lady, donna, belle, matron, dowager, good woman, squaw; wife.

spinster, old maid, bachelor girl, new woman, girl, etc. (*youth*), 129.

mistress, Mrs., *madame* (*pl. mesdames*) [F.], *Frau* [Ger.], *signora* [It.], *señora* [Sp.], *senhora* [Pg.]; miss, *mademoiselle* (*pl. mesdemoiselles*) [F.], *Fräulein* [Ger.], *signorina* [It.], *señorita* [Sp.], *senhorita* [Pg.].

Effeminacy: betty, molly, mollycoddle, old woman, tame cat [*all contemptuous*].

Female animal: hen; bitch, slut; sow, doe, roe, mare; she-goat, nanny goat [*colloq.*], nanny [*colloq.*]; ewe, cow; lioness, tigress; vixen.

harem, seraglio, purdah [India].

Adj. female, feminine, womanly, ladylike, matronly, girlish, maidenly; womanish, effeminate, unmanly.

(2) Sensation

375. PHYSICAL SENSIBILITY.—*N.* sensibility, sensitiveness, feeling, impressibility, susceptibility.

sensation, impression; consciousness.

V. feel, perceive, be sensitive to.

render sensitive, sharpen, refine, excite, stir, cultivate, tutor.

cause sensation, impress, excite (*or* produce) an impression.

Adj. sensitive, sensuous; perceptive, sentient, sensible; conscious, alive, alive to impressions, impressionable, responsive.

acute, sharp, keen, vivid, lively.

Adv. to the quick; on the raw [*slang*].

376. PHYSICAL INSENSIBILITY.—*N.* insensibility, obtuseness, paralysis, anesthesia, hypnosis, stupor, coma, sleep.

anesthetic; opium, ether, chloroform, chloral; nitrous oxide, laughing gas; cocaine, novocain; refrigeration.

V. render insensible, blunt, cloy, satiate; benumb, numb, deaden, freeze, paralyze; anesthetize; put to sleep, hypnotize, stupefy, stun.

Adj. insensible, unfeeling, senseless, callous, hard, hardened, casehardened, proof, obtuse, dull; paralytic, palsied, numb, dead.

377. PHYSICAL PLEASURE.—*N.* pleasure, bodily enjoyment, animal gratification, gusto, relish, delight, sensual delight, sensuality; luxuriousness, dissipation, round of pleasure; comfort, ease, luxury, lap of luxury; creature comforts; purple and fine linen; bed of roses.

treat; diversion, entertainment, banquet, refreshment, feast.

happiness, felicity, bliss, beatitude, etc. (*mental enjoyment*), 827.

V. enjoy, relish; luxuriate in, revel in, bask in, wallow in; feast on, gloat over, smack the lips.

please, charm, delight, enchant, etc., 829.

Adj. comfortable, cosy, snug, luxurious, in comfort, at ease, in clover [*colloq.*].

agreeable, etc., 829; grateful, refreshing, comforting, cordial, genial; gratifying, sensuous; palatable, delicious, sweet; fragrant; melodious, harmonious; lovely, etc. (*beautiful*), 845.

Adv. in comfort, on a bed of roses, on flowery beds of ease.

378. PHYSICAL PAIN.—*N.* pain, suffering, dolor, ache, smart; shoot, shooting, twinge, pang, gripe, hurt, cut; sore, soreness; discomfort.

spasm, cramp; crick, stitch; convulsion, throe; throb, colic, gripes.

torment, torture, agony, anguish, rack, crucifixion, martyrdom.

V. **suffer,** feel (*or* suffer, undergo) pain; ache, smart, bleed, tingle, shoot, twinge; writhe, wince.

pain, give pain, inflict pain; lacerate; hurt, chafe, sting, bite, gnaw, stab, grate, gall, fret, prick, pierce, wring, convulse; torment, torture; rack, agonize; crucify; flog, etc. (*punish*), 972.

Adj. **painful,** aching, poignant, excruciating, biting; on the rack; sore, raw.

(1) *Touch*

379. [Sensation of pressure] **TOUCH.**—*N.* **touch,** contact, tangency, impact, feeling; graze, glance, brush, lick; manipulation, rubbing, kneading, massage.

V. **touch,** feel, handle, finger, thumb, paw, fumble, grope; stroke, massage, rub, knead, manipulate, wield; throw out a feeler.

Adj. **tactual,** tangible, palpable, tangent, lambent.

380. SENSATIONS OF TOUCH.—*N.* **itching,** tickling, titillation.

itch, scabies; mange.

V. **itch,** tingle, creep, thrill, sting; prick, prickle.

tickle, titillate.

Adj. **ticklish,** titillative.

itchy, mangy; creepy, crawly.

381. [Insensibility to touch] **NUMBNESS.**—*N.* **numbness;** physical insensibility, etc., 376; anesthesia.

V. **benumb,** etc., 376; stupefy, drug, deaden, paralyze.

Adj. **numb,** benumbed, insensible, unfeeling, deadened; intangible, impalpable; dazed, comatose, narcotic.

(2) *Heat*

382. HEAT.—*N.* **heat,** caloric; temperature, warmth, incandescence.

summer, dog days, heat wave, broiling sun; sun, etc. (*luminary*), 423.

flush, glow, blush, redness; fever.

fire, spark, scintillation, flash, flame, blaze; bonfire; wildfire; sheet of fire, lambent flame.

hot springs, geysers; thermae, hot baths, Turkish bath; steam.

V. **be hot,** glow, flush, sweat, swelter, bask, smoke, reek, stew, simmer, seethe, boil, burn, singe, scorch, scald, broil, blaze, flame; smolder, parch, pant.

heat, etc. (*make hot*), 384; incandesce.

thaw, fuse, melt, liquefy.

Adj. **warm**, mild, genial; tepid, lukewarm.

hot, heated, fervid, fervent, baking, ardent, sunny, sunshiny, torrid, tropical, thermal.

close, sultry, stifling, stuffy, suffocating, oppressive, sweltering.

fiery; incandescent, ebullient, glowing, aglow, reeking, smoking; live; on fire, blazing, in flames, in a blaze; alight, afire, ablaze, smoldering.

feverish, febrile, inflamed, burning; in a fever.

383. COLD.—*N.* **cold**, coldness, frigidity, inclemency.

winter; depth of winter; hard winter; arctic, antarctic.

ice; sleet; hail, hailstone; frost, rime, hoarfrost, icicle, thick-ribbed ice; iceberg, floe, berg, ice field, ice pack, glacier.

snow, snowflake, snowball, snowdrift, snowstorm, snowslip, snow avalanche.

chill, chilliness, shivering, goose flesh, chilblains, frostbite, chattering of teeth.

V. **be cold**, shiver, quake, shake, tremble, shudder, chill, freeze.

Adj. **cold**, cool, chill, chilly, frigid; fresh, keen, bleak, raw, inclement, bitter, biting, cutting, nipping, piercing, pinching; shivering, anguish; frostbitten.

icy, glacial, frosty, freezing, wintry, boreal, arctic, snowbound, icebound, frost-bound, frozen.

Adv. with chattering teeth.

384. CALEFACTION.—*N.* **calefaction**, tepefaction, heating, melting, fusion, liquefaction, combustion; cremation; calcination; incineration; carbonization; cauterization.

ignition, kindling, inflammation, conflagration; incendiarism, arson; auto-da-fé [Pg.], the stake, burning at the stake; suttee.

incendiary, arsonist, pyromaniac, fire bug.

boiling, ebullition, ebullience, decoction; hot spring, geyser.

crematory, crematorium, incinerator; furnace, etc., 386.

wrap, blanket, flannel, wool, fur; wadding, lining, interlining; clothing, etc., 225.

Products of combustion: cinder, ash, embers, slag, clinker; coke, carbon, charcoal.

V. **heat**, warm, chafe, foment; make hot; sun oneself, bask in the sun.

fire, set fire to, set on fire; kindle, enkindle, light, ignite; rekindle.

melt, thaw, fuse; liquefy, dissolve.

burn, scorch; inflame; roast, toast, fry, grill, singe, parch, bake; brand, cauterize, sear, burn in; corrode, char, carbonize, calcine, incinerate, smelt; reduce to ashes.

take *or* catch fire; blaze, etc. (*flame*), 382.

boil, stew, cook, seethe, scald, parboil, simmer.

Adj. heated, warmed; burnt, scorched; molten; volcanic.

inflammable, inflammatory, combustible.

385. REFRIGERATION.—*N.* refrigeration, cooling, congelation, glaciation; solidification; ice; icebox, ice chest; refrigerator.

fire extinguisher, asbestos; fireman, fire brigade, fire department, fire engine.

V. cool, fan, refresh; ice, refrigerate, congeal, freeze, benumb, chill, petrify, pinch, nip, cut, pierce, bite.

extinguish, put out, stamp out; damp, slack, quench.

Adj. incombustible, asbestic, unflammable, uninflammable; fireproof.

386. FURNACE.—*N.* furnace, stove; cookstove, cooker, oven, brick oven, tin oven, Dutch oven, range, fireless cooker; forge, fiery furnace; volcano; kiln, brickkiln, limekiln.

brasier, tripod, salamander, heater, warming pan, footstove, foot warmer; radiator, register, coil; boiler, caldron, pot; urn, kettle; chafing dish; retort, crucible, alembic, still; flatiron, sadiron; toasting fork, toaster.

galley, caboose; hothouse, conservatory; bakehouse; washhouse, laundry.

fireplace, hearth, grate, firebox; andiron, firedog, fire irons; poker, tongs, shovel, hob, trivet; damper, crane, pothooks, chains, turnspit, spit, gridiron.

hot bath; thermae; Turkish (*or* Russian, vapor, electric, sitz, hip, shower) bath; bathroom, lavatory.

387. REFRIGERATOR.—*N.* refrigerator, icebox, ice chest; cold storage; refrigerating plant; icehouse; ice-cream freezer, freezer; ice bag, ice pack, cold pack; ice pail, cooler, wine cooler.

refrigerant, freezing, mixture, ice, ammonia.

388. FUEL.—*N.* fuel, firing, combustible, coal, anthracite, bituminous coal; carbon, slack, cannel coal *or* cannel, lignite, coke, charcoal; turf, peat; oil, gas, natural gas, electricity; ember, cinder, ash, slag, clinker; tinder, touchwood; punk.

log, backlog, yule log, firewood, fagot, kindling wood, kindlings, brushwood.

fumigator, incense, joss stick; smudge; disinfectant.

brand, firebrand, torch; fuse, wick; spill, match, light.

V. coal, stoke; feed, fire, etc., 384.

Adj. carbonaceous; combustible, inflammable; slow-burning, free-burning.

389. THERMOMETER.—*N.* thermometer, thermometrograph, thermostat, thermoscope; differential thermometer, telethermometer, pyrometer.

(3) *Taste*

390. TASTE.—*N.* taste, flavor, gusto, savor, relish; smack, tang; aftertaste.

palate; tongue; tooth; stomach.

V. taste, flavor, savor, smack; tickle the palate, etc. (*savory*), 394.

Adj. tasty, savory, flavored, spiced; palatable, etc., 394.

391. INSIPIDITY.—*N.* insipidity; tastelessness, unsavoriness.

Adj. insipid; tasteless, unsavory, unflavored, jejune, savorless; weak, stale, flat, vapid, wishy-washy [*colloq.*].

392. PUNGENCY.—*N.* **pungency,** piquancy, poignancy, tang, nip.

sharpness, acridity; sourness, unsavoriness.

dram, cordial, nip, bracer [*colloq.*], pick-me-up [*colloq.*], potion, liqueur.

tobacco, nicotine; smoke, cigar, cheroot, stogy; cigarette, fag [*slang*], Havana, Cuban tobacco; weed [*colloq.*]; snuff.

V. **season,** spice, bespice, salt, pepper, pickle, brine, devil, curry.

Adj. **pungent,** strong, high-flavored, full-flavored, high-seasoned; gamy, high; sharp, piquant, racy; biting, mordant; spicy; seasoned, spiced; hot, peppery; acrid, bitter; sour, acid, etc., 397; unsavory, etc., 395.

salt, saline, brackish, briny.

393. CONDIMENT.—*N.* **condiment,** flavoring, seasoning, sauce, spice, relish; pickle; chutney; appetizer.

V. season, etc. (*render pungent*), 392.

394. SAVORINESS.—*N.* **savoriness,** tastiness, palatability; delectability; relish, zest.

appetizer, hors d'oeuvre [F.].

delicacy, titbit, dainty, ambrosia, nectar.

V. **be savory;** tickle the palate (*or* appetite); tempt the appetite, taste good.

relish, like, smack the lips.

Adj. **savory,** tasty; good, palatable; pleasing, nice, dainty, exquisite, delicate; delectable, toothsome, appetizing, delicious; rich, luscious, ambrosial, nectareous; distinctive.

395. UNSAVORINESS.—*N.* **unsavoriness;** acridness, sourness, etc., 397; acerbity; gall and wormwood.

V. **be unpalatable,** sicken, disgust, nauseate, pall, turn the stomach.

Adj. **unsavory,** unpalatable, ill-flavored; bitter, acrid, acrimonious.

offensive, repulsive, nasty, sickening, nauseous; loathsome; unpleasant, etc., 830.

396. SWEETNESS.—*N.* **sweetness,** saccharinity.

sugar, saccharin; preserve, jam, sugar candy, sugarplum.

sweets, confectionery, caramel, lollipop, bonbon, jujube, comfit, sweetmeat, confection; honey, manna; glucose, sirup, treacle, molasses, maple sirup, maple sugar; taffy, butterscotch.

Sweet beverages: nectar; mead, liqueur, sweet wine.

pastry, cake, pie, tart, puff, pudding.

V. **sweeten,** sugar, sugar off [*local*]; candy.

Adj. **sweet,** sugary, saccharine, candied, honied, luscious, cloying, honey-sweet, nectareous; dulcet, mellifluous.

397. SOURNESS.—*N.* sourness, acerbity, acidity; acid.

V. **render sour,** acidify, acidulate, acetify; ferment.

Adj. **sour;** acid, acidulated; subacid; tart, crabbed; hard, unripe, green; astringent, styptic.

(4) *Odor*

398. ODOR.—*N.* odor, smell, scent; effluvium; emanation, exhalation; fume, trail, redolence.

V. **have an odor** (*or* scent); smell, exhale; give out a smell (*or* odor); scent.

smell, scent, snuff, sniff, inhale.

Adj. **odorous,** odoriferous; strong-scented, redolent, pungent.

Relating to the sense of smell: olfactory; quick-scented, keen-scented.

399. INODOROUSNESS.—*N.* inodorousness, absence (*or* want) of smell.

deodorization; deodorizer, deodorant.

V. **be inodorous** (*or* scentless); not smell.

Adj. **inodorous,** scentless; without smell (*or* odor).

400. FRAGRANCE.—*N.* fragrance, aroma, redolence, perfume, bouquet; sweet smell (*or* odor), scent.

perfumery; incense, frankincense; musk, myrrh, attar, bergamot, balm, civet, potpourri, tuberose, hyacinth, heliotrope, rose, jasmine, lily, lily of the valley, violet, pomander; toilet water; eau de cologne [F.], cologne, cologne water.

bouquet, nosegay, posy [*colloq.*], boutonniere [F.], buttonhole [*colloq.*].

spray; wreath, garland, chaplet.

Scent containers: smelling bottle, scent bottle, vinaigrette; scent bag, sachet; thurible, censer, incense burner, atomizer, spray.

V. **be fragrant** (*or* scented); have a perfume (*or* aroma); smell sweet, scent, perfume; embalm.

Adj. **fragrant,** aromatic, redolent, spicy, balmy, scented; sweet-smelling, sweet-scented; perfumed; incense-breathing, ambrosial.

401. FETOR—*N.* fetor, bad smell (*or* odor), stench, stink, fetidness, fustiness, mustiness; rancidity; foulness.

V. **have a bad smell,** smell, stink, smell strong, smell offensively.

Adj. **fetid;** strong-smelling; high, bad, strong, offensive, noisome, rank, rancid, moldy, tainted, musty; smelling, stinking; putrid, rotten, foul; suffocating.

(5) Sound

402. SOUND.—*N.* sound, noise; sonority, sonorousness; strain; accent, twang, intonation; tune, cadence; audibility; resonance, vibration; voice, etc., 580.

Science of sound: acoustics, phonetics, phonology, phonography; telephony, radiophony.

V. sound, make a noise; give out sound, emit sound; resound.

Adj. sounding, sonorous, resonant, audible, distinct; auditory, acoustic.

phonetic, phonic, sonant.

403. SILENCE.—*N.* silence, stillness, quiet, peace, hush, lull; rest [*music*]; muteness; silence of the tomb (*or* grave).

V. silence, still, hush, stifle, muffle, gag, stop; muzzle, put to silence.

Adj. silent; still, stilly; noiseless, quiet, calm, soundless, hushed; speechless; aphonic, surd, mute.

solemn, soft, awful, deathlike.

Adv. in dead silence.

404. LOUDNESS.—*N.* loudness, power, vociferation, uproariousness.

din, loud noise, clang, clangor, clatter, noise, roar, uproar, hubbub, racket, hullabaloo, pandemonium; fracas; outcry, etc., 411; explosion, detonation.

blare, trumpet blast, flourish of trumpets, fanfare, blast; peal, swell, alarum, boom; resonance, etc., 408.

V. be loud (*or* deafening); peal, swell, clang, boom, thunder, roar; deafen, stun, rend the air, awake the echoes; resound, etc., 408; speak up, shout, etc. (*vociferate*), 411; bellow, etc. (*cry as an animal*), 412.

Adj. loud, sonorous, deep, full, powerful; noisy, blatant; clangorous, thundering, deafening, earsplitting, piercing; shrill, etc., 410; obstreperous, uproarious; clamorous, vociferous, fullmouthed, stentorian.

Adv. loudly, noisily; aloud; at the top of one's lungs, lustily, in full cry.

405. FAINTNESS.—*N.* faintness, inaudibility; faint sound, whisper, breath; undertone; murmur, hum, buzz, purr, lap [*of waves*], plash; sough, moan, rustle; tinkle.

hoarseness, huskiness.

silencer, muffler; soft pedal, damper, mute, sordine [*all music*].

V. whisper, breathe; mutter, etc. (*speak imperfectly*), 583.

murmur, purl, hum, gurgle, ripple, babble, flow; rustle; tinkle.

muffle, deaden, mute, subdue.

Adj. **faint,** low, dull; stifled, muffled; inaudible; hoarse, husky; gentle, soft; floating; purling, flowing; muttered; whispered; liquid; soothing; dulcet, etc. (*melodious*), 413.

Adv. **in a whisper,** with bated breath, *sotto voce* [It.]; between the teeth; aside; piano, pianissimo [*both music*]; out of earshot; inaudibly, faintly.

406. [Sudden and violent sounds] SNAP.—*N.* snap, etc., *v.*; toot, shout, yell, yap [*dial.*], yelp, bark.

report, thump, knock, clap, thud; burst, thunderclap, thunderburst, eruption, blowout [*tire*], explosion, discharge, detonation, firing, salvo, volley.

V. snap, rap, tap, knock; click; clash; crack, crackle; crash; pop; slam, bang, clap; thump, toot, yelp, bark, fire, explode, rattle, burst on the ear.

407. [Repeated and protracted sounds] ROLL.—*N.* roll, etc., *v.*; drumming, rumbling, howl, dingdong; ratatat, rubadub, tattoo; pitapat; quaver, clutter, charivari; racket; peal of bells, devil's tattoo; drumfire, barrage; whir, rattle, drone; reverberation.

V. roll, drum, boom; whir, rustle, tootle, roar, drone, rumble, rattle, clatter, patter, clack.

hum, trill, shake; chime, peal, toll; tick, beat.

408. RESONANCE.—*N.* resonance; ring, chime, ringing, clangor, bell note, tintinnabulation, vibration, reverberation.

bass; basso [It.], basso profundo [It.]; baritone, contralto; pedal point, organ point; snoring, snore.

V. resound, reverberate, re-echo; ring, sound; chink, clink; jingle, tinkle; chime; gurgle, mutter, murmur; plash, echo, ring in the ear.

Adj. resonant, reverberant, resounding, reverberating; deep-toned, deep-mouthed; hollow, sepulchral; gruff, etc. (*harsh*), 410.

408a. NONRESONANCE.—*N.* nonresonance, dead sound; thud, thump, muffled drums, cracked bell; damper, sordine, mute; muffler, silencer.

V. muffle, deaden, mute; sound dead; stop (*or* deaden) the sound.

Adj. nonresonant, dead, mute; muffled, deadened.

409. [Hissing sounds] SIBILATION.—*N.* sibilation, hissing; zip; hiss, buzz; sneezing, sternutation.

V. hiss, buzz, whiz; rustle; fizz, fizzle; wheeze, whistle, sizzle, swish.

Adj. sibilant; hissing; rustling; wheezy.

410. [Harsh or high sounds] STRIDENCY.—*N.* stridency; stridor, harshness, raucousness; sharpness; creak, jar; creaking, grating; discord, dissonance.

high note, shrill note; soprano, treble, tenor, alto, falsetto; head voice, head tone; shriek, yell, cry, wail, pipe.

V. grate, creak, saw, snore, jar, burr, pipe, twang, jangle, clank; scream, etc. (*cry*), 411; set the teeth on edge, pierce (*or* split) the ears; yelp, etc. (*animal sound*), 412; buzz, etc. (*hiss*), 409.

Adj. **grating,** creaking, jangling, jarring, strident, harsh, coarse, hoarse, raucous; metallic; rough, rude; gruff, grum, sepulchral, hollow.

high, sharp, acute, shrill; piercing, high-pitched; cracked; discordant.

411. CRY.—*N.* cry, shout; shriek; hubbub; bark, etc. (*animal*), 412.

outcry, vociferation, ejaculation, hullabaloo, chorus, clamor, hue and cry, plaint; lungs; stentor.

V. **cry,** roar, shout, bawl; halloo, halloa, yo-ho, whoop; yell, bellow; hoot, boo; howl, scream, screech, shriek; shrill, squeak, squeal, squall; whine, pipe.

cheer, huzza, hurrah, yell.

moan, grumble, groan.

snort, snore; grunt, etc., 412.

vociferate, raise (*or* lift) the voice; yell out, call out, sing out, cry out; exclaim, give cry, clamor; rend the air; make the welkin ring; shout at the top of one's voice.

Adj. **clamorous,** clamant, vociferous; stentorian, etc. (*loud*), 404; open-mouthed; full-mouthed.

412. [Animal sounds] ULULATION.—*N.* ululation, howling, cry, roar; call, note, howl, bark, yelp, bowwow, belling; woodnote; insect cry; twittering, drone.

V. **ululate,** howl; cry, roar, bellow; bark, yelp; bay, bay the moon; yap, growl, snarl, howl; grunt, snort, squeak; neigh, bray; mew, purr, caterwaul; bleat, low, moo; crow, screech, croak, caw, coo, gobble, quack, cackle, cluck; chirp, cheep, chirrup, peep, sing, twitter; chatter, hoot, wail; hum, buzz; hiss; blat [*colloq.*].

413. MELODY. CONCORD.—*N.* melody, rhythm, measure; rhyme, etc. (*poetry*), 597; euphony.

Musical terms: pitch, timbre, intonation, tone, overtone.
orchestration, harmonization, modulation, phrasing.
staff *or* stave, line, space, brace; bar, rest; passage, phrase; trill *or* shake, turn, arpeggio [It.].
note, musical note, notes of a scale; sharp, flat, natural; high note, etc., 410; low note, etc., 408; interval; semitone.
breve, semibreve *or* whole note, minim *or* half note, crotchet *or* quarter note, quaver *or* eighth note, semiquaver *or* sixteenth note, demisemiquaver *or* thirty-second note; sustained note, drone.
scale, gamut; diapason; key, clef, chord.
harmony, concord; tonality; consonance; part; unison; chime.
Science of harmony: harmony, harmonics; thorough bass, counterpoint; composer.

opus (*pl. opera*) [L.], piece of music, etc., 415.

V. **harmonize**, chime, symphonize, transpose, orchestrate; blend, put in tune, tune, accord, string.

Adj. **harmonious**, harmonic, in concord, in tune, in concert, in unison.

melodious, musical, tuneful, tunable; sweet, dulcet, mellow, mellifluous; soft; clear, silvery; euphonious; enchanting, etc. (*pleasure-giving*), 829; fine-toned, silver-toned, full-toned, deep-toned.

414. DISCORD.—*N.* **discord**, dissonance, want of harmony; harshness, etc., 410; charivari, racket; Babel, pandemonium.

V. **be discordant** (*or* harsh); jar, etc. (*sound harshly*), 410.

Adj. **discordant**, dissonant, out of tune, tuneless; unmusical, untunable; unmelodious, inharmonious; singsong; harsh, etc., 410; jarring.

415. MUSIC.—*N.* **music**; minstrelsy; strain, tune, air, melody; piece of music; rondo, rondeau, pastoral; cavatina, fantasia, toccata [It.]; fugue, canon; potpourri, medley; incidental music; variations, roulade, cadenza, cadence, trill; serenade, nocturne.

instrumental music; orchestral score, full score; composition, opus (*pl. opera*) [L.]; concert piece; concerto [It.]; symphony, sonata, symphonic poem, tone poem; chamber music; movement; overture, prelude, voluntary; string quartet (*or* quintet).

lively music, polka, reel, etc. (*dance*), 848; ragtime, jazz; syncopation, martial music, march; allegro, presto.

slow music, Lydian measures; adagio, largo, andante; lullaby, cradle song, berceuse [F.]; dirge, etc. (*lament*), 839; dead march; minuet.

vocal music, vocalism; chant; psalm, psalmody; hymnology; hymn; canticle; oratorio; opera, operetta; cantata; song, lay, ballad, ditty, carol; recitative, aria.

solo, duet, trio, quartet, quintet, sestet, septet, double quartet, chorus; part song, descant, glee, madrigal, catch, round, chorale; antiphon; accompaniment; inside part, second, alto, tenor, bass; score, piano score, vocal score.

concert, musicale, recital, chamber concert, popular concert *or* pop [*colloq.*], open-air concert; serenade; community singing, singsong [*colloq.*].

method, solfeggio [It.], tonic sol-fa, sight singing, sight reading.

V. **compose**, write, etc., 416; attune, tune.

perform, execute, play, etc., 416.

Adj. **musical**; instrumental, vocal, choral, lyric, melodic; operatic; classic, modern, orchestral, symphonic, contrapuntal; program, imitative; harmonious, etc., 413.

416. MUSICIAN. [Performance of music]—*N.* **musician**, virtuoso, performer, player, minstrel; bard, etc. (*poet*), 597; accompanist, instrumentalist, organist, pianist, violinist, fiddler; flutist, harpist, fifer, trumpeter, cornetist, piper, drummer.

orchestra; strings, woodwind, brass; band, brass band, military band, German band, jazz band; street musicians.

vocalist, singer, warbler; songbird; songster, songstress; chorister; chorus singer; choir, chorus.

Orpheus, Apollo, the Muses, Polyhymnia, Erato, Euterpe, Terpsichore.

conductor, choirmaster, bandmaster, concertmaster, drum major, song leader, precentor.

performance, execution, touch, expression.

V. **play,** tune, tune up, pipe, pipe up, strike up, sweep the chords, fiddle, strike the lyre, beat the drum; blow (*or* wind) the horn; twang, pluck, pick; pound, thump; drum, thrum, strum, beat time; execute, perform; accompany.

compose, set to music, arrange, harmonize, orchestrate.

sing, troll, chant, intone, hum, warble, twitter, carol, chirp, chirrup, lilt, quaver, trill, shake.

Adj. **musical;** lyric, dramatic; bravura, florid, brilliant.

417. MUSICAL INSTRUMENTS.—*N.* musical instruments; orchestra (*including* strings, woodwind, brass, and percussive instruments); band; string band, military band, brass band.

418. [Sense of sound] HEARING.—*N.* hearing, audition; audibility; acoustics; ear for music.

ear; eardrum, tympanum.

Instruments: ear trumpet, audiphone, dentiphone, speaking trumpet; phonograph, gramophone, graphophone, microphone, victrola; stethoscope; telephone, radiophone, wireless telephone, radio.

hearer, auditor, audience, listener; eavesdropper.

V. **hear,** overhear; hark, hearken; list, listen; strain one's ears, attend to, give attention, prick up one's ears; give ear, give a hearing to.

Adj. **hearing,** auditory, acoustic, phonic; auricular; auditive.

419. DEAFNESS—*N.* **deafness,** hardness of hearing, inaudibility; deaf-mute; deaf-and-dumb alphabet.

V. **deafen,** render deaf, stun, split the ears (*or* eardrum).

Adj. **deaf,** hard (*or* dull) of hearing; stunned, deafened; stone-deaf; inattentive.

inaudible, out of earshot (*or* hearing).

(6) *Light*

420. LIGHT.—*N.* **light,** ray, beam, stream (*of light*), gleam, streak; sunbeam, moonbeam; aurora, dawn, daylight, day, sunshine; glint, glare, glow, afterglow; sun, etc., 423.

reflection, refraction, dispersion.

halo, glory, nimbus, aureole, aura.

spark, scintilla, scintillation, flash, blaze, coruscation; flame, glare, blaze; lightning; phosphorescence.

luster, sheen, shimmer, gloss, brightness, brilliancy, splendor, effulgence; illumination, radiance, radiation.

Science of light: optics, radiometry; photography; phototelegraphy, radiotelegraphy; actinic rays, radioactivity; Röntgen rays, X rays, ultraviolet rays.

illuminant, gas, etc., 423.

V. shine, glow, beam, glitter, glisten, gleam; flare, blaze, glare, shimmer, glimmer, flicker, sparkle, scintillate, coruscate, flash.

daze, dazzle, bedazzle.

lighten, enlighten, light, irradiate, illume, illumine, illuminate; kindle, etc., 384.

Adj. luminous, lucent; light, sunny, bright, vivid, splendid, resplendent, refulgent, lustrous, brilliant, radiant, lambent; aglow.

shiny, glossy, burnished, glassy.

clear, cloudless, unclouded.

421. DARKNESS.—*N.* darkness, duskiness; blackness, swarthiness; obscurity, gloom, murk, murkiness; dusk; dimness, etc., 422.

night; midnight; dead of night.

shadow, shade; obscuration, adumbration; eclipse; radiograph.

V. darken, obscure, shade, dim; lower, overcast, overshadow, cloud, becloud, bedim.

extinguish, put out, blow out, snuff out.

Adj. dark, darkling, obscure; black, etc. (*color*), 431; nocturnal.

somber, dusky; dingy, lurid, gloomy, murky; shady, umbrageous; overcast, etc. (*dim*), 422; cloudy, etc., 426.

422. DIMNESS.—*N.* dimness, paleness, dullness, duskiness, mistiness.

twilight, dusk, nightfall, gloaming; dawn, daybreak, break of day, Aurora; moonlight, moonshine [*poetic*], starlight.

V. cloud over, gloom, lower.

twinkle, glimmer, flicker.

pale, fade, grow dim.

dim, bedim, obscure, shade, shadow, darken, cloud, becloud.

Adj. dim, dull, dingy, dusky, lackluster; cloudy, misty, hazy, leaden, lurid, dun; overcast, dirty.

423. [Source of light] LUMINARY.—*N.* luminary; light, ray, beam; flame, etc. (*fire*), 382; spark, scintilla; phosphorescence.

Heavenly bodies: sun, orb of day, daystar [*poetic*]; star; constellation; galaxy, Milky Way; polestar, Polaris; morning star, Lucifer; evening star, Venus; moon, etc., 318.

sun god, Helios, Phoebus, Apollo, Hyperion, Ra [*Egypt*].

phosphorus; *ignis fatuus* [L.]; jack-o'-lantern, will-o'-the-wisp.

polar lights, northern lights, aurora borealis [L.], aurora australis [L.]; aurora.

Artificial light: gas, gaslight, electric light, electric torch; headlight, searchlight; spotlight, flashlight, limelight, calcium light; lamplight, lamp, lantern, dark lantern, bull's-eye; candle, taper, rushlight; torch, flambeau, brand; gaselier, chandelier; candelabrum, sconce, luster, candlestick; fireworks, pyrotechnics.

signal light, rocket, balefire, beacon fire; lighthouse.

V. illuminate, etc. (*light*), 420.

Adj. self luminous; phosphorescent; radiant, etc. (*light*), 420.

424. SHADE.—*N.* shade; awning, etc. (*cover*), 223.

screen, curtain, portiere [F.]; shutter, blind.

veil, mantle, mask.

cloud, mist, shadow; smoke screen [*mil.*].

blinkers, blinders; smoked glasses, colored spectacles.

V. veil, draw a curtain; cast a shadow, etc. (*darken*), 421.

Adj. shady, umbrageous, shadowy.

425. TRANSPARENCY.—*N.* transparency, transparence, translucence, diaphanousness; lucidity, limpidity; fluorescence; translumination.

V. be transparent (*or* pellucid); transmit light.

Adj. transparent, pellucid, lucid, diaphanous; translucent, limpid, clear, serene, crystalline.

426. OPACITY.—*N.* opacity, opaqueness; cloudiness; film; cloud, etc., 353.

V. be opaque; obstruct the passage of light.

Adj. opaque, impervious to light; dim, etc., 422; turbid, thick, muddy, cloudy, foggy, vaporous; smoky, murky, smeared, dirty.

427. SEMITRANSPARENCY.—*N.* semitransparency, opalescence, milkiness, pearliness; mist, haze, steam.

V. cloud, frost, cloud over, frost over.

Adj. semitransparent, semidiaphanous, semiopaque; opalescent, opaline; pearly, milky; frosted, hazy, misty.

428. [Specific Light] COLOR.—*N.* color, hue, tint, tinge, dye, complexion, shade, tincture; coloration; glow, flush; tone, key.

primary color, complementary color; coloring, keeping, tone, value.

spectrum, spectrum analysis; prism, spectroscope, kaleidoscope.

pigment, coloring matter, paint, dye, wash, distemper, stain; medium.

V. color, dye, tinge, stain, tint, tone; paint, wash, distemper, ingrain, grain, illuminate, emblazon.

Adj. colored, dyed; chromatic, prismatic; double-dyed.

bright, vivid, intense, deep; fresh, rich, gorgeous; bright-colored, gay.

gaudy, florid; garish; showy, flaunting; flashy; many-colored, parti-colored, variegated; raw, crude; glaring, flaring.

mellow, harmonious, pearly, sweet, delicate, subtle, tender.

dull, sad, somber, sad-colored, grave, gray, dark.

429. ABSENCE OF COLOR.—*N.* decoloration, discoloration; pallor, paleness, sallowness.

neutral tint, monochrome, black and white.

V. lose color, fade, become colorless, turn pale; pale, fade out.

deprive of color, decolor, wash out, tone down; whiten, bleach, blanch.

Adj. colorless, uncolored, hueless, pale, pallid; pale-faced, anemic; faint, dull, cold, muddy, leaden, dun, wan, sallow, dingy, ashy, ashen, ghastly, cadaverous, glassy, lackluster; discolored.

light-colored, fair, blond, ash-blond; white, etc., 430; towheaded.

430. WHITENESS.—*N.* whiteness, showiness, hoariness.

whitewash, whiting, whitening, calcimine.

V. whiten, bleach, blanch, silver, frost.

whitewash, calcimine, white.

Adj. white, snow-white, snowy, frosted, hoar, hoary; silvery, silver, milk-white, milky.

whitish, creamy, pearly, ivory, fair, blond, ash-blond; blanched; light.

431. BLACKNESS.—*N.* blackness, darkness, obscurity; swarthiness, swartness; lividness.

Negro, Negress, blackamoor, man of color, colored man, colored woman, nigger [*colloq., usually contemptuous*], darky [*colloq.*], black, Ethiop, Ethiopian, Hottentot, Pygmy, Bushman, African.

V. black, blacken, blot, blotch, smut, smudge, smirch; darken, etc., 421.

Adj. black, sable, somber, livid, dark, inky, ebon, pitchy, sooty; swart, swarthy, dusky, dingy, murky; blotchy, smudgy; low-toned.

432. GRAY.—*N.* gray, etc., *adj.*; grayness; neutral tint, silver, dove color, pepper and salt, chiaroscuro [It.].

V. render gray, gray.

Adj. gray; iron-gray, dun, drab, dingy, leaden, pearly, dove-colored, silver, silvery, silvered; dapple-gray; ashen, ashy; grizzly, grizzled.

433. BROWN.—*N.* brown, etc., *adj.*; brownness.

V. render brown, brown, tan, embrown, bronze.

Adj. brown, nut-brown, seal-brown, mahogany, chocolate; fawn, ecru, tawny; tan, fawn-colored, snuff-colored, liver-colored.

reddish-brown, terra cotta, russet, foxy, bronze, coppery, copper-colored, maroon; bay, roan, sorrel; chestnut, henna, auburn, hazel.

sunburned; tanned, etc., *v.*

434. RED.—*N.* red, etc., *adj.*; flesh color, flesh tint, color, warmth; redness, ruddiness, blush.

V. **redden,** rouge, crimson, incarnadine; ruddle, rust.
blush, flush, color, color up, mantle, redden.

Adj. **red,** scarlet, cardinal, vermilion, carmine, crimson, pink, rose, cerise, cherry, salmon, maroon, carnation, magenta, solferino, damask.

reddish; sanguine, bloody, gory; coral, coralline, rosy, roseate; blood-red, wine-red, wine-colored, ruby, rufous, bricky, reddish-brown, etc., 433; rose (*or* ruby, cherry, claret, flame, flesh, peach, salmon, brick, rust) -colored.

red-complexioned, red-faced, florid, burned, rubicund, ruddy, red, high-colored, glowing, sanguine, blooming, rosy, hectic, flushed, inflamed.

Of hair: sandy, carroty, brick-red, Titian, auburn, chestnut.

435. GREEN.—*N.* green, etc., *adj.*; greenness, verdancy, verdure.

Adj. **green,** verdant, olive; verdurous; emerald (*or* pea, grass, apple, sea, leaf, bottle, Irish, Kelly) green; greenish, aquamarine, blue-green.

436. YELLOW.—*N.* yellow, etc., *adj.*; yellowness; jaundice.
V. **render yellow,** yellow, gild.

Adj. **yellow,** aureate, golden, gold, gilt, gilded, lemon, fallow; sallow, jaundiced; tawny, cream, creamy; flaxen, yellowish, buff; gold (*or* saffron, citron, lemon, amber, straw, primrose, cream) -colored.

437. PURPLE.—*N.* purple, etc., *adj.*; royal purple; gridelin, amethyst; damson, heliotrope.

V. **render purple,** purple, empurple.

Adj. **purple,** violet, plum-colored, lavender, lilac, puce, mauve, purplish, amethystine, magenta, solferino, heliotrope; livid; purplish.

438. BLUE.—*N.* blue, etc., *adj.*; azure [*her.*]; indigo; sapphire, blueness, bluishness; bloom.

Adj. **blue,** azure, cerulean, sky-blue, navy-blue, midnight-blue, cadet-blue, robin's-egg-blue, baby-blue, ultramarine, aquamarine, electric-blue, steel-blue; bluish; cold.

439. ORANGE.—*N.* orange, old gold; gold color, etc., *adj.*
Adj. **orange,** orange (*or* gold, brass, apricot) -colored; warm, hot, glowing, flame-colored.

440. VARIEGATION.—*N.* variegation; iridescence, play of colors, spottiness; tricolor.

check, plaid, tartan, patchwork; marquetry, parquet, parquetry, mosaic, checkerwork; chessboard, checkers; harlequin.

V. **variegate,** stripe, streak, checker, fleck, speckle, besprinkle,

sprinkle; stipple, dot, tattoo, inlay, tessellate; damascene; embroider, quilt.

Adj. **variegated,** many-colored, many-hued, divers-colored, parti-colored, polychromatic; kaleidoscopic.

iridescent, opaline, opalescent, prismatic, pearly, shot, tortoiseshell.

mottled, pied, piebald, skewbald; motley, marbled, pepper-and-salt, dappled.

checkered, checked, plaid, mosaic, tessellated.

spotted, spotty; powdered; speckled, freckled, flea-bitten, studded; flecked.

barred, veined, brindled, tabby, watered.

441. [Perception of light] VISION.—*N.* vision, sight, optics, eyesight.

view, look, glance, ken, glimpse, glint, peep, peek; gaze, stare, leer; contemplation, regard, survey; inspection, reconnaissance, watch, espionage, autopsy; sight-seeing, globe-trotting [*colloq.*].

viewpoint, standpoint, point of view; loophole, watchtower.

field of view; theater, amphitheater, arena, vista, horizon; bird's-eye view, panoramic view.

eye, visual organ, organ of vision, naked eye; clear (*or* sharp, quick, eagle) sight.

V. **see,** behold, discern, perceive, descry, sight, make out; discover, distinguish, recognize, spy, espy, command a view of; witness, contemplate, look on, see at a glance.

look, view, eye, survey, scan, inspect; reconnoiter, glance, cast a glance; observe, etc. (*attend to*), 457; watch, keep watch; watch for, etc. (*expect*), 507; peep, peek, peer, pry, take a peep.

look intently; strain one's eyes; rivet the eyes upon; stare, gaze; pore over, gloat on, gloat over; leer, ogle, glare; goggle; squint, gloat, look askance.

Adj. **ocular,** visual, optic *or* optical; ophthalmic; visible, etc., 446.

clear-sighted, clear-eyed, farsighted; eagle-eyed, hawk-eyed, lynx-eyed, keen-eyed, Argus-eyed.

Adv. **at sight,** at first sight, at a glance, at the first blush.

442. BLINDNESS.—*N.* blindness, sightlessness, benightedness, cataract; dim-sightedness, etc., 443; Braille.

V. **be blind,** not see; lose one's sight; grope in the dark.

blind, blindfold, hoodwink, dazzle; put one's eyes out; throw dust into one's eyes; screen, hide.

Adj. **blind,** eyeless, sightless, visionless; dark; stone-blind, stark-blind, undiscerning; dim-sighted, etc., 443.

Adv. **blindly,** blindfold; darkly.

443. DIM-SIGHTEDNESS.—*N*. **Imperfect vision:** dim (*or* short, near, long) -sightedness; purblindness, blearedness, myopia, astigmatism; color blindness, snow blindness; ophthalmia; cataract.

squint, cross-eye, cast in the eye, swivel eye, cockeye, goggle-eyes.

Limitation of vision: blinker, blinder; screen, curtain, veil.

Fallacies of vision: refraction, distortion, illusion, mirage, phantasm, phantom; vision; specter, apparition, ghost; will-o'-the-wisp, etc., 423.

V. **be dim-sighted,** see double; see through a glass darkly; wink, blink, squint, look askance, screw up the eyes, glare, glower.

dazzle, glare, swim, blur.

Adj. **dim-sighted,** myopic, nearsighted, shortsighted, astigmatic; blear-eyed, goggle-eyed, one-eyed; half-blind, purblind; cockeyed [*colloq*.], dim-eyed, mole-eyed.

444. SPECTATOR.—*N*. **spectator,** beholder, observer, looker-on, onlooker, witness, eyewitness, bystander, passer-by; sightseer; rubberneck [*slang*].

spy, scout; sentinel, etc. (*warning*), 668.

grandstand [*fig*.], bleachers [*fig*.], gallery.

V. **witness,** behold, etc. (*see*), 441; look on, etc. (*be present*), 186.

445. OPTICAL INSTRUMENTS.—*N*. **optical instruments;** lens, magnifier, microscope; spectacles, glasses, goggles, eyeglass, pince-nez; periscope; telescope, glass, lorgnette, binocular; spyglass, opera glass, field glass; burning glass, convex lens; prism.

camera, hand camera, kodak [*trade name*]; moving-picture machine, magic lantern, stereopticon; stereoscope, kaleidoscope.

mirror, reflector, speculum; looking glass, pier glass, cheval glass.

optics, optician; photography, photographer; optometry, optometrist; microscopy, microscopist.

446. VISIBILITY.—*N*. **visibility,** perceptibility, conspicuousness, distinctness, appearance, etc., 448; exposure; manifestation, etc., 525; ocular demonstration; field of view, vista, horizon.

V. **appear,** open to the view; catch the eye; present (*or* show, manifest, reveal, expose, betray) itself; stand forth, stand out; materialize; show; arise; peep out, peer out; start up, spring up; gleam, glimmer; glitter, glow, loom; glare; burst forth; burst upon the view; heave in sight [*naut. or colloq*.]; come into view, come out, come forth, come forward; attract the attention, etc., 457.

expose to view, show, display.

Adj. **visible,** perceptible, discernible, apparent; in view, in full view, in sight; exposed to view.

distinct, plain, clear, definite; obvious, etc. (*manifest*), 525; recognizable; glaring, palpable, staring, conspicuous.

Adv. before one, under one's very eyes, in sight of.

447. INVISIBILITY.—*N.* invisibility, imperceptibility; indistinctness; mystery; latency, obscurity; concealment, mystification.

V. **be invisible** (*or* imperceptible); be hidden, etc. (*hide*), 528; escape notice.

render invisible; conceal, etc., 528; put out of sight.

Adj. **invisible,** imperceptible; out of sight, not in sight, unseen; viewless; inconspicuous; covert, latent.

indistinct; dim; mysterious, dark, obscure; confused, indistinguishable, shadowy, indefinite, undefined, ill-defined, blurred, out of focus; misty, veiled, concealed.

448. APPEARANCE.—*N.* **appearance,** phenomenon, sight, show, scene, view; lookout, outlook, prospect, vista, perspective, bird's-eye view, scenery, landscape, seascape, picture, tableau; display, exposure, rising of the curtain.

spectacle, pageant; peep show, magic lantern, biograph, cinematograph, cinema [*colloq.*], moving pictures, movies [*colloq.*], photoplay, photodrama; panorama.

aspect, angle, phase, shape, form, guise, look, complexion, color, image, mien, air, cast, carriage, port, demeanor; presence, expression, point of view, light.

lineament, feature, trait, lines; outline, outside; contour, silhouette, face, countenance, visage, profile; physiognomy.

V. **appear,** be visible, seem, look, show; cut a figure, figure; present to the view; show, etc. (*make manifest*), 525; look like, resemble.

Adj. **apparent,** seeming, ostensible; on view.

Adv. **to all appearance,** ostensibly, seemingly, on the face of it, at the first blush, at first sight, to the eye.

449. DISAPPEARANCE.—*N.* **disappearance,** evanescence, eclipse; departure, exit; vanishing point.

V. **disappear,** vanish, dissolve, fade, melt away, pass, go, depart, be gone, leave no trace; be lost to view (*or* sight), pass out of sight.

efface, etc., 552.

Adj. **disappearing,** evanescent; missing, lost; lost to sight.

CLASS IV

Words Relating to the INTELLECTUAL FACULTIES

I. FORMATION OF IDEAS

450. INTELLECT.—*N.* **intellect,** mind, understanding, reason; rationality; intellectual faculties (*or* powers); senses, consciousness, observation, intellectuality, mentality, intelligence; conception, judgment, wits, brains, parts, capacity, genius; wit; ability; wisdom; ideality, idealism.

ego, soul, spirit; heart, breast, bosom; subconscious self, subliminal consciousness.

seat of thought, brain; head, headpiece; skull, cranium.

Science of mind: psychology, psychoanalysis; psychophysics; metaphysics; philosophy.

psychical research; telepathy, thought transference, thought reading; clairaudience; clairvoyance, mediumship; spiritualism, etc., 992a.

V. **reason,** understand, think, reflect, cogitate, conceive, judge, contemplate, meditate; ruminate, etc. (*think*), 451.

note, notice, mark; take notice of; be aware of, realize; appreciate.

Adj. **intellectual,** mental, rational; psychological; conscious, percipient, brainy [*colloq.*].

hyperphysical, subconscious, subliminal; telepathic, clairvoyant; psychic *or* psychical, spiritual, metaphysical, transcendental.

450a. ABSENCE OF INTELLECT.—*N.* **want of intellect** (*or* mind, understanding); unintellectuality; imbecility, etc., 490.

Adj. **unendowed with** (*or* void of) reason; unintelligent, etc. (*imbecile*), 499.

451. THOUGHT.—*N.* **thought;** reflection, cogitation, consideration, meditation, study, speculation, deliberation, brainwork, cerebration; close study, application.

mature thought; afterthought, reconsideration, second thoughts; retrospection, examination.

abstraction, abstract thought, contemplation, musing; reverie, etc., 458; depth of thought.

V. **think,** reflect, cogitate, consider, reason, deliberate; contemplate, meditate, ponder, muse, dream, ruminate, speculate; brood over, con over, study; bend (*or* apply) the mind; digest, discuss, hammer at, hammer out; weigh, realize, appreciate; fancy.

harbor, cherish, entertain, nurture (*as an idea*), imagine; bear in mind; reconsider.

suggest itself, present itself, occur to; come into one's head; strike one, come uppermost; enter (or cross, flash across, occupy) the mind.

Adj. **thoughtful,** pensive, meditative, reflective, cogitative, contemplative, speculative, deliberative, studious, introspective, philosophical.

absorbed, rapt; lost in thought; engrossed in, intent.

Adv. all things considered, taking everything into consideration (or account).

452. ABSENCE OF THOUGHT.—*N.* vacancy of mind, poverty of intellect; thoughtlessness, etc. (*inattention*), 458; inanity, fatuity, vacuity.

V. put away thought; relax (or divert) the mind; make the mind a blank, let the mind lie fallow; indulge in reverie, etc. (*be inattentive*), 458.

Adj. **vacant,** inane, unintellectual, unoccupied, unthinking, irrational, unreasoning, thoughtless, inattentive; diverted; bigoted, narrow-minded.

453. [Object of thought] IDEA.—*N.* idea, notion, conception, thought; apprehension, impression, perception; sentiment, reflection, observation, consideration; abstract idea.

view, opinion, theory; conceit, fancy; fantasy, etc., 515.

viewpoint, point of view; aspect, angle; field of view.

454. [Subject of thought] TOPIC.—*N.* subject, subject matter; matter, motif, theme, topic, thesis, text, business, affair, matter in hand, argument; motion, resolution, case, point; proposition, theorem; field of inquiry; moot point, point at issue; problem, etc. (*question*), 461.

V. enter the mind, etc., 451.

Adv. **under consideration,** under advisement; in question, in the mind; at issue, before the house, on foot, on the carpet.

455. [Desire of knowledge] CURIOSITY.—*N.* curiosity; inquisitiveness; interest, thirst for knowledge, mental acquisitiveness; inquiring mind.

investigator, inquirer, etc., 461.

busybody, newsmonger; Peeping Tom, Paul Pry, eavesdropper; gossip.

V. **be curious;** take an interest in, investigate; stare, gape; see the sights.

pry, nose, search, ferret out.

Adj. **curious,** inquiring, etc., 461; inquisitive, burning with curiosity, overcurious, prying; inquisitorial; agape, expectant.

456. [Absence of curiosity] INCURIOSITY.—*N.* incuriosity; incuriousness; apathy, unconcern, indifference.

V. **be incurious** (*or* indifferent); have no curiosity, etc., 455; be bored by, take no interest in.

Adj. **incurious,** uninquisitive, indifferent; impassive, etc., 823; uninterested, bored.

457. ATTENTION.—*N.* **attention;** intentness, alertness; thought, etc., 451; observance, observation; consideration, reflection; heed; heedfulness; notice, regard; circumspection, etc. (*care*), 459; study, scrutiny; inspection, revision, revisal.

minuteness, circumstantiality, attention to detail.

V. **attend,** watch, observe, look, see, view, notice, regard, take notice, mark; pay attention to, give heed to; occupy oneself with; contemplate, etc. (*think of*), 451; look to, see to; heed, mind, take cognizance of, entertain, recognize; make (*or* take) note of; note.

examine, scan, scrutinize, consider; overhaul, revise, pore over; inspect, review.

revert to, hark back to; come to the point.

meet with attention; attract notice, fall under one's notice; be under consideration.

call attention to, bring under one's notice; point out (*or* to, at), indicate; direct attention to; show; bring forward.

Adj. **attentive,** mindful, heedful, observant, regardful; alive to, awake to, on the job [*colloq.*], alert; taken up with, occupied with; engrossed in, wrapped in, absorbed, rapt; watchful; intent on, open-eyed; on the watch.

458. INATTENTION.—*N.* **inattention,** inconsideration, want of consideration, inconsiderateness; oversight; inadvertence, disregard; want of thought; heedlessness, etc. (*neglect*), 460; unconcern.

abstraction; absence of mind, absorption, preoccupation, distraction, reverie, brown study [*colloq.*], woolgathering.

V. **be inattentive** (*or* unobservant); overlook, disregard; pass by, neglect; think little of; pay no attention to; dismiss from one's mind; drop the subject, think no more of; turn a deaf ear to.

confuse, disconcert, discompose, perplex, bewilder, fluster, flurry; call off *or* distract the attention (thoughts, mind); put out of one's head.

Adj. **inattentive,** unobservant, undiscerning, unmindful, unheeding, regardless; listless, apathetic; blind, deaf; volatile, scatter-brained, flighty, giddy; unreflecting; inconsiderate, thoughtless; wild, harum-scarum [*colloq.*], heedless, careless, neglectful.

abstracted, absent, distrait [F.], woolgathering, dreamy; dazed, absent-minded; lost in thought; rapt, in the clouds, daydreaming; preoccupied, engrossed; in a reverie; off one's guard; caught napping.

459. CARE. [Vigilance]—*N.* **care,** solicitude, anxiety; heed, concern, heedfulness; scruple.

vigilance; watchfulness, surveillance, watch, vigil, lookout, watch and ward; espionage, reconnoitering; watching.

alertness, attention, prudence, forethought, circumspection, precaution, caution; accuracy, exactness; minuteness, attention to detail.

watcher, watchman, watchdog.

V. **be careful,** take care, be cautious; take precautions; pay attention to, etc., 457; take care of; look *or* see to, look after, keep an eye upon; chaperon, matronize, keep watch, mount guard, watch.

Adj. **careful,** regardful, heedful; prudent, discreet, cautious; considerate, thoughtful; provident; alert; sure-footed.

guarded, on one's guard; on the alert (*or* watch, lookout); awake, vigilant; watchful, wakeful, Argus-eyed, lynx-eyed.

scrupulous, punctilious, conscientious; tidy, orderly; clean; accurate, exact.

Adv. **carefully,** with care, gingerly.

460. NEGLECT.—*N.* **neglect;** carelessness; negligence; omission, procrastination; supineness, apathy; inattention, etc., 458; imprudence, improvidence, recklessness; slovenliness, untidiness; dirt; inexactness, inaccuracy.

trifler, waiter on providence; Micawber; slacker.

V. **neglect,** take no care of, let slip, let go; lose sight of.

delay, defer, procrastinate, postpone, adjourn, pigeonhole, shelve, table, lay on the table.

overlook, disregard; pass over, pass by; let pass; wink at, connive at.

scamp; trifle, slight, slur; skim, skip, take a cursory view of, run over, dip into; slur *or* slip over; push aside, throw into the background, sink; ignore; forget.

Adj. **neglectful,** negligent, remiss; heedless, careless; thoughtless, inconsiderate; perfunctory, offhand.

unwary, unwatchful, unguarded, off one's guard.

supine, apathetic; inattentive, etc., 458; nonchalant, indifferent; imprudent, reckless; slovenly, disorderly; dirty; inexact, inaccurate; improvident, unthrifty.

neglected, unheeded, uncared for, unattended to; abandoned, shunted, shelved.

461. INQUIRY. [Subject of inquiry. QUESTION.]—*N.* **inquiry;** request, etc., 765; search, research, quest; pursuit, prosecution.

examination, review, scrutiny, investigation; inquest, inquisition; trial; exploration; exploitation, ventilation; sifting; calculation, analysis, dissection; study, consideration.

reconnoitering, reconnaissance, espionage.

questioning, interrogation, interrogatory; challenge, examination, third degree [*colloq.*], cross-examination; discussion; catechism.

question, query, problem, poser, desideratum, point (*or* matter) in dispute; moot point; issue, question at issue; bone of contention, enigma, etc. (*secret*), 533; knotty point.

inquirer, investigator, inquisitor, inspector, querist, examiner, catechist; scrutator, scrutinizer; analyst.

V. **inquire,** seek, search, make inquiry, look for, scan, reconnoiter, explore, sound, rummage, ransack, pry, peer, look round; overhaul; look behind the scenes; nose, nose out, trace up; hunt out, fish out, ferret out; unearth.

track, seek a clue; hunt, trail, shadow, mouse, dodge, trace, pursue, experiment, etc., 463.

examine, study, consider, calculate; dip *or* dive into, probe, sound, fathom, scrutinize, analyze, anatomize, dissect, parse, resolve, sift, winnow, thresh out; investigate, look into, discuss, canvass, subject to examination, quiz, pose; audit, tax, pass in review.

question, ask, demand; interrogate, catechize, pump; cross-question, cross-examine; grill [*colloq*], put through the third degree [*colloq.*].

Adj. **inquiring,** inquisitive, catechetical, inquisitorial, analytic; interrogative.

undetermined, undecided, tentative; in question, in dispute, in issue, under consideration; moot, proposed; doubtful, etc. (*uncertain*), 475.

462. ANSWER.—*N.* **answer,** response, reply, rejoinder; retort, repartee; antiphon, acknowledgment; password; echo; counterstatement, countercharge, contradiction.

[Law] defense, plea, reply, rejoinder, rebutter, surrebutter, surrejoinder.

solution, explanation; discovery, disclosure; cause; clue.

oracle, etc., 513.

V. **answer,** respond, reply, rebut, retort, rejoin; give answer; acknowledge, echo.

[Law] defend, reply, surrejoin, surrebut, plead, rebut.

explain, interpret; solve, etc. (*unriddle*), 522; discover, fathom, hunt out, inquire; satisfy, set at rest, determine.

Adj. **responsive,** respondent, antiphonal; oracular; conclusive.

463. EXPERIMENT.—*N.* **experiment,** essay, trial, attempt;

analysis, investigation; verification, probation, proof, criterion, diagnosis, test, crucial test; assay, ordeal.

speculation, random shot, leap in the dark; feeler, pilot balloon.

experimenter, experimentalist, assayer, analyst; prospector, adventurer; speculator, gambler, stock gambler, plunger [*slang*].

V. experiment, essay, try, venture, make an experiment, make trial of; rehearse; put to the test, prove, verify, test.

grope, grope for, feel one's way, fumble, throw out a feeler; send up a pilot balloon; see how the land lies (*or* wind blows); feel the pulse; fish for, angle, trawl, cast one's net.

Adj. experimental, probationary; analytic, speculative, tentative, empirical.

on trial, on examination, on *or* under probation, under suspicion; on one's trial.

464. COMPARISON.—*N.* comparison, contrast, parallelism, balance; identification; simile, similitude, allegory, etc. (*metaphor*), 521.

V. compare, collate, confront, contrast, balance; parallel.

Adj. comparative, relative, contrastive; metaphorical, etc., 521.

Adv. relatively; as compared with.

465. DISCRIMINATION.—*N.* discrimination, distinction, differentiation, diagnosis, nice perception; estimation; nicety, refinement, taste, judgment; tact, discernment, acuteness, penetration.

V. discriminate, distinguish, separate; draw the line, sift; estimate, etc. (*measure*), 466; sum up, criticize; take into account, weigh carefully.

Adj. discriminating, critical, diagnostic, perceptive, discriminative, distinctive; nice, acute.

465a. INDISCRIMINATION.—*N.* indiscrimination, indistinction; want of discernment; uncertainty, etc. (*doubt*), 475.

V. confound, confuse, jumble, heap indiscriminately; swallow whole.

Adj. indiscriminate, indistinguishable, lacking distinction, undistinguished, undistinguishable; promiscuous, undiscriminating.

466. MEASUREMENT.—*N.* measurement, mensuration, survey, valuation, appraisement, assessment, estimate, estimation; dead reckoning [*naut.*]; reckoning, gauging; horsepower, candle power.

measure, gauge; yard measure, standard, rule, foot rule, spirit level, plumb line; square, T-square, steel square, compass, dividers, calipers; log, log line, patent log [*naut.*]; meter, line, rod, check.

flood mark, high-water mark, load-line mark.

scale; graduation, graduated scale; vernier, quadrant, theodolite; beam, steelyard, weighing machine, balance.

latitude and longitude, altitude and azimuth.

geometry; topography, cartography; surveying, land surveying.

surveyor, land surveyor, topographer, cartographer.

V. **measure,** meter; value, assess, rate, appraise, estimate, form an estimate; standardize; span, pace, step, inch, divide, gauge, balance, poise, weigh; plumb, probe, sound, fathom; survey, plot, block in, block out, rule, draw to scale.

Adj. **metrical,** metric; measurable; topographic *or* topographical, cartographic *or* cartographical.

467. [Materials for reasoning] EVIDENCE.—*N.* **evidence;** facts, premises, data, grounds, proof; confirmation, corroboration, ratification, authentication.

testimony, attestation; affirmation, declaration; deposition.

authority, warrant, credential, diploma, voucher, certificate, document, deed, warranty; autograph, handwriting, signature, seal, countersign; exhibit; citation, reference, quotation; admission, etc. (*assent*), 488.

witness, eyewitness, deponent [*law*]; sponsor.

writ, summons, etc. (*lawsuit*), 696.

V. **evince,** show, betoken, indicate, denote, imply, involve, argue, bespeak.

have weight, carry weight; tell, speak volumes, speak for itself.

testify, bear witness, give evidence, depose, witness, vouch for; certify, attest, acknowledge.

confirm, ratify, corroborate, indorse, support, bear out, vindicate, uphold, warrant.

adduce, evidence, cite, quote; refer to, call, call to witness; bring forward, bring into court; allege, plead.

establish, make out a case; authenticate, substantiate, verify, make good.

Adj. **evidential,** indicative, deducible, inferential, firsthand, authentic, documentary; cumulative, corroborative, confirmatory; significant, weighty, overwhelming, conclusive.

oral, hearsay, circumstantial, presumptive.

Adv. **by inference;** according to, in corroboration of.

468. COUNTEREVIDENCE.—*N.* **counterevidence,** rejoinder, disproof, refutation, negation, denial; plea, etc., 617; vindication.

V. **refute,** rebut, oppose; confute, etc. (*refute*), 479; subvert; destroy, check, weaken; contravene; contradict, deny, alter the case; turn the tables; prove a negative.

Adj. **contradictory,** conflicting; unattested, unauthenticated, unsupported, supposititious, trumped up.

Adv. **on the other hand** (*or* side), in opposition; in rebuttal.

469. QUALIFICATION.—*N.* **qualification,** limitation, modification, coloring; allowance, consideration, extenuating circumstances; mitigation.

condition, proviso, exception; exemption; saving clause.

V. qualify, limit, modify, affect, give a color to, narrow, temper; allow for, take into account.

Adj. qualifying, extenuating, palliative; conditional; exceptional; hypothetical, contingent.

Adv. provided, if, unless, but, yet; according as; conditionally, admitting, supposing; even, although, though.

470. POSSIBILITY.—*N.* possibility, potentiality, practicability, feasibility, workableness; potency; compatibility, etc. (*agreement*), 23.

contingency, chance, etc., 156.

V. be possible, stand a chance; admit of, bear.

render possible, put in the way of, bring to bear, bring together.

Adj. possible, conceivable, imaginable, credible; compatible, etc., 23; likely.

practicable, feasible, workable, achievable; within reach, accessible, surmountable; attainable, obtainable.

Adv. possibly, perhaps, perchance, peradventure, haply.

471. IMPOSSIBILITY.—*N.* impossibility, impracticability, incredibility, hopelessness, infeasibility; discrepancy.

V. attempt impossibilities; square the circle, find the elixir of life, discover the philosopher's stone, discover the grand panacea, find the fountain of youth, discover the secret of perpetual motion; make bricks without straw; weave a rope of sand; be in two places at once; gather grapes from thorns.

Adj. impossible, not possible, absurd, contrary to reason, unlikely, unreasonable, incredible, visionary, impractical, inconceivable, improbable, unimaginable, unthinkable.

impracticable, unachievable, infeasible; insuperable, insurmountable, inaccessible, unattainable, unobtainable; out of the question; incompatible, etc., 24; impassable, impervious, self-contradictory.

472. PROBABILITY.—*N.* probability, likelihood, likeness, verisimilitude, plausibility; color, semblance, show of; presumption; credibility; prospect; chance, etc., 156.

V. be probable, lend color to; point to; imply, bid fair, promise, stand (*or* run) a good chance.

presume, infer, venture, suppose, take for granted, flatter oneself; expect, etc., 507; count upon, etc. (*believe*), 484.

Adj. probable, likely, hopeful, presumable, presumptive, apparent.

plausible, specious, ostensible, colorable, reasonable, credible.

Adv. in all probability, most likely, apparently, seemingly, to all appearance.

473. IMPROBABILITY.—*N.* improbability, unlikelihood; bare possibility; long odds; incredibility.

V. **be improbable,** go beyond reason, strain one's credulity; have a small chance.

Adj. **improbable,** unlikely, rare, unheard of, inconceivable; unimaginable, incredible.

474. CERTAINTY.—*N.* **certainty;** necessity, etc., 601; certitude, sureness, surety, assurance; infallibility, reliability, inevitableness; fact; positive fact, matter of fact.

bigotry, positiveness, dogmatism, dogmatization; fanaticism. **dogmatist,** doctrinaire, bigot; zealot, fanatic.

V. **render certain,** insure, assure; clinch, make sure; determine, decide; know, etc. (*believe*), 484.

Adj. **certain,** sure, inevitable, assured, solid, well founded.

unqualified, absolute, positive, definite, clear, unequivocal, categorical, unmistakable, decisive.

conclusive, undeniable, unquestionable; indisputable, incontestable, indubitable; irrefutable; final; undoubted, unquestioned, undisputed; questionless.

authoritative, authentic, official.

evident, manifest; self-evident, axiomatic.

infallible, unerring; unchangeable, etc., 150; trustworthy, reliable.

dogmatic, opinionated, dictatorial, doctrinaire; fanatical, bigoted.

Adv. **certainly,** undoubtedly, indubitably; for certain, surely, no doubt, doubtless, to be sure, of course, as a matter of course, in truth, truly, without fail.

475. UNCERTAINTY.—*N.* **uncertainty,** incertitude, doubt, doubtfulness, dubiousness.

hesitation, suspense, perplexity, embarrassment, dilemma, bewilderment; puzzle, quandary; timidity, etc. (*fear*), 860; vacillation, wavering, indetermination.

vagueness, haze, fog, obscurity, ambiguity, open question, blind bargain, pig in a poke, leap in the dark.

fallibility, unreliability, untrustworthiness; precariousness.

V. **hesitate,** flounder, miss one's way, wander aimlessly, beat about; lose oneself, lose one's head.

perplex, pose, puzzle, confuse, confound, bewilder, nonplus. **doubt,** etc. (*disbelieve*), 485.

Adj. **uncertain,** unsure; casual, random, aimless, doubtful, dubious; insecure, unstable, indecisive, irresolute; unsettled, undecided, undetermined, in question; experimental, tentative.

vague, indefinite, ambiguous, equivocal, undefined, confused; mysterious, cryptic, veiled, obscure, undefinable; oracular.

perplexing, enigmatic, paradoxical, apocryphal, problematical.

fallible, questionable, debatable, untrustworthy, unreliable.

puzzled, perplexed; lost, astray, adrift, at sea, at fault, at a loss, at one's wit's end, distracted, distraught.

476. REASONING.—*N.* **reasoning,** ratiocination; inference, induction, generalization.

logic, art of reasoning, dialectics; deduction, induction; synthesis, analysis; syllogism.

discussion, comment; ventilation; inquiry, etc., 461.

argumentation, controversy, debate; polemics, wrangling, contention.

argument, case, plea, proposition, terms, premises, data, principle.

arguments, reasons, pros and cons.

reasoner, logician, dialectician, casuist; disputant, controversialist; wrangler, arguer, debater.

V. **reason,** argue, discuss, debate, dispute, contend, wrangle; chop logic; controvert, deny; canvass; consider, examine.

Adj. **reasoning,** rational; argumentative, controversial, dialectic, polemical; disputatious.

logical, syllogistic, inductive, deductive, synthetic *or* synthetical, analytic *or* analytical; relevant, germane.

Adv. **for,** because, hence, whence, seeing that, since, then, thence, so; whereas, considering, therefore, wherefore; consequently, *ergo* [L.], thus, accordingly.

finally, in conclusion, in fine, after all, on the whole.

477. [Absence of reasoning] INTUITION. [Specious reasoning] SOPHISTRY.—*N.* **intuition;** instinct, association of ideas; rule of thumb; presentiment.

sophistry, casuistry, equivocation, evasion, mental reservation, chicanery; perversion, mystification; speciousness; nonsense, etc., 497; hairsplitting, quibbling; begging of the question.

sophism, quibble, quirk, fallacy, subterfuge, shift, subtlety; inconsistency; claptrap.

V. **pervert,** quibble, equivocate, mystify, evade, elude; gloss over, varnish; misteach, etc., 538; mislead, etc. (*error*), 495; misrepresent, etc. (*lie*), 544; cavil, refine, split hairs; misjudge, etc., 481; beg the question, reason in a circle.

Adj. **intuitive,** instinctive, impulsive.

illogical, unreasonable, false, unsound, invalid; unwarranted, gratuitous; incongruous, inconsequent, inconsequential; unconnected; inconsistent; unscientific, untenable, inconclusive, incorrect, fallacious, groundless, unproved.

specious, sophistic *or* sophistical, casuistic; deceptive, illusive, illusory, hollow, plausible; evasive; irrelevant, inapplicable.

weak, feeble, poor, flimsy, loose, vague, irrational; nonsensical, absurd, foolish, etc. (*imbecile*), 499; frivolous; pettifogging, quibbling.

478. DEMONSTRATION.—*N.* demonstration, proof; conclusiveness; evidence, etc., 467; verification, etc., 462.

V. **demonstrate,** prove, establish, make good; show, evince, verify, etc., 467; settle the question.

follow; stand to reason; hold good, hold water [*colloq.*].

Adj. **demonstrative;** demonstrable; unanswerable, conclusive, decisive, convincing; irresistible, irrefutable, undeniable.

demonstrated, proved; unconfuted, unanswered, unrefuted; evident, self-evident, axiomatic.

deducible, inferential, following.

Adv. **of course,** in consequence, consequently, as a matter of course.

479. CONFUTATION.—*N.* confutation, refutation; answer, disproof, conviction, invalidation; exposure, exposé [F.], retort.

V. **confute,** refute, parry, negative, disprove, expose, show up; rebut, defeat, demolish, upset, subvert, overthrow, overturn, confound; invalidate; convince, silence; clinch an argument.

Adj. **confutable,** refutable; capable of refutation.

480. [Results of reasoning] JUDGMENT.—*N.* judgment, decision, determination, finding, verdict, sentence, decree; opinion, etc. (*belief*), 484; good judgment.

result, conclusion, upshot; deduction, inference, corollary.

estimation, valuation, appreciation; arbitrament, arbitration; assessment.

estimate, award; review, criticism, critique, notice, report.

plebiscite, voice, casting vote; vote, suffrage, election.

arbiter, arbitrator; judge, umpire; assessor, referee; inspector; censor.

reviewer, critic; connoisseur; commentator, annotator.

V. **judge,** conclude, opine; come to (*or* arrive at) a conclusion; ascertain, determine.

deduce, derive, gather, collect, infer.

estimate, form an estimate, appreciate, value, count, assess, rate, rank, account; regard, consider, think of; size up [*colloq.*].

decide, settle; try, pronounce, rule; find, pass judgment, sentence, doom, decree; give (*or* deliver) judgment; adjudge, adjudicate; arbitrate, award; confirm.

review, comment, criticize; examine, etc., 457; investigate, etc., 461.

Adj. **judicious,** judicial; determinate, conclusive, confirmatory.

critical, hypercritical, hairsplitting, censorious.

Adv. **on the whole,** all things considered, therefore, wherefore.

480a. [Result of search or inquiry] DISCOVERY.—*N.* discovery, detection, disclosure, find, revelation.

V. **discover,** find, determine, evolve; fix upon; find (*or* trace, make, root) out; spot [*colloq.*], fathom, bring out, draw out, educe, elicit, bring to light, dig up, unearth, disinter.

solve, resolve; unriddle, unravel, find a clue to; interpret; disclose; see through, detect; catch; scent, smell out.

recognize, realize, verify, make certain of, identify.

481. MISJUDGMENT.—*N.* **misjudgment,** obliquity of judgment, warped judgment; miscalculation, misconception, misinterpretation, etc., 523; hasty conclusion.

preconception, prejudgment, foregone conclusion; presumption, preconceived idea; prejudice, predilection, prepossession; presentiment, foreboding; fixed idea, obsession.

partisanship, clannishness; *esprit de corps* [F.], prestige, party spirit, class prejudice, class consciousness, race prejudice, provincialism.

quirk, shift, quibble, equivocation, evasion, subterfuge.

bias, warp, twist; hobby, whim, craze, cult, fad, crotchet, partiality.

V. **misjudge,** misconjecture, misconceive, misunderstand; miscalculate, misreckon; overestimate, etc., 482; underestimate, etc., 483.

prejudge, dogmatize; have a bias, run away with the notion; jump to a conclusion; blunder, etc., 699.

bias, warp, twist; prejudice, prepossess.

Adj. **misjudging,** ill-judging, wrong-headed; superficial; prejudiced, prepossessed; shortsighted, purblind; partial, one-sided; warped.

narrow, narrow-minded, provincial, parochial, insular; mean-spirited, confined, illiberal, intolerant, infatuated, fanatical, positive, dogmatic, dictatorial, pragmatic; egotistical, conceited, opinionated; bigoted, etc. (*obstinate*), 606; unreasonable, stupid, etc., 499; credulous, gullible.

482. OVERESTIMATION.—*N.* **overestimation,** exaggeration, hyperbole; optimism, much ado about nothing; tempest in a teacup; fine writing, rodomontade, gush [*colloq.*], hot air [*slang*].

egoism, egotism, bombast, conceit; vanity; megalomania.

egoist, egotist, megalomaniac; optimist; braggart, boaster, braggadocio, swaggerer.

V. **overestimate,** overrate, overpraise; strain, magnify; exaggerate, etc., 549.

eulogize, gush over [*colloq.*], boost; puff [*colloq.*]; extol.

Adj. **inflated,** puffed up; grandiose, stilted, pompous, pretentious, bombastic.

483. UNDERESTIMATION.—*N.* **underestimation,** undervaluation; depreciation, etc. (*detraction*), 934; pessimism; self-detraction, self-depreciation; modesty, etc., 881.

pessimist, depreciator, knocker [*slang*], crapehanger [*slang*].

V. **underrate,** underestimate, undervalue; depreciate; disparage, detract, decry, ridicule, deride; slight, etc. (*despise*), 930; neglect; slur over.

make light (*or* little) of, belittle, run down [*colloq.*], minimize, set no store by, set at naught, disregard.

Adj. **depreciating,** depreciative, depreciatory; pessimistic.

depreciated, unappreciated, unvalued, unprized.

484. BELIEF.—*N.* **belief,** credence; credit; assurance; faith, trust, confidence, presumption; hope.

conviction, principle; persuasion, certainty, opinion, view, conception, impression, surmise; conclusion.

doctrine, tenet, dogma, articles, canons; view, gospel; article (*or* declaration, profession) of faith, creed; assent, avowal, confession; propaganda.

credibility, probability; plausibility.

V. **believe,** credit, give faith (*or* credit, credence) to; realize; assume, take it; consider, presume; count (*or* depend, rely, build) upon; take for granted.

confide in, believe in, put one's trust in, place reliance on, trust.

think, hold, opine, conceive; have (*or* hold, entertain, adopt, embrace, foster, cherish) a belief *or* an opinion.

persuade, assure, convince, satisfy, bring to reason, convert, indoctrinate; wean, bring round, bring (*or* win) over; carry conviction.

Adj. **certain,** sure, assured, positive, cocksure [*colloq.*], satisfied, confident, unhesitating, convinced, secure.

confiding, trustful, unsuspecting, unsuspicious; credulous, gullible.

believed, trusted, unsuspected, undoubted.

credible, reliable, trustworthy, accredited, satisfactory; probable.

485. UNBELIEF. DOUBT.—*N.* **unbelief,** disbelief, incredulity; infidelity, etc. (*irreligion*), 989; wrangling, nonconformity; dissent, change of opinion; retractation, etc., 607.

doubt, uncertainty, skepticism, misgiving, demur; discredit; distrust, mistrust; misdoubt, suspicion, jealousy, scruple, qualm.

incredibility, incredibleness, unbelievability.

agnostic, skeptic; unbeliever, etc., 487.

V. **disbelieve,** discredit, misbelieve, dissent; refuse to believe.

doubt, distrust, mistrust; question, challenge, dispute; deny, etc., 536; cavil, wrangle; suspect, scent, smell, smell a rat [*colloq.*], harbor suspicions; have one's doubts.

demur, stick at, pause, hesitate, shy at, scruple; waver.

stagger, startle; shake one's faith, stagger one's belief.

Adj. **unbelieving,** skeptical, incredulous; distrustful of, suspicious of.

doubtful, etc. (*uncertain*), 475; disputable, questionable, suspicious; incredible, unbelievable, inconceivable.

Adv. with caution, with grains of allowance.

486. CREDULITY.—*N.* **credulity,** credulousness, gullibility; infatuation; self-delusion, self-deception; superstition; bigotry.

credulous person, dupe, gull.

V. **be credulous;** follow implicitly; swallow, swallow whole, gulp down; take on faith.

impose upon, etc. (*deceive*), 545.

Adj. **credulous,** gullible, easily deceived *or* convinced; simple, silly, childish; infatuated, superstitious; confiding, trustful, unsuspicious.

487. INCREDULITY.—*N.* **incredulity,** incredulousness; skepticism, doubt, disbelief, etc., 989; unbelief, etc., 485.

unbeliever, skeptic, doubting Thomas, disbeliever, agnostic, infidel, misbeliever; heretic, etc. (*heterodox*), 984.

V. **be incredulous,** distrust, doubt, suspect, refuse to believe; turn a deaf ear to.

Adj. **incredulous,** skeptical, suspicious; dissenting, unbelieving; heterodox.

488. ASSENT.—*N.* **assent,** acquiescence, admission; nod; consent, compliance; agreement, understanding; affirmation; recognition, acknowledgment, avowal, confession.

unanimity, common consent, consensus, acclamation, chorus; public opinion; concurrence, accord.

ratification, confirmation, corroboration, approval, acceptance; indorsement.

consenter, indorser, subscriber; upholder, etc. (*auxiliary*), 711.

V. **assent,** give assent, acquiesce, agree, accept, accede, accord, concur, consent, coincide, echo, reciprocate, go with; recognize; subscribe to, conform to, defer to; go with the stream; be in the fashion, join in the chorus.

acknowledge, own, admit, confess; concede, yield; abide by; permit, etc., 760.

confirm, ratify, approve, indorse, countersign; corroborate, etc., 467.

Adj. **assenting,** of one accord (*or* mind); of the same mind, at one with, agreed, acquiescent.

uncontradicted, unchallenged, unquestioned, unanimous.

Adv. **yes,** yea, aye, true; granted; even so, just so; to be sure, as you say; surely, assuredly; exactly, precisely, certainly, of course, unquestionably, no doubt, doubtless.

unanimously, by common consent, to a man, as one man; with one consent (*or* voice, accord).

489. DISSENT.—*N.* **dissent,** nonconsent, discordance, disagreement.

nonconformity, heterodoxy, protestantism, schism; disaffection, secession, recantation.

dissension, discord, caviling, wrangling; discontent, etc., 832.

protest, contradiction, denial; noncompliance, rejection.

dissentient, dissenter, nonconformist; sectary; separatist, protestant; heretic, etc., 984.

V. **dissent,** demur, call in question, disagree, refuse to admit; cavil, wrangle, protest, repudiate; contradict, deny.

secede; recant, etc., 607.

Adj. **dissenting,** negative; contradictory; dissentient; unconvinced, unconverted.

sectarian, denominational, schismatic; heterodox; intolerant.

Adv. at variance with, at issue with; under protest.

490. KNOWLEDGE.—*N.* **knowledge;** cognizance; cognition, acquaintance, experience, ken, insight, familiarity; comprehension, apprehension; recognition; appreciation, judgment, etc., 480; intuition, consciousness, perception.

enlightenment, light; impression, perception, discovery, revelation.

learning, erudition, lore, scholarship; letters, literature; book learning, bookishness, general information; education, culture, cultivation, attainments, acquirements, accomplishments, proficiency.

V. **know,** be aware of; conceive, apprehend, comprehend; realize, understand, appreciate; fathom, make out; recognize, discern, perceive, see, experience.

learn, imbibe knowledge; discover, evolve.

Adj. **aware of,** cognizant of, conscious of; acquainted with, privy to, in the secret; alive to; apprized of, informed of; undeceived.

educated, erudite, instructed, learned, lettered, well informed, well versed, well read, well grounded, well educated; high-brow [*slang*], bookish, scholastic, profound, deep-read, book-learned, accomplished; self-taught, self-educated, knowing, shrewd.

known, ascertained, well known, recognized, noted, received, notorious, proverbial; familiar, hackneyed, trite, commonplace.

Adv. to the best of one's knowledge; as every schoolboy knows.

491. IGNORANCE.—*N.* ignorance, illiteracy, unlearnedness, unacquaintance, unconsciousness, darkness, blindness; incomprehension, simplicity.

sealed book; virgin soil, unexplored ground, dark ages.

Imperfect knowledge: smattering, superficiality, half learning,. shallowness, glimmering; incapacity.

Affectation of knowledge: pedantry, charlatanry, charlatanism.

V. **be ignorant** (*or* uninformed); be uneducated; know nothing of; ignore, be blind to.

Adj. **ignorant;** unknowing, unaware, unacquainted, uninformed, uninitiated, unwitting, unconscious; witless, unconversant.

illiterate, unread, low [*slang*], uncultivated, uninstructed, untaught, untutored, unschooled, uneducated, unlearned, unlettered, empty-headed.

shallow, superficial, green, rude, empty, half-learned, half-baked [*colloq.*], unscholarly.

in the dark; benighted, blinded, blindfold, hoodwinked; misinformed.

unknown, unapprehended, unexplained, uninvestigated, unexplored, unheard of; concealed, etc., 528.

Adv. unawares; for aught one knows; not that one knows.

492. SCHOLAR.—*N.* scholar, savant [F.], pundit [India], schoolman, professor, academician, doctor, fellow, don [Eng.], graduate, postgraduate, classicist, philosopher, scientist, linguist, etymologist, philologist, lexicographer; man of learning.

bookworm, bibliophile, bibliomaniac, bluestocking [*colloq.*], high-brow [*slang*].

pedant, doctrinaire; pedagogue, Dr. Pangloss; instructor, etc., 540.

student, learner, pupil, schoolboy, etc. (*learner*), 541.

Adj. **learned,** etc., 490.

493. IGNORAMUS.—*N.* ignoramus, illiterate, dunce, duffer, numskull [*colloq.*]; no scholar.

smatterer, dabbler, half scholar; charlatan; wiseacre.

novice, greenhorn, plebe [*West Point cant*]; tyro, etc. (*learner*), 541.

Adj. **bookless,** shallow, simple, dull, dumb [*colloq.*], dense, crass; illiterate, etc., 491.

494. [Object of knowledge] TRUTH.—*N.* truth, verity; fact, reality, authenticity, gospel; veracity, etc., 543.

accuracy, exactitude, exactness, preciseness, precision, regularity, fidelity, nicety.

V. hold true, stand the test, have the true ring, hold good.

trace, solve, etc. (*discover*), 480a.

Adj. true, real, actual, veritable; certain, etc., 474; unimpeachable; veracious, etc., 543.

pure, sound, sterling, true-blue; natural, unsophisticated, unadulterated, simon-pure [*colloq.*], unvarnished, undisguised.

exact, accurate, definite, concrete, precise, well defined, just, right, correct, strict, severe, rigid, rigorous, scrupulous, literal, punctilious, mathematical, scientific, unromantic; faithful, constant, unerring; particular, nice, meticulous, delicate, fine; clean-cut, clear-cut.

authentic, genuine, legitimate; orthodox, etc., 983a; official.

valid, well grounded, well founded, solid, substantial, tangible.

Adv. truly, verily, indeed, in reality; in very truth, in fact, as a matter of fact, beyond doubt.

495. ERROR.—*N.* error, fallacy, misconception, misapprehension, misunderstanding; aberration, inexactness, laxity; misconstruction, misinterpretation; misjudgment, heresy, misstatement, anachronism; fable, etc. (*untruth*), 546.

mistake, fault, blunder, oversight, misprint, erratum (*pl.* errata), slip, blot, flaw, trip, stumble, bungle; slip of the tongue, slip of the pen, clerical error; bull, etc. (*absurdity*), 497; spoonerism, malapropism.

delusion, illusion, false impression; bubble; self-deceit, self-deception; hallucination, mirage, etc., 443; dream, etc. (*fancy*), 515.

V. mislead, misguide, lead astray, beguile, misinform, delude; falsify, misstate; deceive, etc., 545; lie, etc., 544.

err, be in error, be mistaken, be deceived; mistake, deceive oneself, blunder, misapprehend, misconceive, misunderstand, miscalculate, misjudge.

trip, stumble, lose oneself, go astray; fail, etc., 732; take the shadow for the substance.

Adj. erroneous, untrue, false, faulty, erring, fallacious, unreal, ungrounded, groundless, unsubstantial, unsound, inexact, inaccurate, incorrect.

illusive, illusory, delusive; mock, imaginary, spurious, etc., 545; deceitful, etc., 544; untrustworthy.

exploded, refuted, discarded.

mistaken, in error, deceived, out in one's reckoning; wide of the mark, at fault, at cross-purposes, at sea, bewildered.

496. MAXIM.—*N.* maxim, aphorism, dictum, saying, adage, saw, proverb, motto, epigram, sentence, mot [*Gallicism*], commonplace, moral.

axiom, theorem, formula, truism.

principle, profession of faith, conclusion, etc. (*judgment*), 480.

Adj. aphoristic, proverbial, axiomatic; hackneyed, trite.

Adv. as the saying is, as they say.

497. ABSURDITY.—*N.* absurdity, absurdness, imbecility, etc., 499; nonsense, paradox, inconsistency.

blunder, muddle, Irish bull; anticlimax, bathos.

farce, burlesque, parody, limerick; farrago, extravagance.

pun, sell [*colloq.*], catch [*colloq.*], verbal quibble, joke.

jargon, gibberish, balderdash, bombast, claptrap, twaddle, moonshine, stuff.

tomfoolery, mummery, monkeyshine [*slang*], monkey trick, frisk, practical joke, escapade.

V. play the fool, blunder, muddle; be guilty of absurdity; romance, talk nonsense, exaggerate; be absurd, frisk, caper, joke, play practical jokes.

Adj. absurd, nonsensical, farcical, burlesque, preposterous, egregious, senseless, inconsistent, ridiculous, extravagant, self-contradictory, paradoxical; foolish, etc., 499; meaningless, fantastic, bombastic, high-flown.

498. [Faculties] INTELLIGENCE. WISDOM.—*N.* intelligence, capacity, comprehension, understanding; intellect, etc., 450; brains, parts, sagacity, mother wit, wit, gumption [*colloq.*], acuteness, acumen, longheadedness, subtlety, penetration, perspicacity, discernment, good judgment; discrimination, cunning, refinement.

wisdom, sapience, sense, common sense, clear thinking, rationality, reason; reasonableness, judgment, solidity, depth, profundity, caliber.

genius, inspiration, talent, etc., 698.

Wisdom in action: prudence, etc., 864; vigilance, etc., 459; tact, etc., 698; foresight, etc., 510; sobriety, self-possession, ballast, mental poise, balance.

V. have all one's wits about one; be brilliant, scintillate, coruscate; understand, etc. (*intelligible*), 518.

penetrate, see through, see at a glance, discern; foresee, etc., 510; discriminate.

Adj. Applied to persons: intelligent, quick of apprehension, keen, acute, alive, awake, bright, quick, sharp, quick-witted, wide-awake; shrewd, astute; clearheaded, long-sighted, calculating, thoughtful, farsighted, discerning, perspicacious, penetrating, piercing; sharp as a needle; alive to, etc. (*cognizant*), 490; clever, etc. (*apt*), 698.

wise, sage, sapient [*often in irony*], sagacious, rational, sensible, judicious, strong-minded; worldly-wise, sophisticated.

impartial, unprejudiced, unbiased, unbigoted, equitable, fair.

prudent, etc. (*cautious*), 864; sober, staid, solid; watchful; provident, prepared, etc., 673.

Applied to actions: wise, sensible, judicious, well judged, well advised; prudent, politic; expedient, etc., 646.

499. IMBECILITY, FOLLY.—*N.* imbecility, want of intelligence (*or* intellect), shallowness, silliness, foolishness, stupidity, stolidity; incompetence.

simplicity, puerility; senility, dotage, second childhood; fatuity; idiocy.

folly, frivolity, irrationality, trifling, ineptitude, inconsistency, giddiness; eccentricity, etc., 503; extravagance, etc. (*absurdity*), 497; rashness, etc., 863.

V. trifle, drivel, dote; ramble, play the fool, fool, stultify oneself, talk nonsense.

Adj. Applied to persons: unintelligent, unintellectual, unreasoning; mindless, brainless; half-baked [*colloq.*], bovine, thick [*colloq.*], blockish, unteachable; ungifted, unenlightened, unwise; thickskulled, muddleheaded, addleheaded, weak-minded, feebleminded.

stupid, dull, heavy, obtuse, blunt, stolid, asinine, inapt.

childish, childlike; infantine, infantile, babyish, puerile, senile, anile; simple, credulous.

imbecile, fatuous, idiotic, driveling; vacant, bewildered.

foolish, silly, senseless, irrational, insensate, nonsensical, maudlin.

narrow-minded, bigoted, etc., 606; rash, etc., 863; eccentric, odd.

Applied to actions: foolish, unwise, injudicious, improper, unreasonable, ill-advised, ridiculous, silly, stupid, asinine; inconsistent, irrational; extravagant, nonsensical, frivolous, trivial; useless, etc., 645; inexpedient, etc., 647.

500. SAGE.—*N.* sage, wise man; master mind, thinker, philosopher, savant [F.], pundit, etc. (*scholar*), 492; wiseacre [*ironical*]; expert, etc., 700.

authority, oracle, mentor, Solon, Solomon, Buddha, Confucius.

Adj. venerable, venerated, reverenced, revered, honored; authoritative, oracular; wise, erudite, etc., 490.

501. FOOL.—*N.* fool, idiot, tomfool, wiseacre, simpleton,

Simple Simon; donkey, ass, owl, goose, dolt, booby, noodle, imbecile, nincompoop [*colloq.*], oaf, lout, blockhead, bonehead [*slang*], calf [*colloq.*], colt, numskull [*colloq.*], clod, clodhopper; soft *or* softy [*colloq. or slang*], mooncalf, saphead [*slang*], gawk, rube [*slang*].

greenhorn, etc. (*dupe*), 547; dunce, etc. (*ignoramus*), 493; lubber, etc. (*bungler*), 701; madman, etc., 504; dotard, driveler, old fogy [*colloq.*].

502. SANITY.—*N.* **sanity,** soundness, rationality, sobriety, lucidity, senses, common sense, horse sense [*colloq.*], sound mind.

V. **become sane,** come to one's senses, sober down, cool down, see things in proper perspective.

render sane, bring to one's senses, sober, bring to reason.

Adj. **sane,** rational, normal, wholesome, right-minded, reasonable, sound, sound-minded, in possession of one's faculties.

Adv. **sanely,** in reason, within reason, within bounds.

503. INSANITY.—*N.* **insanity,** lunacy; madness, mania, dementia, idiocy; delirium tremens, d.t.'s, the horrors [*colloq.*]; frenzy, raving, wandering, delirium, delusion, obsession, hallucination, derangement, unsoundness of mind.

vertigo, dizziness, swimming, sunstroke.

oddity, eccentricity, twist, monomania; fanaticism, infatuation, craze.

V. **be *or* become insane,** lose one's senses (*or* reason), go mad, rave, dote, ramble, wander; lose one's head, drivel.

derange, render *or* drive mad, madden, infatuate, obsess, befool; turn the brain, turn one's head.

Adj. **insane,** mad, lunatic; crazy, crazed, crackbrained, cracked [*colloq.*], touched; bereft of reason; unhinged, insensate, beside oneself, demented, maniacal, daft, frenzied, deranged, maddened, moonstruck, off one's head.

giddy, vertiginous, wild, flighty, distracted, distraught, bewildered.

odd, fanatical, infatuated, eccentric.

delirious, lightheaded, rambling, wandering, frantic, raving, stark mad.

504. MADMAN.—*N.* **madman,** lunatic, maniac; crank [*colloq.*], nut [*slang*].

dreamer, visionary, rhapsodist, seer, enthusiast, fanatic; Don Quixote, Ophelia.

idiot, etc., 501.

505. [The Past] MEMORY.—*N.* **memory,** remembrance; retention, retentiveness; retentive (*or* tenacious, trustworthy, ready) memory.

recollection, retrospect, reminiscence; recognition; afterthought.

reminder, hint, suggestion, memorandum (*pl.* memoranda), token, memento, souvenir, keepsake, relic; memorial, monument; commemoration, jubilee.

mnemonics; art of memory, artificial memory; Mnemosyne.

fame, celebrity, renown, reputation; repute, notoriety.

V. remember, retain the memory of, keep in mind; bear in mind, haunt one's mind (*or* thoughts); rankle; keep the wound open, brood over.

recollect, recall, call up, conjure up, retrace; look back upon, review; call (*or* bring) to mind.

remind, suggest, hint, prompt; put (*or* keep) in mind; bring to mind, call up, summon up, renew; redeem from oblivion; commemorate.

memorize, commit to memory; con, con over; fix in the mind, engrave upon the memory; learn by heart, know by rote, have at one's fingers' ends.

make a note of, put down, record.

Adj. remembering, mindful, reminiscent; fresh, still vivid; enduring, unforgotten; never to be forgotten, indelible; within one's memory; memorable, suggestive.

Adv. by heart, by rote, without book, word for word.

506. OBLIVION.—*N.* oblivion; forgetfulness; Lethe; obliteration of the past; short (*or* treacherous, untrustworthy, slippery, failing) memory; decay (*or* failure, lapse) of memory; amnesia.

amnesty, general pardon.

V. forget, be forgetful; fall (*or* sink) into oblivion; have a short memory; lose, lose the memory of, lose sight of.

efface, from the memory; unlearn; consign to oblivion, think no more of; let bygones be bygones.

Adj. forgotten, unremembered, out of mind; buried (*or* sunk) in oblivion.

forgetful, oblivious; heedless, deaf to the past; Lethean.

507. [The Future] EXPECTATION.—*N.* expectation, expectancy, anticipation, prospect, contingency, reckoning, calculation; foresight; suspense; abeyance.

assurance, confidence, reliance, hope, trust, presumption; prognostication; prediction, etc., 511.

V. expect; look for, look out for, look forward to; hope for, anticipate; have in prospect, keep in view; contemplate; wait for, watch for, await; foresee, prepare for, forestall.

predict, prognosticate, forecast.

Adj. expectant; expecting, in expectation, vigilant; open-eyed, open-mouthed; agape, gaping, on tenterhooks, on tiptoe; ready, prepared, provided for, provident.

expected, foreseen; in prospect, prospective, provisional; future, coming; in view, on the horizon; impending.

Adv. **expectantly,** on the watch, with muscles tense, on edge [*colloq.*], with eyes (*or* ears) strained, with bated breath.

soon, shortly, forthwith, presently.

508. NONEXPECTATION.—*N.* nonexpectation, unforeseen contingency, the unforeseen; miscalculation, false expectation; disappointment; disillusion.

surprise, blow, shock; bolt out of the blue; astonishment, amazement; wonder, bewilderment.

V. **be unexpected,** come unawares, turn up, burst *or* flash upon one; take by surprise, catch unawares.

surprise, startle, stun, stagger, astound; throw off one's guard; spring upon, astonish, etc. (*strike with wonder*), 870.

Adj. **nonexpectant,** surprised; unwarned, unaware; off one's guard.

unexpected, unanticipated, unlooked for, unforeseen; unheard of; startling; sudden.

Adv. **unexpectedly,** abruptly, suddenly, unawares; without notice *or* warning.

509. DISAPPOINTMENT.—*N.* disappointment, blighted hope, disillusion, balk; blow, false (*or* vain) expectation; miscalculation; fool's paradise.

V. **be disappointed;** look blank, look *or* stand aghast; find to one's cost.

disappoint, crush (*or* dash, blight) one's hope, balk *or* disappoint one's expectation, balk, tantalize; dumfounder, dumfound, disconcert, disillusionize; dissatisfy; disgruntle.

Adj. aghast; disgruntled; out of one's reckoning.

510. FORESIGHT.—*N.* foresight, prevision, long-sightedness, farsightedness; anticipation; prudence; forethought.

foreknowledge, prescience; presentiment, foreboding; second sight.

prospect; foregone conclusion; forecast.

V. **foresee;** look forward to, look ahead *or* beyond; look into the future; see one's way; see how the land lies.

anticipate, expect, surmise, contemplate; predict; forewarn.

Adj. **foreseeing,** prescient, anticipatory; farseeing, farsighted, long-sighted; provident; weatherwise; prospective; expectant.

Adv. against the time when; for a rainy day.

511. PREDICTION.—*N.* prediction, announcement; program;

platform; premonition, presage, foreboding; phophecy, prognostication, augury, forecast; omen, etc., 512; horoscope; soothsaying, fortunetelling, divination; oracle, etc., 513.

astrology; spell, charm, etc., 993; sorcery, magic, etc., 992.

V. predict, forecast, prognosticate, prophesy, divine, foretell; tell fortunes, cast a horoscope (*or* nativity); forewarn.

presage, augur, bode, forebode; foretoken, betoken; portend, signify, point to.

herald, usher in, announce; lower; threaten.

Adj. prophetic, oracular, sibylline; weatherwise.

ominous, portentous; auspicious; premonitory, significant of.

512. OMEN.—*N.* omen, portent, presage, augury; sign, token; harbinger; bird of ill omen; halcyon birds; signs of the times; warning, etc., 668.

Adj. auspicious, favorable, halcyon, of good omen.

inauspicious, ill-boding, ill-omened, ill-starred.

513. ORACLE.—*N.* oracle; prophet, seer, soothsayer, prophetess, witch, sibyl; augur, haruspex; medium, clairvoyant, palmist; fortuneteller; sorcerer, etc., 994; interpreter, etc., 524.

Delphic oracle; Cumaean Sibyl, Sibyl, Cassandra, Witch of Endor, Sphinx.

weather prophet, weather bureau.

514. [Creative Thought] SUPPOSITION.—*N.* supposition, assumption, presumption, condition, hypothesis, postulate, theory, data; thesis, theorem; conjecture, guess, guesswork, speculation; surmise, suspicion, inkling, suggestion, hint.

theorist, theorizer, doctrinaire, doctrinarian.

V. suppose, conjecture; surmise, suspect, guess, divine; theorize, speculate; presume, presuppose, assume, predicate; believe, take for granted.

propound, propose, put forth; put a case, submit; move, make a motion; hazard *or* put forward a suggestion (*or* supposition); suggest, allude to, hint.

Adj. assumed, given; conjectural, presumptive, hypothetical; theoretical, academic.

suggestive, allusive, stimulating.

Adv. if, if so be; on the supposition, in case, in the event of; as if, provided; perhaps, for aught one knows.

515. IMAGINATION.—*N.* imagination, originality, invention; fancy; inspiration.

ideality, idealism; romanticism, utopianism, castle-building, dreaming; frenzy, rhapsody, ecstasy, reverie, daydream.

conception; flight of fancy; creation of the brain; imagery; word painting.

fantasy, conceit; figment, myth; romance, extravaganza; dream, vision; shadow, chimera, phantasm, illusion, phantom, fancy, whim, vagary; bugbear, nightmare; flying Dutchman, great sea serpent, man in the moon, castle in the air, castle in Spain, Utopia, fairyland; land of Prester John.

Creative works: work of fiction, etc. (*novel*), 594; poetry, etc., 597; drama, etc., 599; music, etc., 415; painting, sculpture, architecture; art.

idealist, romanticist, visionary, romancer, daydreamer, dreamer, castle-builder; creative artist.

V. **imagine,** fancy, conceive; idealize, realize; dream, dream of; indulge in reverie; fancy (*or* represent, picture, figure) to oneself.

create, originate, devise, invent, make up, coin, fabricate; improvise.

Adj. **imaginative,** original, inventive, creative, productive.

extravagant, romantic, high-flown, flighty, preposterous; unreal; unsubstantial.

ideal; intellectual, impracticable, imaginary, visionary, utopian, quixotic.

fanciful; fantastical; fictitious; fabulous, legendary, mythic *or* mythical, mythological, chimerical; whimsical; fairy, fairylike.

II. COMMUNICATION OF IDEAS

516. MEANING.—*N.* **meaning** [*idea to be conveyed*], signification, significance; sense, import, purport; pith, essence; force; drift, bearing, tenor, spirit; allusion; suggestion, interpretation; acceptation.

Thing signified: matter, subject, subject matter, substance, gist, argument.

V. **mean,** signify, denote, express; import, purport; convey, imply, indicate; tell of, speak of; touch on; point to, allude to; drive at; involve; declare; affirm, state.

paraphrase, state differently; express by a synonym.

Adj. **meaning,** expressive, significant, pithy; intelligible, explicit, clear; suggestive; allusive.

literal, word-for-word, verbatim; exact, real.

synonymous; tantamount, equivalent.

implied; understood, tacit.

Adv. to that effect; that is to say.

517. UNMEANINGNESS.—*N.* **unmeaningness,** absence of meaning, drivel, senselessness; empty sound.

nonsense, jargon, gibberish, mere words, rant, bombast, balderdash, babble, inanity, twaddle, trash, rubbish; absurdity; imbecility, folly; ambiguity, vagueness, etc., 519.

V. **mean nothing;** be unmeaning; gibber; jabber, twaddle, rant, babble.

scribble, scrawl, scratch.

Adj. **unmeaning,** meaningless, senseless; nonsensical; inexpressive; vague; not significant.

trashy, inane, trumpery, trivial, insignificant.

518. INTELLIGIBILITY.—*N.* **intelligibility;** comprehensibility; clearness, clarity, explicitness, lucidity, perspicuity; precision; plain speaking.

V. **render intelligible,** popularize, simplify, elucidate, explain, interpret.

understand, comprehend; take in, catch, grasp, follow; master.

Adj. **intelligible;** clear, lucid; perspicuous, transparent.

plain, distinct, clear-cut, hard-hitting, to the point, explicit; positive; definite, precise; unequivocal, legible, obvious, etc., 525.

graphic, telling, vivid; expressive.

519. UNINTELLIGIBILITY.—*N.* **unintelligibility,** incomprehensibility, vagueness, obscurity, ambiguity, confusion; mystification; jargon.

enigma, riddle; sealed book.

V. **render unintelligible,** conceal, darken, confuse, mystify, perplex.

Adj. **unintelligible,** incomprehensible, unaccountable, undecipherable, unfathomable, inexplicable, inscrutable, insoluble, impenetrable; puzzling, enigmatic; indecipherable, illegible.

obscure, crabbed, dark, muddy, dim, nebulous, mysterious, hidden, latent, occult; abstruse; indefinite, vague, loose, ambiguous.

inexpressible, unutterable, ineffable.

520. [Having a double sense] EQUIVOCALNESS.—*N.* **equivocalness,** equivocation, double meaning; ambiguity; quibble; conundrum, riddle; pun, word play; sphinx, Delphic oracle.

equivocation, etc. (*duplicity*), 544; white lie, mental reservation, etc., 528.

V. **equivocate,** etc. (*palter*), 544; prevaricate; have a double meaning.

Adj. **equivocal,** ambiguous; double-tongued; enigmatical; indeterminate, doubtful.

521. FIGURE OF SPEECH.—*N.* **figure,** trope, phrase, expression; euphemism; image, imagery; personification, metaphor; simile, satire, irony.

allegory, apologue, parable, fable.

V. **employ figures of speech;** personify, allegorize, fable, shadow forth, allude to.

Adj. **figurative,** metaphorical, euphuistic, allusive; allegoric *or* allegorical, ironic, ironical, satiric *or* satirical; euphemistic.

522. INTERPRETATION.—*N.* **interpretation,** definition, explanation; elucidation, diagnosis; solution, answer; meaning, etc., 516; clue.

translation; rendering, rendition; metaphrase, literal (*or* word-for-word) translation; free translation; key; crib, horse, pony, trot [*school cant*].

comment, commentary; exegesis, exposition; inference, deduction; illustration, exemplification; gloss, annotation, note, construction, version, reading.

equivalent, equivalent meaning, synonym; paraphrase, convertible terms.

dictionary, etc., 562.

prediction, etc., 511; chiromancy, palmistry; astrology.

V. interpret, explain, define, construe, translate, render; decipher, make out, unravel, disentangle, solve; read between the lines.

elucidate, account for, throw *or* shed light upon; clear up, popularize, simplify; illustrate, exemplify; unfold, expound, comment upon, annotate.

Adj. explanatory, expository; interpretative, elucidative, inferential, illustrative.

equivalent, convertible, synonymous.

metaphrastic, literal, word-for-word.

Adv. in explanation; that is to say, to wit, namely.

literally, strictly speaking; in plain terms (*or* words).

523. MISINTERPRETATION.—*N.* misinterpretation, misapprehension, misconception, misunderstanding, misconstruction; misapplication; cross-purposes; mistake, etc., 495.

misrepresentation, perversion, misstatement, exaggeration; abuse of terms; play upon words, pun, parody, travesty; falsification, etc. (*lying*), 544.

V. misinterpret, misapprehend, misunderstand, misconceive; misjudge, misspell; mistranslate, misconstrue, misapply; mistake, etc., 495.

misrepresent, pervert, misstate, garble, falsify, distort; travesty, play upon words; stretch (*or* strain, twist, wrest) the sense *or* meaning.

Adj. misinterpreted, mistranslated; confused, tangled, snarled, mixed.

dazed, perplexed, bewildered, rattled [*slang*], benighted.

Adv. at cross-purposes, at sixes and sevens [*colloq.*]; in a maze.

524. INTERPRETER.—*N.* interpreter, translator, expositor, expounder, exponent; demonstrator; commentator, annotator; oracle, etc., 513.

spokesman, speaker, mouthpiece, foreman of the jury, mediator, advocate, delegate, representative, diplomatic agent, ambassador, plenipotentiary.

guide, courier, cicerone, showman, barker [*colloq.*].

525. MANIFESTATION.—*N.* manifestation, indication, expression; plain speaking, candor, openness; showing, exposition, demonstration; séance, materialization; exhibition, production, display, show.

Thing shown: exhibit, exhibition, exposition, show [*colloq.*], performance.

publicity, etc., 531; disclosure, etc., 529; openness, candor; saliency, prominence.

V. make manifest, materialize, express, represent, set forth, evidence, exhibit, produce, show, show up, expose; hold up, show forth, unveil, display, demonstrate, lay open; draw out, bring out; manifest oneself; speak out, proclaim, publish.

indicate, point out; disclose, discover; translate, transcribe, decipher, decode; elicit, bring to light, disinter.

be manifest *or* plain, appear, etc., 446; transpire, come to light, be disclosed; go without saying, be self-evident.

Adj. manifest, apparent; salient, striking, prominent, in the foreground, ostensible, notable, pronounced.

plain, intelligible, clear, defined, definite, distinct, conspicuous, obvious, evident, unmistakable; conclusive, indubitable, palpable, self-evident; open, patent, express, explicit; naked, bare, literal, downright, unreserved, frank, plain-spoken.

barefaced, brazen, bold, shameless, daring, flaunting, loud [*colloq.*]; flagrant, arrant, notorious; glaring.

Adv. manifestly, openly, plainly, above board, in plain sight, in the open, in broad daylight; without reserve.

526. LATENCY.—*N.* latency, hidden meaning; obscurity, ambiguity; secret, mystery, occultism, mysticism, symbolism; reserve, reticence; concealment, mystification, suppression, evasion; Delphic oracle; undercurrent; snake in the grass.

allusion, insinuation, implication; innuendo.

latent influence, power behind the throne, friend at court, wire-puller [*colloq.*], kingmaker.

V. lurk, smolder, underlie, make no sign; escape observation (*or* detection, recognition); lie hid, lie in ambush.

keep back, etc. (*conceal*), 528.

involve, imply, connote, import, allude to, leave an inference; symbolize.

Adj. latent, lurking; dormant, secret, occult; esoteric, recondite, veiled, symbolic, cryptic, mystic, mystical.

unapparent, unknown, unseen, unsuspected; invisible; unexpressed, undisclosed, tacit.

indirect, crooked, underhand, underground; by inference, by implication; implied, implicit, understood, tacit; allusive, covert, undercover, concealed.

Adv. secretly, stealthily, incognito; in the background; behind the scenes, between the lines; below the surface.

527. INFORMATION.—*N.* information, enlightenment, acquaintance, knowledge; publicity, notoriety.

mention; instruction, communicativeness, intercommunication.

notification, intimation, communication, notice, annunciation, announcement, communiqué; representation; message, etc., 532.

report, advice, monition; news, tidings, return, record, account, description; statement, estimate, specification.

informant, authority, teller, harbinger, herald, reporter, exponent, mouthpiece; spokesman, etc. (*interpreter*), 524; spy, informer, eavesdropper, detective, sleuth [*colloq.*]; newsmonger; messenger, etc., 534.

guide, cicerone; pilot; guidebook, handbook; map, plan, chart, gazetteer; itinerary.

hint, suggestion, insinuation, innuendo, inkling, whisper, cue, byplay; gesture; word to the wise.

V. tell, inform, acquaint, impart, apprise, advise, instruct, enlighten.

mention, express, intimate, represent, communicate, make known; publish, disseminate; notify, signify, specify; retail, describe; state, declare, assert, affirm.

announce, report, bring (*or* send, leave) word; telegraph, wire [*colloq.*], telephone, phone [*colloq.*].

disclose, etc., 529; explain.

hint, insinuate, allude to, glance at, let fall, indicate; suggest, prompt, give the cue.

undeceive, set right, correct, disabuse.

Adj. informational, advisory.

expressive, explicit, plain-spoken; declaratory; expository; communicative.

528. CONCEALMENT.—*N.* concealment, mystification; reticence, reserve, reservation; mental reservation, aside; suppression, evasion, white lie; silence, closeness, secretiveness, mystery.

screen, cloak; ambush, ambuscade; stowaway; blind baggage [*slang*].

cipher, code, sympathetic ink.

stealth, stealthiness, slyness, caution, cunning.

secrecy, privacy, secretness; disguise, mask, masquerade; incognito (*fem.* incognita).

masquerader, masker, mask, domino.

V. conceal, hide, secrete; lock up; cover, screen, cloak, veil, shroud; curtain, muffle; mask, camouflage, disguise; ensconce.

keep from, keep to oneself, keep secret; bury; sink, suppress; keep in the background; stifle, hush up; withhold, reserve.

code, use a code *or* cipher, reduce to a code.

hoodwink, blind, blindfold; mystify, puzzle, deceive, lead astray.

be concealed, hide oneself, couch; lie in ambush, lurk, sneak, skulk, slink, prowl, gumshoe [*slang*].

Adj. concealed, hidden, secret, private, privy; recondite, mystic, mystical, occult, dark, cryptic; in secret, tortuous; close, inviolate, confidential, behind a screen, undercover, in ambush, in hiding, in disguise; undisclosed, untold, covert, mysterious.

furtive, stealthy, skulking, surreptitious, underhand, sly, cunning, evasive; secretive, clandestine; reserved, reticent, uncommunicative, close, taciturn.

Adv. secretly, in secret, in private, incognito.

behind closed doors, under the rose, *sub rosa* [L.]; on the sly [*colloq.*]; in a whisper.

confidentially, in strict confidence, between ourselves, between you and me.

underhand, by stealth, like a thief in the night; stealthily.

529. DISCLOSURE.—*N.* disclosure, revelation, divulgence, exposition, exposure, publication, exposé.

acknowledgment, avowal, confession, confessional.

narrator, etc., 594; talebearer, etc., 532; informant, etc., 527.

V. disclose, discover, unmask, unveil, unfold, uncover, unseal, lay bare, expose, bare, bring to light, disabuse, open the eyes of, turn informer.

divulge, reveal, let into the secret, tell, etc. (*inform*), 527; breathe, utter, peach [*slang*]; let slip *or* drop, betray; blurt out, vent, whisper about, speak out, break the news, publish, etc., 531.

acknowledge, allow, concede, grant, admit, own, confess, avow, make a clean breast, unbosom oneself; turn informer.

be disclosed, transpire, come to light, become known, escape the lips; ooze out, leak out, come to one's ears.

530. AMBUSH. [Means of concealment]—*N.* ambush, ambuscade, lurking place, trap, snare, pitfall, etc., 667.

hiding place, secret place, recess, hole, cubbyhole, crypt; safe, safe-deposit box, safety-deposit box.

screen, cover, shade, blinker; veil, curtain, blind, cloak, cloud.

mask, visor, disguise, masquerade, domino.

V. **ambush,** ambuscade, lie in ambush, lie in wait for; set a trap for, ensnare.

531. PUBLICATION.—*N.* **publication,** public announcement, promulgation, propagation, proclamation, pronouncement, edict.

publicity, notoriety, currency, flagrancy, cry, hue and cry, bruit; report, etc. (*news*), 532; telegram, etc., 532.

the press, the fourth estate, public press; newspaper, journal, gazette.

advertisement, placard, bill, flier [*cant*], leaflet, handbill, poster; circular, notice, program, manifesto.

V. **publish,** make public, broach, utter, circulate, propagate, promulgate, spread, spread abroad, rumor, diffuse, disseminate; issue; bring before the public; give to the world; report, voice, bruit; proclaim, herald, blazon, noise abroad, advertise.

telegraph, cable, wireless [*colloq.*], broadcast, wire [*colloq.*].

Adj. **published,** current; public, notorious, flagrant.

Adv. **publicly,** in public, in open court, with open doors.

532. NEWS—*N.* **news,** information, etc., 527; intelligence, tidings; beat *or* scoop [*newspaper cant*], story, copy [*cant*].

message, word, advice, communication, bulletin, broadcast, dispatch; telegram, cable [*colloq.*], wire [*colloq.*], radio, radiogram, wireless telegram, wireless [*colloq.*]; telephone, radiophone, wireless telephone.

report, rumor, hearsay, cry, bruit, fame; talk, scandal, gossip; tittle-tattle.

narrator, historian; newsmonger, scandalmonger; talebearer, telltale, gossip, tattler, tattletale; chatterer, busybody; informer.

V. **transpire,** etc. (*be disclosed*), 529; rumor, etc. (*publish*), 531.

Adj. **rumored,** rife, current, in circulation.

533. SECRET.—*N.* **secret,** mystery; problem, etc. (*question*), 461; unintelligibility, etc., 519.

enigma, riddle, puzzle, conundrum, charade, rebus.

maze, labyrinth, intricacy.

Adj. **secret,** concealed, etc., 528; involved, tortuous, circuitous, labyrinthine; enigmatic *or* enigmatical.

534. MESSENGER.—*N.* **messenger,** intermediary, go-between; envoy, emissary, legate, nuncio, delegate; angel; Gabriel, Hermes, Mercury.

courier, runner; commissionaire, errand boy; herald, crier, trumpeter, bellman.

mail, post, post office; air mail; postman, mailman, letter carrier; carrier pigeon.

telegraph, cable, wire [*colloq.*], radiotelegraph, wireless telegraph, wireless [*colloq.*], radio.

telephone, phone [*colloq.*], radiotelephone, radiophone, wireless telephone.

reporter, newspaperman, journalist; gentleman (*or* representative) of the press; special correspondent; scout, spy, informer.

535. AFFIRMATION.—*N.* affirmation, statement, allegation, profession, assertion, declaration; confirmation; asseveration, swearing, oath, affidavit, deposition; assurance, protest, protestation.

positiveness, emphasis, peremptoriness, dogmatism, weight.

vote, voice; ballot, suffrage.

remark, observation, saying, dictum, sentence.

V. assert, say, affirm, declare, state; protest, profess; acknowledge; put forward; advance, allege, propose, propound; announce, enunciate, broach, set forth, maintain, contend, pronounce.

depose, aver, avow, avouch, asseverate, swear, affirm; take one's oath; make an affidavit; vow, vouch, warrant, certify, assure; attest, adjure.

emphasize, insist upon, lay stress on; lay down the law; dogmatize, repeat, reassert, reaffirm.

Adj. affirmative, declaratory, positive; unmistakable, clear; certain, etc., 474; express, explicit, absolute, emphatic, decided, insistent, dogmatic, formal, solemn, categorical, peremptory.

Adv. with emphasis, ex cathedra, without fear of contradiction.

536. NEGATION.—*N.* negation, denial; disavowal, disclaimer; contradiction, protest; dissent, etc., 489.

qualification, etc., 469; repudiation, rejection, recantation, revocation; retractation, rebuttal, confutation; refusal, etc., 764.

V. deny; contradict, contravene; controvert, gainsay, negative, give the lie to, belie.

disclaim, disown, repudiate, disaffirm, disavow, abjure, forswear, renounce; recant, revoke.

dispute, impugn, confute, rebut, join issue upon; bring (*or* call) in question, set aside, ignore; refuse, etc., 764.

Adj. contradictory; negative; recusant, dissentient, at issue upon.

Adv. no, nay, not, nowise, not at all, not in the least, quite the contrary, by no means.

537. TEACHING.—*N.* teaching, pedagogics, pedagogy, instruction, edification, education, tuition, tutorship, tutelage; direction, guidance.

preparation, qualification, training, schooling, discipline; drill, practice.

lesson, lecture, recitation, sermon, homily, harangue, disquisi-

tion; apologue, parable; discourse; explanation; exercise, task;
curriculum; course.

V. **teach**, instruct, educate, edify, school, tutor, cram [*colloq.*],
grind [*colloq.*], prime, coach; enlighten, inform, etc., 527; direct,
guide.

inculcate, infuse, instill, imbue, impregnate, implant; disseminate, propagate.

expound, etc. (*interpret*), 522; lecture; hold forth, preach; sermonize, moralize.

train, discipline, form, ground, prepare, qualify, drill, exercise,
practice, familiarize with, inure, initiate, graduate.

Adj. **educational**, scholastic, academic, disciplinary, instructive,
pedagogic, didactic; cultural, humanistic, humane; pragmatic,
practical, utilitarian.

538. MISTEACHING.—*N.* **misteaching**, misinformation, misguidance, misdirection, perversion, sophistry; the blind leading
the blind.

V. **misinform**, misteach, misinstruct, misdirect, misguide, pervert; deceive, mislead, misrepresent, lie.

render unintelligible, bewilder, mystify, conceal.

539. LEARNING.—*N.* **learning**, acquisition of knowledge,
acquirement, attainment; mental cultivation, scholarship, erudition; lore; wide reading; study, grind [*colloq.*]; inquiry, etc., 461.

apprenticeship, tutelage, novitiate.

V. **learn**, acquire (*or* gain, imbibe, pick up, obtain) knowledge *or*
learning; master, grind [*college slang*], cram [*colloq.*], get up, learn
by heart.

study, read, peruse; con, pore over, wade through, plunge into.

burn the midnight oil; be taught.

Adj. **studious**; industrious, etc., 682; scholastic, scholarly, well
read, widely read, erudite, learned.

540. TEACHER.—*N.* **teacher**, preceptor, instructor, master,
tutor, schoolmaster, dominie, pedagogue; kindergartner, governess, mistress; coach [*colloq.*], crammer [*colloq.*]; professor, don
[*Univ. cant*], lecturer, reader, preacher; pastor, etc. (*clergy*), 996;
schoolmistress.

guide, counselor, adviser, mentor, pioneer, apostle, missionary,
propagandist; example.

professorship, chair, fellowship, tutorship, mastership, instructorship.

Adj. **pedagogic**, tutorial, professorial; scholastic, etc., 537.

541. LEARNER.—*N.* **learner**, scholar, student, alumnus (*pl.*
alumni; *fem.* alumna, *pl.* alumnae), pupil, schoolboy, schoolgirl;

monitor, prefect; undergraduate, freshman; graduate student, postgraduate student.

class, form, grade, room; promotion, graduation.

disciple, follower, apostle, proselyte.

classmate, fellow student, schoolmate, schoolfellow, fellow pupil.

novice, beginner, tyro, recruit, tenderfoot [*slang or colloq.*], neophyte, probationer; apprentice.

Adj. in leading strings, pupillary, probationary.

542. SCHOOL.—*N.* school, academy, lyceum, seminary, college, educational institution, institute; university, varsity [*colloq.*], alma mater [L.].

General: day (*or* boarding, preparatory, elementary, denominational, secondary, military, naval, technical, library, secretarial, business, correspondence) school; kindergarten, nursery school; Sunday (*or* Sabbath, Bible) school.

United States: district (*or* grade, parochial, public, primary, grammar, junior high, high, Latin) school; private school, normal school, kindergarten training school; summer school; military academy (West Point); naval academy (Annapolis); college, fresh-water college [*colloq. or slang*], state university; graduate school, postgraduate school.

class, division, form, etc., 541; seminar.

classroom, room, schoolroom, recitation room; lecture room, lecture hall, theater, amphitheater.

desk, reading desk, pulpit, forum, stage, rostrum, platform.

schoolbook, textbook; grammar, primer, reader.

Adj. scholastic, academic, collegiate; educational, cultural; gymnastic, athletic, physical, eurythmic.

543. VERACITY.—*N.* veracity, truthfulness, frankness, truth, sincerity, candor, honesty, fidelity, love of truth; probity, etc., 939.

V. speak the truth, tell the truth; speak on oath; speak without equivocation (*or* mental reservation), make a clean breast, disclose, etc., 529; speak one's mind.

Adj. truthful, true; veracious, scrupulous, punctilious; sincere, candid, frank, open, outspoken, straightforward, unreserved, truth-telling, honest, trustworthy; guileless, pure, truth-loving; true-blue, as good as one's word; unfeigned, ingenuous.

544. FALSEHOOD.—*N.* falsehood, falseness, falsity, falsification, misrepresentation, deception, etc., 545; untruthfulness, lying; untruth, etc., 546; mendacity, guile, perjury, false swearing; forgery, invention, fabrication; perversion, distortion, exaggeration, prevarication, equivocation, evasion, fraud; simulation, dissimulation, dissembling; deceit; sham, pretense; malingering.

duplicity, double dealing, insincerity, hypocrisy, cant, pharisaism; casuistry, Machiavellism; lip service, hollowness, mere show; quackery, charlatanism, charlatanry; humbug; cajolery, flattery; Judas kiss; perfidy, etc., 940; cunning, etc., 702; misstatement, false report.

V. **lie,** tell a lie (*or* an untruth), fib, swear falsely, forswear, perjure oneself, bear false witness.

falsify, misstate, misquote; misrepresent, etc., 523; belie; garble, gloss over, disguise, color, varnish, doctor [*colloq.*], dress up, embroider; exaggerate, etc., 549.

prevaricate, equivocate, quibble; trim, shuffle, fence, beat about the bush.

fabricate, invent; trump up; forge; coin; hatch, concoct; romance.

dissemble, dissimulate; feign, assume; pretend, make believe; play false, play a double game; coquet; act *or* play a part; affect, pose; simulate, pass off for; counterfeit, sham; malinger; deceive, etc., 545.

Adj. **false,** untrue, deceitful, mendacious, lying, untruthful, fraudulent, dishonest; faithless, forsworn; evasive, disingenuous, hollow, insincere; artful, cunning, tricky, wily, sly; perfidious, treacherous, perjured; spurious, etc., 545; falsified.

hypocritical, canting, pharisaical; Machiavellian, double-tongued, double-dealing; two-faced, double-faced; smooth-spoken, smooth-tongued; plausible, mealy-mouthed; affected, canting, insincere.

545. DECEPTION.—*N.* **deception;** falseness, etc., 544; untruth, etc., 546; imposition, imposture; fraud, deceit, guile, fraudulence, misrepresentation, bluff; trickery, knavery, sharp practice, collusion, chicanery; treachery, double-dealing.

delusion, jugglery, sleight of hand, legerdemain, conjuring.

trick, cheat, wile, blind, feint, chicane, juggle, swindle; stratagem, artifice; hoax; bunk [*slang*], gold brick [*colloq.*].

snare, trap, pitfall, gin; bait, decoy duck, stool pigeon; cobweb, net, meshes, toils; ambush, ambuscade.

disguise, false colors, camouflage, masquerade, mask, mummery, borrowed plumes; dissembler, hypocrite, etc., 548.

sham, mockery, copy, counterfeit, make-believe, forgery, fraud, untruth, etc., 546; hollow mockery; whited sepulcher, tinsel, paste.

illusion, delusion, self-deception, *ignis fatuus* [L.], mirage, etc., 443.

V. **deceive,** mislead, lead astray, take in, defraud, cheat, cozen, swindle, victimize; betray, play false; lie, etc., 544: mystify; blind, hoodwink; throw dust into the eyes; impose upon, practice upon, palm off on; bluff.

outwit, circumvent, overreach, steal a march on.

insnare, ensnare, entrap, decoy, waylay, lure, beguile, delude, inveigle, trick.

fool, befool, dupe, gull, hoax, humbug, stuff [slang], sell [slang]; trifle with, cajole, flatter; dissemble, dissimulate, sham, counterfeit.

practice chicanery, live by one's wits, juggle, conjure, play off, palm off, foist off.

Adj. deceptive, deceitful, tricky, cunning, etc., 702; elusive, insidious; delusive, illusory.

make-believe; untrue, etc., 546; mock, sham, counterfeit, pseudo, spurious, so-called, pretended, feigned, bogus [colloq.], fraudulent, surreptitious, illegitimate, contraband; adulterated, disguised; unsound, meretricious, jerry-built; tinsel.

Adv. under false colors, under cover of.

546. UNTRUTH.—N. untruth, falsehood, lie, story, fib, whopper [colloq.].

fabrication, forgery, invention; misstatement, misrepresentation, perversion, falsification, false coloring, exaggeration.

fiction; fable, nursery tale, fairy tale, romance, extravaganza; canard; yarn [colloq.], fish story [colloq.], traveler's tale, cock-and-bull story, myth, moonshine, bosh [colloq.].

half truth, white lie, pious fraud; suppression; irony.

pretense, pretext, subterfuge, evasion, shift, shuffle, make-believe, sham, etc., 545; profession, Judas kiss, cajolery, flattery; disguise, etc., 530.

V. feign, make-believe, pretend, sham, counterfeit; lie, etc., 544.

Adj. untrue, false, trumped up; unfounded, invented, fictitious, fabulous, fabricated, fraudulent, forged; evasive.

547. DUPE.—N. dupe, gull, victim, April fool; sucker [slang]; laughingstock, etc., 857; greenhorn; fool, etc., 501; puppet, cat's-paw.

V. be deceived, be the dupe of; fall into a trap; swallow or nibble at the bait; swallow whole; bite.

Adj. credulous, gullible, etc., 486.

mistaken, etc. (error), 495.

548. DECEIVER.—N. deceiver, dissembler, hypocrite, Pharisee; sophist; serpent, snake in the grass, Judas, wolf in sheep's clothing.

liar, storyteller, perjurer, false witness, faker [slang], fraud, four-flusher [slang], confidence man, decoy, stool pigeon; rogue, knave, cheat, swindler.

impostor, pretender, malingerer, humbug; adventurer, adventuress.

trickster, conjurer, juggler, necromancer, sorcerer, magician, wizard, medicine man, witch doctor; quack, charlatan, mountebank.

549. EXAGGERATION.—*N.* exaggeration, expansion, amplification; fringe, embroidery; extravagance, hyperbole, stretch, high coloring, caricature; yarn [*colloq.*], traveler's tale, fish story [*colloq.*]; tempest in a teacup, much ado about nothing; puffery, etc. (*boasting*), 884; rant, etc., 577.

V. exaggerate, magnify, pile up, aggravate; amplify, expand, overestimate, overstate, overdraw, overshoot the mark, overpraise; stretch a point; draw a long bow [*colloq.*], out-Herod Herod; overcolor, heighten; embroider, color; puff, etc. (*boast*), 884.

Adj. exaggerated, overwrought; bombastic, etc. (*magniloquent*), 577; hyperbolical, extravagant; preposterous, egregious.

550. [Means of communication] INDICATION.—*N.* indication, sign, symbol; index, indicator, pointer, cue, note, token, symptom; type, figure, emblem, cipher, device; motto, epitaph.

means of recognition; lineament, feature, trait, trick, earmark, characteristic.

gesture, gesticulation; pantomime; wink, glance, leer; nod, shrug, beck; touch, nudge; byplay, dumb show; deaf-and-dumb alphabet, dactylology.

track, spoor, trail, footprint, scent; clue, key.

signal, rocket, watch fire, beacon fire, watchtower; telegraph, semaphore; fiery cross; calumet, peace pipe; heliograph; searchlight, flashlight.

mark, line, stroke, score, streak, scratch, tick, dot, notch, nick, blaze; red letter, underlining, impression.

Map drawing: hachure, contour line; isobar, isopiestic line, isobaric line; isotherm, isothermal line; latitude, longitude, meridian, equator.

For identification: badge, countercheck, countersign, counterfoil, stub, duplicate, tally; label, ticket, counter, check, chip, voucher, stamp; trade-mark, hallmark; card, visiting card; credentials; handwriting, sign manual, autograph, signature; monogram, seal, signet; fingerprint; brand; caste mark; mortarboard [*colloq.*], cap and gown, hood; shibboleth; watchword, catchword, password, cue; sign, countersign, pass, grip; open-sesame.

Insignia: banner, flag, colors, streamer, pennant, pennon, ensign, standard; eagle, oriflamme, blue peter, jack, Union Jack; Old Glory [*colloq.*], Stars and Stripes.

Heraldry: crest, arms, coat of arms, armorial bearings; hatchment, escutcheon *or* scutcheon; shield, supporters; livery, uniform; cockade, brassard, epaulet, chevron; garland, chaplet, love knot, favor.

Of locality: beacon, flagstaff, hand, pointer, vane, cock, weathercock, weather vane; guidepost, signpost; sign, signboard; North Star, polestar; landmark, seamark; lighthouse; address, direction, name.

Of the future: warning, premonition; omen, portent, sign.

Of the past: trace, record.

Of danger: warning, alarm, fire alarm, burglar alarm.

Of authority: scepter, etc., 747.

Of triumph: trophy, etc., 733.

Of mourning: mourning, etc., 839.

Of quantity: gauge, etc., 466.

Of distance: milestone, milepost.

Of disgrace: brand, foolscap, mark of Cain, stigma, stripes, broad arrow.

call, word of command; bugle call, trumpet call; bell, alarum, battle cry, reveille, taps, last post; sacring bell, Sanctus bell, angelus; dirge.

V. **indicate,** denote, betoken, connote, signify; represent, stand for; typify, symbolize; mark, note, stamp, nick, blaze; label, ticket.

make a sign, signalize; beckon, nod, wink, glance, leer, nudge, shrug, gesticulate.

sign, seal, attest, underscore, underline; call attention to.

Adj. **indicative,** indicatory; connotative, denotative, representative, typical, individual, symbolic *or* symbolical, symptomatic, characteristic, significant, diagnostic, emblematic, armorial.

551. RECORD.—*N.* **trace,** vestige, relic, remains; scar, cicatrix; footstep, footmark, footprint; track, mark, wake, trail, scent, spoor.

monument, hatchment; escutcheon *or* scutcheon; slab, tablet, trophy, obelisk, pillar, column, monolith; memorial; memento; testimonial, medal, Congressional medal; cross, Victoria cross [Eng.], iron cross [Ger.]; ribbon, garter; commemoration, etc. (*celebration*), 883.

record, note, minute; register, registry; roll, list; entry, memorandum, endorsement, inscription, copy, duplicate, docket; mark, etc., 550; deed; document; deposition, affidavit; certificate.

notebook, memorandum book; bulletin, bulletin board, scoreboard, score sheet; card index, file, letter file, pigeonholes.

newspaper, daily, gazette, magazine, paper [*colloq.*].

calendar, diary, log, journal, daybook, ledger, cashbook.

archive, scroll, state paper, return, bluebook; almanac, gazetteer, census report; statistics; Congressional Records; minutes, chronicle, annals; legend; history, biography, etc., 594.

registration; registry, enrollment, tabulation; entry, booking; signature, sign manual; recorder, etc., 553; journalism.

mechanical record, recording instrument; phonograph, etc., 418; speedometer, pedometer, patent log [*naut.*]; ticker, tape; time clock; turnstile; cash register.

V. **record,** put *or* place upon record, chronicle, calendar, hand down to posterity; commemorate, etc. (*celebrate*), 883; report, commit to writing, note, put *or* set down; mark, etc. (*indicate*), 550; sign, etc. (*attest*), 467; enter, book, post, insert; mark off, tick off; register, list, enroll, inscroll; file.

552. [Suppression of sign] OBLITERATION.—*N.* **obliteration,** erasure, cancellation, deletion; blot; effacement, extinction.

V. **efface,** obliterate, erase, expunge, cancel; blot (*or* rub, scratch, strike, wash, wipe) out; deface, render illegible; rule out.

be effaced, leave no trace.

Adj. **obliterated,** erased; unrecorded, unregistered.

553. RECORDER.—*N.* **recorder,** notary, clerk; registrar, register; amanuensis, secretary, recording secretary, stenographer, bookkeeper, scribe.

annalist, historian, historiographer, chronicler; biographer, etc.

(*narrator*), 594; antiquary, antiquarian, archeologist· memorialist.

journalist, newspaperman, reporter, interviewer: publicist, author, editor.

554. REPRESENTATION.—*N.* representation, depiction, imitation, illustration, delineation, imagery, portraiture; design, designing; art, fine arts; painting, etc., 556· sculpture, etc., 557; engraving, etc., 558.

photography; radiography, X-ray photography, skiagraphy.

personation, impersonation; personification; drama, etc., 599.

drawing, picture, sketch, draft; tracing; copy, etc., 21.
photograph, photo [*colloq.*], daguerreotype, print, cabinet, snapshot.
image, effigy, icon, portrait, likeness, facsimile.
figure, figurehead, puppet, doll, manikin, lay figure, model, marionette, statue, statuette, bust.
map, plan, chart; diagram; ground plan, projection, elevation; atlas; outline, view.
radiograph, radiogram, skiagraph, skiagram, X-ray photograph, Xray [*colloq.*].
delineator, draftsman; artist, etc., 559; photographer, radiographer, X-ray photographer, skiagrapher, daguerreotypist.

V. represent, delineate, depict, portray, picture, limn, photograph, snapshot; figure, shadow forth, adumbrate; describe, etc., 594; trace, copy; mold; illustrate, symbolize; paint, etc., 556; sculpture, etc., 557; engrave, etc., 558.

personate, impersonate, dress up [*colloq.*], pose as, act; personify; play, etc. (*drama*), 559; mimic, etc. (*imitate*),19.

Adj. representative; illustrative; imitative, figurative; similar, like, etc., 17; descriptive, etc., 594.

555. MISREPRESENTATION.—*N.* misrepresentation, misstatement, falsification, exaggeration, distortion; bad likeness, daub, scratch.

burlesque, travesty, parody, take-off, caricature, extravaganza.

V. misrepresent, distort, overdraw, exaggerate, daub; falsify, understate, overstate, stretch.

burlesque, travesty, parody, caricature.

556. PAINTING. BLACK AND WHITE.—*N.* painting, depicting, drawing; design; perspective; composition; treatment; arrangement, values, atmosphere, tone, technique.

palette; easel; brush, pencil, stump, black lead, charcoal, crayons, chalk, pastel; paint, etc. (*coloring matter*), 428; water (*or* oil) colors; oils, oil paint; varnish; distemper, fresco, enamel, mosaic, encaustic painting; batik.
style, school; the grand style, high art; futurist, cubist, vorticist.
picture, painting, piece, tableau; canvas; fresco, cartoon; drawing, draft; still life, genre (*or* landscape) painting; sketch, outline, study.
portrait; head; miniature; silhouette; profile.

view, landscape, seascape, sea view, seapiece; scene, prospect; interior; panorama, bird's-eye view.

picture gallery, art gallery, art museum; studio, atelier [F.].

photograph, radiography, etc., 554; photograph, radiograph, etc., 554.

V. **paint,** design, limn, draw, sketch, pencil, color; stencil; depict, etc. (*represent*), 554.

Adj. **pictorial,** graphic; picturesque, historical; futurist, cubist, vorticist; in the grand style.

557. SCULPTURE.—*N.* **sculpture,** carving, modeling, statuary; ceramics.

marble, bronze, terra cotta; ceramic ware, pottery, porcelain, china, earthenware; cloisonné, enamel, faïence.

relief, low relief, bas-relief, high relief; intaglio; cameo; medal, medallion.

statue, statuette, bust; cast.

V. **sculpture,** carve, cut, chisel, model, mold; cast.

558. ENGRAVING.—*N.* **engraving,** etching, chiseling; plate (*or* copperplate, steel, half-tone, wood) engraving; lithography, chromolithography, photolithography.

printing; color printing, lithographic printing; type printing; three-color process. impression, print, engraving, plate; steel-plate, copperplate; etching; aquatint, mezzotint; cut, woodcut; lithograph, chromolithograph, photolithograph. illustration, illumination; half-tone; photogravure; rotogravure; vignette, initial letter, tailpiece.

V. **engrave,** grave, etch; bite; bite in; lithograph; print.

559. ARTIST.—*N.* **artist;** painter, drawer, sketcher, designer, engraver, graver, line engraver, draftsman; chaser; copyist; enameler, enamelist; cartoonist, caricaturist.

historical (*or* landscape, marine, flower, portrait, genre, miniature, scene) painter; carver, modeler, statuary, sculptor.

(1) Language generally

560. LANGUAGE.—*N.* **language;** phraseology, etc., 569; speech, etc., 582; tongue, lingo [*chiefly humorous or contemptuous*], vernacular, mother (*or* vulgar, native) tongue; king's English; dialect, brogue, patois, idiom.

confusion of tongues, Babel; universal language, Esperanto, Ido; pantomime, dumb show.

literature, letters, polite literature, belles-lettres [F.], muses, humanities, republic of letters, dead languages, classics.

linguist, etc. (*scholar*), 492.

V. **express,** say, express by words.

Adj. **lingual,** linguistic; dialectal, dialectic; vernacular, current; bilingual; polyglot; literary; colloquial, slangy.

561. LETTER.—*N.* **letter;** character; hieroglyphic; alphabet,

ABC; consonant, vowel, diphthong, mute, surd, sonant, liquid, labial, palatal, cerebral, dental, guttural.

syllable; monosyllable, dissyllable, polysyllable; prefix, suffix.

spelling, orthography; phonetic spelling, phonetics.

cipher, code; monogram, anagram; acrostic, double acrostic.

V. **spell;** transliterate.

cipher, decipher; code, decode.

Adj. **literal;** alphabetical, syllabic.

phonetic, voiced, tonic, sonant; voiceless, surd; mute, labial, palatal, cerebral, dental, guttural, liquid.

562. WORD.—*N.* **word,** term, vocable; name, etc., 564; phrase, etc., 566; root, derivative; part of speech.

dictionary, lexicon, vocabulary, wordbook, index, glossary, thesaurus.

Science of language: etymology, philology; terminology; pronunciation, orthoëpy; lexicography.

verbosity, verbiage, wordiness; loquacity, etc., 584.

V. **vocalize;** etymologize, derive; index; translate.

Adj. **verbal,** literal; derivative.

verbose, wordy, etc., 573; loquacious, etc., 584.

563. NEOLOGY.—*N.* **neology,** neologism; barbarism; corruption.

dialect, brogue, patois, provincialism, broken English, Anglicism, Briticism, Gallicism, Americanism; gypsy lingo, Romany.

lingua franca, pidgin English, Hindustani; Esperanto, Ido.

jargon, dog Latin, gibberish; confusion of tongues, Babel; lingo, slang, cant, argot, billingsgate.

pseudonym, pen name; nickname; alias.

neologist, word coiner, coiner of words.

V. **coin words;** Americanize, Anglicize, Gallicize.

Adj. **neologic,** neological; slang, cant, barbarous.

564. NOMENCLATURE.—*N.* **nomenclature;** naming, nicknaming; baptism.

name, appellation, appellative, designation, denomination; nickname, etc., 565; epithet; title, head, heading; style, proper name, cognomen, patronymic, surname; title, handle to one's name; namesake.

term, expression, noun; technical term; cant.

V. **name,** call, term, denominate, designate, style, entitle, dub [*colloq. or humorous*], christen, baptize, nickname, characterize, specify, label.

Adj. **named,** yclept [*humorous*]; known as; titular, nominal.

565. MISNOMER.—*N.* **misnomer;** malapropism, Mrs. Malaprop.

nickname, sobriquet, pet name, assumed name, alias; stage name; *nom de guerre* [F.], nom de plume [English formation], pen name, pseudonym.

V. **misname,** miscall, nickname; take an assumed name.

Adj. **misnamed;** self-styled; so-called, quasi.

nameless, anonymous; unacknowledged; pseudo.

566. PHRASE.—*N.* **phrase,** expression, locution; sentence, paragraph; paraphrase, metaphor, euphemism, euphuism; motto, proverb; figure of speech; idiom, turn of expression; phraseology, etc., 569.

V. **express,** phrase; word, voice; put into (*or* express by) words; call, denominate, designate, dub.

Adv. in round (*or* set) terms; in set phrases; by the card.

567. GRAMMAR.—*N.* **grammar,** accidence, syntax, analysis, parts of speech; inflection, case, declension, conjugation; philology.

V. **parse,** analyze, conjugate, decline.

Adj. **grammatical,** syntactic *or* syntactical, inflectional, declensional, synthetic *or* synthetical.

568. SOLECISM.—*N.* **solecism;** grammatical blunder; error, slip; slip of the pen, slip of the tongue, bull; barbarism, impropriety.

V. **solecize,** commit a solecism; murder the king's English.

Adj. **ungrammatical,** incorrect, inaccurate, faulty; improper.

569. STYLE.—*N.* **style,** diction, phraseology, wording; manner, strain; composition; mode of expression, idiom, choice of words; mode of speech, literary power, command of language; authorship, artistry.

V. **word,** phrase, express by words, write; apply the file.

Various Qualities of Style

570. PERSPICUITY.—*N.* **perspicuity,** perspicacity, explicitness, lucidness, lucidity, limpidity, clearness; plain speaking, expression, definiteness, definition; exactness, etc., 494.

Adj. **lucid,** intelligible, etc., 518; limpid, pellucid, clear, explicit; exact, etc., 494.

571. OBSCURITY.—*N.* **obscurity,** unintelligibility, involution, confusion; hard words; ambiguity, indefiniteness, vagueness, inexactness, inaccuracy; darkness of meaning.

Adj. **obscure,** involved, confused.

572. CONCISENESS.—*N.* **conciseness,** terseness, brevity, laconicism, abridgment, compression, condensation, epitome, etc., 596.

Portmanteau word [Lewis Carroll]; brunch [breakfast + lunch], slithy, *adj.* [slimy + lithe], torrible, *adj.* [torrid + horrible].

V. **be concise,** telescope, compress, condense, abridge, abbreviate, abstract, etc., 596; come to the point.

Adj. **concise,** brief, short, laconic, succinct, curt, compact, summary, compendious, etc., 596; terse, to the point; compressed, condensed, pointed; pithy, crisp, trenchant, epigrammatic, sententious.

Adv. **briefly,** summarily; in brief, in short, in a word.

573. DIFFUSENESS.—*N.* **diffuseness,** profuseness, amplification, verbosity, wordiness; verbiage, flow of words, etc. (*loquacity*), 584; looseness; tautology, exuberance, redundance, prolixity, periphrase, expletive; padding [*editors' cant*]; drivel, twaddle.

V. **expand,** expatiate, enlarge, dilate, amplify, inflate, pad [*editors' cant*], rant; maunder, prose; harp upon, dwell on.

digress, ramble, beat about the bush, protract.

Adj. **diffuse,** profuse, wordy, verbose, copious, exuberant; lengthy, long, long-winded, protracted, prolix, diffusive, roundabout, digressive, discursive, loose; rambling, frothy.

574. VIGOR.—*N.* **vigor,** power, force; boldness, intellectual force; spirit, punch [*slang*], point, piquancy, raciness; verve, ardor, enthusiasm, glow, fire, warmth; gravity, weight.

loftiness, elevation, sublimity, grandeur.

eloquence; command of words, command of language.

Adj. **vigorous,** nervous, powerful, forcible, forceful; mordant, biting, trenchant, incisive; graphic, impressive.

spirited, lively, glowing, sparkling; racy, bold, pungent, piquant, pithy.

lofty, elevated, sublime, poetic, grand, weighty, ponderous; eloquent.

vehement, passionate, burning, impassioned, petulant.

575. FEEBLENESS.—*N.* **feebleness,** baldness, enervation, flaccidity, vapidity, poverty.

Adj. **feeble,** tame, meager, insipid, watery, nerveless, vapid, trashy, poor, dull, dry, languid; bald, colorless, enervated; prosy, prosaic, weak, slight; careless, slovenly, loose, lax; slipshod, inexact; puerile, childish; rambling, etc. (*diffuse*), 573.

576. PLAINNESS.—*N.* **plainness,** homeliness, simplicity, severity; household words.

V. **speak plainly,** waste no words, come to the point.

Adj. **plain,** simple, unornamented, unadorned, unvarnished; homely, homespun; neat; severe, chaste, pure, Saxon; commonplace, matter-of-fact, natural, prosaic, sober.

Adv. **point-blank**; in plain English; in common parlance.

577. ORNAMENT.—*N.* **ornament,** floridness, grandiloquence, magniloquence, declamation, well-rounded periods; elegance, etc., 578; flourish, trope; euphuism, euphemism.

bombast, inflation, pretension; rant, fustian, highfalutin [*slang*], buncombe, balderdash; fine writing; purple patches.

V. **ornament,** overcharge, overload; euphuize, euphemize.

Adj. **ornate;** ornamented, beautified, florid, rich, flowery; euphuistic, euphemistic; sonorous, inflated, swelling, tumid; turgid, pedantic, pompous, stilted, high-flown, sententious, rhetorical, declamatory; grandiose; grandiloquent, magniloquent, bombastic; frothy, flashy, flamboyant.

578. ELEGANCE.—*N.* **elegance,** distinction, clarity, purity, grace, felicity, ease; gracefulness, euphony; taste, good taste, restraint, propriety, correctness.

purist, classicist, stylist.

Adj. **elegant,** polished, classic *or* classical, correct, artistic; chaste, pure; graceful, easy, fluent, unaffected, natural, mellifluous, euphonious; restrained.

felicitous, happy, neat; well expressed.

579. INELEGANCE.—*N.* **inelegance,** impurity, vulgarity; poor diction, poor choice of words; loose construction; ill-balanced sentences; barbarism, slang; solecism, mannerism, affectation.

Adj. **inelegant,** graceless, ungraceful; harsh, abrupt; dry, stiff, cramped, formal, forced, labored; artificial, mannered, affected, ponderous, awkward; unpolished; turgid, barbarous, uncouth, rude, crude, halting, vulgar.

(2) *Spoken Language*

580. VOICE.—*N.* **voice;** intonation; utterance; vocalization; cry, exclamation, expletive, ejaculation; vociferation, enunciation, articulation; distinctness; clearness; delivery, attack.

accent, accentuation; emphasis, stress; pronunciation; euphony, etc. (*melody*), 413.

V. **speak,** utter, breathe; cry, etc. (*shout*), 411; ejaculate, rap out; articulate, enunciate, vocalize, pronounce, accentuate, deliver, emit; whisper, murmur.

Adj. **vocal,** phonetic, oral; ejaculatory, articulate, distinct, euphonious, melodious.

581. DUMBNESS.—*N.* **dumbness;** silence, etc. (*taciturnity*), 585; deaf-mutism, deaf-muteness, deaf-dumbness, mute, dummy, deaf-mute.

V. silence, muzzle, muffle, suppress, smother, gag, strike dumb, dumfound.

Adj. dumb, mute, mum; tongue-tied; voiceless, speechless, wordless; silent, etc. (*taciturn*), 585; inarticulate.

582. SPEECH.—*N.* speech, locution, talk, parlance, word of mouth, prattle.

oration, recitation, delivery, speech, address, discourse, lecture, harangue, sermon, tirade, soliloquy, etc., 589; conversation, etc., 588; salutatory; valedictory.

oratory, elocution, eloquence, rhetoric, declamation; grandiloquence.

speaker, spokesman, mouthpiece, orator, rhetorician, lecturer, preacher, elocutionist, reciter, reader; spellbinder.

V. speak, talk, say, utter, pronounce, deliver, breathe, let fall, rap out, blurt out.

soliloquize, etc., 589; tell, etc. (*inform*), 527; address, etc., 586; converse, etc., 588.

declaim, hold forth, harangue, stump [*colloq.*], spout, rant; recite, lecture, sermonize, discourse, expatiate.

Adj. oral, lingual, phonetic, unwritten, spoken.

eloquent, oratorical, rhetorical, elocutionary, declamatory, grandiloquent.

583. [Imperfect Speech] STAMMERING.—*N.* inarticulateness; stammering, hesitation, impediment in one's speech; lisp, drawl, nasal accent; twang; falsetto, brogue.

V. stammer, stutter, hesitate, falter.

mumble, mutter, maunder; mince, lisp; jabber, gabble, gibber; splutter, sputter; drawl, mouth; croak.

murder the language, murder the king's English; mispronounce.

Adj. inarticulate; stammering, guttural, throaty, nasal; tremulous.

584. LOQUACITY.—*N.* loquacity, loquaciousness, effusion; talkativeness, garrulity.

gabble, gab [*colloq.*], jaw [*low*], hot air [*slang*]; jabber, chatter; prate, prattle, twaddle, small talk.

fluency, volubility, flow of words; verbosity, etc. (*diffuseness*), 573; eloquence.

talker; chatterer, chatterbox; babbler, ranter, proser, driveler, gossip, magpie.

V. be loquacious, talk glibly, pour forth, prate, palaver, prose, maunder, chatter, blab, gush, prattle, jabber, jaw [*low*], babble, gabble; expatiate, gossip, talk at random, talk nonsense.

Adj. loquacious, talkative, garrulous, chattering, chatty, declamatory, fluent, voluble, effusive, glib, flippant.

585. TACITURNITY.—*N.* taciturnity, silence, muteness, curtness; reserve, reticence.

man of few words; Spartan.

V. be silent, keep silence; hold one's tongue, say nothing; render mute.

Adj. silent, mute, mum, still, dumb.

taciturn, laconic, concise, sententious, close, close-mouthed, curt; reserved; reticent.

586. ADDRESS.—*N.* address, allocution; speech, etc., 582; appeal, invocation, salutation, salutatory.

V. address, speak to, accost, apostrophize, appeal to, invoke; hail, salute; call to, halloo.

lecture, preach, harangue, spellbind.

587. RESPONSE, etc., *see* Answer 462.

588. CONVERSATION.—*N.* conversation, colloquy, converse, interlocution, talk, discourse, dialogue, duologue.

chat, tattle, gossip, tittle-tattle; babble.

conference, parley, interview, audience, reception; congress, etc. (*council*), 696; powwow.

debate, palaver, war of words, controversy.

talker, gossip, tattler; chatterer, etc. (*loquacity*), 584; speaker, etc., 582; conversationalist.

V. converse, talk together, hold (*or* carry on, join in, engage in) a conversation; parley; palaver; chat, gossip, tattle; prate, etc., 584.

confer with, discourse with, commune with, talk it over.

Adj. conversational, conversable; chatty, colloquial.

589. SOLILOQUY.—*N.* soliloquy, monologue, apostrophe.

V. soliloquize, monologize, talk to oneself; think aloud, apostrophize.

Written Language

590. WRITING.—*N.* writing, chirography, penmanship; typewriting; manuscript; script; character, letter, etc., 561.

shorthand, stenography, phonography; secret writing, cipher, cryptography.

handwriting; signature, mark, autograph, hand, fist [*colloq.*]; calligraphy.

composition, authorship; lucubration, production, work, screed, article, paper; book, etc., 593; essay, theme, thesis; novel, textbook; poem, book of poems (*or* verse), anthology.

writer, scribe; author, etc., 593; amanuensis, secretary, clerk, penman, copyist; stenographer, typewriter, typist.

V. **write,** pen, typewrite, type [*colloq.*]; copy, engross; transcribe; scribble, scrawl, scratch; note down, write down, record.

compose, indite, draw up, draft, formulate; dictate; inscribe.

Adj. **written,** in writing, in black and white; stenographic.

591. PRINTING.—*N.* printing, typography; type, linotype, monotype; composition, print, letterpress, text, context, matter; copy, impression, proof, galley, galley proof, page proof.

printer, compositor; reader, proofreader, corrector of the press; printer's devil; copyholder, copyeditor.

V. **print;** compose; go to press; publish, issue, bring out.

Adj. **typographical,** printed, in type.

592. CORRESPONDENCE.—*N.* correspondence, letter, epistle, missive, note, post card, postal card; dispatch; bulletin, circular.

correspondent, writer, letter writer.

V. **correspond,** write to, send a letter to; communicate, communicate by writing (*or* letter); circularize, follow up, bombard; reply.

593. BOOK.—*N.* **book,** booklet; writing, work, volume, tome, tract, treatise, brochure, monograph, pamphlet, libretto; handbook, manual, novel, etc. (*composition*), 590; publication; magazine, periodical.

work of reference, encyclopedia, cyclopedia, dictionary, thesaurus, concordance, anthology, compilation.

writer, author, essayist, contributor; hack writer, hack; journalist, publicist, reporter, correspondent; editor, scribe, etc., 590; playwright, etc., 599; poet, etc., 597.

publisher, bookseller; librarian; bookworm.

bookstore, bookshop, bookseller's shop, publishing house.

library, public library, lending library.

594. DESCRIPTION.—*N.* description, account, statement, report, record; brief, etc. (*abstract*), 596; delineation, sketch, pastel, vignette; monograph; narration, recital, rehearsal, relation.

narrative, history, memoir; annals, etc., (*chronicle*), 551; journal, letters, biography, autobiography, life, adventures.

Fiction: novel, romance, story, tale, short story, anecdote; detective story, fairy tale, fable, parable, allegory.

narrator, historian, biographer, novelist, storyteller, romancer, anecdotist, word painter; writer, etc., 593.

V. **describe,** set forth, picture, portray, characterize, delineate, narrate, relate, recite, recount, romance, tell, report; detail, particularize.

Adj. **descriptive,** graphic, narrative, epic, romantic, historic *or* historical, biographical, autobiographical; traditional, legendary, mythical, fabulous; anecdotic, idealistic; realistic, true to life.

595. DISSERTATION.—*N.* dissertation, treatise, essay, thesis, theme; tract, discourse, memoir, disquisition, lecture, sermon, homily, investigation, study, discussion, exposition.

commentary, review, critique, criticism, article, leader, editorial.

commentator, critic, essayist, publicist, reviewer, leader writer, editor.

V. comment, explain, interpret, criticize, illuminate; treat of (*or* ventilate, discuss, deal with, go into) a subject.

596. COMPENDIUM.—*N.* compendium, abstract, précis, epitome, analysis, digest, brief, condensation, abridgment, abbreviation, etc., 201; summary, draft, minute, note; excerpt, extract; synopsis, textbook, outlines, syllabus, contents, heads, prospectus.

fragments, extracts, cuttings; fugitive pieces, anthology, miscellany, compilation.

recapitulation, résumé, review; symposium.

V. abridge, abstract, epitomize, summarize; abbreviate, etc. (*shorten*), 201; condense, etc. (*compress*), 195.

compile, etc. (*collect*), 72; note down, collect, edit.

recapitulate, review, skim, run over, sum up.

Adj. compendious, synoptic, abridged, analytic *or* analytical.

Adv. in short, in substance, in few words, in a nutshell.

597. POETRY.—*N.* poetry, poetics, poesy, muse, Apollo, Parnassus, inspiration, fire of genius.

poem; epic, ballad, lyric, ode, idyl, eclogue, pastoral, sonnet, elegy; dramatic (*or* didactic, satirical, narrative, lyric) poetry; satire; anthology.

versification, rhyming, prosody; scansion, scanning.
canto, stanza, verse, line, couplet, triplet, quatrain; refrain, chorus, burden; octave, sextet.
verse, rhyme, assonance, alliteration, meter, measure; foot, numbers, rhythm; ictus, beat, accent, accentuation, iambus, iambic, dactyl, spondee, trochee, anapest, etc.; hexameter, pentameter; Alexandrine; blank verse, heroic verse; doggerel.

poet, genius, creator; poet laureate; laureate; bard, lyrist, sonneteer, rhapsodist, satirist, troubadour; minstrel; minnesinger, Meistersinger; jongleur, versifier, rhymer, rhymester, minor poet, poetaster.

V. poetize, sing, write poetry; string verses together, versify, make verses, rhyme.

Adj. poetic *or* poetical; lyric *or* lyrical; tuneful; metrical; elegiac, iambic, dactylic, spondaic, trochaic, anapestic.

598. PROSE.—*N.* prose, prosaicness; poetic prose; narrative, etc., 594.

prose writer, essayist, novelist, etc., 594.

V. prose; write prose (*or* in prose).

Adj. prosaic, prosy, unpoetical, unrhymed, in prose.

599. THE DRAMA.—*N.* **the drama,** the stage, the theater, the play; theatricals, histrionic art.

play, drama, piece, tragedy, comedy, opera, vaudeville, curtain raiser, interlude, afterpiece, farce, extravaganza, harlequinade, pantomime, burlesque, ballet, spectacle, masque, melodrama; comedy of manners; charade, mystery, miracle play, morality play.

act, scene, tableau, curtain; introduction, prologue, exposition, epilogue; libretto, book, text, prompter's copy.

performance, representation, show [*colloq.*], stage setting, stagecraft; acting; impersonation, stage business; slapstick [*slang*], buffoonery.

theater, playhouse, amphitheater, moving-picture theater, moving pictures, movies [*colloq.*]; puppet show, marionettes, Punch and Judy.

cast, dramatis personae [L.], role, part, character; repertoire, repertory.

actor, player, performer; masker, mime, mimic; star, headliner; comedian, tragedian.

buffoon, mummer, pantomimist, clown; pantaloon, harlequin, columbine; punch.

company, first tragedian, prima donna, leading lady; lead; leading man; comedian, comedienne; juvenile lead, juvenile; villain, heavy lead, heavy, heavy father; ingenue, soubrette; character man, character woman, extra, mute, supernumerary, super [*theat. cant*].

dramatist, playwright, playwriter; dramatic author (*or* writer).
audience, house; orchestra, gallery.

V. act, play, perform; put on the stage, dramatize, stage, produce, set; personate, mimic, enact; rehearse, spout, rant; tread the stage (*or* boards); make one's debut, take a part, star.

Adj. dramatic; theatrical; scenic, histrionic, comic, tragic, farcical, tragicomic, melodramatic, operatic; stagy, spectacular.

Adv. on the stage, on the boards; in the limelight, in the spotlight; before the footlights, before an audience; behind the scenes.

CLASS V

Words Relating to the VOLUNTARY POWERS

I. Individual Volition

600. WILL.—*N.* **will,** volition, free will; freedom, etc., 748; discretion; choice, inclination, intent, purpose, option, etc. (*choice*), 609; spontaneity, spontaneousness; originality.

determination, etc. (*resolution*), 604; force of will, will power, autocracy, bossiness [*colloq.*].

wish, desire, pleasure, mind, disposition, etc., 602; intention, etc., 620.

V. will, see fit, think fit; determine, etc. (*resolve*), 604; enjoin; settle, etc. (*choose*), 609; volunteer; do what one chooses, etc. (*freedom*), 748; have one's own way; use one's discretion; boss, [*colloq.*]; originate.

Adj. **voluntary,** volitional, willful; free, etc., 748; optional, discretionary; autocratic, dictatorial, bossy [*colloq.*].

willing, etc., 602; unbidden, spontaneous; original.

Adv. **voluntarily,** at will, at pleasure.

of one's own accord, on one's own responsibility; by choice, purposely, intentionally.

601. NECESSITY.—*N.* **necessity,** obligation; compulsion, etc., 744; subjection, etc., 749; stern (*or* dire) necessity, last resort.

instinct, blind impulse, natural tendency (*or* impulse), predetermination.

destiny, fatality, fate, kismet, doom, election, predestination; lot, fortune; fatalism.

Fates, God's will, heaven, will of heaven; stars; planets; wheel of fortune.

V. **be obliged,** be forced, be driven; be fated, be doomed, be destined, have no alternative.

destine, doom, foredoom, devote; predestine, preordain; necessitate; compel, etc., 744.

Adj. **necessary,** needful, etc. (*requisite*), 630; compulsory, etc. (*compel*), 744; inevitable, unavoidable, irresistible, irrevocable, inexorable, binding.

fated; destined, fateful, set apart, devoted, elect.

involuntary, instinctive, automatic, blind, mechanical; unconscious, unwitting, unthinking; unintentional.

Adv. **necessarily,** of necessity, of course; willy-nilly.

602. WILLINGNESS.—*N.* **willingness,** disposition, inclination, liking, turn, propensity, leaning, frame of mind, humor, mood, vein, bent, aptitude.

geniality, cordiality, good will; alacrity, readiness, zeal, enthusiasm, earnestness, eagerness.

assent, etc., 488; compliance, etc., 762.

volunteer, unpaid worker, amateur, nonprofessional.

V. **be willing,** incline, lean to, mind, hold to, cling to; desire, etc., 865; acquiesce, assent, comply with; jump at, catch at; take up, plunge into, have a go at [*colloq.*].

volunteer, offer, proffer.

Adj. **willing,** fain, disposed, inclined, favorable, content, well disposed; ready, forward, earnest, eager, zealous, enthusiastic; bent upon, desirous.

docile, amenable, easily persuaded, facile, easygoing, tractable, genial, gracious, cordial.

voluntary, gratuitous, free, unconstrained, spontaneous, unasked, unforced.

Adv. willingly, fain, freely, with pleasure, of one's own accord; graciously, with a good grace, without demur.

603. UNWILLINGNESS.—*N.* unwillingness, indisposition, disinclination, aversion, averseness, reluctance; indifference, etc., 866; backwardness, slowness; obstinacy, etc., 606.

scruple, scrupulousness, delicacy, qualm, shrinking, recoil; hesitation, fastidiousness.

dissent, etc., 489; refusal, etc., 764.

V. be unwilling, dislike, etc., 867; demur, stick at, scruple, stickle; hang fire, shirk, slack, recoil, shrink, hesitate; avoid, etc., 623; oppose, etc., 708; dissent, etc., 489; refuse, etc., 764.

Adj. unwilling, loath, disinclined, indisposed, averse, reluctant, opposed, adverse, laggard, backward, remiss, slack, indifferent, scrupulous; repugnant, restive; grudging, forced, under compulsion, irreconcilable.

Adv. unwillingly, grudgingly, with an ill grace; against one's will, against the grain; under protest.

604. RESOLUTION.—*N.* determination, will, decision, resolution; backbone; clear grit, grit; sand [*slang*]; strength of mind, resolve, firmness, energy, manliness, vigor, resoluteness; zeal, devotion.

self-control, self-mastery, self-command, self-reliance, self-restraint, self-denial.

tenacity, perseverance, etc., 604a; obstinacy, etc., 606; pluck.

V. resolve, will, determine, decide, form a resolution, conclude, fix, bring to a crisis, take a decisive step, take upon oneself.

take one's stand, stand firm, insist upon, make a point of, set one's heart upon; stick at nothing, make short work of, not stick at trifles; persevere, etc., 604a.

Adj. resolved, determined; strong-willed, strong-minded; resolute, self-possessed, earnest, serious; decided, peremptory, unflinching, firm, iron, game, plucky, tenacious, gritty, indomitable, inexorable, relentless; obstinate, etc., 606; unyielding; grim, stern, inflexible, irrevocable.

Adv. resolutely, in earnest, earnestly; on one's mettle, manfully, like a man.

604a. PERSEVERANCE.—*N.* perseverance, continuance, constancy, steadiness, persistence, patience; pertinacity, industry.

grit, bottom, pluck, stamina, backbone, sand [*slang*]; tenacity, staying power, endurance; bulldog courage.

V. persevere, persist, hold on, hold out; stick to, cling to, adhere to; keep on, carry on, hold on; bear up, keep up, hold up; plod; continue, die in harness, die at one's post.

Adj. **persevering,** constant; steady, steadfast, unwavering, unfaltering, unflinching, unflagging, plodding; industrious, etc., 682; strenuous, pertinacious, persistent; indomitable, indefatigable.

Adv. **without fail,** through thick and thin, through fire and water; sink or swim, rain or shine, fair or foul.

605. IRRESOLUTION.—*N.* **irresolution,** indecision, indetermination, instability, uncertainty; demur, suspense, hesitation, hesitancy, vacillation, changeableness, fluctuation; caprice, etc., 608; lukewarmness.

fickleness, levity, pliancy, weakness, timidity; cowardice, etc., 862.

waverer, shilly-shally, turncoat, opportunist, timeserver.

V. **be irresolute,** remain neuter; dilly-dally, hesitate, hover, shilly-shally, hem and haw, demur, debate, balance; dally with, coquet with; go halfway, compromise, be afraid.

vacillate, falter, waver, fluctuate, change, alternate, shuffle, palter, shirk, trim.

Adj. **irresolute,** drifting, halfhearted; undecided, undetermined, uncertain, at a loss; fickle, unreliable, irresponsible, unstable; capricious, etc., 608.

weak, feeble-minded, frail, timid, cowardly, pliant.

Adv. **irresolutely,** in faltering accents; off and on.

606. OBSTINACY.—*N.* **obstinacy,** tenacity, cussedness; perseverance, etc., 604a; immovability, inflexibility, obduracy, doggedness, stubbornness, self-will, contumacy, perversity; resolution, etc., 604.

bigotry, intolerance, dogmatism; fixed idea, fanaticism, zealotry, infatuation, monomania.

bigot, dogmatist, zealot, fanatic, bitter-ender [*colloq.*]; mule.

V. **be obstinate,** stickle, take no denial, be wedded to an opinion, persist, die hard, not yield an inch, stand out.

Adj. **obstinate,** tenacious, stubborn, obdurate, inflexible, balky; immovable, unchangeable, inexorable, determined, mulish, dogged; sullen, sulky; unmoved.

arbitrary, dogmatic, positive, bigoted, opinionated, stiff-necked, hidebound, unyielding; incorrigible.

willful, self-willed, perverse; ungovernable, wayward, refractory, unruly, headstrong; contumacious; cross-grained.

Adv. **with set jaw;** no surrender.

607. APOSTASY.—*N.* **apostasy,** recantation; renunciation; abjuration, defection, retraction, withdrawal, disavowal, revocation, tergiversation, reversal; backsliding.

turncoat, apostate, renegade, pervert, deserter, backslider, crawfish [*slang*].

timeserver, trimmer, double-dealer; weathercock.

V. apostatize, veer round, turn round; change one's mind, abjure, renounce, relinquish, back down, shift one's ground, change sides, go over, recant, retract, revoke, rescind, forswear.

trim, shuffle, blow hot and cold, be on the fence, straddle.

Adj. changeful, irresolute, ductile, slippery, trimming, timeserving.

608. CAPRICE.—*N.* caprice, fancy, humor, whim, fit, crotchet, quirk, freak, fad, vagary, prank, escapade.

V. be capricious, take it into one's head, blow hot and cold, play fast and loose.

Adj. capricious, erratic, eccentric, fitful, inconsistent, fanciful, whimsical, crotchety, freakish, wayward, wanton; contrary, captious, unreasonable, arbitrary; fickle, etc. (*irresolute*), 605.

Adv. by fits, by fits and starts, without rhyme or reason.

609. CHOICE.—*N.* choice, option, selection, pick; discretion, alternative, preference, adoption, decision.

Scylla and Charybdis.

election, poll, ballot, vote, voice, suffrage, plebiscite, referendum; electioneering; voting, elective franchise; ticket; ballot box.

voter, elector, constituent, electorate, constituency.

V. choose; elect, make one's choice; make choice of, fix upon, settle, decide, make up one's mind; adopt, take up, embrace, espouse.

vote, poll, hold up one's hand, give a (*or* the) voting sign; divide.

select, pick, cull, glean, winnow; pitch upon, indulge one's fancy; set apart, mark out for.

prefer, fancy, have rather, had (*or* would) as lief; reserve.

Adj. optional, discretional, at choice, on approval.

chosen, choice, elect, select, popular; preferential.

Adv. optionally, at pleasure, at the option of.

by choice, by preference; in preference; rather, before.

609a. ABSENCE OF CHOICE.—*N.* no choice; Hobson's choice; first come first served; necessity, etc., 601.

neutrality, indifference; indecision, etc. (*irresolution*), 605.

V. be neutral, have no preference, waive, not vote.

Adj. neutral, neuter; indifferent; undecided, etc. (*irresolute*), 605.

610. REJECTION.—*N.* rejection, repudiation, exclusion; refusal, etc., 764.

V. reject, set (*or* lay) aside, give up; decline, etc. (*refuse*), 764; exclude, except; pluck up, spurn, cast out; repudiate, scout, disclaim, discard.

Adv. neither, neither the one nor the other.

611. PREDETERMINATION.—*N.* predetermination, predestination, premeditation, foregone conclusion; resolve, project; intention, etc., 620; fate, necessity.

list, schedule, calendar, docket, slate [*pol. cant*], register, roster, poll, muster, draft.

V. predetermine, predestine, premeditate, resolve beforehand.

list, schedule, docket, slate, register, poll, empanel, draft.

Adj. premeditated, predesigned, prepense [*as,* malice *prepense*], studied, designed, calculated, aforethought; foregone.

well laid, well devised, well weighed; maturely considered; cut-and-dried.

Adv. deliberately, with eyes open, in cold blood; intentionally.

612. IMPULSE.—*N.* impulse, sudden thought; impromptu, improvisation; inspiration, flash, spurt.

V. improvise, extemporize; say what comes uppermost, act on the spur of the moment, rise to the occasion; spurt.

Adj. extemporaneous, impulsive, snap, improvised, unpremeditated, unprompted, natural, unguarded; spontaneous.

Adv. extempore, extemporaneously; offhand, impromptu.

613. HABIT.—*N.* habit, addiction, wont, run, way, matter of course, beaten path, second nature; trick, knack, skill.

custom, use, usage, prescription, practice; prevalence, observance; conventionalism, conventionality, mode, fashion, vogue, etiquette.

rule, standing order, precedent, routine, red tape, rut, groove.

V. habituate, inure, harden, season, caseharden; accustom, familiarize; acclimatize.

cling to, adhere to; acquire a habit; follow the beaten track (*or* path), move in a rut.

prevail; come into use, become a habit, take root; grow upon one.

Adj. habitual, customary, accustomed, wonted, usual, general, ordinary, common, frequent, everyday, household, familiar, trite, hackneyed, commonplace, conventional, regular, set, stock, established, stereotyped; fixed, rooted, permanent, inveterate, besetting, ingrained, current.

wont; used to, given to, addicted to, in the habit of; seasoned, imbued with, devoted to, wedded to.

Adv. as usual, as things go, as the world goes; as you were [*mil.*].

as a rule, for the most part, generally, most frequently.

614. DESUETUDE.—*N.* desuetude, disusage; disuse, etc., 678; want of practice.

V. **be unaccustomed,** leave off (*or* break off, shake off, violate) a habit *or* custom; be weaned from; disuse, etc., 678; wear off.

Adj. **unaccustomed,** unused, unwonted, unseasoned, untrained; new, fresh, original; unskilled.

unconventional, unfashionable, unusual; disused, etc., 678.

615. MOTIVE.—*N.* **motive,** reason, ground, call, principle, mainspring, pro and con, reason why; ulterior motive; intention, etc., 620.

inducement, consideration; attraction, loadstone, magnet, magnetism, temptation, enticement, allurement, glamour, witchery; charm, spell; fascination, blandishment, cajolery; seduction.

influence, prompting, dictate, instance; impulse, incitement, press, insistence, instigation; inspiration, persuasion, encouragement, exhortation, advice, solicitation, pull [*slang*].

incentive, stimulus, spur, fillip, whip, goad, provocative, whet.
bribe, lure, sop, decoy, bait, bribery and corruption.

tempter, prompter, instigator, coaxer, wheedler, siren; firebrand.

V. **induce,** move, draw, inspire; put up to [*slang*], prompt; stimulate, rouse, arouse, animate, whet, incite, provoke, instigate, actuate, encourage, advocate.

influence, bias, sway, incline, dispose, predispose; lead, lobby.
persuade, prevail upon, overcome, carry, bring round, conciliate, win (*or* talk) over; enlist, engage; invite, court.

tempt, overpersuade, entice, allure, captivate, fascinate, bewitch, hypnotize, charm, magnetize, wheedle, coax, lure, inveigle.
bribe, tamper with, suborn, grease the palm, corrupt.

enforce, force, impel, propel, whip, lash, goad, spur, prick, urge, egg on, hound on, hurry on.

Adj. **persuasive,** inviting, tempting, suasive, seductive, attractive, fascinating; provocative.

Adv. **because,** therefore, for, by reason of, for the sake of, on account of; out of, from, as, forasmuch as.

615a. ABSENCE OF MOTIVE.—*N.* **absence of motive;** caprice, etc., 608; chance, etc. (*absence of design*), 621.

V. **scruple,** etc. (*be unwilling*), 603; have no motive.

Adj. **aimless,** capricious, without rhyme or reason.

Adv. **capriciously,** out of mere caprice.

616. DISSUASION.—*N.* **dissuasion,** expostulation, remonstrance; deprecation, etc., 766; discouragement, damper, wet blanket.

curb, restraint, constraint, check.

V. **dissuade,** cry out against, remonstrate, expostulate, warn.
disincline, indispose, shake, stagger; discourage, dishearten,

disenchant; deter, hold back, restrain, repel, turn aside, damp, cool, chill, blunt, calm, quiet, quench.

Adj. averse, etc. (*unwilling*), 603; repugnant, etc. (*dislike*), 867.

617. [Ostensible motive, ground, or reason] PLEA.—*N.* plea, pretext; allegation, excuse, vindication, justification; color; gloss, guise.

pretense, subterfuge, dust thrown in the eye; blind, lame excuse, makeshift, shift.

V. **plead,** allege, excuse, vindicate; color, gloss over, make a pretext of, use as a plea, take one's stand upon; pretend.

Adj. ostensible, alleged, pretended.

Adv. ostensibly; under the plea of, under the pretense of.

618. GOOD.—*N.* **good,** benefit, advantage; improvement, etc., 658; interest, service, behoof, behalf; commonweal; gain, profit, harvest; boon, etc. (*gift*), 784; good turn, blessing, prize, windfall, godsend, good fortune; happiness, etc., 827; goodness, etc., 648.

V. **benefit,** profit, advantage, serve, help, avail, do good to.

gain, prosper, flourish, thrive.

Adj. commendable, etc., 931; useful, etc., 644; good, beneficial, etc., 648.

Adv. **well,** aright, satisfactorily, favorably, in one's interest.

619. EVIL.—*N.* **evil,** ill, harm, hurt, mischief, nuisance, drawback, disadvantage; ills that flesh is heir to, mental suffering, pain; bane, etc., 663.

badness, etc., 649; painfulness, etc., 830; evildoer, etc., 913.

blow, buffet, stroke, scratch, bruise, wound, gash, mutilation; mortal blow (*or* wound); damage, loss.

disaster, accident, casualty, mishap, misfortune, calamity, woe, fatal mischief, catastrophe, tragedy, ruin; adversity, etc., 735.

outrage, wrong, injury, foul play; bad turn, disservice, grievance.

V. **harm,** injure, hurt, do disservice to.

Adj. disastrous; hurtful, etc., 649; disadvantageous, injurious, harmful.

Adv. **amiss,** wrong, ill; to one's cost.

620. INTENTION.—*N.* **intention,** intent, purpose; project, etc., 626; undertaking, design, ambition; view, proposal; contemplation.

object, aim, end; drift, tendency; destination, mark, point, goal, target, prey, quarry, game.

decision, determination, resolve; fixed purpose, resolution; ultimatum.

V. **intend,** purpose, design, mean, have in view, bid for, labor for, aspire to, aim at; contemplate, meditate, think of, dream of, talk of; premeditate, destine, propose; project, etc. (*plan*), 626; desire, etc., 865; pursue, etc., 622.

Adj. intentional, advised, express, determinate; bound for; disposed, inclined, bent upon, at stake; in prospect.

Adv. intentionally, advisedly, wittingly, knowingly, designedly, purposely, on purpose, by design, studiously, pointedly; deliberately.

621. [Absence of purpose] CHANCE.[1]—*N.* chance, etc., 156; lot, destiny, etc., 601; luck; hoodoo [*colloq.*], jinx [*slang*], Jonah, voodoo; wheel of chance, fortune's wheel; mascot.

speculation, venture, random shot, blind bargain, leap in the dark; fluke [*sporting cant*], flier [*slang*]; flutter [*slang*]; futures.

gambling, betting, drawing lots; wager; gamble, risk, stake, bet.

gambler, gamester, speculator; bookmaker, man of the turf.

V. chance, etc., 156; toss up, cast (*or* draw) lots; tempt fortune; speculate.

risk, venture, hazard, stake; wager, bet, gamble, game, play for.

Adj. chance; fortuitous, etc., 156; unintentional, unintended, accidental; random, undesigned, purposeless.

Adv. at random, at a venture, by chance, as it may happen.

622. [Purpose in action] PURSUIT.—*N.* pursuit, prosecution; pursuance, enterprise, undertaking, business, etc., 625; adventure, quest, hobby.

chase, hunt, race, steeplechase; hunting, coursing, sport, shooting, angling, fishing.

pursuer; hunter, huntsman, the field; sportsman, Nimrod; hound.

V. pursue, prosecute, follow, shadow; carry on, undertake, engage in, set about, endeavor, seek, trace, aim at, fish, fish for; press on, follow up, take up; go in for.

chase, give chase, stalk, course, hunt, hound.

Adj. in quest of, in pursuit, in full cry, on the scent.

623. [Absence of pursuit] AVOIDANCE.—*N.* avoidance, evasion, flight; escape, retreat, recoil, departure.

abstention, abstinence; forbearance; inaction, etc., 681; neutrality.

shirker, slacker [*colloq.*], shirk, quitter, truant; fugitive, refugee, runaway, deserter, renegade, backslider.

V. abstain, refrain, spare; eschew, keep from, let alone.

avoid, shun, steer (*or* keep) clear of; fight shy of, evade, elude, shirk.

shrink, hang (*or* hold, draw) back; recoil, retire, flinch, shy, dodge, parry.

[1] See note on 156.

beat a retreat; turn tail, take to one's heels; run, run away, cut and run [*colloq.*]; fly, flee, take flight; desert, make off, sneak off, sheer off; slip, play truant, decamp, flit, bolt, abscond; escape, etc., 671; abandon, etc., 624.

Adj. elusive, evasive; fugitive, runaway; shy, wild.

624. RELINQUISHMENT.—*N.* relinquishment, abandonment; desertion, defection, secession, withdrawal; discontinuance, renunciation, abrogation, resignation, retirement; cession, etc. (*of property*), 782.

V. **relinquish**, give up, abandon, desert, forsake, leave in the lurch; go back on [*colloq.*]; leave, quit, vacate, resign.

renounce, forego, have done with, drop, discard, give up the point (*or* argument), table, table the motion.

625. BUSINESS.—*N.* **business**, occupation, employment, undertaking, pursuit; affair, concern, matter, case.

task, work, job, chore, errand, commission, mission, charge, duty; avocation, hobby.

function, part, role, capacity, province, department, sphere, field, line; walk, round, routine; race, career.

office, place, position, post, incumbency, living; situation, berth, billet, appointment, engagement; undertaking, etc., 676.

vocation, calling, profession; cloth, faculty; craft, handicraft; trade.

V. **occupy oneself with**; employ oneself in *or* upon; undertake, etc., 676; turn one's hand to; be engaged in, be occupied with, be at work on; have in hand; ply one's trade.

officiate, serve, act, do duty; discharge (*or* perform) the duties of; hold (*or* fill) an office; hold a portfolio.

Adj. businesslike; workaday; professional, official, functional; busy.

in hand, on hand, afoot, on foot, going on; acting.

626. PLAN.—*N.* **plan**, scheme, design, project, proposal, proposition, suggestion; resolution, motion; organization, arrangement, system.

outline, sketch, skeleton, draft, rough draft, copy; forecast, program, prospectus; order of the day, memoranda, platform, plank, slate, ticket; role; policy.

contrivance, invention, expedient, receipt, nostrum, artifice, device; stratagem, trick; shift.

measure, step; stroke, master stroke; trump, trump card.

intrigue, cabal, plot, conspiracy, machination; mine.

promoter, designer, organizer, founder, projector; author, artist.

V. **plan**, scheme, design, frame, contrive, project, forecast, sketch, devise, invent, hatch, concoct; hit upon; map out, shape out a course; prepare, etc., 673.

systematize, organize; cast, recast, arrange; digest, mature.

plot, intrigue; counterplot, mine, countermine, lay a train.

Adj. under consideration, on the carpet, on the table.

627. METHOD. [Path]—*N.* method, way, manner, form, mode, fashion, guise; procedure.

path, road, route, course, tack; trajectory, orbit, track, beat.

means of access, entrance, approach, passage, cloister, covered way, lobby, corridor, aisle; alley, lane, avenue, artery, channel; gateway, door; secret passage; covert way.

roadway, thoroughfare; highway, turnpike, state road, causeway, king's highway; parkway, boulevard, speedway; walk, footpath, pathway, pavement, sidewalk, byroad, crossroad; railroad, railway, trolley track, tramway; towpath; street, etc. (*abode*), 189; bridge, viaduct.

Adv. how; in what way, in what manner; by what mode; so, thus; anyhow.

628. MID-COURSE.—*N.* mid-course, middle way, middle course; moderation; mean, etc., 29; golden mean.

compromise, half measures, neutrality.

V. keep the golden mean, steer a middle course; go straight.

compromise, make a compromise, concede half, go halfway.

Adj. neutral, average, even; impartial, moderate; straight.

Adv. in the mean; in moderation.

629. CIRCUIT.—*N.* circuit, roundabout way, digression, detour, loop, winding.

V. go round about, make a circuit, make a detour; meander, deviate.

Adj. circuitous, indirect, roundabout; zigzag.

Adv. in a roundabout way; by an indirect course.

630. REQUIREMENT.—*N.* requirement, need, wants, necessities; stress, exigency, pinch, case of need; desideratum; necessity, indispensability, urgency.

requisition, demand, request, claim; run, call for.

charge, command, injunction, precept, mandate, order, ultimatum.

V. require, need, want, stand in need of, lack; desire, etc., 865.

Adj. necessary, requisite, needful, imperative, essential, indispensable, called for; in demand, in request.

urgent, exigent, pressing, instant, crying.

Adv. of necessity; at a pinch.

631. INSTRUMENTALITY.—*N.* instrumentality; aid, etc., 707; subservience, mediation, intervention; pull [*slang*], influence; medium, intermediary, vehicle, tool, agency; instrument, expedient; means, etc., 632.

minister, handmaid, servant; friend at court, go-between.

V. **mediate,** minister, intervene, come (*or* go) between; interpose; use one's influence, be instrumental; subserve.

Adj. **instrumental;** useful, etc., 644; subservient, serviceable; intermediary, intermediate, intervening; conducive.

Adv. **through,** by, whereby, thereby, hereby; by the agency of, by dint of; by (*or* in) virtue of; by means of.

somehow, by fair means or foul; somehow or other; by hook or by crook.

632. MEANS.—*N.* **means,** resources, wherewithal, ways and means; capital, etc. (*money*), 800; revenue, income; stock in trade, provision, reserve, remnant, last resource, appliances, conveniences; expedients, wheels within wheels; sheet anchor; aid, etc., 707; medium, etc., 631.

V. **provide the wherewithal,** find (*or* possess) means, have powerful friends, have friends at court; have something to draw on.

Adj. **instrumental,** etc., 631; **mechanical,** etc., 633.

trustworthy, reliable, efficient; honorable, etc. (*upright*), 939.

Adv. **by means of,** with; wherewith, herewith, therewith; wherewithal.

633. INSTRUMENT.—*N.* **instrument,** organ, tool, implement, utensil, machine, engine, lathe, gin, mill; motor; machinery, mechanism.

equipment, gear, tackle, tackling; rigging, apparatus, appliances; plant, harness, trappings, fittings, accouterments, appointments, furniture, upholstery; chattels; paraphernalia.

mechanical powers; leverage; fulcrum, lever, crow, crowbar, jimmy, marline spike, handspike; arm, limb, wing; wheel and axle; wheelwork, clockwork; wheels within wheels; pinion, crank, winch, capstan, wheel, flywheel, turbine, water wheel, pump; pulley, crane, derrick; inclined plane; wedge; screw; jack; spring, mainspring; loom, shuttle, jenny.
handle, hilt, haft, shaft, shank; tiller, rudder, helm; treadle, pedal.

Adj. **mechanical;** propulsive, driving, hoisting, elevating, lifting.

useful, labor-saving, ingenious; well made, well fitted, well equipped.

634. SUBSTITUTE.—*N.* **substitute,** etc., 147; proxy, alternate, understudy; deputy, etc., 759.

635. MATERIALS.—*N.* **material,** raw material, stuff, stock, staple; ore.

636. STORE.—*N.* **store,** accumulation, hoard; stock, fund, mine, vein, lode, quarry; spring, fount, fountain; well; orchard, garden, farm; stock in trade, supply; treasure; reserve, reserve fund, savings.

crop, harvest, vintage, yield, product, gleaning.

storehouse, storeroom, store closet; depository, depot, cache, warehouse, magazine; garner, granary, grain elevator, silo; safe-deposit vault; armory; arsenal; stable, barn.

reservoir, cistern, tank, pond, millpond; gasometer.

V. **store,** put by, lay by, set by, stow away, store up, hoard up, treasure up, lay up, save, preserve, save up, bank; cache, deposit; stow, stack, load; harvest; accumulate, amass, hoard.

reserve; keep back, hold back; husband, husband one's resources.

Adj. in store, in reserve, spare, supernumerary.

Adv. for a rainy day, for a nest egg, to fall back upon; on deposit.

637. PROVISION.—*N.* **provision,** supply; grist, resources, etc. (*means*), 632; groceries, purveyance, commissariat.

caterer, purveyor, commissary, quartermaster, steward, purser, housekeeper; innkeeper, landlord, mine host; grocer, fishmonger, provision merchant.

V. **provide,** make provision, lay in, lay in a stock (*or* store).

supply, furnish; cater, victual, provision, purvey, forage; stock, make good, replenish, fill; recruit, feed.

store, etc., 636; conserve, keep, preserve, lay by, gather into barns.

638. WASTE.—*N.* **consumption,** expenditure, exhaustion; dispersion, leakage, loss, wear and tear, waste; prodigality.

V. **consume,** spend, expend, use, swallow up; exhaust, spill, drain, empty, deplete; disperse, etc., 73; waste; squander.

labor in vain, etc. (*useless*), 645; cast pearls before swine; waste powder and shot.

run to waste; ebb, leak, melt away, run dry, dry up.

Adj. **wasted,** gone to waste, useless, run to seed; dried up.

wasteful, etc. (*prodigal*), 818; penny wise and pound foolish.

639. SUFFICIENCY.—*N.* **sufficiency,** adequacy, enough, wherewithal, competence.

abundance, plenitude, plenty, copiousness, amplitude, profusion, full measure; fill; luxuriance, affluence, fat of the land.

rich man, etc. (*wealth*), 803; financier, banker, plutocrat.

V. **suffice,** do, just do [*both colloq.*], satisfy, pass muster; have enough, have one's fill.

abound, teem, flow, stream, rain, shower down; pour, pour in; swarm; bristle with.

Adj. **sufficient,** enough, adequate, up to the mark, commensurate, competent, satisfactory; ample; plenty, plentiful, plenteous; copious, abundant; replete, unstinted, inexhaustible.

rich, affluent, etc. (*wealthy*), 803; luxuriant, etc. (*fertile*), 168.

Adv. without stint; to the good.

640. INSUFFICIENCY.—*N.* insufficiency, inadequacy, incompetence, deficiency, imperfection, shortcoming; paucity, stint, bare subsistence; poverty, etc., 804.

scarcity, dearth; want, need, lack, poverty, starvation, famine, drought.

dole, mite, pittance; short allowance; half rations.

depletion, emptiness, vacancy; ebb tide; low water; insolvency, etc. (*nonpayment*), 808.

poor man, pauper, etc., 804; bankrupt.

V. want, lack, need, require; be in want, etc. (*poor*), 804; live from hand to mouth.

impoverish, drain, drain of resources; stint, etc., 819.

Adj. insufficient, inadequate, too little, not enough; incompetent, perfunctory, deficient, wanting; imperfect; ill-furnished, ill-provided, ill-stored.

short of, out of, destitute of, devoid of, bereft of, slack, at a low ebb; empty, vacant, bare; dry, drained.

unprovided, unsupplied, unfurnished; unfed; empty-handed.

meager, poor, thin, spare, stinted, starved, emaciated, undernourished, underfed, half-starved, famine-stricken, famished.

scarce, scant, not to be had, scurvy, stingy, etc., 819; at the end of one's tether; without resources, in want.

Adv. in default of, for want of; failing.

641. REDUNDANCE.—*N.* redundance, too much, too many, superabundance, superfluity, exuberance, profuseness; profusion, plenty, repletion, plethora, glut, congestion, surfeit, overdose, oversupply, overflow; excess, surplus, remainder.

V. superabound, overabound, swarm; bristle with, overflow, run over; run riot; overrun, overstock, overdose, overfeed, overload, overburden, overwhelm, overshoot the mark; gorge, glut, load, drench, inundate, deluge, flood; send (*or* carry) coals to Newcastle.

cloy, choke, suffocate; pile up, lay on thick, lavish.

Adj. redundant, turgid; exuberant, inordinate, superabundant, excess, overmuch, replete, profuse, lavish, prodigal; exorbitant, extravagant, overflowing; gorged, stuffed.

superfluous, unnecessary, needless, over and above, supernumerary, spare, duplicate, supererogatory.

Adv. over and above; over much, too much; too far; over, too; over head and ears, over one's head; up to one's eyes; extra.

642. IMPORTANCE.—*N.* importance, consequence, moment, prominence, consideration, mark; weight, influence; value, usefulness; greatness, etc., 31; superiority, etc., 33; notability.

salient point, outstanding feature; cardinal point: substance, gist, sum and substance, cream, salt, core, kernel, heart, nucleus; key, keynote; keystone.

import, significance, concern; emphasis, interest.

gravity, seriousness, solemnity; pressure, urgency, stress.

V. be important, be somebody, be something; import, signify, matter, carry weight; come to the front, lead the way, take the lead.

value, care for, set store upon *or* by.

accentuate, emphasize, lay stress on; mark, underline, underscore.

Adj. important, of importance, momentous, material, considerable, weighty, influential, notable, prominent, salient, signal; memorable, remarkable; stirring, eventful.

grave, serious, earnest, grand, solemn, impressive, commanding, imposing.

urgent, pressing, critical, crucial, instant.

foremost, principal, leading, chief, main, prime, primary; capital; superior, etc., 33; marked, rare; paramount, essential, vital, radical, cardinal.

significant, telling, trenchant, emphatic, pregnant.

Adv. in the main; above all, in the first place, before everything else.

643. UNIMPORTANCE.—*N.* unimportance, insignificance, nothingness, immateriality.

triviality, levity, frivolity, paltriness, smallness, matter of indifference; no object.

nothing, small (*or* trifling) matter; joke, jest, snap of the fingers, fudge, fiddlestick, incident, mere nothing, nonentity.

toy, plaything, gewgaw, bauble, trinket, bagatelle, kickshaw, knickknack.

trumpery, trash, rubbish, stuff, frippery; chaff, dross, froth, scum, bubble, smoke; weed; refuse.

trifle, straw, pin, fig, button, feather, continental, jot, mote, rap, old song; cent, red cent; picayune [*colloq.*].

nine days' wonder, flash in the pan, much ado about nothing, tempest in a teapot.

minutiae, details, minor details.

V. be unimportant, not matter, matter (*or* signify) little, not matter a straw.

make light of, catch at straws, make mountains out of molehills.

Adj. unimportant, immaterial; nonessential, unessential, irrelevant; indifferent, mediocre, passable, fair, tolerable, commonplace; mere, common, ordinary, insignificant.

trifling, trivial; slight, slender, light, airy, flimsy, idle, shallow, weak, powerless, frivolous, petty, finical.

paltry, poor, pitiful, contemptible, puerile; sorry, mean, meager, shabby, miserable, wretched, vile, niggardly, scurvy, beggarly, worthless, two-by-four [*colloq.*], cheap, trashy, catchpenny, gimcrack, trumpery; one-horse [*colloq.*]

Adv. rather, somewhat, fairly, fairly well, tolerably.

644. UTILITY.—*N.* utility, usefulness, efficacy, efficiency, adequacy; helpfulness, service, use, help, aid, applicability, subservience; value, worth, productiveness, utilization.

commonweal, public good; utilitarianism.

V. **avail,** serve, conduce, tend, answer (*or* serve) one's turn; benefit, bear fruit, profit, remunerate.

act a part, etc. (*action*), 680; discharge a function, render a service; bestead, stand one in good stead; help, etc., 707.

Adj. **useful,** of use, serviceable, subservient, conducive, helpful.

advantageous, beneficial, profitable, gainful, remunerative, valuable; invaluable, beyond price; prolific.

adequate; efficient, efficacious; effective, effectual.

applicable, available, ready, handy, at hand, commodious, adaptable.

645. INUTILITY.—*N.* inutility, uselessness, inefficacy, futility; ineptitude, inadequacy, unfitness; inefficiency, incompetence, unskillfulness, labor in vain; worthlessness; triviality, etc., 643.

rubbish, junk, lumber, litter, odds and ends, shoddy; rags, leavings, dross, trash, refuse, sweepings, offscourings, waste, rubble, debris; chaff, stubble, dregs, weeds, tares.

V. **labor in vain;** seek (*or* strive) after impossibilities; use vain efforts, beat the air, pour water into a sieve, bay at the moon; cast pearls before swine, carry coals to Newcastle.

render useless, dismantle, dismast, disqualify; disable, hamstring, cripple, lame; spike guns, clip the wings; put out of gear.

Adj. **useless,** inutile, futile, unavailing, bootless; inoperative, inadequate, inept, inefficient, ineffectual, incompetent.

worthless, valueless, unsalable; not worth a straw, good for nothing, dear at any price; vain, empty, inane; gainless, profitless, fruitless; unserviceable, unprofitable; ill-spent; effete, barren, sterile, impotent, worn out, unproductive; uncalled for; unnecessary, unneeded, superfluous.

646. EXPEDIENCE.—*N.* expedience, desirability, fitness, propriety, utility, advantage, opportunity; opportunism; pragmatism.

V. **be expedient,** suit, befit; suit (*or* befit) the occasion.

Adj. **expedient,** desirable, advisable, acceptable; convenient; worth while, meet; fit, fitting, due, proper, eligible, seemly, becoming, befitting; opportune, advantageous, etc., 644; suitable.

practical, practicable, effective, pragmatic, pragmatical.

Adv. in the nick of time; in the right place.

647. INEXPEDIENCE.—*N.* inexpedience, undesirability, impropriety, unfitness, inutility, disadvantage, inconvenience, inadvisability.

V. be inexpedient, come amiss, embarrass, put to inconvenience.

Adj. inexpedient, undesirable; inadvisable, ill-advised, unsuitable, troublesome, objectionable, ineligible, inadmissible, inconvenient, discommodious, disadvantageous; inappropriate, unfit; unsatisfactory, unprofitable, inept, inopportune, improper, unseemly.

clumsy, awkward; cumbrous, cumbersome, lumbering, unwieldy, hulky.

648. [Good qualities] **GOODNESS.**—*N.* goodness, excellence, merit; beneficence, benevolence, etc., 906; virtue, etc., 944; value, worth, price.

perfection, quintessence; superiority, etc., 33; prime, flower, cream, elite, pick, A 1 *or* A number 1 [*colloq.*], pick of the crop, salt of the earth; prodigy, wonder; gem of the first water, treasure, one in a thousand.

good man, etc., 948.

V. be beneficial, produce (*or* do) good, profit, benefit, improve, be the making of, make a man of; do a good turn, confer an obligation.

be good, be pure gold, look good to [*colloq.*]; excel, transcend, stand the test; pass muster, pass an examination.

vie, challenge, comparison, emulate, rival.

Adj. beneficial, valuable, of value; useful, etc., 644; advantageous, profitable; edifying, salutary.

harmless, innocuous, innocent, inoffensive.

favorable; propitious, etc. (*hope-giving*), 858; fair.

good, excellent; better; superior, etc., 33; above par; nice, fine; genuine, etc. (*true*), 494.

choice, best, select, picked, elect, rare, priceless, matchless, peerless, unequaled, unparalleled, inimitable, crack [*colloq.*], crackajack [*slang*], gilt-edge [*colloq.*]; superfine, of the first water; first-rate, first-class; high-wrought, exquisite, admirable, capital, estimable, precious, priceless, invaluable, inestimable.

satisfactory, up to the mark, unexceptionable, unobjectionable.

Adv. for one's benefit.

649. [Bad qualities] **BADNESS.**—*N.* badness, hurtfulness, virulence; abomination, pestilence, guilt, depravity, vice, etc., 945; malignity, malevolence.

bane, etc., 663; plague spot, evil star, ill-wind; hoodoo [*colloq.*], jinx [*slang*], Jonah; snake in the grass, skeleton in the closet; thorn in the flesh.

ill-treatment, annoyance, molestation, abuse, oppression, persecution, outrage, misusage, scathe, injury.

bad man, etc., 949; evildoer, etc., 913.

V. hurt, harm, scathe, injure; pain, etc., 830.

wrong, aggrieve, oppress, persecute, trample upon; overburden, weigh down; victimize.

maltreat, abuse; ill-use, ill-treat; buffet, bruise, scratch, maul; smite, molest, do violence; stab, pierce.

Adj. hurtful, harmful, baneful, baleful, injurious, deleterious, detrimental, noxious, pernicious, mischievous, mischief-making, malignant, prejudicial; oppressive, burdensome, onerous; malign.

corrupting, virulent, venomous, corrosive; poisonous, deadly, destructive.

bad, ill, arrant, dreadful; horrid, horrible; dire; rank, foul, rotten.

unsatisfactory, indifferent, deteriorated, below par, imperfect, ill-conditioned.

deplorable, wretched, sad, grievous, lamentable, pitiful, pitiable, woeful.

evil, wrong; depraved, wicked, etc., 945; shocking; reprehensible.

hateful, abominable, vile, base, villainous, detestable, execrable, cursed, accursed, damnable, diabolic.

Adv. to one's cost; where the shoe pinches.

650. PERFECTION.—*N.* perfection; paragon, pink, pink (*or* acme) of perfection.

model, standard, pattern, mirror.

masterpiece, master stroke, prize winner, prize; superexcellence.

V. perfect, bring to perfection, ripen, mature; consummate, crown, put the finishing touch to (*or* upon); complete.

Adj. perfect, faultless, immaculate, spotless, impeccable, unblemished, sound, scathless, intact; consummate, finished.

best, model, standard; inimitable, unparalleled, beyond all praise.

Adv. clean as a whistle; with a finish; to the limit.

651. IMPERFECTION.—*N.* imperfection; deficiency, inadequacy, defection, badness, immaturity.

fault, defect, weak point; screw loose; flaw, taint, blemish, weakness, shortcoming, drawback.

V. be imperfect, have a defect, lie under a disadvantage; not pass muster, fall short.

Adj. imperfect, deficient, defective, faulty, unsound, tainted, out of order; warped, injured; inadequate, crude, incomplete, below par.

indifferent, middling, ordinary, mediocre, average, tolerable, fair, passable; decent; not bad, not amiss; admissible, bearable.

inferior, secondary, second-rate, one-horse [*colloq.*]; two-by-four [*colloq.*].

Adv. to a limited extent, pretty, moderately, considering.

652. CLEANNESS.—*N.* **cleanness**, purity, purification, purgation; ablution, lavation; disinfection, drainage, sewerage.

bath, bathroom, swimming pool, swimming bath, public bath, baths, bathhouse, lavatory; laundry, washhouse.

cleaner, washerwoman, laundress, laundryman, washerman; scavenger, sweeper; street sweeper, white wing [*local*]; dustman.

brush; broom, vacuum cleaner, carpet sweeper; mop, swab, hose.

cathartic, purgative, aperient, laxative.

V. **clean**, cleanse; rinse, flush, mop, sponge, scour, swab, scrub; wash, lave, launder; purify; purge, expurgate, clarify, refine.

strain, separate, filter, filtrate, drain; percolate.

sift, winnow, sieve, bolt, screen, riddle; pick, weed.

comb, rake, scrape, rasp; card.

sweep, brush, brush up, rout out; clean house, spruce up [*colloq.*].

disinfect, fumigate, ventilate, deodorize; whitewash.

Adj. **clean**, cleanly, pure, immaculate, spotless, stainless, unspotted, unsoiled, unsullied, untainted, sweet.

neat, spruce, tidy, trim, cleaned.

653. UNCLEANNESS.—*N.* **uncleanness**, impurity; defilement, contamination, abomination; taint.

decay, putrefaction; corruption; mold, mildew, dry rot, caries [*med.*].

squalor, squalidness, slovenliness.

dirt, filth, soil, slop; dust, smoke, soot, smudge, smut, grime.

dregs, grounds, lees, sediment, heeltap; dross, ashes, cinders; scum, froth.

sty, pigsty, lair, den, Augean stable, sink of corruption; slum, rookery.

mud, mire, quagmire, silt, slime, slush.

V. **rot**, putrefy, fester, rankle, reek; mold, molder, go bad.

soil, smoke, tarnish, spot, smear; daub, blot, blur, smudge, smutch, smirch; drabble, besmear, befoul, splash, stain, sully.

pollute, defile, debase, contaminate, taint, corrupt.

Adj. **unclean**, dirty, filthy, grimy, soiled, dusty, smutty, sooty; mussy [*colloq.*].

uncleanly, slovenly, slatternly, untidy, frowzy, sluttish, unkempt, unwashed, squalid.

offensive, nasty, coarse, foul, impure, abominable, beastly, reeky, fetid; moldy, musty, rancid, bad, touched, rotten, corrupt, tainted, putrid; gory, bloody.

654. HEALTH.—*N.* health, sanity; soundness, vigor; good (*or* perfect, excellent, robust) health; bloom, convalescence, strength, poise.

V. **be in health,** bloom, flourish, enjoy good health.

return to health; recover, etc., 660; get better, convalesce, be convalescent, recruit; restore to health, cure.

Adj. **healthy,** healthful, in health, well, sound, whole, strong, blooming, hearty, hale, fresh, green, florid, hardy, robust, vigorous, in fine fettle; chipper [*colloq.*].

uninjured, unscathed, unmarred, without a scratch, safe and sound.

655. DISEASE.—*N.* disease; illness, sickness; infirmity, ailment, indisposition; complaint, disorder, malady, loss of health, delicacy, delicate health, invalidism, malnutrition, want of nourishment; prostration, decline, collapse, decay.

visitation, attack, seizure, stroke, fit, epilepsy, apoplexy, palsy, paralysis; shock; shell shock.

taint, virus, pollution, infection, contagion; epidemic, plague, pestilence.

Science of disease: pathology, therapeutics; diagnostics, diagnosis.

V. **ail,** suffer, be affected with, droop, flag, languish, sicken, pine, dwindle; waste away, fail, lose strength, be laid by the heels; lie helpless.

Adj. **sick,** ill, not well, indisposed, ailing, squeamish, poorly, seedy [*colloq.*], laid up, confined, bedridden, in hospital, on the sick list; out of health, out of sorts [*colloq.*], under the weather [*colloq.*]; valetudinary.

sickly, infirm, unsound, unhealthy, weakly, drooping, flagging, lame, halt, crippled, halting.

diseased, morbid, tainted, poisoned, septic; mangy, leprous, cankered; rotten, withered; palsied, paralytic; consumptive, tubercular, tuberculous.

656. HEALTHINESS.—*N.* healthiness, wholesomeness; healthfulness, salubrity.

Preservation of health: hygiene, pure air, exercise, nourishment, tonic; immunity; sanitarium, sanatorium.

V. **be salubrious,** make for health, conduce to health; be good for, agree with.

Adj. **healthy,** healthful; salubrious, salutary, wholesome, sanitary, prophylactic; benign, bracing, tonic, invigorating, nutritious; hygienic.

innocuous, innocent; harmless, uninjurious, immune.

657. UNHEALTHINESS.—*N.* unhealthiness, plague spot; malaria, insalubrity; contagion; poisonousness.

V. **be unhealthy,** disagree with; shorten one's days.

Adj. **unhealthy,** insalubrious, unwholesome, noxious, noisome; pestiferous, pestilential; virulent, venomous, poisonous, septic, toxic, deadly.

infectious, contagious, catching, communicable, epidemic, sporadic, endemic; epizootic [*of animals*].

658. IMPROVEMENT.—*N.* **improvement,** amelioration, betterment; recovery, mend, amendment, emendation; advancement, advance, promotion, preferment, elevation, increase.

cultivation, culture, march of intellect, civilization.

reform, reformation; revision, radical reform; correction, refinement, elaboration; purification, repair.

reformer, progressive, radical.

V. **improve,** mend, amend, better, ameliorate, relieve; correct, repair, restore.

improve upon; rectify; enrich, mellow, elaborate, fatten.

refresh, revive; invigorate, strengthen, recruit, renew, revivify, freshen.

promote, cultivate, advance, forward, enhance, bring forward, foster.

revise, edit, review, make corrections, make improvements.

reform, remodel, reorganize, reclaim, civilize, lift, uplift, inspire.

Adj. **better,** better off, all the better for; improving, progressive, improved.

corrigible, improvable, curable.

Adv. **on consideration,** on reconsideration, on second thought.

659. DETERIORATION.—*N.* **deterioration,** debasement; wane, ebb, recession, retrogradation, decrease.

degeneracy, degeneration, degradation, depravation, depravity, demoralization.

injury, damage, loss, detriment, harm, impairment, outrage, havoc, inroad, ravage, vitiation, discoloration, pollution, poisoning, contamination, canker, corruption, adulteration, alloy.

decline, declension, declination; decadence, falling off; senility, decrepitude.

decay, dilapidation, wear and tear, erosion, corrosion, rottenness; moth and rust, dry rot, blight, atrophy.

V. **deteriorate,** degenerate, fall off, wane, ebb; retrograde, decline, droop, run to seed *or* waste, lapse, break down, crack, shrivel, fade, wither, molder, rot, rankle, decay, go bad; rust, crumble, shake, totter, perish.

corrupt, taint, infect, contaminate, poison, envenom, canker, blight, rot, pollute, defile, vitiate, debase, deprave, degrade; alloy, adulterate, tamper with, prejudice; pervert, demoralize, brutalize.

embitter, exasperate, irritate.

injure, impair, damage, harm, hurt, spoil, mar, despoil, waste; overrun, ravage, pillage.

wound, stab, pierce, maim, lame, cripple, hamstring, mangle, mutilate, disfigure, blemish, deface, warp.

Adj. deteriorated, unimproved, injured, degenerate, imperfect; battered, weathered, weather-beaten, stale, dilapidated, faded, worn, wasted, wilted, shabby, threadbare, frayed.

decayed, moth-eaten, worm-eaten, mildewed, rusty, moldy, seedy [*colloq.*], timeworn, effete, crumbling, moldering, rotten, cankered, blighted, tainted; decrepit, broken-down, worn-out, used up [*colloq.*].

stagnant, backward, unprogressive.

Adv. on the downgrade, on the downward track; beyond hope.

660. RESTORATION.—*N.* restoration, replacement, rehabilitation, reconstruction, reproduction, renovation, renewal, revival, resuscitation, reanimation, reorganization; redemption, restitution, relief, redress, retrieval, reclamation, recovery, convalescence, resumption.

renaissance, renascence, rebirth, new birth, regeneration, regeneracy, resurrection.

repair, repairing, reparation, mending; recruiting.

mender, repairer, tinker, cobbler.

V. recover, rally, revive; come to, come round, come to oneself; pull through, weather the storm, be oneself again; get well, survive, reappear.

restore, put back, reinstate, replace, rehabilitate, re-establish, reconstruct, rebuild, reorganize, convert, recondition, renew, renovate; regenerate; rejuvenate.

redeem, reclaim, recover, retrieve; rescue, etc. (*deliver*), 672.

cure, heal, remedy, doctor, bring round, set on one's legs.

resuscitate, revive, reanimate, revivify, reinvigorate, refresh.

repair, mend, put in repair, retouch, tinker, cobble, patch up, darn; stanch, calk, splice.

Adj. restored, convalescent, rejuvenated, renascent.

restorative, recuperative, curative, remedial.

restorable, remediable, retrievable, curable.

661. RELAPSE.—*N.* relapse, lapse; falling back, retrogradation; deterioration, etc., 659; backsliding.

V. relapse, lapse, fall (*or* slip) back, have a relapse, be overcome, be overtaken, yield again to, fall again into, return, retrograde.

Adj. backsliding, retrograde.

662. REMEDY.—*N.* remedy, help, redress, febrifuge; antipoison, antidote, emetic; stimulant, tonic; prophylactic, antiseptic, germicide, disinfectant; restorative; specific; cure, sovereign remedy, panacea.

materia medica, pharmacy, pharmaceutics; pharmacopoeia.

narcotic, opium, morphine, cocaine, hashish, dope [*slang*]; sedative.

physic, medicine, simples, drug, potion, draft, dose, pill, medicament; recipe, receipt, prescription; patent medicine, nostrum; elixir, balm, balsam, cordial.

salve, ointment, oil, lenitive, lotion, embrocation, liniment.

treatment, regimen, diet; dietary, dietetics; operation, the knife [*colloq.*], surgical operation; major operation.

healing art, practice of medicine, therapeutics; allopathy, homeopathy, osteopathy, eclecticism, surgery; faith cure, faith healing, mind cure, psychotherapy, psychotherapeutics; vocational therapy; dentistry.

hospital, surgery, infirmary, clinic, sanitarium, sanatorium; springs, baths, spa; asylum, home; Red Cross; ambulance.

dispensary, drugstore.

doctor, physician, medical man, general practitioner; specialist, consultant; surgeon.

intern, anesthetist, aurist, oculist, dentist, dental surgeon; osteopath, osteopathist; nurse, sister, nursing sister; apothecary, druggist, pharmacist, pharmaceutical chemist, Hippocrates, Galen; masseur (*fem.* masseuse), rubber.

V. **apply a remedy,** doctor [*colloq.*], dose, physic, nurse, minister to, attend, dress the wounds; relieve, palliate, heal, cure, remedy, restore.

Adj. **remedial,** restorative, corrective, palliative, healing; sanatory, sanative; prophylactic; medical, medicinal; therapeutic, surgical; tonic, sedative, lenitive; allopathic, homeopathic, eclectic; aperient, laxative, cathartic, purgative; septic; aseptic, antiseptic.

dietetic, dietary, alimentary; nutritious, nutritive; digestive, digestible.

663. BANE.—*N.* **bane,** curse, thorn in the flesh; bête noir [F.], bugbear; evil, scourge; fungus, mildew; dry rot; canker, cancer; poison, virus, venom; stench, fetor, poison gas.

sting, fang, thorn, bramble, brier, nettle.

Science of poisons: toxicology.

Adj. baneful, poisonous, etc. (*unwholesome*), 657.

664. SAFETY.—*N.* **safety,** security, surety, impregnability, invulnerability, escape, means of escape; safeguard, palladium; sheet anchor; rock, tower.

guardianship, wardship, wardenship; tutelage, custody, safekeeping, protection; auspices.

protector, guardian; warden, warder: preserver, lifesaver, custodian, duenna, chaperon.

safe-conduct, escort, convoy; guard, shield, guardian angel; tutelary deity (*or* saint).

watchman, patrolman, policeman, police officer, officer [colloq.]; cop, copper [both slang], bluecoat [colloq.], constable; detective, spotter [slang]; sheriff, deputy; sentinel, sentry, scout.

armed force, garrison, lifeguard, state guard, militia, regular army, navy; volunteer; marine, etc., 726; battleship, man-of-war, etc., 726.

judge, justice, judiciary, magistrate, justice of the peace.

V. **protect**, watch over, take care of, preserve, cover, screen, shelter, shroud, flank, ward, guard; defend, take precautions.

escort, support, accompany, convoy.

watch, mount guard, patrol, scout, spy.

Adj. **safe**, secure, sure, on terra firma [L.]; on the safe side; undercover, under lock and key; out of danger, protected; at anchor, high and dry, above-water; safe and sound.

snug, seaworthy, watertight, weatherproof, waterproof, fireproof; bombproof, shellproof.

defensible, tenable, proof against, invulnerable, unassailable, impregnable.

guardian, tutelary, protective.

Adv. with impunity.

665. DANGER.—*N.* **danger**, peril, insecurity, jeopardy, risk, hazard, venture, precariousness, instability; exposure, vulnerability, vulnerable point, heel of Achilles; forlorn hope.

Sense of danger: apprehension, etc., 860.

V. **endanger**, expose to danger, imperil, jeopardize, beard the lion in his den; sail too near the wind.

risk, hazard, venture, adventure, stake, set at hazard; run the gantlet.

Adj. **dangerous**, hazardous, perilous, unsafe, unprotected, insecure.

defenseless, guardless, unsheltered, unshielded; vulnerable, exposed; at bay.

precarious, critical, ticklish; slippery, between Scylla and Charybdis, between two fires; under fire; at stake, in question.

unsteady, unstable, shaky, tottering, top-heavy, tumble-down, ramshackle, crumbling, helpless, trembling in the balance; nodding to its fall.

threatening, ominous, ill-omened, alarming.

666. [Means of safety] REFUGE.—*N.* **refuge**, sanctuary, retreat, fastness, stronghold, fortress, castle, keep; asylum, shelter, covert, ark, home, hiding place.

anchorage, roadstead; breakwater, port, haven, harbor, pier, jetty, embankment, quay, wharf.

anchor, sheet anchor, grapnel, grappling iron, mainstay, support, safeguard.

667. [Source of danger] PITFALL.—*N.* pitfall, ambush, trap, snare, mine, spring gun.

rocks, reefs, sunken rocks, snags; sands, quicksands; breakers, shoals, shallows, lee shore, rockbound coast.

abyss, abysm, pit, void, chasm.

whirlpool, eddy, vortex, rapids, undertow; current, tiderace, maelstrom; eagre, bore, tidal wave.

pest, ugly customer, incendiary, firebug [*slang*]; firebrand; hornet's nest.

sword of Damocles; wolf at the door, snake in the grass, snake in one's bosom.

668. WARNING.—*N.* warning, caution, notice, premonition, prediction; symptom; lesson, admonition; handwriting on the wall, monitor, warning voice; stormy petrel, bird of ill omen, gathering clouds.

watchtower, beacon, signal post; lighthouse, etc., 550.

sentinel, sentry; watch, watchman; watch and ward; watchdog; patrol, picket, scout, spy, lookout, flagman.

V. warn, caution; forewarn, admonish, forbode, give warning; put on one's guard; sound the alarm.

beware, take warning, look out, keep watch and ward.

Adj. premonitory, cautionary; ominous, threatening, lowering, minatory; symptomatic.

Adv. with alarm, on guard, after due warning, with one's eyes open.

669. [Indication of danger] ALARM.—*N.* alarm; alarum, alarm bell, tocsin, beat of drum, sound of trumpet, hue and cry; signal of distress, SOS; fog signal, siren; yellow flag; danger signal; red light, red flag; fire alarm, still alarm; burglar alarm; police whistle.

V. alarm, give (*or* raise, sound) an alarm, warn, ring the tocsin.

670. PRESERVATION.—*N.* preservation, safekeeping, conservation, economy, maintenance, support, salvation, deliverance, etc., 672.

Means of preservation: prophylaxis; preserver, preservative; hygiene, hygienics; ensilage; dehydration, evaporation, drying, canning, pickling.

V. preserve, maintain, keep, sustain, support; save, rescue, make safe, take care of, guard; husband, economize.

embalm, dry, cure, salt, pickle, season, bottle, pot, tin, can; dehydrate, evaporate.

Adj. preserved, unimpaired, unbroken, uninjured, unhurt, unmarred; safe, safe and sound, intact, with a whole skin.

671. ESCAPE.—*N.* escape, flight, evasion, loophole, retreat; narrow (*or* hairbreadth) escape; close call [*colloq.*]; impunity.

refugee, etc. (*fugitive*), 623.

V. escape, make one's escape; break jail; get off, get clear off, elude, make off, give one the slip; wriggle out of; break loose, break away.

Adj. stolen away; fled; scot-free.

672. DELIVERANCE.—*N.* deliverance, extrication, rescue, ransom, reprieve, respite; armistice, truce; liberation, emancipation; redemption, salvation.

V. deliver, extricate, rescue, save, free, liberate, set free, release, emancipate, redeem, ransom; come to the rescue.

673. PREPARATION.—*N.* preparation, provision, arrangement, anticipation, precaution, forecast, rehearsal; dissemination, propaganda.

groundwork, steppingstone; foundation; scaffold, scaffolding.

elaboration, ripening, evolution; concoction, digestion; hatching, incubation.

Preparation of men: training, education, equipment, inurement; novitiate.

Preparation of food: cooking, cookery, culinary art; brewing.

Preparation of the soil: tilling, plowing, sowing, cultivation.

preparedness, readiness, ripeness, mellowness; maturity.

preparer, trainer, coach, teacher, pioneer; prophet; forerunner, etc. (*precursor*), 64; sappers and miners.

V. prepare, prime, get (*or* make) ready, arrange, make preparations, settle preliminaries, get up; prepare the ground, lay the foundations, erect the scaffolding.

elaborate, mature, ripen, mellow, season, bring to maturity; nurture; cook, brew.

equip, arm, man; fit out, fit up; furnish, rig, dress, accouter, array.

prepare for, guard against, forearm; make provision for; provide, provide against; set one's house in order, make all snug; clear decks, clear for action.

be prepared, be ready, watch and pray, keep one's powder dry, lie in wait for, anticipate, foresee.

Adj. preparatory, precautionary, provident; provisional, preliminary; in embryo, in hand, in train; afoot, afloat; on foot, brewing, hatching, forthcoming.

prepared, ready, cut and dried; available, at one's elbow, ready for use, all ready; handy.

ripe, mature, mellow; seasoned, practiced, experienced.

elaborate, labored, high-wrought, worked up.

Adv. **in preparation,** in anticipation of; afoot, astir, abroad.

674. NONPREPARATION.—*N.* **nonpreparation,** unpreparedness; improvidence.

immaturity, crudity, rawness; disqualification.

Absence of art: nature, state of nature; virgin soil, unweeded garden; rough diamond; raw material.

improvisation, etc. (*impulse*), 612.

V. **be unprepared;** lie fallow; live from hand to mouth.

extemporize, improvise; cook up, fix up.

surprise, drop in [*colloq.*], take (*or* catch) unawares; take by surprise.

Adj. **unprepared,** incomplete, premature, rudimental, embryonic, immature, unripe, callow, unfledged, unhatched; uncooked, raw, green, crude; coarse; rough, roughhewn; in the rough.

untaught, uneducated, untrained, untutored, unlicked.

fallow, unsown, untilled, uncultivated.

unfitted, disqualified, unqualified, ill-digested; unready, unorganized, unfurnished, unprovided, unequipped.

shiftless, improvident, unthrifty, thriftless, happy-go-lucky; slack, remiss.

Adv. **inadvertently,** by surprise, without premeditation; extempore.

675. ESSAY—*N.* **essay,** trial, endeavor, attempt; aim, struggle, venture, adventure, speculation, probation, experiment.

V. **try,** essay; experiment, etc., 463; endeavor, strive; tempt, attempt, venture, adventure, speculate, tempt fortune.

Adj. **tentative,** experimental, empirical, problematic, probationary.

Adv. **on examination,** on trial, at a venture; by rule of thumb.

676. UNDERTAKING.—*N.* **undertaking,** adventure, venture, engagement, compact, enterprise; pilgrimage.

V. **undertake,** engage in, embark in, launch (*or* plunge) into, volunteer; apprentice oneself to; engage, contract, devote oneself to, take up, take on, take in hand; tackle [*colloq.*]; set about; launch forth; betake oneself to, turn one's hand to, have in hand, begin, broach, institute.

Adj. **energetic;** full of pep [*slang*]; enterprising, adventurous, venturesome.

677. USE.—*N.* **use,** employ, exercise, application, appliance; disposal; consumption; agency, usefulness, etc., 644; benefit, recourse, resort, avail.

Conversion to use: utilization, utility, service, wear.

Way of using: usage, employment, *modus operandi* [L.].

user, consumer, market, demand.

V. **use,** make use of, employ, put to use, apply, put in action, set in motion, set to work; ply, work, wield, handle, manipulate; exert, exercise, practice, avail oneself of, profit by; resort to, have recourse to, recur to, take up, try.

utilize, turn to account (*or* use); exploit; administer, apply, bring into play; task, tax, put to task; devote, dedicate, consecrate.

consume, use up, devour, swallow up; absorb, expend; wear.

Adj. **useful,** etc., 644; instrumental, subservient, utilitarian, pragmatic.

678. DISUSE.—*N.* **disuse;** forbearance, abstinence; relinquishment, abandonment; desuetude, disusage.

V. **not use;** do without, dispense with, let alone, forbear, abstain, spare, waive, neglect; keep back, reserve.

disuse; lay up, lay by, shelve; set aside, lay aside, leave off, have done with; supersede, discard, throw aside, relinquish; destroy, make away with, cast (*or* throw) overboard; dismantle.

Adj. **disused,** done with, run down, worn out; unemployed, unapplied, unexercised, uncalled for, not required.

679. MISUSE.—*N.* **misuse,** misusage, misapplication, misappropriation; abuse, profanation, desecration; waste.

V. **misuse,** misemploy, misapply; exploit; misappropriate; desecrate, abuse, profane.

overtask, overtax, overwork; squander, waste.

680. ACTION.—*N.* **action,** performance, perpetration, exercise, movement, operation, evolution, work, employment; labor, exertion, execution; procedure, conduct; handicraft; business, agency.

deed, act, stitch, touch, transaction, job, doings, dealings, proceeding, measure, step, maneuver, bout, passage, move, stroke, blow; feat, exploit, achievement; handiwork, craftsmanship, workmanship; manufacture; stroke of policy.

doer, worker, agent, etc., 690.

V. **do,** perform, execute, achieve, transact, enact; commit, perpetrate, inflict; exercise, prosecute, carry on, work, labor, practice, play; employ oneself, ply one's task; officiate, have in hand; shape one's course.

act, operate, take action, take steps, take in hand, put in practice, carry into execution, act upon.

Adj. **in action,** acting, in harness, on duty; at work; operative.

Adv. **in the act,** in the midst of; red-handed.

681. INACTION.—*N.* **inaction,** passiveness, watchful waiting; noninterference; neglect, etc., 460; inactivity, etc., 683; stagnation, vegetation, rest, loafing, want of occupation, unemployment; sinecure; soft snap, cinch [*both slang*].

V. **not do,** not act, not attempt; be inactive, abstain from doing, do nothing, hold, spare; leave (*or* let) alone; let be, let pass, let things take their course, live and let live; rest upon one's oars; stand aloof; refrain, relax one's efforts; desist, stop, pause, wait; waste time.

undo, do away with; take down, take to pieces; destroy, etc., 162.

Adj. **passive;** unoccupied, unemployed, out of employ (*or* work, a job); uncultivated, fallow.

Adv. at a stand.

682. ACTIVITY.—*N.* **activity,** animation, life, vivacity, spirit, verve, pep [*slang*], dash, go [*colloq.*], energy, snap, vim.

smartness, nimbleness, agility; quickness, velocity, alacrity, promptitude; dispatch, expedition, haste, etc., 684; punctuality.

eagerness, zeal, ardor, enthusiasm, earnestness, intentness, vigor, devotion, exertion.

industry, assiduity, assiduousness, sedulousness, laboriousness, drudgery, diligence, perseverance, etc., 604*a.*

vigilance, etc., 459; wakefulness; sleeplessness, restlessness; insomnia.

bustle, hustle [*colloq.*], movement, stir, fuss, ado, bother, fidget, flurry.

officiousness, dabbling, meddling; interference, intermeddling; butting in [*slang*], intrusiveness, intrigue.

man of action, busy bee; new broom; devotee, enthusiast, fanatic, zealot, hustler [*colloq.*], live wire, human dynamo [*both colloq.*].

meddler, intriguer, busybody.

V. **be active,** busy oneself in; stir, stir about, bestir oneself; speed, hasten, bustle, fuss; push, go ahead, push forward; make progress; toil, moil, drudge, plod, persist, persevere, hustle [*colloq.*], push [*colloq.*], keep moving, seize the opportunity, lose no time, dash off, make haste.

have a hand in, take an active part, put in one's oar, have a finger in the pie, dabble, intrigue; agitate.

meddle, tamper with, interfere, interpose; obtrude; butt in, horn in [*both slang*].

Adj. **active,** brisk, lively, animated, vivacious, alive, frisky, spirited; nimble, agile, light-footed, nimble-footed.

quick, prompt, instant, ready, alert, spry [*colloq. and dial.*], sharp, smart; fast, etc. (*swift*), 274; capable, expeditious, awake, go-ahead [*colloq.*], live [*colloq.*], hustling [*colloq.*], wide-awake.

enterprising, eager, ardent, strenuous, zealous, resolute.

industrious, assiduous, diligent, sedulous, painstaking, intent, indefatigable, persevering, unwearied, sleepless; busy, occupied; hard at work, hard at it; plodding, hard-working, businesslike.

bustling, restless, fussy, fidgety, pottering.

meddlesome, pushing, officious.

astir, stirring, afoot, on foot, in full swing; on the alert.

Adv. with life and spirit, with might and main, full tilt.

683. INACTIVITY.—*N.* **inactivity;** inaction, etc., 681; inertness, lull, quiescence; rust.

idleness, remissness, sloth, indolence, dawdling, puttering, relaxation.

languor, dullness, sluggishness, procrastination, torpor, stupor, somnolence, drowsiness, heaviness, hypnotism, lethargy.

sleep, slumber; Morpheus; coma, trance, catalepsy, hypnosis, dream; nap, doze, siesta; hibernation.

idler, drone, dawdler, truant; dead one [*slang*], dummy, bum [*slang*], tramp, hobo, beggar, lounge lizard [*slang*], lounger, loafer, slow-poke, laggard, sluggard.

V. **be inactive,** do nothing; dawdle, drawl, lag, hang back, slouch, loll, lounge, loaf, loiter; sleep at one's post; take it easy.

dally, dilly-dally, idle (*or* fritter, fool) away time; putter, dabble.

sleep, slumber, be asleep, oversleep hibernate; doze, drowse, nap, take a nap; fall asleep, drop asleep; get sleepy, nod, go to bed, turn in.

languish, expend itself, flag, hang fire; relax.

Adj. **inactive,** motionless; unoccupied, unemployed.

indolent, lazy, slothful, idle, remiss, slack, inert, torpid, sluggish, logy, languid, listless; lackadaisical, maudlin; heavy, dull, leaden; dilatory, laggard, slow, flagging; puttering.

sleeping, asleep, comatose; in the arms (*or* lap) of Morpheus.

sleepy, dozy, drowsy, somnolent, lethargic, heavy, heavy with sleep; soporific, hypnotic; dreamy.

Adv. with half-shut eyes, half asleep; in dreams, in dreamland.

684. HASTE.—*N.* **haste,** urgency, dispatch, acceleration, spurt, forced march, rush, scurry, scuttle, dash; velocity, etc., 274; precipitancy, precipitation, impetuosity; hurry, drive, scramble, bustle, fidget, flurry.

V. **haste,** hasten, make haste, dash on, push on, press on *or* forward, hurry, scurry, bustle, flutter, scramble, plunge, dash off, rush, express; bestir oneself, etc. (*be active*), 682; lose no time, make short work of; work against time, work under pressure.

quicken, accelerate, expedite, precipitate, urge, whip, spur, flog, goad.

Adj. **hasty,** hurried, cursory, precipitate, headlong, furious, boisterous, impetuous, hotheaded; feverish, pushing.

in haste, in a hurry, in hot haste, breathless, hard-pressed, urgent.

Adv. **with haste,** with speed, in haste, apace, amain; at short notice, immediately, posthaste; by cable, by telegraph, by wireless [*colloq.*], by airplane, by return mail, by forced marches.

hastily, precipitately, helter-skelter, hurry-scurry, slapdash, slap-bang; full-tilt, full-drive; heels over head, headlong.

685. LEISURE.—*N.* leisure, convenience; spare time, vacant hour; time, time to spare; holiday, ease.

V. **have leisure,** take one's time (*or* leisure, ease); repose, etc., 687; move slowly, while away the time, be master of one's time, be an idle man.

686. EXERTION.—*N.* exertion, effort, strain, stress, tug, pull, throw, stretch, struggle, spell, spurt; dead lift, heft [*dial.*]; trouble, pains, duty; energy, etc. [*physical*], 171.

exercise, practice, play, gymnastics, field sports; breather [*colloq.*].

labor, work, toil, manual labor, sweat of one's brow, drudgery, slavery.

worker, plodder, laborer, drudge, slave; man of action; Hercules.

V. **labor,** work, toil, sweat, fag, drudge, slave, strive, strain; pull, tug, ply; ply the oar; exert oneself, bestir oneself (*be active*), 682.

work hard; rough it; put forth one's strength, buckle to, set one's shoulder to the wheel, do double duty; burn the candle at both ends, work (*or* fight) one's way; do one's best, do one's utmost; take pains; strain every nerve; spare no efforts *or* pains.

Adj. **laborious,** elaborate; strained; toilsome, wearisome, burdensome; uphill; herculean.

hard-working, painstaking, strenuous, energetic, never idle.

Adv. with might and main, with all one's might, to the best of one's abilities, tooth and nail, hammer and tongs, heart and soul.

687. REPOSE.—*N.* repose, rest, sleep, etc., 683; relaxation, breathing time; halt, stay, pause, respite.

day of rest, Sabbath, Lord's day, Sunday; holiday, red-letter day, gala day; vacation, recess.

V. **repose,** rest, take rest, take one's ease; lie down, recline, go to rest (*or* bed, sleep).

relax, unbend, slacken, take breath, rest upon one's oars; pause, etc. (*cease*), 142; stay one's hand.

take a holiday, shut up shop; lie fallow.

Adj. **holiday,** festal; sabbatic *or* sabbatical.

688. FATIGUE.—*N.* fatigue; weariness, etc., 841; yawning, drowsiness, lassitude, tiredness, sweat.

faintness, fainting, swoon, exhaustion, collapse, prostration.

V. **be fatigued,** yawn, droop, sink; flag; gasp, pant, puff, blow, drop, swoon, faint, succumb.

fatigue, tire, bore, weary, flag, jade, harass, exhaust, wear out, prostrate.

tax, task, strain; overtask, overwork, overburden, overtax, overstrain, fag, fag out.

Adj. **fatigued**; weary, etc., 841; drowsy, haggard, toilworn, way-worn, footsore, faint; done up [*colloq.*], exhausted, prostrate, spent, ready to drop, all in [*slang*], dog-tired, tired to death, played out.

worn, worn out; battered, shattered, seedy [*colloq.*], enfeebled.

breathless, short of (*or* out of)breath, blown, puffing and blowing, short-breathed, broken-winded.

689. REFRESHMENT.—*N.* recuperation; recovery of strength, restoration, revival, etc., 660; repair, refreshment; relief, etc., 834.

V. **refresh,** brace, strengthen, reinvigorate; air, freshen up, recruit, regale, repair, restore, revive; get better, recover (*or* regain) one's strength, recuperate.

Adj. refreshing, recuperative.

690. AGENT.—*N.* agent, doer, actor, performer, perpetrator, operator; executor, executrix; practitioner, worker; minister, etc. (*instrument*), 631; representative, etc. (*commissioner*), 758, (*deputy*), 759; factor, steward; servant, etc., 746; factotum.

workman, artisan, craftsman, handicraftsman, mechanic, operative; working-man, laboring man; hewers of wood and drawers of water; laborer; hand, man, day laborer, journeyman, hack, drudge, roustabout.

maker, artificer, artist, wright, manufacturer, architect, contractor, builder, smith.

machinist, engineer, electrician.

workwoman, charwoman, dressmaker, modiste, seamstress, needlewoman, milliner, laundress, washerwoman.

coworker, associate, fellow worker, co-operator, colleague, confrere; force, staff, personnel.

691. WORKSHOP.—*N.* workshop, laboratory, manufactory, armory, arsenal, mill, factory, studio, atelier; hive, hive of industry, beehive; bindery; dock, dockyard, slip, yard, wharf; foundry, forge, furnace.

melting pot, crucible, caldron, mortar, alembic; matrix.

692. CONDUCT.—*N.* **conduct,** behavior; deportment, carriage, demeanor, guise, bearing, manner; course of conduct, line of action; role; process, ways, practice, procedure, method; dealing, transaction, business.

policy, tactics, game, generalship, statesmanship, strategy, plan.

management; government, etc., 693; stewardship, husbandry; housekeeping, ménage, regime, regimen, economy; economics, political economy.

career, life, course, walk, province, race, record; execution, treatment; campaign.

V. **transact,** execute; dispatch, proceed with, discharge; carry on (*or* through, out, into effect); work out; go through, get through; enact.

adopt a course, shape one's course, play one's part; shift for oneself, paddle one's own canoe; conduct; manage, etc. (*direct*), 693.

behave, conduct (*or* acquit, carry, comport, bear, demean) oneself.

Adj. **directive,** methodical, businesslike, practical, executive, strategic, economic.

693. DIRECTION.—*N.* **direction;** management, government, conduct, legislation, regulation, guidance, reins; steerage, pilotage, helm, rudder, needle, compass; guiding star, lodestar, polestar, cynosure.

ministry, administration; stewardship, proctorship; chair; agency.

supervision, superintendence; surveillance, oversight; eye of the master; control, charge; auspices; command, etc. (*authority*), 737.

statesmanship, statecraft, kingcraft, reins of government; director, etc., 694; seat, portfolio.

V. **direct,** manage, govern, conduct; order, prescribe, head, lead, regulate, guide, steer, pilot, take the helm, be at the helm; hold the reins, drive.

superintend, supervise; overlook, oversee, control, handle, look after, see to, administer, patronize; rule, etc. (*command*), 737; hold office.

Adj. **directing,** executive, gubernatorial, supervisory; statesmanlike.

Adv. **in charge of,** under the guidance of, under the auspices of; in control of, at the helm, at the head of.

694. DIRECTOR.—*N.* **director,** manager, governor, controller, superintendent, supervisor, overseer, supercargo, inspector, foreman, surveyor, taskmaster; master, etc., 745; leader, ringleader, agitator, demagogue, conductor, precentor, bellwether, file leader.

guide, pilot; helmsman, steersman; adviser, etc., 695.

driver, whip, charioteer; coachman, carman, cabman; postilion, muleteer, teamster; chauffeur, motorman, engine driver.

head, headman, chief, principal, president, speaker; chair, chairman; captain, etc. (*master*), 745; superior; prime minister, premier.

officer, functionary, minister, official, bureaucrat, officeholder.

statesman, strategist, legislator, lawgiver, politician, boss [*slang*], political dictator, wirepuller [*colloq.*], power behind the throne, kingmaker.

steward, factor, agent, bailiff, factotum, major-domo, seneschal, housekeeper, shepherd; proctor, curator, librarian.

695. ADVICE.—*N.* advice, counsel, word to the wise, suggestion, recommendation, advocacy; consultation; exhortation, expostulation, dissuasion, admonition; guidance.

instruction, charge, injunction, message, speech from the throne.

adviser, prompter; counsel, counselor; monitor, mentor, sage, wise man; teacher, etc., 540; physician; arbiter, referee, judge.

consultation, conference, parley, powwow; reference.

V. advise, counsel, suggest, prompt, recommend, prescribe, advocate, exhort, persuade.

enjoin, enforce, charge, instruct, call, call upon, request, dictate.

expostulate, dissuade, admonish, warn.

confer, consult, refer to, call in; follow, take (*or* follow) advice.

696. COUNCIL.—*N.* council, committee, privy council, court, chamber, cabinet, board, directorate, syndicate, bench, staff.

Ecclesiastical: convocation, synod, congregation, church, chapter, vestry. consistory, conventicle, conclave, convention.

legislature, parliament, congress, national council, states-general, diet.

Duma [Russia], Storthing *or* Storting [Norway], Rigsdag [Denmark], Riksdag [Sweden], Cortes [Spain], Reichsrath *or* Reichsrat [Austria], Volksraad [Dutch], Dail Eireann [Sinn Fein].

upper house, upper chamber, first chamber, senate, legislative council, House of Lords, House of Peers; Bundesrath *or* Bundesrat [Ger.], federal council, Lagting [Nor.], Landsthing [Den.].

lower house, lower chamber, second chamber, house of representatives, House of Commons, the house, legislative assembly, chamber of deputies; Odelsting [Nor.], Folkething [Den.], Reichstag [Ger.].

assembly, caucus, clique; meeting, sitting, séance, conference, hearing, session, palaver; council fire, powwow.

Representatives: congressman, M.C., senator, representative; member, member of parliament, M.P., assemblyman, councilor.

Adj. curule, congressional, senatorial, parliamentary; synodic *or* synodical.

697. PRECEPT.—*N.* precept, direction, instruction, charge; prescript, prescription; recipe, receipt; golden rule; maxim, etc., 496.

rule, canon, law, code, convention; unwritten law; canon law; act, statute, rubric, stage direction, regulation; model, form, formula, technicality.

order, etc. (*command*), 741.

698. SKILL.—*N.* skill, skillfulness, address, dexterity, adroitness, expertness, proficiency, competence, craft; facility, knack, trick, sleight; mastery, excellence, sleight of hand, etc. (*deception*), 545.

accomplishment, acquirement, attainment; art, science; finish, technique.

worldly wisdom, knowledge of the world, *savoir-faire* [F.]; tact; mother wit, discretion, finesse; management.

cleverness, talent, ability, ingenuity, capacity, talents, faculty, endowment, forte, turn, gift, genius, intelligence, sharpness, readiness, aptness, aptitude, resourcefulness; felicity, capability, qualification.

expert, adept, etc., 700.

masterpiece, masterwork, chef-d'oeuvre [F.].

V. **be skillful,** excel in, be master of; have a turn for.

take advantage of, make the most of, profit by, make a hit, make a virtue of necessity, make hay while the sun shines.

Adj. **skillful,** dexterous, adroit, expert, apt, handy, quick, deft, ready, smart, proficient, good at, at home in, master of, conversant with; masterly, crack [*colloq.*], crackajack [*slang*], accomplished.

experienced, practiced, skilled, up in, in practice, competent, efficient, qualified, capable, fitted, fit for, trained, initiated, sophisticated, prepared, primed, finished.

clever, able, ingenious, felicitous, gifted, talented, resourceful, inventive; shrewd, sharp, cunning; neat-handed, fine-fingered; nimble-fingered, ambidextrous, sure-footed.

technical, artistic, scientific, workmanlike, businesslike, statesmanlike.

Adv. **skillfully,** artistically, with skill, with fine technique, with consummate skill; like a machine.

699. UNSKILLFULNESS.—*N.* **unskillfulness,** want of skill, incompetence, inability, infelicity, clumsiness, inaptitude, inexperience; disqualification.

mismanagement, misconduct, bad policy, impolicy; maladministration; misrule, misgovernment.

blunder, act of folly, bungle, botch, bad job, sad work.

bungler, etc., 701; fool, etc., 501.

V. **bungle,** blunder, muff [*esp. baseball*], boggle, fumble, botch, mar, spoil, flounder, stumble, trip; mismanage, misdirect, misapply.

mistake, take the shadow for the substance, bark up the wrong tree; be in the wrong box [*colloq.*]; lose one's way, miss one's way; fall into a trap.

Adj. **unskillful,** unskilled, inexpert, incompetent, bungling, awkward, clumsy, gawky, unhandy, maladroit; stupid, ill-qualified, unfit; raw, green, inexperienced; rusty, out of practice.

unaccustomed, unused, untrained, uninitiated; unbusinesslike, unpractical, shiftless; unstatesmanlike.

ill-advised, misadvised; ill-devised, ill-judged, ill-contrived, ill-conducted; misguided, foolish, wild; infelicitous.

700. EXPERT.—*N.* **expert,** adept, proficient, connoisseur, master, master hand; top sawyer; prima donna, first fiddle; past master.

picked man; medalist, prizeman.

veteran, old stager, old campaigner, man of business, man of the world.

genius; mastermind, master spirit; prodigy of learning, walking encyclopedia, mine of information.

man of cunning, diplomatist, diplomat, Machiavellian; politician, tactician strategist.

701. BUNGLER.—*N.* **bungler,** blunderer, blunderhead; fumbler, lubber, clown, lout, duffer [*colloq.*]; butter-fingers, muff, muffer [*all colloq.*]; awkward squad; novice, greenhorn.

landlubber, fresh-water sailor, fair-weather sailor, horse marine.

sloven, slattern, slut.

702. CUNNING.—*N.* **cunning,** craft, subtlety, maneuvering, temporization; circumvention; chicane, chicanery; sharp practice, knavery, jugglery, concealment, a nigger in the woodpile [*colloq.*], guile, duplicity, foul play.

diplomacy, politics, Machiavellianism; gerrymander, jobbery, back-stairs influence.

artifice, art, device, machination; plot, maneuver, stratagem, dodge, wile, trick, trickery, ruse, finesse, subterfuge, evasion, white lie, gold brick [*colloq.*], imposture, deception, net, trap.

schemer, trickster, sly boots [*humorous*], fox, reynard; intriguer, man of cunning.

V. **intrigue,** live by one's wits; maneuver, gerrymander, finesse, double, temporize, circumvent, outdo, get the better of, throw off one's guard; surprise, waylay, undermine, flatter; have an ax to grind.

Adj. **cunning,** crafty, artful, skillful; subtle, feline, deep, profound, designing, timeserving, tricky, wily, sly, insidious, stealthy, underhand, double-faced, shifty, deceptive; deceitful, crooked; shrewd, acute; sharp, canny, astute, knowing.

703. ARTLESSNESS.—*N.* **artlessness,** unsophistication, simplicity, innocence, candor, sincerity, singleness of purpose, honesty.

rough diamond, matter-of-fact man; *enfant terrible* [F.].

V. **be artless,** think aloud; speak one's mind; be free with one, call a spade a spade; tell the truth, the whole truth, and nothing but the truth.

Adj. **artless,** natural, pure, confiding, simple, plain, unsophisticated, unaffected, naïve; sincere, frank, open, candid, ingenuous, guileless; unsuspicious, honest, childlike; innocent. straightforward, aboveboard; single-minded.

matter-of-fact, plain-spoken, outspoken; blunt, downright, direct, unflattering, unvarnished.

Adv. in plain words (*or* English); without mincing the matter.

704. DIFFICULTY.—*N.* difficulty, hardness, impracticability, uphill work, herculean task; dead weight, dead lift.

dilemma, predicament, fix [*colloq.*], quandary, embarrassment, deadlock, perplexity, intricacy, entanglement, knot, Gordian knot, maze, coil, strait, pass, pinch, rub, critical situation, exigency, crisis, trial, emergency, scrape, slough, quagmire, hot water [*colloq.*], pickle, stew, imbroglio, mess, muddle, botch, hitch, stumbling block.

vexed question, poser, puzzle, knotty point, paradox; hard nut to crack, crux.

V. be difficult, go against the grain, try one's patience, go hard with one, pose, perplex, bother, nonplus.

flounder, boggle [*local*], struggle, stick fast; come to a deadlock.

render difficult, enmesh, encumber, embarrass, entangle; spike one's guns.

Adj. difficult, hard, tough [*colloq.*]; troublesome, toilsome, irksome; laborious, onerous, arduous, herculean, formidable.

awkward, unwieldy, unmanageable, intractable, stubborn, perverse, refractory, knotted, knotty, thorny; pathless, trackless, intricate.

embarrassing, perplexing, delicate, ticklish, critical, thorny.

in difficulty, in hot water [*colloq.*], in a fix [*colloq.*], in a scrape, between Scylla and Charybdis; on the horns of a dilemma; on the rocks; reduced to straits; hard-pressed; run hard; pinched, straitened; hard up [*slang*]; puzzled, at a loss, at one's wits' end, at a standstill; nonplused, stranded, aground.

Adv. with much ado; uphill, upstream; in the teeth of; against the grain.

705. FACILITY.—*N.* facility, ease, easiness, capability, feasibility, practicability; flexibility, pliancy, smoothness, plain sailing; mere child's play; cinch, snap [*both slang*].

V. be easy, run smoothly; have full play, obey the helm, work well, work smoothly.

facilitate, smooth, ease, lighten, free, clear, disencumber, disembarrass, disentangle, extricate, unravel, unknot; humor, leave a loophole, leave the matter open; give full play, make way for, pave the way, bridge over.

Adj. easy, facile; feasible, practicable, within reach, gettable, accessible.

manageable, tractable; submissive; yielding, ductile, tractable, pliant.

unburdened, unencumbered, unloaded, unobstructed, untrammeled; unrestrained, free, at ease, light.

Adv. **easily,** readily, expertly, adroitly, smoothly, swimmingly, with no effort.

706. HINDRANCE.—*N.* **prevention,** obstruction, stoppage, interruption, interception, hindrance, embarrassment, constriction, restriction, restraint, etc., 751.

interference, interposition, obtrusion; discouragement, disapproval, disapprobation, opposition.

impediment, obstacle, obstruction, knot, snag, hitch, contretemps, stumbling block, lion in the path.

check; encumbrance; clog, brake, anchor; bit, snaffle, curb; drag, load, burden, onus, impedimenta; dead weight; lumber, pack; nightmare, incubus; stay, stop; preventive, prophylactic.

drawback, objection; difficulty, etc., 704; obstacle; ill-wind, head wind; trammel, tether.

damper, wet blanket, kill-joy, dog in the manger, usurper, interloper, opponent; filibusterer.

V. **hinder,** impede, filibuster, embarrass.

avert, keep off, stave off, ward off; obviate; turn aside, draw off, prevent, nip in the bud; retard, slacken, check, counteract, countercheck, preclude, debar, inhibit, restrict.

obstruct, stop, stay, bar, bolt, lock; block, barricade; dam up, put on the brake, put a stop to, interrupt, intercept, oppose, interfere, interpose.

encumber, cramp, hamper; clog, cumber, handicap; choke, saddle with, load with, overload, overwhelm, lumber, entrammel, trammel, incommode, discommode, discompose, corner.

thwart, frustrate, disconcert, balk, foil; circumvent, baffle, override, defeat, spoil, mar, clip the wings of, cripple, damp, dishearten, discountenance, undermine.

Adj. **obstructive,** intrusive, meddlesome; onerous, burdensome; cumbrous, cumbersome.

Adv. **in the way,** with everything against one, through all obstacles, under many difficulties.

707. AID.—*N.* **aid,** assistance, help, succor; support, lift, advance, furtherance, promotion.

patronage, auspices, countenance, favor, interest, advocacy.

sustenance, maintenance, nutrition, nourishment; manna in the wilderness, food, means, subsidy, bounty.

relief, rescue; ministry, ministration; supernatural aid; *deus ex machina* [L.].

supplies, re-enforcements, contingents, recruits, support, ally.

V. **aid,** assist, help, succor, lend a hand; contribute, subscribe to;

take by the hand, take in tow; relieve, rescue; set on one's legs, give new life to, be the making of; re-enforce, recruit; promote, further, forward, advance; speed, expedite, quicken, hasten.

support, sustain, uphold, prop, hold up, bolster.

nourish, nurture, nurse, cradle, dry-nurse, suckle, foster, cherish, cultivate.

serve; do service to, tender to, pander to, minister to; tend, attend, wait on; take care of; entertain, regale.

oblige, accommodate, consult the wishes of; humor, cheer, encourage.

second, stand by, back, back up; abet, work for, stick up for [*colloq.*], stick by, take up (*or* espouse) the cause of; advocate, countenance, patronize, smile upon, favor, befriend, side with.

Adj. aiding, auxiliary, adjuvant, helpful, subservient, accessary, accessory, subsidiary.

friendly, amicable, favorable, propitious, well disposed, neighborly, obliging, at one's beck.

Adv. in aid of, on (*or* in) behalf of, in favor of, in the name of, in furtherance of, on account of, for the sake of.

708. OPPOSITION.—*N.* opposition, antagonism, contrariness, contrariety; contravention, counteraction; resistance, etc., 719; hindrance, restraint, etc., 751.

collision, conflict, discord, want of harmony; filibuster, clashing.

competition, rivalry, emulation, race, contest; tug of war.

V. oppose, counteract, withstand, etc. (*resist*), 719; hinder, restrain; obstruct, etc., 706; antagonize, cross, thwart, pit against, face, confront, cope with; protest (*or* vote) against; disfavor; contradict, contravene, belie.

encounter, meet, stem, breast, resist, grapple with, kick against the pricks; contend with (*or* against), do battle with (*or* against).

compete, emulate, rival; force out, drive one out of business.

Adj. adverse, antagonistic, oppugnant, contrary, at variance, at issue, at war with, in opposition, at daggers drawn.

unfavorable, unpropitious, unfriendly, hostile, inimical, cross.

competitive, emulous, cutthroat; in rivalry with, in friendly rivalry.

Adv. against, counter to, in conflict with, at cross-purposes.

in spite, in despite, in defiance; in the teeth (*or* face) of; across; athwart.

709. CO-OPERATION.—*N.* co-operation, concert, concurrence, complicity, collusion; participation; union, combination.

association, alliance, joint stock, partnership, pool, gentleman's agreement; confederation, coalition, federation, fusion; logrolling; freemasonry.

unanimity, *esprit de corps* [F.], party spirit, school spirit; clanship, partisanship; concord.

V. co-operate, concur; conduce, combine, pool, unite one's efforts, pull together, stand shoulder to shoulder; act in concert, join forces, fraternize; conspire, concert.

side with, take sides with, go along with, join hands with, make common cause with, unite with, join with, take part with, cast in one's lot with; rally round.

participate, be a party to, lend oneself to; chip in [*colloq.*], bear part in, second, espouse a cause.

Adj. co-operating, in league, hand in glove with; favorable to, unopposed.

Adv. unanimously, as one man, shoulder to shoulder.

710. OPPONENT.—*N.* opponent, antagonist, adversary; opposition; assailant, enemy, etc., 891.

oppositionist, wrangler, disputant; filibuster, filibusterer, extremist, bitter-ender, irreconcilable, obstructionist.

malcontent; demagogue, reactionist; anarchist, Red.

rival, competitor, contestant; the field.

711. AUXILIARY.—*N.* auxiliary, recruit, assistant, help, helper, helpmate, helping hand; colleague, partner, confrere, co-operator, coadjutor, collaborator, associate, right hand, right-hand man.

ally; friend, etc., 890; confidant (*fem.* confidante), alter ego [L.], pal [*slang*], chum [*colloq.*], mate.

puppet, cat's-paw, creature, tool; satellite, adherent, parasite, dependent.

confederate; accomplice; accessory.

upholder, seconder, backer, supporter, abettor, advocate, partisan, champion, patron, friend at court, mediator.

friend in need, special providence, guardian angel, fairy godmother, tutelary genius.

712. PARTY.—*N.* party, faction, denomination, class, communion, side, crew, team, band, horde, posse, phalanx; caste, family, clan.

community, body, fellowship, party spirit, solidarity, freemasonry; fraternity, sodality, brotherhood, sisterhood, sorority; fraternal order.

gang, tong [Chin.], bolsheviki, bolshevists, ring, machine, junto, cabal.

clique, knot, circle, set, coterie; club, casino.

corporation, corporate body, guild, company, partnership, firm, house; combine [*colloq.*], trust; holding company, merger.

society, association; institute, institution; union; trade-union;

league, syndicate, alliance, combination, coalition, federation, confederation, confederacy.

staff; cast, dramatis personae [L.].

V. unite, join, band together, club together, co-operate, etc., 709; associate, federate, federalize.

Adj. joint, federal, corporate, confederated, organized, leagued, syndicated; fraternal, Masonic, institutional, denominational; cliquish, cliquy.

Adv. side by side, hand in hand, shoulder to shoulder, in the same boat.

713. DISCORD.—*N.* discord, dissidence, dissonance, disagreement, jar, clash, break, shock.

variance, difference, dissension, misunderstanding, cross-purposes, odds, division, split, rupture, disruption, disunion, breach, schism, feud, faction.

polemics; litigation, strife, warfare, outbreak, open rupture, declaration of war.

quarrel, dispute, tiff, bicker, squabble, altercation, words, high words, family jars.

broil, brawl, row [*colloq.*], racket, hubbub, imbroglio, fracas, scrimmage, rumpus [*colloq.*], squall, riot, disturbance, commotion.

subject of dispute, ground of quarrel, battleground, disputed point, bone of contention, apple of discord, question at issue.

V. disagree, clash, jar, conflict, misunderstand, live like cat and dog; differ; dissent, etc., 489.

quarrel, fall out, dispute, litigate; controvert, squabble, altercate, row [*colloq.*], wrangle, bicker, nag, spar, brawl.

split, break with; declare war, try conclusions, join issue, pick a quarrel; sow dissension, embroil, entangle, disunite, widen the breach; set (*or* pit) against.

Adj. discordant, dissident, out of tune, dissonant, harsh, grating, jangling, unmelodious; on bad terms, dissentient, unreconciled, unpacified; inconsistent, contradictory, incongruous.

quarrelsome, heated, unpacific, controversial, polemic, disputatious, factious.

at strife, at odds, at loggerheads, at daggers drawn, at variance, at issue, at cross-purposes, at sixes and sevens, embroiled, torn, disunited.

714. CONCORD.—*N.* concord, accord, harmony, homologue, correspondence, agreement, sympathy, response; union, unison, unity, peace, unanimity; happy family.

amity, etc. (*friendship*), 888; alliance, *entente cordiale* [F.], good understanding, conciliation, arbitration, reunion.

peacemaker, intercessor, interceder, mediator.

V. **agree,** accord, harmonize with, fraternize, go hand in hand, run parallel, concur, co-operate, pull together, sing in chorus.

side with, sympathize with; go with, chime in with, fall in with; assent, etc., 488; reciprocate.

smooth, pour oil on the troubled waters, keep in good humor, meet halfway; mediate, intercede.

Adj. **concordant,** congenial; in accord, harmonious, united, cemented, allied, friendly, fraternal, conciliatory, of one mind.

Adv. **unanimously,** with one voice, in concert with, hand in hand.

715. DEFIANCE.—*N.* **defiance,** dare, defial; challenge; threat, etc., 909; war cry, war whoop.

V. **defy,** dare, beard, brave, set at defiance, set at naught, hurl defiance at; laugh to scorn; disobey, etc., 742; threaten; challenge.

Adj. **defiant;** rebellious, bold, insolent, reckless, contemptuous, greatly daring, regardless of consequences.

Adv. in the teeth of; under one's very nose; in open rebellion.

716. ATTACK.—*N.* **attack,** assault, onset, onslaught, charge.

aggression, offense; incursion, inroad, invasion; irruption, outbreak; sally, sortie, raid, foray.

storm, storming, boarding, escalade; siege, investment, bombardment, cannonade, barrage; zero hour.

fire, volley, fusilade; sharpshooting, broadside, cross-fire.

thrust, lunge, pass, home thrust; cut.

assailant, aggressor, invader; sharpshooter, dead shot.

V. **attack,** assault, assail; set upon, pounce upon, fall upon, charge; enter the lists.

show fight, take the offensive; strike at, thrust at; aim (*or* deal) a blow at; be the aggressor, strike the first blow, fire the first shot; advance (*or* march) against, march upon, invade, harry.

close with, come to close quarters, bring to bay, come to blows.

fire upon, fire at, draw a bead on, shoot at, pop at, level at, open fire, pepper, bombard, shell, fire a volley.

besiege, beset, beleaguer, invest; sap, mine; storm, board, scale the walls, go over the top.

cut and thrust, bayonet, butt; kick, strike, etc., 276; horsewhip, whip.

Adj. **aggressive,** offensive; up in arms; amuck.

Adv. on the warpath; over the top; at bay.

717. DEFENSE.—*N.* **defense,** protection, guard, ward; guardianship.

self-defense, self-preservation; resistance, etc., 719.

safeguard, screen, fortification, bulwark, trench, mine, dugout;

moat, ditch, intrenchment; rampart, dike; parapet, battlement, bastion, redoubt, embankment, mound, bank, breastwork, earthwork, fieldwork; buttress, abutment, fence, wall, paling, palisade, stockade; barrier, barricade, boom; portcullis, barbed-wire entanglements.

stronghold, hold, fastness, asylum, keep, donjon, citadel, capitol, castle; tower, fortress, fort, barrack; blockhouse.

[protective devices] buffer, fender, cowcatcher, armor; mail, shield, buckler.

defender, protector, guardian, bodyguard, champion; knight-errant, paladin; garrison.

V. **defend,** guard, ward (*or* beat) off, shield, screen, shroud; garrison, man; fence, intrench, arm, accouter.

repel, parry, put to flight; hold (*or* keep) at bay; resist invasion, stand siege, stand (*or* act) on the defensive, show fight; stand one's ground, hold, stand in the gap.

Adj. **defensive;** armed, armed at all points (*or* to the teeth); panoplied, accoutered; iron-plated, ironclad; bulletproof, bombproof; protective.

Adv. on the defensive, in defense, in self-defense; at bay.

718. RETALIATION.—*N.* **retaliation,** reprisal, retort; counterstroke, counterblast; retribution.

requital, desert; tit for tat, give-and-take, blow for blow, an eye for an eye; boomerang.

recrimination, accusation; revenge, etc., 919; compensation.

V. **retaliate,** retort, turn upon; pay, pay off, pay back; cap, match; reciprocate, turn the tables upon, return the compliment; exchange blows; give and take, be quits, be even with; pay off old scores.

Adj. **retaliatory,** retaliative, retributive, recriminatory, reciprocal.

719. RESISTANCE.—*N.* **resistance,** stand, front, opposition, recalcitrance, repugnance, repulsion.

repulse, rebuff, snub.

insurrection, revolt, etc., 742; strike, lockout; boycott; riot.

V. **resist;** withstand; stand, stand firm (*or* fast, one's ground), stick it out [*colloq.*].

face, confront, breast the wave, stem the tide; grapple with; show a bold front, make a stand.

oppose, etc., 708; fly in the face of; withstand an attack, rise up in arms, strike, turn out, boycott; revolt, rebel; repel, repulse.

Adj. **resistant,** resistive, refractory, repugnant, recalcitrant, repulsive, repellent; up in arms.

unconquerable, stubborn, unconquered; indomitable, unyielding.

720. CONTENTION.—*N.* **contention,** strife, contest, struggle; belligerency, pugnacity, opposition.

controversy, polemics; debate, war of words, paper war, high words, quarrel, litigation.

competition, rivalry, match, race; athletics, athletic sports; games of skill.

conflict, skirmish; encounter, rencounter, rencontre, collision, affair, brush, fracas, etc. (*discord*), 713; clash of arms; tussle, scuffle, bout, broil, fray, affray, fight, battle, combat, action, engagement, joust, tournament, tourney; pitched battle; guerrilla (*or* irregular) warfare; death struggle, Armageddon.

duel, single combat, satisfaction, passage of arms, affair of honor; hostile meeting, appeal to arms.

V. **contend,** contest, strive, struggle, scramble, wrestle; spar, exchange blows, tussle, tilt, box, fence; skirmish, fight; wrangle; oppose, etc., 708; join issue.

compete (*or* cope, vie, race) with, emulate, rival; run a race.

Adj. **contentious,** combative, bellicose, belligerent, warlike, quarrelsome, pugnacious, pugilistic.

athletic, gymnastic, competitive, rival.

721. PEACE.—*N.* **peace,** amity, etc. (*friendship*), 888; harmony, concord, tranquillity, truce, pipe of peace, calumet.

piping time of peace, quiet life; neutrality; pacifism.

V. **be at peace,** keep the peace, make peace, pacify; be a pacifist.

Adj. **pacific;** peaceable, peaceful; calm, tranquil, untroubled, halcyon; bloodless; neutral, pacifistic.

722. WARFARE.—*N.* **warfare,** fighting, hostilities; war, arms, the sword, bloodshed; Mars.

appeal to arms (*or* the sword); ordeal (*or* wager) of battle; declaration of war.

battle array, campaign, crusade, expedition; warpath.

art of war, rules of war, the war game, tactics, strategy, generalship.

battle, conflict, etc. (*contention*), 720; service, campaigning, active service, tented field; war to the death (*or* knife).

war medal, military medal, Congressional Medal, Victoria Cross, V. C. [Eng.], *Croix de guerre* [F.], *Médaille militaire* [F.], Iron Cross [Ger.].

V. **war,** make war, go to war, declare war, wage war, arm, take up (*or* appeal to) arms; take the field, give battle, engage, fight, combat, contend, battle with.

serve; enroll, enlist; be on service (*or* active service), campaign;

smell powder, be under fire; be on the warpath, keep the field; take by storm; go over the top [*colloq.*]; sell one's life dearly.

Adj. **armed,** in (*or* under) arms, in battle array, in the field; embattled; battled.

warlike, belligerent, combative, bellicose, martial, military, militant; soldierly, chivalrous; civil, internecine; irregular, guerrilla.

Adv. in the thick of the fray, in the cannon's mouth; at the sword's point, at the point of the bayonet.

723. PACIFICATION.—*N.* **pacification,** conciliation, reconciliation, reconcilement; accommodation, arrangement, adjustment; terms, compromise; amnesty.

peace offering; olive branch; calumet, peace pipe.

truce, armistice; suspension of arms (*or* hostilities); truce of God; flag of truce, white flag.

V. **pacify,** tranquillize, compose, allay, reconcile, propitiate, placate, conciliate, meet halfway, hold out the olive branch, heal the breach, make peace, restore harmony, bring to terms.

raise a siege, sheathe the sword, bury the hatchet, lay down one's arms, turn swords into plowshares.

Adj. **conciliatory,** pacificatory.

724. MEDIATION.—*N.* **mediation,** mediatorship, intervention, interposition, interference, intercession; parley, negotiation, arbitration, good offices.

mediator, intercessor, peacemaker, negotiator, go-between, diplomatist, propitiator; umpire, arbitrator.

V. **mediate,** intercede, interpose, interfere, intervene; step in, negotiate; meet halfway; arbitrate, propitiate.

Adj. **mediatory,** propitiatory, diplomatic.

725. SUBMISSION.—*N.* **submission,** yielding, acquiescence, compliance, submissiveness, deference, nonresistance, obedience.

surrender, cession, capitulation, resignation, backdown [*colloq.*].

obeisance, homage, kneeling, genuflection, curtsy, kowtow [Chinese], salaam [Oriental], prostration.

V. **submit,** succumb, yield, defer to; bend, stoop; accede, resign oneself.

surrender, cede, capitulate, come to terms, lay down one's arms, strike one's flag, give way (*or* ground, in, up); obey.

yield obeisance, kneel to, bow to, pay homage to, cringe to, truckle to; kneel, bow submission, curtsy, kowtow [Chinese].

Adj. **submissive,** resigned, crouching, prostrate; unresisting, humble.

untenable, indefensible, insupportable, unsupportable.

726. COMBATANT.—*N.* **combatant;** belligerent, assailant, swashbuckler, duelist, swordsman; competitor, rival.

fighter, fighting man, prize fighter, pugilist, bruiser; gladiator.

soldier, warrior, brave, man at arms, guardsman, gendarme [F.]; campaigner, veteran; military man; knight; myrmidon, mercenary, irregular, free lance, franctireur; private, Tommy Atkins [Brit.], doughboy [slang], rank and file; sepoy [India], spearman, pikeman; archer, bowman; musketeer, rifleman, sharpshooter, skirmisher; grenadier, fusileer, infantryman, foot soldier, chasseur, zouave, artilleryman, gunner, cannoneer, engineer; cavalryman, trooper, dragoon; cuirassier, hussar, lancer; recruit, rookie [slang], conscript, drafted man, enlisted man.

officer, etc. (commander), 745; subaltern, ensign, standard-bearer.

horse and foot; cavalry, horse, light horse; infantry, foot, rifles; artillery, horse artillery, field artillery, gunners; military train.

armed force, troops, soldiery, military, forces, the army, standing army, regulars, the line; militia, national guard, state guard, yeomanry, volunteers, minutemen [Am. hist.]; posse; guards, yeomen of the guard, beefeaters [Eng.], lifeguards, household troops, bodyguard.

levy, draft; raw levies, awkward squad.

army, army corps; division, column, wing, detachment, garrison, flying column, brigade, regiment, battalion, squadron, company, battery, section, platoon, squad; picket, guard, legion, phalanx, cohort.

navy, first line of defense, wooden walls, naval forces, fleet, flotilla, armada, squadron; man-of-war's man, etc. (sailor), 269; marines.

man-of-war, line-of-battle ship, ship of the line, battleship, warship, ironclad, war vessel, superdreadnought, dreadnought, cruiser; torpedo boat, destroyer, gunboat, submarine, submersible, U-boat [Ger.]; submarine chaser, monitor; frigate, sloop of war, corvet, flagship; privateer; troopship, transport, tender.

airplane, hydroplane, seaplane, flying boat; glider; divebomber, bomber, Flying Fortress; dirigible, blimp [cant]; zeppelin, etc. (aeronautics), 273.

727. ARMS.—N. arms; arm, weapon, deadly weapon; armament; armor.

side arms, sword, cold steel, naked steel, steel, blade; broadsword, saber, cutlass, scimitar, rapier, foil, dagger, poniard, dirk, stiletto, bowie knife, bayonet.

ax, battle-ax, poleax, halberd, tomahawk, bill, partisan.

spear, lance, pike, assagai, javelin, dart, arrow; harpoon, boomerang; oxgoad, ankus.

club, war club, mace, truncheon, staff, bludgeon, cudgel, shillelagh, quarterstaff; billy, life preserver, blackjack.

bow, crossbow, long bow; catapult, sling.

firearms; gun, piece; artillery, ordnance; park, battery; cannon, fieldpiece, field gun, siege gun, mortar, howitzer, pompom, seventy-five [French rapid-fire 75-mm. field gun]; Lewis gun.

small arms; musketry; musket, firelock, fowling piece, rifle, carbine, blunderbuss, matchlock, harquebus, shotgun, breechloader, muzzle-loader, magazine rifle, automatic pistol, automatic, revolver, repeater; shooting iron [slang], six-shooter [colloq], gun [colloq. for revolver or pistol], pistol.

missile, bolt, projectile, shot, ball, slug; grape, shrapnel, grenade, shell, bomb, depth bomb, smoke bomb, gas bomb; bullet; dumdum (or explosive, expanding) bullet; torpedo.

ammunition; powder, powder and shot; explosive; gunpowder; dynamite, cordite; cartridge; poison gas, mustard gas, chlorine gas, tear gas, etc.

728. ARENA.—N. arena, field, platform; scene of action, theater, walk, course; hustings; stage, boards, amphitheater, coliseum, colosseum; hippodrome, circus, race course, turf, cockpit, bear garden, gymnasium, ring, lists; campus, playing field, playground.

battlefield, battleground, field of battle; no man's land [*First World War*]; theater (*or* seat) of war.

729. COMPLETION.—*N.* completion; accomplishment, achievement, fulfillment, performance, execution; dispatch, consummation, culmination; finish, conclusion; limit, close, finale, denouement, issue, upshot, result.

V. complete, perfect, effect, accomplish, achieve, compass, consummate, bring to maturity (*or* perfection); elaborate.

do, execute, make, work out, enact, dispatch, knock off [*colloq.*], finish off, dispose of, perform, discharge, fulfill, realize; carry out (*or* into effect).

do thoroughly, not do by halves, drive home; carry through, deliver the goods [*colloq.*].

finish, bring to a close, wind up, clinch, seal, put the last (*or* finishing) touch to; crown, crown all; cap.

Adj. conclusive, final, crowning, exhaustive, complete, mature, perfect, consummate, thorough.

Adv. to crown all, as a last stroke, as a fitting climax.

730. NONCOMPLETION.—*N.* noncompletion, nonfulfillment, nonperformance, neglect, etc., 460; shortcoming, incompleteness; drawn battle, drawn game.

V. leave unfinished, leave undone, neglect, etc., 460; let alone, let slip; lose sight of.

fall short of, do things by halves, hang fire; collapse.

Adj. incomplete, uncompleted, unfinished, unaccomplished, unperformed, unexecuted; sketchy; sterile.

Adv. without (*or* lacking) the final touches.

731. SUCCESS—*N.* success, successfulness; progress; advance; good fortune, prosperity, etc., 734; profit.

trump card; hit, stroke, master stroke; ten-strike [*colloq.*]; checkmate; prize.

mastery, advantage over; upper hand, whip hand; ascendancy, conquest, victory, walkover [*colloq.*], triumph.

victor, conqueror, master, champion, winner; master of the situation (*or* position).

V. succeed, be successful, gain one's end (*or* ends); crown with success; gain (*or* attain, carry, secure) a point *or* an object; get there [*slang*]; manage to, contrive to; accomplish, effect; come off successfully, take (*or* carry) by storm; gain the day (*or* prize, palm); carry all before one, score a success.

make progress, etc. (*advance*), 282; win (*or* make, work) one's way; speed; turn to account, prosper, etc., 734; strike oil [*slang*], make one's fortune.

triumph, be triumphant, gain a victory (*or* an advantage); surmount (*or* overcome) a difficulty, stem the torrent, weather the storm, master; distance, surpass, win.

defeat, conquer, discomfit, vanquish, overcome, overthrow, overpower, overmaster, outwit, outdo, outmaneuver, outgeneral, checkmate, beat, rout, floor, worst, lick to a frazzle [*colloq.*]; settle [*colloq.*], do for [*colloq.*], subdue, subjugate, reduce.

quell, silence, put down, confound, nonplus, baffle, circumvent, elude; drive to the wall.

avail, answer, answer the purpose; prevail, take effect, do, turn out well, take [*colloq.*], tell, bear fruit.

Adj. successful; prosperous, etc., 734; triumphant, crowned with success, victorious; unbeaten.

Adv. successfully, with flying colors, in triumph, swimmingly.

732. FAILURE.—*N.* failure, unsuccess, nonsuccess, nonfulfillment; labor in vain, no go [*colloq.*], inefficacy; vain attempt; frustration, disappointment.

blunder, error, etc., 495; fault, omission, miss, oversight, slip, trip, stumble; step, *faux pas* [F.]; scrape, mess, muddle, botch, fiasco.

mishap, etc. (*misfortune*), 735; split, collapse, smash, blow, explosion.

repulse, rebuff, defeat, rout, overthrow, discomfiture; beating, drubbing; subjugation, checkmate.

fall, downfall, ruin, perdition, wreck; deathblow; bankruptcy.

V. fail, be unsuccessful, make vain efforts, labor in vain; flunk [*colloq.*]; bring to naught, make nothing of, fall short of, go to the wall [*colloq.*], lick the dust; be defeated, have the worst of it, lose the day, lose; succumb.

miss, miss one's aim (*or* the mark), slip, trip, stumble, blunder, miscarry.

flounder, falter, limp, halt, hobble, fall, tumble, run aground, split upon a rock, break down, sink, drown, founder, come to grief.

come to nothing, end in smoke; flat out [*colloq.*]; fall through, hang fire, flash in the pan, collapse, go to wrack and ruin.

Adj. unsuccessful, successless, at fault; unfortunate, etc., 735; abortive, sterile, fruitless, bootless; ineffectual, ineffective, inefficient, lame, insufficient, unavailing.

stranded, aground, grounded, swamped, wrecked, shipwrecked, foundered, capsized.

undone, lost, ruined, broken, bankrupt, played out; done up, done for [*colloq.*]; broken down, overborne, overwhelmed; all up with [*colloq.*].

frustrated, thwarted, crossed, disconcerted; unhorsed, hard hit, stultified, befooled, dished [*colloq.*], foiled, defeated, victimized, sacrificed.

Adv. to little or no purpose, in vain.

733. TROPHY.—*N.* trophy; medal, prize, palm, laurel, laurels, bays, crown, chaplet, wreath; eulogy, citation; scholarship; garland; triumphal arch; war medal, etc., 722; Carnegie medal, Nobel prize; blue ribbon; decoration, etc., 877.

734. PROSPERITY.—*N.* prosperity, welfare, well-being; affluence, etc. (*wealth*), 803; success, etc., 731; luck, good fortune, good luck, blessings, godsend; bed of roses; fat of the land.

upstart, parvenu, *nouveau riche* [F.], mushroom.

V. **prosper,** thrive, flourish, swim with the tide; rise (*or* get on) in the world; light on one's feet; bask in the sunshine; have a run of luck; make one's fortune, feather one's nest, make one's pile [*slang*].

flower, blossom, bloom, fructify, bear fruit; fatten, batten.

Adj. **prosperous,** thriving, well off, well to do, at one's ease; rich, etc., 803; fortunate, lucky; palmy, halcyon.

auspicious, propitious, providential.

Adv. prosperously, swimmingly; as good luck would have it.

735. ADVERSITY.—*N.* adversity, evil, etc., 619; failure, etc., 732; bad (*or* ill, evil, adverse, hard) fortune *or* luck, frowns of fortune; broken fortunes; slough of despond; evil day, hard times, rainy day, cloud, gathering clouds, ill-wind; affliction, trouble, hardship, curse, blight, load, pressure, humiliation.

misfortune, mishap, mischance, misadventure, disaster, calamity, catastrophe; accident, casualty, blow, trial, sorrow, visitation, infliction, reverse, check, setback, contretemps [F.].

downfall, fall; losing game; ruin, undoing, extremity.

V. **come to grief,** go downhill, go to wrack and ruin, go to the dogs [*colloq.*]; fall, decay, sink, decline, go down in the world; have seen better days; be all up with [*colloq.*].

Adj. **unfortunate,** unblest, unhappy, unlucky, unprosperous, hoodooed [*colloq.*], luckless, hapless, out of luck; under a cloud; badly off; in adverse circumstances; poor, etc., 804; decayed, undone, on the road to ruin.

ill-fated, ill-starred, ill-omened; devoted, doomed; inauspicious, ominous, sinister, unpropitious, unfavorable.

adverse, untoward; disastrous, calamitous, ruinous, dire, deplorable.

Adv. from bad to worse, out of the frying pan into the fire.

736. MEDIOCRITY.—*N.* mediocrity, golden mean, moderation; moderate (*or* average) circumstances; respectability.

middle classes, *bourgeoisie* [F.].

V. strike the golden mean; preserve a middle course.

jog on, get along [*colloq.*], get on tolerably (*or* respectably).

Adj. middling, so-so, fair, medium, moderate, mediocre, ordinary.

Adv. with nothing to brag about.

II. INTERSOCIAL VOLITION[1]

737. AUTHORITY.—*N.* authority; influence, patronage, power, prestige, prerogative, jurisdiction.

right, divine right, authoritativeness, royalty, absolutism, despotism, tyranny.

command, empire, sway, rule; dominion, domination; sovereignty, supremacy, suzerainty, kingship; lordship, headship, leadership, mastership, government, dictation, control, hold, grasp; grip, iron sway, rod of empire.

reign, dynasty, administration; dictatorship, protectorate, presidency, presidentship, consulship, magistracy.

Governments: empire; monarchy; limited (*or* constitutional) monarchy; aristocracy; oligarchy, democracy, republic; triumvirate; autocracy; dictatorship, totalitarian state.

representative government, constitutional government, home rule, dominion rule [Brit.], colonial government; self-government, autonomy, self-determination; republicanism, federalism; socialism; communism; authoritarianism; totalitarianism; bureaucracy; martial law; feudal system, feudalism.

state, realm, commonwealth, country, power, body politic.

ruler, person in authority, lord, etc., 745; judicature, etc., 965; cabinet, etc. (*council*), 696; seat of government, headquarters.

V. **authorize,** empower, etc., 760; warrant, dictate.

rule, sway, command, control, administer, govern, direct, lead, preside over, be at the head of, reign.

dominate, have the upper (*or* whip) hand; preponderate, boss [*colloq.*]; override, overrule, overawe; lord it over, keep under, bend to one's will, have it all one's own way, be master of the situation, take the lead, lay down the law.

Adj. **ruling,** regnant, dominant, paramount, supreme, predominant, preponderant, in the ascendant, influential; imperious, dictatorial, peremptory; authoritative, executive, administrative, official, gubernatorial, bureaucratic, departmental.

sovereign; regal, royal, royalist, monarchical, kingly; dynastic, imperial, autocratic; oligarchic, democratic, republican.

[1]Implying the action of the will of one mind over the will of another.

Adv. in the name of, by the authority of, at one's command, in virtue of, under the auspices of.

738. [Absence of authority] LAXITY.—*N.* laxity; laxness, looseness, slackness; toleration, lenity, etc., 740; relaxation; freedom, etc., 748.

anarchy, interregnum; misrule, license, insubordination, mob rule, mob law, lynch law, nihilism, reign of violence.

Deprivation of power: dethronement, impeachment, deposition, abdication; usurpation.

V. be lax, hold a loose rein; give the reins to, give rope enough, give free rein to; tolerate; relax; misrule.

have one's fling, act without authority, act on one's own responsibility, usurp authority.

dethrone, depose; abdicate.

Adj. lax, loose; slack, remiss, negligent, etc., 460; weak.

relaxed, licensed, unbridled; anarchic *or* anarchical, nihilistic; unauthorized.

739. SEVERITY.—*N.* severity; strictness, harshness, rigor, stringency, austerity, inclemency; arrogance, etc., 885.

arbitrary power; absolutism, despotism; dictatorship, autocracy, tyranny, domination, oppression, assumption, usurpation; inquisition, reign of terror, iron rule, coercion, etc., 744; martial law.

bureaucracy, red-tapism, officialism.

tyrant, disciplinarian, martinet, stickler, despot, autocrat, oppressor, inquisitor, extortioner.

V. arrogate, assume, usurp, take liberties; domineer, bully, tyrannize, put on the screw, be hard upon, ill-treat, rule with a rod of iron, oppress, override, trample under foot, ride roughshod over; coerce, etc., 744.

Adj. severe, strict, hard, harsh, dour [Scot.], rigid, stern, rigorous, uncompromising, exacting, searching, inexorable, inflexible, obdurate, austere, relentless, stringent, strict, strait-laced, peremptory, absolute, arbitrary, imperative, coercive, tyrannical, extortionate, oppressive, cruel, arrogant; formal, punctilious.

Adv. with a high (*or* strong, tight, heavy) hand.

740. MILDNESS.—*N.* mildness, lenity, moderation, temperateness; tolerance, toleration, mildness, gentleness; favor; indulgence, clemency, mercy, forbearance, quarter, compassion, etc., 914.

V. be lenient, tolerate, bear with; spare the vanquished, give quarter; indulge, spoil.

Adj. lenient, mild, gentle, tolerant, indulgent, easy, moderate, complaisant, easygoing; clement, compassionate, forbearing; long-suffering.

741. COMMAND.—*N.* command, order, ordinance, act, fiat, bidding, word, call, beck, nod; direction, injunction, charge, instructions; dispatch, message.

demand, exaction, imposition, requisition, claim, requirement, ultimatum; request, etc., 765.

decree, dictate, dictation, mandate, precept; prescript, writ, ordination, bull, edict, dispensation, prescription, enactment, law, act; warrant, passport, summons, subpoena, citation; word of command, order of the day.

V. command, order, decree, enact, ordain, dictate, direct, give orders, issue a command; call to order; assume the command.

prescribe, set, appoint, mark out; set (*or* prescribe, impose) a task; set to work.

bid, enjoin, charge, instruct; require, demand, exact, impose, tax.

claim, lay claim to, reclaim.

cite, summon, call for, send for; subpoena; beckon.

Adj. commanding, authoritative, imperative, decisive, final.

Adv. in a commanding tone; by a stroke (*or* dash) of the pen; by order.

742. DISOBEDIENCE.—*N.* disobedience, insubordination, contumacy; infraction, infringement, violation.

revolt, rebellion, mutiny, outbreak, rising, uprising, insurrection, riot, tumult, strike.

sedition, treason; lese majesty; defection, secession, revolution; bolshevism.

insurgent, mutineer, rebel, traitor, communist, Fenian, Sinn Feiner, Red, Bolshevist, seceder, Secessionist [esp., U. S. hist.] *or* Secesh [*colloq. or slang*, U. S.]; apostate, renegade, anarchist.

V. disobey, violate, infringe; shirk, slack; defy, set at defiance, run riot, take the law into one's own hands; kick over the traces; refuse to support, bolt [*politics*].

resist, strike, rise, rise in arms; secede, mutiny, rebel.

Adj. disobedient, unruly, ungovernable; insubordinate, restive, refractory, defiant, contumacious; recusant, recalcitrant.

lawless, riotous, mutinous, seditious, insurgent, revolutionary.

743. OBEDIENCE.—*N.* obedience, observance, compliance; submission, subjection; nonresistance, passivity, resignation, submissiveness, ductility, obsequiousness, servility.

allegiance, loyalty, fealty, homage, deference, devotion; constancy, fidelity.

V. obey, submit, etc., 725; comply, do one's bidding, attend to orders, serve faithfully (*or* loyally, devotedly, without question); be resigned to, be submissive to; serve, etc., 746; play second fiddle.

Adj. obedient, law-abiding, complying, compliant; loyal, faithful, devoted; under beck and call, under control.

resigned, passive; submissive, etc., 725; unresisting, pliant.

Adv. as you please, if you please; in compliance with, in obedience to.

744. COMPULSION.—*N.* compulsion, coercion, constraint; restraint, etc., 751; enforcement, draft, conscription; eminent domain.

force; brute (*or* main, physical) force; the sword; mob law, martial law.

necessity, etc., 601; spur of necessity, Hobson's choice.

V. compel, force, make, drive, dragoon, coerce, constrain, enforce, necessitate, oblige.

extort, wring from, force upon, drag into; bind, pin down; require; tax, put in force; commandeer; restrain, etc., 751.

Adj. compelling, coercive, inexorable, compulsory, obligatory, stringent, peremptory, binding.

Adv. forcibly, by force, by force of arms; on compulsion, perforce, under protest, in spite of, in one's teeth; against one's will.

745. MASTER.—*N.* master, lord, commander, commandant, captain, chief, chieftain; paterfamilias [*Rom. law*], patriarch; sahib [India], head, senior, governor, ruler, dictator, leader, director, boss; sachem, sagamore.

potentate; liege, liege lord, suzerain, overlord, sovereign, monarch, crowned head, emperor, king, majesty, protector, president; autocrat, despot, tyrant, oligarch, dictator.

caesar, kaiser, czar, sultan, caliph, mogul, great mogul, mikado, inca; prince, duke, etc. (*nobility*), 875; archduke, doge; maharaja, raja, emir, nizam, nawab [*Indian ruling chiefs*].

empress, queen, sultana, czarina, princess, infanta, duchess, maharani, rani [both Hindu], begum [Moham.].

regent, viceroy, khedive, pasha, bey, mandarin.

the authorities, the powers that be, the government; staff, official, man in office, person in authority.

Military authorities: marshal, field marshal, generalissimo; commander in chief, general, brigadier general, brigadier, lieutenant general, major general, colonel, lieutenant colonel, major, captain, lieutenant, sublieutenant; officer, staff officer, aide-de-camp, adjutant, ensign, cornet, cadet, subaltern; noncommissioned officer; sergeant, top sergeant, corporal.

Civil authorities: mayor, prefect, chancellor, magistrate, syndic; burgomaster, seneschal, alderman, warden, constable.

Naval authorities: admiral, admiralty; commodore, captain, commander, lieutenant; skipper, master, mate.

746. SERVANT.—*N.* servant, retainer, follower, henchman, servitor, domestic, menial, help [*local*], employee; attaché [F.], official.

subject, liege, liegeman.

retinue, suite, cortege, staff, court; office force, clerical staff, clerical force, workers, associate workers, employees, the help.

attendant, squire, usher, apprentice; page, buttons [*colloq.*]; trainbearer, cupbearer; waiter, butler, lackey, footman, flunky [*colloq.*]; boy [*any colored male servant, as in the Orient, South Africa, etc.*]; valet, equerry, groom, jockey, hostler *or* ostler, orderly, messenger, caddie; secretary, stenographer, clerk, agent, underling, understrapper; man.

maid, maidservant; girl, help [*local*], handmaid, lady's maid, nurse, ayah [India], nursemaid; cook, scullion, Cinderella; general servant [Brit.], general-housework maid [U. S.], general [*colloq.*]; washerwoman, laundress, charwoman.

dependent, hanger-on, satellite, parasite, protégé [F.], ward, hireling, mercenary, puppet, creature; serf, vassal, thrall, slave, Negro, helot; bondsman, bondswoman; bondslave; villein [*hist.*], churl [*hist.*].

V. **serve,** minister to, help, co-operate; wait (*or* attend, dance attendance) upon; squire, valet, tend, do for [*colloq.*].

Adj. **serviceable,** useful, helpful, co-operative; at one's call.

servile, slavish, subject, thrall, bond; subservient, obsequious, base, fawning, truckling, sycophantic, parasitic, cringing.

747. [Insignia of authority] SCEPTER.—*N.* Regal: scepter, orb; pall; robes of state, ermine, purple; crown, coronet, diadem; triple plume; flail [Egyptian]; signet seal.

Ecclesiastical: tiara, triple crown; ring, keys; miter, crozier, crook, staff; cardinal's hat; bishop's apron (*or* sleeves, lawn, gaiters), fillet.

Military: epaulet, star, bar, eagle, crown [Brit.], oak leaf, Sam Browne belt; chevron, stripe.

caduceus; Mercury's staff (*or* rod, wand); mace, fasces, ax, truncheon, staff, baton, wand, rod; flag, etc. (*insignia*), 550; regalia; toga, mantle; decoration, title, etc., 877; portfolio.

throne, divan; woolsack [*seat of English Lord Chancellor in the House of Lords*], chair, seat, dais.

talisman, amulet, charm, sign.

748. FREEDOM.—*N.* **freedom,** liberty, independence; license, indulgence.

scope, range, latitude, play, free play (*or* scope), swing, full swing, elbowroom, margin, rope, wide berth.

franchise; prerogative, etc., 924.

freeman, freedman, citizen, denizen.

immunity, exemption; emancipation, etc., 750; right, privilege.

autonomy, self-government; free trade; self-determination, non-interference; Monroe Doctrine [U. S.].

independent, free lance, freethinker, free trader.

V. **be free,** have scope (*or* one's own way), do what one likes, go at large, feel at home, stand on one's rights.

free, liberate, set free, etc., 750; give the reins to; make free of, enfranchise.

Adj. **free,** independent, at large, loose, scot-free; unconstrained, unconfined, unchecked, unhindered, unobstructed, uncontrolled, ungoverned, unchained, unshackled, unfettered, unbridled, uncurbed, unmuzzled, unvanquished.

unrestricted, unlimited, unconditional; absolute; with unlimited power (*or* opportunity); discretionary.

unbiased, unprejudiced, uninfluenced; spontaneous.

free and easy, at ease, at one's ease; quite at home.

exempt, immune, freed, freeborn; autonomous, freehold.

gratuitous, gratis, etc., 815; for nothing, for love.

Adv. freely, at will, with no restraint.

749. SUBJECTION.—*N.* subjection; dependence, subordination; thrall, thralldom, subjugation, bondage, serfdom; feudalism, vassalage, slavery, enslavement; conquest.

service; servitude, employ, tutelage, constraint, yoke, submission, obedience.

V. be subject, be at the mercy of, depend upon; fall a prey to, fall under, play second fiddle; serve, etc., 746; obey, etc., 743; submit, etc., 725.

subjugate, subject, tame, break in; master, tread down, weigh down, keep under, enthrall, enslave, lead captive, rule, etc., 737; hold in bondage (*or* leading strings).

Adj. subject, dependent, subordinate; feudal, feudatory; under control; in leading strings, in harness; servile, slavish, enslaved, downtrodden; henpecked; under one's thumb, tied to one's apron strings, at one's beck and call; liable.

Adv. under; under orders (*or* command), at one's orders.

750. LIBERATION.—*N.* liberation, disengagement, release, emancipation, Emancipation Proclamation; enfranchisement, manumission; discharge, dismissal.

deliverance, etc., 672; redemption, extrication, acquittance, absolution, acquittal, escape.

V. liberate, free, set free, emancipate, release; enfranchise, manumit; demobilize, disband, discharge, dismiss; let go, let loose, let out, deliver, etc., 672; absolve, acquit.

unfetter, untie, loose, loosen, relax; unbolt, unbar, unhand, unbind, unchain, disengage, disentangle; clear, extricate; reprieve.

Adj. liberated, freed; foot-loose, one's own master.

Adv. at large, at liberty; adrift.

751. RESTRAINT.—*N.* restraint; hindrance, etc., 706; coercion, compulsion, constraint, repression; discipline, control; limitation, restriction, protection, monopoly; prohibition, economic pressure.

confinement, durance, duress; imprisonment, incarceration, thrall, thralldom, limbo, captivity; blockade.

keep, care, charge, custody, ward.

repressionist, monopolist, protectionist.

V. **restrain,** check, restrict, debar, hinder, constrain, coerce, compel, curb, harness, control; hold in leash, withhold, repress, suppress, keep under; smother, pull in, rein in, hold, prohibit.

fasten, enchain, fetter, shackle, trammel; bridle, muzzle, gag, pinion, manacle, handcuff, hobble, bind, swathe, swaddle; tether, picket, tie, secure.

confine, shut up (*or* in), lock up, box up, bottle up, cork up, seal up, blockade, hem in, bolt in, wall in, rail in; impound, pen, coop; inclose, cage, imprison, immure, incarcerate, entomb; put in irons, cast into prison.

arrest, take into custody; take (*or* make) prisoner, lead captive, send to prison, commit; give in charge (*or* custody).

Adj. **restrained,** constrained, repressive, suppressive; imprisoned, pent up, wedged in; on parole; doing time [*colloq. or slang*], in custody.

stiff, narrow, prudish, strait-laced, hidebound.

Adv. **under restraint** (*or* lock and key, hatches), under discipline; in prison, in jail, in durance vile, in confinement; behind bars, in captivity, under arrest.

752. [Means of restraint] PRISON.—*N.* **prison,** prisonhouse; jail, cage, coop, den, cell; stronghold, fortress, keep, donjon, dungeon, Bastille, penitentiary, state prison, lockup, station house, station [*colloq.*], pen [*also slang for penitentiary*], pound; penal settlement; workhouse [U. S.; *in England, a workhouse is a poorhouse*], reformatory, reform school.

Restraining devices: shackle, bond, gyve, fetter, irons, pinion, manacle, handcuff, straight jacket, stocks, pillory; vise, bandage, splint, strap; yoke, collar, halter, harness; muzzle, gag, bit, curb, snaffle, bridle; rein, reins, lines [U. S. and dial. Eng.], ribbons [*colloq.*]; tether, picket, band, chain, cord.

bar, bolt, lock, padlock; rail, paling, palisade; wall, fence, barrier, barricade.

drag, brake, check, etc. (*hindrance*), 706.

753. KEEPER.—*N.* **keeper,** custodian, ranger, gamekeeper, warder, jailer, turnkey, castellan, guard; watch, watchdog, watchman, concierge [F.], sentry, sentinel; coastguard.

escort, bodyguard; convoy.

guardian, protector, governor; duenna, governess, nurse.

754. PRISONER.—*N.* **prisoner,** convict, captive, close prisoner.

V. **stand committed;** be imprisoned.

Adj. **imprisoned,** in prison, in custody, in charge, behind bars, under lock and key, under hatches.

755. [Vicarious authority] COMMISSION.—*N.* **commission,**

delegation; consignment, assignment; proxy, power of attorney, deputation, legation, mission, embassy; agency.

errand, charge, brevet, diploma, permit.

appointment, nomination, charter; ordination; installation, inauguration, investiture; accession, coronation, enthronement.

V. commission, delegate, depute; consign, assign, commit, charge, intrust, authorize.

accredit, engage, hire, bespeak, appoint, name, nominate, return; ordain, install, induct, inaugurate, invest, crown; enroll, enlist; employ, empower.

Adv. instead of, in one's stead, in one's place; as proxy for.

756. ANNULMENT.—*N.* annulment, nullification, cancellation, abrogation, revocation, repeal.

dismissal, *congé* [F.], sack [*slang*], deposition, dethronement; disestablishment, disendowment.

countermand, repudiation, retractation, recantation; abolition, abolishment; dissolution.

V. annul, cancel, destroy, abolish, abrogate, revoke, repeal, rescind, reverse, retract, recall; overrule, override; set aside; disannul, dissolve, quash, nullify, nol-pros [*law, short for nolle prosequi*], disestablish; countermand, counterorder, throw overboard.

disclaim, deny, ignore, repudiate; recant, break off.

dismiss, discard; turn out, cast off (*or* adrift, aside, away); send off, send away, discharge, get rid of, bounce [*slang*]; fire, sack [*both slang*].

cashier, oust, unseat, dethrone, depose, unfrock, strike off the roll, disbar.

757. RESIGNATION.—*N.* resignation, retirement, abdication; renunciation, retractation, retraction, disclaimer, abandonment, relinquishment.

V. resign, give up, throw up, lay down, abjure, renounce, forego, disclaim, retract, deny, desert.

vacate, abdicate, retire, tender (*or* hand in) one's resignation.

758. CONSIGNEE.—*N.* consignee, trustee, nominee; committee.

functionary, curator; treasurer, etc., 801; agent, factor, steward, bailiff, clerk, secretary, attorney, solicitor, proctor, broker, underwriter, commission agent, factotum, caretaker, employee; servant, etc., 746.

negotiator, go-between; middleman.

delegate, commissioner; emissary, envoy, messenger.

diplomatist, diplomat, ambassador, plenipotentiary, diplomatic agent, representative, resident, consul, legate, etc., 534; attaché [F.].

salesman, traveler, traveling salesman, commercial traveler, drummer, traveling man.

759. DEPUTY.—*N.* deputy, substitute, proxy, delegate, representative, alternate; vice-president.

regent, vicegerent, viceroy, minister, premier, chancellor, provost, warden, lieutenant, consul, ambassador; delegate, etc., 758.

team, eight, nine, eleven; captain, champion.

V. **represent,** stand for, appear for, hold a brief for, answer for; stand in the shoes of; stand in the stead of.

delegate, depute, empower, commission, substitute, accredit.

Adj. **acting,** vice, viceregal; accredited to; delegated, representative.

Adv. **in behalf of,** in the place of, as representing, by proxy.

760. PERMISSION.—*N.* permission, leave, allowance, sufferance, tolerance, toleration, connivance; liberty, law, license, concession, grace; indulgence, favor, dispensation, exemption, release; authorization, accordance, admission.

permit, warrant, sanction, authority, pass, passport; license, carte blanche [F.], grant, charter, patent.

V. **permit,** let, allow, admit; suffer, tolerate, recognize; concede, etc., 762; accord, vouchsafe, favor, humor, gratify, indulge, wink at, connive at.

grant, empower, charter, enfranchise, privilege, license, authorize, warrant, sanction; intrust, commission.

absolve, release, exonerate, dispense with.

Adj. **permitted,** permissible, allowable, lawful, legitimate, legal, legalized, chartered, unforbidden.

Adv. by (*or* with) leave, under favor of, by all means.

761. PROHIBITION.—*N.* prohibition, inhibition; veto, interdict, interdiction, injunction, embargo, ban, taboo, proscription, restriction; contraband; forbidden fruit; Volstead Act, 18th amendment [all U. S.].

V. **prohibit,** inhibit, forbid, disallow; bar, debar, hinder, restrain, etc., 751; withhold, limit, circumscribe, clip the wings of, restrict; interdict, taboo, proscribe; exclude, shut out.

Adj. **prohibitive,** prohibitory; proscriptive; restrictive, exclusive.

prohibited, unlicensed, contraband, taboo, illegal, unauthorized.

762. CONSENT.—*N.* consent; assent, etc., 488; acquiescence, approval, compliance, agreement, concession, accession, acknowledgment, acceptance; permit, etc. (*permission*), 760; promise, etc., 768.

settlement, adjustment, ratification, confirmation.

V. **consent;** assent, etc., 488; yield assent, admit, allow, con-

cede, grant, yield; acknowledge, give consent, comply with, acquiesce, agree to, accede, accept, close with, satisfy, settle, come
to terms; deign, vouchsafe, promise.

Adj. willing, compliant, agreeable [*colloq.*], eager.

763. OFFER.—*N.* **offer,** proffer, tender, bid, overture, proposal, proposition; motion, invitation, offering.

V. **offer,** proffer, present, tender; bid; propose, move, make a
motion, start, invite, place at one's disposal; make possible, put
forward, press, urge upon, hold out.

volunteer, come forward, be a candidate, offer (*or* present) oneself, stand for, bid for; seek; be at one's service.

Adj. in the market, for sale, to let, disengaged, on hire; at one's
disposal.

764. REFUSAL.—*N.* **refusal,** rejection, denial, declension, flat
(*or* point-blank) refusal; repulse, rebuff; discountenance, disapprobation.

negation, abnegation, protest, renunciation, disclaimer; dissent, etc., 489; revocation, annulment.

V. **refuse,** reject, deny, decline, turn down [*slang*], dissent, etc.,
489; negative, withhold one's assent, grudge, begrudge; stand
aloof, be deaf to, turn one's back upon, discountenance, forswear,
set aside.

resist, repel, repulse, rebuff, deny oneself, discard, repudiate,
rescind, disclaim, protest.

Adj. **uncomplying,** deaf to, noncompliant, unconsenting; recusant, dissentient.

Adv. on no account, not for the world, not on your life! [*colloq.*].

765. REQUEST.—*N.* **request,** requisition; claim, demand, etc.,
741; petition, suit, prayer, solicitation, invitation, entreaty, im-
portunity, supplication, invocation.

motion, overture, application, canvass, address, appeal, imprecation; proposal, proposition.

V. **request,** ask, beg, crave, sue, pray, petition, solicit, canvass,
invite, beg leave, beg a boon, apply to, call to, call for; make a
request, make application, claim, demand; offer up prayers.

entreat, beseech, plead, supplicate, implore; conjure, adjure;
apostrophize, cry to, kneel to, appeal to; invoke, evoke; press,
urge, importune, dun, clamor for, cry aloud, cry for help.

Adj. **importunate,** clamorous, urgent, solicitous; cap in hand.

Adv. **please,** prithee, do, pray; be so good as, be good enough;
have the goodness, vouchsafe, will you, I pray thee, if you please.

766. [**Negative request**] **DEPRECATION.**—*N.* **deprecation,**
expostulation; intercession, mediation, protest, remonstrance.

V. **deprecate,** protest, expostulate, enter a protest, remonstrate.

Adj. **deprecatory,** expostulatory, intercessory.

unsought, unbesought; unasked.

767. PETITIONER.—*N.* petitioner, solicitor, applicant, suppliant, supplicant, suitor, candidate, claimant, aspirant, competitor, bidder; place hunter.

salesman, drummer, etc., 758; canvasser.

beggar, mendicant, panhandler [*slang*], cadger.

hotel runner, runner [*both cant*], steerer [*colloq.*], barker [*colloq.*].

sycophant, parasite, etc. (*servility*), 886.

768. PROMISE.—*N.* promise, undertaking, word, troth, plight, pledge, parole, word of honor, vow, oath, profession, assurance, warranty, guarantee, insurance, obligation, contract, stipulation.

engagement, affiance, betrothal, marriage contract (*or* vow); plighted faith.

V. **promise,** undertake, engage; make (*or* form, enter into) an engagement; bind (*or* pledge) oneself; vow, swear, give (*or* pledge) one's word; betroth, plight faith.

assure, warrant, guarantee, covenant, agree, vouch for, attest; answer for, be answerable for; secure, give security, underwrite.

Adj. **promissory,** votive, under hand and seal, upon oath, upon affirmation.

promised, affianced, pledged, bound, committed, compromised.

Adv. as true as I live; in all soberness; upon my honor; my word for it.

769. COMPACT.—*N.* compact, contract, specialty, deal [*colloq.*], agreement, bargain; pact, bond, covenant, indenture [*law*]; stipulation, settlement, convention; compromise, negotiation.

treaty, protocol, concordat, charter, Magna Charta, pragmatic sanction.

ratification, completion, signature, seal, bond.

V. **contract,** covenant, agree for; engage, etc. (*promise*), 768.

negotiate, treat, stipulate, make terms; bargain.

conclude, close, close with, complete, strike a bargain; come to terms (*or* an understanding); compromise, settle; confirm, ratify, clinch, subscribe, underwrite; indorse, sign, seal.

Adj. **contractual,** complete, agreed; signed, sealed, and delivered.

Adv. **as agreed upon,** as promised, according to the contract.

770. CONDITIONS.—*N.* conditions, terms, articles, articles of agreement; memorandum, clauses, provisions, proviso, covenant, stipulation, obligation, ultimatum.

V. **condition,** stipulate, insist upon, make a point of; bind, tie up; fence in, hedge in, make (*or* come to) terms.

Adj. **conditional**, provisional, guarded, fenced, hedged in.

Adv. **conditionally**, provisionally, on condition; with a string to it [*colloq.*], with a reservation.

771. SECURITY.—*N.* **security**, guaranty, guarantee; gage, bond, tie, pledge, mortgage, debenture; bill of sale, lien, collateral, bail, stake, deposit, earnest.

promissory note; bill, bill of exchange; I O U; personal security; covenant.

acceptance, indorsement, signature, execution, stamp, seal.

sponsor, surety, bail, hostage; godchild, godfather, godmother.

authentication, verification, warrant, certificate, voucher, receipt.

deed, instrument, title deed, indenture; charter, paper, parchment, settlement, will, testament, codicil.

V. **give security,** give bail, go bail; pawn, put in pawn pledge, mortgage.

guarantee, warrant, assure; accept, indorse, underwrite, insure.

execute, stamp; sign, seal.

Adj. **pledged,** pawned, in pawn, at stake, on deposit, as earnest.

772. OBSERVANCE.—*N.* **observance,** performance, compliance, acquiescence, concurrence; obedience, etc , 743; fulfillment, satisfaction, discharge; acquittance, acquittal; adhesion, ackowledgment; fidelity.

V. **observe,** comply with, respect, acknowledge, abide by; cling to, adhere to, be faithful to, act up to; meet, fulfill, carry out, execute, perform, discharge, keep one's word (*or* pledge).

Adj. **observant,** faithful, true, loyal, honorable, etc., 939; punctual, punctilious, scrupulous, as good as one's word.

Adv. to the letter.

773. NONOBSERVANCE.—*N.* **nonobservance,** noncompliance, evasion, failure, omission, neglect, slackness, laxness, laxity, informality; lawlessness, disobedience, etc., 742; bad faith, etc., 940.

infringement, infraction; violation, transgression; piracy, literary theft.

V. **evade,** fail, neglect, omit, elude, cut [*colloq.*], set aside, ignore; shut (*or* close) one's eyes to.

infringe, transgress, violate, steal, pirate [*a book, etc.*].

discard, repudiate, protest, nullify, declare null and void, cancel, forfeit.

Adj. **elusive,** evasive, slack, lax, casual, slippery; nonobservant.

774. COMPROMISE.—*N.* **compromise,** composition, middle term, compensation, adjustment, mutual concession.

V. **compromise,** commute, compound, split the difference, meet one halfway, give and take, come to terms, submit to arbitration, patch up, arrange, straighten out, adjust, agree, make the best of, make a virtue of necessity.

POSSESSIVE RELATIONS[1]

(1) Property

775. ACQUISITION.—*N.* **acquisition,** procurement; purchase, nheritance; gift, etc., 784.

recovery, redemption, salvage, find.

gain, thrift, money-making, pelf, lucre, filthy lucre, the main chance.

profit, earnings, wages, salary, emolument, income, remuneration; winnings, pickings, perquisite; proceeds, produce, product; outcome, output; return, fruit, crop, harvest; benefit; prize; wealth, etc., 803.

V. **acquire,** get, gain, win, earn, obtain, procure, gather; collect, pick, pick up, glean, find, light upon, come across, come at; scrape up (*or* together); get in, net, bag, secure; derive, draw, get in the harvest.

profit, turn to profit (*or* account), make capital out of, make money by, obtain a return, reap the fruits of; gain an advantage; make (*or* coin, raise) money, raise funds; realize, clear, produce, take, receive, come by, inherit.

recover, get back, regain, retrieve, redeem.

Adj. **profitable,** productive, advantageous, gainful, remunerative, paying, lucrative.

Adv. in the way of gain; for money; at interest.

776. LOSS.—*N.* **loss,** forfeiture, lapse; privation, bereavement, deprivation, riddance; damage, squandering, waste.

V. **lose,** incur a loss, miss, mislay, let slip, be deprived of, be without, forfeit.

squander, lavish, get rid of, waste.

Adj. **bereft,** bereaved, deprived of, shorn of, denuded, minus [*colloq., exc. in math.*], cut off; rid of, quit of, out of pocket, lost.

777. POSSESSION.—*N.* **possession,** ownership, proprietorship, occupancy, hold, holding, tenure, tenancy, dependency.

exclusive possession, monopoly, retention, corner.

future possession, heritage, inheritance, heirship, reversion; primogeniture.

V. **possess,** have, hold, occupy, enjoy, be possessed of, own, command, inherit.

[1]That is, relations which concern property.

monopolize, corner, engross, forestall, appropriate.

belong to, appertain to, pertain to; be in one's possession, vest in.

Adj. possessing, worth, possessed of, master of, in possession of; endowed (*or* blest, fraught, laden, charged) with.

possessed, on hand, in hand, in store, in stock; at one's command, at one's disposal.

777a. EXEMPTION.—*N.* exemption, exception, immunity, privilege, release.

V. not have, not possess, not own, be without.

Adj. devoid of, exempt from, without, unpossessed of, unblest with; immune from.

unpossessed; untenanted, vacant, without an owner.

778. [Joint possession] PARTICIPATION.—*N.* participation, joint tenancy; joint (*or* common) stock; partnership; communion; community of possessions, communism, collectivism, socialism; co-operation.

participator, sharer, partner; shareholder; joint tenant; tenants in common; coheir.

communist, communalist, collectivist, socialist.

V. participate, partake, share, share in, join in, go shares, go cahoots [*slang*], go halves; share and share alike.

communize, communalize; have (*or* possess) in common.

Adj. communistic, socialistic; co-operative, profit-sharing.

Adv. in common, share and share alike; on shares.

779. POSSESSOR.—*N.* possessor, holder, occupant, occupier, tenant, tenant at will, lessee, lodger.

owner; proprietor, proprietress, master, mistress, lord.

landholder, landowner, landlord, landlady; lord of the manor, laird [*Scot.*], landed gentry.

Future possessor: heir, heir apparent, heir presumptive; inheritor, heiress, inheritrix.

780. PROPERTY.—*N.* property, possession, tenure; ownership, etc., 777.

estate, interest, right, title, claim, demand, holding, vested interest; use, trust, benefit; term, lease, settlement; remainder, reversion.

dower, dowry, jointure, inheritance, heritage, patrimony, legacy.

assets, belongings, means, resources, circumstances; wealth, etc., 803; money, etc., 800; estate and effects.

realty, real estate, land, lands, landed (*or* real) property; tenements; plant, fixtures; ground; freehold, copyhold, leasehold.

manor, domain, demesne; farm, plantation, ranch.

territory, state, kingdom, principality, realm, empire, protectorate, dependency, sphere of influence, mandate.

personalty, personal property (*or* estate, effects), chattels, goods, effects, movables; stock, stock in trade, things, paraphernalia, equipage, appurtenances; income, etc., 810.

baggage, luggage [esp. in Eng.], impedimenta, bag and baggage; cargo.

V. **possess,** etc., 777; be the possessor, own; inherit.

Adj. landed, hereditary, entailed, real, personal.

Adv. **to one's credit,** to one's account; to the good.

781. RETENTION.—*N.* retention, detention, custody; tenacity, firm hold, grasp, gripe, grip, clutches, talon, claw, fang, tentacle.

captive, prisoner, bird in hand.

V. **retain,** keep, hold, hold fast, clinch, clench, clutch, grasp, gripe, hug; secure, withhold, detain; hold (*or* keep) back; husband, reserve; have (*or* keep) in stock; entail, tie up, settle.

Adj. **retentive,** tenacious.

782. RIDDANCE.—*N.* riddance, relinquishment, abandonment, renunciation, dereliction; cession, surrender, dispensation; resignation.

derelict, jetsam; abandoned farm [U. S.]; waif, foundling.

V. **relinquish,** give up, surrender, yield, cede; let go, let slip; spare, drop, resign, forego, renounce, abandon, give away, dispose of, part with; lay aside, set aside, discard, cast off, dismiss; maroon.

cast (*or* throw, fling) away, jettison.

supersede, give notice to quit, give warning; be (*or* get) rid of; eject.

divorce, cut off, desert, disinherit; separate.

Adj. **relinquished,** cast off, derelict; disowned, disinherited, divorced.

783. TRANSFER [of property].—*N.* transfer, conveyance, assignment, alienation, conveyancing, transmission, sale, lease, release, exchange, barter; succession, reversion.

V. **transfer,** convey, alienate, assign, grant, consign; make over, hand over, transmit, negotiate; hand down; exchange.

change hands, devolve, succeed; require, come into possession.

disinherit; dispossess, etc., 789; substitute.

Adj. **transferable,** alienable, negotiable, reversional, transmissive; inherited.

784. GIVING.—*N.* giving, bestowal, presentation, concession, cession; delivery, consignment, dispensation, endowment; investment, investiture; award, recompense, etc., 973.

charity, almsgiving, liberality, generosity.

gift, donation, present, boon, favor, benefaction, grant, offering, bonus, oblation, sacrifice.

allowance, contribution, subscription, subsidy, tribute.

bequest, legacy, devise, will, dot, dowry, dower.

gratuity, alms, largess, bounty, dole, help, offertory, honorarium, Christmas box, tip, baksheesh, consideration.

bribe, bait, peace offering; graft [*colloq.*].

giver, grantor, donor, testator; investor, subscriber, contributor; fairy godmother.

V. **deliver,** hand, pass, assign, hand (*or* make, deliver, turn) over.

pay, etc., 807; render, impart, communicate.

concede, cede, yield, part with, shed; spend, sacrifice.

give, bestow, donate, confer, grant; accord, award, assign, offer; present, give away, dispense, dispose of; give (*or* deal) out, fork out [*slang*]; allow, contribute, subscribe.

invest, endow, settle upon; bequeath, leave, devise.

furnish, supply, help, administer to, afford, spare, accommodate with, indulge with, favor with; lavish, pour on, thrust upon.

bribe, tip; grease the palm [*slang*].

Adj. **charitable,** eleemosynary, tributary; gratis, etc., 815; donative.

785. RECEIVING.—*N.* **receiving,** acquisition, etc., 775; reception, acceptance, admission.

recipient, receiver; assignee, legatee, grantee, lessee; beneficiary, pensioner.

income, etc. (*receipt*), 810.

V. **receive;** take, etc., 789; pocket; acquire, etc., 775; admit, take in, catch, accept.

be received; come in, come to hand, go into one's pocket; fall to one's lot (*or* share), accrue.

Adj. **receiving,** recipient; stipendiary, pensionary.

received, given, allowed; secondhand.

786. APPORTIONMENT.—*N.* **apportionment,** allotment, consignment, assignment, allocation, appropriation; distribution, division, deal; partition, administration.

portion, dividend, share, allotment, lot, measure, dose; dole, meed, pittance; ration; ratio, proportion, quota, modicum, allowance.

V. **apportion,** divide; distribute, administer, dispense; allot, allocate, detail, cast, share, mete; portion (*or* parcel, dole) out; deal, carve.

partition, assign, appropriate, appoint.

Adv. **respectively,** each to each; by lot; in equal shares.

787. LENDING.—*N.* **lending,** loan, advance, accommodation, mortgage, etc., 771; investment.

lender, pawnbroker, my uncle [*slang*], moneylender, usurer, Shylock.

V. **lend,** advance, accommodate with; lend on security; loan; pawn.

invest, intrust, place (*or* put) out to interest; place, put; embark, risk, venture, sink.

let, lease, sublet, sublease.

Adv. in advance; on loan, on security.

788. BORROWING.—*N.* borrowing, pledging, pawning.

V. **borrow,** pledge, pawn, put up the spout [*slang*], raise money, raise the wind [*slang*]; run into debt.

hire, rent, farm; take a lease.

appropriate, adopt, apply, imitate, make use of, take; plagiarize, pirate.

789. TAKING.—*N.* taking, reception, appropriation, capture, apprehension, seizure; abduction, abstraction.

dispossession; deprivation, bereavement, disinheritance; attachment, execution, sequestration, confiscation, eviction.

rapacity, rapaciousness, extortion, bloodsucking; theft, etc.,791.

taker, captor, capturer; extortioner *or* extortionist; vampire.

V. **take,** catch, hook, bag, sack, pocket, receive, accept.

reap, crop, cull, pluck, gather, draw.

appropriate, assume, possess oneself of; commandeer [*colloq.*]; help oneself to, make free with, lay under contribution; intercept, scramble for; deprive of.

seize, snatch, abstract, take away (*or* off), run away with; abduct, kidnap, capture, steal, pounce (*or* spring) upon; swoop down upon; take by storm; take prisoner; grapple, embrace, grip, gripe, clasp, grab [*colloq.*], clutch, collar, throttle, claw.

dispossess, take from, take away from; tear from, tear away from, wrench (*or* wrest, wring) from; extort; deprive of, bereave; disinherit, oust, evict, eject, divest; levy, distrain [*law*], confiscate; sequester, sequestrate, usurp; despoil, strip, fleece, bleed [*colloq.*].

Adj. **predatory,** wolfish, rapacious, ravening, ravenous; parasitic; all-devouring, all-engulfing.

790. RESTITUTION.—*N.* restitution, return, restoration, reinstatement, reinvestment, rehabilitation, reparation, atonement; compensation, indemnification; recovery.

V. **restore,** return, give back, render, give up, let go, release, remit; disgorge, recoup, reimburse, compensate, indemnify, reinvest, reinstate, rehabilitate, repair, make good.

recover, get back, retrieve, redeem; take back again.

Adj. **compensatory,** indemnificatory; reversionary, redemptive.

Adv. in full restitution; as partial compensation; to atone for.

791. STEALING.—*N.* stealing, theft, thievery, robbery, rapacity, thievishness, abstraction, appropriation, plagiarism, depredation; kidnaping.

pillage, spoliation, plunder, sack, rapine, brigandage, highway robbery, holdup [*slang*]; raid, foray, piracy, privateering, buccaneering, filibustering; burglary, housebreaking; shoplifting, blackmail.

peculation, embezzlement, fraud, forgery, larceny, pilfering; kleptomania.

V. steal, thieve, rob, purloin, pilfer, filch, bag, crib [*colloq.*], palm; abstract; appropriate, plagiarize.

abduct, convey away, carry off, kidnap, impress, make (*or* run) off with, run away with, spirit away, seize.

plunder, pillage, filibuster, rifle, sack, loot, ransack, spoil, despoil, strip, sweep, gut, forage, levy blackmail, maraud, poach, smuggle, bunko; hold up.

swindle, peculate, embezzle; sponge, pluck, fleece, defraud, obtain under false pretenses.

counterfeit, forge, coin, circulate bad money.

Adj. thievish, light-fingered, piratical; predatory, raptorial.

792. THIEF.—*N.* thief, robber, spoiler, depredator, pillager, marauder; pilferer, plagiarist; harpy, shark [*slang*], smuggler, poacher, kidnaper; crook [*slang*], shoplifter.

pirate, corsair, viking, buccaneer, privateer.

brigand, bandit, filibuster, freebooter, thug, cattle thief, bushranger, mosstrooper [*hist.*], highwayman, footpad, strong-arm man.

pickpocket, cutpurse, light-fingered gentry; sharper; cardsharper, trickster.

swindler, peculator, forger, coiner, counterfeiter; fence, receiver of stolen goods.

burglar, housebreaker, yegg [*slang*], cracksman [*slang*], sneak thief; second-story thief (*or* man).

793. BOOTY.—*N.* booty, spoil, plunder, prize, prey, loot, swag [*cant*]; perquisite, boodle [*polit. cant*], graft [*colloq.*], pork barrel [*polit. cant*], pickings; blackmail; stolen goods.

Adj. looting, plundering, spoliative.

794. BARTER.—*N.* barter, exchange, interchange, Indian gift [*colloq.*].

trade, commerce, buying and selling, traffic, business, custom, transaction, negotiation, bargain; speculation, jobbing, stock-jobbing.

free trade [*opp. to* protection].

V. barter, exchange, truck, swap *or* swop [*colloq. and dial.*]; interchange.

trade, traffic, buy and sell, give and take, carry on (*or* ply) a trade; deal in, speculate.

bargain; drive (*or* make, strike) a bargain; negotiate, bid for; haggle, stickle, dicker, cheapen, beat down, underbid; outbid.

Adj. **commercial,** mercantile, trading; marketable, staple, in the market, for sale; at a bargain, marked down; retail; wholesale.

Adv. across the counter; in the marts of trade.

795. PURCHASE.—*N.* **purchase,** buying, purchasing, shopping.

buyer, purchaser, client, customer, patron, clientele.

V. **buy,** purchase, invest in, procure; shop, market, go a-shopping; rent, hire, repurchase, buy in.

796. SALE.—*N.* **sale,** disposal; auction, custom.

salableness, salability, marketability, vendibility.

seller, vender, vendor [*law*]; merchant, auctioneer.

salesmanship, selling ability.

V. **sell,** vend, dispose of, make a sale, effect a sale; auction, sell at auction, put up to (*or* at) auction; hawk, dump, unload, place, undersell; dispense, offer, retail; deal in, sell off (*or* out), turn into money, realize.

Adj. **salable,** marketable, staple, in demand, popular.

unsalable, unpurchased, unbought, on the shelves, on one's hands.

797. MERCHANT.—*N.* **merchant,** trader, dealer, salesman; money-changer, shopkeeper, shopman; tradesman, tradespeople, tradesfolk.

peddler, hawker, huckster, sutler, vivandière; costermonger; canvasser, solicitor; faker [*slang*].

moneylender, usurer, banker; money-changer, money broker.

jobber, broker; buyer, seller; bear, bull [*Stock Exchange*].

firm, company, house, corporation, concern, trust.

798. MERCHANDISE.—*N.* **merchandise,** ware, commodity, effects, goods, article, stock, produce, staple commodity; stock in trade, cargo.

799. MART.—*N.* **mart,** market, market place; fair, bazaar, exchange, stock exchange, Wheat Pit [*Chicago*]; bourse, curb.

shop, store, department store, chain store, warehouse, depot, emporium, establishment; stall, booth; office, chambers, counting-house, bureau; counter.

(2) Monetary Relations

800. MONEY.—*N.* **money,** finance, funds, treasure, capital, stock; assets, wealth, etc., 803; supplies, ways and means, wherewithal *or* wherewith, sinews of war, almighty dollar, cash.

solvency, responsibility, reliability, solidity, soundness.

sum, amount; balance, balance sheet; sum total; proceeds, receipts.

currency, circulating medium, specie, coin, piece, hard cash; dollar, sterling; pounds, shillings, and pence, £ s. d.; guinea; wallet, roll, wad [*slang*], purse, ready money.

precious metals, gold, silver, copper, bullion, ingot, bar, nugget.

petty cash, pocket money, pin money, spending money, change, small coin.

wampum.

great wealth, money to burn [*colloq.*]; power *or* mint of money [*colloq.*], good sum, millions, thousands.

Science of coins: numismatics.

paper money; bill, money order; note, note of hand; bank note, promissory note; I O U, bond; bill of exchange; draft, check, order, warrant, coupon, debenture, greenback.

V. total, amount to, come to, mount up to.

issue, utter, circulate; fiscalize, monetize.

demonetize, deprive of standard value; cease to issue.

Adj. monetary, pecuniary, fiscal, financial; sterling.

solvent, sound, substantial, good, reliable, responsible, solid, having a good rating; able to pay 100 cents to the dollar.

801. TREASURER.—*N.* treasurer, bursar, purser, banker, financier; receiver, liquidator, steward, trustee, accountant, expert accountant, almoner, paymaster, cashier, teller; money-changer.

802. TREASURY.—*N.* treasury, bank, exchequer, bursary; strongbox, stronghold, strong room; coffer, chest, safe, depository, cash register, cashbox, money box, till.

purse, moneybag, pocketbook, wallet; pocket.

securities, stocks; public stocks (*or* funds, securities); bonds, government bonds, Liberty bonds [U. S.], gilt-edged securities.

803. WEALTH.—*N.* wealth, riches, fortune, opulence, affluence; easy circumstances; independence, competence.

capital, money; great wealth, bonanza, El Dorado; philosopher's stone; the golden touch.

pelf, mammon, lucre, filthy lucre.

means, resources, substance, command of money; property, income, livelihood.

rich man, moneyed man, man of substance; capitalist, millionaire, multimillionaire, plutocrat; nabob, Croesus, Midas.

V. be rich, roll (*or* wallow) in wealth, have money to burn [*colloq.*]; afford, well afford, command money.

become rich, fill one's pocket, feather one's nest, make a fortune; make money; worship mammon, worship the golden calf.

Adj. wealthy, rich, affluent, opulent, moneyed, well-to-do, well off, rolling in riches.

804. POVERTY.—*N.* poverty, indigence, penury, pauperism, destitution, want; need, neediness; lack, necessity, privation, distress, difficulties, wolf at the door, straits; low water [*slang*], impecuniosity.

mendicancy, beggary, mendicity; broken (*or* loss of) fortune; insolvency.

poor man, pauper, mendicant, beggar.

V. **be poor,** want, lack, starve, live from hand to mouth, have seen better days, go to rack and ruin; beg one's bread, run into debt.

impoverish, reduce, reduce to poverty, pauperize, fleece, ruin.

Adj. **poor,** indigent; poverty-stricken, badly off, moneyless, penniless; impecunious, short of money, hard up, seedy [*colloq.*]; barefooted, beggarly, beggared, destitute, reduced, needy, necessitous, distressed, pinched, straitened, embarrassed, involved, insolvent.

805. CREDIT.—*N.* **credit,** trust, score, tally, account.

paper credit, letter of credit, circular note; duplicate; mortgage. lien, draft, securities.

creditor, lender, lessor [*law*], mortgagee; dun, usurer.

V. **credit,** accredit, intrust, keep (*or* run up) an account with; place to one's credit (*or* account); give (*or* take) credit.

Adj. **accredited;** of good credit, of unlimited credit; well rated; credited.

Adv. on credit, to the account of, to the credit of.

806. DEBT.—*N.* **debt,** obligation, liability, debit, score.

arrears, deferred payment, deficit, default, insolvency; bad debt.

interest; premium, usury.

debtor; mortgagor, defaulter, borrower.

V. **be in debt,** owe; incur (*or* contract) a debt, run up a bill, (*or* an account); borrow, run into debt, be in difficulties.

answer for, go bail for; back one's note.

Adj. **liable,** chargeable, answerable for.

indebted, in debt, in embarrassed circumstances, in difficulties; encumbered, involved; insolvent.

unpaid; unrequited, unrewarded; owing, due, in arrear, outstanding.

807. PAYMENT.—*N.* **payment,** discharge, settlement, clearance, liquidation, satisfaction, reckoning, arrangement.

acknowledgment, release; receipt, voucher.

repayment, reimbursement, retribution; pay, money paid.

V. **pay,** defray, make payment; pay one's way, expend, put down, lay down; discharge, settle, foot the bill [*colloq.*]; settle with, satisfy, pay in full, clear, liquidate, pay up; cash, honor a bill, acknowledge; redeem.

repay, refund, reimburse, disgorge, make repayment.

Adj. out of debt, owing nothing, all clear, clear of debt, above-water; solvent.

Adv. money down, cash down, cash on delivery, C.O.D.

808. NONPAYMENT.—*N.* nonpayment; default, defalcation; protest, repudiation.

insolvency, bankruptcy, failure; run upon a bank; overdrawn account.

defaulter, bankrupt, insolvent, insolvent debtor; absconder, welsher [*slang*].

V. not pay, fail, break, stop payment; become insolvent (*or* bankrupt), swindle, run up bills.

protest, dishonor, repudiate, nullify.

Adj. in debt, behindhand, in arrear; beggared, insolvent, bankrupt, ruined.

809. EXPENDITURE.—*N.* expenditure, outgoings, outlay, expenses, disbursement; circulation.

Money paid: payment, etc., 807; pay, etc. (*remuneration*), 973; fee, footing, subsidy, tribute, ransom, bribe, donation, gift; investment; purchase.

deposit, earnest, installment.

V. expend, spend; run (*or* get) through, pay, disburse; lay out, fork out [*slang*]; invest, sink money.

reward, fee, remunerate; give, subscribe, subsidize; bribe.

Adj. lavish, free, liberal; beyond one's income.

expensive, costly, dear, high-priced, precious, high.

810. RECEIPT.—*N.* receipt, value received, income, revenue, return, proceeds; earnings.

rent, rent roll; rental.

premium, bonus, prize, drawings, handout [*slang*].

pension, annuity, pittance, jointure, alimony.

V. receive, get, be in receipt of, have coming in; take money; draw from, derive from; acquire, take.

yield, bring in, afford, pay, return; accrue.

Adj. remunerative, profitable, gainful, well paying, interest-bearing, well invested.

Adv. within one's income.

811. ACCOUNTS.—*N.* accounts, money matters, finance, budget, bill, score, reckoning, account.

bookkeeping, audit, single entry, double entry; ledger, cash-book, journal; balance sheet; receipts, assets; expenditure, liabilities; profit and loss account (*or* statement).

accountant, auditor, actuary, bookkeeper; expert accountant, certified accountant; bank examiner.

V. **keep accounts,** enter, post, post up, book, credit, debit, balance.

812. PRICE.—*N.* price, amount, cost, expense, charge, figure, demand, fare, hire; wages.

dues, duty, toll, tax, impost, tariff, levy; capitation, poll tax; custom, excise, assessment, taxation, tithe, ransom, salvage, towage; brokerage, wharfage, freightage.

worth, rate, value, par value, valuation, appraisement, money's worth; price current, market price, quotation.

V. **price,** set (*or* fix) a price, appraise, assess, charge, demand, ask, require, exact.

fetch, sell for, cost, bring in, yield, afford.

Adj. **taxable,** dutiable, assessable.

813. DISCOUNT.—*N.* discount, abatement, concession, reduction, depreciation, allowance, qualification, setoff, drawback, percentage, rebate.

V. **discount,** bate, rebate, abate, deduct, strike off, mark down, reduce, take off, allow, give, make allowance; depreciate.

Adv. **at a discount,** at a bargain, below par.

814. DEARNESS.—*N.* dearness, expensiveness, costliness, high price; overcharge, extravagance, exorbitance, extortion.

V. **overcharge,** bleed [*colloq.*], skin [*slang*], fleece, extort, profiteer.

pay too much, pay dearly, pay through the nose [*colloq.*].

Adj. **dear,** high, high-priced, expensive, costly, precious; extravagant, exorbitant, extortionate.

at a premium, beyond price, above price; priceless, of priceless value.

Adv. **dear,** dearly; at great cost, at heavy cost, at a high price.

815. CHEAPNESS.—*N.* cheapness, low price, depreciation, bargain, drug in the market.

V. **be cheap,** cost little; come down (*or* fall) in price, be marked down.

buy at a bargain, buy dirt-cheap, have one's money's worth; beat down, cheapen.

Adj. **cheap,** low-priced, low, moderate, reasonable, inexpensive, cheap at the price; dirt-cheap, catchpenny.

reduced, half-price, depreciated, shopworn, marked down, unsalable.

gratuitous, gratis, free, for nothing; costless, without charge, scot-free, complimentary, honorary.

Adv. **at a bargain,** for a mere song; at cost price, at prime cost.

816. LIBERALITY.—*N.* liberality, generosity, munificence;

bounty, bounteousness, hospitality, charity, open (or free) hand, open (or large) heart.

cheerful giver, free giver, patron; benefactor.

V. **be liberal,** spend freely; shower down upon, spare no expense, give with both hands; keep open house.

Adj. **liberal,** free, generous. charitable, hospitable; bountiful, bounteous, ample, handsome; unsparing, ungrudging; unselfish; open-handed large-hearted; munificent, princely.

Adv. ungrudgingly; with open hands, with both hands.

817. ECONOMY.—*N.* economy, frugality; thrift, thriftiness; care, husbandry, retrenchment.

savings; prevention of waste, save-all; parsimony, etc., 819.

V. **economize,** save; retrench, cut down expenses; make both ends meet, meet one's expenses, pay one's way; husband, save (or invest) money; provide against a rainy day.

Adj. **economical,** frugal, careful, thrifty, saving, chary, spare, sparing; parsimonious, etc., 819; sufficient; plain.

818. PRODIGALITY.—*N.* prodigality, wastefulness, unthriftiness, waste; profusion, profuseness; extravagance, lavishness.

prodigal, spendthrift, waster, high roller [*slang*], squanderer, spender, prodigal son.

V. **squander,** lavish, sow broadcast, pay through the nose, spill, waste dissipate, exhaust, drain, overdraw, spend money like water.

Adj. **prodigal,** profuse, thriftless, unthrifty, improvident, wasteful, extravagant, lavish, dissipated; penny-wise and pound-foolish.

Adv. with an unsparing hand.

819. PARSIMONY.—*N.* parsimony, parsimoniousness, stinginess, stint, illiberality, avarice, avidity, rapacity, extortion, venality, cupidity, selfishness.

miser, niggard, churl, screw, skinflint, curmudgeon, harpy, extortioner, extortionist, usurer.

V. **grudge,** begrudge, stint, pinch, gripe, screw, dole out, hold back, withhold, starve, famish.

drive a bargain, cheapen, beat down; have an itching palm, grasp, grab.

Adj. **parsimonious,** penurious, stingy, miserly, mean, shabby, near, niggardly, close, sparing, grudging, illiberal, ungenerous, churlish, sordid, mercenary, venal, covetous, avaricious; greedy, grasping, extortionate, rapacious.

Adv. with a sparing hand.

CLASS VI

WORDS RELATING TO THE SENTIENT AND MORAL POWERS

I. AFFECTIONS IN GENERAL

820. AFFECTIONS.—*N.* **character,** qualities, disposition, affections, nature, spirit, temper, temperament, idiosyncrasy, predilection, turn of mind, bent, bias, predisposition, proneness, proclivity, propensity, vein, humor, mood, sympathy.

soul, heart, bosom, inner man; inmost recesses of the heart.

passion, pervading spirit; ruling passion, fullness of the heart.

energy, fervor, fire, verve, force.

Adj. **characterized,** affected, formed, molded, cast, tempered; framed.

prone, predisposed, disposed, inclined; having a bias.

inborn, inbred, ingrained; deep-rooted, congenital, inherent.

Adv. at heart; in the vein, in the mood.

821. FEELING.—*N.* **feeling,** suffering, endurance, sufferance, response; sympathy, impression, inspiration, affection, sensation, emotion, pathos.

fervor, unction, gusto, vehemence, heartiness, cordiality, earnestness, eagerness, gush [*colloq.*], ardor, warmth, zeal, passion, enthusiasm, ecstasy.

excitement; thrill, shock, agitation, quiver, flutter, flurry, fluster, twitter, tremor, throb, throbbing, pulsation, palpitation, panting; blush, flush.

V. **feel,** receive an impression, be impressed with, respond, enter into the spirit of.

bear, suffer, support, sustain, endure, brook, brave, stand, abide, experience, taste, prove.

be agitated, be excited, glow, flush, blush, crimson, change color, mantle; darken, whiten, pale, tingle, thrill, heave, pant, throb, palpitate, tremble, quiver, flutter, shake, stagger, reel; wince.

Adj. **sentient,** sensuous, emotional; of (*or* with) feeling.

keen, sharp, lively, quick, acute, cutting, piercing, incisive, trenchant, pungent, racy, piquant, poignant, caustic.

impressive, deep, profound, indelible, deep-felt, heartfelt, soul-stirring, electric, thrilling, rapturous, ecstatic, rapt; pervading, penetrating, absorbing.

earnest, wistful, eager, fervent, fervid, gushing [*colloq.*], warm, passionate, hearty, cordial, sincere, zealous, enthusiastic, glowing, ardent.

rabid, raving, feverish, fanatical, hysterical, impetuous.

Adv. **heartily,** heart and soul, from the bottom of one's heart, devoutly.

822. SENSITIVENESS.—*N.* **sensitiveness,** sensibleness, sensibility, impressibility, susceptibility, vivacity, tenderness, sentimentality. sentimentalism.

excitability, etc., 825; physical sensibility, etc., 375.

V. **be sensitive,** have a tender heart; take to heart, shrink, wince, blench, quiver.

Adj. **sensitive,** sensible, impressible, impressionable; susceptive, susceptible; warmhearted, tenderhearted, softhearted, tender; sentimental, romantic; enthusiastic, impassioned, spirited, mettlesome, vivacious, lively, expressive, mobile, excitable, oversensitive, thin-skinned, fastidious.

Adv. to the quick, on the raw.

823. INSENSITIVENESS.—*N.* **insensitiveness,** insensibility, insensibleness, inertness, inertia, impassibility, impassivity, apathy, dullness, insusceptibility, lukewarmness.

coldness, coolness, frigidity, stoicism, nonchalance, unconcern, indifference, callousness, heart of stone.

torpor, torpidity, lethargy, coma, trance; sleep, stupor, stupefaction; paralysis, numbness.

stoic, Indian, man of iron.

V. **be insensitive,** not mind, not care, not be affected by; take no interest in; disregard.

blunt, numb, benumb, paralyze, deaden, stun, stupefy; brutalize.

inure; harden, steel, caseharden, sear.

Adj. **insensitive,** insensible, unconscious, impassive, insusceptible, unimpressible; passionless, spiritless, heartless, soulless, unfeeling.

apathetic, unemotional, phlegmatic; dull, frigid, cold, coldblooded, coldhearted; inert, supine, sluggish, torpid, sleepy, languid, halfhearted; numb, numbed; comatose.

indifferent, lukewarm, careless, mindless, inattentive, unconcerned, nonchalant.

unaffected, unruffled, unimpressed, unexcited, unmoved, unstirred, untouched, unshocked, unblushing.

callous, thick-skinned, impervious, hard, hardened, inured, casehardened; imperturbable, unfelt.

Adv. in cold blood; with dry eyes.

824. EXCITEMENT.—*N.* **excitement,** excitation, stimulation, piquancy, provocation, inspiration, animation, agitation, perturbation; fascination, intoxication, impressiveness; irritation, passion, thrill.

emotional appeal, melodrama, sensationalism, yellow journalism.

V. **excite,** affect, touch, move, impress, strike, interest, animate, inspire, smite, infect, awake, wake; awaken, waken; call forth; evoke, provoke; raise up, summon up, call up, wake up, raise; rouse, arouse, stir, fire, kindle, enkindle, illumine, illuminate, inflame.

stimulate, inspirit; stir up, infuse life into, give new life to; introduce new blood, quicken; sharpen, whet, fillip; fan, foster, heat, warm, foment, revive, rekindle.

penetrate, pierce; go to one's heart, touch to the quick, possess the soul, rivet the attention; prey on the mind.

agitate, perturb, ruffle, fluster, flutter, flurry, shake, disturb, startle, shock, stagger, strike dumb, stun, astound, electrify, galvanize, petrify.

irritate, sting, cut, pique, infuriate, madden, lash into fury.

flare up, flash up, seethe, boil, simmer, foam, fume, flame, rage, rave.

Adj. **excited,** wrought up, overwrought, hot, red-hot, flushed, feverish; raging, flaming, ebullient, seething, foaming, fuming, stung to the quick; wild, raving, frantic, mad, distracted, beside oneself.

exciting, impressive, telling, warm, glowing, fervid, spirit-stirring, thrilling; soul-stirring, heart-stirring, agonizing, sensational, yellow [*colloq.*], melodramatic, hysterical; overpowering, overwhelming.

piquant, spicy, appetizing, stinging, provocative, tantalizing.

Adv. at a critical moment, under a sudden strain.

825. [Excess of sensitiveness] **EXCITABILITY.**—*N.* **excitability,** impetuosity, vehemence, boisterousness, turbulence; impatience, intolerance, irritability; disquiet, disquietude, restlessness, fidgets, agitation.

trepidation, perturbation, ruffle, hurry, fuss, flurry, fluster, flutter; ferment; whirl; stage fright, thrill.

passion, excitement, flush, heat, fever, fire, flame, fume, tumult, effervescence, ebullition; gust, storm, tempest; burst, fit, paroxysm, explosion, outbreak, scene, outburst; agony.

fury; violence, fierceness, rage, furor, desperation, madness, distraction, raving, delirium; frenzy, hysterics; intoxication; towering rage, anger, etc., 900.

fixed idea, monomania; fascination, infatuation; fanaticism; quixotism, quixotry.

V. fidget, fuss.

fume, rage, foam; bear ill, wince, chafe, champ the bit, lose one's temper, break out, burst out, fly out, explode, flare up, flame up, fire up, boil, rave, rant, tear, go into hysterics; run riot, run amuck; raise Cain [*slang*].

Adj. **excitable,** easily excited, mettlesome, high-mettled, skittish, high-strung, nervous, irritable, hasty, impatient, intolerant, moody; feverish, hysterical, delirious, mad.

restless, unquiet, mercurial, galvanic, fidgety, fussy.

vehement, demonstrative, violent, wild, furious, fierce, fiery, hotheaded; overzealous, enthusiastic, impassioned, fanatical; rabid, rampant, clamorous, uproarious, turbulent, tempestuous, boisterous.

impulsive, impetuous, passionate, uncontrolled, uncontrollable, ungovernable, irrepressible, volcanic.

Adv. in confusion, pellmell.

826. INEXCITABILITY.—*N.* **inexcitability,** imperturbability, even temper, tranquil mind, dispassion; toleration, tolerance, patience; passiveness, inertia, etc., 172; impassibility, etc. (*insensibility*), 823; stupefaction.

calmness, composure, placidity, *sang-froid* [F.], coolness, tranquillity, serenity, content; quiet, quietude; peace of mind.

equanimity, poise, staidness, gravity, sobriety, philosophy, stoicism, self-possession, self-control, self-command, self-restraint; presence of mind.

resignation, submission, sufferance, endurance, long-sufferance, forbearance, longanimity, fortitude, patience of Job, moderation, restraint.

V. **endure,** bear, go through, support, brave, disregard; tolerate, suffer, stand, bide; abide, bear with, put up with, acquiesce, submit, resign oneself to, brook, digest, eat, swallow, pocket, stomach; carry on, carry through; make light of, make the best of, put a good face on.

compose, appease, assuage, propitiate, repress, restrain, master one's feelings, set one's mind at ease (*or* rest), calm down, cool down.

Adj. **inexcitable,** imperturbable; unsusceptible, dispassionate, cold-blooded, enduring, stoical, philosophical, staid, sober, grave; sedate, demure, coolheaded, levelheaded.

easygoing, peaceful, placid, calm; quiet, tranquil, serene, cool, undemonstrative.

composed, collected, temperate, unstirred, unruffled, unperturbed.

meek, mild, tame, subdued, unoffended, unresisting, submissive, gentle, patient, tolerant, clement, long-suffering.

Adv. in cold blood; more in sorrow than in anger.

II. PERSONAL AFFECTIONS[1]

827. PLEASURE.—*N.* **pleasure,** gratification, enjoyment, delectation, relish, zest, gusto, satisfaction, complacency; well-being; good, etc., 618; comfort, ease, luxury: physical pleasure, etc., 377.

joy, gladness, delight, glee, cheer, sunshine; cheerfulness, etc., 836; treat, luxury; amusement, etc., 840.

happiness, felicity, bliss, beatitude, enchantment, transport, rapture, ecstasy; paradise, heaven.

V. **enjoy oneself,** joy, be in clover [*colloq.*], tread on enchanted ground; go into raptures; feel at home, breathe freely, bask in the sunshine.

enjoy, like, relish, be pleased with, derive pleasure from, take pleasure in, delight in, rejoice in, indulge in, gloat over, love; take to, take a fancy to [*both colloq.*].

Adj. **pleased,** gratified, glad, gladsome; comfortable, etc. (*physical pleasure*), 377; at ease; content, etc.. 831.

happy, blessed, blissful, beatified, joyful, in raptures, in ecstasies.

overjoyed, entranced, enchanted; raptured, enraptured, ravished, transported; fascinated, captivated.

pleasing, delightful, ecstatic, beatific, painless, unalloyed, cloudless.

828. PAIN.—*N.* **pain,** mental suffering, dolor, suffering, ache; physical pain, etc., 378.

displeasure, dissatisfaction, discomfort, discomposure, disquiet; inquietude, uneasiness, discontent.

annoyance, irritation, worry; infliction, visitation; plague, bore; bother, vexation, mortification, chagrin.

care, anxiety, solicitude, concern, trouble, trial, ordeal, shock, blow, fret, burden, load.

grief, sorrow, distress, affliction, woe, bitterness, heartache, heavy (*or* aching, bleeding, broken) heart.

misery, unhappiness, infelicity, tribulation, wretchedness, desolation; despair, etc., 859; extremity, prostration, depth of misery, slough of despond; nightmare, incubus.

anguish, pang, agony, torture, torment; crucifixion, martyrdom, rack, hell upon earth; reign of terror.

sufferer, victim, prey, martyr, wretch, shorn lamb.

V. **suffer,** ail, feel (*or* suffer, undergo, bear, endure) pain, smart, ache, bleed, bear the cross; fall on evil days, come to grief.

fret, chafe, sit on thorns, wince, worry oneself, fret and fume; take to heart.

[1]Or those which concern one's own state of feeling.

grieve, mourn, lament, etc., 839; yearn, repine, pine, droop, languish, sink, despair, break one's heart.

Adj. **pained,** afflicted, suffering, worried, displeased, aching, griped, sore, raw, on the rack.

uneasy, uncomfortable, ill at ease; disturbed; discontented; weary, etc., 841.

unfortunate, etc., 735; doomed, devoted, accursed, undone, crushed, lost, stranded; victimized, ill-used.

unhappy, infelicitous, poor, wretched, miserable, woebegone, comfortless, cheerless, etc. (*dejected*), 837; careworn; heavy-laden, stricken.

sorry, concerned, sorrowful, cut up [*colloq.*], chagrined, horrified, horror-stricken; heartbroken, brokenhearted.

829. [Capability of giving pleasure] PLEASURABLENESS.— *N.* **pleasurableness,** pleasantness, agreeableness, pleasure giving, amusement, etc., 840; treat, etc. (*physical pleasure*), 377; dainty titbit, sweets, sweetmeats, nuts, salt, savor.

attraction, attractiveness, charm, fascination, captivation, enchantment, witchery, seduction, winning ways, winsomeness; loveliness, beauty, etc., 845.

V. **delight,** charm, gladden, bless, captivate, fascinate; enchant, entrance, enrapture, transport, bewitch, ravish.

please, satisfy, gratify, satiate, quench, indulge, humor, flatter, tickle; tickle the palate, refresh, enliven, treat, amuse, take one's fancy; attract, allure; stimulate, excite, interest.

Adj. **pleasurable,** pleasure-giving, pleasing, pleasant, amiable, agreeable, grateful, gratifying; acceptable; dear, beloved, welcome, favorite.

refreshing, comfortable, cordial, genial, glad, gladsome; sweet, delectable, nice, dainty, delicate, delicious.

attractive, inviting, prepossessing, engaging; winning, winsome, magnetic, fascinating, seductive; alluring, enticing, appetizing, cheering, bewitching, enchanting, entrancing.

delightful, charming, felicitous, exquisite, lovely, ravishing, rapturous; heartfelt, thrilling, ecstatic, heavenly.

Adv. to one's delight, in utter satisfaction; at one's ease; in clover [*colloq.*].

830. [Capability of giving pain] PAINFULNESS.— *N.* **painfulness,** trouble, care, trial, affliction, infliction, misfortune, mishap; cross, blow, stroke, burden, load, curse.

annoyance, pique, grievance, nuisance, vexation, mortification, worry, bore, bother, hornet's nest, plague, pest, wound; sore subject, skeleton in the closet; thorn in the flesh.

V. **pain,** hurt, wound, cause (*or* occasion, give, inflict) pain;

pierce, prick, cut, etc. (*physical pain*), 378; pierce (*or* break, rend) the heart; make the heart bleed.

sadden, make unhappy, grieve, afflict, distress; cut up [*colloq.*], cut to the heart.

annoy, incommode, displease, discompose, trouble, disturb, cross, thwart, perplex, molest; tease, tire, irk, fret, vex, mortify, worry, plague, bother, pester, bore, harass, harry, badger, heckle [*Brit.*], bait, beset, infest, persecute.

torment, wring, harrow, torture, rack, crucify, convulse, agonize.

irritate, provoke, sting, nettle, pique, fret, roil, rile [*colloq. & dial.*], chafe, gall; aggrieve, affront, enrage, ruffle, give offense.

maltreat, bite, snap at, assail, smite, etc., 972.

repel, revolt, sicken, disgust, nauseate, disenchant, offend, shock, rankle, gnaw, corrode, horrify, appall.

Adj. **painful,** hurtful, dolorous; distressing, cheerless, dismal, disheartening, depressing, dreary, melancholy, grievous, piteous, woeful, mournful, deplorable, pitiable, lamentable, sad; affecting, touching, pathetic.

unpleasant, unpleasing, displeasing, disagreeable, unpalatable, bitter, distasteful, uninviting, unwelcome, undesirable, obnoxious; unacceptable.

inauspicious, unlucky, ill-starred, unsatisfactory; untoward.

irritating, provoking, annoying, aggravating [*colloq.*], exasperating, galling, vexatious; troublesome, tiresome, irksome, wearisome.

importunate, pestering, bothering, harassing, worrying, tormenting.

insufferable, intolerable, insupportable, unbearable, unendurable.

shocking, terrific, grim, appalling, crushing; dreadful, fearful, frightful, tremendous, dire, heartbreaking, heart-rending, harrowing, rending.

odious, hateful, execrable, repulsive, repellent, horrid, horrible; offensive; nauseous, disgusting, revolting, nasty, loathsome, vile, hideous.

acute, sharp, sore, severe, grave, hard, harsh, cruel, biting, caustic; cutting, corroding, consuming, excruciating, agonizing.

cumbrous, cumbersome, burdensome, onerous, oppressive.

desolating, withering, tragical, disastrous, calamitous, ruinous.

Adv. in agony, out of the depths.

831. CONTENT.—*N.* content, contentment, contentedness; complacency, satisfaction, ease, peace of mind, serenity, cheerfulness; comfort.

patience, moderation, endurance; conciliation, reconciliation; resignation.

V. **be content,** rest satisfied, let well enough alone; take in good part; be reconciled to, take heart, take comfort.

content, set at ease, comfort; conciliate, reconcile, win over, propitiate, disarm, beguile; content, satisfy; gratify, etc., 836.

Adj. **content,** contented, satisfied, at ease, at one's ease, easygoing, not particular; conciliatory, unrepining, resigned, cheerful, serene, at rest; snug, comfortable.

satisfactory, adequate, sufficient, ample, equal to; satisfying.

Adv. to one's heart's content.

832. DISCONTENT.—*N.* **discontent,** dissatisfaction; disappointment, mortification; cold comfort; regret, repining, inquietude, vexation of spirit, soreness; heartburning.

malcontent, grumbler, growler, grouch [*slang*], croaker, faultfinder.

the opposition; bitter-enders [*politics*, U. S.], die-hards.

V. **be discontented,** repine, regret, take to heart, make a wry face, look blue, look black, look glum.

grumble, take ill, take in bad part; fret, chafe, croak; lament. **dissatisfy,** disappoint, mortify, put out [*colloq.*], disconcert, dishearten.

Adj. **discontented,** dissatisfied, unsatisfied, regretful, dejected, etc., 837; dissentient, malcontent, exacting.

glum, sulky, in high dudgeon, in a fume, in the sulks (*or* dumps), in bad humor; sour, soured, sore; out of humor, out of temper.

833. REGRET.—*N.* **regret,** repining; homesickness, nostalgia; bitterness, heartburning; lamentation, penitence, etc., 950.

V. **regret,** deplore, bewail, lament, etc., 839; repine, rue, rue the day; repent, etc., 950; leave an aching void.

Adj. **regretful,** rueful; homesick.

834. RELIEF.—*N.* **relief,** deliverance, alleviation, mitigation, palliation, solace, consolation, comfort, unction; encouragement.

V. **relieve,** ease, alleviate, mitigate, palliate, soothe; salve; soften, assuage, allay; remedy, cure, restore, refresh.

cheer, comfort, console; enliven; encourage, give comfort, inspirit, invigorate.

Adj. **soothing,** assuaging, balmy, lenitive, palliative, curative.

835. AGGRAVATION.—*N.* **aggravation,** heightening, intensification, overestimation, exaggeration.

V. **aggravate,** render worse, heighten, embitter, sour, intensify, enhance [*Note:* aggravate *in the sense of* provoke *is colloquial*].

Adj. **aggravated,** worse, unrelieved, aggravative.

Adv. from bad to worse, worse and worse.

836. CHEERFULNESS.—*N.* cheerfulness, geniality, gayety, cheer, good humor, spirits; high spirits, animal spirits, glee, high glee, light heart.

liveliness, life, alacrity, vivacity, animation, joviality, jollity, levity, jocularity.

mirth, merriment, hilarity, exhilaration, laughter, merrymaking, rejoicing, etc., 838.

optimism, hopefulness, etc., 858.

V. **be cheerful,** have the mind at ease, smile, keep up one's spirits, cheer up, take heart, cast away care, perk up; rejoice, etc., 838; carol, chirp, chirrup, lilt.

cheer, enliven, elate, exhilarate, gladden, delight, inspirit, animate, inspire.

Adj. **cheerful;** happy, etc., 827; cheery, sunny, smiling; blithe, in good spirits, chipper [*colloq.*], gay, debonair, light, lightsome, lighthearted; buoyant, bright, airy, jaunty, sprightly, spirited, lively, animated, vivacious, sparkling, sportive.

merry, joyful, joyous, jocund, jovial; jolly, blithesome, gleeful, hilarious.

winsome, bonny, hearty, buxom.

playful, tricksy, frisky, frolicsome, jocose, jocular, waggish, mirthful, rollicking.

elate, elated; exulting, jubilant, flushed, rejoicing.

cheering, inspiriting, exhilarating, pleasing, palmy, flourishing.

Adv. **cheerfully,** cheerily, with relish, with zest.

837. DEJECTION.—*N.* dejection, depression, mopishness, low (*or* depressed) spirits; heaviness, gloom; weariness, disgust of life; prostration, broken heart; despair, hopelessness.

melancholy, sadness, melancholia, blue devils [*colloq.*], blues [*colloq.*], dumps [*chiefly humorous*], doldrums, horrors, hypochondria, pessimism; despondency, slough of despond; disconsolateness, hope deferred.

gravity; demureness, solemnity; long face, grave face.

hypochondriac, self-tormentor, croaker, pessimist, damper, wet blanket.

V. **be dejected,** grieve, mourn, lament, give way, lose heart, despond, droop, sink, despair.

lower, frown, pout; look blue, lay to heart, take to heart.

mope, brood over, fret, sulk, pine, pine away; yearn, repine.

depress, discourage, dishearten, dispirit, damp, dull, deject, sink, dash, unman, prostrate, break one's heart; sadden, dash one's hopes, prey on the mind, damp the spirits.

Adj. **cheerless,** joyless, spiritless; unhappy, etc., 828; melancholy, dismal, dreary, depressing, somber, dark, gloomy, lowering, frowning, funereal, mournful, lamentable, dreadful.

downcast, downhearted, down in the mouth [*colloq.*], down on one's luck [*colloq.*], heavyhearted; sullen, mopish, moody, glum; sulky, etc. (*discontented*), 832; out of heart (*or* spirits); low-spirited; weary, etc., 841; discouraged, disheartened, despondent, crestfallen.

sad, pensive, doleful, woebegone, melancholic, bilious, jaundiced, saturnine, lackadaisical.

serious, sedate, staid, earnest, grave, sober, solemn, demure, grim, grim-faced, rueful, wan, long-faced.

disconsolate, forlorn, comfortless, desolate, sick at heart, heart-sick.

overcome, broken-down, prostrate, cut up [*colloq.*], unnerved, unmanned; downfallen, downtrodden; brokenhearted; careworn.

Adv. with a long face, with tears in one's eyes.

838. [Expression of pleasure] REJOICING.—*N.* rejoicing, exultation, triumph, jubilation, heyday, flush, reveling, merry-making, pæan, *Te Deum* [L.]; congratulation.

smile, simper, smirk, grin; broad grin, sardonic grin.

laughter, giggle, titter, snicker, snigger, crow, cheer, chuckle, shout; guffaw, burst (*or* fit, shout, roar, peal) of laughter.

cheer, huzza, hurrah, cheering; shout, yell [U. S. and Can.], college yell; tiger [*colloq.*].

V. rejoice, congratulate oneself, hug oneself, clap one's hands; skip; sing, carol, chirrup, chirp, hurrah, cry for joy, leap with joy; exult, triumph; make merry.

smile, simper, smirk, grin, laugh in one's sleeve.

laugh, giggle, titter, snigger, snicker, chuckle, cackle; burst out, shout, roar, shake (*or* split) one's sides.

Adj. rejoicing, jubilant, exultant, triumphant, flushed, elated; laughing, convulsed with laughter.

laughable, ludicrous, etc. 853.

Adv. in fits of laughter; in triumph.

839. [Expression of pain] LAMENTATION.—*N.* lamentation, lament, wail, complaint, plaint, murmur, mutter, grumble, groan, moan, whine, whimper, sob, sigh; frown, scowl.

cry, scream, howl; outcry, wail of woe.

weeping, flood of tears, fit of crying, crying; melting mood. plaintiveness; languishment; condolence, etc., 915.

mourning, weeds [*colloq.*], widow's weeds, crape, deep mourning; sackcloth and ashes; death song, dirge, requiem, elegy, threnody, jeremiad, keen [Ir.].

mourner, keener [Ir.]; Niobe.

V. lament, mourn, deplore, grieve, keen [Ir.], weep over; bewail, bemoan, condole with, etc., 915; fret.

sigh, give (*or* heave) a sigh; wail.

cry, weep, sob, blubber, snivel, whimper, shed tears, burst into tears.

scream, groan, moan, whine, yelp, howl, yell, roar; rend the air.

complain, murmur, mutter, grumble, growl, clamor, croak, grunt.

Adj. lamenting, in mourning, in sackcloth and ashes, clamorous, sorrowing, sorrowful, mournful, lamentable, tearful, lachrymose, plaintive, querulous; in tears.

840 AMUSEMENT.—*N.* amusement, entertainment, diversion, recreation, relaxation, solace; pastime, sport; labor of love; pleasure, etc.. 827.

fun, frolic, merriment, jollity, joviality, laughter, etc., 838; pleasantry, quip, jocoseness; drollery, buffoonery, tomfoolery; mummery, pageant.

play, game, gambol, romp, prank, antic, lark [*colloq.*], spree, skylarking, vagary, monkey trick, escapade, practical joke.

dance, hop [*colloq.*]; ball, masquerade, ballet; step dance, skirt dance, folk dance, morris dance; gavot, minuet, Highland fling, reel jig, hornpipe, sword dance, cakewalk; country dance, Scotch reel, Virginia reel, quadrille, lancers, cotillion; waltz, polka, mazurka, schottische, one-step, fox-trot.

festivity, fete, festival, merrymaking; party, etc. (*social gathering*), 892; revels, revelry, reveling, carnival, saturnalia, jollification [*colloq.*], junket, picnic.

holiday, red-letter day, play day; high days and holidays; high holiday.

place of amusement, theater; concert hall, ballroom, dance hall, assembly room; moving-picture theater; movies [*colloq.*]; music hall; vaudeville theater; circus, hippodrome.

Sports and games: athletic sports, track events, gymnastics; tournament.
skating, tobogganing; cricket, tennis, lawn tennis, rackets, squash, fives; croquet, golf, curling, hockey, polo, football, Rugby, rugger [*colloq.*]; association, soccer [*colloq.*]; quoits, discus, putting the weight (*or* shot), tug of war; baseball, basketball, pushball, lacrosse
billiards, pool, pyramids, bagatelle; bowls, skittles, ninepins, tenpins; chess, draughts, checkers, dominoes; dice; card games, etc.

toy, plaything, doll, bauble.

sportsman (*fem.* sportswoman), hunter, Nimrod.

gamester, sport, gambler; dicer, punter, plunger.

devotee, enthusiast, follower, fan [*slang*], rooter [*slang or cant*].

V. amuse, entertain, divert, enliven, raise a smile, excite (*or* convulse with) laughter; cheer, rejoice, solace, please, interest.

amuse oneself, sport, disport, revel, junket, feast, carouse.

banquet, make merry; frolic, gambol, frisk, romp, caper, dance.

Adj. amusing, entertaining, diverting, recreative, pleasant, laughable, etc. (*ludicrous*), 853; witty, etc., 842; festive, festal, jovial, jolly, roguish, arch, playful, sportive.

Adv. at play, in sport.

841. WEARINESS.—*N.* weariness, ennui, boredom, lassitude, fatigue, etc., 688; drowsiness, languor.

disgust, nausea, loathing, sickness; satiety, repletion.

tedium, wearisomeness, tediousness, monotony.

bore, buttonholer, proser, dry-as-dust, fossil [*colloq.*], wet blanket.

V. weary, tire, fatigue, bore, send to sleep; buttonhole.

pall, sicken, nauseate, disgust; harp on the same string.

Adj. wearying, wearing, wearisome, tiresome, irksome, uninteresting, stupid, monotonous, dull, dry, arid, tedious, humdrum, flat; prosy, prosing; slow, soporific, somniferous.

weary, tired, drowsy, sleepy, etc., 683; uninterested, flagging, used up, worn out, blasé [F.].

842. WIT.—*N.* wit, wittiness, Attic salt, Atticism; point, fancy, whim, humor, drollery, pleasantry.

buffoonery, fooling, farce, tomfoolery, broad farce, fun.

jocularity, jocoseness, facetiousness, waggishness, comicality.

smartness, ready wit, banter, persiflage, retort, repartee.

witticism, smart saying, sally, flash, scintillation, flash of wit; jest, joke, epigram, conceit.

wordplay, play upon words, pun, riddle, conundrum, quibble.

V. joke, jest, cut jokes; crack a joke, pun; make merry with.

retort, flash back, flash, scintillate; banter, etc. (*ridicule*), 856.

Adj. witty, clever, keen, keen-witted, brilliant, pungent, quick-witted, smart, jocular, jocose, funny, waggish, facetious, comic, whimsical, humorous, sprightly, sparkling, epigrammatic.

843. DULLNESS.—*N.* dullness, heaviness, flatness, stupidity, want of originality, dearth of ideas; matter of fact, commonplace, platitude.

V. be dull, hang fire, fall flat, platitudinize, prose.

depress, damp, throw cold water on, lay a wet blanket on.

Adj. dull, jejune, dry, uninteresting, heavy-footed, elephantine; insipid, tasteless, unimaginative; prosy, prosaic, matter-of-fact, commonplace, platitudinous, pointless.

stupid, slow, flat, humdrum, monotonous, stolid.

844. HUMORIST.—*N.* humorist, wag, wit, epigrammatist, punster; life of the party; joker, jester, buffoon, comedian, merry-andrew, mime, tumbler, acrobat, mountebank, harlequin, pantaloon, punch, punchinello, clown; motley fool; caricaturist.

845. BEAUTY.—*N.* beauty, form, elegance, grace, symmetry, bloom, delicacy, refinement, charm, style; comeliness, fairness, polish, gloss; good effect, good looks.

brilliancy, radiance, splendor, gorgeousness, magnificence; sublimity.

beau ideal, Venus, Aphrodite, Hebe, the Graces, peri, houri, Cupid, Apollo, Hyperion, Adonis; Helen of Troy, Cleopatra; Venus de Milo, Apollo Belvedere.

loveliness, pleasurableness, etc., 829.

beautifying, decoration, ornamentation, etc., 847.

V. beautify, set off, grace; decorate, etc., 847.

Adj. beautiful, beauteous, handsome; pretty; lovely, graceful, elegant, exquisite, delicate, dainty.

comely, fair, goodly, bonny, good-looking, well favored, well formed, well proportioned, shapely, symmetrical, harmonious.

bright, bright-eyed; rosy-cheeked, rosy, ruddy, blooming, in full bloom.

trim, trig, tidy, neat, spruce, smart, jaunty, dapper.

brilliant, shining, sparkling, radiant, splendid, resplendent, dazzling, glowing, glossy, sleek; rich, gorgeous, superb, magnificent, grand, fine.

artistic, aesthetic, picturesque, pictorial, enchanting, attractive, becoming, ornamental.

perfect, unspotted, spotless, immaculate; undeformed, undefaced.

passable, presentable, tolerable, not amiss.

846. UGLINESS.—*N.* ugliness, deformity, inelegance, disfigurement, blemish, want of symmetry, distortion; squalor.

eyesore, object, figure, sight [*colloq.*], fright, scarecrow, hag, harridan, satyr, witch, monster.

V. deface, disfigure, deform, distort, blemish, injure, spoil; soil.

Adj. ugly, inartistic, unsightly, unseemly, uncomely, unshapely, unlovely; unbeautiful; coarse, plain, homely.

misshapen, misproportioned, shapeless, monstrous, gross; ill-made, ill-shaped, ill-proportioned, crooked, distorted.

unprepossessing, hard-featured, ill-favored, ill-looking; squalid, haggard; grim, grisly, ghastly, cadaverous, gruesome.

uncouth, ungainly, graceless, inelegant, ungraceful, stiff, rough, gross, rude, awkward, clumsy, gawky, lumbering, unwieldy.

repellent, forbidding, frightful, hideous, odious, repulsive; horrid, horrible, shocking.

disfigured, tarnished, smeared, besmeared, discolored, spotted, spotty.

showy, specious, pretentious, garish.

847. ORNAMENT.—*N.* ornament, ornamentation, ornateness, adornment, decoration, embellishment.

embroidery, needlework; lace, trimming, drapery; tapestry, arras; millinery.
wreath, festoon, garland, chaplet, flower, nosegay, bouquet, posy [*colloq.*].
tassel, knot; shoulder knot, epaulet, star, rosette, bow; feather, plume, fillet, snood.
jewelry: tiara, crown, coronet, diadem; jewel, gem, precious stone, trinket.

finery, frippery, tinsel, spangle, excess of ornament; pride, show, ostentation.

illustration, illumination; purple patches.

virtu, article of virtu, work of art, bric-a-brac, curio; rarity, a find.

V. ornament, embellish, enrich, decorate, adorn, beautify; garnish, furbish, polish, gild, varnish, enamel, paint.

spangle, bespangle, bead, embroider, chase, tool; emblazon, blazon, illuminate.

smarten, trim, bedizen, prink, trick up, trick out, deck, bedeck, array; spruce up [*colloq.*]; smarten up, dress, dress up.

Adj. ornamental, ornate, ornamented, rich, gilt, begilt, festooned.

smart, gay, flowery, glittering, new-spangled, fine, well groomed.

showy, gorgeous, flashy, gaudy, garish, tawdry, etc., 851.

848. BLEMISH.—*N.* blemish, disfigurement, deformity, defect, flaw, injury, eyesore.

stain, blot, spot, speck, speckle, blur, freckle, patch, blotch, smudge, birthmark, scar, mole, pimple, blister.

V. disfigure, etc. (*injure*), 659.

Adj. disfigured, imperfect, injured; discolored, specked, speckled, freckled, pitted, bruised.

849. SIMPLICITY.—*N.* simplicity, plainness, homeliness; chasteness, chastity, restraint, severity, naturalness, unaffectedness.

V. simplify, reduce to simplicity, strip of ornament, chasten, restrain.

Adj. simple, plain, homelike, homely, homespun [*fig.*], ordinary. unaffected, natural, native; inartificial, free from affectation; chaste, severe; unadorned, unornamented.

simple-minded, childish, credulous, etc., 486.

850. [Good taste] TASTE.—*N.* taste, good (*or* refined, cultivated) taste; delicacy, refinement, fine feeling, discrimination, tact, polish, elegance, grace, culture, cultivation.

Science of taste: aesthetics.

man of taste, connoisseur, judge, critic, virtuoso, amateur, dilettante; purist, precisián.

V. **display taste,** appreciate, judge, criticize, discriminate.

Adj. **in good taste,** tasteful, unaffected, pure, chaste, classical, cultivated; graceful, attractive, charming, aesthetic, artistic.

refined, elegant, prim, precise, formal.

Adv. with quiet elegance; with elegant simplicity; without ostentation.

851. [Bad taste] VULGARITY.—*N.* vulgarity, vulgarism, barbarism, vandalism, bad taste; want of tact; ill-breeding, coarseness, indecorum, misbehavior, boorishness.

lowness, low life, brutality, blackguardism, rowdyism, ruffianism; ribaldry.

Excess of ornament: gaudiness, tawdriness, cheap jewelry; flashy clothes (*or* dress), finery, frippery, trickery, tinsel.

vulgarian, rough diamond, clown, Goth, vandal; snob, cad [*colloq.*], cub; parvenu, upstart; frump [*colloq.*], dowdy, slattern.

V. **be vulgar,** misbehave; show a want of tact (*or* consideration); be a vulgarian.

Adj. **in bad taste,** vulgar, unrefined, coarse, indecorous, ribald, gross; unseemly, unpresentable, ungraceful; dowdy, slovenly; low, extravagant, monstrous, horrid, shocking.

ill-mannered, ill-bred, underbred, snobbish, uncourtly, uncivil, discourteous, ungentlemanly, unladylike.

uncouth, unkempt, unpolished, plebeian; rude, awkward; homely, homespun, provincial, countrified, rustic; boorish, clownish; savage, brutish, blackguardly, rowdy, wild; barbarous, barbaric, outlandish; uncultivated.

antiquated, obsolete, out of fashion, old-fashioned, out of date, unfashionable.

newfangled, fantastic, fantastical, odd, affected.

tawdry, gaudy, meretricious, obtrusive, flaunting, loud, crass, showy, flashy, garish.

852. FASHION.—*N.* fashion, style, society, good (*or* polite) society, civilized life, civilization; court, high life, world, fashionable world; upper ten [*colloq.*], elite, smart set [*colloq.*], the four hundred; Vanity Fair; Mayfair.

manners, breeding, politeness; air, demeanor, *savoir-faire* [F.], gentility, decorum, propriety, Mrs. Grundy; convention, conventionality, the proprieties, punctiliousness, form, formality, etiquette.

mode, vogue, style, the latest thing, the rage, prevailing taste; custom.

V. **be fashionable,** be the rage, have a run, pass current, follow the fashion, go with the stream

Adj. **fashionable,** in fashion, *à la mode* [F.], presentable; punctilious, genteel, decorous, conventional; well bred, gentlemanly, ladylike.

polished, refined, thoroughbred, gently bred, courtly, distinguished, aristocratic, self-possessed, poised, easy, frank, unconstrained.

modish, stylish, swell [*slang*], all the rage, all the go [*colloq.*].

Adv. for fashion's sake; in the latest style (*or* mode).

853. RIDICULOUSNESS.—*N.* ridiculousness, comicality, oddity, drollery; farce, comedy, burlesque, buffoonery, bull, Irish bull, spoonerism; bombast, anticlimax, bathos; absurdity, laughingstock.

V. be ridiculous, play the fool, make a fool of oneself, commit an absurdity.

Adj. ridiculous, ludicrous, comic *or* comical, waggish, quizzical, droll, funny, laughable, farcical, seriocomic, tragicomic.

odd, grotesque, whimsical, fanciful, fantastic, queer, quaint, bizarre, eccentric, strange, outlandish, out-of-the-way.

extravagant, monstrous, preposterous, absurd, bombastic, inflated, stilted, burlesque, mock heroic.

854. FOP.—*N.* fine gentleman, fop, swell [*colloq.*], dandy, exquisite, coxcomb, beau, man about town, spark, popinjay, puppy [*contemptuous*], prig, jackanapes, carpet knight; dude [*colloq.*].

fine lady, belle, flirt, coquette, toast.

855. AFFECTATION.—*N.* affectation, affectedness, pretense, pretension, airs, pedantry, stiffness, formality, mannerism, euphuism; boasting, charlatanism, quackery.

prudery, demureness, mock modesty, false shame; sentimentalism.

foppery, dandyism, coxcombry, puppyism, conceit; coquetry.

poser, actor; pedant, pedagogue, doctrinaire, purist, euphuist, mannerist; bluestocking, prig, charlatan; prude, puritan, precisian, formalist.

V. affect, act a part, give oneself airs, boast, simper, mince, attitudinize, pose, languish; overact, overdo.

Adj. affected, pretentious, pedantic, stilted, stagy, theatrical, canting, insincere, unnatural; self-conscious, artificial; overdone, overacted.

stiff, formal, prim, smug, complacent; demure, puritanical, prudish.

priggish, conceited, foppish, finical, finicking, mincing, simpering, namby-pamby, sentimental, languishing.

856. RIDICULE.—*N.* ridicule, derision, snicker *or* snigger, grin, scoffing, mockery, banter, irony, persiflage, raillery, chaff.

squib, satire, skit, quip.

burlesque, parody, travesty, farce, caricature.

buffoonery, practical joke, horseplay, roughhouse [*slang*].

V. ridicule, deride; laugh at, grin at, smile at; snicker *or* snigger; banter, chaff, joke, guy [*colloq.*], rag [*slang*], haze [*colloq.*].

burlesque, satirize, parody, caricature, travesty.

Adj. derisive, sarcastic, ironical, satirical, quizzical, burlesque, mock.

Adv. as a joke, to raise a laugh.

857. [Object and cause of ridicule] LAUGHINGSTOCK.—*N.* laughingstock, butt, game, fair game, April fool, original, oddity; queer fish [*colloq.*], figure of fun [*colloq.*]; monkey; buffoon.

858. HOPE.—*N.* hope; desire, etc., 865; trust, confidence, reliance, faith, assurance, security; reassurance.

hopefulness, buoyancy, optimism, enthusiasm, aspiration; assumption, presumption; anticipation.

optimist, utopian.

daydream, castles in the air, utopia, millennium; golden dream, airy hopes, fool's paradise, fond hope.

mainstay, anchor, sheet anchor; staff.

V. hope, trust, confide, rely, lean upon; live in hope, rest assured.

hope for, etc. (*desire*), 865; anticipate; presume, aspire; promise oneself; expect.

be hopeful, look on the bright side of, make the best of it, hope for the best; hope against hope, take heart, flatter oneself.

encourage, hearten, inspirit, hold out hope, cheer, assure, reassure, buoy up, embolden; promise, bid fair, augur well.

Adj. hopeful, confident, in hopes, secure, sanguine, buoyant, elated, flushed, exultant, enthusiastic.

fearless, unsuspecting, unsuspicious, undespairing, self-reliant; dauntless, etc. (*courageous*), 861.

propitious, promising; probable, auspicious, reassuring; encouraging, cheering, inspiriting, bright, roseate.

859. HOPELESSNESS.—*N.* hopelessness, despair, desperation; despondency, dejection, etc., 837; pessimism, hope deferred, dashed hopes.

pessimist, hypochondriac; bird of ill omen.

V. despair; lose (*or* give up, abandon) all hope, give up, give over, yield to despair; falter; despond.

Adj. hopeless, desperate, despairing, gone, in despair, forlorn, inconsolable, brokenhearted.

undone, ruined; incurable, cureless, incorrigible; irreparable, irrecoverable, irretrievable, irreclaimable, irredeemable, irrevocable.

unpropitious, unpromising, inauspicious, ill-omened, threatening, lowering, ominous.

860. FEAR.—*N.* **fear,** timidity, diffidence, apprehensiveness, fearfulness, solicitude, anxiety, care, apprehension, misgiving, mistrust, suspicion, qualm; hesitation.

trepidation, flutter, fear and trembling, perturbation, tremor, quivering, shaking, trembling, palpitation, nervousness, restlessness, disquietude, funk [*colloq.*].

fright, alarm, dread, awe, terror, horror, dismay, consternation, panic, scare; stampede [*of horses*].

intimidation, bullying; terrorism, reign of terror; terrorist, bully.

V. **fear,** be afraid, apprehend, dread, distrust; hesitate, falter, funk [*colloq.*], cower, crouch, skulk, take fright, take alarm; start, wince, flinch, shy, shrink, fly.

tremble, shake, shiver, shudder, flutter, quake, quaver, quiver, quail.

frighten, fright, terrify, inspire (*or* excite) fear, bulldoze [*colloq.*], alarm, startle, scare, dismay, astound; awe, strike terror, appall, unman, petrify, horrify.

daunt, intimidate, cow, overawe, abash, deter, discourage; browbeat, bully, threaten, terrorize.

haunt, obsess, beset, besiege; prey (*or* weigh) on the mind.

Adj. **afraid,** frightened, alarmed, fearful, timid, timorous, nervous, diffident, fainthearted, tremulous, shaky. afraid of one's shadow, apprehensive; aghast, awe-struck, awe-stricken, horror-stricken, panic-stricken.

dreadful, alarming, redoubtable, perilous, dread, fell, dire, direful, shocking, frightful, terrible, terrific, tremendous; horrid, horrible, ghastly, awful, awe-inspiring, revolting.

861. [Absence of fear] **COURAGE** —*N.* **courage,** bravery, valor, resoluteness, boldness, spirit, daring, gallantry, intrepidity, prowess, heroism, chivalry, audacity, rashness, dash, defiance, confidence, self-reliance; manhood, manliness, nerve, pluck, mettle, grit, virtue, hardihood, fortitude, firmness, backbone, resolution, tenacity.

exploit, feat, deed, act, achievement.

brave man, man of courage, a man, hero, demigod; Hercules, Achilles, Sir Galahad.

brave woman, heroine; Amazon, Joan of Arc.

V. **dare,** venture, make bold; face (*or* front, confront, brave, defy, despise) danger; face; meet, brave, beard, defy.

nerve oneself, summon up (*or* pluck up) courage, take heart, stand to one's guns, bear up, hold out; present a bold front, show fight, face the music.

hearten, inspire courage, reassure, encourage, embolden, inspirit, cheer, nerve, rally.

Adj. **courageous,** brave, valiant, valorous, gallant, intrepid, spirited, high-spirited, mettlesome, plucky; manly, manful, stouthearted, lionhearted, bold, daring, audacious, fearless, dauntless, undaunted, undismayed, unflinching, unshrinking, confident, self-reliant.

enterprising, adventurous, venturous, venturesome; dashing, chivalrous, warlike, soldierly, heroic.

fierce, savage, pugnacious, bellicose.

strong-minded, strong-willed, hardy, doughty [*archaic or humorous*]; firm, resolute, determined, dogged, indomitable.

862. [Excess of fear] COWARDICE.—*N.* cowardice, pusillanimity, cowardliness, timidity, effeminacy; baseness, abject fear, funk [*colloq.*]; fear, etc., 860; white feather, cold feet [*slang*], yellow streak [*slang*].

coward, poltroon, dastard, sneak, recreant, cur [*contemptuous*], craven.

alarmist, terrorist, pessimist.

shirker, slacker; fugitive, etc., 623.

V. **quail,** funk [*colloq.*], cower, skulk, sneak; flinch, shy, fight shy, slink, run away; show the white feather.

Adj. **cowardly,** coward, fearful, shy, timid, timorous, spiritless, soft, effeminate, fainthearted; white-livered; dastard, dastardly, base, craven, sneaking, recreant; unwarlike.

Adv. **with fear and trembling,** in fear of one's life, in a blue funk [*colloq.*].

863. RASHNESS.—*N.* rashness, temerity, imprudence, indiscretion; overconfidence, presumption, audacity, precipitancy, impetuosity, foolhardiness, heedlessness, thoughtlessness, carelessness, desperation.

gaming, gambling; blind bargain, leap in the dark.

desperado, madcap, daredevil; scapegrace, Don Quixote, knight-errant, adventurer; fire-eater, bully, bravo.

gambler, gamester, etc. (*chance*), 621.

V. **be rash,** stick at nothing, play a desperate game, run into danger, play with fire (*or* edged tools); rush on destruction, tempt providence, go on a forlorn hope.

Adj. **rash,** incautious, indiscreet, injudicious, imprudent, improvident, uncalculating, impulsive, heedless, careless, without ballast.

reckless, wild, madcap, desperate, devil-may-care, death-defying, hotheaded, headlong, headstrong; breakneck, foolhardy, harebrained, precipitate.

overconfident, overweening; venturesome, venturous, adventurous, quixotic.

Adv. posthaste, headforemost.

864. CAUTION.—*N.* caution, cautiousness, discretion, prudence, heed, circumspection, calculation, deliberation, foresight, etc., 510; vigilance, etc., 459; warning, etc., 668.

worldly wisdom; safety first, Fabian policy, watchful waiting.

coolness, self-possession, self-command; presence of mind, *sang-froid* [F.].

V. be cautious, take care, take heed, mind, be on one's guard; think twice, look before one leaps, count the cost, feel one's way, see how the land lies; pussyfoot [*colloq.*], keep out of harm's way, stand aloof; keep (*or* be) on the safe side.

warn, caution, etc., 668.

Adj. cautious, wary, guarded, on one's guard, suspicious, vigilant, careful, heedful, chary, sure-footed, circumspect, prudent, noncommittal, canny [Scot.], discreet, politic, strategic.

unenterprising, unadventurous, cool, steady, self-possessed; overcautious.

865. DESIRE.—*N.* desire, wish, fancy, inclination, leaning, bent, mind, whim, partiality, predilection, propensity, liking, love, fondness, relish.

longing, hankering, yearning, aspiration, ambition, eagerness, zeal, ardor, solicitude, anxiety.

need, want, exigency, urgency, necessity.

appetite, keenness, hunger, stomach, thirst, drought.

avidity, greed, greediness, covetousness, ravenousness, grasping, craving, rapacity, voracity.

mania, passion, rage, furor, frenzy, itching palm, cupidity, kleptomania, dipsomania; monomania.

Person desiring: lover, votary, devotee, aspirant; parasite, sycophant.

attraction, magnet, loadstone, lure, allurement, fancy, temptation, fascination; hobby.

V. desire, wish, wish for, care for, affect, like, take to, cling to, fancy; prefer, have an eye to, have a mind to; have a fancy for, have at heart, be bent upon; set one's heart (*or* mind) upon, covet, crave, hanker after, pine for, long for; hope, etc., 858.

woo, court, ogle, solicit; fish for.

want, miss, need, lack, feel the want of.

attract, allure, whet the appetite; appetize, take one's fancy, tempt, tantalize, make one's mouth water.

Adj. desirous, desiring, appetitive, inclined, fain, wishful, longing, wistful; anxious, solicitous, sedulous.

eager, keen, burning, fervent, ardent; agog; breathless; impatient.

ambitious, aspiring, vaulting.

craving, hungry, sharp-set, peckish [*colloq.*], ravening, famished; thirsty, athirst, dry [*colloq. when meaning thirsty*], droughty.

greedy, voracious, ravenous, omnivorous, covetous, rapacious, grasping, extortionate, exacting, sordid, insatiable, insatiate.

desirable, desired, in demand, popular, pleasing, appetizing.

Adv. fain; with eager appetite.

866. INDIFFERENCE.—*N.* indifference, neutrality; unconcern, nonchalance, apathy, supineness, disdain, inattention, coldness.

V. be indifferent, stand neuter, take no interest in, have no desire for, have no taste for, not care for, care nothing for (*or* about); not mind; spurn, disdain.

Adj. indifferent, cold, frigid, lukewarm; cool, neutral, unconcerned, phlegmatic, easygoing, careless, listless, halfhearted, unambitious, undesirous, unsolicitous.

unattractive, unalluring, undesired, undesirable, unwished.

867. DISLIKE.—*N.* dislike, distaste, disrelish, disinclination, unwillingness, reluctance, backwardness.

repugnance, disgust, nausea, loathing, aversion, abomination, antipathy, abhorrence, horror, hatred, detestation; hate, etc., 898.

V. dislike, disrelish; mind, object to, have no taste for, shudder at, turn up the nose at, look askance at; shun, avoid, eschew, shrink from.

loathe, abominate, detest, abhor; hate, etc., 898.

repel, disincline, sicken, pall, nauseate, disgust, shock, make one's blood run cold.

Adj. loath, averse; shy of, sick of, disinclined, heartsick.

repugnant, repulsive, repellent, abhorrent, insufferable, fulsome, nauseous, loathsome, offensive, disgusting.

unpopular, undesirable, uncared for, disliked, out of favor.

uneatable, inedible, unappetizing, unsavory.

Adv. to satiety, to one's disgust.

868. FASTIDIOUSNESS.—*N.* fastidiousness, nicety, hypercriticism, epicurism.

discrimination, discernment, perspicacity, keenness, sharpness, insight.

epicure, gourmet.

Excess of delicacy: prudery, prudishness, primness.

V. be fastidious, split hairs; mince the matter; turn up one's nose at, disdain.

discriminate, have nice discrimination; have exquisite taste; be discriminative.

Adj. **fastidious,** nice, delicate, meticulous, finicking *or* finicky, exacting, hard to please, difficult, dainty, squeamish, thin-skinned; querulous; particular, scrupulous; critical, hypercritical, overcritical.

prudish, strait-laced, prim.

discriminative, discriminating, discerning, judicious, keen, sharp, perspicacious.

869. SATIETY.—*N.* **satiety,** satisfaction, saturation, repletion, glut, surfeit, satiation.

V. **sate,** satiate, satisfy, saturate, cloy, quench, slake, pall, glut, gorge, surfeit; bore, tire, spoil.

Adj. **satiated,** overgorged, overfed, blasé [F.], sick of.

870. WONDER.—*N.* **wonder,** astonishment, amazement, wonderment, bewilderment, admiration, awe; stupor, stupefaction, fascination, surprise.

V. **wonder,** marvel, admire, be surprised, start, stare; gape, hold one's breath, stand aghast.

astonish, surprise, amaze, astound; dumfound, dumfounder, startle, dazzle, daze, strike, electrify, stun, stupefy, petrify, confound, bewilder, stagger, fascinate, take away one's breath, strike dumb.

Adj. **astonished,** surprised, aghast, breathless, agape, openmouthed, thunderstruck, spellbound; lost in amazement (*or* wonder, astonishment).

wonderful, wondrous, surprising, striking, marvelous, miraculous; unexpected, mysterious, monstrous, prodigious, stupendous, inconceivable, incredible, strange.

indescribable, inexpressible, ineffable; unutterable, unspeakable.

Adv. for a wonder, strange to say, to one's great surprise.

871. [Absence of wonder] EXPECTANCE.—*N.* **expectance,** expectancy, expectation, etc., 507.

calmness, imperturbability, *sang-froid* [F.], coolness, steadiness, lack of nerves, want of imagination.

V. **expect,** etc., 507; not wonder, make nothing of, take it coolly.

Adj. **expecting,** unamazed, astonished at nothing, blasé [F.], expected, foreseen.

calm, imperturbable, nerveless, cool, coolheaded, unruffled, steady, unimaginative.

common, ordinary, etc. (*habitual*), 613.

872. PRODIGY.—*N.* **prodigy,** phenomenon, wonder, wonderment, marvel, miracle; freak, freak of nature, monstrosity, monster; curiosity, infant prodigy, lion, sight, spectacle; sign, portent.

873. REPUTE.—*N.* **repute,** reputation, distinction, mark, name, figure, note, notability, éclat, vogue, celebrity, fame, renown, popularity; credit, prestige, account, regard, respect, fair name.

dignity, stateliness, solemnity, grandeur, luster, splendor, nobility, majesty, sublimity, glory, honor.

rank, standing, precedence, station, place, status, position, order, degree, caste, condition.

eminence, greatness, height, importance, pre-eminence, supereminence, elevation, exaltation.

celebrity, worthy, hero, man of mark (*or* rank), lion, notability, somebody.

scholar, savant; paragon, star; elite.

ornament, honor, feather in one's cap, halo, aureole, nimbus; laurels.

posthumous fame, memory, celebration, canonization, enshrinement, glorification, immortality, immortal name.

V. **be distinguished,** shine, etc. (*light*), 420; shine forth, figure, cut a figure, flourish, flaunt, play first fiddle, bear the palm, take precedence; win laurels (*or* golden opinions).

surpass, outshine, outrival, outvie, eclipse; throw into the shade, overshadow.

rival, emulate, vie with.

honor, give (*or* do, pay) honor to, accredit, dignify, glorify, pledge, toast, look up to, exalt, aggrandize, elevate, enthrone, signalize, immortalize, deify.

consecrate; dedicate to, devote to; enshrine, inscribe, blazon, lionize.

Adj. **distinguished,** noted, of note, honored, popular, remarkable, notable, celebrated, renowned, famous, famed, far-famed, conspicuous, foremost.

reputable, in good odor, in favor, in high favor, respectable, creditable, worthy.

imperishable, deathless, immortal, never fading, fadeless.

illustrious, glorious, splendid, brilliant, radiant; bright, etc.,420.

eminent, prominent, high, etc., 206; peerless, pre-eminent, great, dignified, proud, noble, honorable, lordly, grand, stately, august, princely, imposing, solemn, transcendent, majestic, sacred, sublime.

874. DISREPUTE.—*N.* **disrepute,** discredit, ill-repute, illfavor, ingloriousness, derogation, abasement, debasement, degradation; odium, obloquy, opprobrium, ignominy, dishonor, disgrace, shame, humiliation, scandal, infamy.

stigma, brand, reproach, imputation, slur, stain, blot, spot, blur, tarnish, taint, badge of infamy.

V. **be inglorious**, have a bad name; disgrace oneself, lose caste; fall from one's high estate, cut a sorry figure.

shame, disgrace, put to shame, dishonor; tarnish, stain, blot, sully, taint; discredit, degrade, debase, expel.

stigmatize, vilify, defame, slur, brand, post, send to Coventry, snub, show up [*colloq.*], reprehend.

disconcert, put out [*colloq.*], upset, discompose; put to the blush.

Adj. **disgraced**, overcome, downtrodden, in bad repute, under a cloud, in the shade (*or* background); down in the world, down and out [*colloq.*].

inglorious, nameless, obscure, unknown to fame, unnoticed, unnoted, unhonored, unglorified.

discreditable, questionable, shameful, disgraceful, disreputable, despicable; unbecoming, unworthy, derogatory, degrading, humiliating, scandalous, infamous, opprobrious, arrant, shocking, outrageous, notorious, ignominious, base, abject, vile.

beggarly, pitiful, mean, petty, shabby.

875. NOBILITY.—*N.* **nobility**, rank, condition, distinction, blood, birth, high descent, order, quality.

high life, upper classes, upper ten [*colloq.*], the four hundred; elite, aristocracy, fashionable world.

celebrity, bigwig [*humorous*], magnate, great man, star, great gun [*colloq.*].

The nobility: peerage, baronage; House of Lords (*or* peers); lords, noblesse.

peer, noble, nobleman; lord, grandee, don, hidalgo; aristocrat, swell [*colloq.*], gentleman, squire, patrician.

gentry, gentlefolk, magnates.

king, etc., 745; prince, duke, marquis, earl, viscount, baron, baronet, knight, chevalier, count, esquire, laird [Scot.]; signior, seignior; *signor* [It.], *señor* [Sp.], *senhor* [Pg.]; sheik, pasha, sahib.

empress, queen, princess, duchess, marchioness, viscountess, countess; lady, *doña* [Sp.], *dona* [Pg.]; *signora* [It.], *señora* [Sp.], *senhora* [Pg.].

Hindu titles: raja, rana (*fem.* rani), maharaja, maharana (*fem.* maharani), Gaekwar [*lit.* cowherd; *Baroda*].

Mohammedan titles: nawab, sultan (*fem.* sultana), amir.

Rank or office: kingship, dukedom, marquisate, earldom; viscountship, county, lordship, baronetcy, knighthood.

Adj. **noble**, exalted, princely, titled, patrician, aristocratic; highborn, well born, courtly.

Adv. in high quarters.

876. THE PEOPLE.—*N.* **the people**, commonalty, democracy; obscurity; *bourgeoisie* [F.], the four million; lower classes (*or* orders), common herd, rank and file, the many, the general, the crowd, the ruck, the populace, the multitude, the million, the masses, the mobility [*humorous*], the peasantry, proletariat; *hoi polloi* [Gr.].

rabble, horde, canaille, dregs of society, mob, trash, riffraff, ragtag and bobtail.

commoner, one of the people, democrat, plebeian, republican, bourgeois [F.].

peasant, countryman, boor, churl, serf; swain, clown, clodhopper, yokel, lout, bumpkin; plowman, hayseed [*slang*], rustic, lunkhead [*colloq.*], rube [*slang*]; tiller of the soil; hewers of wood and drawers of water; gamin, street Arab.

rough, rowdy, roughneck [*slang*], ruffian, tough [*colloq.*], scullion, low fellow, cad.

upstart, parvenu, nobody, snob, mushroom, adventurer, *nouveau riche* (*pl. nouveaux riches*) [F.].

vagabond, beggar, caitiff, ragamuffin, pariah, outcast, tramp, panhandler [*slang*], bum [*slang*], hobo.

Adj. ignoble, common, mean, low, base, vile, sorry, scrubby, beggarly; vulgar, low-minded; snobbish, parvenu, low-bred; menial, servile.

plebeian, proletarian, lowborn, baseborn, risen from the ranks, obscure, untitled.

rustic, country, uncivilized; loutish, boorish, clownish, churlish, rude.

barbarous, barbarian, barbaric.

Adv. below the salt.

877. TITLE.—*N.* title, honor; earldom, etc. (*nobility*), 875.

highness, excellency, grace, lordship, reverence; reverend; esquire, sir, master, Mr., *signor* [It.], *señor* [Sp.], etc., 373; your (*or* his) honor.

madam, etc. (*mistress*), 374; empress, queen, etc., 875.

decoration, laurel, palm, wreath, garland, bays; medal, ribbon, cordon, cross, crown, coronet, star, garter; epaulet, chevron, colors, cockade; livery; order, arms, coat of arms, shield, escutcheon *or* scutcheon, crest; handle to one's name.

878. PRIDE.—*N.* pride, haughtiness, high notions, hauteur, vainglory, arrogance, self-importance, pomposity, side [*slang*], swagger, toploftiness [*colloq.*].

dignity, self-respect, self-esteem, decorum, stateliness, seemliness.

V. be proud, presume, swagger, strut, hold one's head high, look big, carry with a high hand; ride the high horse, give oneself airs.

Adj. dignified, stately, lordly, lofty-minded, high-souled, high-minded, high-mettled, high-flown.

proud, haughty, lofty, high, mighty, swollen, puffed up, flushed, vainglorious; purse-proud, fine.

supercilious, disdainful, bumptious, magisterial, imperious, high and mighty, overweening, consequential; pompous, toplofty [*colloq.*]; arrogant.

stiff, stiff-necked; starched, stuck up [*colloq.*]; strait-laced, prim, affected, etc., 855.

Adv. with head erect, with nose in air, with nose turned up; with a sneer, with curling lip.

879. HUMILITY.—*N.* humility, humbleness, meekness, lowliness, abasement, self-abasement, submission, resignation.

modesty, timidity; confusion, humiliation, mortification.

V. **be humble,** deign, vouchsafe, condescend, humble oneself, stoop, submit, yield the palm, sing small [*colloq.*], hide one's face.

be humiliated, be put out of countenance, be shamed, be put to the blush, receive a snub, eat humble pie.

humble, humiliate, snub, abash, abase, strike dumb, lower, cast into the shade, put to the blush, confuse, shame, mortify, disgrace, crush.

Adj. **humble,** lowly, meek, modest, etc., 881; humble-minded, sober-minded; submissive, servile.

humbled, bowed down, abashed, ashamed, dashed, crestfallen, shorn of one's glory.

Adv. with downcast eyes, with bated breath, on bended knee.

880. VANITY.—*N.* vanity, conceit, conceitedness, self-conceit, self-sufficiency, self-praise, self-glorification, self-applause, self-admiration; selfishness, etc., 943.

pretension, airs, affected manner, mannerism; egoism, egotism, priggishness; vainglory, arrogance, pride, ostentation.

egoist, egotist; peacock; coxcomb.

V. **be vain,** pique oneself, have too high opinion of oneself, strut, put oneself forward; give oneself airs, boast, etc., 884.

render vain, inflate, puff up, turn one's head.

Adj. **vain,** conceited, overweening, forward, vainglorious, high-flown, ostentatious, etc., 882; puffed up, inflated, flushed, elate.

self-satisfied, complacent, self-confident, self-sufficient, self-admiring, pretentious, priggish, egotistic *or* egotistical, arrogant, assured.

881. MODESTY.—*N.* modesty; humility, etc., 879; diffidence, demureness, timidity, bashfulness, retiring disposition, unobtrusiveness; blush, blushing; reserve, constraint.

V. **be modest,** retire, give way to, hide one's face; keep in the background; hide one's light under a bushel.

Adj. **modest,** diffident, retiring, humble, etc., 879; timid, timorous, bashful, shy, coy, demure, sheepish, shamefaced, blushing.

unpretending, unpretentious, unobtrusive, unassuming, unostentatious; reserved, constrained.

Adv. **modestly,** quietly, privately; without ceremony.

882. OSTENTATION.—*N.* ostentation, display, show, flourish, parade, pomp, magnificence, splendor, pageantry, array, state, solemnity; dash [*colloq.*], splash [*colloq.*], glitter, pomposity, pretense, pretensions.

demonstration, pageant, spectacle, exhibition, exposition, procession, turnout [*colloq.*]; fete, field day, review, march past, promenade.

ceremony, ceremonial, ritual, form, formality, etiquette, punctilio.

V. flaunt, show off, parade, display, exhibit, brandish, blazon forth; dangle, emblazon.

Adj. ostentatious, showy, dashing, pretentious, grand, pompous; garish, gaudy, flaunting, glittering, gay.

splendid, magnificent, sumptuous, palatial.

theatrical, theatric, dramatic, spectacular, scenic.

ceremonial, ceremonious, ritualistic; solemn, stately, majestic, formal, punctilious.

Adv. with flourish of trumpet, with beat of drum, with flying colors.

883. CELEBRATION.—*N.* celebration, solemnization, commemoration; jubilation, ovation, triumph; inauguration, installation, presentation; coronation; debut, coming out [*colloq.*].

birthday, anniversary, biennial, triennial, etc.; centenary, centennial; bicentenary, bicentennial; tercentenary, tercentennial, etc.; festivity, festival, fete, holiday.

triumphal arch; salute, salvo, salvo of artillery; flourish of trumpets, fanfare; colors flying; illuminations.

jubilee, 50th anniversary; diamond jubilee.

V. celebrate, keep, signalize, do honor to, commemorate, solemnize; rejoice, etc., 838; paint the town red [*colloq.*].

inaugurate, install, instate, induct, chair.

Adj. commemorative, celebrated, kept in remembrance; immortal.

Adv. in honor of, in commemoration of, in celebration of, in memory of, in memoriam [L.].

884. BOASTING.—*N.* boasting, boast, vaunt, pretensions, braggadocio, puff [*colloq.*], flourish, bluff, highfalutin, swagger, jingoism, chauvinism, brag, bounce, bluster, bravado, buncombe [*cant or slang*]; rodomontade, bombast, hot air [*slang*], tall talk [*colloq.*], exaggeration, magniloquence, heroics.

boaster, braggart, pretender, bluffer, hot-air artist [*slang*]; chauvinist, jingo, jingoist; blusterer, swaggerer.

V. boast, brag, vaunt, puff, show off, flourish, strut, swagger, bluff; talk big, draw the long bow, blow one's own trumpet.

exult, crow [*colloq.*], triumph, glory, rejoice, cheer; gloat, gloat over, chuckle.

Adj. boastful, braggart, pretentious, vainglorious, highfalutin.

elate, elated, jubilant, triumphant, exultant; in high feather.

885. [Undue assumption of superiority] INSOLENCE.—*N.* in-

solence, brazenness, haughtiness, arrogance, airs; bumptiousness, assumption, presumption; disdain, insult, bluster, swagger.

impertinence, cheek [*colloq. or, slang*], nerve [*slang*], sauce [*colloq.*], abuse; flippancy.

impudence, self-assertion, assurance, audacity, hardihood, gall [*slang*], shamelessness, effrontery.

V. be insolent, bluster, swagger, give oneself airs, arrogate, assume, presume; make bold, make free, take a liberty.

outface, outlook, outstare, outbrazen, brazen out; look big.

domineer, bully, dictate, hector; lord it over; snub, browbeat, intimidate; dragoon, bulldoze [*colloq.*], terrorize.

Adj. insolent, haughty, arrogant, imperious, dictatorial, arbitrary, highhanded, supercilious, overbearing, toplofty [*colloq.*], intolerant, domineering, overweening, bumptious.

pert, flippant, fresh [*slang*], saucy, forward, impertinent, assuming, impudent, audacious, presumptuous.

brazen, shameless, unblushing, unabashed; barefaced, brazen-faced; lost to shame.

blustering, swaggering, hectoring, rollicking, roistering, devil-may-care.

jingo, jingoistic, chauvinistic.

Adv. with nose in air; with arms akimbo; with a high hand.

886. SERVILITY.—*N.* servility, slavery, obsequiousness, toadying, subserviency; abasement, prostration, toadeating, fawning, flunkyism, sycophancy; humility, etc., 879.

sycophant, parasite, toady, toadeater, flunky, hanger-on, timeserver, flatterer, tool; beat [*slang*], dead beat [*slang*]; heeler, ward heeler [*both polit. cant*]; sponge, sponger, truckler.

V. cringe, bow, stoop, kneel; fawn, crouch, cower, sneak, crawl, sponge, toady, grovel; be servile.

go with the stream, follow the crowd, worship the rising sun; be a timeserver.

Adj. servile, obsequious, oily, pliant, cringing, fawning, slavish, groveling, sniveling, mealy-mouthed; sycophantic, parasitical; abject, prostrate, base, mean, sneaking, timeserving.

887. BLUSTERER.—*N.* blusterer, swaggerer, braggart; roisterer, brawler, bully, terrorist, rough, ruffian, roughneck [*slang*], tough [*colloq.*], rowdy, hoodlum [*colloq.*], hooligan [*slang*], swashbuckler; desperado, daredevil, fire-eater [*colloq.*], jingo.

dogmatist, doctrinaire, stump orator.

III. SYMPATHETIC AFFECTIONS

888. FRIENDSHIP.—*N.* friendship, amity, friendliness; harmony, concord, peace, etc., 721; cordiality, *entente cordiale* [F.], good understanding, sympathy, fellow feeling, response; affection, etc. (*love*), 897; benevolence, good will; partiality, favoritism.

brotherhood, fraternization, association; acquaintance, familiarity, intimacy, intercourse, fellowship.

fraternity, sodality; sisterhood, sorority, sorosis.

V. **be friendly,** be friends, be acquainted with, know; have dealings with, sympathize with, have a leaning to, bear good will, love, befriend.

become friendly, make friends with, break the ice, be introduced to, make (*or* scrape) acquaintance with, get into favor, gain the friendship of; shake hands with, fraternize.

Adj. **friendly,** amicable, neighborly; brotherly, fraternal, sisterly; ardent, devoted, sympathetic, harmonious, hearty, cordial, warmhearted.

friends with, at home with, on good (*or* friendly, amicable, cordial, familiar, intimate) terms, on speaking terms, on visiting terms.

acquainted, familiar, intimate, hail fellow well met, free and easy; welcome.

Adv. with open arms; arm in arm.

889. ENMITY.—*N.* enmity, hostility, antagonism, unfriendliness; discord, etc., 713; bitterness, rancor; heartburning, animosity; malevolence, etc., 907.

alienation, estrangement; dislike, aversion, hate, etc., 898.

V. **be unfriendly,** keep (*or* hold) at arm's length; be at loggerheads, bear malice, fall out; take umbrage; alienate, estrange.

Adj. **unfriendly,** inimical, hostile; at enmity, at variance, at daggers drawn, up in arms against.

on bad terms, not on speaking terms; cool, cold, estranged, alienated, disaffected, irreconcilable.

890. FRIEND.—*N.* friend, alter ego [L.], other self; intimate, confidant (*masc.*), confidante (*fem.*); best (*or* bosom, fast) friend, well-wisher; neighbor, acquaintance.

patron, backer, tutelary saint, good genius, advocate, partisan, sympathizer; ally, friend in need.

associate, comrade, mate, companion, confrere, colleague, partner, consort, chum [*colloq.*], pal [*slang*], buddy [*slang, First World War*]; playfellow, playmate, schoolmate, schoolfellow, classmate; bedfellow, bunkie [*colloq.*], roommate, shopmate, shipmate, messmate; fellow (*or* boon) companion.

Famous friendships: Pylades and Orestes, Castor and Pollux, Achilles and Patroclus, Damon and Pythias, David and Jonathan; Soldiers Three, the Three Musketeers.

host, hostess (*fem.*).

guest, visitor, frequenter, habitué, protégé.

compatriot, countryman, fellow countryman; fellow townsman.

891. ENEMY.—*N.* enemy, antagonist, foe, foeman, open (*or* bitter) enemy, opponent; mortal aversion (*or* antipathy); snake in the grass.

public enemy, enemy to society; anarchist, seditionist, traitor, traitress (*fem.*).

892. SOCIALITY.—*N.* sociality, sociability, social intercourse, intercourse, companionship, comradeship, fellowship; urbanity, intimacy, familiarity, condescension, *esprit de corps* [F.]; morale.

conviviality, good fellowship, joviality, jollity, festivity, merry-making; hospitality, heartiness; cheer.

welcome, greeting; hearty (*or* warm) reception; hearty welcome (*or* greeting), the glad hand [*slang*].

social gathering, social reunion, assembly, barbecue; bee; cornhusking, corn shucking [U. S.]; husking, husking-bee [U. S.]; hen party [*colloq.*]; house raising, housewarming, hanging of the crane, smoker [*colloq.*]; Dutch treat [*colloq.*]; stag, stag party [*both colloq.*]; sociable [U. S.], party, entertainment, reception, levee, at home, soiree, matinee; garden party, coming-out party [*colloq.*], surprise party; ball, hunt ball, dance festival.

Social meals: breakfast, wedding breakfast, hunt breakfast; luncheon, lunch; picnic lunch, basket lunch, picnic; tea, afternoon tea, five-o'clock tea, cup of tea, dish of tea [esp. Brit.], coming-out tea [*colloq.*]; tea party, tea fight [*slang*]; dinner, potluck, bachelor dinner, stag dinner [*colloq.*], hunt dinner; church supper, high tea, banquet.

visit, visiting; round of visits; call, morning call, interview; tryst, appointment.

V. be sociable, know, be acquainted, associate with, consort with, club together, join; make advances, fraternize.

visit, pay a visit, call at, call upon, leave a card, drop in, look in.

entertain, give a party; see one's friends, keep open house, do the honors, receive, welcome; kill the fatted calf.

Adj. sociable, companionable, clubbable [*colloq.*], cozy, chatty, conversational; convivial, festive, festal, jovial, jolly, hospitable.

free and easy, hail fellow well met, familiar, intimate, social, neighborly.

Adv. en *famille* [F.], in the family circle; on terms of intimacy; in the social whirl.

893. SECLUSION. EXCLUSION.—*N.* seclusion, privacy, retirement, concealment, rustication, solitude, isolation, loneliness, voluntary exile, aloofness.

retreat, cell, hermitage, cloister, convent; sanctum sanctorum [L.], study, library, den [*colloq.*].

exclusion, excommunication, banishment, exile, ostracism, cut.

unsociability, unsociableness, inhospitality, domesticity, self-sufficiency.

recluse, hermit; caveman, cave dweller, troglodyte, cynic, Diogenes.

outcast, pariah, leper; outsider, rank outsider; castaway, foundling.

V. **seclude oneself,** keep aloof, shut oneself up; deny oneself, rusticate, retire, retire from the world; take the veil.

exclude, repel, cut; send to Coventry, turn one's back upon, shut the door upon; blackball, excommunicate, exile, expatriate; banish, outlaw, maroon, ostracize, keep at arm's length; boycott, embargo, blockade, isolate.

Adj. **secluded,** sequestered, retired, private, out of the world.

unsociable, unsocial, inhospitable; domestic, stay-at-home.

excluded, unfrequented, unvisited, uninvited, unwelcome, under a cloud.

friendless, homeless, desolate, lorn, forlorn; solitary, lonely, lonesome, isolated, single, estranged; derelict, outcast, deserted, banished.

uninhabited, unoccupied, untenanted, tenantless, abandoned.

894. COURTESY.—*N.* courtesy; respect, etc., 928; good manners (*or* behavior, breeding); manners, politeness, urbanity, gentility, breeding, gentle breeding, cultivation, culture, polish, civility, amenity, suavity; good temper, good humor, amiability, complacency, affability, complaisance, compliance, gallantry, chivalry.

pink of courtesy, pink of politeness; flower of knighthood; Chesterfield; Lancelot.

ceremonial; salutation, reception, presentation, introduction, welcome, greeting; respects, regards, remembrances; deference, love.

Forms of greeting: bow, curtsy, salaam, kowtow [China], obeisance, bowing and scraping; kneeling, genuflection; capping, pulling the forelock, nod, shaking hands; embrace, hug, squeeze, kiss; salute, accolade.

V. **be courteous,** show courtesy; behave oneself, conciliate, speak one fair, take in good part.

do the honors, usher, usher in, receive, greet, hail, bid welcome, welcome; bid Godspeed; speed the parting guest.

salute; nod to; smile upon; uncover, touch (*or* raise) the hat, doff the cap, bow, make one's bow, curtsy, bob a curtsy, kneel; bow (*or* bend) the knee; salaam, kowtow [China], prostrate oneself.

Adj. **courteous,** polite, civil, mannerly, urbane; well behaved, well mannered, well bred, gently bred, of gentle breeding; polished, cultivated, refined; gallant, chivalrous, chivalric, knightly.

tactful, ingratiating, winning; gentle, mild; good-humored, cordial, gracious, amiable, familiar; neighborly; obliging, complacent, conciliatory.

bland, suave, affable, honey-tongued; oily, unctuous, obsequious.

Adv. with a good grace; with open arms, with outstretched arms, with perfect courtesy, in good humor.

895. DISCOURTESY.—*N.* discourtesy, ill-breeding, bad manners; tactlessness; discourteousness, rusticity, incivility, lack (*or* want) of courtesy, disrespect, impudence, misbehavior, barbarism, barbarity; vulgarity, brutality, blackguardism, conduct unbecoming a gentleman.

bad temper, ill-temper, peevishness, surliness, churlishness, perversity; moroseness, etc., 901*a*; sternness, austerity; moodishness, captiousness, tartness, acrimony, asperity.

scowl, black looks, frown; sulks, short answer, rebuff; hard words, unparliamentary language, personality.

bear, brute, blackguard, beast; unlicked cub; crosspatch [*colloq.*], grouch [*slang*].

V. **be rude,** insult, treat with discourtesy, make bold with, make free with; take a liberty; stare out of countenance, ogle, point at.

sulk, frown, scowl, glower, pout; snap, snarl, growl.

cut; turn one's back upon, turn on one's heel; give the cold shoulder, keep at a distance.

Adj. **discourteous,** uncourteous, uncourtly, ill-bred, ill-mannered, ill-behaved, unmannerly, uncivil, impolite, unaccommodating, unneighborly, ungallant, ungracious, unpolished; ungentlemanly; unladylike; vulgar.

pert, forward, obtrusive, impudent, rude, saucy, flippant.

rough, rugged, bluff, blunt, short, gruff; churlish, boorish, bearish; brutal, brusque, stern, harsh, austere; cavalier.

bad-tempered, ill-tempered, ill-humored, crusty, tart, sour, crabbed, sharp, trenchant, sarcastic, caustic, virulent, bitter, acrimonious, venomous, contumelious, snarling, surly, perverse, grim, sullen, peevish, bristling, thorny.

Adv. with a bad grace.

896. CONGRATULATION.—*N.* **congratulation,** felicitation, compliment; compliments of the season; good wishes, best wishes.

V. **congratulate,** felicitate, wish one joy, compliment, tender (*or* offer) one's congratulations; wish many happy returns of the day.

897. LOVE.—*N.* **love,** affection, sympathy, fellow feeling; tenderness, heart, brotherly love; charity, good will, benevolence; attachment, fondness, liking, inclination; regard, admiration, fancy.

yearning, tender passion, gallantry, passion, flame, devotion, fervor, enthusiasm, rapture, enchantment, infatuation, adoration, idolatry.

mother love, maternal love, natural affection.

attractiveness, charm; popularity; idol, favorite, etc., 899.

god of love, Cupid, Eros, Venus; myrtle.

lover, suitor, fiancé [F.], follower [*colloq.*], admirer, adorer, wooer, beau, sweetheart, swain, young man [*colloq.*], flame [*colloq.*], love, truelove.

ladylove, sweetheart, mistress, inamorata, darling, idol, angel, goddess; betrothed, fiancée [F.].

flirt, coquette.

V. **love,** like, fancy, care for, take an interest in, sympathize with; be in love with, regard, revere, take to, set one's affections on, adore, idolize, dote on (*or* upon), make much of, hold dear, prize; hug, cling to, cherish, caress, fondle, pet.

charm, attract, attach, fascinate, captivate, bewitch, enrapture, turn the head.

Adj. **loving,** affectionate, tender, sympathetic, amorous, love-sick, fond, ardent, passionate, rapturous, devoted, motherly.

loved, beloved, well beloved, dearly beloved; dear, precious, darling, pet; favorite, popular.

lovable, adorable, lovely, sweet, attractive, winning, winsome, charming, enchanting, captivating, fascinating, bewitching, amiable.

898. HATE.—*N.* **hate,** hatred, vials of hate; hymn of hate; disaffection, disfavor; alienation, estrangement, coolness; enmity, etc., 889; animosity, malice, implacability.

umbrage, pique, grudge, spleen, bitterness, bitterness of feeling; ill-blood, bad blood; acrimony.

repugnance, etc. (*dislike*), 867; odium, unpopularity; detestation, abhorrence, loathing, execration, abomination, aversion, antipathy.

object of hatred, an abomination, an aversion, bête noire [F.]; enemy, etc., 891; bitter pill.

V. **hate,** detest, abominate, abhor, loathe; recoil at, shudder at; shrink from, revolt against, execrate; dislike, etc., 867.

alienate, estrange, repel, horrify, set against, sow dissension, set by the ears, envenom, incense, irritate, ruffle, vex.

Adj. **abhorrent,** averse from, set against; bitter, etc. (*acrimonious*), 895; implacable.

unloved, unbeloved, unlamented, undeplored, unmourned, uncared for, unvalued; disliked.

lovelorn, jilted, crossed in love, forsaken, rejected.

hateful, obnoxious, odious, abominable, repulsive, offensive, shocking; disgusting, reprehensible.

invidious, spiteful; malicious, etc., 907.

899. FAVORITE.—*N.* favorite, pet, idol, jewel, spoiled child, apple of one's eye, man after one's own heart.

love, dear, darling, duck, honey, sweetheart, etc. (*ladylove*), 897.

general (*or* universal) favorite; idol of the people; matinee idol.

900. RESENTMENT.—*N.* resentment, displeasure, animosity, anger, wrath, ire, indignation; exasperation, vexation, wrathful, indignation.

pique, umbrage, huff, soreness, acerbity, virulence, bitterness, acrimony, asperity; irascibility, etc., 901; sulks, etc., 901a; hate, etc., 898; revenge.

irritation; warmth, ferment, excitement, ebullition; angry mood, pet, tiff, passion, fit, tantrum [*colloq.*].

rage, fury, towering rage, passion; outburst, explosion, paroxysm, storm, violence, vials of wrath; hot blood, high words.

Furies, Erinyes (*sing.* Erinys), Eumenides.

provocation, affront, offense, indignity, insult, grudge; last straw, sore subject; ill-turn, outrage; buffet, blow, box on the ear, rap on the knuckles.

V. **resent,** take amiss, take offense (*or* umbrage, exception); pout, frown, scowl, lower, snarl, growl, gnash, snap; redden, color; look black, look daggers.

be angry, fly into a rage, bridle up, fire up, flare up; chafe, mantle, fume, kindle, fly out, boil, boil with indignation (*or* rage); rage, storm, foam; hector, bully, bluster; lose one's temper; raise Cain [*slang*]; breathe revenge.

anger, affront, offend, give offense (*or* umbrage); hurt the feelings; insult, ruffle, heckle [Brit.], nettle, huff, pique; excite, irritate, fret, sting, provoke, chafe, wound, incense, inflame, enrage, envenom, embitter, exasperate, infuriate, madden; rankle.

Adj. **angry,** wroth, irate, ireful, wrathful; irascible, etc., 901; bitter, virulent, acrimonious, offended, indignant, hurt, sore.

fuming, raging, hot under the collar [*slang*]; convulsed with rage; fierce, wild, furious, fiery, rabid, savage, violent.

Adv. in the height (*or* heat) of passion; in an ecstasy of rage.

901. IRASCIBILITY.—*N.* irascibility, temper; crossness, petulance, irritability, tartness, acerbity, acrimony, asperity, pugnacity, excitability.

shrew, vixen, virago, dragon, scold, spitfire, fury.

V. **be irascible,** have a temper, be possessed of the devil, have the temper of a fiend; fire up, flare up.

Adj. **irascible,** bad-tempered, irritable, excitable; thin-skinned, sensitive; hasty, quick, warm, hot, testy, touchy, huffy, pettish, petulant, fretful, querulous, captious, moody, cross, fractious, peevish.

quarrelsome, contentious, disputatious, pugnacious, cantankerous [*colloq.*], cross-grained; waspish, peppery, fiery, passionate, choleric, shrewish.

901a. SULLENNESS.—*N.* sullenness, moroseness, spleen; churlishness, irascibility, moodiness, perversity, obstinacy, crabbedness.

sulks, dudgeon, dumps [*humorous*], doldrums; black looks, scowl; grouch [*slang*], huff.

V. sulk, frown, scowl, lower, glower, pout, grouch [*slang*].

Adj. sullen, sulky, ill-tempered, ill-humored, ill-disposed; crusty, crabbed, sour, sore, surly, moody, cross, cross-grained; perverse, wayward, refractory, restive, ungovernable, cussed [*vulgar or euphemistic*]; grumpy, glum, grum, grim, morose, grouchy [*slang*].

902. [Expression of affection] ENDEARMENT.—*N.* endearment, caress, blandishment, fondling, billing and cooing, dalliance, caressing, embrace, salute, kiss, smack, osculation.

courtship, wooing, suit, addresses, love-making; calf love [*colloq.*]; amorous glances, ogle, side glance, sheep's eyes, goo-goo eyes [*slang*].

flirting, flirtation, gallantry; coquetry, spooning [*slang*].

engagement, betrothal; marriage, etc., 903; honeymoon; love letter, billet-doux; valentine.

flirt, coquette; male flirt, philanderer; spoon [*slang*].

V. caress, fondle, pet; smile upon, coax, wheedle, coddle, make much of, cherish, foster.

clasp, hug, cuddle; fold to the heart, press to the bosom, fold in one's arms; snuggle, nestle, nuzzle; embrace, kiss, salute.

court, make love, bill and coo, spoon [*slang*], toy, dally, flirt, coquet, philander, pay court to; serenade; woo.

propose, make (*or* have) an offer, pop the question [*colloq.*]; become engaged, become betrothed; plight one's troth.

Adj. lovesick, spoony [*slang*].

903. MARRIAGE.—*N.* marriage, matrimony, wedlock, union, intermarriage; nuptial tie, nuptial knot; match; betrothment.

wedding, nuptials, Hymen, bridal, espousals; leading to the altar; honeymoon.

bridesmaid, maid of honor, matron of honor; attendant, usher, best man, bridesman, groomsman; bride, bridegroom.

married man, partner, spouse, mate, husband, man [*dial.*], consort.

married woman, wife, wedded wife, spouse, helpmeet, help-mate, better half, lady [*obs. or uncultivated*]; squaw; matron.

married couple, man and wife, wedded pair, wedded couple, Darby and Joan.

Kinds of marriage: monogamy, bigamy, polygamy, polyandry; Mormonism; morganatic (*or* left-handed) marriage, *mésalliance* [F.].

matchmaker, matrimonial agency (*or* agent, bureau).

V. **marry**, wive, take to oneself a wife; be married, be spliced [*colloq.*]; wed, espouse, lead to the altar, join, couple, be made one.

Adj. **engaged**, betrothed, plighted, affianced.

Matrimonial, marital, conjugal, connubial, wedded; nuptial, hymeneal, spousal, bridal.

904. CELIBACY.—*N.* **celibacy**, singleness, single blessedness; bachelorhood, bachelorship; misogyny.

virginity, maidenhood, maidenhead.

unmarried man, bachelor, old bachelor; misogamist, misogynist; monk, priest, celibate, religious.

unmarried woman, maid, maiden, virgin, spinster, old maid; nun, sister, vestal, vestal virgin; Diana.

Adj. **unmarried**, unwedded; wifeless, spouseless; single, celibate, virgin.

905. DIVORCE. WIDOWHOOD.—*N.* **divorce**, divorcement; separation, judicial separation, separate maintenance.

widowhood, weeds.

widow, relict, dowager; divorcée; grass widow.

widower; grass widower.

V. live separate; separate, divorce, put away.

906. BENEVOLENCE.—*N.* **benevolence**, Christian charity; God's grace; good will, philanthropy, unselfishness, kindness, kindliness, good nature, loving-kindness, benignity, brotherly love, charity, humanity, kindly feelings, fellow feeling, sympathy, goodness of heart, warmheartedness, kindheartedness, amiability, tenderness, love, friendship; tolerance, consideration; mercy.

charitableness, bounty, almsgiving; good works, beneficence, generosity, a good turn.

philanthropist, salt of the earth; good Samaritan, sympathizer, well-wisher, altruist.

V. bear good will, wish well, take (*or* feel) an interest in; be interested in, sympathize with, feel for; treat well, give comfort, do good, do a good turn, benefit, assist, render a service, render assistance, aid.

enter into the feelings of others, practice the golden rule, do as you would be done by.

Adj. **benevolent,** kind, kindly, well meaning, amiable, cordial, obliging, accommodating, indulgent, gracious, tender, considerate, warmhearted, kindhearted, tenderhearted, largehearted, softhearted, merciful; sympathizing, sympathetic.

full of natural affection, fatherly, motherly, brotherly, sisterly; paternal, maternal, fraternal; friendly.

charitable, beneficent, philanthropical, generous, humane, benignant, unselfish, altruistic, bountiful.

Adv. with the best intentions; out of deepest sympathy.

907. MALEVOLENCE.—*N.* **malevolence,** bad intent, bad intention, unkindness, uncharitableness, ill-nature, ill-will, enmity, hate, malice, malignance, malignity, maliciousness; spite, resentment; gall, venom, rancor, virulence, hardness of heart, heart of stone, obduracy; evil eye, cloven foot (*or* hoof).

ill-turn, bad turn; affront, indignity; tender mercies (*ironical*).

cruelty, brutality, savagery, ferocity; outrage, atrocity, ill-usage, persecution; barbarity, inhumanity, truculence, ruffianism; inquisition, torture.

V. **bear malice,** harbor a grudge; hurt, annoy, injure, harm, wrong, outrage, malign; molest, worry, harass, harry, bait, hound, persecute, oppress, grind, maltreat, ill-treat; give no quarter, have no mercy.

Adj. **malevolent,** ill-disposed, ill-intentioned, ill-natured, ill-conditioned, evil-minded, evil-disposed, venomous, malicious, malign, malignant, maleficent; rancorous, spiteful, treacherous, caustic, bitter, envenomed, acrimonious, virulent; grinding, galling, harsh; disobliging, unkind, unfriendly; ungracious, churlish, surly, sullen.

cold-blooded, coldhearted, hardhearted, stonyhearted, cold, unnatural; ruthless, pitiless, relentless.

cruel, brutal, brutish, savage, ferocious, inhuman; barbarous, fell, truculent, bloodthirsty, atrocious, fiendish, diabolic *or* diabolical, devilish, infernal, hellish.

Adv. with bad intent; with the ferocity of a tiger.

908. MALEDICTION.—*N.* **malediction,** malison, curse, imprecation, denunciation, execration; anathema, ban, proscription, excommunication, commination, fulmination; disparagement, vilification, vituperation.

abuse, evil speaking, foul (*or* bad, strong, unparliamentary) language, billingsgate, blackguardism, cursing, profane, swearing, expletive, oath, foul invective, ribaldry, scurrility, invective.

V. **curse,** imprecate, damn, swear at; execrate, vituperate, scold; anathematize, denounce, proscribe, excommunicate, fulminate, thunder against.

909. THREAT.—*N.* **threat,** menace, defiance, abuse, intimidation, denunciation, fulmination, etc., 908; gathering clouds.

V. **threaten,** threat, menace; snarl, growl, mutter, bully; defy, intimidate, shake the fist at; thunder, fulminate, bluster.

Adj. **threatening,** menacing, minatory, abusive; ominous, defiant.

910. PHILANTHROPY.—*N.* **philanthropy,** altruism, humanity, humanitarianism, benevolence; public welfare.

public spirit, patriotism, nationality, love of country.

philanthropist, altruist, etc., 906; humanitarian, patriot.

Adj. **philanthropic,** altruistic, humanitarian, public-spirited, patriotic; humane, largehearted, benevolent, etc., 906; generous, liberal, etc., 942.

911. MISANTHROPY.—*N.* **misanthropy,** hatred of mankind; selfishness, egoism, egotism; sullenness, moroseness, cynicism; want of patriotism.

misanthrope, misanthropist, egoist, egotist, cynic, man hater.

woman hater, misogynist.

Adj. **misanthropic,** antisocial, unpatriotic; egoistical, egotistical, selfish; morose, sullen, cynical, etc., 901*a*.

912. BENEFACTOR.—*N.* **benefactor,** savior, protector, good genius, tutelary saint, guardian angel, good Samaritan; friend in need; salt of the earth; philanthropist, etc., 910; fairy godmother.

913. [Maleficent being] EVILDOER.—*N.* **evildoer,** evil worker, wrongdoer, etc., 949; mischiefmaker, marplot; oppressor, tyrant; incendiary, etc., 384; anarchist, nihilist, destroyer, vandal, iconoclast, terrorist.

savage, brute, ruffian, barbarian, desperado; apache, gunman, hoodlum [*colloq.*], redskin, tough [*colloq.*], bully, rough, hooligan [*slang*], dangerous classes; thief, etc., 792; cutthroat.

wild beast, tiger, leopard, panther, hyena, catamount [U. S.], catamountain, lynx, cougar, jaguar, puma; bloodhound, hellhound, sleuthhound; gorilla; vulture.

cockatrice, adder; snake, serpent, cobra, asp, viper, rattlesnake, boa; alligator, crocodile, octopus.

hag, hellhag, beldam, Jezebel.

monster, fiend, demon, etc., 980; devil incarnate, Frankenstein's monster; cannibal; bloodsucker, vampire, ogre, ghoul.

914. PITY.—*N.* **pity,** compassion, commiseration, sympathy, fellow feeling, tenderness, softheartedness, yearning, forbearance, humanity, mercy, clemency; leniency, lenity, charity, ruth, longsuffering; quarter, grace.

sympathizer; advocate, friend, partisan, patron, well-wisher, defender, champion.

V. pity, have (*or* take) pity, commiserate, condole, sympathize, feel for, be sorry for.

forbear, relent, relax, give quarter.

excite pity, touch, soften, melt, melt the heart; propitiate.

Adj. pitying, pitiful, compassionate, sympathetic, touched. merciful, clement, humane, humanitarian; tender, tender-hearted, softhearted, lenient, forbearing.

914a. PITILESSNESS.—*N.* pitilessness, inclemency, inexorability, inflexibility, hardness of heart; want of pity, severity, malevolence, etc., 907.

V. **be pitiless,** turn a deaf ear to; claim one's pound of flesh; have no mercy, give no quarter.

Adj. pitiless, merciless, ruthless, unpitying, unmerciful, inclement, grim-faced, grim-visaged; inflexible, relentless, inexorable, harsh, cruel, etc., 907.

915. CONDOLENCE.—*N.* condolence, sympathy, consolation; lamentation, etc., 839.

V. condole with, console, sympathize, express pity; afford consolation; lament with, express sympathy for, feel for, send one's condolences; share one's sorrow.

916. GRATITUDE.—*N.* gratitude, gratefulness, thankfulness; sense of obligation; acknowledgment, recognition, thanksgiving, giving thanks.

thanks, praise, benediction; paean; *Te Deum* [L.], grace, requital, thank offering.

V. **be grateful,** thank; give (*or* render, return, offer, tender) thanks, acknowledge, requite; lie under an obligation; never forget; overflow with gratitude.

Adj. grateful, thankful, obliged, beholden, indebted to, under obligation.

917. INGRATITUDE.—*N.* ingratitude, thanklessness, unthankfulness; thankless task, thankless office.

V. **be ungrateful,** feel no obligation, owe one no thanks, forget benefits, have a short memory for.

Adj. ungrateful, unmindful, unthankful; thankless, ingrate. forgotten; unacknowledged, unthanked, unrequited, unrewarded; ill-requited; ill-rewarded.

918. FORGIVENESS.—*N.* forgiveness, pardon, grace, remission, absolution, amnesty, oblivion; reprieve.

conciliation; reconciliation, forbearance, propitiation.

exoneration, excuse, quittance, release, indemnity; acquittal, exculpation.

V. **forgive,** pardon, think no more of, let bygones by bygones, bury the hatchet. start afresh.

remit, exculpate, exonerate, absolve, give absolution; blot out one's sins (*or* offenses, transgressions), wipe the slate clean; reprieve, acquit.

excuse, pass over, overlook; condone, wink at; bear with, allow for, make allowances for; pocket the affront.

conciliate, propitiate, placate; beg (*or* ask) pardon, make up a quarrel.

Adj. forgiving, placable, conciliatory.

919. REVENGE.—*N.* revenge, vengeance; vendetta, death feud, eye for an eye, tooth for a tooth, retaliation; day of reckoning.

rancor, vindictiveness, implacability, ruthlessness; malevolence, etc., 907.

avenger, nemesis, Eumenides.

V. **revenge**, avenge, take revenge, have one's revenge; breathe vengeance; give no quarter, take no prisoners.

keep the wound open, harbor revenge, bear malice; rankle, rankle in the breast.

Adj. **revengeful**, vengeful, vindictive, rancorous; pitiless, ruthless, rigorous, avenging, retaliative; unforgiving, unrelenting, inexorable, implacable, relentless, remorseless.

920. JEALOUSY.—*N.* **jealousy**, distrust, mistrust, heartburn; envy, etc., 921; doubt, suspicion; green-eyed monster.

V. **be jealous**, view with jealousy, grudge, begrudge.

doubt, distrust, mistrust, suspect, misdoubt.

Adj. **jealous**, jaundiced, yellow-eyed, envious.

921. ENVY.—*N.* **envy**, enviousness; rivalry; ill-will, spite; jealousy, etc., 920.

V. **envy**, covet, grudge, begrudge, break the tenth commandment.

Adj. **envious**, invidious, covetous, grudging, begrudged; belittling.

IV. MORAL AFFECTIONS

922. RIGHT.—*N.* right; what ought to be, what should be; fitness.

justice, equity, equitableness, propriety, fairness, fair play, square deal [*colloq.*], impartiality; lawfulness, legality.

morals, etc. (*duty*), 926; law, etc., 963; honor, etc., 939; virtue, etc., 944.

V. **be right**, stand to reason.

do right, see justice done, see fair play; do justice to, recompense, hold the scales even, give everyone his due.

Adj. **right,** good; just, reasonable; fit, etc., 924; equal, equable, equitable; even-handed, fair, square.

legitimate, justifiable, rightful, as it ought to be; lawful, legal.

Adv. in justice, in equity, in reason; upon even terms.

923. WRONG.—*N.* **wrong,** iniquity; what ought not to be, what should not be; unreasonableness, grievance; shame.

injustice, unfairness, foul play, partiality, leaning, favor, favoritism, partisanship; undueness, unlawfulness, illegality.

dishonor, etc., 939; vice, etc., 945.

V. **do wrong,** be inequitable, show partiality, favor, lean toward; encroach; impose upon; reap where one has not sown.

Adj. **wrong,** wrongful, iniquitous, bad, unjust, unfair, inequitable, unequal, partial, one-sided; injurious.

unjustifiable, unreasonable, unwarrantable, objectionable, improper, unfit, unjustified; unlawful; illegal, immoral.

924. AUTHORIZATION.—*N.* **authorization,** sanction, authority, charter, warrant; constitution; bond.

right, dueness, due, privilege, prerogative, prescription, title, claim, pretension, legality, demand, birthright.

immunity, license, liberty, franchise; vested interest (*or* right).

deserts, merits, dues.

claimant, appellant; plaintiff, etc., 938.

V. **deserve,** merit, be worthy of, make good.

demand, claim, lay claim to, reclaim, exact; insist on (*or* upon), make a point of, require, assert, assume, arrogate.

entitle, give (*or* confer) a right, authorize, sanction, legalize, ordain, prescribe, allot.

Adj. **privileged,** allowed, sanctioned, warranted, authorized; ordained, prescribed, constitutional, chartered, enfranchised.

prescriptive, presumptive, absolute, inalienable, inviolable, sacrosanct.

merited, due to, deserved, condign [*archaic, except of punishment*].

right, creditable, fit, fitting, correct, square, due, proper, meet, befitting, becoming, seemly; decorous.

lawful, legitimate, legal, legalized, allowable.

Adv. by right, by divine right; on the square [*colloq.*].

925. [Want of authorization] IMPROPRIETY.—*N.* **impropriety,** undueness, unrightfulness, illegality, unlawfulness; falseness, invalidity of title; illegitimacy.

loss of right, disfranchisement, forfeiture.

assumption, usurpation, tort [*law*], violation, breach, encroachment, seizure, exaction, imposition.

usurper, pretender, impostor.

V. **infringe,** encroach, trench on, exact, arrogate, usurp, violate; get under false pretenses, sail under false colors.

disentitle, disfranchise, disqualify; invalidate.

Adj. **undue,** unlawful, illegal, illicit, unconstitutional, unauthorized, unwarranted, unsanctioned, unjustified; disqualified, unqualified; unprivileged, unchartered.

undeserved, unmerited, unearned.

illegitimate, bastard, spurious, false; usurped.

improper, unfit, unbefitting, unseemly, unbecoming, misbecoming; preposterous, pretentious, would-be.

926. DUTY.—*N.* **duty,** moral obligation, accountability, liability, onus, responsibility.

allegiance, fealty, tie; engagement; function, part, calling.

observance, fulfillment, discharge, performance, acquittal, satisfaction, redemption; good behavior.

morality, morals, decalogue; conscientiousness, conscience, inward monitor, still small voice within, sense of duty.

propriety, fitness, seemliness, decorum, the thing, the proper thing.

Science of morals: ethics, moral (*or* ethical) philosophy, casuistry, polity.

V. **behoove,** become, befit, beseem; belong to, pertain to; rest with, fall to one's lot, devolve on.

take upon oneself, be (*or* become) sponsor for, incur a responsibility; perform (*or* discharge) a duty *or* an obligation; act one's part, redeem one's pledge, be at one's post, do one's duty.

impose a duty, enjoin, require, exact; bind, bind over; saddle with, prescribe, assign, call upon, look to, oblige.

Adj. **obligatory,** binding, imperative, peremptory, stringent, incumbent on.

amenable, liable, accountable, responsible, answerable.

right, meet, etc. (*due*), 924; moral, ethical, conscientious.

Adv. with a safe conscience, as in duty bound, on one's own responsibility, at one's own risk.

927. DERELICTION OF DUTY.—*N.* **dereliction,** nonobservance, nonperformance, nonco-operation; indolence, neglect, infraction, violation, transgression, failure, evasion; fault, etc. (*guilt*), 947.

slacker, loafer, time killer; eyeserver, eyeservant; striker; nonco-operator.

V. **violate,** break, break through; infringe, set aside, set at naught; encroach upon, trench upon, trample on; slight, get by [*slang*], neglect, evade, escape, transgress, fail.

927a. EXEMPTION.—*N.* **exemption,** freedom, irresponsibility,

immunity, liberty, license, release, discharge, excuse, dispensation, absolution, exculpation, exoneration.

V. **exempt**, release, acquit, discharge, remit; free, set at
liberty, let off [*colloq.*], pass over, spare, excuse, dispense with,
license; absolve, exonerate.

Adj. **exempt**, free, immune, at liberty, scot-free, released,
unbound; irresponsible, not accountable, excusable.

928. RESPECT.—*N.* **respect**, regard, consideration, courtesy,
attention, deference, reverence, honor, esteem, estimation, veneration, admiration; approbation, etc., 931.

homage, fealty, obeisance, genuflection, kneeling, prostration;
salaam, etc., 894.

V. **respect**, regard; revere, reverence, honor, venerate, hallow;
esteem, think much of, entertain respect for, look up to, defer to,
pay attention to, pay respect to, do honor to; do the honors, hail,
show courtesy, pay homage to.

command respect, inspire respect; awe, impose, overawe, dazzle.

Adj. **respectful**, deferential, decorous, reverential, ceremonious,
bareheaded, cap in hand; prostrate.

respected, estimable; time-honored, venerable.

Adv. **in deference to**; with all respect, with due respect, with
the highest respect; with submission.

929. DISRESPECT.—*N.* **disrespect**, disfavor, disrepute, want
of esteem, low estimation, disparagement, detraction; irreverence,
slight, indignity, contumely, affront, dishonor, insult, outrage,
discourtesy, scoffing; hiss, hissing, hoot, derision; mockery.

gibe, flout, jeer, scoff, taunt, sneer, fling.

V. **slight**, disregard, undervalue, humiliate, depreciate, trifle
with, pass by, push aside, overlook, be discourteous.

disparage, call names; throw mud at; point at, indulge in personalities.

dishonor, desecrate; insult, affront, browbeat, outrage.

deride, scoff, sneer, laugh at, ridicule, gibe, mock, jeer, taunt,
twit, flout, roast [*colloq.*], guy [*colloq.*], rag [*dial. Eng.* and *college
slang*], burlesque, scout, hiss, hoot.

Adj. **disrespectful**, disparaging, etc., 934; insulting, supercilious, rude, derisive, sarcastic, scurrilous, contemptuous, insolent, disdainful; irreverent.

unrespected, unregarded, disregarded, unenvied, unsaluted.

930. CONTEMPT.—*N.* **contempt**, disdain, scorn, contemp-
tuousness, derision, etc. (*disrespect*), 929; contumely; slight,
sneer, spurn, byword.

V. **despise**, contemn, scorn, disdain, disregard, scout, slight,
pass by, look down upon, sneer at, laugh at, curl up one's lip, think

nothing of, make light of, underestimate, esteem slightly, care nothing for, set no store by; pooh-pooh, damn with faint praise.

spurn, turn one's back upon, trample underfoot; kick; fling to the winds, repudiate.

Adj. **contemptuous,** disdainful, scornful, withering, supercilious, cynical, haughty, cavalier; derisive; with the nose in air.

contemptible, despicable, despised, pitiable, pitiful, downtrodden.

931. APPROBATION.—*N.* **approbation,** approval, sanction, advocacy; esteem, estimation, good opinion, admiration; love, etc., 897; appreciation, regard, account, popularity, credit, repute.

commendation, compliment, praise, laud, laudation; good word; encomium, eulogy, eulogium, panegyric, blurb [*slang*]; benediction, blessing, benison.

applause, plaudit, clap, clapping, acclaim, acclamation; cheer; paean, shout (*or* peal, chorus, thunders) of applause.

V. **approve,** esteem, value, prize, set great store by; honor, hold in esteem, look up to, admire, like, appreciate; stand up for, stick up for [*colloq.*], uphold, countenance, sanction, indorse, recommend.

commend, praise, laud, compliment, applaud, clap, cheer, acclaim, encore; eulogize, boost [*colloq.*], root for [*slang*], cry up, puff; extol, magnify, glorify, exalt, sing the praises of.

Adj. **commendatory,** complimentary, laudatory, panegyrical, eulogistic, lavish of praise, uncritical.

approved, praised, popular, in good odor; in high esteem, in favor, in high favor.

praiseworthy, commendable, worthy of praise, good, meritorious, estimable, creditable, unimpeachable.

Adv. with credit, to admiration.

932. DISAPPROBATION.—*N.* **disapprobation,** disapproval, disesteem, odium, dislike, black list, blackball, ostracism, boycott.

disparagement, depreciation, dispraise, detraction, etc., 934; denunciation, condemnation, stricture, objection, exception, criticism; blame, censure, obloquy, sarcasm, satire, insinuation, innuendo, sneer, taunt.

reproof, reprehension, remonstrance, expostulation, reprobation, admonition, reproach; rebuke, reprimand, lecture, curtain lecture; wigging, dressing down [*both colloq.*]; rating, scolding, correction, rebuff, home thrust, hit; frown, scowl, black look.

abuse, personalities, personal remarks, vituperation, invective, contumely, hard words; bad language.

diatribe, tirade, philippic.

clamor, outcry, hue and cry; hiss, hissing, catcall; execration.

V. **disapprove,** dislike, object to, take exception to, think ill of, view with disfavor, frown upon, look askance, look black upon, set one's face against.

blame, censure, reproach, reprobate, impugn, impeach, accuse, denounce, expose, brand, gibbet, stigmatize; show up [*colloq.*].

reprove, reprehend, chide, admonish, berate, take to task, overhaul, lecture, rebuke, blow up [*colloq.*], correct, reprimand, snub; chastise, castigate, lash, trounce.

remonstrate, expostulate, recriminate.

abuse, scold, rate, upbraid, fall foul of; jaw [*low*], rail, rail at, call names, execrate, revile, vilify.

decry, cry down, run down, backbite; insinuate, damn with faint praise; hiss, hoot, catcall, mob; ostracize, blacklist, boycott, blackball.

disparage, depreciate, knock [*colloq.*], dispraise, deprecate, speak ill of, condemn, scoff at, sneer at, satirize, lampoon, defame, criticize.

incur blame, scandalize, shock, revolt; get a bad name, forfeit one's good opinion, be under a cloud.

Adj. **disparaging,** condemnatory, denunciatory, reproachful, abusive, vituperative, defamatory.

critical, satirical, sarcastic, sardonic, cynical, dry, sharp, cutting, biting, severe, withering, trenchant, censorious, captious, hypercritical.

blameworthy, reprehensible, blamable, answerable, bad; vicious, etc., 945.

Adv. with a wry face.

933. FLATTERY.—*N.* **flattery,** adulation, cajolery, fawning, wheedling, obsequiousness, sycophancy, flunkeyism, toadyism.

honeyed words, flummery, buncombe [*cant or slang*]; blarney, soft soap [*both colloq.*].

V. **flatter,** overpraise, puff, wheedle, cajole, fawn upon, humor, pet, coquet, butter [*colloq.*], jolly [*slang or colloq.*]; truckle to, pander to, court, curry favor with.

Adj. **flattering,** adulatory; mealy-mouthed, honeyed, smooth, smooth-tongued; oily, unctuous, specious, plausible, servile, sycophantic, fulsome.

934. DETRACTION.—*N.* **detraction,** disparagement, depreciation, vilification, obloquy, scandal, defamation, slander, calumny, evil-speaking, backbiting; sarcasm, cynicism, criticism; invective.

personality, libel, lampoon, skit, squib.

V. **detract,** derogate, decry, depreciate, disparage, run down, cry down, belittle, criticize, pull to pieces, asperse, bespatter, blacken, vilify, brand, malign, backbite, libel, lampoon, traduce, slander, defame, calumniate.

Adj. **detracting,** defamatory, detractory, derogatory, disparaging, libelous; scurrilous, abusive, foul-mouthed; slanderous, calumnious.

935. FLATTERER.—*N.* **flatterer,** adulator, eulogist, euphemist; optimist; puffer, booster [*colloq.*], whitewasher.

toady, sycophant, parasite, hanger-on; courtier.

936. DETRACTOR.—*N.* **detractor,** censor, censurer; cynic, critic, caviler, carper.

defamer, knocker [*colloq.*], backbiter, slanderer, lampooner, satirist, traducer, libeler, calumniator, reviler, vituperator.

Adj. defamatory, etc., 934.

937. VINDICATION.—*N.* **vindication,** justification, warrant; exoneration, exculpation, acquittal; whitewashing, extenuation, palliation, softening, mitigation.

plea, apology, gloss, varnish; excuse, extenuating circumstances; allowance; reply, defense; recrimination.

apologist, vindicator, justifier; defendant, etc., 938.

V. **justify,** warrant, lend a color, vindicate, exculpate, acquit, clear, exonerate, whitewash.

extenuate, palliate, excuse, soften, apologize.

advocate, defend, plead one's cause; contend for, speak for; bear out, make good; support, plead, say in defense.

Adj. **vindicative,** vindicatory, palliative, extenuating, exculpatory, apologetic.

excusable, defensible, pardonable; venial, plausible, justifiable.

938. ACCUSATION.—*N.* **accusation,** charge, imputation, slur, incrimination, recrimination, denunciation.

libel, challenge, citation, arraignment, impeachment, indictment, true bill, lawsuit, condemnation.

accuser, prosecutor, plaintiff, complainant, libelant, informant, informer.

accused, defendant, prisoner, respondent, litigant.

V. **accuse,** charge, tax, impute, twit, taunt with, reproach, stigmatize, slur; incriminate, inculpate, implicate.

inform against, indict, denounce, arraign; charge with, saddle with; impeach, show up [*colloq.*], challenge, cite, prosecute; blow upon [*colloq.*], squeal [*slang*].

Adj. **accusatory,** denunciatory, recriminatory.

inexcusable, indefensible, unpardonable, unjustifiable.

939. PROBITY.—*N.* **probity,** integrity, rectitude, uprightness, respectability, honesty, faith, honor, good faith; constancy, faithfulness, fidelity, loyalty, trustworthiness, truth, veracity, candor, singleness of heart.

fairness, fair play, justice, equity, impartiality, principle.

punctiliousness, punctilio, delicacy, scrupulosity, scrupulousness, scruple; point of honor.

man of honor, man of his word, gentleman, trump [*slang*], brick [*slang or colloq.*].

V. **be honorable,** speak the truth, draw a straight furrow, make a point of; do one's duty, play the game [*colloq.*]; redeem one's pledge, keep one's promise (*or* word), keep faith with.

Adj. **upright,** honest, veracious, truthful, virtuous, noble, honorable, reputable, respectable; fair, right, just, equitable, impartial, square, white [*slang*].

manly, straightforward, frank, candid, openhearted.

loyal, constant, faithful, stanch; true; trusty, trustworthy; incorruptible.

conscientious, right-minded, high-principled, high-minded, scrupulous, religious, strict; nice, punctilious.

stainless, unstained, unsullied, inviolate, untainted, incorrupt, innocent, pure, undefiled, undepraved.

chivalrous, jealous of honor, high-spirited.

Adv. on the square [*colloq.*], in good faith, in all honor, by fair means, with clean hands.

940. IMPROBITY.—*N.* **improbity,** dishonesty, dishonor, disgrace; fraud, lying; bad faith, infidelity, faithlessness; Judas kiss, betrayal, perfidy, treachery, double-dealing; villainy, baseness, degradation, turpitude, moral turpitude.

breach of trust (*or* faith), disloyalty, divided allegiance, hyphenated allegiance [*cant*], treason, high treason; apostasy.

knavery, roguery, rascality, foul play; jobbing, jobbery, graft [*colloq.*], venality, corruption, sharp practice.

V. **play false;** break one's word (*or* promise), jilt, betray, forswear; grovel, sneak, lose caste; sell oneself, squeal [*slang*], go back on [*colloq.*].

Adj. **dishonest,** dishonorable; unconscientious, unscrupulous; fraudulent, knavish, falsehearted; unfair, one-sided; double, double-tongued, double-faced; timeserving, crooked, slippery; fishy [*colloq.*], questionable.

infamous, arrant, foul, base, vile, low, ignominious, perfidious, treacherous, perjured; contemptible, abject, mean, shabby, paltry, dirty, sneaking, groveling, rascally, corrupt, venal.

derogatory, degrading, undignified, unbefitting, ungentlemanly, unchivalric, unmanly, recreant, inglorious.

faithless, false, unfaithful, disloyal; untrustworthy; trustless, lost to shame, dead to honor.

Adv. like a thief in the night, by crooked paths, by foul means.

941. KNAVE.—*N.* **knave,** rogue, villain, rascal, etc., 949; shyster.

traitor, betrayer, archtraitor, conspirator, Judas; reptile, serpent, snake in the grass, wolf in sheep's clothing, sneak, squealer [*slang*], telltale, mischiefmaker; renegade, recreant, slacker.

942. DISINTERESTEDNESS.—*N.* disinterestedness, unselfishness, generosity; liberality, altruism, benevolence, loftiness of purpose, exaltation, magnanimity; honor, chivalry, heroism, sublimity.

self-denial, self-control, stoicism, self-abnegation, self-sacrifice, devotion, self-devotion; labor of love.

Adj. **disinterested,** unselfish, self-denying, self-sacrificing, altruistic.

magnanimous, high-minded; princely, great, high, elevated, lofty, exalted, greathearted, largehearted; generous, liberal; chivalrous, heroic, sublime.

943. SELFISHNESS.—*N.* **selfishness,** self-love, self-indulgence, self-worship, self-seeking, self-interest; egotism, egoism; illiberality, meanness.

self-seeker, timeserver, fortune hunter, monopolist, dog in the manger, trimmer; hog, roadhog [*colloq.*].

V. **be selfish,** feather one's nest; have an eye to the main chance, live for oneself alone.

Adj. **selfish,** self-seeking, self-indulgent, self-interested; self-centered; egotistic, egoistic.

illiberal, mean, ungenerous, narrow-minded; mercenary, venal; covetous.

worldly, unspiritual, earthly, earthly-minded, mundane, worldly-minded, worldly-wise; timeserving, interested.

Adv. from selfish motives.

944. VIRTUE.—*N.* **virtue,** morality, moral rectitude; integrity, probity, nobleness, well-doing, good actions, good behavior, well-spent life, innocence.

merit, worth, desert, excellence, credit; self-control, self-denial. morals; ethics, duty, etc., 926; cardinal virtues.

V. **be virtuous,** practice virtue, do one's duty, fight the good fight; acquit oneself well, keep in the right path.

Adj. **virtuous,** good, innocent, meritorious, deserving, worthy, dutiful, duteous; moral, right, righteous, right-minded; creditable, laudable, commendable, praiseworthy; sterling, pure, noble; whole-souled.

exemplary; matchless, peerless; saintly, saintlike; angelic, god-like.

945. VICE.—*N.* vice, evildoing, wrongdoing, wickedness, viciousness, iniquity, sin, immorality, want of principle, knavery, obliquity, backsliding, infamy, brutality.

depravity, demoralization, corruption, profligacy, flagrancy.

weakness, infirmity, frailty, imperfection, error; foible; failing, failure; besetting sin; defect, defection.

fault, crime; guilt, etc., 947.

reprobate; sinner, etc., 949.

V. be vicious, sin, commit sin, err, transgress; misconduct one-self, misbehave; fall, lapse, slip, trip, offend, trespass, go astray; sow one's wild oats.

demoralize, brutalize; corrupt, degrade, etc., 659.

Adj.[1] vicious, sinful; wicked, iniquitous, immoral, unrighteous, wrong, criminal; unprincipled, lawless, disorderly, disgraceful, recreant, disreputable; demoralized, corrupt, depraved, degener-ate; evil-minded, heartless, graceless, shameless, abandoned.

base, sinister, foul, gross, vile, black, felonious, nefarious, shame-ful, scandalous, infamous, villainous, heinous; flagrant, atrocious.

diabolic *or* diabolical, devilish, fiendish, fiendlike, demoniacal, Mephistophelian, satanic, hellish, infernal, hellborn.

incorrigible, irreclaimable, obdurate, reprobate, reprehensible.

unjustifiable, indefensible, inexcusable, inexpiable, unpardon-able.

improper, unseemly, indecorous, indiscreet, unworthy, blame-worthy, discreditable; incorrect, undutiful, naughty.

weak, frail, lax, infirm, imperfect; spineless, invertebrate [*both fig.*].

946. INNOCENCE.—*N.* innocence; guiltlessness, incorrup-tion, impeccability; clean hands, clear conscience.

innocent, newborn babe; lamb, dove.

Adj. innocent, not guilty, unguilty; guiltless, faultless, sinless, stainless, spotless, clear, immaculate, unerring, undefiled, inculp-able, blameless, above suspicion, irreproachable, unimpeachable; virtuous, etc., 944.

harmless, inoffensive, innocuous, pure.

Adv. with clean hands; with a clear conscience.

947. GUILT.—*N.* guilt, guiltiness, culpability, criminality; vice, sinfulness, misconduct, misbehavior, misdeed; fault, sin, error, transgression; dereliction, delinquency.

indiscretion, lapse, slip, trip, flaw, blot, omission, failing, failure, blunder, break [*colloq.*].

[1]Most of these adjectives are applicable both to the act and to the agent.

offense, trespass: misdemeanor, malefaction, malversation, corruption, malpractice; crime, felony, capital crime.

enormity, atrocity, outrage; deadly sin, mortal sin.

Adj. guilty, blamable, culpable, reprehensible, blameworthy.

Adv. in the very act, red-handed.

948. GOOD MAN. GOOD WOMAN.—*N.* good man, worthy, model, paragon, pattern, good example; hero, demigod, angel, saint; benefactor, etc., 912; philanthropist, etc., 910.

salt of the earth; one in ten thousand; a man among men, white man [*slang*].

good woman, virgin, innocent; goddess, queen, Madonna, ministering angel, heaven's noblest gift.

949. BAD MAN. BAD WOMAN.—*N.* bad man, wrongdoer, worker of iniquity; evildoer, etc., 913; sinner, transgressor; bad example.

rascal, scoundrel, villain, knave, etc., 941; miscreant, wretch, reptile, viper, serpent, monster, devil, demon, devil incarnate, fallen angel, lost sheep, black sheep, castaway, prodigal.

bad woman, jade, Jezebel, hellcat.

ruffian, rowdy, bully, etc., 887; thief, murderer.

culprit, delinquent, criminal, malefactor, felon, convict, outlaw.

riffraff, scum of the earth; blackguard, loafer, sneak, vagabond.

scamp, scapegrace, ne'er-do-well, good for nothing, reprobate, scalawag [*colloq.*], limb [*colloq.*], rapscallion [*all the words in this paragraph are commonly applied jocularly or lightly*].

950. PENITENCE.—*N.* penitence, contrition, compunction, repentance, remorse, regret, self-reproach, self-reproof, self-accusation, self-condemnation, qualms of conscience.

acknowledgment, confession, apology, recantation; penance.

penitent, Magdalen, prodigal son, returned prodigal.

V. repent, be sorry for, rue, regret, think better of, recant; plead guilty, acknowledge, confess, humble oneself, beg pardon, apologize; turn over a new leaf.

reclaim, reform, regenerate, redeem, convert, amend, make a new man of, restore self-respect.

Adj. penitent, repentant, contrite, softened, melted, touched, conscience-stricken; self-accusing, self-convicted.

951. IMPENITENCE.—*N.* impenitence, irrepentance, recusancy, hardness of heart, heart of stone, seared conscience, obduracy.

V. be impenitent, steel the heart, harden the heart; die and make no sign.

Adj. impenitent, obdurate, hard, hardened, seared, recusant, unrepentant; relentless, remorseless, graceless.

lost, incorrigible, irreclaimable; unreclaimed, unreformed.

952. ATONEMENT.—*N.* atonement, reparation, compromise, composition, compensation, quittance, expiation, redemption, reclamation, conciliation, propitiation; indemnification, redress, amends, apology, satisfaction; sacrifice.

penance, fasting, sackcloth and ashes, shrift, purgation, purgatory.

V. atone, atone for, expiate, propitiate, make amends; reclaim, redeem, repair, ransom, absolve, purge, shrive, do penance, pay the penalty.

apologize, express regret, beg pardon, give satisfaction.

Adj. propitiatory, expiatory, sacrifice, sacrificial.

953. [Moral Practice] TEMPERANCE.—*N.* temperance, moderation, frugality, sobriety, soberness, forbearance, abnegation; self-denial, self-restraint, self-control.

abstinence, abstemiousness, asceticism; vegetarianism, prohibition, teetotalism, total abstinence.

abstainer; teetotaler, etc., 958; vegetarian, fruitarian; ascetic.

V. be temperate, abstain, forbear, refrain, deny oneself, spare.

Adj. temperate, moderate, sober, frugal, sparing, abstemious.

954. INTEMPERANCE.—*N.* intemperance, sensuality, animalism, pleasure, luxury, luxuriousness, freeliving, indulgence, high living, dissipation, self-indulgence; voluptuousness, debauchery.

revel, revels, revelry, orgy; drunkenness, debauch, carousal, drinking bout, saturnalia.

V. be intemperate, indulge, exceed; live high (*or* on the fat of the land), dine not wisely but too well; plunge into dissipation, revel, carouse, run riot, sow one's wild oats.

Adj. intemperate, excessive; sensual, self-indulgent, voluptuous, wild, dissipated, dissolute, fast.

brutish, swinish, piggish, hoggish, beastlike, beastly.

luxurious, epicurean, sybaritical; nursed in the lap of luxury; indulged, pampered; full fed, high fed.

intoxicated, drunk, etc., 959.

954a. SENSUALIST.—*N.* sensualist, sybarite, voluptuary, man of pleasure, epicure, epicurean, gourmet; gourmand, glutton, pig, hog; free liver, hard liver.

955. ASCETICISM.—*N.* asceticism, puritanism, austerity; total abstinence; mortification, sackcloth and ashes, penance, fasting; martyrdom.

ascetic, anchorite, hermit, recluse; puritan, yogi [Hindu]; dervish, fakir [both Moham.]; martyr.

Adj. ascetic, austere, puritanical.

956. FASTING.—*N.* fasting, famishment, starvation.

fast, fast day, Lent, spare (*or* meager) diet, lenten diet, Barmecide feast; short rations.

V. fast, starve, famish, perish with hunger.

Adj. fasting, lenten, unfed; starved, half-starved, hungry.

957. GLUTTONY.—*N.* gluttony; greed, greediness, voracity; epicurism, gastronomy; high living; guzzling.

feast, banquet, good cheer, blow out [*slang*].

glutton, gormandizer, cormorant, hog, etc. (*sensualist*), 954a.

epicure, *bon vivant* [F.], gourmand [*obs. as* glutton], gourmet.

V. gormandize, gorge; overeat, glut, satiate, indulge, eat one's fill, cram, stuff, guzzle, bolt, devour, gobble up, gulp, raven, eat out of house and home.

Adj. gluttonous, greedy, gormandizing, omnivorous, voracious, devouring, overfed, gorged.

958. SOBRIETY.—*N.* sobriety; total abstinence, teetotalism.

water drinker; prohibitionist, dry [*slang*], teetotaler, total abstainer.

V. take the pledge; abstain, etc., 953.

Adj. sober, temperate, moderate, abstemious.

959. DRUNKENNESS.—*N.* drunkenness, intemperance, drinking, inebriety, inebriation, intoxication, winebibbing; bacchanalia; libations.

alcoholism, dipsomania; delirium tremens, d.t.'s [*colloq.*].

drink, alcoholic drinks, alcohol, blue ruin [*slang*], booze [*colloq.*]; grog, punch; punchbowl, cup, rosy wine, flowing bowl; liquor, dram, beverage, beer, etc.; cocktail, highball, peg [*slang*, orig. India]; stirrup cup, parting cup.

illicit distilling; bootlegging [*slang*], moonshining, moonshine *or* moonshine whisky [*colloq.*], hooch [*slang*], home-brew; moonshiner [*colloq.*]; bootlegger [*slang*].

drunkard, sot, toper, tippler, winebibber, hard drinker, soaker [*slang*], sponge [*slang*], boozer [*colloq.*], bum [*slang*]; reveler, carouser; dipsomaniac.

V. get (*or* be) drunk, see double; take a drop (*or* glass) too much; drink, tipple, booze [*colloq.*], soak [*slang*], have a jag on [*slang*], carouse; drink hard (*or* deep, like a fish).

liquor, liquor up [*both slang*], wet one's whistle [*colloq. or humorous*]; raise the elbow, hit the booze [*slang*], crack a bottle.

inebriate, fuddle [*colloq.*], befuddle.

sell illicitly, bootleg [*slang*].

Adj. drunk, tipsy, intoxicated, inebriate, inebriated; in a state of intoxication, overcome, fuddled [*colloq.*], boozy [*colloq.*], full [*vulgar*], lit up [*slang*], elevated [*colloq.*]; groggy [*colloq.*]; screwed, tight, primed [*all slang*], muddled, maudlin; blind drunk, dead drunk.

960. PURITY.—*N.* purity; decency, decorum, delicacy; continence, chastity, virtue, modesty; virginity.

virgin, vestal, prude; Diana.

Adj. **pure,** undefiled, modest, delicate, clean, decent, decorous; chaste, continent, virtuous, honest.

961. IMPURITY.—*N.* impurity, uncleanness; immodesty; grossness; indelicacy, indecency, obscenity; dissipation.

Adj. **impure,** unclean; immodest, shameless, indelicate, indecent, coarse, gross.

962. LIBERTINE.—*N.* libertine, voluptuary, rake, roué [F.], fast man.

5. Institutions

963. LEGALITY.—*N.* legality, legitimacy, legitimateness; legitimization.

law, code, constitution, charter, act, enactment, statute, rule, canon, ordinance, institution, regulation, bylaw, decree, standing order.

equity, common law; unwritten law; law of nations, international law; constitutionality; justice, etc., 922; jurisprudence; legislation.

V. **legalize,** legitimize; enact, ordain, decree, authorize, pass a law, legislate; codify, formulate, regulate.

Adj. **legal,** legitimate; according to law; vested, constitutional, chartered, legalized, lawful, statutory; legislative; judicial, juridical.

Adv. in the eye of the law.

964. [Absence or violation of law] ILLEGALITY.—*N.* lawlessness, illicitness; breach (*or* violation) of law; disobedience, violence, brute force, despotism, tyranny, outlawry; mob (*or* lynch) law.

illegality, informality, unlawfulness, illegitimacy; smuggling.

V. **violate the law,** set the law at defiance, make the law a dead letter, take the law into one's own hands.

smuggle, run, poach, bootleg [*slang*].

Adj. **illegal,** prohibited, unlawful, illegitimate, illicit, contraband, actionable.

unchartered, unconstitutional, lawless, unwarranted, unauthorized; unofficial.

arbitrary, despotic, summary, irresponsible.

Adv. with a high hand, in violation of law.

965. JURISDICTION. [Executive]—*N.* jurisdiction, judicature, administration of justice; judge, etc., 967; tribunal, etc., 966.

city government, municipal government, commission government, Oregon plan [U. S.]; municipality, corporation; police, police force, constabulary.

executive, officer, commissioner, lord lieutenant [Brit.], city manager, mayor, alderman, councilor, selectman; bailiff, beadle; sheriff, constable, policeman, police constable, police sergeant, patrolman, gendarme [F.].

bureau, department, portfolio, secretariat.

V. **judge,** adjudge, adjudicate, sit in judgment; have jurisdiction over.

Adj. **executive,** administrative; municipal; judiciary, judicial, juridical.

966. TRIBUNAL.—*N.* **tribunal,** court, board, bench, judicature, court of justice (*or* law), judgment seat, mercy seat; bar, bar of justice; town hall, statehouse, townhouse, courthouse; forum; sessions.

United States courts: U. S. Supreme Court, U. S. District Court, U. S. Circuit Court of Appeal; Federal Court of Claims, Court of Private Land Claims; Supreme Court, Superior Court, court of sessions, criminal court, police court, juvenile court.

court-martial, (*pl.* courts-martial), drumhead court-martial.
Adj. **judicial,** etc., 965; appellate; curial.

967. JUDGE.—*N.* **judge,** justice, justice (*or* judge) of assize; magistrate, police magistrate, beak [*slang*]; his worship [Eng.], his honor, his lordship [Brit.], the court.

Lord Chancellor, Master of the Rolls, Vice-Chancellor, Lord Chief Justice [all Brit.], Chief Justice.

arbiter, arbitrator; moderator, receiver, master; umpire, referee; censor.

jury, grand jury, petty jury, inquest, panel.

juror, juryman, talesman; grand juror, grand juryman; petty juror, petty juryman.

V. **adjudge,** etc. (*determine*), 480; try a case, try a prisoner.
Adj. **judicial,** etc., 965.

968. LAWYER.—*N.* **lawyer,** jurist, legal adviser, advocate; barrister, barrister-at-law [Eng.]; counsel, counselor; king's counsel [Eng.]; pleader, special pleader.

attorney, solicitor; conveyancer, notary, notary public; pettifogger, shyster.

bar, legal profession; Inns of Court [Eng.].

V. **practice law;** practice at (*or* within) the bar, plead; be called to (*or* within) the bar; admitted to the bar.

disbar, degrade.

Adj. **learned in the law;** at the bar; forensic.

969. LAWSUIT.—*N.* **lawsuit,** suit, action, cause; litigation; suit in law.

writ, summons, subpoena, citation; habeas corpus [L.].

arraignment, prosecution, impeachment, accusation; presentment, true bill, indictment.

arrest, apprehension, committal, commitment; imprisonment.

pleadings; declaration, bill, claim; affidavit, libel; answer, plea, demurrer, rebutter, rejoinder; surrebutter, surrejoinder.

litigant, suitor, libelant; plaintiff, defendant, etc., 938.

hearing, trial; judgment, sentence, finding, verdict; appeal, writ of error.

case, decision, decided case, precedent.

V. litigate, go to law, appeal to the law; bring to justice (*or* trial, the bar), put on trial, accuse, prefer (*or* file) a claim.

cite, summon, summons, serve with a writ, arraign; sue, prosecute, indict, impeach; attach, distrain; commit, apprehend, arrest, give in charge.

try, hear a cause; sit in judgment; adjudicate, etc., 480.

970. ACQUITTAL.—*N.* acquittal, exculpation, acquittance, clearance, exoneration, discharge, release, absolution, reprieve, respite, pardon.

Exemption from punishment: impunity, immunity.

V. acquit, exculpate, exonerate, clear; absolve, whitewash, discharge, release, liberate, reprieve, respite, pardon.

Adj. acquitted, uncondemned, unpunished; recommend to mercy.

971. CONDEMNATION.—*N.* condemnation, conviction, judgment, penalty, sentence; death warrant.

V. condemn, convict, find guilty, damn, doom, sentence, pass sentence on, attaint, confiscate, sequestrate.

proscribe, interdict; disapprove, etc., 932; accuse, etc., 938.

Adj. condemnatory, damnatory, condemned, self-convicted.

972. PUNISHMENT.—*N.* punishment, punition, chastisement, chastening, correction, castigation; discipline, infliction, trial; judgment, penalty, retribution, nemesis, retributive justice.

Forms of punishment: lash, scaffold, etc. (*instrument of punishment*), 975; imprisonment; transportation, banishment, expulsion, exile, involuntary exile, ostracism, penal servitude, hard labor, galleys; beating, flagellation, bastinado, blow, stripe, cuff, kick, buffet, pummel; torture, rack.

capital punishment, execution; hanging, shooting, electrocution, decapitation, strangling, strangulation, crucifixion, impalement, martyrdom, auto-da-fé (*pl.* autos-da-fé) [Pg.], hara-kiri [Jap.], happy dispatch [*jocular*], lethal chamber, hemlock.

V. punish, chastise, chasten, castigate, correct, inflict punishment; tar and feather; masthead, keelhaul.

visit upon, pay, settle, settle with, do for [*colloq.*], get even with, make an example of; give it one [*both colloq.*].

strike, etc., 276; smite; spank, thwack, thump, beat, buffet, thrash, pommel, drub, trounce, belabor; trim [*colloq.*], cowhide, lambaste [*slang*], lash, flog, scourge, whip, birch, cane, switch, horsewhip, lay about one, beat black and blue; sandbag, blackjack; pelt, stone.

execute; bring to the block (*or* gallows), behead, decapitate, guillotine; hang [*p. p.* hanged, *not* hung, *for the death penalty*], electrocute, shoot, burn, crucify, impale, lynch.

torture, agonize, rack, put on (*or* to) the rack, martyr, martyrize.

banish, exile, transport, deport, expel, ostracize; rusticate; drum out; dismiss, disbar; unfrock [*as a priest*].

Adj. punitive, penal, punitory, inflictive, castigatory.

973. REWARD.—*N.* reward, recompense, remuneration, prize, meed, guerdon, indemnity, indemnification; quittance, compensation, reparation, redress, acknowledgment, requital, amends, sop, consideration, return; atonement.

perquisite, perks [*slang*]; donation, etc., 784; tip, bribe, hush money, blackmail.

allowance, salary, stipend, wages; pay, payment, emolument; tribute; premium, fee, honorarium; hire; mileage.

V. reward, recompense, repay, requite, remunerate, compensate; fee, tip, bribe; pay, etc., 807; make amends, indemnify, redress, atone, satisfy, acknowledge.

Adj. remunerative, compensatory; retributive.

974. PENALTY.—*N.* penalty; retribution, etc. (*punishment*), 972; pain, penance.

fine, mulct, forfeit, forfeiture, damages, sequestration, confiscation.

V. penalize, fine, mulct, confiscate, sequestrate, sequester; forfeit.

975. [Instrument of punishment] SCOURGE.—*N.* scourge, whip, lash, strap, thong, cowhide, knout, cat, cat-o'-nine-tails; rope's end; black snake, bullwhack, quirt, rawhide.

rod, cane, stick, rattan, birch, birch rod; rod in pickle; switch, ferule, cudgel, truncheon.

Various instruments: pillory, stocks, whipping post, ducking stool, iron maiden; thumbscrew, boot, rack, wheel; treadmill, crank, galleys; bed of Procrustes.

scaffold; block, ax, guillotine; stake; cross, gallows, gibbet, tree; noose, rope, halter, bowstring; death chair, electric chair.

prison, jail, etc., 752; jailer.

executioner; electrocutioner, headsman, hangman; lyncher, torturer.

malefactor, criminal, culprit, felon, victim, gallows bird [*slang*].

V. RELIGIOUS AFFECTIONS

976. DEITY.—*N.* Deity, Divinity, Godhead, Omnipotence, Omniscience, Providence.

GOD, Lord, Jehovah, The King of Kings, The Lord of Lords, The Almighty, The Supreme Being, The Absolute, The First Cause, Author of all things, Creator of all things, The Infinite, The Eternal, The All-powerful, The Omnipotent, The All-wise, The All-merciful, The All-knowing, The Omniscient.

Deus [L.], *Theos* [Gr. Θεος], *Dieu* [F.], *Gott* [Ger.], *Dio* [It.], *Dios* [Sp.], *Deos* [Pg.], *Gud* [Nor., Sw., and Dan.], *God* [Du.], *Bog'* Russ.], Brahma [Skr.], *Deva* [Skr.], *Khuda* (Hind.), Allah (Ar.).

THE TRINITY, The Holy Trinity, The Trinity in Unity, Triunity, Threefold Unity.

I. GOD THE FATHER, The Maker, The Creator, The Preserver.

Functions: creation, preservation, divine government, thearchy.

II. GOD THE SON, Jesus Christ; The Messiah, The Anointed, The Saviour, The Redeemer, The Mediator, The Intercessor, The Advocate, The Judge; The Son of God, The Son of Man; The Only-Begotten, The Lamb of God, The Word, Logos; The Man of Sorrows; Jesus of Nazareth, King of the Jews, The Son of Mary, The Risen, Immanuel, The King of Kings and Lord of Lords, The King of Glory, The Prince of Peace, The Good Shepherd, The Way, The Door, The Truth, The Life, The Bread of Life, The Light of the World, The Vine, The True Vine.

The Incarnation, The Word made Flesh.

Functions: salvation, redemption, atonement, propitiation, mediation, intercession, judgment.

III. GOD THE HOLY GHOST, The Holy Spirit, Paraclete, The Comforter, The Consoler, The Intercessor, The Spirit of God, The Spirit of Truth, The Dove.

Functions: inspiration, regeneration, sanctification, consolation, grace.

The Deity in other religions: Brahmanism *or* **Hinduism:** Brahma (*neuter*), the Supreme Soul *or* Essence of the Universe; Trimurti *or* Hindu trinity *or* Hindu triad: (1) Brahma (*masc.*), the Creator; (2) Vishnu, the Preserver; (3) Siva, the Destroyer and Regenerator.

Buddhism: the Protestantism of the East; Buddha, the Blessed One, the Teacher.

Zoroastrianism: Zerâna-Akerana, the Infinite Being; Ahuramazda *or* Ormazd, the Creator, the Lord of Wisdom, the King of Light (*opposed by* Ahriman, the King of Darkness).

Mohammedanism *or* **Islam:** Allah.

V. create, fashion, make, form, mold, manifest.

preserve, uphold, keep, perpetuate, immortalize.

atone, redeem, save, propitiate, expiate; intercede, mediate.

predestinate, predestine, foreordain, preordain; elect, call, ordain.

bless, sanctify, hallow, justify, absolve, glorify.

Adj. **almighty,** all-powerful, omnipotent; omnipresent, all-wise, all-seeing, all-knowing, omniscient, supreme.

divine, heavenly, celestial; holy, hallowed, sacred, sacrosanct.

supernatural, superhuman, spiritual, ghostly, unearthly.

Adv. **by God's will,** by God's help, *Deo volente* [L.], God willing; in Jesus' name, in His name, to His glory.

977. [Beneficent spirits] ANGEL.—*N.* **angel,** archangel, messenger of God, guardian angel; ministering spirits, invisible helpers, choir invisible, heavenly host, sons of God; saint; seraphim (*sing.,* seraph, *E. pl.,* seraphs), Cherubim (*sing.,* cherub, *E. pl.,* cherubs· cherubim or cherubin *are often treated as sing.*).

Madonna, Our Lady, *Notre Dame* [F.], Holy Mary, The Virgin, The Blessed Virgin, The Virgin Mary.

Adj. **angelic,** seraphic, cherubic, archangelic.

978. [Maleficent spirits] SATAN.—*N.* Satan, the Devil, Lucifer, Belial, Beelzebub, Mephistopheles, Mephisto, Asmodeus, *le Diable* [F.], Deil [Scot.].

fallen angels, unclean spirits, devils; rulers of darkness, the powers of darkness; demon, etc.,980.

Moloch, Mammon; Belial, Beelzebub; Loki [*Norse Myth*].

diabolism, devil worship, demonism, demonology; Black Mass, black magic, demonolatry, witchcraft.

diabolist, demonologist.

V. **demonize;** bewitch, bedevil, etc. (*sorcery*), 992; possess, obsess.

Adj. **satanic,** diabolic *or* diabolical, devilish, demoniac *or* demoniacal, infernal, hellborn.

979. MYTHIC AND PAGAN DEITIES.—*N.* god, goddess; heathen gods and goddesses; pantheon.

Greek and Latin: Zeus, Jupiter *or* Jove (*King*); Apollo *or* Phoebus Apollo (*the sun*); Ares, Mars (*war*); Hermes, Mercury (*messenger*); Poseidon, Neptune (*ocean*); Hephaestus, Vulcan (*smith*); Dionysus, Bacchus (*wine*); Hades [Gr.], Pluto *or* Dis [L.] (*King of the lower world*); Kronos, Saturn (*time*); Eros, Cupid (*love*); Pan, Faunus (*flocks, herds, forests, and wild life*).

Hera, Juno (*Queen*); Demeter, Ceres (*fruitfulness*); Persephone, Proserpina *or* Proserpine (*Queen of the lower world*); Artemis, Diana (*the moon and hunting*); Athena, Minerva (*wisdom*); Aphrodite, Venus (*love and beauty*); Hestia, Vesta (*the hearth*); Rhea *or* Cybele ("Mother of the gods," *identified with* Ops, *wife of Saturn*); Gaea *or* Ge, Tellus (*earth goddess, mother of the Titans*).

Norse: Ymir (*primeval giant*), Odin *or* Woden (*the All-father* = *Zeus*); the Æsir: Thor (*the Thunderer*), Balder (= *Apollo*), Freyr (*fruitfulness*), Tyr (*war*), Bragi (*poetry and eloquence*), Höder (*blind god of the winter*), Heimdall (*warder of Asgard*), Loki (*evil*).

the Vanir: Njorth (*the winds and the sea*), Frey (*prosperity and love*), Freya (*goddess of love and beauty* = *Venus*).

Frigg or Frigga (*wife of Odin*), Hel (*goddess of death* = *Persephone*), Idun (*goddess of spring, wife of Bragi*), Sigyn (*wife of Loki*).

Egyptian: Ra or Amon-Ra (*the sun god*), Osiris (*judge of the dead*), Isis (*wife of Osiris*), Horus (*the morning sun; son of Osiris and Isis*), Anubis (*jackal-god, brother of Horus, a conductor of the dead*), Nephthys (*sister of Isis*), Set (*evil deity, brother of Osiris*), Thoth (*clerk of the underworld*), Bast or Bubastis (*a goddess with head of a cat*), the Sphinx (*wisdom*).

Various: Baal [Semitic]; Astarte or Ashtoreth (*goddess of fertility and love*) [Phoenician]; Bel [Babylonian]; The Great Spirit [N. Amer. Indian].

nymph, dryad, hamadryad, wood nymph; naiad, fresh-water nymph; oread, mountain nymph; nereid, sea nymph; Oceanid, ocean nymph; Pleiades, Hyades.

fairy, fay, sprite; nix (*fem.* nixie), water sprite; the good folk, brownie, pixy, elf (*pl.* elves), banshee; the Fates; kobold, troll, hobgoblin, gnome, kelpie; faun; peri, undine, sea maid, mermaid (*masc.* merman); Mab, Oberon, Titania, Ariel; Puck, Robin Goodfellow.

familiar spirit, familiar, genius, guide, good genius, daimon, demon.

mythology, mythical lore, folklore, fairyism, fairy mythology.

Adj. **mythical,** mythic, mythological, fabulous, legendary.

fairylike, sylphlike, elfin, elflike, elfish, nymphlike.

980. EVIL SPIRITS.—*N.* demon, fiend, devil, etc. (*Satan*), 978; evil genius, familiar, familiar spirit; bad (*or* unclean) spirit; incubus; ogre, ogress, ghoul, vampire, harpy; Fury, the Furies, the Erinyes, the Eumenides.

imp, bad fairy, sprite, jinni (*pl.* jinn), genius (*pl.* genii), dwarf.

changeling, elf child, werewolf; satyr.

elemental, sylph, gnome, salamander, nymph [*Rosicrucian*].

siren, nixie, undine, Lorelei.

bugbear, bugaboo, bogy, goblin, hobgoblin.

Adj. **demoniac,** demoniacal, fiendish, fiendlike, evil, ghoulish; pokerish [*colloq.*], bewitched.

980a. SPECTER.—*N.* specter, ghost, apparition, vision, spirit, sprite, shade, shadow, wraith, banshee, spook [*now humorous*], phantom, phantasm, materialization [*spiritualism*], double.

will-o'-the-wisp, etc., 423.

Adj. **spectral,** ghostly, ghostlike, spiritual, wraithlike, weird, uncanny, eerie, spooky [*colloq.*] haunted; unearthly, supernatural.

981. HEAVEN.—*N.* heaven; kingdom of heaven (*or* God), heavenly kingdom; heaven of heavens, God's throne, throne of God; Paradise, Eden, Zion, Holy City, New Jerusalem, Heavenly City, City Celestial, abode of the blessed.

Mythological heaven or paradise: Olympus; Elysium, Elysian fields, Islands (*or* Isles) of the Blessed, Happy Isles, Fortunate Isles, garden of the Hesperides; third heaven, seventh heaven; Valhalla [Scandinavian]; Nirvana [Buddhist]; happy hunting grounds [N. Amer. Indian].

future state, life after death, eternal home, resurrection, translation; apotheosis, deification.

Adj. **heavenly,** celestial, supernal, unearthly, paradisaic, beatific; Elysian, Olympian.

982. HELL.—*N.* **hell,** bottomless pit, place of torment; pandemonium; hell-fire, everlasting fire (*or* torment); worm that never dies.

purgatory, limbo, Gehenna, abyss.

Mythological hell: Tartarus, Hades, Avernus; infernal regions, inferno, shades below, realms of Pluto.
Pluto, Rhadamanthus, Erebus, Charon, Cerberus; Persephone, Proserpina; Minos, Osiris.
Rivers of hell: Styx, Acheron, Cocytus, Phlegethon, Lethe.

Adj. **hellish,** infernal, stygian.

983. [Religious Knowledge] THEOLOGY.—*N.* theology, theosophy, divine wisdom, divinity, hagiography; monotheism, theism, religion; religious persuasion (*or* sect, denomination, affiliation); creed, articles (*or* declaration, profession, confession) of faith.

theologian, scholastic, divine, schoolman, the Fathers; monotheist, theist.

Adj. **theological,** religious, divine, canonical; denominational; sectarian.

983a. ORTHODOXY.—*N.* **orthodoxy;** strictness, soundness, religious truth, true faith; truth, etc., 494; soundness of doctrine; Christianity, Catholicism.

the church, Holy Church, Church Militant, Church Triumphant; Catholic (*or* Universal, Apostolic) Church; Established (*or* State) Church; The Bride of the Lamb; temple of the Holy Ghost; Church of Christ; Christians, Christendom.

canons; thirty-nine articles; Apostles' (*or* Nicene, Athanasian) Creed.

Adj. **orthodox,** sound, strict, faithful, catholic, Christian, evangelical, scriptural, literal, divine, monotheistic, true, etc., 494.

984. HETERODOXY. [Sectarianism]—*N.* **heterodoxy;** error, false doctrine, heresy, schism, recusancy, backsliding, apostasy; materialism, atheism; idolatry, superstition.

bigotry, fanaticism, iconoclasm; precisianism; sabbatarianism, puritanism, bibliolatry.

sectarianism, nonconformity, dissent, secularism; religious sects, the clash of creeds, the isms.

[*Generally speaking, each sect is* orthodox *to itself and* heterodox *to others.*]

paganism, heathenism, heathendom; animism, polytheism, pantheism; dualism.

pagan, heathen, paynim; kafir, non-Mohammedan; gentile; pantheist, polytheist, animist.

misbeliever, heretic, apostate; backslider; antichrist; idolater; skeptic, etc., 989.

bigot, dogmatist, fanatic, dervish, iconoclast.

sectarian, sectary; seceder, separatist, recusant, dissenter, nonconformist.

materialist, positivist, deist, agnostic, atheist, etc., 989.

Adj. **heterodox,** heretical, unorthodox, unscriptural, uncanonical, unchristian, apocryphal; antichristian; schismatic, recusant, iconoclastic; sectarian, dissenting, secular; agnostic, atheistic; skeptical, etc., 989.

bigoted, dogmatical, fanatical; superstitious, credulous; idolatrous.

pagan, heathen, heathenish, gentile, paynim; polytheistic, pantheistic, animistic.

985. REVELATION. [Biblical]—*N.* **revelation,** inspiration.

The Bible, the Book, the Book of Books, The Good Book, the Word, the Word of God, Scripture, the Scriptures, Holy Writ, Holy Scriptures, inspired writings, Gospel.

Old Testament, Septuagint, Vulgate, Pentateuch; the Law, the Prophets; Apocrypha.

New Testament; Gospels, Evangelists, Acts, Epistles, Apocalypse, Revelation; Good Tidings, Glad Tidings.

inspired writers, prophet, evangelist, apostle, disciple, saint; the Fathers, the Apostolic Fathers; Holy Men of old.

Adj. **scriptural,** biblical, sacred, prophetic; evangelical, evangelistic, apostolic, apostolical; inspired, apocalyptic, revealed; ecclesiastical, canonical.

986. SACRED WRITINGS. [Non-Biblical]—*N.* The Vedas, Upanishads, Puranas, Sutras, Bhagavad Gita [all Brahmanic]; Zendavesta, Avesta [Zoroastrian]; The Koran *or* Alcoran [Mohammedan]; Tripitaka, Dhammapada [Buddhist]; Granth, Adigranth [*Sikh*]; the Kings [Chinese]; the Eddas [Scandinavian].

Non-Biblical prophets and religious founders: Gautama (Buddha); Zoroaster, Confucius, Mohammed.

987. PIETY.—*N.* **piety,** religion, theism, faith; religiousness, religiosity, holiness, saintship; reverence, humility, veneration, devotion, worship, grace, sanctity, consecration.

beatification, regeneration, conversion, sanctification, salvation, inspiration, bread of life; Body and Blood of Christ.

believer, convert, theist, Christian, devotee, pietist, saint.

V. **be pious,** have faith, believe, receive Christ; venerate, adore, worship, revere, be converted, be on God's side, stand up for Jesus, fight the good fight, keep the faith, let one's light shine.

regenerate, convert, edify, sanctify, hallow, keep holy, beatify, inspire, consecrate, enshrine.

Adj. pious, religious, devout, devoted, reverent, godly, humble, pure, pure in heart, holy, spiritual, saintly, saintlike; believing, faithful, Christian.

regenerated; inspired, consecrated, converted, unearthly.

elected, adopted, justified, sanctified.

988. IMPIETY.—*N.* impiety, sin, irreverence; profaneness, profanity, blasphemy, profanation; desecration, sacrilege; scoffing.

Assumed piety: hypocrisy, pietism, cant, pious fraud; lip devotion, lip service; formalism, austerity; sanctimony, sanctimoniousness, pharisaism, sabbatarianism; sacerdotalism; bigotry; blue laws.

apostasy, recusancy, backsliding, perversion, reprobation.

bigot, pharisee, sabbatarian, formalist, pietist, precisian, devotee, ranter, fanatic.

sinner, scoffer, blasphemer, sabbath breaker; worldling; hypocrite.

the wicked, the evil, the unjust, the reprobate.

V. profane, desecrate, blaspheme, revile, scoff, swear; commit sacrilege.

dissemble, simulate, play the hypocrite, snuffle.

Adj. impious, irreligious, etc., 989; profane, irreverent, sacrilegious, blasphemous.

unhallowed, unsanctified, unregenerate; hardened, perverted, reprobate.

hypocritical, canting, pietistical, sanctimonious, unctuous, pharisaical, overrighteous.

bigoted, fanatical, hidebound, narrow, narrow-minded, illiberal, prejudiced, little; provincial, parochial, insular.

989. IRRELIGION.—*N.* irreligion, impiety, ungodliness, laxity, apathy, indifference.

skepticism, doubt; unbelief, disbelief, incredulity, agnosticism, freethinking; materialism, rationalism, positivism; atheism, infidelity.

unbeliever, infidel, atheist, heretic, heathen, alien, gentile, Nazarene; freethinker, skeptic, rationalist; materialist, positivist, nihilist, agnostic.

V. disbelieve, lack faith; doubt, question, deny the truth.

Adj. irreligious; undevout, godless, graceless, ungodly; unholy, unsanctified, unhallowed; atheistic.

skeptical, freethinking, unbelieving, unconverted; incredulous, faithless.

worldly, mundane, earthly, carnal, worldly, worldly-minded, unspiritual.

990. WORSHIP.—*N.* **worship,** cult, adoration, devotion, vow, aspiration, homage, service; kneeling, genuflection, prostration.

prayer, invocation, supplication, intercession, orison, petition; collect, litany, Lord's prayer, paternoster; *Ave Maria* [L.], Hail, Mary.

thanksgiving; grace, praise, glorification, paean, benediction, doxology, hosanna, hallelujah, alleluia, *Te Deum* [L.], *Gloria* [L.]. psalm, hymn, chant, response, anthem.

offering, oblation, sacrifice, incense, libation, offertory, collection.

divine service, office, duty; exercises; morning prayer; Mass, matins, evensong, vespers, vigils, lauds.

worshiper, congregation, communicant, celebrant.

V. **worship,** lift up the heart, aspire; revere, adore, do service, pay homage, offer one's vows, vow; bow down and worship.

pray, invoke, supplicate; beseech; offer up prayers, say one's prayers, tell one's beads, recite the rosary.

give thanks, say grace, bless, praise, laud, glorify, magnify, sing praises.

Adj. devout, devotional, reverent, solemn, fervid.

991. IDOLATRY.—*N.* **idolatry,** idolatrousness, demonism, demonology, devil worship, fetishism.

idolization, deification, apotheosis, canonization; hero worship.

sacrifice, hecatomb, holocaust; human sacrifices, immolation, self-immolation, suttee.

idol, golden calf, graven image, fetish, joss [Chinese], *lares et penates* [L.]; god (*or* goddess) of one's idolatry; Baal, Moloch, Juggernaut.

idolater, idolatress, idolizer, fetishist.

V. **idolize,** idolatrize, worship idols, worship, put on a pedestal, prostrate oneself before; make sacrifice to, deify, canonize.

Adj. **idolatrous,** idolistic, prone before, prostrate before, in the dust before, at the feet of.

992. SORCERY.—*N.* **sorcery,** magic, black magic, the black art, necromancy, demonology, witchcraft, witchery, wizardry, fetishism, hoodoo, voodoo, voodooism; fire worship, incantation, enchantment, bewitchment, glamour; obsession, possession.

divination, etc. (*prediction*), 511; sortilege, ordeal, hocus-pocus.

V. **practice sorcery,** cast a nativity (*or* horoscope), conjure, charm, enchant, bewitch, bedevil, witch, voodoo, hoodoo [*colloq.*]; entrance, fascinate, hypnotize, cast a spell; call up spirits.

Adj. **magic,** magical, witching, weird, cabalistic, talismanic.

992a. PSYCHICAL RESEARCH.—*N.* **psychical research,** psychical (*or* psychic) investigation; abnormal (*or* mediumistic) phenomena; mysticism.

the subconscious, the subconscious self, the subliminal self, the higher self, ego, astral body; aura; subconsciousness, subliminal consciousness; intuition; dual personality, multiple personality, obsession, possession.

psychotherapy, psychotherapeutics, psychoanalysis; hysteria, neurasthenia, dreams, visions, apparitions, hallucinations.

mesmerism, animal magnetism; mesmeric trance; hypnotism; hypnosis.

Phenomena: **telepathy,** thought transference, thought transmission, telepathic transmission; second sight, clairvoyance, clairaudience, psychometry.
premonitions, previsions, premonitory apparition, fetch, wraith, double; death lights, ominous dreams.
automatism, automatic writing, planchette, ouija board, trance writing, spirit writing; trance speaking, inspirational speaking.
spiritualism, spiritism, spirit manifestations; trance, spirit control, spirit possession; mediumistic communications; séance; materialization.
medium, seer, clairvoyant, clairaudient, telepathist; guide, control; mesmerist, hypnotist.

V. **psychologize;** investigate the abnormal (*or* supernormal, subconscious, subliminal), traverse the borderland, know oneself.

mesmerize, magnetize, hypnotize, place under control, subject to suggestion, place in a trance, induce hypnosis.

Adj. **psychical,** psychic, psychological; spiritistic, spiritualistic, spiritual; subconscious, subliminal, supernormal, abnormal; mystic *or* mystical.

993. SPELL.—*N.* **spell,** charm, incantation, exorcism, abracadabra, open-sesame; evil eye.

talisman, amulet, phylactery, philter, fetish, wishbone; mascot, rabbit's foot, hoodoo [*colloq.*], jinx [*slang*], scarabaeus *or* scarab; veronica, swastika.

wand, caduceus, rod, divining rod, witch hazel, Aaron's rod.

Magic wish-givers: **Aladdin's lamp,** Aladdin's casket, magic casket, magic ring, magic belt, magic spectacles, wishing cap, Fortunatus' cap; seven-league boots; magic carpet; cap of darkness.

994. SORCERER.—*N.* **sorcerer,** magician, wizard, necromancer, conjuror, prestidigitator; charmer, exorcist, voodoo medicine man, witch doctor; astrologer, soothsayer, etc., 513.

sorceress, witch, hag; siren, harpy.

Cagliostro, Merlin; Circe, weird sisters, witch of Endor.

995. CHURCHDOM.—*N.* **churchdom;** church, ministry, priesthood, prelacy, hierarchy, church government; clericalism, sacerdotalism, episcopalianism.

monasticism, monkhood, monachism; celibacy.

Ecclesiastical offices and dignities: cardinalate, cardinalship; primacy, archbishopric, archiepiscopacy; prelacy, bishopric, episcopate, episcopacy, see, diocese; benefice, incumbency, living, cure, charge, cure of souls; rectorship, vicariate, vicarship; pastorate, pastorship, pastoral charge; deaconry, deaconship; curacy; chaplaincy, chaplainship, presbytery.

holy orders, ordination, institution, consecration, induction, installation, preferment, translation, presentation.

papacy, pontificate, See of Rome, the Vatican, the apostolic see.

V. call, ordain, induct, install, translate, consecrate, present, elect, bestow.

Adj. ecclesiastical, clerical, sacerdotal, priestly, pastoral, ministerial, hierarchical, episcopal, canonical; pontifical, papal, apostolic.

996. CLERGY.—*N.* clergy, clericals, ministry, priesthood, presbytery, the cloth, the pulpit, the desk.

clergyman, divine, ecclesiastic, priest, pastor, shepherd, minister, preacher, clerk in holy orders, parson, sky pilot [*slang*]; father, padre, *abbé* [F.], *curé* [F.]; reverend.

Dignitaries of the church: Pope, pontiff, Holy Father; cardinal, primate, metropolitan, archbishop, bishop, prelate, dean, archdeacon, canon, rector, vicar, beneficiary, incumbent, chaplain, curate; elder, deacon.

religious, abbot, prior, monk, friar, lay brother, pilgrim, palmer.

nun, sister, priestess, abbess, prioress, canoness; mother superior, the reverend mother; novice.

Adj. ordained, in orders, in holy orders, called to the ministry.

997. LAITY.—*N.* laity, flock, fold, congregation, assembly, brethren, people; society [U. S.]; class [Methodist].

layman, parishioner, catechumen.

V. laicize, secularize.

Adj. secular, lay congregational, civil, temporal, profane.

998. RITE.—*N.* rite, ceremony, observance, function, duty, form, solemnity, sacrament; service, ministry, ministration.

sermon, preaching, preachment, exhortation, religious harangue, homily, lecture, discourse.

worship, etc., 990; invocation of saints, confession, the confessional; absolution, remission of sins; reciting the rosary, telling one's beads.

Seven Sacraments: (1) baptism, immersion, christening; baptismal regeneration; font.

(2) confirmation, laying on of hands.

(3) Eucharist, Mass, Lord's supper, communion; the sacrament, the holy sacrament; consecrated elements, bread and wine, celebration; transubstantiation, real presence.

(4) penance, fasting, sackcloth and ashes, flagellation.

(5) **extreme unction,** last rites, viaticum.

(6) **holy orders,** ordination, etc. (*churchdom*), 995.

(7) **matrimony,** marriage, wedlock, etc., 903.

Sacred articles: relics, rosary, beads, reliquary, host, cross, rood, crucifix; pyx, censer, thurible; prayer wheel [Buddhist]; Sangraal, Holy Grail.

ritual, liturgy, rubric, canon, ordinal, missal, breviary, Mass book, beadroll, litany, prayer book, Book of Common Prayer; psalter, psalmbook, hymnbook, hymnal.

ritualism, ceremonialism; sabbatism, sabbatarianism; ritualist, sabbatarian.

V. **perform service,** do duty, minister, officiate, celebrate.

excommunicate; ban with bell, book, and candle.

preach, sermonize, address the congregation.

Adj. **ritual,** ritualistic, ceremonial, liturgic *or* liturgical; paschal.

999. CANONICALS.—*N.* **canonicals,** vestments, robe, gown, surplice, etc.

1000. TEMPLE.—*N.* **temple,** fane, place of worship; house of God, house of prayer; cathedral, minster, church, kirk [Scot.], chapel, meetinghouse.

synagogue, tabernacle; mosque [Moham.]; pagoda, Chinese temple, joss house [*colloq.*]; pantheon, shrine.

monastery, priory, abbey, friary, convent, nunnery, cloister.

parsonage, rectory, vicarage, manse, deanery, clergy house; bishop's palace; Vatican.

Adj. **churchly,** cloistered, monastic, monasterial, conventual.

The numbers refer to the headings under which the words or phrases occur. When the same word or phrase can be used in various senses, the several headings under which it or its synonyms will be found are indicated by *italics*.

When the word given in the Index is itself the title or heading of a category, the word is printed in capitals and the reference number in bold-faced type, thus: ACTIVITY 682. When the word is the keyword to a group of synonyms, the reference number is also in bold-faced type.

Derivatives likewise have been sparingly admitted, since the allied or basic term will serve as a key to the various derived forms; thus *alarm* is given, but not *alarmed* or *alarming*. Adverbs ending in -*ly* should be looked for under the adjective, if not found in the Index.

IMPORTANT NOTE

The numbers following all references in this Index Guide refer to the *section* numbers in the text, and *not* to pages.

INDEX

A

abandon 624, 782
abandoned
  forsaken 893
  vicious 945
abandonment 757, 782
abase 879
abasement 874
abash 879
abashed 879
abatement 36
abbess 996
abbey 1000
abbot 996
abbreviation 201
abdicate 757
abdomen 250
abduct *repel* 289
  steal 791
aberration 83
abet 707
abhor 867, 898
abhorrence 867, 898
abhorrent *painful* 830
  hateful 898
abide *endure* 1, 106
  remain 110
  dwell 186
ability 157, 698
abject *vile* 874
  servile 886
abjure *deny* 536
  renounce 607
ablaze 382
able *capable* 157
  skillful 698
able-bodied 159
ablution 652
abnormal 83
aboard *present* 186
  afloat 273
abode 189
abolish 756
abolition 2, 162, 756
abominable *bad* 649
  hateful 898
abominate *dislike* 867
  hate 898
abomination 867
aboriginal 66, 124
aborigine 188
abound 639
about *nearly* 32, **197**
  around 227

above 206
abracadabra 993
abrade 330,331
abrasion 330,331
abreast 216, 236
abridge 36, 201
  in writing 596
abridgment 35, **201**
abroad 57, 196
abrupt *sudden* 113
  steep 217
abscond 623
ABSENCE 187
  -of mind 458
  -of time 107
absent 187, 458
absentee 187
absent-minded 458
absolute *not relative* 1
  great **31**
  certain 474
absolution 918
absolve 918, 952
absorb *combine* 48
  take in 296
absorbed 451
absorption 296
abstain *refrain* 623
  be temperate 953
abstainer **953, 958**
abstemious **953, 958**
abstention 623
abstinence 623, **953**
abstract, *v. take* 789
abstract, *n. epitome* 195, 596
abstracted *inattentive* 458
abstraction 38, 451, **458**
absurd 471, **497**, 583
ABSURDITY
  impossibility 471
  nonsense **497**
  ridiculousness 853
abundance 31, **639**
abundant *great* 31
  enough 639
abuse, *v. illtreat* 649
  misuse 679
abuse, *n. in-vective* **908, 932**
abusive **909, 932**
abut 197
abysmal *deep* 208

abyss 198, **667**
academic 537
academy 542
accede *assent* 488
  submit 725
  consent 762
accelerate 132, 274, 684
accent 402, 580
accentuate 580, **642**
accept *assent* 488
  receive **785**
acceptable
  expedient 646
  agreeable 829
acceptance *security* **771**
access *approach* 286
accessible *possible* 470
  easy 705
accession *increase* 35
accessory *extrinsic* 6
  adjunct 37, 39
  accompanying 88
accident 151, 619, 735
accidental *extrinsic* 6
  occasional 134
  fortuitous 156
acclaim 931
acclamation 488, 931
acclivity 217
accommodate *suit* 23
  aid 707
accommodation
  adaptation 23
  space 180
ACCOMPANIMENT
  adjunct 37, 39
  coexistence 88
  musical 415
accompany
  coexist 88
  escort 664
accomplice 711
accomplish *execute* 161
  complete 729
accomplishment
  learning 490
  talent 698
accord
  agree 23
  assent 488
  grant 760, 784
accordance 16, 23
accordingly 8, 476

altar 903
alter 15, 140
alteration *difference* 15
   variation 20a
   change 140
alternate *reciprocal* 12
   vary 20a
   periodic 138
   substitute 147
   oscillate 314
alternation 12, 138, **314**
alternative 147
although 179, 469
altitude 206
altogether 50, 52
altruism 910, 942
altruist 906, 910
alumnus 541
always *uniformly* **16**
   generally 78
   perpetually 112
amain *violent* 173
amalgamate 41, 48
amass 50, 72
amateur 602
amateurish 643
amaze 870
amazement 870
ambassador 534, 758
ambidexter 238
ambiguous *uncertain* 475
   unintelligible 519
   equivocal 520
ambition 620, 865
ambitious 865
amble 266
ambuscade 530
AMBUSH *hiding* **530**
   pitfall 667
amenable 602, 926
amend *improve* 658
amendment 658
amends 952
amenity 894
amiable 894, 906
amicable 888
amidst 41, 228
amiss 619
amity 714, 888
ammunition 727
amnesty 918
among 41, 228
amorous 897
amount *quantity* 25
   sum of money 800
amphitheater 728
ample *much* 31
   spacious 180
   large 192
   broad 202
amplify 194, 549
amputate 38
amulet *talisman* 747
   charm 993
amuse 840
AMUSEMENT 840

ANACHRONISM 115,
135
anemia 160
anesthesia 376, 381
anesthetic 376
anesthetize 376
analogous 17
analogy 9, 17
analysis
   decomposition 49
   inquiry 461
   reasoning 476
analyst 463
analytical [see analysis]
analyze [see analysis]
anarchist 891, 913
anarchy *disorder* 59
   social 738
anathema 908
anathematize 908
anatomize *dissect* 44
   investigate 461
anatomy 44, 329
ancestor 166
ancestral 166
ancestry 69, **122**, 166
anchor *moor* 184
   stop 265
   safeguard 666
   hope 858
anchorage *location* 184
   roadstead 189
   refuge 666
anchorite 893, 955
ancient *old* 124
and 37
anecdote 594
anew 104, 123
ANGEL 977
angelic 977
anger 900
angle 244, 448
angry 900
anguish *physical* 378
   moral 828
angular 244
ANGULARITY 244
ANIMAL 366, 370
   -life 364
animalcule 193
animalism 954
animate 824, 836
animation *activity* 682
   vivacity 836
animosity 889, 900
annalist 553
annals 594
annex 37, 43
annihilate 2, 162
annihilation 2
anniversary 138, 883
annotation 522
announce *predict* 511
   inform 527
announcement
   [see announce]

annoy *molest* 907
   disquiet 830
annoyance 828, 830
annual 138
annul 756
ANNULMENT 756
anoint 332, 355
anointment 332, 355
anomaly 83
anonymous 565
another 15
ANSWER *reply* **462**
   go bail 806
answerable 177, 926
ant 366
antagonism *different* 24
   enmity 889
antagonist 710
antagonistic 14, 24, **179**
antecedence 62
antecedent 64
antedate 115
antediluvian 124
antelope 366
anthem 990
anthology *collection* 596
anthropology 368, 372
antic 840
anticipate
   foresee 121, **510**
   be early **132**
   expect 507
   hope 858
anticipation 115, 121
   [see anticipate]
anticlimax 853
antipathy *contrariety* 14
   repulsion 289
   dislike 867
   enemy 891
   hate 898
antipodes 14, 237
antiquary 122
antiquated
   aged 122, **124**, 128
   out of fashion 851
antique 124
antiquity 122, 124
antiseptic 662
antisocial 911
antithesis 14, 15
anxiety *solicitude* 459
   pain 828
   fear 860
anxious [see anxiety]
any 25
anybody 78
anyhow 627
apace 132
apache 361, 913
apart *irrelative* 10
   separate 15, 44
   singleness 87
   asunder 96
apartment 191
apathetic 275, 462, **823**

attendant 88, 281, **746**
ATTENTION 457
attentive *mindful* 457 [*see*
   attend]
attenuate *decrease* 36
   reduce 195
   make rare 322
attenuated 203
attest *bear testimony* 467
   guarantee 768
attic 191, 210
attire 225
attitude 240
attitudinize 855
attorney 968
attract *bring towards* 288
   allure 865
   excite love 897
ATTRACTION *pull* 288
   pleasure 829
   lure 865
attractive [*see* attract]
   pleasing 829
attribute 88
attribute to 155
attribution 155
attune *music* 415
   prepare 673
attuned to *habit* 613
auburn 433
auction 796
audacity *courage* 861
   rashness 863
   insolence 885
audible 402
audience *hearers* 418
   drama 599
audit 85, 461, 811
auditor *hearer* 418
   accountant 811
auditorium 189
auditory 402
auger 262
aught 51
augment *increase* 35, 37
   expand 194
augur *soothsayer* 513
augury 512
august 31
aura 992a
aureole 873
auricular 418
aurist 662
aurora 125, 423
auspices 175, 664
auspicious *opportune* 134
   favorable 512
   prosperous 734

hopeful 858
austere 739, 955
austerity 739, 955
authentic *well founded* 1
   evidential 467
   certain 474
   true 484
authentication
   evidence 467
   security 771
author *writer* 593
   projector 626
authoritative *certain* 474
   commanding 741
authorities 745
AUTHORITY *power* 737
   influence 157, 175
   testimony 467
   sage 500
   informant 527
   permission 760
   right 924
AUTHORIZATION 924
authorize *empower* 737
   permit 760
   entitle 924
authorized 924
authorship
   composition 54
   production 161
   writing 590
auto 272
autocar 272
autocracy 737
autocrat 739, 745
autocratic *will* 600
   ruling 737
auto-da-fé *burning* 384
   execution 972
autograph *evidence* 467
   signature 550
   writing 590
automatic 601
   pistol 727
automatism 992a
automobile 266, 272
automobilist 268
autonomy 748
autopsy 363
autumn 126
AUXILIARY 711
   extra 37
   aiding 707
avail *be useful* **644**
   succeed 731
available 673
avalanche 306
avarice 819

Ave Maria 900
avenge 919
avenger 919
avenue 627
aver 535
average *balance* **29**
   mediocre 651
averse *contrary* 14
   unwilling 603, 867
aversion *dislike* 867
avert 706
aviate 267
aviation 267
aviator 269
avidity *avarice* 819
   desire 865
avocation 625
avoid 623, 867
AVOIDANCE 623
avouch 535
avow 535
avowal 535
await *foresee* 121
   be kept waiting 133
   expect 507
awake *attentive* 457
   intelligent 498
   excite 824
awaken *excite* 824
award *adjudge* 480
   give 784
aware 490
away *distant* 196
awe *fear* 860
   wonder 870
awe-struck 860, 870
awful *fearful* 860
awhile 111
awkward *inexpedient* 647
   unskillful 699
   difficult 704
   ugly 846
awkwardness
   [*see* awkward]
awning 223
awry *oblique* 217
   distorted 243
ax *edge tool* 253
   weapon 727
axiom 496
axiomatic 496
axis 222
axle 312
ay 488
aye *ever* 112
   yes 488
azure 438

B

babble *gurgle* 348
   jabber 517, 584
babe 129

Babel 560, 563
baby 129, 167
babyhood 127

babyish 499
bachelor 904
back, *n. rear* 235

betroth 768, 903
betrothal 902
betrothed 897, 903
better *improve* **658**
between 228
betwixt 228
beverage 298
bevy 102
bewail 839
beware 668
bewilder *put out* 458
  perplex 475
  astonish 870
bewitch *fascinate* 615
  diabolize 978
  hoodoo 992
beyond *superior* **33**
  further 196
bias *influence* 175
  tendency 176
  slope 217
  prepossession **481**
bib *pinafore* 225
Bible **985**
bicentenary 98, 138
bicentennial 98, 138
bicker *quarrel* 713
bicycle 272
bid *order* 741
  offer 763
bide *wait* 133
  remain 141
biennial 138
bier 363
big *in degree* 31
  in size 192, 206
bigot *dogmatist* 474
  mule 606
  heterodox **984**
  impious **988**
bigoted **988**
bigotry 474, 606, **984**
bill *money account* 811
  -of fare 86, 298
billet, *n. office* 625
billet, *v. locate* **184**
billingsgate 908
billows 341
bind *connect* 43
  compel 744
biography 594
biologist 357
biology 357, 359
biplane 273
bird 366
birth *beginning* 66
  production 161
birthday 138
birthright 924
bisect **91**
bisection **91**
bishop 996
bishopric 995
bit *small quantity* 32
  part 51
  curb 752

bite *eat* 298
biting *cold* 383
  pungent 392
bitter *cold* 383
  acrid 395
  malevolent 907
bitterness [*see* bitter]
bivouac 265
bizarre 83, 853
black *color* **431**
  -sheep 949
blackball 893, 932
blacken 431
  defame 934
blacklist 932
blackmail 793
BLACKNESS 431
blade *edge tool* 253
blamable 932, 947
blame 155, **932**
blameless 946
blameworthy **932**, 947
blanch 429, 430
bland 894
blandishment 902
blank *inexistent* 2
  unsubstantial 4
blanket 223
blare 404
blarney 933
blasé 869, 871
blasphemy 988
blast, *n. destroy* 162
  explosion 173
blast, *v. wind* 349
blatant *loud* 404
blaze *heat* 382
  mark 550
blazer *coat* 225
blazon *publish* 531
  inscribe 873
  -forth 882
bleach 429
bleachers 444
bleak 383
blear-eyed 443
bleat 412
bleed *extort money* 814
  suffer 828
bleeding *hemorrhage* 299
BLEMISH *deface* 241
  imperfection 651
  defect **848**
blench *shrink* 821
blend *mix* 41
  combine 48
  harmonize 413
bless *sanctify* 976
blessed **827**
blessing 618, 931
blight 659
blighted 659
blind, *n. shade* 530
  pretext 617
blind, *adj. sightless* **442**
blind, *v. conceal* 528

blinders 443
blindfold 442, 491, 528
BLINDNESS 442
blink *wink* 443
blinker 424, 443, 530
bliss 827
blister 848
blithe 836
blithesome 836
blizzard 349
bloat *inflate* 194
bloated *expanded* 194
  convex 250
block, *n. houses* 189
  mass 192
block, *v. hinder* 706
  execution 975
blockade *surround* 227
  close 261
  seclude 893
blockhead 501
blonde 429
blood *consanguinity* 11
  -relation 11
bloodlessness 160
bloodshed 361
bloodthirsty 361
bloody *killing* 361
bloom *blossom* 367
  health 654
  flower 734
blossom
  flower 161, 365, 367
  flower 734
blot *blacken* 431
  blemish 848
  disgrace 874
blotch *black* 431
  blemish 848
blotchy 431
blouse 225
blow *knock* 276
  waft 349
  disappointment 509
  evil 619
  -up *explode* 173
  inflate 194, 349
  objurgate 932
blowhole 260, 351
bludgeon 727
BLUE *color* 438
bluestocking 492
bluff *high* 206
  brag 884
blunder *error* 495
  absurdity 497
  bungle 699
  failure 732
  indiscretion 947
blunt *obtuse* 254
  benumb 376
  plain-spoken 703
BLUNTNESS 254
blur *dim* 443
  blemish 848
blurred *invisible* 447

curb 752
brake, v. retard 275
bramble 253
branch, n. 51, 367
branch, v. ramify 244
brand, n. fuel 388
  torch 423
  mark 550
  sword 727
brand, v. sear 384
  defame 874
brandish 315
brass alloy 41
bravado 884
brave, adj. 861
  -man 861
  -woman 861
brave, v. defy 234
  bear 826
bravery 861
brawl discord 713
brawny strong 159
brazen unreserved 525
  -insolent 885
breach crack 44
  gap 198
  quarrel 713
  violation 925
bread 298
BREADTH 202
break fracture 44
  discontinuity 70
  gap 198
  faux pas 947
break, v. crumble 328
  train animals 370
  -in domesticate 370
  -out begin 66
  -up disjoin 44
  destroy 162
breakdown 162
breakers surf 348
breakneck
  rash 863
breast, n. 221
breast, v. confront 234
breath breeze 349
  life 359
breathe exist 1
  blow 349
breathing 349
breathless
  out of breath 688
  astonished 870
breeches 225
breed, n. race 11
breed, v. multiply 161
breeding politeness 894
breeze wind 349
brethren 997
brevity 201, 572
brew 48
bribe, n. gift 784
bribe, v. tempt 615
  buy 795
  reward 973

bribery [see bribe]
bric-a-brac 847
bridal 903
bride 903
bridegroom 903
bridesmaid 903
bridge link 45
  -over join 43, 45
bridle depart 293
  restrain 751
brief time 111
  space 201
  concise 572
briefly awhile 111
  anon 132
  shortly 572
brier 253
brigade 726
brigand 792
bright shining 420
  color 428
  intelligent 498
  cheery 836
  beautiful 845
  cheering 848
brilliant shining 420
  witty 842
  beautiful 845
  glorious 873
brim 231
brimful 52
brindled 440
brine salt 392
bring 270
  -about cause 153
  -forth produce 161
  -forward adduce 467
  -over persuade 484
  -round persuade 615
  -together assemble 72
  -to mind 505
  -to terms 723
  -up develop 161
brink 231
briny 392
brisk prompt 111
  active 274, 682
bristle 253
bristling thorny 253
  discourteous 895
bristly rough 256
brittle 328
BRITTLENESS 328
broach begin 66
  tap 297
broad general 78
  space 202
broadcast
  disperse 73, 291
  publish 531
broaden 78
broadside side 236
  cannonade 716
broadsword 727
broil, n. fray 713
broil, v. heat 382

fry 384
broken divided 51
  discontinuous 70
  weak 160
  of horses 370
  -heart 837
broker 758
brokerage 812
bromide
  conventionalist 82
broncho 271
  -buster 370
bronze brown 433
brood multitude 102
  family 167
brook, n. stream 348
brook, v. bear 826
broom undergrowth 367
  sweeper 652
brother 17, 27
brotherhood 11, 17, 888
brotherly 888
brow top 210
  front 234
browbeat 860
BROWN 433
  -study 458
brownie 979
brownness 433
browse 298
bruise powder 330
  injure 649
bruised blemished 848
brunt 66, 276
brush, n. tail 235
  fight 720
brush, v. groom 370
  touch 379
  clean 652
brushwood 367
brusque 895
brutal savage 907
brutalize 945
brute animal 366
  rude person 895
  evildoer 913
  -force 964
brutish intemperate 954
BUBBLE, n.
  transience 111
  air 353
bubble, v. boil 315
bubonic plague 655
buccaneer 792
buck, n. stag 366
buck, v. leap 309
bucket receptacle 191
buckle, n. tie 43
buckle, v. distort 243
  -to labor 686
buckler 717
bucolic 371
bud, n. blossom 367
bud, v. expand 194
Buddhism 976
buddy chum 890

budge 264
budget *finance* 811
buff *color* 436
buffer 717
buffet *strike* 276
  smite 972
buffet *café* 189
  cupboard 191
buffoon *actor* 599
  humorist 844
  butt 857
buffoonery
  humor 840, 842, 853
  horseplay 856
bug 193, 366
bugaboo 980
bugbear 980
build *construct* 161
  form 240
building 189
bulb 249, 250
bulge 250
bulk, *n. quantity* 25
  whole 50
  size 192
bulk, *v* 31
bulkhead 228
bulky 31, 192
bull *animal* 366
  absurdity 495, 497
  stock exchange 797
bulldoze 860
bullet 727
bulletin *list* 86
  news 532
bullion 800
bully, *n* 863, 887
bully, *v frighten* 860
  bluster 885
  threaten 909
bulwark 717
bump, *n.* 250
bump, *v.* 276

bumptious *proud* 878
bunch *collection* 72
  protuberance 250
buncombe *bombast* 577
  boast 884
  flattery 933
bundle *packet* 72
bung 263
bungle 495, **699**
bungler 701
bunkum
  [*see* buncombe]
buoy *raise* 307
buoyant
  floating 305
  light 320
  elastic 325
  hopeful 858
bur 53
burden *clog* 706
bureau *chest* 191
  department 965
bureaucracy **737**
burgess 188
burgher 188
burglar 792
burglary 791
burial 363
  -place **363**
burlesque, *n.*
  travesty 555, **853**
  absurdity 497
  ridicule 856
burlesque, *v. imitate* 19
  ridicule 856
burn *heat* 382
  consume 384
burnish *polish* 255
burrow *excavate* 208, 252
burst, *n. sound* 406
  paroxysm 825
burst, *v.*
  -forth *begin* 66

expand 194
  be seen 446
bury 229, 363
bush *shrub* 367
bushy 256
BUSINESS 151, **625**
businesslike
  orderly 58
  business 625
  practical 692
bustle *energy* 171
  agitation 315
  activity **682**
bustling 682
busy 625, **682**
busybody **455**
but 30
butcher *kill* 361
butchered 53
butler 746
butt, *n. cask* 191
  laughingstock 857
butt, *v.* 276
butter 356
button *fasten* 43
buttonhole, *n.*
  bouquet 400
buttonhole, *v.*
  to bore 841
buttress 717
buxom 836
buy 795
buyer 795
buzz 409
by 236, 631
  -and by 132
  -means of **632**
  -the by 134
  -the way **134**
bygone *past* 122
byplay 550
bystander 197, 444
byword, *contempt* 930

C

cab 272
cabin *room* 189
cabinet *receptacle* 191
  council 696
cable, *n. link* 45
  dispatch 532
cable, *v* 534
cabman 268
cackle (*of geese*) 412
  laugh 838
cad 851
cadaverous *pale* 429
  hideous 846
cadence *sound* 402
  music 415
cadet *junior* 129
  officer 745
caesura 44, 198

café 189, 298
cage, *n. prison* 752
cage, *v. restrain* 751
caisson 191, 252
cajole *flatter* 933
  [*see* cajolery]
cajolery *imposition* 544
  persuasion 615
  flattery 933
cake, *n.* 396
cake, *v. stick* 46
  consolidate 321
calamitous
  adverse 735, 935
  disastrous 830
calamity *killing* 361
  evil 619
  adversity 735

calcine 384
calculate 85
calculation 85
caldron 191
CALEFACTION **384**
calendar *list* 86, 611
  chronicle 114
calf *animal* 366
  fool 501
caliber *measure* 26, 192
  intellectual capacity 498
calipers 466
calisthenics 159
calk 660
call *signal* 550
  name 564
  visit 892
  ordain 995

catechism *inquiry* 461
catechize 461
categorical *positive* 474
category *state* 7
  class 75
cater 298, 637
caterer 637
cathartic 652
cathedral 1000
catholic *universal* 78
  religious 987
Catholicism 983a
cattle *animals* 366
caucus *assemblage* 72
  council 696
causal 153
causative 153
CAUSE *source* 153
causeway 627
caustic *energetic* 171
  keen 821
  painful 830
CAUTION *warn* 668
  prudence 864
  with - 485
cautious 864
cavalcade 266
cavalier *horseman* 268
cavalry 726
cavalryman 726
cave 189, 252
caveman 893
cavern [see cave]
cavernous 252
cavil *dissent* 489
cavity 252
cavort 315
cease 142
ceaseless 112
cede *surrender* 725
  relinquish 782
ceiling 223
celebrate 883
CELEBRATION 883
celebrity 873
  nobility 875
celerity 274
celestial *physical* 318
  heavenly 976, 981
CELIBACY 904
celibate 904
cell *abode* 189, 191, 893
  organism 357
cellar 207
cement, *n. glue* 45
cement, *v. unite* 46
cemetery 363
censor *critic* 480
  detractor 936
censure 932
census 85, 86
centenary 98
centennial 98
center, *n. in order* 68
  focus 74
  in space 222

center, *v. converge* 290
central 68, 222
CENTRALITY 222
centralize 48, 222
centuple 98
century *hundred* 98
  period 108
  long time 110
ceremonial 882
ceremonious 882, 928
ceremony 882, 998
certain 474, 484
certainly 474, 488
CERTAINTY 474
certificate *evidence* 467
  security 771
certify 467
certitude 474
CESSATION 142
chafe *warm* 384
  fret 828, 830
chaff *ridicule* 856
chafing dish 386
chagrin 828
chain, *n. vinculum* 45
  series 69
chain, *v. fasten* 43
chair *support* 215
  professorship 540
  president 694
chairman 694
chalet 189
challenge *doubt* 485
  accuse 938
chamber *room* 191
champ 298
champion *auxiliary* 711
  victor 731
  defender 914
CHANCE
  absence of cause 156
  absence of aim 621
chancellor *judge* 967
chandelier 214
CHANGE, *n.*
  alteration 20a, 140
  small coin 800
change, *v. differ* 15
  -for 147
  -hands 783
changeable 140, 149
CHANGEABLENESS
  140, 149
changeful 140, 607
changeling 147
channel *furrow* 259
  opening 260
chant, *n.* 415, 990
chant, *v.* 416
chaos 59
chap *fellow* 373
chapel 1000
chaperon 88, 459
chaplain 996
chaplet *circle* 247
  trophy 733

chapter *part* 51
  council 696
char 384
character *state* 7
  class 75
  oddity 83
  letter 561
  disposition 820
characteristic
  intrinsic 5
  distinctive 15
  special 79
  mark 550
characterize *name* 564
  describe 594
charge, *n. mandate* 630
  advice 695
  precept 697
  price 812
  accusation 938
charge, *v. fill* 52
  enjoin 695
  attack 716
charger *horse* 271
chariot 272
charitable 784, 906
charity *giving* 784
  beneficence 906
  pity 914
charlatan *impostor* 548
  poser 855
charm, *n. talisman* 747
  beauty 845
  love 897
  spell 993
charm, *v. draw* 288
  please 377, 829
  conjure 992
charming [see charm]
chart 183, 527
charter *permit* 760
  privilege 924
charwoman 690, 746
chary *cautious* 864
chase *drive away* 289
  pursue 622
chasm 198, 208, 350
chaste *shapely* 242
  simple 849
  pure 960
chasten *moderate* 174
  punish 972
chasteness [see chaste]
chastise 972
chastity 960
chat 588
chattels 780
chatter 412, 584
chatterbox 584
chauffeur 268
cheap 815
cheapen *haggle* 794, 819
CHEAPNESS 815
cheat, *n. deceiver* 548
cheat, *v. deceive* 545
check, *n. plaid* 440

clash, *v. disagree* 24
  cross 179
  -of arms 720
clashing *contrariety* 14
clasp *fasten* 43
  stick 46
  embrace 902
CLASS, *n. category* 75
  learners 541
  school 542
  party 712
  laity 997
class, *v. arrange* 60
classfellow 890
classic *old* 124
  symmetry 242
classics 560
classification 60
classify 60
classmate 541
classroom 542
clatter *noise* 404
  rattle 407
clause 51
claw 781
clay *earth* 342
clean *perfect* 650
  unstained 652
  -cut 494
cleaner 652
cleanly 652
cleanness 652
cleanse 652
clear *simple* 42
  light 420
  transparent 425
  certain 474
  intelligible 518
  manifest 525
  distinct 535
  perspicuous 570
clear, *v. leap* 309
  vindicate 937, 970
clear-cut *true* 494
clear-sighted 441
clearness [see clear]
cleavage *cutting* 44
cleave *sunder* 44
  adhere 46
  bisect 91
clef 413
cleft *chink* 198
clement *lenient* 740
  compassionate 914
CLERGY 996
clergyman 996
clerical 995
clerk *recorder* 553
  writer 590
clever 698
cleverness 698
click 406
client *dependent* 711
  customer 795
clientele 795
cliff *height* 206

verticality **212**
  steep 217
  crag 342
climate 338
climax *supremacy* 33
  summit 210
climb 305
clime 181
clinch *fasten* 43
cling *adhere* 46
  -to
    persevere **604a**
    desire 865
    love 897
clink *resound* 408
clip *shorten* 201
clique 75, **712**
cliquish 712
cloak, *n. dress* 225
cloak, *v. conceal* 528
  disguise 530
clock 114
clod *lump* 192
  earth 342
  fool 501
clog *hinder* 706
cloister *arcade* 189
  seclusion 893
close, *n. end* 67
close, *adj. similar* 17, 21
  tight 43
  near 197
  dense 321
  warm 382
  taciturn 585
  stingy 819
close, *v. shut* 261
  conclude 769
closely [see close]
closet 191
CLOSURE 261
clot 321
clothe 225
CLOTHING 225
cloture 142
CLOUD, *n. mist* 353
cloud, *v. darken* 421
  dim 422, 427
  -over **422**, 427
cloudy *dim* 422
  opaque 426
clown 599, 844
cloy 641, 869
club, *n. place of meeting* 74
  association 712
  weapon 727
club, *v. combine* 48, 892
clue *answer* 462
  indication 550
clump 72, 250
  -of trees 367
clumsiness [see clumsy]
clumsy *unfit* 647
  awkward 699
cluster 72
clutch *seize* 781

  throttle 789
clutter 59
coach, *n. carriage* 272
  tutor 540
coach, *v. teach* 537
coachman 268
coagulate *cohere* 46
  densify 321
coal 388
coalesce 13, 48
coalition 709, 712
coarse *harsh* 410
  vulgar 851
coast, *n. border* 231
coast, *v. glide* 266
  navigate 267
  land 342
coat *layer* 204
  paint 223
  dress 225
  -of arms 550
coating, inner - 224
coax *persuade* 615
  wheedle 902
cobble *mend* 660
cobbler 660
cobra 366
cobweb 205
cock *vane* 338
  bird 366
cockeyed 443
cockle 258
cocksure 484
coddle 902
code *concealment* **528**
  cipher 561
  law 963
codicil *addition* 37
  testament 771
codify *arrange* 60
  legalize 963
coequal 27
coequality 27
coerce *compel* 744
  restrain 751
coeval 120
coexist *exist* 1
  concur 120
coexistence 120
coffer *chest* 191
  money chest 802
coffin 363
cog *tooth* 253
cogency 157
cogent *powerful* 157
cogitate 450, 451
cogitative 451
cognate *related* 9
  similar 17
cognition 490
cognizance 490
cohere 46
COHERENCE 46
coherent 23
cohesion 46
cohesive 46

coil *convolution* 248
  circuit 311
coin, n. 800
coin, v. *fabricate* 161
coincide 13, 120, 488
coincidence *identity* 13
  in time 120
coincident 13, 120, 178
coiner 792
COLD, n. *frigidity* 383
cold, adj.
  frigid 383
  insensible 823
  indifferent 866
cold-blooded 907
cold-bloodedness 871
coldhearted
  unfeeling 823
  malevolent 907
coldness *cold* 383
  unconcern 823
  indifference 866
collaboration 178
collaborator 711
collapse, n.
  prostration 158
  failure 732
collapse, v. *fail* 304
collar *dress* 225
  circlet 247
collateral *relative* 9
colleague
  associate 88, 690
  friend 890
collect *assemble* 72
  compile 596
collected *calm* 826
collection *assemblage* 72
  offertory 990
collective 78
collectively 50
college 542
collide 276
collision *clash* 179
  percussion 276
  opposition 708
  encounter 720
colloquial 588
collusion *deceit* 545
  complicity 709
colonel 745
colonial 188
colonist 188, 294, 295
colonization 184
colonize 184
colony *region* 184
  settlement 188
COLOR, n *hue* 428
color, v. *redden* 434
  be angry 900
colored 428
colorless *pale* 429
colors *ensign* 550
colossal 106, 192
colossus 206
colt *horse* 271

column *height* 206
  support 215
  monument 551
coma 683
comb, n. 253
comb, v. *clean* 652
combat 720
COMBATANT 726
combative 720, 722
COMBINATION 48
combine *unite* 48
  compose 56
  co-operate 709
combustible 384, 388
combustion 384
come *arrive* 292
  -after *succeed* 117
  -amiss 135
  -of age 131
  -out *come of age* 131
  -together *assemble* 72
  converge 290
  -to nothing
  fail 732
  -to pass 151
comedian 844
comedy 599, 853
comely 845
comfort *pleasure* 377
  delight 827
  relief 834
comfortable 377
Comforter 976
comforter *wrap* 223
comfortless 837
comic 842, 853
coming [see come]
  impending 152
  -out *debut* 883
COMMAND, n.
  requirement 630
  authority 737
  order 741
command, v. *tower* 206
  order 737, 741
  possess 777
commandant 745
commander 744, 789
commander
  mariner 269
  chief 745
commander-in-chief 745
commemorate 883
commemorative 883
commence 66
commend 931
commendable 944
commendatory 931
comment 522, 595
commentary 522, 595
commentator 595
commerce 794
commercial 794
commingle 41
commiserate 914
commissariat 637

COMMISSION
  task 625
  delegate 755
commissioner 745, 758
commit *do* 680
  delegate 755
  arrest 969
  -to memory 505
commitment 969
committee 696, 758
commodious 644
commodity 798
commodore 745
common, n. 367
common, adj.
  general 78
  ordinary 82
  habitual 613
  base 876
  -run 78
  -sense 498, 502
  in - *participated* 778
commonalty 876
commoner 876
commonplace *mediocre* 29
  plain 576
  habit 613
  unimportant 643
commonweal
  mankind 372
  good 618
  utility 644
commonwealth *region* 181
  mankind 372
  state 737
commotion 315
commune *township* 181
commune with 588
communicate *tell* 527
communication 43, 527
communicative 527
communion
  participation 778
  sacrament 998
communist 778
communistic 778
community *party* 712
communize 778
commutation
  substitution 147
  interchange 148
commute 774
commuter 268
COMPACT *joined* 43
  compressed 195
  compendious 201
  dense 321
  bargain 769
compactness
  [see compact]
companion *match* 17
  accompaniment 88
  friend 890
companionable 892
companionship 892
company *assembly* 72

actors 599
  partnership 797
  troop 726
comparative 464
comparatively 32
compare 464
COMPARISON 9, 464
compartment 182, 191
compass, n. degree 26
  space 180
  circuit 311
  measure 466
compass, v. surround 227
  circumscribe 233
  guide 693
  achieve 729
compassion 914
compassionate 914
compatible 23
compatriot 890
compeer equal 27
compel 744
compendious 596
COMPENDIUM 596
compensate
  make up for 30
  requite 973
COMPENSATION 30,
  952
compensatory 30, 790
complete 708, 720
competence power 157
  sufficiency 639
  skill 698
  wealth 803
competition
  opposition 708
  contention 720
competitor
  opponent 710
  candidate 767
compile 54, 72, 596
complacent vain 880
  courteous 894
complain 839
complainant 938
complaint illness 655
  murmur 839
complement
  counterpart 14
  adjunct 39
complete, fill up 52
  accomplish 729
  conclude 769
COMPLETENESS 50, 52
  unity 87
COMPLETION 67, 87,
  729
complex 59
complexion color 428
  appearance 448
complexity 59
compliance
  submission 725
  consent 762
  observance 772

compliant [see compli-
  ance]
complicate derange 61
complicity 709
compliment 896, 931
complimentary 931
comply [see compliance]
COMPONENT 56
compose, make up 54, 56
  produce 161
  music 415, 416
  write 590
  printing 591
  assuage 826
composed
  self-possessed 826
composer music 413
composite 41
COMPOSITION 54
  [see compose]
  combination 48
  embodiment 76
  style 569
  writing 590
  compromise 774
  atonement 952
compositor 591
composure 174, 826
compound mix 41
  combination 48
  compromise 774
comprehend include 76
  know 490
  understand 518
comprehensibility 518
comprehension
  [see comprehend]
comprehensive
  wholesale 50
  inclusive 56, 76
  general 78
compress contract 195
  condense 321
compressed 572
compression 195
comprise 76
compromise 774
  mean 29
  compensation 30
  mid-course 628
  compound 774
COMPULSION 744
compulsory 601
compunction 950
computable 85
compute 37, 85
computation 85
comrade 890
comradeship 892
con learn 505, 539
concave 252
CONCAVITY 252
conceal hide 528
CONCEALMENT 528
concede admit 529
  consent 762

give 784
conceit overestimation 482
  imagination 515
  wit 842
  affectation 855
  vanity 880
conceited 481, 855, 880
conceivable 470
conceive note 450
  believe 484
  understand 490
  imagine 515
concentrate assemble 72
  centralize 222
  converge 290
concentric 222
conception [see conceive]
  intellect 450
  idea 453, 515
concern relation 9
  event 151
  care 459
  business 625
  importance 642
  firm 797
concerning 9
concert agreement 23
  music 415
concession permission 760
  giving 784
  discount 813
conciliate pacify 723
  satisfy 831
  forgive 918
conciliatory [see concili-
  ate]
  concordant 714
  courteous 894
concise 572
  taciturn 585
CONCISENESS 201, 572
conclude infer 480
  complete 769
conclusion [see conclude]
  sequel 65
  eventuality 151
  effect 154
  judgment 480
conclusive [see conclude]
  final 67, 729
  evidential 467
  certain 474
  proved 478
concoct 544, 626
CONCORD agreement 23
  music 413
  harmony 714
concordance
  dictionary 593
concordant 714
concourse assemblage 72
  convergence 290
concrete hard 321
  definite 494
concur coexist 120
  agree 178

consonance 16
consort *associate* 892
  spouse 903
conspicuous *visible* 446
  famous 873
conspiracy 626
conspirator *traitor* 941
conspire *concur* 178
  co-operate 709
constable *safety* 664
  officer 965
constancy 16, 141, 939
constant *uniform* 16
  regular 80
  frequent 136
  periodic 138
  immutable 150
  persevering 604a
  faithful 939
constellation 318
consternation 860
constituency 609
constituent 56, 609
constitute *compose* 56
constitution *nature* 5
  state 7
  composition 54
  charter 924
  law 963
constitutional 963
constrain *compel* 744
  restrain 751
constraint [see constrain]
constrict 195
construct *compose* 54
  produce 161
  organize 357
construction
  production 161
  form 240
  structure 329
  meaning 522
constructive *creative* 161
construe 522
consult *advise* 695
consultant 662
consultation 695
consume *destroy* 162
  waste 638
  use 677
consumer *user* 677
consummate, *adj.*
  great 31
  completed 729
consummate, *v.* 650
consummation *end* 67
  completion 729
consumption
  [see consume]
  waste 638
  disease 655
consumptive 655
CONTACT *contiguity* 199
  touch 379
contagion 270, 657
contagious 655, 657

contain *be composed of* 54
  include 76
contaminate *soil* 653
  spoil 659
contamination 653, 659
contemplate *view* 441
  think 450, 451
  expect 507
  purpose 620
contemplation
  [see contemplate]
contemporary 120
CONTEMPT 930
contemptible
  despicable 930
  dishonorable 940
contemptuous
  disrespectful 929
  disdainful 930
contend *reason* 476
  assert 535
  fight 720
CONTENT, *n.*
  calmness 826
  contentment 831
content, *adj.* 602
CONTENTION 720
contentious 720, 901
CONTENTS
  ingredients 56
  list 86
  components 190
contest 708, 720
contestant 710
context 591
contiguity 199
contiguous 197
continent 342
contingency
  junction 43
  event 151
  expectation 470, 507
contingent *extrinsic* 6
  conditional 8
  liable 177
  aid 707
continual *perpetual* 112
  frequent 136
CONTINUANCE 110,
  117, 143
continuation *sequence* 63
  continuance 143
  sequel 65
continue *exist* 1
  endure 106
  persist 143
continued 69
continuing 143
CONTINUITY 16, 69
continuous 69
contortion *distortion* 243
  convolution 248
contour *outline* 230, 240
  appearance 448
contraband, *n.* 761
contraband, *adj.*

deceitful 545
  prohibited 761
  illicit 964
contraclockwise 283
contract *shrink* 195
  shorten 201
  covenant 769
CONTRACTION 195
contractor 690
contradict *contrary* 14
  deny 468, 536
  dissent 489
contradiction 15, 536
contradictoriness 15
contradictory 468, 536
contrapuntal 415
CONTRARIETY 14, 15,
  708
contrariness 708
contrary *opposite* 14
  captious 608
  opposing 708
  be - oppose 14
contrast *contrariety* 14
  difference 15
  comparison 464
contravene
  go contrary 14
  counteract 179
  deny 536
  oppose 708
contretemps
  hindrance 706
  misfortune 735
contribute *cause* 153
  tend 176
  concur 178
  give 784
contribution 784
contributor *author* 593
  giver 784
contributory *extra* 37
contrition *penitence* 950
contrivance 626
contrive *produce* 161
  plan 626
control, *n.* *power* 157
  influence 175
  aviation 273
control, *v.* *regulate* 693
  restrain 751
controversial 476, 713
controversialist 476
controversy *discussion* 476
  contention 720
controvert *deny* 536
contumacy *obstinacy* 606
  disobedience 742
contumely *scorn* 930
  reproach 932
conundrum 533
convalesce 654
convalescence 654, 660
convene 72
convenience 685
conveniences 632

cottager 188
couch, n. bed 215
couch, v. lurk 528
cough 349
COUNCIL senate 696
councilor 696
counsel advice 695
   lawyer 968
count, n. item 79
   lord 875
count, v.
   compute 37, 85
   estimate 480
countenance, n. face 234
   appearance 448
   favor 707
countenance, v. approve
   931
counter, n. token 550
counter, adj. contrary 14
   reverse 237
counteract 179, 706
COUNTERACTION 179
counterbalance 30, 179
countercharge 462
counterclaim 30
COUNTEREVIDENCE
   468
counterfeit imitate 19
   copy 21
   sham 545
   swindle 791
counterfeiter 792
countermand 756
countermarch 283
countermotion 283
counterpane 223
counterpart identity 13
   complement 14
   match 17
   copy 21
counterpoise
   compensate 30
countersign n.
   evidence 467
   mark 550
countersign, v. 488
countess 875
countless 105
countrified 189
country region 181
   abode 189
   land 342
   state 737
countryman 876
county 181
coupé 272
couple, n. two 89
couple, v. unite 43
   combine 48
COURAGE 861
courageous 861
courier traveler 268
   messenger 534
COURSE order 58
   continuity 69

time 106, 109
   layer 204
   locomotion 267
   direction 278
   lesson 537
   pursue 622
courser horse 271
court, n. house 189
   hall 191
   retinue 746
court, v. invite 615
   tribunal 966
   woo 902
   flatter 933
courteous 894
COURTESY
   politeness 894
courtier 935
courtly 852
court-martial 966
courtship 902
courtyard 182
cousin 11
cove hollow 252
   bay 343
covenant compact 769
   condition 770
   security 771
cover, n. dress 225
   lid 223
cover, v. include 76
   superpose 223
   conceal 528
   keep safe 664
covered 223
COVERING 220, 223
coverlet 223
covert abode 189
   invisible 447
   latent 526
   refuge 666
coverture 903
covet desire 865
   envy 921
covetous miserly 921
covey 102
cow, n. animal 366
cow, v. intimidate 860
coward 862
COWARDICE 862
cowardly 862
cowboy 370
cower stoop 308
   fear 860
   quail 862
   fawn 886
cowherd 370
cowhide, n. whip 975
cowhide, v. lash 972
coworker 690
cowpuncher 370
coxcomb 854, 880
coxcombry affectation 855
coxswain 269
coy 881
cozy 377, 892

crabbed sour 397
   unintelligible 519
   uncivil 895
crack, n. fissure 44, 198
   furrow 259
crack, v. split 44
   crush 328
   sound 406
crack, adj. excellent 648
crack-brained insane 503
cracked unmusical 410
   mad 503
crackle 406
cracksman 792
cradle beginning 66
   infancy 127
   origin 153
   bed 215
   aid 707
craft shipping 273
   calling 625
   cunning 702
craftsman 690
craftsmanship 680
crag cliff 212, 253, 342
craggy rough 256
crake 884
cram stuff 194
   choke 261
   teach 537
   learn 539
   gorge 957
cramp, n. spasm 315
cramp, v. paralyze 158
   weaken 160
   hinder 706
crane lever 307
cranium 450
crank fanatic 504
   instrument 633
cranny 198
crash, n. collision 276
   sound 406
crash, v. destroy 162
   crack 328
crass unintelligent 493
   bad taste 851
cravat 225
crave ask 765
   desire 865
craven cowardly 862
craving 865
craw 191
crawl elapse 109
   creep 275
   cower 886
crazy weak 160
   mad 503
creak 410
cream, n. 356
   important part 642
   best 648
cream, adj. yellow 436
creamy 430
crease 258
create cause 153

produce 161, **976**
imagine **515**
creation [*see* create]
    effect 154
    production 161
    world 318
creative 20, 153, 162
creativeness 20
Creator 976
creator *cause* 153
    producer 164
    poet 597
creature *thing* 3
    animal 366
    man 372
    slave 746
credence *belief* 484
credential 467
credibility 484
credible *possible* 470
    believable 484
CREDIT *belief* 484
    pecuniary 805
    repute 873
    approbation 931
    desert 944
creditable *right* 924
creditor 805
CREDULITY 486
credulous 486
    -person *dupe* 486
creed *belief* 484
    theology 983
creek 343
creep *crawl* 275
    tingle 380
cremation 363
crematory 384
crescendo 35
crescent 35
    curve 245
crest *climax* 33
    summit 210
    tuft 256
    sign 550
    armorial 877
crestfallen 879
crevasse 198
crevice 198
crew *assemblage* 72
    mariners 269
    party 712
crib *bed* 215
    translation 522
crime *guilt* 947
criminal *vicious* 945
    culprit 949
    malefactor 975
criminality 947
crimson *color* 434
cringe *fawn* 886
cringing *servile* 746
crinkle *ruffle* 256
    fold 258
cripple *disable* 158
    weaken 160

crisis *conjuncture* 8
    contingency 43
    opportunity **134**
    event 151
    strait 704
crisp 328
crisscross 219
criterion *test* 463
critic *judge* 480, 595, 850
    detractor 936
critical *discriminating* 465
    judicious 480
    important 642
    censorious 932
criticism *judgment* 480
    dissertation 595
    disapprobation 932
    detraction 934
criticize *discriminate* 465
    judge 480, 595, 850
    disapprove 932
    detract 934
critique 480, 595
croak *cry* 412
    grumble 832
    lament 839
croaker 832, 837
crocodile 366
crone *veteran* 130
crony *friend* 890
crook *support* 215
    curve 245
    thief 792
crooked *distorted* 243
    angular 244
    latent 526
    crafty 702
croon 405
crop, *n. harvest* 154
    store 636
crop, *v. shorten* 201
    produce 775
    -up *begin* 66
    take place 151
cropped *fragmentary* 51
cross, *n.* 215
    decoration 877
cross, *v. mix* 41
    intersect 219
    pass 302
    oppose 708
    vex 830
cross, *adj. fretful* 901
cross, *adv.* 219
crossbow 727
crossbreed 41
crossed 219
cross-examine 461
cross-eye 443
cross-fire *interchange* 148
    attack 716
cross-grained
    obstinate 606
    irascible 901
CROSSING 219
cross-purposes

misinterpretation 523
    discord 713
cross-question 461
crossroad 627
crosswise 219
crotch 91, 244
crotchet *music* 413
    misjudgment 481
    caprice 608
crouch *be low* 207
    stoop 308
    fear 860
    fawn 886
crow, *n.*
    laughter 838
crow, *v. cry* 412
    boast 884
crowbar 633
crowd, *n. assemblage* **72**
    multitude 102
    the masses 876
crowd, *v. huddle* 197
crowded 102, 197 [*see* crowd]
crown *top* **210**
    trophy 733
    scepter 747
    jewel 847
    decoration 877
crown, *v. complete* 729
    install 755
crowning [*see* crown]
    superior 33
    final 67
crozier 747
crucial 478, 642
crucible 386, 691
crucifix 219, 998
crucifixion *anguish* 828
    [*see* crucify]
cruciform 219, 1000
crucify *torture* 378
    agonize 830
    execute 972
crude *immature* 53
    gay 428
    inelegant 579
    unprepared 674
cruel *painful* 830
    inhuman 907
cruelty 907
cruise 267
cruiser 726
crumb *small* 32
    bit 51
crumble *decrease* 36
    be weak 160
    perish 162
    splinter 328
    pulverize 330
    decay 659
crumple *ruffle* 256
crunch *pulverize* 330
crusade 722
crush *crowd* 72
    destroy 162

compress 195
  shatter 328
  humble 879
crushed *unhappy* 828
crust 223
crusty *discourteous* 895
crutch *support* 215
crux *difficulty* 704
CRY *stridor* 410
  human 411
  animal 412
  weep **839**
crying [*see* cry]
  urgent 630
crypt *cell* 191
  grave 207, 363
cryptic *uncertain* 475
  concealed 528
crystalline *dense* 321
  transparent 425
crystallization 321, 323
crystallize 321
cub *cad* 851
cubicle 191
cubist 556
cuddle 902
cudgel, *n.* 727
cudgel, *v. beat* 276
cue *hint* 527
  watchword 550
cuff *blow* 276
cuirass 717
cuisine 298
cul-de-sac 261
culinary 298
cull *choose* 609
  take 789
culminate *cap* 33
  tower 206
  crown 210
culprit **949**, **975**
cult 481, 990
cultivate *till* 371
  improve 658, 707
cultivated *courteous* 894
cultivation *tillage* 371
  knowledge 490
  improvement **658**
  courtesy 894
cultivator 371
cultural 537, 542
culture *knowledge* 490
  improvement 658
  courtesy 894
cumber 706
cumbersome *heavy* 319
  disagreeable 830
cumbrous 319, **830**
cumulative 467
CUNNING *artfulness* **702**
cup *vessel* 191

hollow 252
cupboard **191**
cupidity *avarice* 819
  desire 865
cupola *dome* 223, 250
cupping 662
cur *dog* 366
curable 658, 660
curate 996
curb, *n. bit* 752
curb, *v. moderate* 174
  slacken 275
  .*check* 706
  restrain 751
curd 321
curdle *condense* 321
cure *reinstate* 660
  remedy 662
curio 847
CURIOSITY **455**
  phenomenon 872
curious *exceptional* 83
  inquisitive **455**
curl *bend* 245
  convolution 248
  hair 256
curly 248
currency *publicity* 531
  money 800
current, *n.*
  of air 349
current, *adj. existing* 1
  general 78
  present 118
  happening 151
  rife 531, 532
currycomb 253
curse, *n. bane* 663
  adversity 735
curse, *v. execrate* **908**
cursory *transient* 111
  hasty 684
curt *short* 201
  concise 572
curtail *retrench* 38
  shorten 201
curtailment
  decrease 36
  [*see* curtail]
curtain *shade* 424
  screen 530
curtsy 308
CURVATURE **245**
curve 245, 252, 279
curved **245**
curvet *leap* 309
cushion *pillow* 215
cussedness 606
custodian 753
custody 664, 751
custom, *rule* 80

habit 124, **613**
  barter 794
  sale 796
  fashion 852
customary [*see* custom]
  regular 80
customer 795
cut, *n. bit* 51
  notch 257
  blow 276
  path 627
cut, *v. divide* 44
  absent 187
  curtail 201
  form 240
  depart 293
  reap 371
  carve 557
  ignore 893
  snub 895
  -*across* 302
  -*adrift* 44
  -*away* 38
  -*off subduct* 38
  disjoin 44
  bereft 776
  divorce 782
  -*out surpass* 33
  substitute 147
  -*short stop* 142
cuticle 223
cutlass 727
cutlery 253
cutter 273
cutthroat 361, 913
cutting *sharp* 253
  affecting 821
  painful 830
  -*edge* **253**
cuttings 596
cycle *period* 138
  circle 247
  vehicle 272
cyclic 138
cyclist 268
cyclone *rotation* 312
  wind 349
cyclonic 349
cyclopedia 593
cylinder 249, 272
cylindrical 249
cynic *recluse* 893
  misanthrope 911
  detractor 936
cynical *morose* 911
  contemptuous 930
  censorious 932
cynicism
  misanthropy 911
  discourtesy 895
czar 745

D

DESCENT 69
 lineage 166
 fall 306
describe 594
DESCRIPTION *kind* 75
 narration 594
descriptive 594
desecrate *misuse* 679
 profane 988
desert, *n. waste* 169, 180,
  344
 merit 924
desert, *v. run away* 187
 relinquish 624
deserted *empty* 187
 outcast 893
deserter 623
DESERTION 624
deserve *be entitled to* 924
deserving 924
deshabille
 [see dishabille]
desiccate 340
desideratum 630
design *prototype* 22
 delineation 554
 painting 556
 intention 620
 plan 626
designate *specify* 79
 call 564
designation *kind* 75
designer 559, 626
designing *cunning* 702
desirability 646
desirable 646, 865
DESIRE 865
 will 600
desirous *desiring* 865
desist *discontinue* 142
desk *box* 191
 school – 542
desolate, *adj. dejected* 837
 secluded 893
desolate, *v. ravage* 162
desolating *painful* 830
desolation
 [see desolate]
despair *grief* 828
 hopelessness 859
despatch [see dispatch]
desperado 863, 887
desperate *great* 31
 violent 173
 hopeless 859
 rash 863
despicable *shameful* 874
 contemptible 930
despise 930
despite 30
despoil *injure* 659
 take 789
 rob 791
despond *despair* 859
 fear 860
despot 739, 745

despotism *severity* 739
 tyranny 964
destination *end* 67
 rest 265
 arrival 292
destine 152, 601, 620
DESTINY *chance* 152
 fate 601
destitute 640, 804
destroy 2, 162
DESTROYER 165
 naval 726
DESTRUCTION 21, 162
destructive *ruinous* 162
 bad 649
DESUETUDE 614
desultory *fitful* 70
 irregular *in time* 139
 changeable 149
 deviating 279
detach 44
detached *irrelated* 10
 loose 47
detachment *separation* 44
 part 51
 army 726
detail, *n. item* 79
detail, *v. describe* 594
 allot 786
 in – 51
details *minutiae* 32
 particulars 79
detain 781
detect 480a
detective 527
detention 781
deter *dissuade* 616
deteriorate 659
DETERIORATION 659
determine *define* 79
 cause 153
 satisfy 462
 make sure 474
 judge 480
 discover 480a
 resolve 604
determinant 153
determined *resolute* 604
detest *dislike* 867
 hate 898
detestable 649
dethrone 738
dethronement 738, 756
detour 279, 629
detract *subduct* 38
 underrate 483
 defame 934
DETRACTION 934
DETRACTOR 936
detriment 619, 659
detrimental 649
devastate *destroy* 162
 make havoc 659
 depopulate 893
devastation 162
develop *produce* 161

evolve 313
development 35, 154
deviate *change* 140
 turn 279
DEVIATION 20a,140,279
device *motto* 550
 expedient 626
 artifice 702
devil *Satan* 978
 -worship 978
devious *changeful* 140
 deviating 279
 circuitous 311
devise *imagine* 515
 plan 626
 bequeath 784
devoid 777a
devolve 783
devote *destine* 601
 employ 677
 consecrate 873
devoted *ill-fated* 735
 obedient 743
 loving 897
devotee *zealot* 682
 enthusiast 840
 fanatic 988
devotion *obedience* 743
 love 897
 piety 987
 worship 990
devour *destroy* 162
 eat 298
 cram 957
devout 987, 990
dew 339
dewy 339
dexter 238
dexterous 238, 698
dextral 238
dextrality 238
diabolic *malevolent* 907
 wicked 945
 satanic 978
diabolism 978
diabolist 978
diadem 747, 847
diagnosis 465, 522, 655
diagnostic 15, 465, 550
diagonal 217
diagram 554
dial 114
dialect 560, 563
dialogue 588
diameter 202
diametrical 237
diamond *lozenge* 244
diaphragm 68, 228
diary *journal* 114
diatribe 932
dichotomy 91
dicker *haggle* 794
dictate *write* 590
 advise 695
 command 741
dictator 745

disclaim *deny* **536**
  repudiate **756**
disclaimer **536**
disclamation
  [*see* disclaim]
disclose **529**
DISCLOSURE 529
  discovery **480a**
discoloration 429
discolored 848
discomfiture 732
discomfort *physical* 378
  mental 828
discommode *hinder* 706
discompose *derange* 61
  put out 458
  pain 830
  disconcert 874
disconcert *derange* 61
  distract 458
  dishearten 832
  confuse 874
disconnect 44
disconnected
  unrelated 10
  interrupted 70
disconnection
  irrelation 19
  disjunction 44
  discontinuity 70
disconsolate 837
DISCONTENT 832
discontinuance 142
DISCONTINUITY 70
discontinuous 44, 70
DISCORD
  disagreement 24
  of sound 414
  dissension 713
discordance 414, 713
DISCOUNT *decrease* 36
  decrement 40a
  money 813
discountenance 706
discourage *dissuade* 616
  dishearten 837
  frighten 860
discourse, *n. speech* 582
  talk 588
discourse, *v. speak* 582
  talk 588
discourteous 895
DISCOURTESY 895
discover *perceive* 441
  find 480a
  disclose 529
DISCOVERY 480a
discredit *disbelieve* 485
  dishonor 874
discreditable 874
discreet 459, 864
discrepancy 20a, 24
discretion *will* 600
  choice 609
  caution 864
discriminate 15, 465, 868

DISCRIMINATION
  difference 15
  nice perception **465**
  fastidiousness 868
discriminative 868
discursive *wandering* 279
discuss *inquire* 461
  reason 476
discussion 476
disdain, *n. pride* 878
  contempt 930
disdain, *v. spurn* 866
disdainful *proud* 878
  disrespectful 929
DISEASE 655
diseased 655
disembark 342
disembody
  spiritualize **317**
disembogue
  flow out 348
disencumber 705
disengage *detach* 44
  liberate 750
disengaged *to let* 763
disentangle *separate* 44
  arrange 60
  facilitate 705
  liberate 750
disestablish *displace* 185
  abrogate 756
disfavor *oppose* 708
  disrespect 929
disfigure *deface* 241
  deform 846
  blemish 848
disfranchise 925
disgorge *emit* 297
  restore 790
disgrace *shame* 879
  dishonor 940
disgraceful 945
disgruntle 509
disgruntled 509
disguise, *n. mask* 530
  deception 545
disguise, *v. conceal* 528
disgust, *n.*
  weariness 841
  dislike 867
disgust, *v. nauseate* 395
  offend 830
disgusting 867
dish *plate* 191
dishabille *undress* 225
dishearten *dissuade* 616
  disappoint 832
  deject 837
dishevel *disorder* 61
dishonest *false* 544
  base 940
dishonor *protest* 808
  disrepute 874
  disrespect 929
  baseness 940
disillusion 509

disinclination 867
disincline *dissuade* **616**
  dislike 867
disinclined 603, 867
disinfect *purify* 652
disinfectant 388, 662
disinherit 782, **783**
disintegrate *separate* **44**
  decompose 49
disintegration 49
disinter *exhume* **363**
  discover 480a
disinterment 363
disinterested 942
DISINTERESTEDNESS
  542
disjoin **44**
DISJUNCTION 10, **44**
disjunctive 44
disk 247
DISLIKE 867
dislocate *separate* 44
  put out of joint 61
dislodge *displace* 185
  eject 297
disloyal 940
dismal *depressing* 830
  dejected 837
dismantle *destroy* 162
  divest 226
  render useless 645
dismast 645
dismay 860
dismember 44
dismiss *discharge* 297
  liberate 750
  abrogate **756**
dismissal 746
dismount 306
DISOBEDIENCE 742
disobey 742
DISORDER, *n.*
  confusion 59
  turbulence 173
  disease 655
disorder, *v. derange* 61
disorderly 59, 945
disorganize *derange* 61
disown 536
disparage
  underrate 483, **929**
  dispraise **932**
  detract 934
disparagement 908, 934
disparate 15, 18
disparity *difference* 15
  dissimilarity 18
  disagreeing **24**
  inequality 28
dispassionate 826
dispatch, *n. message* 527
  news 532
  epistle 592
  expedition 682
  haste 684
  command 741

DIVERGENCE 291
difference 15
nonuniformity 16a
dissimilarity 18
variation 20a
disagreement 24
diverse 15, 81
diversified 16a
diversify [see diversity]
vary 18, 20a
change 140
diversion change 140
deviation 279
pleasure 377
amusement 840
diversity difference 15
irregularity 16a
dissimilarity 18
multiformity 81
divert turn 279
deceive 545
amuse 840
divest denude 226
-oneself of
DIVESTMENT 226
divide separate 44
part 51
bisect 91
apportion 786
dividend part 51
portion 786
divination 511, 992
divine, n. clergyman 996
divine, v. predict 511
guess 514
divine, adj. perfect 650
of God 976, 983, 983a
-service 990
Divinity God 976
theology 983
divisible 51
[see divide]
division [see divide]
separation 44
part 51
class 75
interval 198
discord 713
DIVORCE, n. 44, 905
divorce, v. relinquish 782
divulge 529
dizziness [see dizzy]
dizzy confused 458
vertigo 503
do suit 23
produce 161
act 680
complete 729
-for destroy 162
kill 361
docile willing 602
dock, n. wharf 231
tribunal 966
dock, v. shorten 201
docket list 86

schedule 611
doctor learned man 492
physician 662
doctrinaire 855
doctrine tenet 484
document 551
documentary 467
dodder 160
dodge, n. stratagem 702
dodge, v. change 140
deviate 279
avoid 623
doer 680, 690
doff 226
dog, n. 366
dog, v. follow 281
dogged obstinate 606
valorous 861
doggerel verse 597
ridiculous 851, 853
dogma 484
dogmatic certain 474
positive 481
dogmatism 474
dogmatist 474, 887
doings events 151
actions 680
doldrums sulks 901a
dole, n. mite 640
dole, v. give 784
doleful 837
doll 554
dollar 800
dolor physical 378
moral 828
dolorous 830
domain 75, 181
dome 206, 223, 250
domestic, n. servant 746
domestic, adj.
native 188, 367
tame 370
home 189, 221
secluded 893
-animals 366
domesticate locate 184
acclimatize 613
-animals 370
domestication 184, 370
domesticize 370
domicile 189
domiciled
inhabiting 186
domiciliary 188
-visit 461
dominant 175
dominate influence 175
rule 737
domination 175, 737
domineer 739, 885
dominion 181, 737
-rule 737
domino dress 225
mask 530
don, n. scholar 492
tutor 540

noble 875
don, v. put on 225
donate 784
donation 784
done
-for 732
failed 732
-up tired 688
donjon defense 717
prison 752
donkey ass 271
fool 501
donor 784
doom, n. fate 152
destruction 162
death 360
necessity 601
doom, v. sentence 971
door entrance 66, 260
brink 231
barrier 232
doorkeeper 263
dormancy 172
dormant inert 172
dormitory 191
dory 273
dose quantity 25
medicine 662
dot speck 32, 193
dot dowry 784
dotage age 128
dotard 130, 501
dote drivel 499, 503
-upon 897
double similar 17
increase 35
duplex 90
substitute 147
fold 258
wraith 992a
double-dealing 544, 940
double-faced 940
DOUBT, n. uncertainty
475
disbelief 485
skepticism 989
doubtful 475, 485
doubtless 474, 488
douceur gift 784
doughboy 726
doughty 159, 861
dour 739
douse 310
dovetail agree 23
join 43
insert 228
dowdy 851
dower property 780
bequest 784
down, n. upland 180
down, adj. below 207
down, v. cast down 308
downcast dejected 837
downfall destruction 162
failure 732
misfortune 735

duet 415
duffer *ignoramus* 493
  bungler 701
dugout *boat* 273
  defense 717
duke 875
dukedom 877
dulcet *sweet* 396
  melodious 413
dull *unintelligent* 493
  inert 172
  blunt 254
  slow 275
  somber **428**
  stolid 499
  weary 841
  prosing **843**
dullard 501
DULLNESS 254, **843**
duma 696
dumb *voiceless* **581**
  -animal 366
  strike - *astonish* 870
DUMBNESS **581**
dumfound *disappoint* 509
  astonish 870
dummy *substitute* 147
  idle 683

dump *unload* 297
dumps 837, 901*a*
dumpy *short* 201
  thick 202
dun, *n. creditor* 805
dun, *adj. gray* 432
dun, *v. importune* 765
dunce 493
dungeon 752
duologue 588
DUPE, *n.* 547
dupe, *v. deceive* 545
duplex 90
duplicate *copy* 21
  double 90
DUPLICATION 19, 90,
  104
duplicity 544
DURABILITY 110, 141
durable 110, 141
duration 106
duress *restraint* 751
during 106
dusk 126, 422
dusky *dark* 421
  dim 422
dust *powder* 330
  dirt 653

throw - in the eyes
  blind 442
  deceive 545
dusty 330, 653
dutiable 812
dutiful 944
DUTY
  business 625
  work 686
  tax 812
  obligation 926
dwarf, *n.* 193
dwarf, *v. lessen* 36
dwell *reside* 186, 188
  abide 141, 265
  -upon *repeat* 573
dweller 188
dwelling *location* 184
  abode 189
dwindle *lessen* 36
  shrink 195
dye 428
dying 360
dyke [*see dike*]
dynamic 157, 276
dynamite 727
dynasty 106, 737

E

each 79
eager *willing* 602
  active 682
  ardent 821
  desirous 865
eagerness 682
eagle *bird* 366
ear *hearing* 418
earl 875
earldom 877
EARLINESS 132
early 121, 132
earn 775
earnest, *n. pledge* 771
earnest *willing* 602
  determined 604
  emphatic 642
  eager 821
  serious 837
earnings 775
earsplitting 404
earth *ground* 211
  world 318
  land 342
earthenware 384
earthly 318, 342
earthquake 146
earthwork 717
earthly 342
ease, *n. leisure* 377, 685
  facility 705
ease, *v. abate* 36
easel *support* 215

easily [*see easy*] 705
east 236
eastern 236
easy *gentle* 275
  facile 705
easy-going
  inexcitable 826
  contented 831
  indifferent 866
eat 298
eatable 298
eatables 298
eating 298
eaves 250
eavesdropper 455
ebb, *n. decline* 36
  tide 348
ebb, *v.*
  decrease 36
  regress 283
  recede 287
ebb tide 36, 207
ebullient *hot* 382
ebullition *violence* 173
  ferment 315
  boiling 384
eccentric *irregular* 83
  crazed 503
  capricious 608
ecclesiastical **995**
echelon 279
echo, *n. similarity* 17
  copy 21

  resonance 408
echo, *v. imitate* 19
  repeat 104
  recoil 277
éclat 873
eclipse, *n.* 421
eclipse, *v. surpass* 33
  outshine 873, 527
economical 817
economics 692
economize 817
ECONOMY *order* 58
  management 692
  frugality 817
ecstasy *frenzy* 515
  rapture 827
ecstatic 827, 829
EDDY *whirlpool* 348
  current 312
Eden *heaven* 827
EDGE *brink* 231
  -in 228
edible 298
edict 531, 741
edification 537
edifice 161
edifying 648
edit *publish* 531
  compile 596
  revise 658
edition 531
editor 593, 595
editorial 595

educate *teach* 537
educated 490
education *teaching* 537
  knowledge 490
educational 537
educe *extract* 301
efface *destroy* 162
  obliterate 552
EFFECT *consequence* 154
  complete 729
effective *capable* 157
  influential 175
  useful 644
effects *property* 780
  goods 798
effectual 157, 175
effectually 52
effeminacy
  [*see* effeminate]
effeminate *weak* 160
  womanish 374
  timorous 862
effervesce 173, 353
effervescence 353
effervescent 338, 353
effete *old* 128
  weak 160
  useless 645
efficacious [*see* efficient]
efficient *powerful* 157
  operative 170
  reliable 632
  useful 644
effigy *copy* 21
efflorescence 161
effluence 295
effluvium *vapor* 334
  odor 398
efflux *egress* 295
effort 686
effrontery 885
effulgence 420
effusion
  loquacity 584
  -of blood 361
effusive 584
egg *embryo* 153
  -on 615
egg-shaped 247
ego 317, 450, 980a
egoism 482, 880, 911
egoist 482, 880, 911
egotism *overestimation* 482
  vanity 880
  cynicism 911
  selfishness 943
egotist 482, 880, 911
egotistical [*see* egotism]
  narrow 481
egregious *exceptional* 83
  absurd 497
EGRESS 295
Egyptian -deities 979
eight *number* 98
ejaculate *utter* 580
eject 284, 297

EJECTION
  displacement 185
  propulsion 284
  emission 297
eke
  -out *complete* 52
  spin out 110
elaborate, *adj.* 686
elaborate, *v. improve* 658
  prepare 673
  work out 729
elaboration 673
elapse *flow* 109
  pass 122
elastic 325
  [*see* elasticity]
ELASTICITY
  strength 159
  energy 171
  spring 325
elate, *adj. exulting* 836
  vain 880
  boastful 884
elate, *v. gladden* 836
elated 838
  [*see* elate]
elbow, *n. angle* 244
elbow, *v. push* 276
elbowroom 180, 748
elder, *adj.* 124, 128
elder, *n.* 996
elderly 128
elect *choose* 609
  predestinate 976
election 609
elector 609
electorate 609
electric *swift* 274
electricity 388
electrify *strengthen* 157
  motorize 226
  excite 824
  astonish 870
electron 32
ELEGANCE *in style* 578
  beauty 845
elegy *poetry* 597
element *component* 56
  beginning 66
  cause 153
elemental, *adj. simple* 42
elemental, *n.*
  Rosicrucian 980
elementary *simple* 42
elephantine *huge* 192
elevate 307
elevated 206
ELEVATION
  height 206
  raising 307
  repute 873
elevator 307
elf *fairy* 979
elicit *cause* 153
  draw out 301
  discover 480a

eligible 646
eliminate *subduct* 38
  simplify 42
  exclude 55
  weed out 103, 297
  extract 301
elimination 42
eliminative 299, 350
elision 201
elixir 5
ellipse 247
ellipsis 201
elliptic 247
elocution 582
elocutionist 582
elongate 200
elongation 200
eloquence *style* 569, **574**
  speech 582
eloquent 574, **582**
elsewhere 187
elucidate 522
elude *avoid* 623
  escape 671
  palter 773
elusive 623, 773
elysian 981
Elysium 981
emaciated 203, 640
emaciation 203
emanate 295
emanation *egress* 295
  odor 398
emancipate *deliver* 672
  free 750
embalm 400
embankment
  esplanade 189
  fence 717
embargo 761
embark *sail* 267
  depart 293
  -in *engage in* 676
embarrass 704
embarrassed *poor* 804
  in debt 806
embarrassing 704
embarrassment 704
embassy 755, 758
embellish 847
embers 384
embezzle 791
embitter *deteriorate* 659
  aggravate 835
emblazon *color* 428
  ornament 847
emblem 550
embody *join* 43
  combine 48
  form a whole 50
  include 76
  materialize 316
embolden 861
emboss 550
embrace, *n.* 892, 902
embrace, *v. compose* 54

erudite 490, 500, 539
erudition 490, 539
eruption *revolution* 146
  violence 173
  egress 295
  ejection 297
  explosion 406
eruptive [*see* eruption]
escalade 305
escalator 305, 307
escapade 608, 840
ESCAPE, *n. flight* 671
escape, *v.* 671, 927
eschew *avoid* 623
  dislike 867
escort *companion* 88
  safeguard 664
  keeper 753
esculent 298
escutcheon 550, 551
esophagus 350
esoteric 528
especial 79
especially 33
espionage 441, 461
esplanade 189
espouse *choose* 609
  marry 903
  -a cause *aid* 707
  co-operate 709
esprit de corps 709
espy 441
esquire 875
essay, *n.*
  experiment 463
  dissertation 595
ESSAY, *v.*
  endeavor 675
essence *being* 1
  nature 5
  meaning 516
essential *real* 1
  intrinsic 5
  inherent 56
  important 642
establish *settle* 150
  create 161
  place 184
  evidence 467
  demonstrate 478
established 141
  church 983a
establishment
  fixture 150
  location 184
  shop 799
estate *condition* 7
  property 780
esteem 928, 931
estimable 648
estimate *number* 85
  measure 466
  adjudge 480
estimation 480, **928**, 931
estrange *disjoin* 44
  alienate 889

hate 898
estuary 343
etch 259, 558
etching 558
Eternal, The - 976
eternal 112
eternalize **112**
eternity 112
  an - 110
ether *space* 180
  vapor 334
  anaesthetic 376
ethereal 4, 820
etheric body 980a
ethical 926
ethics 926
ethnology 372
etiquette *custom* 613
  fashion 852
etymology 562
Eucharist 998
eulogist 935
eulogize **482**
eulogy 931
Eumenides 173, 900
euphemism *metaphor* 521
  phrase 566
  style 577
euphemist 935
euphony *melody* 413
  elegant style 578
euphuism 579, 855
eurythmic 542
eurythmics 242
evacuate *vacate* 185
  quit 293
  emit 297
evade *elude* 477
  not observe 773
  exempt 927
evanescent 111
evangelical 983a, 985
Evangelists 985
evaporate *vanish* 4
  vaporize 336
  dry up 340
evaporation
  vaporization 336
  dryness 340
evasion *sophistry* 477
  quirk 481
  concealment 528
  falsehood 544
  avoidance 623
evasive [*see* evasion]
eve 126
even, *adj.*
  uniform 16
  equal 27
  level 213
  parallel 216
  straight 246
  flat 251
  smooth 255
even, *v. level* 213
even, *adv.* 469

EVENING 126
evenness
  [*see* even]
  symmetry 242
evensong 126, 990
event 151
  in the - of
    circumstance 8
    eventuality 151
    destiny 152
    supposition 514
  justified by the - 937
eventful **151**, 642
eventide 126
eventual 121
EVENTUALITY **151**
eventually 121, **151**, 154
eventuate 151
ever 16, 112
everlasting 112
evermore 16, 112
every 78, 138
  -other 138
everybody 78
every one 78
everywhere 180, 186
evict 297, 789
EVIDENCE **467**
evident *visible* 446
  certain 474
  proved 478
  manifest 525
evidential **467**
EVIL *harm* 619
  badness 649
  -spirits **980**
  -star 649
EVILDOER **913**, 949
evildoing 945
evil-minded 907, 945
evil speaking 908, 934
evince *show* 467
  prove 478
evoke *cause* 153
  call upon 765
  excite 824
evolution 161, 311, **313**
evolutionary 313
evolve 161, **313**
ewer 191
exact, *adj. similar* 17
  copy 21
  true 494
  literal 516
exact, *v. require* 741
  claim 924, 926
exacting *discontented* 832
  fastidious 865
exaction 741
exactly *literally* 19
exactness [*see* exact]
  repetition 13
exaggerate *increase* 35
  overestimate 482
  magnify **549**
  misrepresent 555

F

fable 546, 594
fabric 329
fabricate *compose* 54
  make 161
  invent 515
  falsify **544**
fabrication *lie* 546
fabulous *inexistent* **2**
  enormous 31
  imaginary 515
  mythical **979**
façade 234
face, *n. exterior* 220
  front 234, 861
  aspect 448
  -*to face* 237
face, *v. cover* 223
  line 224
  oppose 708
  resist **719**
facet 220
facetious 842
facile *willing* 602
  easy 705
facilitate 705
FACILITY *skill* 698
  ease 705
facing *covering* 223
  lining 224
facsimile 21, 90
fact *existence* 1
  event 151
  certainty 474
  truth 494
faction *party* 712
  feud 713
factious 24, 713
factor *agent* 690
factory 691
factotum *agent* 690
  employee 758
faculty *power* 157
  profession 625
  skill 698
fad 481, 608
fade *vanish* 2, 4, 111
  become old 124
  droop 160
  grow dim 422
  lose color 429
fag *labor* 686
  overwork 688
  -*end* 67
fagot *bundle* 72
fail *droop* 160
  collapse 304
  go wrong 495
  not succeed **732**
  not pay 808
failing, *adj.* [*see fail*]
  incomplete 53
ailing, *n. guilt* 947

FAILURE **304**, **732**, 947
fain *willing* 602
  wishful 865
faint *impotent* 158
  weak 160
  low 405
  colorless 429
  exhausted 688
fainthearted 860, 862
FAINTNESS *sound* **405**
  swoon 688
  [*see faint*]
fair, *n. mart* 799
fair, *adj. pale* 429
  impartial 498, 922
  favorable 648
  moderate 651
  beautiful 845
  honorable 939
  -*play* 922, 939
fairly 643
fairy 515, **979**
  -*tale* 594
  fabrication 546
fairyland 515
faith *belief* 484
  hope 858
  piety 987
faithful [*see faith*]
  like 17
  copy **21**
  exact 494
  obedient 743
  -*memory* 505
  loyal 939
faithless *false* 544
  dishonorable **940**
faker 548
fakir 955
fall, *n. autumn* 126
  slope 217
  descent 306
  adversity 735
fall, *v. perish* **162**
  descend 306
  die 360
  fail 732
  -*away* 195
  -*back recede* 287
  relapse 661
  -*in order* 58
  -*off deteriorate* 659
  -*out happen* 151
  quarrel 713
  -*short of* **304**, **730**
  -*through fail* 732
  let - *hint* 527
fallacy *sophistry* 477
  error 495
fallible **475**
fallow *unproductive* 169
  yellow 436

  unready 674
false *imitative* 19, 477
  faulty 495
  untrue 544, 546
  dishonorable 940
FALSEHOOD 544, 546
falsetto 410
falsify *delude* 495
  misrepresent **544**, 555
falsity [*see false*]
falter *go slow* 275
  stammer 583
  hesitate 605
  slip 732
  despair 859
fame *greatness* **31**
  memory 505
  renown 873
familiar, *n. spirit* 979
familiar, *adj. known* 490
  habitual 613
  affable 894
familiarity [*see familiar*]
familiarize 537, 613
family *kin* **11**
  pedigree 69
  class 75
  ancestors 166
  posterity 167
  -*likeness* 17
famine 640
famine-stricken 640
famish 956
famous 873
fan, *n.* 349
  enthusiast 840
fan, *v. blow* 349
  cool 385
fanatic *dogmatist* 474
  madman 504
  zealot 682
fanatical *dogmatic* 474
  insane 503
  emotional 821
  heterodox 984
fanaticism 474, 984
fanciful *imaginative* **515**
  capricious 608
  odd 853
fancy, *n. idea* 453
  caprice 608
  choice 609
fancy, *v.*
  think 451
  believe 484
  suppose 514
  imagine 515
  desire 865
  love 897
fane 1000
fanfare 404, 888
fang 663, 781

fence, *n enclosure* **232,** 752
  thief 792
  on the - 607
fence, *v, evade* 544
  fight 720
fender 717
ferment, *n. disorder* 59
  agitation 171, **315**
  lightness **320**
  excitement 825
ferment, *v. effervesce* **353**
  sour 397
fermentation
  [see ferment]
fern 367
ferocity *violence* **173**
  brutality 907
ferret
  -out *be curious* 455
ferry 270
ferryman 269
fertile 168
fertilization 161, 168
fertilize 168
ferule 975
fervent *hot* 382
  desirous 865
fervid *hot* 382
  heartfelt 821
fervor *passion* 820
  animation 821
festal 687, 840
fester *corrupt* 653
festival 138, 883
festivity 840, 883
festoon 245
fetch *bring* 270
  sell for 812
fete 840, 882
fetid 401
fetish 991, 993
FETOR 401, 663
fetter *restrain* 43, **751**
  shackle 752
feud *discord* 713
feudal 749
feudatory 749
fever *heat* 382
  disease 655
  excitement 825
feverish *hot* **382**
  hurry 684
  excited 824
few 103, 137
FEWNESS 32, **103**
fez 225
fiancée 897
fiasco 732
fiat 741
fib *falsehood* 546
fiber *filament* 205
fibrous 205
fickle *changeable* 149
  irresolute 605
fickleness 605

fiction *untruth* 546
  work of - 594
fictitious 515, 546
fiddle 417
fiddler 416
fidelity *identity* **13**
  truth 494
  veracity 543
  obedience 743
  honor 939
fidget 682, 825
field *scope* 180
  region 181
  plain 344
  agriculture **371**
  business 625
field day 882
field glass 445
field marshal 745
fiend *ruffian* 913
  demon 980
fiendish 907, 945, 980
fierce *violent* 173
  daring 861
  angry 900
fiery *violent* **173**
  hot **382**
  excitable 825
  angry 900
fifer 416
fight *contention* 720
  warfare 722
  -shy *avoid* 623
  turn tail 862
fighter 726
figment 515
figurative **521**
FIGURE, *n. number* **84**
  form 240
  metaphor 521
  price 812
  cut a - *repute* 873
  - of speech **521**
figure, *v. represent* **554**
figurehead *sign* 550
  representation 554
FILAMENT **205**
filch 791
file, *v. pare* 38
  arrange 60
  smooth 255
  pulverize 330
  record 551
  -off *march* **266**
file, *n. row* 69
  list 86
  on - 60
filial 167
filibuster, *n.*
  obstructionist 710
  freebooter 792
filibuster, *v. delay* 133
  impede 706
  pillage 791
filibusterer 706, 710
filigree 219

fill *complete* 52
  occupy 186
  load 190
  stuff 224
  -up *complete* 52
  close 261
fillet *band* 45
  filament 205
  ornament 847
filling *stuffing* 224
fillip *impulse* 276
  stimulus 615
film *layer* 204
  opacity 426
filmy *scaly* 204
filter *percolate* **295**
  clean 652
filth 653
filthy 653
final 67, 729
finale *end* 67, 729
finality 67, 729
finally *eventually* 151
  on the whole **476**
finance 800
financier 639
find *experience* 151
  adjudge 480
  discover 480a
  -out 480a
finding *judgment* 480
fine, *adj. rare* 322
  not raining 340
  delicate 329
  exact 494
  good 648
  beautiful 845
  adorned 847
  proud 878
  -arts 554
  -gentleman *fop* **854**
  -lady **854**
  -writing 482, 577
  in end 67
  after all 476
fine, *v. mulct* 974
fineness [see fine)]
finery 847
finesse *tact* 698
  artifice 702
finger *touch* 379
finical 855, 868
finicking 855, 868
finis 67
finish, *n. end* 67
  symmetry 242
finish, *v. complete* 729
finished *symmetrical* 242
  perfect 650
  skilled 698
finite 32
fire, *n. energy* 171
  heat **382**
  fuel 388
fire, *v. make hot* **384**
  shoot **716**

flourishing [*see* flourish]
flout 929
flow *course* 109
   motion 264
   stream 348
   -from *result* 154
   -into *river* 348
flower, *n. plant* 367
   ornament 847
flower, *v. produce* 161
   prosper 734
flowery *ornamental* 847
flowing [*see* flow] 348
fluctuate *change* 149
   oscillate 314, 605
fluctuation 314
flue 351
fluency 584
fluent *flowing* 348
   loquacious 584
fluffy 324
fluid 333
   -in *motion* 347
fluidity 333
fluke *chance* 156
flume 350
flunk 732
flunky *servant* 746
flunkyism 933
fluorescence 425
flurry, *n.*
   agitation 821, 824
   excitability 825
flurry, *v.* 458
flush, *n. heat* 382
   glow 420, 428
flush, *adj. even* 213
   flat 251
flush, *v. glow* 382
   redden 434
   wash 652
   blush 821
fluster, *n.* 821
fluster, *v.* 824, 825
flutter, *n. agitation* 315
flutter, *v. vary* 149
   excite 821
   tremble 860
flux *conversion* 144
   motion 264
   flow 348
fly, *n. insect* 366
fly, *v. vanish* 4
   elapse 109
   be *transient* 111
   aviate 267
   hasten 274
   recede 287
   depart 293
   soar 338
   shun 623
   -at 716
   -off 291
   -open 260
flying [*see* fly] 267
foal 271

foam, *n.* 353
foam, *v. boil* 315
   rage 824, 825
foamy 320
focal 222
FOCUS 74
   center 222
fodder *food* 298
foe 891
fog *mist* 353
   uncertainty 475
foggy *opaque* 426
fogy *fool* 501
   laughingstock 857
foible 945
foil, *n. weapon* 727
foil, *v. contrast* 14
   baffle 706
   defeat 731
FOLD, *n. inclosure* 232
   plait 258
   congregation 997
fold, *v.* 91, 258
foliage 367
folio 593
folk 372
folklore 124, 979
follow *be similar* 17
   -in *order* 63
   -in *time* 117
   pursue 235
   -in *motion* 281
   hold good 478
   understand 518
   pursue 622
   obey 743
   -up *continue* 143
follower [*see* follow]
   successor 65
   pursuer 281
   disciple 541
   servant 746
   lover 897
FOLLOWING 282
FOLLY 499
foment *stimulate* 173
   warm 384
   promote 707
   excite 824
fond 897
fondle 897, 902
fondness *desire* 865
FOOD *eatables* 298
FOOL, *n.* 501
fool, *v deceive* 545
   trifle 499
   ridicule 856
foolhardy 863
foolish 499, 699
foot *length* 200
   base 211
   on - *existing* 1
   preparing 673
   active 682
footfall *motion* 264
footing *circumstances* 8

influence 175
   situation 183
   support 215
foot-loose *liberated* 750
footman 746
footpad 792
footpath 627
footprint 550, 551
foot soldier 726
foot-sore 688
footstep 551
footstool 215
FOP 854
foppery 855, 882
foppish *affected* 855
for *because* 476
forage *food* 298
foray *attack* 716
   robbery 791
forbear *avoid* 623
   spare 678
   tolerate 826
   pity 914
   abstain 953
forbearance 826, 918
forbid 761
forbidding *ugly* 846
force, *n. assemblage* 72
   power 157
   strength 159
   energy 171
   violence 173
   significance 516
   troops 726
force, *v. urge* 615
   compulsion 744
forced *irrelative* 10
   unwilling 603
forceful 171, 574
forcible [*see* force]
forcibly 744
ford 302
fore 234
fore-and-aft 200
fore-and-after 273
forebears 166
forebode 511
forecast *foresight* 510
   prediction 507, 511
   plan 626
forefathers 166
forefront 234
forego 624, 757
foregoing 116, 122
foregone *past* 122
foreground 234
forehead 234
foreign *alien* 10
   extraneous 57
foreigner 57
foreknow 510
foreknowledge 510
foreland 206
foreman 694
foremost *superior* 33
   beginning 66

front 234
  important **642**
forenoon 125
forensic 968
foreordain *destine* 152
forerun 62, 116, 280
forerunner 64, 673
foresee *expect* 121, 507
  foreknow 510
foreseen 871
foreshadow 511
foreshorten 201
FORESIGHT 510
forest 367
forestall 132
forester 371
forestry 371
foretaste 510
foretell 511
forethought 510
forever 16, 112
forewarn *predict* 511
  warn 668
foreword 64
forfeit, *n.* 974
forfeit, *v. lose* 776
forgather 72
forge *imitate* 19
  swindle 791
  -ahead 282
forger 792
forgery 21, 791
forget 506
forgetful 506
forgive **918**
FORGIVENESS 918
forgo [*see* forego]
forgotten 122, 506
fork *divide* 91
  branch 244
forlorn *dejected* 837
  hopeless 859
  deserted 893
  -hope 859
FORM, *n. state* 7
  likeness 21
  bench 215
  shape **240**
  school class 541
  manner 627
  beauty 845
  fashion 852
  etiquette 882
form, *v. make up* 54
  compose **56**
  order 58
  arrange 60
  convert 144
  produce 161
  shape **240**
  organize 357
formal [*see* form]
  regular 62
  severe 739
  affected 855
  stately 882

formalism 739, 988
formalist 82, 988
formality [*see* formal]
  ceremony 882
formation
  composition 54, 76
  production 161
  shape 240
formative *causal* 153
former *in order* 62
  prior in time 116
  past **122**
formerly 119, **122**
formidable 704
formless **241**
formula 80, 697
formulate 590
forsake 624
forsaken 898
forswear *deny* 536
  lie 544
  refuse 764
fort 666, 717
forth 282
forthwith 132
fortification 717
fortify 159
fortitude *endurance* 826
  courage 861
fortress 666, 717
fortuitous 6, 156, 621
fortuity 156
fortunate *opportune* 134
  prosperous 734
fortune *destiny* 152, 601
  chance 156
  wealth 803
fortune teller 513
forum *place* 182
  tribunal 966
forward, *adj. early* 132
  front 234
  onward **282**
  active 682
  insolent 885
  uncourteous 895
forward, *v. transmit* 270
  improve 658
  help 707
fossil 40, **357**
fossilize **357**
foster *aid* 707
  excite 824
  caress 902
foul, *adj. bad* 649
  dirty 653
  ugly 846
  base 940
  vicious 945
  -play *wrong* 923
  improbity 940
foul, *v. collide* 276
foul-mouthed 895
foulness [*see* foul]
foul-spoken 934
found *cause* 153

colonize 184
foundation *stability* 150
  base 211
  support 215, 215
founder, *n.* 164, 626
founder, *v. sink* **310**
  fail 732
foundling 782, 893
fountain 153, 348
four 95
fourfold **96**
Four Hundred 852, 875
fowl 366
fox *animal* 366
fox trot *dance* 840
fracas *noise* 404
  discord 713
FRACTION *part* 51
  less than one **100a**
fractional 51, 100a
fractious 901
fracture *disjunction* 44, 70
  fissure 198
fragile *weak* 160
  brittle 328
fragment *small part* 32
  part 51, 100a
  extract 596
fragmentary 100a
FRAGRANCE 400
fragrant **400**
frail *weak* **160**
  brittle 328
  irresolute 605
  failing 945
frailty [*see* frail]
frame, *n. condition* 7
  support **215**
  border 231
  form 240
  structure 329
frame, *v. make* 161
framework 215, 329
franchise *freedom* **748**
  right 924
frangible 328
frank *open* 525
  sincere 543
  artless 703
frantic *violent* 173
  delirious 503
  excited 824
fraternal *brotherly* 11
  leagued 712
  friendly 888
  -order 711
fraternity *brothers* 11
  party 712
  friends 888
fraternize *combine* 48, 709
  sympathize 888
  associate 892
fraud *deception* 545
  impostor 548
fraudulent [*see* fraud]
fraught *full* 52

futile 645
futility 499, 645
FUTURE 117, **121**, 152

expected 507
-events 152
-state *destiny* 152

heaven 981
futurity 121

G

gab 584
gabble **584**
gable *side* 236
gad 266
gag 403, 581
　muzzle 751
gage *measure* 466
gain *increase* **35**
　prosper 618
　acquisition 775
-time *protract* 110
-upon *approach* 286
　pass 303
gainsay 536
gairish [see garish]
gait *walk* 264
galaxy *multitude* 102
　stars 318
gale 349
gall, *n. bitterness* 395
　insolence 885
gall, *v. hurt* 378
　annoy 830
gallant *brave* 861
　courteous 894
gallantry 861, 902
gallery *room* 191
　passage 260
　spectators 444
galley *ship* 273
　cookroom 386
　printing 591
gallop 266, 274
gallows 361, 975
galore 102
galvanic *excitable* 825
galvanize 157
gamble 156, 621, 840
gambler 463, **621**, 863
gambling *chance* 621
　rashness 863
gambol 309
game, *n. animal* **366**
　amusement 840
game, *adj. resolute* 604
game, *v. gamble* 621
gamester 840
gaming 156
gang 72, **712**
gangway 260
gaol [see jail]
gap 70, 198
gape, *yawn* **198**, 260
　stare 455
garage 191, 272
garb 225
garble *misinterpret* 523
　falsify 544

garden 371
gardener 371
gargle 337
garish 851
garland *circle* 247
　fragrance 400
　ornament 847
garment 225
garner *store* 636
garnish 847
garret 210
garrison 717, 726
garrote 361
garrulity 584
garter *fastening* 45
gas *gaseity* 334
GASEITY **334**
gaseous *unsubstantial* 4
　vaporous **334**, 336
gash *cut* 44
　interval 198
gasify 334
gasoline 356
gasp 688
gastronomy 957
gate 66, 232, 260
gather *collect* 72
　fold 258
　conclude 480
gathering *assemblage* 72
gaudy **428**, 851
gauge 466
gaunt 203
gauntlet *glove* 225
gawky *awkward* 699
　ugly 846
gay *bright* 428
　cheerful 836
　showy 882
gayety [see gay] 836
gaze 441
gazelle 366
gazette 531
gazetteer 86
gear *clothes* 225
　harness 633
gelatinous 352
gem *excellence* 648
　ornament 847
gendarme 726, 965
gender 75
genealogy 69
general, *adj. generic* **78**
　habitual 613
general, *n.* 745
GENERALITY **78**
generalize 78, 476
generally 16, 78

generalship 692, 722
generate 161, 168
generation
　consanguinity 11
　period 108
　production 161
generic 78
generosity *liberality* 816
　benevolence 906
　disinterestedness 942
generous [see generosity]
genesis *beginning* 66
　production 161
genial *cordial* 377
　warm 382
　willing 602
geniality 602
　[see genial]
genius *intellect* 450
　talent 498
　skill 698
　adept 700
　familiar spirit 979
genteel 852
gentile *heterodox* 984
gentility 852
gentle *moderate* 174
　lenient 740
　meek 826
　courteous 894
-breeding 894
gentlefolk 875
gentleman 373, 939
gentleness [see gentle]
gentry 875
genuflexion 308
genuine *true* 494
　good 648
genus 75
geography 183
geometry 466
germane *relevant* 23
germinate 194, 365
gesticulate 550
gesture 550
get *acquire* 775
-back *regain* 775
-down *descend* **306**
-in 775
-on *advance* 282
　prosper 734
gewgaw *trifle* 643
geyser 382, 384
ghastly *pale* 429

hideous 846
ghost 362, 980a
ghoul *demon* 980
giant 192, 206
gibber *stammer* 583
gibberish 563
gibbet 975
gibbous 249, 250
gibe *disrespect* 929
giddy *inattentive* 458
   wild 503
gift *power* 157
   transference 270
   talent 698
   thing given 784
gifted 698
gigantic *large* 192
   tall 206
giggle 838
gild 223, 436
gilt 436
gimcrack *weak* 160
   trifling 643
gimlet 262
gingerly 459
gipsy 268
gird *bind* 43
   strengthen 159
   surround 227
girder *beam* 215
girdle *bond* 45
   tie 225
   circumference 230
   circle 247
girl 129
   servant 746
girlhood 127
girlish 374
girt 229
girth 45, 230
gist *essence* 5
   meaning 516
give *yield* 324
   bestow 784
   -up *relinquish* 624
   surrender 782
   restore 790
giver 784
GIVING 784
glacial 383
glacier 383
glad *pleased* 827
   pleasing 829
gladden 836
glade 260
gladiator 726
glamour 615, 992
glance *touch* 379
   look 441
   -at *take notice of* 457
   allude to 527
   -off 279
glare *light* 420
   stare 441
glaring [*see glare*]
   great 31

gaudy 428
   manifest 525
glass 255
   vessel 191
   lens 445
glassy 255
glaze 255
gleam *light* 420
   shine 446
glean *choose* 609
   acquire 775
glee 827, 836
glen 252
glib *voluble* 584
   facile 705
glide *lapse* 109
   move 264
   travel 266
   aviation 267
glimmer *light* 420
   flicker 422
   be visible 446
glimpse *sight* 441
glint 420, 441
glisten 420
glitter *shine* 420
   be visible 446
gloaming 126
gloat
   -over *delight* 827
   brag 884
globe *sphere* 249
   world 318
globe-trotter 268
globularity 249
gloom *darkness* 421
   dimness 422
   sadness 837
gloomy *dark* 421
   sad 837
glorification
   [*see glorify*]
glorify *honor* 873
   worship 976, 990
glorious 873
glory *light* 420
   honor 873
gloss *smoothness* 255
   sheen 420
   -over 477
glossary *list* 86
   dictionary 562
glossy [*see gloss*]
glove 225
glow *warm* 382
   shine 420
   appear 446
glower *glare* 443
   be sullen 901a
glowing [*see glow*]
   red 484
   exciting 824
glue *cement* 46
glum *discontented* 832
   sulky 901a
glut 957

glutinous 327, 352
glutton 954a 957
GLUTTONY 957
gnarled *crooked* 243
   rough 250, 256
gnaw 298
go, *n. energy* 171, 682
go, *v. move* 264
   progress 282
   depart 293
   disappear 449
   -about *turn around* 311
   -by *elapse* 109
   outrun 303
   -off *explode* 173
   depart 293
   -on *continue* 143
   advance 282
   -through *meet with* 151
   endure 826
   -to *travel* 266
goad, *n.* 370
goad, *v. quicken* 684
go-ahead 171, 282, 682
goal *end* 67, 292
   haven 265
   object 620
gob *sailor* 269
gobble *cry* 412
   gormandize 957
go-between
   intermediary 228, 758
   instrument 631
goblet 191
goblin 980
GOD 976
god 979
goddess 979
Godhead 976
godly 944
godsend 618, 734
Godspeed *farewell* 293
goggle 441
gold, *adj. yellow* 436
gold, *n. money* 800
golden 436
   -mean 628
gondola 273
gondolier 269
gone [*see go*]
   extinct 2
   past 122
   absent 187
   dead 360
   -by 124
GOOD, *n.* 618
   for - *permanent* 141
good, *adj. palatable* 394
   beneficial 648
   virtuous 944
   pious 987
   -at 698
   -humor 836
   -looks 845
   -luck 734
   -man *worthy* 948

-nature 906
-offices *mediation* 724
-taste 578, 850
-turn *kindness* 906
-will *benevolence* 906
-woman **948**
-word 931
make - *restore* 790
  substantiate 924
  vindicate 937
good-for-nothing 158, 949
good-looking 845
goodly *great* 31
  handsome 845
good-natured 906
GOODNESS **648**
goods *effects* 780
  merchandise 798
goose *bird* 366
gore, n. *gusset* 43
  blood 361
gore, v. 260
gorge, n. *ravine* 198
gorge, v. *glut* 869
  gormandize 957
gorgeous *gay* 428
  beautiful 845
gorilla 366
gormandize **957**
gorse 367
gory *murderous* 361
  red 434
gospel *doctrine* 484
  truth 494
Gospels **985**
gossamer 205
gossamery 320
gossip *news* 532
  babbler 584
  conversation 588
gouge 262
gourmand *glutton* 957
gourmet 868, 954*a*
govern 693, 737
governess 540
government 737, 745, 965
governor *director* 694
  ruler 745
gown *dress* 225
grab *take* 789
grace *elegance* 845
  polish 850
  pity 914
  forgiveness 918
  worship 990
graceful *elegant* 578
  beautiful 845
  tasteful 850
graceless *inelegant* 579
  ugly 846
  impenitent 951
Graces 845
gracious *courteous* 894
  kind 906
gradation *degree* 26
  order **58**

grade *degree* 26
  classify 60
  term 71
  obliquity 217
  ascent 305
  class 541
  crossing 219
gradual *degree* 26
  continuous 69
  slow 275
gradually **275**
graduate, *n.* 492
graduate, v. *adjust* 23
  measure 26
  arrange 60
  initiate 537
graduation 541
graft, v. *insert* **300**
graft, n. *loot* 784
  improbity 940
grain *humor* 5
  tendency 176
  roughness 256
  texture 329
  powder 330
  against the- 704
GRAMMAR **567**
grammatical **567**
gramophone 418
grand *august* 31
  important 642
  handsome 845
  glorious 873
  ostentatious 882
-juror **967**
grandee 875
grandeur *greatness* 31
  repute 873
grandfather 130, 166
grandmother 166
grandness [*see* grand]
granny 30
grant *admit* 529
  permit 760
  consent 762
  confer 784
granular 330
graphic *intelligible* **518**
  vigorous 574
  descriptive 594
graphophone 418
grapnel 666
grapple 789
-with
  -*a question* 461
  -*difficulties* 704
  oppose 708
  resist 719
grasp, *n. power* 737
grasp, *v. comprehend* 518
  retain 781
  -*at* 865
grasping *miserly* 819
  covetous 865
grass 367
-widow 905

grassland 367
grassplot 371
grassy 367
grate, *n. fireplace* 386
grate, v. *rub* 330
-on the ear
  harsh sound 410
grateful *enjoyable* 377
  agreeable 829
  thankful **916**
gratification 377, 827
gratify *permit* 760
  please 829
grating *lattice* 219
  stridor 410
gratis 815
GRATITUDE **916**
gratuitous
  inconsequent 477
  free 748, 815
gratuity *gift* 784
grave, *n.* 363
grave, *adj. somber* 428
  important 642
  distressing 830
  sad 837
graveclothes 363
gravedigger 363
gravestone 363
gravitate *descend* 306
  weigh 319
  -*towards* 176
GRAVITY *weight* **319**
  importance 642
  seriousness 837
  [*see* grave]
GRAY *old* 128
  color 428, **432**
graybeard 130
graze *touch* 199, 379
  browse 298
  rub 331
grease *lubricate* 332
  oil 355, 356
greasy 355
great *much* **31**
  big 192
  glorious 873
greater 33
greatness 33
GREATNESS **31**
greed *desire* 865
  gluttony 957
greedy 819, 865, 957
Greek - deities **970**
GREEN, *n. lawn* 344, 37
  color **435**
green, *adj. new* 123
  young 127
  sour 397
  credulous 486
  novice 701
  immature 674
greenhorn *novice* **493**
  bungler 701
greenness **435**

gut, n. 260
gut, v. destroy 162
gutter groove 259
guttural 561
guy chaff 856

guzzle gourmandize 957
gybe 279
gymnasium 189, 728
gymnast 159
gymnastic strong 159

athletic 720
gymnastics 159
gypsy 268
gyrate 312
gyve 752

H

habiliment 225
HABIT, n. dress 225
  custom 613
habitat 189
HABITATION 189
habitual normal 80
  ordinary 82
  customary 136, 613
habituate 613
habitude 613
hack, n. horse 271
  vehicle 272
  writer 593
hack, v. cut 44
hackneyed trite 496
  habitual 613
Hades 982
haft 633
hag 846, 913
haggard tired 688
  ugly 846
haggle chaffer 794
ha-ha ditch 198
hail, n. 383
hail, v. welcome 292
  call 586
  greet 894
hair 205, 256
hairless 226
hair-splitting 480
hairy 256
halcyon calm 174
  prosperous 734
hale 654
half 91
  -truth 546
half-baked ignorant 491
half-blood mixture 41
half-breed 41
half-caste 41
halfhearted
  irresolute 605
  insensible 823
  indifferent 866
half-starved 640, 956
halfway 68
half-witted 499, 501
hall chamber 189
hallelujah 990
halloo 411, 586
hallow 976, 987
hallowed 976
hallucination 495, 992a
halo light 420
  glory 873
halt cessation 142

rest 265
halt, adj. lame 655
halter 752
halve 91
hamadryad 979
hamlet 189
hammer repeat 104
hammock 215
hamper, n. basket 191
hamper, v. obstruct 706
hand, n. side 236
  mariner 269
  man 372
  organ of touch 379
  indicator 550
  writing 590
  at - present 118
  destined 152
  near 197
  in - incomplete 53
hand, v. transfer 270
  grasp 781
handbag 191
handbook travel 266
  information 527
  book 593
handcuff 751
handful 25
handicap, n. race 720
handicap, v. equalize 27
  incumber 706
handicraft 625
handiwork 154, 680
handkerchief 225
handle, n. 633
handle, v. touch 379
  use 677
  manage 693
handmaid 631, 746
handsome liberal 816
  beautiful 845
handwriting 590
handy near 197
  useful 644
  ready 673
  dexterous 698
hang loiter 133
  be pendent 214
  kill 361
  execute 972
  -back 623
  -fire be late 133
  not finish 730
  fail 732
  -together 178
hangar 273

hanger-on
  accompaniment 88
  dependent 746
  flunky 886
hangman 975
hanker 865
hansom 272
hap 156
haphazard 156
hapless 735
haply possibly 470
happen, 1, 151
happening 151
happiness 377, 827
  [see happy]
happy fit 23
  opportune 134
  glad 827
  cheerful 836
harangue speech 582
harass vex 830
  worry 907
harbinger precursor 64
  omen 512
harbor, n. haven 189, 292
  refuge 666
harbor, v. cherish 451
hard strong 159
  firm 323
  difficult 704
  severe 739
  grievous 830
  impenitent 951
  -by 197
  -pressed 684, 704
  -up 704, 804
harden 323 [see hard]
  strengthen 159
  accustom 613
hardened impenitent 951
hardheaded 498
hardhearted 907
hardihood courage 861
  insolence 885
hardiness [see hardy]
hardly scarcely 32, 137
  -ever 137
HARDNESS 323
hardpan 211
hardship 735
hard-working 686
hardy strong 159
  brave 861
harebrained 863
harem 374
hark hear 418

hollow, *n.* 207, 252
hollow, *adj.*
  unsubstantial 4
  resonant 408
  gruff 410
  specious 477
hollowness [*see* hollow]
holocaust 991
Holy *of God* 976
  pious 987
  -Ghost **976**
  -orders **995, 998**
  -Scriptures 985
homage *submission* 725
  respect 928
home *habitation* 189
  interior 221
  country 342
  refuge 666
  -rule 737
  -thrust
  attack 716
  censure 932
homeless *unhoused* 185
  banished 893
homelike 849
homeliness 851
  [*see* homely]
homely *unadorned* 849
  common 851
homesick 833
homestead 189
homicide 361
homily *teaching* 537
  sermon 998
homogeneity *relation* 9
  identity 13
  uniformity 16
  simplicity 42
hone 253
honest 939
honeycomb 252
honeymoon, 902, 903
honor, *n. glory* **873**
  respect 928
  approbation 931
  probity 939
honor, *v.* 873
honorable 873, 939
honorarium 784, 973
honorary 815
honored 873
hood *cap* 225
hoodoo 621, 992, 993
hoodwink *blind* 442
  hide **528**
hoof 211
hook *fasten* 43
  hang 214
  fork 244
  curve 245
hooligan 887, 913
hoop *circle* 247
  cry 411
hoot *cry* 411, 412
  deride 929

censure 932
hop *leap* 309
HOPE 858
hopeful 858
hopeless 859
HOPELESSNESS 859
horde 72
horizon 196, 230
horizontal **213**, 251, 308
HORIZONTALITY 213
horny 323
horoscope 511
horrible *noxious* 649
  dire 830
  ugly 846
  fearful 860
horrid 649, 830, 846
horrify *terrify* 860
horror *fear* 860
  dislike 867
horror-stricken 828
horse *animal* 271
  translation 539
  cavalry 726
horseman 268
horsemanship 266
horseplay 856
horse *power* 466
horticulture 371
horticulturist 369
hosanna 990
hose *stockings* 225
  pipe 350
hospitable 816, 892
hospital 662
hospitality 816, 892
host *multitude* 102
  army 726
  friend 890
hostage 771
hostel 189
hostess 890
hostile 14, 24, 889
hostility 889
hot *warm* 382
  pungent 392
  excited 824
  irascible 901
  -air *bombast* 884
  -bath **386**
  -springs 382
hotbed 153
hotel 189
  -runner **767**
hotheaded 825, 863
hothouse *conservatory* 371
hound, *n. animal* 366
hound, *v. hunt* 622
  persecute 907
hourglass 114
house *lineage* 69
  family 166
  abode **189**
  council 696
  firm 712
  -of Commons 966

  -of Lords 875
  -of Representatives 696
house, *v.* 184
housebreaker 792
housebreaking 791
household *inhabitants* 188
  abode 189
householder 188
housemaid 746
housing *lodging* 189
hovel 189
hover *soar* 206, 267
  vacillate 605
how 627
however 30
howitzer 727
howl *cry* 411, 412
  lamentation 839
hoyden *tomboy* 129
hub 122, 247
hubbub 315, 404
huddle 72, 197
hue 428
huff 900
hug, *v. clasp* 46
  border on 197
  love 897
huge 192
hulking 193
hulky *big* 192
  unwieldy 647
hullabaloo *noise* 404
hum *sound* 405, 407
  sing 416
human 364, 372
humane *benevolent* 906
  merciful 914
humanitarian 910
humanitarianism 910
humanity 906, 910
humble *inferior* 34
  meek 879
humbug, *n. falsehood* 544
  deceiver 548
humbug, *v.* 545
humdrum *dull* 843
humid 339
humiliate 879, 929
humiliation 735, 879
HUMILITY
  meekness 879
hummock 206, 250
humor, *n. essence* 5
  tendency 176
  disposition 602
  caprice 608
  wit 842
humor, *v. indulge* 760
  please 829
  flatter 933
HUMORIST 844
humorous 842
hump 250
humpbacked 243
Hun *destroyer* 165
hunch 250

hunchbacked 243
hundred 98
hunger 865
hungry 865, 956
hunt *pursuit* 286, 622
  inquiry 461
hunter *horse* 271
  pursuer 622
hurl 284
hurrah 838
hurricane *tempest* 349
hurry 274, 684
hurt, *n. physical pain* 378
  evil 619
hurt, *v.*
  cause (physical) pain 378
  maltreat 649
  injure 659, 907
  pain 830
  more frightened than-
   860
hurtful 649
hurtle 276
hurtless 648

husband *store* 636
  director 694
  spouse 903
husbandman 371
husbandry *agriculture* 371
  conduct 692
  economy 817
hush *moderate* 174
  stop 265
  silence 403
  taciturn 585
-up *conceal* 528
  pacify 723
husk *covering* 223
husky *strong* 159
  hoarse 405, 581
hussar 726
hustings 728
hustle 682
hustler 682
hut 189
hybrid 41
hydroplane 273
hydroplaning 267

hygiene 656
hygienic 656
hygienics 670
Hymen 903
hymeneal 903
hymn *song* 415
  worship 990
hyperbole 549
hypercriticism 868
hyperphysical **450**
hyphen 45
hypnosis 376, 992a
hypnotic 683
hypnotism 683, 992a
hypnotize 615, 992
hypochondriac **837**, 859
hypocrisy 544, 988
hypocrite 548
hypocritical **544**, **988**
hypothesis 514
hypothetical 514
hysteria 992a
hysterical 821
hysterics 173

I

ice 383, 387
iceberg 383
ice chest 385
icon 554
iconoclasm 984
iconoclast 165
icy 383
IDEA *notion* **453**
ideal 515
idealism 450, 515
idealist 515
ideality 450, 515
idealize 515
identical 13
identification 13
IDENTITY **13**, 27
idiocy 503
idiom 560, 566
idiosyncrasy 5, 79, 83
idiot 501
idiotic *foolish* 499
idle *trivial* 643
  slothful 683
idler 683
idol *favorite* 899
  fetich 991
idolatry 991
IDOLATRY **991**
idolize *love* 897
  idolatrize **991**
idyl 597
if 8, 469, **514**
igneous 382
ignis fatuus 4, 443
ignite 384
ignition *calefaction* **384**
ignoble 876

ignominious 940
ignominy *shame* 874
  dishonor 940
IGNORAMUS **493**
IGNORANCE **491**
ignorant 491
ignore *neglect* 460
  not known 491
ill, *n. evil* 619
  badness 649
  sick 655
ill, *adj. bad* 649
-usage 807
-will 907, 921
ill-adapted 24
ill-advised *inexpedient* 647
  unskillful 699
ill-assorted 24
ill-behaved 895
ill-bred *vulgar* 851
  rude 895
ill-disposed 907
illegal 964
ILLEGALITY **964**
illegible 519
illegitimate 925, 964
ill-fated 135, 735
ill-favored 846
illiberal *stingy* 819
  selfish **943**
  bigoted 988
illicit 925, 964
illiteracy 491
illiterate 491, 493
ill-made 243
ill-mannered 851
ill-natured 907

illness 655
illogical **477**
ill-omened 135, 735
ill-proportioned 846
ill-spent 645
ill-starred 135
ill-timed 24, **135**
ill-treat 649, 907
ill-treatment 649
illuminant 420
illuminate *enlighten* 420
  comment 595
illumine *lighten* 420
  excite 824
ill-use 649
illusion
  fallacy of vision 443
  error 495
  deception 545
illusive 4, **495**
illusory 4, 495
illustrate *exemplify* 82
  interpret 522
  represent 554
illustration 558
illustrious 873
image *likeness* 17
  appearance 448
  metaphor 521
imagery *fancy* 515
  metaphor 521
imaginable 470
imaginary 2, 4, 515
IMAGINATION **515**
imaginative 515
imagine 515
imbecile, *adj. ignorant* 493

inconvenience 647
inconvenient 135, 647
incorporate, *v. combine* 48
  include 76
  materialize 316, 364
incorporate, *adj.* 317
incorporation
  [*see* incorporate]
incorrect 477, 495, 568
incorrigible *obstinate* 606
  vicious 945
  impenitent 951
incorruption *probity* 939
  innocence 946
INCREASE
  -*in degree* 35
  -*in number* 102
  -*in size* 194
incredibility 485
incredible *impossible* 471
  improbable 473
  doubtful 485
  wonderful 870
INCREDULITY 485, **487**
incredulous 485, **487**
increment 35, 37, 39
incriminate 938
incrust 223
incubate 370
incubus *hindrance* 706
inculcate 537
inculcated 6
incumbency *office* 625
  benefice 995
incumbent, *adj. overhang-*
  ing 206
  binding 926
incumbent, *n. clergyman*
  996
incumber 706
incumbrance 706
incur 177
incurable 859
INCURIOSITY 456
incursion *ingress* 294
  attack 716
indebted 806, 916
indecent 961
indecipherable 519
indecision 149, 605
indecisive 475
indecorous *vulgar* 851
indeed 1, 31, 494
indefatigable 604*a*
indefensible 938
indefinite *every* 78
  misty 447
  uncertain 475
  vague 519
indelible 150
indelicate 961
indemnification 30, 790
indemnity 30, 973
indent *list* 86
  notch 257
indentation 252, 257

indenture *compact* 769
independence *freedom* 748
  wealth 803
independent 748
indescribable *great* 31
  wonderful 870
indestructible 150
index 86, 875
indicate *specify* 79
  direct attention to 457
  denote 467
  mean 516
  disclose 525
  mark 550
INDICATION 550
indict *accuse* 938
  arraign 969
INDIFFERENCE
  incuriosity 456
  insensibility 823
  unconcern 866
indifferent 462, 823
  [*see* indifference]
  imperfect 651
  cold 866
indigence 804
indigenous *intrinsic* 5
  native 188, 367
indignation 900
indignity *affront* 900
  insult 929
indirect *devious* 279
  latent 526
  circuitous 629
indiscreet *rash* 863
  blamable 945
indiscrete 48
indiscretion *guilt* 947
  [*see* indiscreet]
indiscriminate *mixed* 41
  multiform 81
  indistinguishable 465*a*
INDISCRIMINATION
  465*a*
indispensable 630
indisposed *unwilling* 603
  sick 655
indisputable 474
indissoluble *joined* 43
  whole 50
  dense 321
indistinct *dim* 447
indistinguishable
  identical 13
  invisible 447
indite 590
individual *special* 79
  unit 87
  person 372
individuality 79, **83**, 87
individualize 79
indivisible *whole* 50
  dense 321
indolence 683, 927
indolent **683**
indomitable *strong* 159

  determined 604, 604*a*
  courageous 861
indoor 221
indoors 221
indorse 467, 488, 769
indorsement 551
indubitable 474, 525
induce *cause* 153
  produce 161
  move 615
inducement 615
induct *receive* 296
  inaugurate 883
induction *reasoning* 476
  -*of a priest* 995
inductive 476
indue 157
indulge *bear with* 740
  please 829
  be intemperate 954
indulgence 740, 954
indulgent *kind* 740, 906
industrious 682
  studious 539
industry *business* 625
  activity **682**
indweller 188
indwelling 5
inedible 867
ineffable *great* 31
  wonderful 870
ineffectual *incapable* 158
  useless 645
  failing 732
inefficient 158, 732
inelastic 326
INELASTICITY 326
INELEGANCE
  in language 579
  ugly 846
inept *incapable* 158
  inappropriate 24
  useless 645
INEQUALITY 15, 24, **28**
ineradicable *intrinsic* 5
  stable 150
inert 172
inertia 172, 823
INERTNESS
  physical **172**
  moral 823
inessential 10
inestimable 648
inevitable 474, 601
inexact *erroneous* 495
INEXCITABILITY 826
inexcusable *accusable* 938
inexhaustible 639
inexistence 2
inexistent 2
inexorable *unavoidable*
  601
  stern 739
  compelling 744
  pitiless 914*a*
inexpectation 508

inoffensive *innocent* 946
inofficious 907
inoperative *powerless* 158
  useless 645
inopportune 135
inordinate 31, 641
inorganic 358
INORGANIZATION 358
inquest 461, 967
inquietude 828, 832
inquire 461
inquirer **461**
inquiring **461**
INQUIRY 461
inquisition *inquiry* 461
  severity 739
inquisitive 455
inroad *ingress* 294
  trespass 303
  invasion 716
insane 503
INSANITY 61, 503
insatiable 865
inscribe *write* 590
inscription 590
inscrutable 519
insect 193, **366**
insecure 665
insensate *foolish* 499
  insane 503
INSENSIBILITY
  physical **376**
  moral 823
insensible 376, **381**
INSENSITIVENESS 823
inseparable *junction* 43
  coherence 46
insert *interpose* 228
  enter 294
  put in **300**
  record 551
INSERTION 37, 228, 300
inside 221
  -out 218
insidious *deceitful* 545
  cunning 702
insight 490
insignia **550**
insignificance 32
insignificant 517, 643
insincere 544, 855
insinuate *intervene* 228
  insert **300**
  hint 527
  blame 932
insipid *tasteless* **391**
INSIPIDITY 391
insist *argue* 476
  command 741
  -upon *affirm* 535
  be determined 604
insistence [*see* insist]
insaner 545
INSOLENCE 885
insolent *defiant* 715
  arrogant **885**

disrespectful 929
insoluble *dense* 321
  unintelligible 519
insolvable 519
insolvency 808
insolvent 804, 806, 808
insomnia 682
inspect *look* 441
  attend to 457
inspector 694
inspiration *breathing* 349
  wisdom 498
  imagination 515
  motive 615
  revelation 985
inspire *breathe* 349
  prompt 615
  animate 824
  cheer 836
inspired 615
  -writers **985**
inspirit *incite* 615
  animate 824
  cheer 834
instability 149, 605
install 184, 883
installment *portion* 51
  payment 809
instance *example* 82
instant 113, 152
instantaneity 113
instantaneous **113**
instanter 113
instate 883
instead **147**
  -of **755**
instigate 615
instigator 615
instill *introduce* 296
  insert **300**
  teach 537
instinct *intuition* 477
  impulse 601
instinctive 5, 477
institute, *n.* 542, 712
institute, *v. begin* 66
  cause 153
  produce 161
institution 542, 712
instruct *teach* 537
  advise 695
  order 741
instruction 537, **695**
instructive 537
instructor 540
INSTRUMENT
  implement **633**
  security 771
  musical - 417
  optical - 445
instrumental 631, **632**
  -music **415**
INSTRUMENTALITY
  170, 631
insubordinate 742
insufferable 830, 867

INSUFFICIENCY 53, 640
insufficient **640**
insufficiently 32
insular *apart* 44, **346**
  narrow 481
  bigoted 988
insulate 44, 87, **346**
  dull 843
insult *insolence* 885
  rudeness 895
  disrespect 929
insuperable 471
insupportable 830
insurance 768
insure *make sure* 474
  obtain security 771
insurgent 146, **742**
insurmountable 471
insurrection 719, 742
insurrectionary 146
insusceptible 823
intact 52, 141
intaglio 22, 252
intangible 381
integer 50
integral 50
integrity *whole* 50, 52
  probity 939
integument 223
INTELLECT 450
  absence of - **405a**
intellectual 450
INTELLIGENCE
  mind 450
  capacity **498**
  news 532
intelligent 498
INTELLIGIBILITY 518
intelligible **518**
INTEMPERANCE 954
  drunkenness 959
intemperate **954**
intend 620
intense *great* 31
  energetic 171
intensify 35, 835
intensity *degree* 26
  greatness 31
  energy 171
intensive 35
intent, *adj.* 457
intent, *n. design* 620
INTENTION 620
intentional **620**
inter 363
interact 12
interaction 170
intercalate 228
intercede *mediate* 724, 976
intercept *hinder* 706
  take 789
intercession 724, 976
  [*see* intercede]
intercessor 714
INTERCHANGE 12, 148
  barter 794

J

K

L

libel *detraction* 934
   accusation 938
libelant 938
libeler 936
liberal *ample* 639
   expending 809
   generous 816
LIBERALITY 784, 816
liberate *disjoin* 44
   deliver 672
   free 748, 750
LIBERATION 750
LIBERTINE 962
liberty *freedom* 748
   permission 760
   right 924
library 593
lice 366
license *laxity* 738
   permission 760
   right 924
lid 223
lie, *n. untruth* 546
lie, *v. be situated* 183
   be present 186
   recline 213
   fib 544
   -in *be* 1
lien *security* 771
   credit 805
lieutenant *officer* 745
   deputy 759
LIFE *essence* 5
   events 151
   vitality 359
   biography 594
   activity 682
   -to come 152
lifeboat 273
life-giving 168
lifeless *inert* 172
   dead 360
lifelike 17, 21
lifelong 110
lifetime 108
lift *raise* 307
ligament 45
ligature 45
LIGHT, *n. window* 260
   luminosity 420
   luminary 423
   aspect 448
   knowledge 490
light, *adj. not heavy* 320
   luminous 420
   trivial 643
   unburdened 705
   gay 836
light, *v. arrive* 292
   descend 306
   kindle 384
   illumine 420
light-colored 429
lighten *illume* 420
   facilitate 705
light-fingered 791

light-footed *fleet* 274
   active 682
lightheaded 503
lighthearted 836
lighthouse 550
lightning 420
like, *adj. similar* 17
like, *v. relish* 394
   enjoy 827
   wish 865
   love 897
likely 472
likeness *similarity* 17, 21
   portrait 556
likewise 37
lilac *color* 437
Liliputian 193
limb *member* 51
limber *pliable* 324
LIMIT, *n. end* 67
   boundary 233
limit, *v. circumscribe* 195, 229
   qualify 469
   restrain 751
limitation [see limit]
limited 32
limitless 105
limp, *adj. weak* 160
   supple 324
limp, *v.* 275
limpid 425, 570
line, *n. fastening* 45
   row 69
   lineage 69, 167
   length 200
   direction 278
   mark 550
   vocation 625
   armed force 726
line, *v.* 224
lineage *kindred* 11
   series 69
   ancestry 122, 166
   posterity 167
lineament *outline* 230
   appearance 448
linear 200
linen 225
liner 273
linger *delay* 133
   loiter 275, 281, 291
   -on *time* 106
lingo 563
lingua franca 563
lingual 560
linguistic 560
liniment *ointment* 356
LINING 224
link, *n. tie* 9
   vinculum 45
link, *v. connect* 43
lion *animal* 366
   celebrity 873
lion-hearted 861
lionize 873

lip 231
LIQUEFACTION 335
liquefy 335
liquid *fluid* 333
liquidate 807
liquidity 333
liquor 298
lisp 583
LIST, *n. catalogue* 86
   leaning 217
   schedule 611
   arena 728
list, *v. classify* 69
   hear 418
   record 551
listen 418
listless *inactive* 683
   indifferent 866
literal *exact* 516
literally 19
literary 560
literature 490, 560
lithe 324
litigant 938, 969
litigate 969
litigation 969
litigious 713
litter, *n. disorder* 59
litter, *v. derange* 61
   bed cattle 370
little -in *degree* 32
   -in *size* 193
   bigoted 988
LITTLENESS 32, 193
liturgy 998
live *exist* 1, 359
   continue 141
   dwell 186
livelihood 803
liveliness 836 [see lively]
livelong 110
lively *frisky* 309
   keen 375
   active 682
   acute 821
   sensitive 822
   sprightly 836
livery 225
livid 431, 437
living *alive* 359
   benefice 995
lizard 366
load, *n. quantity* 31
   cargo 190
   hindrance 706
   anxiety 828
load, *v. fill* 52
   lade 184, 190
loadstar [see lodestar]
loadstone *attraction* 288
loaf *dawdle* 683
loafer 268, 927
loan 787
loath 603, 867
loathe *dislike* 867
   hate 898

relinquish 624
lure *charm* **288**
  deceive 545
  entice 615
lurid *dark* 421
  dim 422
lurk 526, 528
luscious *savory* 394
luster 420, 873

lustily *loud* 404
lustrous *shining* 420
lusty *strong* 159
  big 192
luxuriant *fertile* 168
  rank 365
luxurious *pleasant* 377
  intemperate **954**
luxury

enjoyment 377, 827
  sensuality 954
lying 544
lymphatic *slow* 275
lynch 972
  -law 964
lyncher 975
lyric 597
lyrist 597

M

mace *weapon* 727
  scepter 747
machination 626, 702
machine *automobile* 272
  instrument 633
  party 712
machinery 633
machinist 690
mackintosh 225
mad *violent* 173
  insane 503
  excited 824
madam 374, 877
madden 824
MADMAN 504
madness 503
Madonna 977
maelstrom *whirl* 312
magazine *book* 593
  store 636
magenta 434, 437
magic 992
magician 548, 994
magisterial 878, 885
magistrate 967
magnanimity 942
magnanimous 942
magnate 875
magnet *attraction* 288
  desire 865
magnetic 157, 829
magnetism *power* 157
  influence 175
  attraction 288
magnetize 157, 288
magnificent *fine* 845
  grand 882
magnify *increase* 31, 35
  enlarge 194
  overrate 549
magnitude 25, 31, 192
maharajah 875
mahogany *color* 433
maid *girl* 129
  servant 746
  spinster 904
maiden *first* 66
  girl 129
maidenly 374
mail *post* 270, **534**
  armor 717
maim *injure* 659

main, *n. ocean* 341
  land 342
  conduit 350
  in the - *principally* **642**
main, *adj. principal* 642
  -force strength 159
  violence 173
  compulsion 744
mainland 342
mainspring *cause* 153
mainstay *support* 215
  refuge 666
  hope 858
maintain *keep* 141
  continue 143
  sustain 170
  assert 535
  preserve 670
maintenance
  [see maintain]
majestic *grand* 31
  glorious 873
  stately 882
majesty 745, 873
major, *adj. greater* 33
major, *n. officer* 745
majority *superiority* 33
  plurality 100
  age 131
make *constitute* 54, 56
  render 144
  produce 161
  form 240
  complete 729
  compel 744
  create 976
  -believe 545
  -good
  demonstrate 478
  -out discover 480a
  know 490
  interpret 522
  -up complete 52
maker *artificer* 690
Maker, the - 976
makeshift *substitute* 147
  excuse 617
make-up *composition* 54
makeweight 30
malady 655
malcontent 710, **832**
male *man* 373

MALEDICTION 908
malefaction 947
malefactor 975
maleficent 907
MALEVOLENCE 907
malevolent 907
malformation 243
malformed 241
malice *hate* 898
  spite 907
  bear - 907
malign, *adj. malevolent* 907
malign, *v detract* 934
malignant 907
malignity 907
malinger 544
malison 908
malleable *soft* 324
maltreat *injure* 649
  aggrieve 830
  molest 907
mamma 166
mammal 366
Mammon 803
mammoth 192
MAN, *n. mankind* 372
  male 373
  workman 690
  servant 746
  -of action 682
man, *v. prepare* 673
  defend 717
manacle *fetter* 752
manage 175, 693
manageable *easy* 705
management 692, 693
manage *director* 694
mandate *requirement* 630
  command 741
mane 256
manege 370
maneuver *operation* 680
  stratagem 702
manful *strong* 159
  resolute 604
  brave 861
manger 191
mangle *smooth* 255
  injure 659
manhood 131, 861
mania *insanity* 503
  desire 865

maniac 504
manifest, n. list 86
manifest, adj. visible 446
  obvious 525
MANIFESTATION 525
manifold 81
manipulate handle 379
  use 677
MANKIND 372
manly adolescent 131
  strong 159
  male 373
  brave 861
  upright 939
manna food 396
manner kind 75
  style 569
  way 627
  conduct 692
mannerism special 79
  affectation 855
manners breeding 852
man-of-war 726
manse 1000
mansion 189
manslaughter 361
mantle, n. dress 225
mantle, v. redden 434
manual schoolbook 542
  book 593
  -labor 686
manufactory 691
manufacture 161
manufacturer 690
manuscript 590
many 102
many-colored 428, 440
many-sided 81
map 554
mar deface 241
  botch 699
maraud 791
marauder 792
marble ball 249
  sculpture 557
marbled 440
march journey 266
  music 415
  -with 199
marchioness 875
mare 271
margin space 180
  edge 231
marine, n. 269, 726
marine, adj 273, 341
MARINER 269
marital 903
maritime 267, 273, 241
mark, n. degree 26
  indication 550
  object 620
  repute 873
mark, v. take cognizance
  450
  attend to 457
  -out choose 609

command 741
-time halt 265
marked [see mark]
  special 79
market consumer 677
  mart 799
marksman 284, 700
maroon, adj. 433, 434
maroon, v. 782
marquis 875
marriage 43, 903, 998
marriageable 131
married 903
-man 903
-woman 903
marrow 5, 221, 222
marry combine 43, 48
  wed 903
MARSH 345
marshal, n. auxiliary 711
  officer 745
marshal, v. 60
marshy 345
MART 799
martial 722
martinet 739
martyr 828
  ascetic 955
martyrdom 828, 972
marvel wonder 870
  prodigy 872
marvelous 870
mascot 993
masculine strong 159
  male 373
mash soften 324
  squash 352
mask dress 225
  shade 424
  concealment 528
Masonic 712
masquerade 530, 840
masquerader 528
Mass worship 990
  Eucharist 998
mass quantity 25
  much 31
  whole 50
  heap 72
  size 192
  density 321
massacre 361
massage 324, 331, 379
masses, the 876
masseur 662
massive huge 192
  heavy 319
  dense 321
mast 206
MASTER, n. teacher 540
  ruler 745
  adept 700
  owner 779
master, v. influence 175
  understand 518
  learn 539

succeed, conquer 731
-of the situation 731
masterpiece 650, 698
mastery success 731
masticate 298
mastiff 366
mat 215
match fellow 17
  copy 19
  equal 27
  contest 720
  marriage 903
matchless unequal 28
  supreme 33
mate similar 17
  equal 27
  duality 89
  auxiliary 711
  friend 890
material, n. substance 316
  stuff 635
material, adj.
  important 642
materialism 984
materialist, 316, 984
MATERIALITY 3, 316
materialize 316
MATERIALS 635
materia medica 662
maternal 166
maternity 166
mathematical precise 494
mathematician 85
mathematics 25
matin 125
matinée 892
matrimonial 903
matrimony 903, 998
matrix mold 22
matron 374, 903
matronly 131
matter, n. affair 151
  material world 316
  topic 454
  -of fact 1
matter, v. signify 642
matter-of-fact prosaic 576
  blunt 703
  dull 843
mature, adj. old 124
  adolescent 131
  ripe 673
  -thought 451
mature, v mellow 144
  perfect 650
  prepare 673
maturity 124
  [see mature]
maul hurt 649
maunder prose 573
  mumble 583
mausoleum 363
mauve 437
maw 191
MAXIM 80, 496
maximum supreme 33

summit 210
mayor 745
maze *convolution* 248
  enigma 533
  difficulty 704
mazy 248
mead 344
meadow 344, 371
meager *small* 32
  thin 203
  scanty 640
meal *repast* 298
MEAN, *n. average* 29
  middle 68
mean, *adj. middle* 68
  contemptible 643
  stingy 819
  shabby 874
  ignoble 876
  selfish 943
mean, *v. signify* 516
  intend 620
meander *wind* 248
  stroll 266
  deviate 279
MEANING 516
meaningless 517
meanness *inferiority* 34
  [*see* mean]
MEANS *appliances* 632
  wealth 803
meantime 106
meanwhile 106
measurable 466
measure, *n. extent* 25
  degree 26
  proceeding 626
measure, *v.* 466
measureless 105
MEASUREMENT 25,
  466
meat 298
mechanic 690
mechanical 601
  -powers 633
mechanics 276
mechanism 633
medal *record* 551
  palm 733
meddle 682
meddlesome 682, 706
medial 68
mediate *intervene* 631
  intercede 724, 976
MEDIATION
  instrumentality 631
  intercession 724
  Christ 976
Mediator *Saviour* 976
mediator 724
medical 662
medicine 662
  -man 548, 994
medieval 124
mediocre *mean* 29
  ordinary 736

MEDIOCRITY
  average 29
  smallness 32
  -of fortune 736
meditate *think* 450, 451
meditation 451
medium, *n. mean* 29
  middle 68
  instrument 631
  seer 992a
medium, *adj.* 736
medley *mixture* 41
  disorder 59
meed *reward* 973
meek *gentle* 826
  humble 879
meet, *v. agree* 23
  assemble 72
  converge 290
  fulfill 772
  -with *experience* 151
meeting [*see* meet]
  junction 43
  convergence 290
  arrival 292
  assembly 696
melancholy 830, 837
mellow, *adj. old* 128
  soft 324, 428
  ripe 673
mellow, *v.* 673
melodious 413
melodrama 599, 824
melody 413
melt *vanish* 111
  convert 144
  liquefy 335
  heat 382
  fuse 384
  pity 914
  -away *cease to exist* 2
  vanish 4
melting pot 691
member *part* 51
  component 56
  councilor 696
membrane 204
membranous 204
memento 505
memoir 594, 595
memorable 151
memorandum 551
memorial *record* 551
memorialize 505
memorize 505
MEMORY 505
  fame 873
menace 909
ménage 692
menagerie 370
mend *improve* 658
  repair 660
mendacity 544
mendicancy 804
mendicant 800
menial *servant* 746

mensuration 466
mental 450
  -reservation 528
mentality 450
mention 527
menu 86, 298
mercantile 794
mercenary, *n. soldier* 726
  servant 746
mercenary, *adj.* 943
MERCHANDISE 798
MERCHANT 797
merciful 914
merciless 914a
mercurial *mobile* 264
  excitable 825
mercy *lenity* 740
  pity 914
mere *simple* 32
  trifling 643
meretricious 851
merge *combine* 48
  insert 300
  -into *become* 144
merit *goodness* 648
  due 924
  virtue 944
merited 924
meritorious 931
mermaid 979
merriment 836, 840
merry *cheerful* 836,
mesh 219
mesmerism 992
mesmerist 992a
mess *mixture* 41
  disorder 59
  derangement 61
  difficulty 704
message *dispatch* 527
  intelligence 532
  command 741
MESSENGER
  traveler 268
  envoy 534
Messiah 976
messmate 890
metallic *harsh* 410
metaphor *figure* 521
metaphorical 521
metaphysics 450
mete *measure* 466
  distribute 786
metempsychosis 140
meteoric *transient* 111
meteorology 338
meter *length* 200
  versification 597
METHOD *order* 58
  agency 170
  way 627
methodical *orderly* 58
  regular 80, 138
  businesslike 692
methodize 60
meticulous *exact* 494

fastidious 868
metrical *measured* **466**
metropolis 189, 222
mettle *energy* 171
  spirit 820
  courage 861
mew *cry* 412
microbe 193
microscopic 32
mid 68
MID-COURSE **628**
midday 125
MIDDLE *-in degree* 29
  -in order 68
  -in space 222
  -age **131**
middle-aged 131
middle-class 29
middleman 228
middling 736
midmost 68
midnight **126**
midriff 228
midshipman 269
midst 68
midsummer 125
midway **68**
mien 448
might 31, 157
mighty *much* 31
  strong 157, 159
migrate 266
mild *moderate* 174
  warm 382
  lenient 740
  calm 826
MILDNESS **740**
mile 200
militant 722
military 722
  soldiers 726
  -authorities **745**
militia 726
milksop *coward* 862
milky 430
mill, *n.* 691
mill, *v. indent* 257
  pulverize 330
millennium *period* 108
  hope 858
millinery *ornament* 847
million 98, 876
millionaire 803
mimic *imitate* **19**
mince *step short* 275
  lisp 583
  affect 855
mind, *n. intellect* 450
  will 600
  purpose 620
  desire 865
  bear in - 505
mind, *v. attend to* 457
  dislike 867
mindful 457, 505
mine, *n.* 545, 636

mine, *v. sap* 162, 252, **717**
miner 252
  sapper and - 726
mineral 358
mineralize 358
mingle 41
miniature *small* 32
minimize 36
minimum 32, 34
minister *deputy* 759
  clergy 996
  -to help 707, 746
ministerial 995
ministration *aid* 707
ministry *direction* 693
  aid 707
  church 995
  clergy 996
minor *inferior* 34
  infant 129
minority *few* 103
  youth 127
minster 1000
minstrel 416, 597
mint 22
minuend 38
minus *subtracted* 38
  absent 187
minute, *n. period* 108
  record 551
minute, *adj. -in degree* 32
  -in size 193
minutemen 726
minuteness 457, 459
minutiae 32, **643**
miracle *exceptional* 83
  prodigy 872
miraculous *wonderful* 870
mirage 443
mire 653
mirror, *n. reflector* **445**
mirror, *v. imitate* 19
mirth 836
misadventure 735
misanthrope 911
MISANTHROPY **911**
misapply *misinterpret* 523
  misuse 679
  mismanage 699
misapprehend *mistake* 495
  misinterpret 523
misappropriate 679
misbehave 851, 945
misbehavior
  discourtesy 851, 895
  guilt 947
misbelief 485
misbeliever **984**
miscalculate 481, 495
miscall 565
miscarry 732
miscellany 41, 72, 78
mischance *misfortune* 735
mischief 619
mischief-maker 913
mischievous 649

misconceive *mistake* 481, 495
  misinterpret 523
misconception 481, 495
misconduct *guilt* 947
misconstrue 523
miscreant 949
misdate 115
misdeed 947
misdemeanor 947
misdoubt 485
misemploy 679
miser 819
miserable *unhappy* 828
miserably 32
miserly 819
misery 828
misfire 732
misfortune *adversity* **735**
misgiving 485, 860
misguide 495, 538
misguided 699
mishap *failure* 732
  misfortune 735
misinform 495, 538
misinstruct 538
MISINTERPRETATION **523**
MISJUDGMENT 481, 495
mislay *derange* 61
  lose 776
mislead 495
mismanage 699
mismatch 15
misname 565
MISNOMER **565**
misplace *derange* 61
  displace 185
misprint 495
mispronounce 583
misproportioned *ugly* 846
misreckon 481
misrepresent
  misinterpret **523**
  misteach 538
  lie 544
  distort **555**
MISREPRESENTATION **523, 555**
misrule 699, 738
miss, *n. girl* 129
  error 495
miss, *v. neglect* 460
  fail 732
  lose 776
  want 865
misshapen *shapeless* 241
  distorted 243
  ugly 846
missile 284, **727**
missing 2, 187
mission 625, 755
missionary 540
missive 592
misspell 523
misspend 818

misstate 495
misstatement *error* 495
  untruth 546
  misrepresentation 555
mist *cloud* 353
  semitransparency 427
mistake 495, 699
mistaken 495
MISTEACHING 538
mister 373
mistime 135
mistress *lady* 374
mistrust 485
misty [*see* mist]
misunderstand 495, 523
misunderstanding
  disagreement 24
  error 495
MISUSE 679
mite *bit* 32
  infant 129
  small 193
mitigate *decrease* 36
  abate 174
  relieve 834
mitigation
  [*see* mitigate]
mitten 225
mix 41
mixed 41
mixture 41, 335
mizzen 235
mnemonics 505
moan *cry* 411
  lament 839
moat *inclosure* 232
  canal 350
mob 72, 102, 876
  -law 738
mobile *inconstant* 149
  movable 264
  sensitive 822
mobilization 264, 722
mobilize 264
moccasin 225
mock, *v imitate* 17, 19
mock, *adj. derisive* 856
  -modesty 855
mockery 19, 856
mode *state* 7
  habit 613
  method 627
  fashion 852
model *copy* 21
  prototype 22
  form 240
  sculpture 557
  perfection 650
  good man 948
moderate, *adj. small* 32
  slow 275
  lenient 740
  cheap 815
  temperate 953
moderate, *v. allay* 174
MODERATION 174

  patience 831
  [*see* moderate]
moderator *lenitive* 174
  judge 967
modern 123
modernism 123
modernization 123
modest *small* 32
  humble 879
  diffident 881
MODESTY 879, 881
modicum *little* 32
modification *difference* 15
  variation 20a
  change 140
  qualification 469
modify 469
modish 852
modulation 140
Mohammedanism 976
moiety 51
moil 682
moist 339
moisten 339
MOISTURE 339
mold, n. *matrix* 22
  form 240, 554
  structure 329
  earth 342
mold, *v. convert* 144
  carve 557
  decay 653
  create 976
moldy *fetid* 401
molecular 32
molecule 32, 193
molest 907
mollify *allay* 174
  soften 324
mollycoddle 158
molten *liquefied* 384
moment 113
momentous 151, 642
momentum 276
monarch 745
monarchy 737
monastery 1000
monasticism 995
monetary 800
MONEY 800
money-changer 797
moneylender 797
monger 797
mongrel 41, 83
monitor *oracle* 513
  director 694
  adviser 695
  warship 726
monitory *prediction* 511
  dissuasion 616
  warning 668
monk 996
monkey *imitator* 19
  ape 366
  butt 857
monocycle 272

monograph 594
monologue 589
monoplane 273
monoplanist 269a
monopolist 751, 943
monopolize 777
monopoly *restraint* 751
  possession 777
monotone 104
monotonous *uniform* 16
  equal 27
  repetition 104
  weary 841
monotony 13
  [*see* monotonous]
monsoon 348, 349
monster *exception* 83
  giant 192
  prodigy 872
  evildoer 913
  ruffian 949
monstrosity
  [*see* monster]
  distortion 243
monstrous *excessive* 31
  exceptional 83
  huge 192
  wonderful 870
month 108
monument *tomb* 363
  record 551
moo 412
mood *nature* 5
  state 7
  tendency 176
  humor 602
moody *sad* 837
  sullen 901a
moon 108, 318
  -shaped 245
moonbeam *light* 420
moonlight 422
moonshine *absurdity* 497
moonstruck *insane* 503
moor, n *open space* 180
  plain 344
moor, *v. fasten* 43
  locate 184
moorings 184
moot *-point topic* 454
  question 461
mop 256, 652
mope 837
moraine 270
moral, n. *maxim* 496
moral, *adj. right* 922, 926
  virtuous 944
  -courage 604
  -obligation 926
morality 926, 944
moralize 476
morals *duty* 926
  virtue 944
morass 345
moratorium 133
morbid 655

mordant *keen* 171
  pungent 392
  vigorous 574
more *superior* 33
  extra 37
moreover 37
moribund *dying* 360
MORNING 125
morose 901a, 911
morris chair 215
morrow 121
morsel 32, 51
mortal, *n. man* 372
mortal, *adj. transient* 111
  fatal 361
mortality *evanescence* 111
  death 360
mortar *cement* 45
  pulverizer 330
  crucible 691
  cannon 727
mortgage *security* 771
  lend 787
  sale 796
  credit 805
mortification
  vexation 830
  humiliation 879
mortify 879
mortise *intersect* 219
mosaic 41, 440
mosque 1000
moss 367
most 31
mote 32
mother *parent* 166
  -tongue 560
motherhood 166
motherland 181, 189
motherly 897, 906
MOTION
  change of place 264
  topic 454
  proposal 763
  request 765
motionless 265
MOTIVE 264, 615
  absence of -615a
  -power 264
motley 41, 81
motor, *n. vehicle* 272
motor, *adj. motion* 264
motor, *v. journey* 266
motor car 272
motorcycle 266, 272
motorist 268
motorize 266
motorman 268
mottled 440
motto *maxim* 496
  device 550
mould [*see* mold]
mound *hill* 206
mount, *n.* 206, 250
mount, *v. increase* 35
  ascend 305

raise 307
mountain 206
mountainous 206
mountebank *quack* 548
  buffoon 844
mourn *grieve* 828
  lament 839
mourner 363, 839
mournful *sad* 837
mourning 839
mouth *entrance* 66
  opening 260, 294
  jaws 298
  estuary 343
mouthful *quantity* 25
  food 298
movable 264, 270
movement 264, 680
movies *theater* 599
moving 185, 264
  -pictures 448, 599
mow *shorten* 201
  -down *destroy* 162
  level 213
much 31
mud 345, 352, 653
muddle *disorder* 59
  derange 61
  blunder 497, 732
muddle-headed 499
muddy *moist* 339
  opaque 426
muff
  dress 225
  bungler 701
muffle *wrap* 225
  silence 403
  deaden 405, 408a
  gag 581
muffler *dress* 225
  silencer 408a
mufti *undress* 225
mug *cup* 191
muggy *moist* 339
mulatto 41
mulct 974
mule 41, 271
mulish 606
multifarious
  diverse 16a
multifold 81
MULTIFORMITY 81
multiplex 81
multiplication
  productiveness 168
multiplicity 102
multiply 163, 168
MULTITUDE 31, 102
mum *mute* 581

mumble *mutter* 583
mummy 362
munch 298
mundane *worldly* 318
  irreligious 989
municipal 965
munificent 816
munition 717
murder 361
murderer 361
murderous 361
murky *dark* 421
murmur 405
muscle 159
muscular 159
muse, *v.* 451
Muse *poetry* 597
Muses, the - 416
mushroom *upstart* 734
MUSIC 415
musical 413, 415, 416
  -instruments 417
  -terms 413
musicale 415
music hall 840
MUSICIAN 416
musing *thought* 451
musket 727
musketeer 726
musketry 727
muss 61
mussy 653
mustache 256
mustang 271
muster 72, 85
muster roll *list* 86
mutable *changeable* 149
mutation 20a 140
mute, *adj. silent* 403
  letter 561
  speechless 581
  sordine 408a
mutescence 408a
mutilate *retrench* 38
  deform 241
mutilated 53
mutilation 38, 619
mutineer 742
mutiny 146, 742
mutter 583
mutual 12, 148
muzzle *silence* 403, 581
  restrain 751
  gag 752
myriad 102
myrmidon 726
mysterious *uncertain* 475
  obscure 519
  concealed 528
mystery
  [*see* mysterious]
  latency 526
  secret 533
mystic 528, 992a
mysticism 992a
mystify *perplex* 519

hide 528
deceive 545

myth *fancy* 515
MYTHIC DEITIES 979

mythical 515, **979**
mythology **979**

N

nadir 211
nag, *n. horse* 271
nag, *v. quarrel* 713
nail *fasten* 43
naked **226**
namby-pamby
  affected 855
name *indication* 550
  appellation **564**
nameless 565
namely 79
namesake 564
nap *texture* **256, 329**
  sleep 683
narcotic 662
narration 594
narrative 594
narrator 529, **532, 594**
narrow *thin* 203
  bigoted 481, **988**
narrow-minded
  bigoted 481
  foolish 499
  selfish 943
NARROWNESS 203
nasty *foul* 653
  offensive 830
nation 372
national 372
  -guard 726
nationality 372, 910
nationwide 78
native, *n.* 188
native, *adj.* 5, 367
  -land 342
nativity *birth* 66
natural *intrinsic* 5
  true 494
  artless 703
  simple 849
  -history 357
  -philosophy 316
naturalist 357
naturalization 184
naturalized 188
nature *essence* 5
  tendency 176
  world 318
naught 4, 101
naughty 945
nausea 841, 867
nauseate *sicken* 395, 867
  give pain 830
nauseous *unsavory* 395
  unpleasant 830
  disgusting 867
nautical 267, 273
naval 267, 273
  -authorities **745**

NAVIGATION 267
navigator 269
navvy *laborer* 690
navy 273, **726**
nay 536
neap *low* 207
  -tide 36
near *like* 17
  -in space **197**
  -in time 121
  soon 132
  impending 152
  approach 286
  stingy 819
  nearly 32
NEARNESS 9, 197
nearsighted 443
neat *orderly* 58
  trim 240, 845
  clean 652
nebula 353
nebulous *misty* 353
  obscure 519
necessarily 154
necessary 601, 630
necessitate 630
NECESSITY *fate* 601
  predetermination 611
  compulsion 744
  indigence 804
  need 865
necromancy 511
necropolis 363
nectar 394, 396
need *necessity* 601
  requirement 630
  want 640
  indigence 804
  desire 865
needful 601, 630
needle 262
needless 641
needlework 847
nefarious 945
NEGATION 536, 764
negative, *n.* 22
negative, *adj. inexisting* 2
  denying 536
negative, *v. confute* 479
  deny 536
NEGLECT 460
  leave undone 730
  omit 773
  evade 927
negligence 460
negligent 460
negotiable 270
negotiate *mediate* **724**
  bargain **769**

negotiator 724, 758
Negro *black* 431
neigh 412
neighbor *near* 197
  friend 890
neighborhood 197, 227
neighborly *aiding* 707
  friendly 888
  social 892
nemesis 972
neologist 563
NEOLOGY 563
Nereid 979
nerve *strength* 159
  courage 861
nerveless *impotent* 158
  imperturbable 871
nervous *excitable* 825
  timid 860
nest 102, **153**
nestle 186, 902
net, *adj.* 40
net, *n.* 219, 232
nether 207
netlike 219
netting 219
nettle 830
network 59, **219**
neutral *mean* 29
  no choice 609a
  mid-course 628
  indifferent 866
neutrality
  indifference 609a, 866
  [see neutral]
neutralize 179
never 107
  -more 107
new *different* 18
  novel 123
newcomer 294
newfangled 851
NEWNESS 123
NEWS 532
newsmonger *gossip* 532
newspaper 531, 551
next 63, 121
nib *end* 67
nibble *eat* 298
nice *discriminative* 465
  exact 494
  pleasing 829
  fastidious 868
niceness [see nice]
nicety 494
niche 191, 244
nick *notch* 257
nickel 800
nickname 565

O

God 976
omnipresence 1, 186
omniscience 976
omnivorous 957
on *forward* 282
once 119
one 13, 87
onerous *difficult* 704
　burdensome 706
oneself 13
one-sided 481, 923
onlooker 444
only 32
onset *beginning* 66
　attack 716
onslaught 716
ontology 1
onus *burden* 706
　duty 926
onward 282
oodles 102
ooze *emerge* 295
　flow 348
OPACITY 426
opaque 426
open, n. *begin* 66
　unclose 260
　reveal 529
open, adj. *frank* 543
　artless 703
opener 260
OPENING *beginning* 66
　opportunity 134
　aperture 260
opera *music* 415
operate *produce* 161
　act 170
　work 680
operation [*see* operate]
operative, adj. *acting* 170
operative, n. *workman* 690
operator *doer* 690
opiate 174
opine 484
opinion 484
opinionated 474, 606
OPPONENT
　antagonist 710
　enemy 891
opportune *well timed* 134
　expedient 646
opportunism 646
opportunist 605
opportunity 134, 646
oppose *be contrary* 14
　counteract 179
　front 234
　refute 468
　clash 708, 719
OPPOSITE 14, 237
OPPOSITION 708
　[*see* oppose]
oppositionist 710
oppress *molest* 649
　domineer 739
　harry 907

oppressive *hot* 382
　painful 649, 830
oppressor 739, 913
opprobrium 874
optic 420
OPTICAL 441
　-instruments **445**
optics *light* 420
　optical instruments **445**
optimism 858
optimist 858, 935
option 609
optional 609
opulence 803
ORACLE *prediction* 511
　prophet 513
oracular *ambiguous* 475
　wise 500
　predicting 511
oral 467, 582
ORANGE *color* 439
oration 582
orator 582
oratorical 582
oratory *speaking* 582
orb *circle* 247
orbit *circle* 247
　path 627
orchestra *musicians* 416
　instruments 417
orchestration 413
ordain *command* 741
　install 755, 995
ordained 996
ordeal 463, 828
ORDER *regularity* 58
　requirement 630
　command 741
orderly, adj. *regular* 58,
　60, 80
ordinance *command* 741
　law 963
ordinary *usual* 82
　imperfect 651
　mediocre 736
ordination *commission* 755
　church 995
ordnance 727
organ *instrument* 633
organic *structural* 329
　organized 357
organism 367
ORGANIZATION
　arrangement 60, 626
　production 161
　animated nature 357
organize *arrange* 60
　produce 161
　form 357
　plan 626
organizer 626
orgy 954
Orient *East* 236
orifice *opening* 260
origin *beginning* 66
　cause 153

original *dissimilar* 18
　not imitated 20
　model 22
　individual 79
　exceptional 83
　causal 153
　invented 515
originality [*see* original]
　will 600
originate *begin* 66
　cause 153
　invent 515
　-in 154
originative 153
originator 164
orison *request* 765
　worship 990
ORNAMENT
　in writing 577
　adornment 847
　glory 873
ornamentation 847
ornate *in writing* 577
　ornamental 847
orthodox 82, 983a
ORTHODOXY 983a
orthography 561
oscillate 314
OSCILLATION *perio-*
　dicity 138
　change 149
　motion 314
osseous 323
ossify 323
ostensible *probable* 472
　manifest 525
　alleged 617
OSTENTATION 880, **882**
ostentatious 880, **882**
ostracism [*see* ostracize]
ostracize *exclude* 55
　banish 893
　censure 932
other *different* **15**
　extra 37
otherwise 18
ottoman 215
ouija board 992a
Our Lady 977
oust *eject* 297
　dismiss 756
　deprive 789
out *exterior* 220
　-of the way
　distant 196
outbalance 33
outbound 295
outbreak *beginning* 66
　violence 173
　egress 295
　revolt 742
outburst *violence* 173
　egress 295
　rage 825
outcast 83, 876, **893**
outcome *effect* 154

pertinent *relative* 9
 congruous 23
perturbation *agitation* 315
 excitation 824, 825
 fear 860
peruse 539
pervade *influence* 175
 extend 186
perverse *reactionary* 283
 obstinate 606
 sulky 901a
perversion *sophistry* 477
 misinterpretation 523
 misteaching 538
 falsehood 544
perversity [see perverse]
pervert *quibble* 477
 distort 523
pervious 260
pessimism *dejection* 837,
 859
pessimist 482, 862, 859
pest *bane* 663
pester 830
pestilence 655
pestle 330
pet, n. *favorite* 899
 anger 900
pet, v. *love* 897
 fondle 902
petal 367
petition *ask* 765
 pray 990
PETITIONER 767
pet name 565
petrify *thicken* 321
 harden 323
 organization 357
 thrill 824
 astonish 870
petroleum 356
petticoat 225
pettifogger 968
pettifogging 477
pettish 901
petty 643
 -cash 800
petulance 901
petulant 901
pew 191
pewter 41
phalanx 712, 726
phantasm 443
phantom *unreality* 4
 specter 980a
pharisaical 544, 988
Pharisee 988
pharmacy 662
phase *aspect* 8
 apperance 448
phenomenon *event* 151
 prodigy 872
phial 191
philander 902
philanderer 902
philanthropic 906, 910

philanthropist 906, 910
PHILANTHROPY 906,
 910
Philistine 82
philosopher 500
philosophical
 thoughtful 451
 calm 826
philosophy *intellect* 450
 calmness 826
phlegmatic 823
phonetic *sonant* **402**
 tonic 561
 voice 580
 vocal 582
phonograph 418
phonography 402
phosphorescence *light* 420
 luminary 423
phosphorus 423
photograph 554
photographer 554
photography 554, 556
PHRASE 566
phraseology 569
physic *remedy* 662
physical 316
 -pain **378**
 -pleasure **377**
physician 662, 695
physics 316
physiognomy 234
physiology 357, 359
physique 159, 364
piazza 189
picayune 643
pick, n. *best* 648
pick, v. *select* 609
 -a quarrel 713
 -up *learn* 539
 get better 658
 gain 775
pickaninny 129
picket, n. *fence* 229
 guard 668
picket, v. *join* 43
 locate 184
 restrain 751
pickings *gain* 775
 booty 793
pickle 670
pickpocket 792
picnic 298, 840
pictorial 556
picture *appearance* 448
 representation 554
 painting 556
picture gallery 556
picturesque 556, 845
pie 396
piebald 440
piece, n. *bit* 51
piece, v. 140
 cannon 727
 -together 43
piecemeal 51

pied 440
pierce *perforate* 260
 chill 385
 wound 659
 affect 824
piercer 262
piercing *cold* 383
 shrill 410
 acute 821
PIETY 987
pig *animal* 366
 glutton 954a
pigeonhole, n. 191
pigeonhole, v. *shelve* 460
piggish 954
pigment 428
pigmy [see pygmy]
pike 727
pikestaff 206
pilaster 215
pile *heap* 72
 edifice 161
pilfer *steal* 791
pilferer 792
pilgrim 268, 996
pilgrimage *journey* 266
 undertaking 676
pill 249
pillage *theft* **791**
pillar 206, 215
pillory 975
pillow 215
pilot 269, 269a
pimple 250
pin 43
pinch, n. *emergency* 8
 need 630
 difficulty 704
pinch, v. *contract* 195
 chill 385
pinched [see pinch]
 thin 203
pine *mope* 837
 -for 865
pinion *restrain* 751
 fetter 752
pink, adj. 434
pink, v. *pierce* 260
pinnace 273
pinnacle 210
pioneer *precursor* 64
pious 987
pipe, n. *tube* 260
pipe, v. *sound* 410
piper 416
piquant *pungent* 392
 impressive 821
pique *excite* 824
 pain 830
 hate 898
piracy 773
pirate, n. 792
pirate, v. *plagiarize* 788
pirouette 312
pistol 727
piston 263

point *small* 32
　　end 67
　　place 182
　　sharpness **253**
　　topic 454
　　mark 550
　　intention 620
　　wit 842
　　-at *direct attention* 457
　　disparage 929
　　-of view 441
　　-out *indicate* 79
　　-to *direct* 278
　　predict 511
point-blank *direct* 278
　　plain **576**
pointed *sharp* 253
　　marked 550
　　concise 572
pointedly 620
pointer 550
pointless 254
poise *balance* 27
　　weight 319
　　inexcitability 826
poison 659, 663
　　-gas 727
poisonous 657
poke 191
polar 210
　　-lights **423**
polarity 89, 237
pole *pikestaff* **206**
　　axis 222
　　oar 267
polemic 713
polestar *attraction* 288
　　luminary 423
　　indication 550
police 965
policeman 664
policy 626, **692**
polish, *n. smooth* 255
　　gloss 332
　　taste 850
　　politeness 894
polish, *v. rub* 331
　　furbish 658
polished *fashionable* **852**
　　polite 894
polite 894
politeness 894
politic *wise* 498
　　cautious 864
politician 694, **700**
politics 702
polity 926
poll *count* 85
　　list 86
　　vote 609
pollute *soil* 653
　　corrupt 659
pollution *disease* 655
poltroon 862
pommel, *n.* 215

pommel, *v. beat* 972
pomp 882
pompom 727
pomposity 878, 882
pompous *inflated* 577
　　proud 878
　　ostentatious 882
pond 343
ponder 451
ponderous *heavy* 319
poniard 727
pontiff 996
pontificate 995
pony 271
　　translation 522
poodle 366
pool, *n. lake* 343
pool, *v. co-operate* 709
poor *feeble* 477
　　insufficient 640
　　indigent **804**
　　-man 640, 804
poorness [*see* poor]
　　inferiority 34
pop *noise* 406
pope 996
popinjay 854
populace 876
popular *choosing* 609
　　desirable 865
　　celebrated 873
　　approved 931
popularize 518
population 188, 372
populous 72, 102, 186
porch 66, 191, 260
pore, *n.* 260
pore over
　　apply the mind 457
　　learn 539
porous 252, 295, 322
port *harbor* 189, 666
　　left 239
　　gait 448
portable 270
portage 270
portal 66, **260**
portend 511
portent 512
portentous *prophetic* 511
　　fearful 860
porter 263, 271
portfolio *case* 191
　　authority 747
　　jurisdiction 965
portico 191
portion *part* 51
　　allotment **786**
portly 192
portmanteau 191
　　-word **572**
portrait 554, **556**
portraiture 554
portray 554
pose, *n. situation* 183
　　form 240

pose, *v. inquire* 461
　　puzzle 475
　　affect 855
poser 855
position *circumstances* 8
　　situation 183
　　post 625
　　status 873
positive *real* 1
　　great 31
　　certain 474
　　narrow-minded 481
　　assertive 535
posse 72
possess 777, 780
　　bedevil 978, 992
POSSESSION 777, 780
POSSESSOR 779
POSSIBILITY *chance* 156
　　liability 177
　　likelihood 470
possible 177, 470
post, *n. situation* 183
　　support 215
　　mail 534
　　employment 625
post, *v. list* 86
　　send 270
　　publish 531
　　enter accounts 811
postal 592
post card 592
postdate 115
poster 531
posterior *in time* 117
　　in space 235
POSTERIORITY 117
POSTERITY 121, **167**
posthaste *swiftly* 274
　　rash 863
posthumous 117, 133
postilion *rider* 268
postman 271, 534
post-mortem 363
post office 534
postpone 133, 460
postscript 37, 65
posture *situation* 183
　　form 240
posy *bouquet* 400
pot *mug* 191
potency 157
potent 157, 159
potentate **745**
potential 2, 157
potentiality *power* 157
　　possibility 470
potion *beverage* 298
potpourri *mixture* 41
pouch 191
poultry 366
pounce upon *attack* 716
　　seize 789
pound *bruise* 330
　　-the piano 416
pour *emerge* 295

presuppose 514
pretend 544, 546
pretender *deceiver* 548
pretense *imitation* 19
  untruth 546
  excuse 617
  ostentation 882
pretension 855, 880, 882
pretentious *affected* 855
  vain 880
  ostentatious 882
pretext *untruth* 546
  plea 617
pretty *much* 31
  beautiful 845
prevail *exist* 1
  be superior 33
  be general 78
  succeed 731
  -upon 615
prevailing 78
prevalence 33, 175
prevaricate **544**
prevent 706
prevention 706
preventive 55
previous 116
prevision 510
prey *quarry* 620
  booty 793
  victim 828
PRICE 812
  consideration 147
priceless *valuable* 648
  dear 814
prick *pierce* 260
  sting 378, 830
  incite 615
prickly 253
PRIDE 878
priest 904, 996
priesthood 995
prig 855, 887
priggish *affected* 855
prim 855, 868, 878
prima donna 599
primacy *superiority* 33
  church 995
primal 66
primary *initial* 66
  causal 153
prime, *adj. initial* 66
  primeval 124
  important 642
prime, *v. teach* 537
  prepare 673
primeval 124
primitive 124
primogeniture 128
primordial *original* 20
prince 745
princely *liberal* 816
  noble 875
  generous 942
princess 745
principal, *adj.* 642

principal, *n.* 694
principality 181
principally 33
principle *nature* **5**
  tenet 484
  maxim 496
  probity 939
prink *adorn* 847
print, *n. engraving* 558
  letterpress 591
print, *v.* 591
printer, 591
PRINTING 558, 591
prior, *adj.* 62, 116
prior, *n. monk* 996
PRIORITY 62, 116, 280
prismatic 440
PRISON 752
PRISONER *captive* **754**
  accused 938
pristine 122
privacy 893
private, *n. soldier* 726
private, *adj. special* 79
  secluded 893
privation *loss* 776
  poverty 804
privilege 748, 924
privileged 924
privy *hidden* 528
prize, *n.* 733, 775
prize, *v. love* 897
PROBABILITY 472
  chance 156
probable 472
probation *trial* 463
probationary 463
probationer 541
probe, *n. perforator* 262
probe, *v. investigate* 461
  measure 466
PROBITY 939
problem 461
problematical
  uncertain 475
proboscis 250
procedure 170, 627
proceed *flow* 109
  advance 282
proceeding, *n.* 680
proceeding, *adj.*
  incomplete 53
proceedings *records* 551
proceeds 775, 800
process *conduct* 692
procession *continuity* 69
  march 266
proclaim 531
proclivity *tendency* 176
  proneness 820
procrastination *delay* 133
  neglect 460
procure *cause* **153**
  get 775
  buy 795
prod 276

prodigal *lavish* 641
  extravagant 818
PRODIGALITY 818
prodigious *much* 31
  wonderful 870
• PRODIGY *exception* 83
  genius 492
  wonder 872
produce, *n.* 775, 798
produce, *v. increase* 35
  cause 153
  create 161
PRODUCER 164
product *increase* 35
  effect 154
  gain 775
PRODUCTION 161
  effect 154
  composition 54
  [*see produce*]
productive *causal* 153
  creative 161, 168
PRODUCTIVENESS 168
profane 988
profess [*see profession*]
profession *assertion* 535
  pretense 546
  business 625
professional *business* 625
professor 492, 540
professorship 540
proffer 763
proficient 698, 700
profile *outline* 230
profit *increase* 35
  advantage 618
  acquisition 775
profitable *useful* 644
  gainful 775
  paying 810
profiteer 814
profitless 646
profound *great* 31
  deep 208
  learned 490
  wise 498
  heartfelt 821
profundity 208
  [*see profound*]
profuse *redundant* 641
  prodigal 818
profusion 102, 639
progenitor 166
progeny 167
prognosticate 511
program *catalogue* 86
  plan 626
progress *growth* 144
  motion 264
  advance 282
PROGRESSION
  gradation 58
  series 69
  motion 282
progressive *continuous* 69
  advancing 282

improving 658
prohibit 761
PROHIBITION 761
  exclusion 55
prohibitionist 958
prohibitive 55, 761
project *bulge* 250
  impel 284
  intend 620
  plan 626
projectile 284, 727
projecting 214, 250
projection 250, 283
projector *promoter* 626
proletariat 876
prolific 168
prolix 573
prolixity 573
prologue 64, 599
prolong *protract* 110
  delay 133
  continue 143
  lengthen 200
prolongation 117
  [*see* prolong]
prolonged 110
promenade *walk* 266
prominence
  [*see* prominent]
prominent *convex* 250
  important 642
  eminent 873
promiscuous *mixed* 41
  indiscriminate 465a
PROMISE 768
promissory 768
  -note *security* 771
promontory 206
promote *improve* 658
promoter *planner* 626
promotion 541, 658
prompt, *adj. early* 132
  active 682
prompt, *v. remind* 505
  tell 527
promulgate 531
pronounce *judge* 480
  assert 535
  voice 580
  speak 582
pronounced 525
pronouncement 531
pronunciation 580
proof *test* 463
  demonstration 478
  printing 591
  -against 664
prop *support* 215
propaganda 673
propagate 161
propel 284

propensity *tendency* 176
  inclination 820
proper *individual* 79
  due 924
PROPERTY 342, 780
prophecy 511
prophet *seer* 513
prophetic 511
prophylactic *healthful* 656
  preventive 706
propinquity 197
propitiate *pacify* 723
  mediate 724
  atone 952, 976
propitiator 724
propitiatory 952
propitious *timely* 134
  prosperous 734
  auspicious 858
proportion *relation* 9
  symmetry 242
proportions *space* 180
  size 192
proposal 763, 765
propose *suggest* 514
  offer 763
  offer marriage 902
proposition *supposition*
  454
  reasoning 476
  project 626
  offer 763
propound *suggest* **514**
proprietor 779
propriety *agreement* 23
  elegance 578
  fashion 852
  duty 924
PROPULSION 284
propulsive 284
prorogue 133
prosaic *sober* 576
  dull 843
proscribe *interdict* 761
  curse 908
  condemn 971
PROSE, n. 598
prose, *v.* 584
prosecute *pursue* 622
  arraign 969
prosecutor 938
proselyte 144, 607
prospect *destiny* 152
  futurity 121
  view 448
  expectation 507
prospector 463
prospective 120, 507
prospectus *list* 86
  scheme 626
prosper 618, **734**
PROSPERITY 734
prostrate, *adj. powerless*
  158
  low 207
  horizontal 213, 251

submissive 725
  dejected 837
prostrate, *v. depress* 308
prostration
  [*see* prostrate]
  sickness 655
prosy *weary* 841
  dull 843
protect 664
protection *influence* 175
  defense 717
protectionist 751
protective 717
protector 664, 717, 912
protectorate 737
protest *dissent* **489**
  deprecate 766
  not pay 808
protestant
  dissenting 489
protoplasm 357
PROTOTYPE 22
protract *prolong* 110
  delay 133
  lengthen 200
protrude 250
protrusive 250
protuberance 250
proud *dignified* 873
  lofty 878
prove *arithmetic* 85
  demonstrate 478
  indicate 550
proverb 496
proverbial 490
provide *furnish* **637**
provided 8, **469**
providence 976
provident *careful* 459
  prepared 673
providential
  opportune 134
  fortunate 734
province *department* 75
  region 181
  office 625
provincial *rural* **189**
  narrow 481
provincialism 563
PROVISION *food* 298
  supply **637**
  preparation 673
provisional
  conditional 8, 770
  temporary 111
  contingent 134
proviso 469, 770
provocation 900
provoke *cause* 153
  excite 824
  vex 830
  anger 900
prow 234
prowess 861
prowl *walk* 266
  lurk 528

Q

R

rostrum 542
rosy 434, 845
rosy-cheeked 845
rot *decay* 49, 659
  putrefy 653
rotate 312
ROTATION 138, **312**
rotten *foul* 653
  decayed 659
rotound 249
ROTUNDITY 249
rough, *n. bully* 876, 887
  913
rough, *adj. violent* 173
  shapeless 241
  uneven 256
  harsh 410
  churlish 895
roughen 256
roughew 240
roughly *nearly* 197
ROUGHNESS 256
  [see *rough*]
roughrider 268
round, *n. series* 69
  revolution 138
round, *adj.*
  circular 247, 249
round, *v.* 245, 311
roundabout 279, 311
roundup 72
rouse *stimulate* 615
  excite 502
rout, *n. tumult* 315
rout, *v. overcome* 731
  discomfit 732
route 266, 627
routine *order* 58, 138
  custom 613
  business 625
rove *travel* 266
rover 268
roving 266
row, *n. series* 69
  violence 173
  street 189
row, *v* 267
rowdy, *n. blusterer* 887
rowdyism 851
rower 269

royal 737
royalist 737
royalty 737
rub, *n. difficulty* 704
rub, *v.* 331, 379, 662
rubber *overshoe* 225
  eraser 331
  masseur 662
rubbish 645
rube 876
Rubicon *limit* 233
rubicund 434
rubric *liturgy* 998
ruby *red* 434
ruck 876
rudder 273, 633, 693
ruddy *red* 434
rude *violent* 173
  shapeless 241
  vulgar 851
  uncivil 895
rudiment *beginning* 66
  cause 153
rudimentary 66
rudiments 66
rue *regret* 833
rueful *regretful* 833
  sad 837
ruff 225
ruffian *rough* 876, 913
  scoundrel 949
ruffianism 907
ruffle *disorder* 59
  derange 61
  roughen 256
  fold 258
  excite 824, 825
  irritate 898
rug *covering* 223
rugged
  shapeless 241
  rough 256
ruin *destruction* 162
  failure 732
  adversity 735
ruined 732, 859
ruinous *painful* 830
ruins *remains* 40
RULE *average* 29

regularity 80
  influence 175
  measure 466
  decide 480
  custom 613
  precept 697
  reign 737
ruler 737, 745
rumble 407
ruminate *chew* 298
  think 451
rummage 461
rumor 532
rump *remainder* 40
rumple *disorder* 59
  derange 61
  roughen 256
rumpus *confusion* 59
run, *n. rule* 29
  repetition 104
  motion 264
  speed 274
  habit 613
run, *v. flow* 109, 264, 348
  race 274
  -down *depreciate* 932
runaway 623
rung 215
runner *branch* 51
  courier 268, 271, 534
rupture 44
  quarrel 713
rural 189, **371**
ruse *cunning* 702
rush *crowd* 72
  dash 274
  haste 684
russet 433
rust *decay* 659
rustic, *n.* 876
rustic, *adj.* 189, **371**
rustle 405, 407
rusty *decayed* 659
  unskillful 699
rut *regularity* 80
  furrow 259
ruthless
  savage 907
  revengeful 919

S

Sabbath 687
saber 727
sable 431
sabotage 162
saccharin 396
sacerdotal 995
sack, *n. bag* 191
  dismissal 756
sack, *v. plunder* 791
sacrament 998
SACRED *holy* 976

-writings 986
sacrifice, *n. worship* 990
  holocaust 991
sacrifice, *v.* 162
sacrilege 988
sad *dull* 428
  painful 830
  dejected 837
sadden 830, 837
saddle 155, 293
  -with *quarter on* 184

sadness 837
safe, *n.* 530
safe, *adj. secure* 664
safeguard 717
SAFETY 664
sag *curve* 245
sagacious 498
SAGE, *n.* 500
sage, *adj.* 498
said *repeated* 104
sail *navigate* 267

set out 293
sailor 269
saint 987
saintly *virtuous* 944
  pious 987
salable 796
salary 775, 973
SALE 796
salesman 758
salesmanship 796
salient *projecting* 250
  sharp 253
  manifest 525
sallow *yellow* 436
sally, *n. attack* 716
  wit 842
sally, *v. issue* 293
salmon-colored 434
salon 191
saloon 191
salt, *adj. pungent* 392
salt, *v. preserve* 670
salubrity 656
salutary *healthful* 656
salutation [see salute]
salute *accost* 586
  greet 894
salvation 976, 987
salve *remedy* 662
salver 191
salvo 406
same 13
sameness 13, 16
samovar 191
sample 82
sanatorium 189, 662
sanctification 976
sanctify 976, 987
sanctimony 988
sanction 924
sanctitude 987
sanctity 987
sanctuary 666
sanctum *chamber* 191
sand *powder* 330
  resolution 604
sandal 225
sandy *red* 434
sane 502
sang-froid 871
sangraal 998
sanguinary 361
sanguine *red* 434
  hopeful 858
sanitarium 189, 662
sanitary 656
SANITY 502
sap, *n.* 333
sap, *v. weaken* 160
  excavate 252
sapper *excavator* 252
  soldier 726
sapphire 438
sarcasm 932, 934
sarcastic 856, 932
sash 247

SATAN 978
satanic *diabolic* 978
satchel 191
sate 869
satellite *companion* 88
  heavenly body 318
satiate 869, 957
SATIETY 869
satire *metaphor* 521
  ridicule 856
satirical 521, 856, 932
satirize 856, 932
satisfaction [see satisfy]
satisfactory 831
  [see satisfy]
  good 648
satisfy *convince* 484
  suffice 639
  gratify 829
  satiate 869
saturate *fill* 52
  moisten 339
  satiate 869
sauce 393
saucepan 191
saucer 191
saucy *insolent* 885
  flippant 895
saunter *ramble* 266
  dawdle 275
savage, *n.* 913
savage, *adj. violent* 173
  brave 861
  angry 900
  malevolent 907
savagery 907
savanna 344
savant *learned man* 492
  sage 500
save, *adv. except* 38
save, *v. preserve* 670
  deliver 672
  economize 817
savings *economy* 817
savior *benefactor* 912
Saviour 976
savor 390
SAVORINESS 394
savory 390, 394
saw, *n. notch* 257
  adage 496
saw, *v. cut* 44
say *assert* 535
  express 560
  speak 582
saying *maxim* 496
  assertion 535
scabbard 191
scaffold *support* 215
  execution 975
scald *burn* 382
scale, *n. series* 69
  slice 204
  skin 223
  weight 319
  gamut 413

measure 466
scale, *v. mount* 305
scallop *notch* 257
scalp 226
scaly 223
scamp, *n. rascal* 949
scamp, *v. neglect* 460
scamper *speed* 274
scan *see* 441
  attend to 457
  inquire 461
scandal *news* 532
  obloquy 934
scandalize 932
scandalmonger 532
scandalous 874
scant *small* 32
  few 103, 137
  narrow 203
scanty [see scant]
scapegoat 147
scapegrace 949
scar *blemish* 848
scarce *few* 103
  infrequent 137
  insufficient 640
scarcely 32, 137
scarcity 103, 640
scare 860
scarecrow 846
scarf 225
scarlet 434
scathe 649
scatheless *perfect* 650
scatter *derange* 61
  disperse 73
  diverge 291
scatterbrained 458
scavenger 652
scene *appearance* 448
  drama 599
  excitement 825
scenery 448, 599
scenic 599, 882
scent *smell* 398, 400
  trail 551
scentless 399
SCEPTER 747
sceptic [see skeptic]
scepticism
  [see skepticism]
schedule 86, 611
scheme *plan* 626
schemer 702
schism *dissent* 489
  heterodoxy 984
SCHOLAR
  learned man 492, 873
  learner 541
scholarly 539
scholarship 539
scholastic 490, 537, 542
SCHOOL *herd* 72
  academy 542
schoolbook 542
schoolboy *lad* 129

seductive 288, 829
sedulous *active* 682
  desirous 865
see, *n. bishopric* 995
see, *v. view* **441**
  look 457
  know 490
seed *cause* 153
  grain 330
seedy *weak* 160
  exhausted 688
  needy 804
seeing 441
  -*that* 476
seek *inquire* 461
  pursue 622
seem 448
seemly *expedient* 646
  due 924
seep 295, 337
seer *oracle* 513
seesaw 12
seethe *moisten* 339
  simmer 382
  boil 384
  fume 824
segment 51
segregate 44
segregated 47
seine *net* 232
seize *take* **789**
  -*an opportunity* 134
seizure 315, 925
seldom **137**
select *specify* 79
  choose 609
selection 75
self *identity* 13
  -*assertion* 885
  -*command*
    resolution 604
  -*conscious* 855
  -*control* 604, 826
  -*convicted* 950
  -*deceit error* 495
  -*deception* 495
  -*defense* 717
  -*delusion* 486, 347
  -*denial* 604, **942**
  -*determination* 737, 748
  -*educated* 490
  -*esteem* 878
  -*government* 737
  -*importance* 878
  -*indulgence*
    intemperance 954
  -*interest* 943
  -*luminous* **423**
  -*moving* 266
  -*possessed* 852
  -*possession*
    inexcitability 826
    caution 864
  -*preservation* 717
  -*reliance*
    resolution 604

  courage 861
  -*reproach* 950
  -*respect* 878
  -*restraint* 826
  -*sacrifice* 942
  -*satisfied* 880
  -*seeker* **943**
  -*seeking* 943
  -*sufficiency* 880
  -*sufficient* 880
selfish 943
SELFISHNESS 911, 943
selfsame 13
sell *vend* 796
seller 796
selvage 231
semblance *similarity* 17
  imitation 19
  copy 21
semester 108
semicircle 247
semifluid 352
SEMILIQUIDITY 352
seminar 542
seminary 542
SEMITRANSPARENCY
  427
senate 72, 696
senator 696
send *transfer* 270
  propel 284
senile 128, 158
senior 128
seniority **128**
sensation 375
sensational 824
SENSATIONS OF
  TOUCH 380
sense *wisdom* 498
  meaning 516
senseless *insensible* 376
  absurd 497
  foolish 499
  unmeaning 517
senses *sanity* 502
SENSIBILITY
  physical - 375
  moral - 822
sensible *wise* 498
sensitive 375, 822
SENSITIVENESS 822
sensual 954
SENSUALIST 954a
sensuous 821
sentence *decision* 480
  phrase 566
  judgment 969
  condemnation 971
sententious *concise* 572
  taciturn 585
sentient - *physically* 375
  -*morally* **821**
sentiment *idea* 453
sentimental *sensitive* 822
  affected 855
sentinel 263, **668**

sentry 668
separable 44
separate *disjoin* 44
  bisect 91
  diverge 291
  divorce 782
separation 54, 55, 905
septic 655, 657, 662
sepulcher 363
sepulchral 408
SEQUEL *adjunct* 39
  following 65
  -*in time* 117
  sequence 281
SEQUENCE
  -*in order* 63
  -*in time* 117
  motion 281
sequester *take* 789
  confiscate 974
seraph 977
Seraphim 977
serenade 415
serene *calm* 826
serf *slave* 746
serfdom 749
sergeant 745
serial *continuous* 69
  periodic 138
series *continuity* 69
serious *important* 642
  sedate **837**
sermon 537, **998**
serpent *snake* 366
serpentine 248
serrated *notched* 257
serried *dense* 321
serum *lymph* 333
SERVANT *minister* 631
  help 711
  retainer 746
serve *benefit* 618
  officiate 625
  avail 644
  aid 707
  help 746
service *good* 618
  utility 644
  use 677
  warfare 722
  servitude 749
  worship 990
serviceable
  instrumental 631
  useful 644, 746
servile *serving* 746
  obsequious 879, **886**
SERVILITY 886
  [*see* servile]
servitude 749
session 696
sessions *law* 966
set, *n. group* 72
  class 75
  tendency 176
  direction 278

seethe 824
simoom 349
simper *smile* 838
 affect 855
simple *mere* 32
 unmixed 42
 credulous 486
 ignorant 493
 silly 499
 artless 703
 unadorned 849
simple-minded 849
SIMPLENESS 42
simpleton 501
SIMPLICITY 849
 ignorance 499
 [*see* simple]
simplify 849 [*see* simple]
simply *little* 32
simulate *resemble* 17
 imitate 19
 cheat 544
simulation 19
simultaneous 120
SIMULTANEOUSNESS
 120
sin, *n. guilt* 947
sin, *v. transgress* 945
since *under the circum-
 stances* 8
 after 117
 because 155, 476
sincere *veracious* 543
 ingenuous 703
 earnest 821
sinecure 681
sinew 159
sinewy 159
sinful 945
sing *chant* 416
 rejoice 838
singe 382
singer *musician* 416
single *unmixed* 42
 sole 87
 unmarried 904
single-handed 87
single-minded 703
singleness [*see* single]
singsong 16
singular *exceptional* 83
 one 87
sinister *left* 239
 bad 649
 adverse 735
sink *disappear* 4
 destroy 162
 lower 308
 submerge 310
 fail 732
sinless 946
sinner 949, 988
Sinn Feiner 712, 742
sinuous 248
sip *drink* 298
sir *man* 373

title 877
sire 166
siren *sea nymph* 341
 tempter 615
 alarm 669
 evil spirit 980
sirocco *wind* 349
sirup 396
sissy *milksop* 158
sister *likeness* 17
 nurse 662
sisterhood 11, 712, 888
sisterly 888
sit 308
site 182, 183
sitting [*see* sit]
 assembly 696
sitting room 191
situate 183, 184
SITUATION
 circumstances 8
 place 183
 location 184
 business 625
six 98
SIZE *magnitude* 31
 glue 45
 dimensions 192
sizzle 409
skate, *n.* 272
skate, *v.* 266
skeleton, *remains* 40
 essential part 50
 outline 626
skeptic *agnostic* 485, 989
skeptical 989
skepticism *doubt* 485
 irreligion 989
sketch *form* 240
 represent 554
 paint 556
 outline 626
sketchy *incomplete* 53
 unfinished 730
ski 225, 272
skid, *v.* 217, 306
skiff 273
SKILL 698
skillful 698
skim *move* 266
 neglect 460
 summarize 596
skin *tegument* 223
 peel 226
skin-deep 220
skinny *thin* 203
skip *jump* 309
 rejoice 838
skipper *sea captain* 269
 captain 745
skirmish 720
skirt, *n. dress* 225
 edge 231
skirt, *v. environ* 227
 flank 236
skit *ridicule* 856

detraction 934
skittish *excitable* 825
skulk *hide* 528
 sneak 862
skull 450
sky 318
skylight 260
skyscraper 210
slab 251
slack *loose* 47
 inert 172
 slow 275
 unwilling 603
 insufficient 640
 shiftless 674
 lax 738
 nonobservant 773
slacken *loosen* 47
 moderate 174
 retard 275
slacker 623, **927**
slake *quench* 174
 satiate 869
slam *shut* 261
slander 934
slanderer 936
slang 563
slant 217
slap 276
slapdash 684
slash 44
slate, *n. schedule* 611
 plan 626
slate, *v. list* 86
slatternly 653
slaughter 361
slave 746
slavery *toil* 686
 subjection 749
slavish *servile* 746, 886
 subject 749
slay 361
slayer 361
sled 272
sledge 272
sleek *smooth* 255
sleep 376, 683
sleepy 683
sleet 383
sleigh 272
sleight *skill* 698
 -of hand *deception* 545
slender 203
sleuth 527
slice, *n.* 51
slice, *v. cut* 44
 shave 204
slide *elapse* 109
 pass 264
 glide 266
 descend 306
slight, *n.* 929, 930
slight, *adj. shallow* 209
 rare 322
 feeble 575
slight, *v. neglect* 460

specific, *n. remedy* 662
specific, *adj. special* 79
specification *class* 75
specify *particularize* 79
  tell 527
  name 564
specimen 82
specious *probable* 472
  sophistical 477
  showy 846
speck 32, 193
speckle *variegate* 440
spectacle *show* 599, 882
  appearance 448
  prodigy 872
spectacles 445
spectacular 599, 882
SPECTATOR 197, **444**
SPECTER 4, 361, **980a**
spectral 980a
spectrum 428
speculate *think* 451
  suppose 514
  chance 621
speculation *chance* 156
  experiment 463
  venture **621**
speculative
  thoughtful 451
  experimental 463
speculator 463
SPEECH **582**
speechless 581
speed *journey* 266
  velocity 274
speedily *soon* 132
SPELL, *n. period* 106
  influence 175
  exertion 686
  charm **993**
spell, *v.* 561
spellbind 586
spellbound 870
spelling 561
spend *waste* 638
  give 784
  expend 809
spendthrift 818
spent *weak* 160
  tired 688
sphere *rank* 26
  class 75
  space 180
  region 181
  ball **249**
  function 625
sphinx 513, 520
spice, *n.* 41, 393
spice, *v. season* 392
spicy *fragrant* 400
  exciting 824
spike, *n.* 253, 263
spike, *v. pierce* 260
spill *shed* 297
  waste 638
spin, *n. journey* 266

aviation 267
spin, *v. rotate* 312
  -out *protract* 110
  prolong 200
spindle-shanked 203
spine 253
spineless *weak* 945
spinster 374, 904
spiny 253
spiral 248, 311
spire *height* 206
  peak 253
SPIRIT *essence* 5
  immateriality 317
  intellect 450
  vigorous language 574
  activity 682
  courage 861
  ghost 980a
  evil - 980a
spirited *vigorous* **574**
  active 682
  brave 861
spiritism 317, 992a
spiritist 317
spiritual *immaterial* 317
  psychical 450
  divine 976
  pious 987
spiritualism
  immateriality 317
  psychical research **992a**
spiritualist 317
spiritualize 317
spit, *n. saliva* 299
spit, *v. pierce* 260
spite 907
spiteful 907
spitfire *shrew* 901
splash 348, 653
splendid 873
splendor *luster* 420
  beauty 845
  glory 873
  display 882
splice *join* 43, 228
  cross 219
splinter, *n.* 205
splinter, *v.* 44, 328
split, *n. quarrel* 713
split, *v. divide* 44
  bisect 91
  break 328
  -hairs 477
spoil, *n. booty* 793
spoil, *v. botch* 699
  hinder 706
spokesman 524, 582
sponge, *n. stopper* 263
  pulpiness 354
  drunkard 959
sponge, *v. moisten* 339
  dry 340
  clean 652
  cringe 886
sponger 886

sponsor *witness* 467
  security 771
spontaneous
  voluntary 600
  willing 602
  impulsive 612
spoon, *n.* 191
spoon, *v. court* 902
spoonerism 495
spoonful 25
spoor 550
sporadic *infrequent* 137
  infectious 657
spore 330
sport *killing* 361
  amusement 840
sportive *gay* 836
  frolicsome 840
sportsman 361, **840**
spot, *n. place* 182
  mark 550
  blemish 848
spot, *v. discover* 480a
  soil 653
spotless *perfect* 650
  clean 652
  innocent 946
spotted *variegated* **440**
spouse 88, 903
spout, *n.* 295
spout, *v. declaim* 582
sprain 160
sprawl 200, 308
spray, *n. sprig* 51
  foam 353
  flowers 400
spray, *v. atomize* 336
spread, *n. expanse* 180
  meal 298
spread, *v. disperse* 73
  universalize 78
  expand 194
  diverge 291
  publish 531
spree 840
sprig *branch* 51
sprightly *cheerful* 836
  witty 842
spring, *n. early* **125**
  source **153**
  strength 159
  elasticity 325
  rivulet 348
spring, *v. leap* 309
springy 325
sprinkle *scatter* 73
  wet 337
sprinkler **337**
sprint 274
sprout *grow* 365
  expand 194
spruce *neat* 652
  beautiful 845
spur, *n. projection* 250
  prick 253
spur, *v incite* 370, 615

straggle *stroll* 266
  deviate 279
straggler 268
straight, *adj.* 246
straight, *adv.* 278
straighten 246
straightforward
  truthful 543
  honorable 939
STRAIGHTNESS 246
straightway 132
strain, *n. race* 11
  melody 415
strain, *v. weaken* 160
  percolate 295
  overrate 482
  clarify 652
  tax 688
  effort 686
strainer *sieve* 260
strait *interval* 198
  water 343
  difficulty 704
straitened *poor* 804
strait-laced *severe* 739
  fastidious 868
  haughty 878
strand *thread* 205
  land 342
stranded *stuck fast* 150
  ruined 732
  lost 828
strange *unrelated* 10
  exceptional 83
  ridiculous 853
  wonderful 870
  -bedfellows 713
  -to say 870
stranger *alien* 57
strangle *contract* 195
  kill 361
strangulation 361
strap, *n.* 45
strap, *v. fasten* 43
strapping *strong* 159
stratagem *plan* 626
  artifice 702
strategic 692, 864
strategist 694, 700
strategy *conduct* 692
  warfare 722
stratification 204
stratum 204, 251
stray, *adj.* 73
stray, *v.* 279
streak 440
STREAM, *n. -of fluid* 347
  -of water 348
  -of air 349
  -of light 420
stream, *v.* 72, 264
streamer *flag* 550
street, 189, 627
STRENGTH *quantity* 25
  degree 26
  greatness 31

vigor **159**
  energy 171
  tenacity 327
strengthen *reinforce* 37
  invigorate **159**
strenuous *energetic* 171
  persevering 604a
  active 682
stress *emphasis* 580
  importance 642
  strain 686
stretch, *n. expanse* 180
  exertion 686
stretch, *v. expand* 194
  extend 200
  misrepresent 555
stretcher 272
strew 73
strict *rigid* 82
  exact 494
  severe 739
  conscientious 939
  orthodox 983a
stricture 932
stride, *n.* 264
stride, *v.* 266
STRIDENCY **410**
strident **410**
strife *discord* 713
  contention 720
strike *hit* 276
  resist 719
  disobey 742
  impress 824
  beat 972
  -off exclude 55
  -root 150
striking 525, 890
string **205**
stringent *energetic* 171
  strict 739
  compulsory 744
stringy *filamentous* 205
  tough 327
strip, *n.* 205
strip, *v. divest* 226
  take 789
  rob 791
stripe, *n, line* 200
  insignia 747
  blow 972
stripe, *v.* 440
stripling 129
strive *endeavor* 675
  exert 686
  content 720
stroke *impulse* 276
  mark 550
  blow 619
  expedient 626
  disease 655
  action 680
  success 731
stroke, *v.* 379
stroll 266
strong *powerful* **159**

energetic 171
  tough 327
  pungent 392
  fetid 401
  healthy 654
stronghold **717**
strong-minded 604, **861**
strong-willed 604, **861**
strop *253*
structural 240, 329
STRUCTURE 329
  production 161
  organization 357
struggle, *n. essay* 675
  exertion 686
struggle, *v. flounder* 704
  contend 720
strum 416
strut *walk* 266
  swagger 878, 880
  boast 884
stub 550
stubble *remains* 40
stubborn *hard* 323
  obstinate 606
stubby 201
stucco 223
stuck [*see stick*]
  -fast firm 150
stuck-up 878
studded *spiked* 253
  variegated 440
student 492, 541
studio *room* 191
  workshop 691
studious *thoughtful* 451
  docile **539**
study, *n copy* 21
  room 191
  learning **539**
study, *v. think* 451
  examine 461
stuff, *n matter* 316
  absurdity 497
  material 635
stuff, *v. fill* 190
  pad 194
  line 224
  fool 545
  overeat 957
stuffing *lining* 224
  stopper 263
stuffy *sultry* 382
stultify 499
stumble *fall* 306
  flounder 315
  trip 495
stumbling block
  difficulty 704
  hindrance 706
stump *remainder* 40
  trunk 51
stumpy *short* 201
stun *stupefy* 376
  deafen 419
  startle 508

affect 823, 824
  astonish 870
stunt shorten 201
stunted 32, 195
stupefy stun 376
  affect 823
  astonish 870
stupendous 31, 192
stupid unintelligent 499
  dull 843
stupor insensibility 376,
  823
  wonder 870
sturdy strong 159
stutter 583
sty inclosure 232
  dirt 653
STYLE state 7
  name 564
  diction 569
  fashion 852
stylish 852
suave 894
suavity 894
subaltern 745
subconscious 450, 992a
  -self 450, 992a
subdivide 44
subdivision 44, 51
subdue calm 174
  succeed 731
subject, n. topic 454
  meaning 516
  servant 746
subject, adj. liable 177
  enthrall 749
subject, v. dominate 175
SUBJECTION 749
subjective intrinsic 5
  immaterial 317
SUBJECTIVENESS 5
subjoin 37, 63
subjugate 731, 749
sublet 787
sublease 787
sublime
  great 31
  high 206
  eminent 873
  magnanimous 942
subliminal 450
  -consciousness 450, 992a
  -self 317, 992a
sublimity [see sublime]
submarine, adj. 208
submarine, n. boat 726
submerge, 310, 337
submergible 310
submersible 310
submersion 310
SUBMISSION 725
  obedience 743
  humility 879
submissive 725, 879
submit propound 514
  yield 725

subordinate 34
subpoena writ 960
subscribe agree to 769
  give 784
subscriber [see subscribe]
subscription gift 784
subsequent
  -in order 63
  -in time 117
subserviency 886
subservient
  instrumental 631
  aiding 707
  servile 746
subside decrease 36
  sink 306
subsidence 36
subsidiary 707
subsidy aid 707
  gift 784
subsist exist 1
  continue 141
subsistence food 298
substance thing 3
  gist 5
  quantity 25
  matter 316
  meaning 516
  wealth 803
substantial existing 1, 3
  material 316
  dense 321
  true 494
SUBSTANTIALITY 3,
  316
substantially 5, 50
substantiate
  materialize 316
  verify 467
SUBSTITUTE, n. 634,
  759
substitute, v. 147
SUBSTITUTION 147
substratum 204
subterfuge sophistry 477
  quirk 481
  cunning 702
subterranean 208
subtle light 320
  rare 322
  cunning 702
subtlety rarity 322
  sophistry 477
  wisdom 498
subtraction 36, 38
subtrahend 38
suburb 197, 227
suburban 227
subversion 14
subvert destroy 162
  invert 218
succeed follow 63, 117
  triumph 731
  acquire 783
SUCCESS 731
successful 731

succession sequence 63,
  117
  continuity 69
  repetition 104
successor 65, 117
succinct 572
succor 707
succulent nutritive 298
  juicy 333
succumb yield 725
suckle 707
suckling infant 129
suction 296
sudden transient 111
  instantaneous 113
  soon 132
suds froth 353
sue 969
suffer endure 151, 826
  ail 378, 655
  allow 760
  feel 821
  ache 828
sufferance 826
suffering 639
SUFFICIENCY 31, 639
sufficient enough 639
  satisfactory 831
suffix adjunct 39
suffocate kill 361
suffocation 361
suffrage 535, 609
sugar 396
sugary 396
suggest suppose 514
  inform 527
  advise 695
  -itself 451
suggestion hint 527
  plan 626
  advice 695
suggestive 505, 514
suicidal destructive 162
suicide 361
suit, n. clothes 225
  petition 765
  courtship 902
  lawsuit 969
suit, v. accord 23
  befit 646
  -the occasion 134, 646
suitable 23, 134, 646
suite sequel 65
  series 69
  retinue 88, 746
suitor petitioner 767
  lover 897
sulk 901a
sulkiness [see sulky]
sulky obstinate 606
  discontented 832
  dejected 837
  sullen 901a
sulks 895
sullen obstinate 606
  gloomy 837

swarm, *n. crowd* 72
  multitude 102
swarm, *v. climb* 305
swarthy 431
swath 72
swathe *clothe* 225
sway, *n. power* 157
  influence 175
  agitation 315
  authority 737
sway, *v. influence* 175, 615
  lean 217
  oscillate 314
swear *affirm* 535
  promise 768
sweat, *n. excretion* 299
  fatigue 688
sweat, *v.* 295, 382, 686
sweater 225
sweep, *n. space* 180
  curve 245
sweep, *v. curve* 245
  speed 274
  clean 652
sweeping *whole* 50
  complete 52
  inclusive 76
  general 78
sweepings 645
sweet *saccharine* **396**
  melodious 413
  clean 652
  lovely 897
sweeten 396
sweetheart 897
SWEETNESS 396
sweets 396
swell, *n. bulge* 250
  wave 348
  blare 404
  fop 854

swell, *v. increase* 31
  expand 194
swelter 382
swerve *change* 140
  deviate 279
swift 274
swim 267, 320
swindle *cheat* 545
  peculate 791
swindler *cheat* 548
  thief **792**
swine 366
swing, *n. operation* 170
  space 180
  freedom 748
swing, *n. hang* 214
  oscillate **314**
swirl 348
swish 409
switch, *n. rod* 975
switch, *v. deviate* 279
  flog 972
swollen 194, 250
swoon 158, 688
swoop *descend* 274
  seize 789
sword 727
swordsman 726
Sybarite 954a
sycophant 65, 886
syllable 561
syllabus *list* 86
  compendium 596
sylvan 367
symbol *sign* 550
symbolic *latent* 526
  indicative 550
symbolize *involve* 526
  indicate 550
  represent 554
symmetrical 27, **242**

SYMMETRY
  equality 27
  regular form **242**
  beauty 845
sympathetic
  [*see sympathy*]
sympathizer 914
sympathize with 906
sympathy
  feeling 821
  love 897
  kindness 906
  pity 914
  condolence 915
symphony *music* 415
symposium 72, 596
symptom 550
synagogue 1000
synchronism 120
syndicate *council* 696
  league 712
synod 696
synodic (al) 696
synonym 522
synonymous 27, **516**
synopsis 86, 596
syntax 567
synthesis
  combination 48
  reasoning 476
synthetic 476
syringe, *v.* 337
syrup [*see* sirup]
system *order* 58
  rule 80
  plan 626
systematic 60, 80
systematize *order* 58
  arrange 60
  organize 357
  plan 626

T

tabernacle 189, 1000
table, *n. arrangement* 60
  list 86
  support 215, 251
  repast 298
table, *v. defer* 133, 460
tableau 448, 599
tableland 344
tablet 251, 551
taboo *prohibited* 761
tabular 60
tabulate 60, 69, 86
tabulation 551
tacit *implied* 516
  latent 526
TACITURNITY 585
tack, *n. direction* 278
tack, *v. change course* 140
  turn 279
tackle, *n. fastening* 45
  gear 633

tackle, *v. undertake* 676
  manage 693
tact *discrimination* 465
  wisdom 498
  skill 698
tactful [*see tact*]
  affable 894
tactics *conduct* 692
  warfare 722
tactlessness 895
tactual 379
tag, *n. addition* 37
  sequel 65
  end 67
tag, *v. follow* 63, 235
tail 65, 67, 235
taint, *n. imperfection* 651
  disease 659
  disgrace 874
taint, *v.* 659
take *receive* 785

  appropriate 788, **789**
  -after 17
  -away *subtract* 38
  remove 185
  seize 789
  -from *subtract* 38
  seize 789
  -in *shorten* 201
  admit 296
  understand 518
  deceive 545
  -place 1, 151
  -to *like* 827
  desire 865
  love 897
  -up *pursue* 622
  undertake 676
  use 677
taker 789
TAKING 789
tale *counting* 85

agitate 315
throe *revolution* 146
  violence 173
  agitation 315
  physical pain 378
throne 215, **747**
throng 72
throttle
  render powerless 158
  close 261
  kill 361
through *via* 278
  by means of 631
throughout 52, 106
throw 284
  -up *resign* 757
throwback 145
thrust *push* 276
  attack 716
thud 406, 408a
thug *murderer* 361, 792
thumb, *v.* 379
thump, *n. noise* 406
thump, *v. beat* 276
thunder, *n.* 404
thunder, *v.* 173
thunderstorm 173
thunderstruck 870
thus 8, 233
thwack *beat* 276
  punish 972
thwart *across* 219
  obstruct 706
  oppose 708
tiara *insignia* 747
  jewelry 847
tick *sound* 407
  mark 550
ticket 550
  slate 626
tickle *touch* 380
  please 829
ticklish 380
  dangerous 665
  difficult 704
tidbit 298
tide 52, 348
  -over 106
tidings 532
tidy *orderly* 58
  clean 652
tie, *n. relation* 9
  equality 27
  fastening 45
  neckcloth 225
  obligation 926
  -s *of blood* 11
tie, *v. fasten* 43
tier *layer* 204
tiff *quarrel* 713
  anger 900
tiger *cheer* 838
  wild beast 913
tight *fast* 43
  closed 261
tighten 43, 195

tights 225
tile *roof* 223
till, *n. coffer* 191, 802
till, *v. cultivate* 371
till, *adv.* 106
tiller *rudder* 633
tilt *slope* 217
  fall 218, 306
  contentior 720
timber *trees* 367
TIME, *n.* 106
  leisure 685
  in - 109, 152
time, *v. adjust* 58
timekeeper 114
TIMELINESS **134**
timely *early* 132
  opportune **134**
timepiece 114
times *present* 118
  events 151
timeserver 605, 607, 943
timeserving **607**, 702
timid *weak* 605
  fearful 860
  cowardly 862
  humble 881
timidity [see timid]
timorous [see timid]
tincture *mixture* 41
  color 428
tinder *fuel* 388
tinge *mixture* 41
  color 428
tingle 378, 380
tinker *repair* 660
tinkle 405, 408
tinsel *sham* 545
  ornament 847
  frippery 851
tint 428
tintinnabulation 408
tiny 193
tip *end* 67
  summit 210
  gift 784, 973
tipple 298, 959
tippler 959
tipsy 959
tirade *speech* 582
  censure 932
tire, *n.* 230
tire, *v. fatigue* 688
  bother 841
  weary 841
tiresome 830, 841
tissue *whole* 50
  texture 329
titanic 31, 192
titbit 394
tit for tat 718
tithe *tenth* 99
TITLE *name* 564
  right to property **780**
  distinction 877
  right 924

titter 838
tittle-tattle *news* 532
  small talk 588
titular 564
to *towards* 278
  -and fro 12, **314**
toadying 886
toadyism 933
toast *roast* 384
  honor 873
tobacco **392**
toboggan 272
tocsin 669
today 118
toddle 266, 275
toe 211
toga 225
together *accompanying* 88
  simultaneously 120
toil 686
toilet 225
token 550
tolerable *trifling* 643
  passable 651, 845
toleration *laxity* 738
  lenity 740
  permission 760
  calmness 826
toll, *n. tax* 812
toll, *v. ring* 407
tomahawk 727
tomb 363
tomboy 129
tombstone 363
tomfoolery **497**
tomorrow 121
tone *state* 7
  sound 402
  color 428
tongue *taste* 390
  language 560
tonic, *n. medicine* 662
tonic, *adj. phonetic* 561
  bracing 656
tonnage 192
too *also* 37
  over and above 641
tool *instrument* 631, 633
  cat's-paw 711
toot 406
tooth 250, 253
  taste 390
toothed 257
top *summit* 210
top-heavy 28
TOPIC **454**
topical 183
topmost 210
topography 183
topple 162
topsy-turvy 218
torch 388
torment *physical* 378
  moral 828, **830**
tornado 312, 349
torpedo 727

traveling **266**
traverse 302
travesty *imitate* 19
  copy 21
  misinterpret 523
  burlesque 555
trawl 285
trawler 273
tray 191
treacherous 907, 940
treachery *deception* 545
  dishonesty 940
tread 266
treason *revolt* 742
  treachery 940
treasure 636, 800
TREASURER 801
TREASURY 802
treat
  physical pleasure **377**
  bargain 769
  delight 827, 829
  -of 595
treatise 593, 595
treatment
  conduct 692
  medical - 662
treaty **769**
treble *three* 93
  shrill 410
tree *pedigree* 166
  plant 367
trellis 219
tremble *totter* 160
  shake 315
  fear 860
tremendous *painful* 830
  fearful 860
tremor *agitation* 315
  emotion 821
  fear 860
tremulous *changeable* 149
  agitated 315
  fearful 860
trench *dike* 232
  furrow 259
  defense 717
trenchant *energetic* 171
  concise 572
  vigorous 574
  keen 821
trend *tendency* 176
  bend 278
trepidation *agitation* 315
  excitement **825**
  fear 860
trespass *go beyond* 303
  sin 945
tress 256
triad 92
trial *inquiry* 461
  experiment 463
  essay 675
  adversity 735
  suffering 828
  lawsuit 969

TRIALITY 92
triangle 92
tribe *race* 11
  assemblage 72
  clan 166
tribulation 828
TRIBUNAL 966
tributary, *n. river* 348
tributary, *adj. giving* 784
tribute *donation* 784
  money paid 809
  reward 973
trick *deception* **545**
  habit 613
  contrivance 626
  skill 698
  artifice 702
trickery *deceit* 545
trickiness [see tricky]
trickle 295, 348
trickster *deceiver* **548**
  schemer 702
tricky *deceiving* 545
  cunning 702
tricycle 272
trident 92
trifle, *n.* 32, **643**
trifle, *v. neglect* 460
  fool 499
  -with *deceive* 545
trifler 460
trifling 643
trig 845
trill *sound* 407
  sing 416
trim, *n. state* 7
trim, *adj. neat* 652, **845**
trim, *v. adjust* 27
  form 240
  lie 544
  waver 605
  change sides 607
  adorn 847
trimmer
  timeserver 607, 943
trimming *border* 231
  ornament 847
trinity 92
Trinity, Holy - **976**
trinket 643, 847
trio 92
trip, *n. jaunt* 266
  fall 306
trip, *v. run* 274
  leap 309
  mistake 495
triple 93
triplet 92
TRIPLICATION 93
triplicity 92
TRISECTION 94
trite *known* 490
  conventional 613
triumph *succeed* **731**
  exult 838
trivial *unmeaning* 517

trifling 643
triviality **643**
troglodyte 893
troll, *n.* 980
troll, *v.* 416
trolley 272
  -car 272
troop *assemblage* 72
  soldiers 726
trooper 726
troopship 726
trope 521
TROPHY 733
tropical 382
trot *run* 266, 274
  translation 522
troth 768
troubadour 597
trouble, *n. turmoil* 59
  exertion 686
  adversity 735
  care 828
trouble, *v. derange* 61
troublesome
  inexpedient 647
  difficult 704
  painful 830
troublous **59**
trough 259
trounce *censure* 932
  punish 972
trousers 225
trousseau 225
trow 484
truant 187, 623
truce 133, 142, **723**
truck *vehicle* 272
  barter 794
truckman 268
truculent 907
trudge *walk* 266
  move slowly 175
true *real* 1
  straight 246
  accurate **494**
  veracious 543
  faithful 772
trueness [see true]
truism *axiom* 496
truly *really* **494**
trumpery 517, **643**
truncheon 727
trundle 284
trunk *stem* 166
  box 191
truss *bundle* 72
  support 215
trust, *n. belief* 484
  firm 712
  property 780
  credit 805
  hope 858
trust, *v.* 484, 858
trustee 758, 801
trustful 484, 486
trustworthy *certain* **474**

reliable 484, **632**
veracious 543
honorable 939
TRUTH *reality* 1
exactness **494**
veracity 543
truthful 543
truthless 544
try *experiment* 463
adjudge 480, **969**
endeavor 675
use 677
tryst 74, **892**
tub 191
tube 260
tubular 260
tuck *fold* 258
tuft 256
tug, *n. ship* 273
effort 686
-*of war* 720
tug, *v. pull* 285
tuition 537
tumble 162, **306**
tumbledown 160
tumbler *glass* 191
buffoon 844
tumbrel 272
tumult *disorder* 59
agitation 315
revolt 742
emotion 825
tumultuous [see tumult]
tumulus 363
tundra 344
tune 413, 415, 416
tuneful 413
tuneless 414
tunic 225
tunnel 260
turban 225
turbine 633
turbulence *violence* 173
agitation 315
excitability 825
turbulent 173
[see turbulence]
turf *lawn* 344
grass 367

race course 728
turgid 641
inflated 577
turmoil *confusion* **59**
agitation 315
turn, *n. crisis* 134
period of time 138
tendency 176
stroll 266
circle 311
inclination 602
aptitude 698
-*of mind beat* 820
by -s **138,** 148
in - 138
turn, *v. change* 140
curve 245
blunt 254
deviate 279
rotate 312
-*about interchange* 148
-*into convert* 144
-*out become* 144
happen 151
eject 297
dismiss 756
-*topsy-turvy* 61
-*up happen* 151
chance 156
turncoat 144, **607**
turning point 134, 145
turnout 882
turnpike 627
turpitude 940
turquoise *blue* 438
turret 206
tusk 253
tussle 720
tutelage *teaching* 537
learning 539
tutor, *n. teacher* 540
tutor, *v. teach* 537
tutorship 537
Tuxedo 225
twaddle 497, 517
twain 89
twang 402, 410
sound 402
stridor 410

twelve 98
twenty 98
twice **90**
twig 51
twilight *dusk* **422**
twin *similar* 17
accompanying 88
two 89
duplicate 90
twine, *n. string* 205
twine, *v. intersect* 219
wind 248
twinge *pain* 378
twinkle 420, **422**
twirl 248, 311
twist, *n.* 248
twist, *v. cross* 219
distort 243
deviate 279
bend 311
twit 938
twitching 315
twitter
agitation 315
cry 412
emotion 821
two 89
two-faced *deceitful* 544
two-step *dance* 840
type *similarity* 17
pattern 22
class 75
printing 591
typesetting 54
typewrite 590
typhoon 349
typical *special* 79
conformable **82**
significant 550
typify 550
typist 590
typography 590
tyranny *severity* 739
illegality 964
tyrant 739
tyro *ignoramus* 493
learner 541

U

ubiquity 1, 186
U-boat 208, 726
UGLINESS 846
ugly 846
ulster 225
ulterior -*in time* 121
-*in space* 196
ultimate 67
ultimately 121, 133
ultimatum
requirement 630
terms 770

ultra *superior* 33
ululate 412
ULULATION 407, 412
umbrella 223
umpire 480, 724
unable 158
unaccompanied 87
unaccustomed *unused* **614**
unskillful 699
unadorned 576, 849
unadulterated *genuine* 494
unaffected *artless* 703

insensible **823**
simple **849**
unallied 10
unalterable 150
unaltered 150
unambitious 866
unanimity *agreement* 23
assent **488**
accord 714
unanimously **709, 714**
unanswerable 478
unappetizing 867

neutralize 179
  not do 681
undoing *ruin* 735
undone *ruined* **732**
  hopeless **859**
undress, *n. clothes* 225
undress, *v. strip* 226
undue 925
undulate *wave* 248
  oscillate 314
undutiful 945
undying *perpetual* 143
unearth *eject* 297
  disinter 363
  discover 480a
unearthly *immaterial* 317
  spectral 980a
  heavenly 981
uneasy 828
uneatable 867
uneducated *ignorant* 491
  unprepared 674
unemotional 823
unemployed *not used* 678
  inactive 681
unemployment 681
unenterprising 864
unequal 28, 139
unequaled 28, 33
unequivocal *great* 31
  sure 474
unerring *certain* 474
  exact 494
unessential *extrinsic* 6
  irrelative 10
  unimportant 643
uneven *diverse* 16a
  unequal 28
  irregular 139
  rough 256
unexampled
  unimitated 20
unexpected *sudden* 132
  unforeseen 508
unfading 112
unfailing 141
unfair *unjust* 923
unfaithful 940
unfamiliar 83
unfashionable
  unconventional 614
  vulgar 851
unfasten 44
unfathomable *infinite* 105
  deep 208
  mysterious 519
unfavorable
  out of season 135
  obstructive **708**
  adverse 735
unfeeling *insensible* 376
  numb 381
  heartless 823
unfeigned 543
unfetter *release* **750**

unfettered *free* 748
unfinished 53, 730
unfit *inappropriate* 24
  impotence 158
  inexpedient 647
  unskillful 699
  wrong 923
  undue 925
unfitness *inaptitude* **24**
  [*see* unfit]
unfitted *not prepared* 674
unfledged *young* 127
  callow 674
unflinching
  persevering 604a
  brave 861
unfold *evolve* 313
  interpret 522
  disclose 529
UNFOLDMENT 313
unforeseen
  unexpected 508
unforgiving 919
unfortunate *ill-timed* 135
  unlucky 735
  unhappy 828
unfriendly *opposed* 708
  hostile **889**
  malevolent 907
unfruitful 169
unfurl *unfold* 313
ungainly 846
ungenerous *stingy* 819
  selfish 943
ungentlemanly *rude* 895
  dishonorable 940
ungodly 989
ungovernable *violent* 173
  passionate 825
ungraceful 846
ungracious *uncivil* 895
  unfriendly 907
ungrammatical 568
ungrateful 917
ungrounded
  unsubstantial 4
unguarded *neglected* 460
  spontaneous 612
unguilty 946
unhallowed 988
unhappy *unlucky* 735
  wretched 828
  dejected 837
UNHEALTHINESS 657
unhealthy *ill* 655
  unwholesome **657**
unheard of
  exceptional 83
  improbable 473
  ignorant 491
unhinge *derange* 61
  make powerless 158
unholy 989
unhonored 874
unhurt 670
uniform, *n.* 225, 550

uniform, *adj.*
  homogeneous **16**
  regular 80
  dress 225
  symmetrical 242
UNIFORMITY 16, 80, 242
unimitated 20
UNIMPORTANCE 643
unimportant 643
unimpressed 838
uninhabitable 187
uninhabited 187, 893
uninitiated *ignorant* 491
  unskillful 699
uninjured *healthy* **654**
  preserved 670
unintellectual 452
unintelligent 499
UNINTELLIGIBILITY
  519
unintelligible 519
unintentional 601
  undesigned 621
uninteresting 841
uninterrupted
  continuous 69
  perpetual 112
uninvited 893
uninviting 830
union *agreement* 23
  junction 43
  combination 48
  party 712
  concord 714
unique *dissimilar* 18
  original 20
  unequal 28
  exceptional 83
  alone 87
unison *agreement* 23
  melody 413
unit 87
unite *join* 43, **712**
  combine 48
  compose 56
  assemble 72
  concur 178
  converge 290
United States courts 966
UNITY *identity* 13
  uniformity 16
  agreement 23
  completeness 52
  oneness 87
  concord 714
universal 78
  -language 560
universe 318
university 542
unjust *wrong* 923
unjustifiable *wrong* **923**
  inexcusable 938
  wicked **945**
unkempt *rough* 256
  vulgar 851
unkind 907

publish 531
speak 580, 582

money 800
utterance [see utter]

V

vacancy [see vacant]
vacant void 4
 absent 187
 thoughtless 452
 scanty 640
vacate displace 185
 depart 293
 resign 757
vacation 687
vacillate change 149
 waver 605
vacuity 452
vacuous unsubstantial 4
 absent 187
vacuum 2, 187, 197
vagabond 268, 876
vagary fantasy 515
 whim 608
vagrant, n. 268
vagrant, adj. 266
vague unsubstantial 4
 uncertain 475
 obscure 519
vagueness 475
vain unprofitable 645
 conceited 880
vainglorious 878
vale 252
valediction adieu 293
valedictorian 293
valedictory 293, 582
valentine 902
valet 746
valiant 861
valid powerful 157
 true 494
valise 191
valley 252
valor 861
valuable useful 644
 good 648
value, n. color 428
 importance 642
 utility 644
 goodness 648
 price 812
value, v. 466, 480
valve 263, 350
vampire evildoer 913
 demon 980
van front 234
 wagon 272
vandal 165, 913
vandalism 851
vane 349
vanguard 234
vanish disappear 2, 4, 449
 be transient 111
VANITY conceit 880

vanquish 731
vapid insipid 391
vapor gas 334, 353
VAPORIZATION 336
vaporize 336
vaporizer 336
vaporous unsubstantial 4
 volatile 336
variable irregular 120
 changeable 140, 149
variance difference 15
 disagreement 24
 discord 713
VARIATION
 difference 15
 dissimilarity 18
 diverseness 20a
 chance 140
varied 15, 16a
variegated 428, 440
VARIEGATION 440
variety difference 15
 class 75
 multiformity 81
various different 15
 many 102
varnish, n. resin 356a
varnish, v. overlay 223
 decorate 847
vary differ 15, 18, 20a
 change 140
 fluctuate 149
vase 191
vassal 746
vast great 31
 spacious 180
 large 192
vat 191
vaudeville 599
vault, n. cellar 191, 207
 dome 250
 tomb 363
vault, v. leap 309
vaunt 884
veer change 140
 deviate 279
 go back 283
VEGETABLE 367
 -kingdom 367
 -life 365
vegetarian 953
vegetarianism 298
vegetate exist 1
 grow 365, 367
VEGETATION 365
 inaction 681
vegetative 365, 367
vehemence violence 173
 emotion 825

vehement violent 173, 825
 impassioned 574
VEHICLE carriage 272
 instrument 631
veil, n. covering 225, 424
veil, v. shade 424
 conceal 528
vein conduit 350
 humor 602, 820
 mine 636
VELOCITY
 rate of motion 264
 swiftness 274
vender 796
vendetta 919
vendor 796
veneer 204, 223
venerable old 124, 128
 sage 500
 respected 928
veneration respect 928
 piety 987
vengeance 919
venom bane 663
 malignity 907
venomous bad 649
 poisonous 657
 rude 895
 maleficent 907
vent, n. opening 260, 295
vent, v. disclose 529
ventilate air 338
 discuss 595
venture, n. chance 621
 trial 675
 undertaking 676
venture, v. experiment 463
 presume 472
 risk 665
 try 675
 dare 861
venturesome
 enterprising 676
 brave 861
 rash 863
VERACITY 494, 543
veranda 191
verbal 562
verbatim 19, 516
verbiage 562, 573
verbosity words 562
 diffuseness 573
verdant green 435
verdict opinion 480
 lawsuit 969
verdure vegetation 367
 green 435
verge, n. edge 231
 limit 233

verge, *v. tend* 176
  incline 278
  -upon 197
verification *test* 463
  warrant 771
verify *test* 463
  evidence 467
  find out 480a
verily *truly* 494
veritable 1, 494
verity 1, 494
vermin 366
vernacular, *n.* 560
vernacular, *adj. native* 188
  lingual 560
vernal 125
versatile *changeable* 149
verse *poetry* 597
versify 597
version 522
vertical 212, 246
VERTICALITY 212
vertigo 503
very 31
vesper 126
vespers 126
vessel *receptacle* 191
  ship 273
vest 225
vested *fixed* 150
  legal 963
vestibule *entrance* 66
vestige 551
vestment *dress* 225
  canonicals 999
vestry *council* 696
vesture 225
VETERAN *old* 130
  adept 700
  warrior 726
veterinarian 370
veto 761
vex 830, 898
vexation 830, 900
vexatious 830
vexed question 704
viaduct 627
vial 191
viands 298
vibrate 149, 314
vibration 138, 314, 408
vicar 996
vicarage 1000
vicarious *substitute* 147
VICE 945
vice-president 759
viceroy *governor* 745
vicinity 227
vicious 945
vicissitude 149
victim *dupe* 547
  sufferer 828
  culprit 975
victimize *deceive* 545
  injure 649
victor 731

victoria *carriage* 272
victory 731
victual *provide* 637
victuals 298
videlicet *namely* 79, 522
vie 648
view, *n. sight* 441
  appearance 448
  opinion 453, 484
  landscape 556
view, *v.* 441, 457
viewpoint 441, 453
vigil *care* 459
vigilance *care* 459
  activity 682
vigilant 459, 864
VIGOR *energy* 157, 171
  strength 159
  style 574
  resolution 604
  health 654
vigorous 574
vile *hateful* 649
  disgraceful 874
  plebeian 876
  dishonorable 940
  vicious 945
vilification 908
vilify *censure* 932
  detract 934
villa 189
village 189
villager 188
villain *actor* 599
  rascal 949
villainous *evil* 649
  wicked 945
villainy 940
vim 171, 682
VINCULUM 45
vindicate *justify* 937
VINDICATION 937
vindictive *revengeful* 919
vine 367
violate *disobey* 742
  infringe 925
  fail 927
VIOLENCE 173, 825
violent 173, 825
violet 437
violinist 416
viper *snake* 366, 913
virago 901
Virgin, The 977
virgin, *n. girl* 129
  spinster 904
  good woman 948, 960
virgin, *adj. new* 123
virile *adolescent* 131
  strong 159
  manly 373
virtu 847
virtual *inexistent* 2
  unsubstantial 5
virtually 5
VIRTUE *power* 157

  goodness 944
  purity 960
virtuous 944, 960
virulence *noxiousness* 649
  anger 900
  malevolence 907
virulent *energetic* 171
  corrupting 649, 657
  angry 900
  malevolent 907
virus *disease* 655
visage *front* 234
  appearance 448
viscount 875
VISIBILITY 446
visible 446
vision *phantom* 4, 980a
  sight 441
  dream 515
visionary *inexistent* 2
  unsubstantial 4
  imaginary 515
visit *arrival* 292
  sociality 892
visitation *disease* 655
  adversity 735
  suffering 828
visitor *friend* 890
vista *glade* 260
  sight 441
  appearance 448
visual 441
  -organ 441
visualize 220
vital *living* 359
  important 642
  -principle 1
vitality *stability* 150
  strength 159
  life 359
vitalize 359
vitiate *deteriorate* 659
vituperate 908, 932
vituperation 908, 932
vivacious *active* 682
  sensitive 822
  cheerful 836
vivid *bright* 420, 428
  graphic 518
vivification 359
vivify 359
vixen *fox* 366
  shrew 901
viz. [*see* videlicet]
vizor 530
vocabulary 86, 562
vocal *musical* 415
  oral 580
  -music 415
vocalist 416
vocalize 562, 580
vocation *business* 625
vociferate 411
vociferation *loudness* 404
  cry 411
  voice 580

W

X

Y

Z

FOREIGN WORDS AND PHRASES

à bas. [F.] Down, down with.

ab initio. [L.] From the beginning.

à bon marché. [F.] Cheap; a good bargain.

ab origine. [L.] From the origin.

ab ovo. [L.] From the egg; from the beginning.

à cheval. [F.] On horseback.

addenda. [L.] Things to be added; list of additions.

ad finem. [L.] To the end.

ad hoc. [L.] To or with respect to this (object); said of a body elected or appointed for a definite work (as a school board for education).

ad infinitum. [L.] To infinity.

ad libitum. [L.] At pleasure; as much as one pleases.

ad nauseam. [L.] To the point of disgust or satiety.

ad rem. [L.] To the purpose; to the point.

adsum. [L.] I am present; here!

ad valorem. [L.] According to the value.

advocatus diaboli. [L.] Devil's advocate; a person chosen to dispute before the papal court the claims of a candidate for canonization.

æquo animo. [L.] With an equable mind; with equanimity.

ære perennius. [L.] More lasting than brass (or bronze).

affaire d'amour. [F.] A love affair.

affaire de cœur. [F.] An affair of the heart.

affaire d'honneur. [F.] An affair of honor; a duel.

a fortiori. [L.] With stronger reason.

Agnus Dei. [L.] Lamb of God.

à haute voix. [F.] Aloud.

à la belle étoile. [F.] Under the stars; in the open air.

à la bonne heure. [F.] In good time; very well.

à la carte. [F.] According to the bill of fare.

à la mode. [F.] According to the custom (or fashion).

al fresco. [It.] In the open air.

alter ego. [L.] Another self.

amende honorable. [F.] Satisfactory apology; reparation.

à merveille. [F.] Admirably; marvelously.

amour propre. [F.] Self-love; vanity.

ancien régime. [F.] The former order of things.

anglice. [NL.] In the English language or fashion.

anguis in herba. [L.] A snake in the grass; an unsuspected danger.

anno urbis conditæ. [L.] In the year (or from the time) of the founded city (Rome).

à outrance. [F.] To the utmost.

aperçu. [F.] A general sketch or survey.

à perte de vue. [F.] Till beyond one's view.

à peu près. [F.] Nearly.

à pied. [F.] On foot.

a posteriori. [L.] From effect to cause; empirical.

a priori. [L.] From cause to effect; presumptive.

arbiter elegantiarum. [L.] A judge or supreme authority in matters of taste.

arcana imperii. [L.] State secrets.

argumentum ad hominem. [L.] An argument to the individual man; *i.e.*, to his interests and prejudices.

arrière-pensée. [F.] Mental reservation.

ars est celare artem. [L.] It is true art to conceal art.

ars longa, vita brevis. [L.] Art is long, life is short.

au contraire. [F.] On the contrary.

au courant. [F.] Fully acquainted with matters.

au désespoir. [F.] In despair.

au fait. [F.] Well acquainted with; expert.

au fond. [F.] At bottom.

au reste. [F.] As for the rest; besides.

au revoir. [F.] Until we meet again.

autant d'hommes, autant d'avis. [F.] So many men, so many minds.

avant-propos. [F.] Preliminary matter; preface.

à votre santé! [F.] To your health!

ballon d'essai. [F.] A trial balloon; a device to test opinion.

bas bleu. [F.] A bluestocking; a literary woman.

beau idéal. [F.] The ideal of perfection.

beau monde. [F.] The world of fashion.

beaux esprits. [F.] Men of wit.

beaux yeux. [F.] Fine eyes; good looks.

bel esprit. [F.] A person of wit or genius; a brilliant mind.

ben trovato. [It.] Well found.

bête noire. [F.] A bugbear; a special aversion; *lit.*, black beast.

bis dat qui cito dat. [L.] He gives twice who gives quickly.

bona fides (bona fide). [L.] Good faith (in good faith).

bon ami. [F.] Good friend.

bon gré, mal gré. [F.] With good or ill grace; willing or unwilling.

bon jour. [F.] Good day; good morning.

bon mot. [F.] A witty saying.

bonne foi. [F.] Good faith.

bon naturel. [F.] Good nature.

bon soir. [F.] Good evening.

bon ton. [F.] Fashionable society; good style.

bon vivant. [F.] A lover of good living; a gourmet.

bon voyage! [F.] A good voyage or journey to you!

campo santo. [It.] A burying-ground; *lit.*, a holy field.

canaille. [F.] Rabble.

carpe diem. [L.] Enjoy the present day; improve the time.

casus belli. [L.] That which causes or justifies war.

catalogue raisonné. [F.] A catalogue arranged according to subjects.

cause célèbre. [F.] A celebrated or notorious case (in law).

caveat emptor. [L.] Let the purchaser beware (*i.e.*, he buys at his own risk).

cave canem. [L.] Beware of the dog.

cela va sans dire. [F.] That goes without saying; that is a matter of course.

c'est-à-dire. [F.] That is to say.

c'est égal. [F.] It's all one.

c'est magnifique, mais ce n'est pas la guerre. [F.] It is magnificent, but it is not war.

c'est autre chose. [F.] That's quite another thing.

ceteris paribus. [L.] Other things being equal.

chacun à son goût. [F.] Every one to his taste.

chef-d'œuvre. [F.] Masterpiece.

cherchez la femme. [F.] Look for the woman (who is at the bottom of the affair).

chère amie. [F.] A dear (female) friend.

chevalier d'industrie. [F.] One who lives by his wits; a swindler.

ci-gît. [F.] Here lies.

circa. [L.] About.

cogito, ergo sum. [L.] I think, therefore I exist.

comme il faut. [F.] As it should be; in good form.

compte rendu. [F.] An account rendered; a report.

con amore. [It.] With love; very earnestly.

confrère. [F.] Colleague.

contretemps. [F.] An unex-pected or untoward event; a hitch.

coram populo. [L.] Publicly; in public.

corpus delicti. [L.] The body of the crime.

corrigenda. [L.] Things to be corrected; a list of errors.

coup. [F.] A stroke.—**coup d'essai,** a first attempt.—**coup d'état,** a sudden decisive blow in politics; a stroke of policy.—**coup de grâce,** a finishing stroke.—**coup de main,** a sudden attack or en-terprise.—**coup de maître,** a master stroke.—**coup d'œil,** a rapid glance of the eye.—**coup de pied,** a kick.—**coup de soleil,** sunstroke.—**coup de théâtre,** a theatrical effect.

coûte que coûte. [F.] Cost what it may.

credat Judæus Apella. [L.] Let Apella, the superstitious Jew, believe it; I won't.

credo quia absurdum. [L.] I believe because it is absurd, or contrary to reason.

cui bono? [L.] For whose ad-vantage?

cul-de-sac. [F.] A blind alley (often used figuratively).

cum grano salis. [L.] With a grain of salt; with some al-lowance.

d'accord. [F.] In agreement.

débâcle. [F.] The break-up of ice in a river; *hence*, a general, confused rout.

de bonne grâce. [F.] With good grace; willingly.

de facto. [L.] In point of fact; actual or actually.

dégagé. [F.] Free; easy; unconstrained.

de gustibus non est disputandum. [L.] There is no disputing about tastes.

Dei gratia. [L.] By the grace of God.

de jure. [L.] From the law; by right.

delenda est Carthago. [L.] Carthage must be destroyed.

de mortuis nil nisi bonum. [L.] (Say) nothing but good of the dead.

dénoûement. [F.] The issue; the end of a plot.

de novo. [L.] Anew.

Deo gratias. [L.] Thanks to God.

de profundis. [L.] Out of the depths.

de rigueur. [F.] Indispensable; obligatory.

dernier ressort. [F.] A last resort.

de trop. [F.] Too much; more than is wanted; out of place.

deus ex machina. [L.] A god from a machine; used in reference to forced or unlikely events introduced in a drama, novel, etc., to resolve a difficult or awkward situation; derived from the use of deities in the ancient drama.

dies iræ. [L.] Day of wrath.

Dieu et mon droit. [F.] God and my right (British royal motto).

distingué. [F.] Distinguished; of elegant appearance.

dolce far niente. [It.] Sweet doing-nothing; sweet idleness.

Dominus vobiscum. [L.] The Lord be with you.

double entente (or, esp. in English, **entendre**). [F.] A double meaning; a play upon words.

dramatis personæ. [L.] Characters of the drama or play.

dulce et decorum est pro patria mori. [L.] It is sweet and glorious to die for one's country.

dum spiro, spero. [L.] While I breathe, I hope.

dum vivimus, vivamus. [L.] While we live, let us live.

ecce homo. [L.] Behold the man!

édition de luxe. [F.] A splendid and expensive edition of a book.

editio princeps. [L.] The first printed edition of a book.

ego et rex meus. [L.] I and my king.

élite. [F.] The best part; the pick.

emeritus. [L.] Retired or superannuated after long service.

en avant. [F.] Forward.

en déshabillé. [F.] In undress.

en effet. [F.] In effect; substantially; really.

en famille. [F.] With one's family; in a domestic state.

enfant gâté. [F.] A spoiled child.

enfants perdus. [F.] Lost children; a forlorn hope.

enfant terrible. [F.] A terrible child, *that is*, one who makes disconcerting remarks.

enfant trouvé. [F.] A foundling.

enfin. [F.] In short; at last; finally.

en masse. [F.] In a mass (or body).

en rapport. [F.] In harmony; in agreement.

en route. [F.] On the way.

en suite. [F.] In company; in a set.

entente cordiale. [F.] Cordial understanding, especially between two states.

entourage. [F.] Surroundings; friends, confidants, etc., closely associated with a person.

entre nous. [F.] Between ourselves.

en vérité. [F.] In truth; verily.

e pluribus unum. [L.] One out of many; one composed of many (motto of the United States).

errata. [L.] Errors; list of errors.

esprit de corps. [F.] The animating spirit of a collective body, as a regiment.

est modus in rebus. [L.] There is a medium in all things.

et cætera (or **et cetera**.) [L.] And the rest.

et id genus omne. [L.] And everything of the sort.

et tu, Brute! [L.] And thou also, Brutus!

eureka! [Gr.] I have found (it)!

Ewigkeit. [G.] Eternity.

ex cathedra. [L.] From the chair; with high authority.

excelsior. [L.] Higher, *that is,* taller, loftier.

exeunt omnes. [L.] All go out (or retire).

exit. [L.] He goes out.

ex nihilo nihil fit. [L.] Out of nothing, nothing comes.

ex officio. [L.] In virtue of (his) office.

ex parte. [L.] From one party or side.

ex pede Herculem. [L.] From the foot we recognize a Hercules; we judge of the whole from the specimen.

experto crede. [L.] Trust one who has had experience.

exposé. [F.] A statement; a recital.

ex post facto. [L.] After the deed is done; retrospective.

extra muros. [L.] Beyond the walls.

ex uno disce omnes. [L.] From one judge of the rest.

facile princeps. [L.] Easily pre-eminent; indisputably the first.

facilis est descensus Averni. [L.] The descent to Avernus (or hell) is easy.

façon de parler. [F.] Way of speaking.

fait accompli. [F.] A thing already done.

faux pas. [F.] A false step; a slip in behavior.

femme de chambre. [F.] A chambermaid; lady's maid.

festina lente. [L.] Hasten slowly.

feu de joie. [F.] A discharge of firearms as a sign of rejoicing.

fiat justitia, ruat cœlum. [L.] Let justice be done though the heavens should fall.

fiat lux. [L.] Let there be light.

fides Punica. [L.] Punic (or

Carthaginian) faith; treachery.

fidus Achates. [L.] Faithful Achates; a true friend.

fin de siècle. [F.] End of the (nineteenth) century.

finis coronat opus. [L.] The end crowns the work.

flagrante delicto. [L.] In the commission of the crime; red-handed.

fons et origo. [L.] The source and origin.

force majeure. [F.] Greater force or strength; overwhelming force; compulsion.

fortiter in re. [L.] With firmness in acting.

fortuna favet fortibus. [L.] Fortune favors the bold.

furor loquendi. [L.] A rage for speaking.

furor scribendi. [L.] A rage for writing.

gaucherie. [F.] Awkwardness.

gaudeamus igitur. [L.] So let us be joyful.

genius loci. [L.] The genius (*or* guardian spirit) of a place.

gens d'armes. [F.] Men at arms.

gloria in excelsis (Deo). [L.] Glory (to God) in the highest.

gloria Patri. [L.] Glory be to the Father.

goût. [F.] Taste; relish.

grâce à Dieu. [F.] Thanks to God.

habitué. [F.] One in the habit of frequenting a place.

hic et ubique. [L.] Here and everywhere.

hic jacet. [L.] Here lies.

hinc illæ lacrimæ. [L.] Hence these tears.

hodie mihi, cras tibi. [L.] Mine today; yours tomorrow.

hoi polloi. [Gr.] The many; the vulgar; the rabble.

homme d'esprit. [F.] A man of wit or genius.

homo sum; humani nihil a me alienum puto. [L.] I am a man; I count nothing human indifferent to me.

honi soit qui mal y pense. [O. F.] Shamed be he who thinks evil of it (motto of the Order of the Garter).

horribile dictu. [L.] Horrible to relate.

hors de combat. [F.] Out of the combat; disabled.

hors d'œuvre. [F.] A relish.

hôtel de ville. [F.] A town hall.

hôtel-Dieu. [F.] A hospital.

humanum est errare. [L.] To err is human.

ibidem. [L.] At the same place (in a book).

ich dien. [G.] I serve (motto of the Prince of Wales).

ici on parle français. [F.] French is spoken here.

ignotum per ignotius. [L.] The unknown (explained) by the still more unknown.

il n'y a pas de quoi. [F.] Don't mention it; it's not worth speaking of.

il n'y a que le premier pas qui coûte. [F.] It is only the first step that costs.

il penseroso. [It.] The pensive man.

impasse. [F.] A deadlock; an insurmountable difficulty.

impedimenta. [L.] Encumbrances; luggage; baggage.

in æternum. [L.] Forever.

in articulo mortis. [L.] At the point of death; in the last struggle.

index expurgatorius. [L.] A list of prohibited works.

in esse. [L.] In being; in actuality.

in extenso. [L.] At full length.

in extremis. [L.] At the point of death.

infra dignitatem. [L.] Below one's dignity.

in loco. [L.] In the place; in the natural (*or* proper) place.

in loco parentis. [L.] In the place of a parent.

in medias res. [L.] Into the midst of things.

in memoriam. [L.] To the memory of; in memory.

in nomine. [L.] In the name of.

in omnia paratus. [L.] Prepared for all things.

in perpetuum. [L.] Forever.

in posse. [L.] In possible existence; in possibility.

in præsenti. [L.] At the present moment.

in propria persona. [L.] In one's own person.

in puris naturalibus. [L.] Quite naked.

in re. [L.] In the matter of.

in rerum natura. [L.] In the nature of things.

in sæcula sæculorum. [L.] For ages on ages.

in situ. [L.] In its original position.

in statu quo. [L.] In the former state.

inter alia. [L.] Among other things.

inter nos. [L.] Between ourselves.

in terrorem. [L.] As a warning.

in toto. [L.] In the whole; entirely.

intra muros. [L.] Within the walls.

in transitu. [L.] In course of transit.

in vacuo. [L.] In empty space; in a vacuum.

in vino veritas. [L.] There is truth in wine; truth is told under the influence of liquor.

invita Minerva. [L.] Against the will of Minerva; without genius or natural abilities.

ipse dixit. [L.] He himself said it; a dogmatic saying or assertion.

ipsissima verba. [L.] The very words.

ipso facto. [L.] By that very fact.

ipso jure. [L.] By the law itself.

jacquerie. [F.] French peasantry; a revolt of peasants.

je ne sais quoi. [F.] I know not what; a something or other.

jeu de mots. [F.] A play on words; a pun.

jeu d'esprit. [F.] A display of wit; a witticism.

jeunesse dorée. [F.] Gilded youth; rich and fashionable young men.

jubilate Deo. [L.] Rejoice in God; be joyful in the Lord.

jure divino. [L.] By divine law.

jure humano. [L.] By human law.

juste milieu. [F.] The golden mean.

laborare est orare. [L.] To labor is to pray; work is worship.

labor omnia vincit. [L.] Labor conquers everything.

laissez-faire. [F.] Let alone; noninterference.

l'allegro. [It.] The merry man.

lapsus calami. [L.] A slip of the pen.

lapsus linguæ. [L.] A slip of the tongue.

lapsus memoriæ. [L.] A slip of the memory.

lares et penates. [L.] Household gods.

lasciate ogni speranza voi ch'entrate. [It.] All hope abandon ye who enter here (inscription on the entrance to the hell of Dante's Inferno).

laudator temporis acti. [L.] A praiser of past times.

laus Deo. [L.] Praise to God.

l'avenir. [F.] The future.

le beau monde. [F.] The fashionable world.

lebe wohl. [G.] Farewell.

la grand monarque. [F.] The great monarch; Louis XIV of France.

le pas. [F.] Precedence in place or rank.

le roi est mort, vive le roi! [F.] The king is dead, long live the king (his successor)!

le roy le veult. [Norm. F.] The king wills it; the formula used by the sovereign in assenting to a bill.

le roy s'avisera. [Norm. F.] The king will consider; the formula formerly used by the sovereign in rejecting a bill.

lèse-majesté. [F.] High treason.

l'état c'est moi. [F.] It is I who am the state.

le tout ensemble. [F.] The whole (taken) together.

lettre de cachet. [F.] A sealed letter containing private orders; a royal warrant.

lex non scripta. [L.] Unwritten law; common law.

lex scripta. [L.] Statute law.

l'homme propose, et Dieu dispose. [F.] Man proposes, and God disposes.

l'inconnu. [F.] The unknown.

littera scripta manet. [L.] The written word remains.

locum tenens. [L.] One occupying the place of another; a substitute.

longo intervallo. [L.] By or at a long interval.

lucus a non lucendo. [L.] Used as typical of an absurd derivation—*lucus*, a grove, having been derived by an old grammarian from *luceo*, to shine—"from not shining."

lusus naturæ. [L.] A sport or freak of nature.

ma chère. [F.] My dear (fem.).

ma foi. [F.] Upon my faith.

magna est veritas, et prevalebit. [L.] Truth is mighty, and will prevail.

magnum opus. [L.] A great work.

maison de santé. [F.] A private asylum *or* hospital.

maître d'hôtel. [F.] A house steward.

mala fide. [L.] With bad faith; treacherously.

mal-à-propos. [F.] Ill-timed; out of place.

mal de mer. [F.] Seasickness.

malgré nous. [F.] In spite of us.

mañana. [Sp.] Tomorrow.

mardi gras. [F.] Shrove Tuesday.

mare clausum. [L.] A closed sea; a sea belonging to a single nation.

mariage de convenance. [F.] Marriage from motives of interest rather than of love.

materfamilias. [L.] Mother of a family.

matériel. [F.] Baggage and munitions of an army; material equipment as opposed to men.

mauvaise honte. [F.] Bashfulness; shamefacedness.

mauvais goût. [F.] Bad taste.

mauvais sujet. [F.] A bad subject; a worthless scamp.

mea culpa. [L.] My fault; by my fault.

me judice. [L.] I being judge; in my opinion.

mêlée. [F.] A confused conflict.

memento mori. [L.] Remember that you must die; a reminder of death.

mens sana in corpore sano. [L.] A sound mind in a sound body.

mens sibi conscia recti. [L.] A mind conscious of rectitude.

meo periculo. [L.] At my own risk.

mésalliance. [F.] A bad match; marriage with one of a lower rank.

meum et tuum. [L.] Mine and thine.

mirabile dictu. [L.] Wonderful to relate.

mirabile visu. [L.] Wonderful to see.

mise en scène. [F.] Stage setting.

modus operandi. [L.] Manner of working.

modus vivendi. [L.] Manner of living; used of a temporary working agreement or compromise.

mon ami. [F.] My friend (masc.).

mon cher. [F.] My dear (masc.).

mont-de-piété. [F.] A public or municipal pawnshop.

monumentum ære perennius. [L.] A monument more lasting than brass.

more majorum. [L.] After the manner of our ancestors.

morituri te salutamus. [L.] We, about to die, salute thee:— said by the Roman gladiators to the emperor.

mot d'ordre. [F.] Watchword.

motu proprio. [L.] Of his own accord.

moyen âge. [F.] Middle Ages.

multum in parvo. [L.] Much in little.

mutatis mutandis. [L.] With the necessary changes.

natura non facit saltum. [L.] Nature does not make a leap.

née. [F.] Born; used in giving

the maiden name of a married woman.

négligé. [F.] Morning dress; an easy loose dress.

nemine contradicente. [L.] No one speaking in opposition; without opposition.

nemine dissentiente. [L.] No one dissenting; with a dissenting voice.

nemo me impune lacessit. [L.] No one assails me with impunity (motto of Scotland).

ne plus ultra. [L.] Nothing further; the uttermost point; perfection.

ne quid nimis. [L.] Avoid excess.

n'est-ce pas? [F.] Isn't that so?

nicht wahr? [G.] Isn't that so?

nil admirari. [L.] To be astonished at nothing.

nil desperandum. [L.] There is no reason for despair.

n'importe. [F] It matters not.

nisi Dominus, frustra. [L.] Except the Lord (build the house, they labor) in vain (that build it). Ps. cxxvii. (motto of Edinburgh).

noblesse oblige. [F.] Rank imposes obligations.

Noël. [F.] Christmas.

nolens volens. [L.] Unwilling or willing.

noli me tangere. [L.] Touch me not.

nom de guerre. [F.] A war name; a pseudonym; a pen name.

nom de plume. [F.] A pen name. (Incorrect for *Nom de guerre*.)

non Angli sed angeli. [L.] Not Angles but angels.

non compos mentis. [L.] Not of sound mind.

non est. [L.] He (*or* it) is not.

non est inventus. [L.] He has not been found.

non libet. [L.] It does not please (me).

non liquet. [L.] The case is not clear.

non multa, sed multum. [L.] Not many things, but much.

non nobis solum. [L.] Not for ourselves alone.

non omnis moriar. [L.] I shall not wholly die.

non sequitur. [L.] It does not follow.

nosce te ipsum. [L.] Know thyself.

nota bene. [L.] Note well; take notice.

Notre Dame. [F.] Our Lady.

nous avons changé tout cela. [F.] We have changed all that.

nous verrons. [F.] We shall see.

novus homo. [L.] A new man; one who has raised himself from obscurity.

nuance. [F.] Shade; tint.

nulla dies sine linea. [L.] Not a day without a line; no day without something done.

nunc aut nunquam. [L.] Now or never.

obiit. [L.] He (*or* she) died.

obiter dictum. [L.] A thing said by the way.

odi profanum vulgus. [L.] I loathe the profane rabble.

odium theologicum. [L.] The hatred of theologians.

œuvres. [F.] Works.

ohne Hast, ohne Rast. [G.] Without haste, without rest: —motto of Goethe.

omnia vincit amor. [L.] Love conquers all things.

on dit. [F.] They say.

onus probandi. [L.] The burden of proof.

operæ pretium est. [L.] It is worth while.

ora et labora. [L.] Pray and work.

ora pro nobis. [L.] Pray for us.

ore rotundo. [L.] With round full voice; well-turned speech.

O! si sic omnia. [L.] Oh, if all things (were) so; Oh, if he had always so spoken or acted.

O tempora! O mores! [L.] Alas for the times! Alas for the manners (or morals)!

otium cum dignitate. [L.] Ease with dignity.

ouï-dire. [F.] Hearsay.

ouvrage de longue haleine. [F.] A work of long breath; a long work or one which lasts.

pace. [L.] By leave of; not to give offence to.

palmam qui meruit ferat. [L.] Let him who has won the palm wear it.

pardonnez-moi. [F.] Pardon me; I beg your pardon.

par excellence. [F.] Pre-eminently.

par exemple. [F.] For example.

par hasard. [F.] By chance.

pari passu. [L.] With equal pace; side by side.

par nobile fratrum. [L.] A noble pair of brothers; two just alike.

parole d'honneur. [F.] Word of honor.

particeps criminis. [L.] An accomplice in a crime.

parti pris. [F.] Preconceived opinion.

parvenu. [L.] A person of low origin who has risen suddenly to wealth or position; an upstart.

pas. [F.] A step; precedence.

passim. [L.] Everywhere; throughout; in all parts of the book, chapter, etc.

pâté de foie gras. [F.] Goose-liver pie.

paterfamilias. [L.] Father of a family; head of a household.

pater patriæ. [L.] Father of his country.

pax vobiscum. [L.] Peace be with you.

peccavi. [L.] I have sinned (or been to blame).

peine forte et dure. [F.] Strong and severe punishment; a kind of judicial torture.

penchant. [F.] A strong liking.

pensée. [F.] A thought.

per. [L.] For; through; by.— **per contra.** On the contrary. —**per annum.** By the year; annually.—**per capita.** By heads; for each individual.— **per centum.** By the hundred. —**per diem.** By the day; daily.—**per fas et nefas.** Through right and wrong.— **per se.** By itself.

persona non grata. [L.] An unacceptable person.

peu à peu. [F.] Little by little.

peu de chose. [F.] A trifle.

pièce de résistance. [F.] A resistance piece; the main dish of a meal.

pied-à-terre. [F.] A resting-place; a temporary lodging.

pis aller. [F.] The worst or last shift.

place aux dames. [F.] Make room for the ladies.

plebs. [L.] The common people.

poco a poco. [It.] Little by little.

point d'appui. [F.] Point of support; basis.

pons asinorum. [L.] The asses' bridge; a name for the fifth proposition of the first book in Euclid.

poste restante. [F.] To remain in the post office till called for.

post hoc ergo propter hoc. [L.] After this, therefore, on account of this; subsequent to, therefore due to this—an illogical way of reasoning.

pour faire rire. [F.] To excite laughter.

pour le mérite. [F.] For merit.

pour passer le temps. [F.] To pass the time.

preux chevalier. [F.] A brave knight.

prima donna. [It.] First lady; the chief female singer in an opera, etc.

prima facie. [L.] At first view (or consideration).

primo. [L.] In the first place.

primum mobile. [L.] The source of motion; the mainspring.

principia, non homines. [L.] Principles, not men.

pro bono publico. [L.] For the good of the public.

procès-verbal. [F.] An authenticated minute or statement.

pro et contra. [L.] For and against.

profanum vulgus. [L.] The profane herd.

pro forma. [L.] For the sake of form.

pro patria. [L.] For our country.

pro rata. [L.] According to rate or proportion.

pro tanto. [L.] For so much; as far as it goes.

protégé. [F.] One under the protection of another.

Punica fides. [L.] Punic (or Carthaginian) faith; treachery.

qualis rex, talis grex. [L.] Like king, like people.

quand même. [F.] Even if; whatever may happen.

quantum libet. [L.] As much as you please.

quantum sufficit. [L.] As much as suffices.

quelque chose. [F.] Something; a trifle.

quid pro quo. [L.] Something in return; an equivalent.

quién sabe? [Sp.] Who knows?

quis custodiet ipsos custodes? [L.] Who shall guard the guards themselves?

qui s'excuse s'accuse. [F.] He who excuses himself accuses himself.

qui va là? [F.] Who goes there?

qui vive? [F.] Who lives? Who goes there? To be on the qui vive means to be alert or watchful.

quoad hoc. [L.] To this extent.

quoad sacra. [L.] As far as sacred things are concerned; for ecclesiastical purposes only.

quem Deus vult perdere, prius dementat. [L.] Those whom God wishes to destroy, he first makes mad.

quod erat demonstrandum. [L.] Which was to be proved or demonstrated.

quod vide. [L.] Which see.

quorum pars magna fui. [L.] Of which things, I was an important part.

quot homines, tot sententiæ. [L.] Many men, many minds.

raconteur. [F.] A teller of stories.

raison d'être. [F.] The reason for a thing's existence.

rapprochement. [F.] The act of bringing (*or* coming) together.

rara avis. [L.] A rare bird; a paragon.

réchauffé. [F.] *Lit.*, something warmed up; *hence*, old literary material worked up into a new form.

reductio ad absurdum. [L.] A reducing to the absurd; a method of proof in which a proposition is shown to be true by demonstrating the absurdity of its contradictions.

rencontre. [F.] An encounter; a hostile meeting.

répondez, s'il vous plaît. [F.] Please reply. *R. S. V. P.*

requiescat in pace. [L.] May he rest in peace.

res angusta domi. [L.] Narrow circumstances at home; poverty.

res gestæ. [L.] Things done; exploits; history.

respice finem. [L.] Look to the end.

résumé. [F.] A summary or abstract.

resurgam. [L.] I shall rise again.

revenons à nos moutons. [F.] Let us return to our sheep; let us return to our subject.

rôle. [F.] A character represented on the stage; also other similar meanings.

rouge et noir. [F.] Red and black; a game of chance.

rus in urbe. [L.] The country in town.

salle à manger. [F.] Dining room

sanctum sanctorum. [L.] Holy of holies.

sang froid. [F.] Coolness; indifference.

sans façon. [F.] Without ceremony.

sans peur et sans reproche. [F.] Without fear and without reproach.

sans souci. [F.] Without care.

sartor resartus. [L.] The patcher repatched; the tailor patched (*or* mended).

satis superque. [L.] Enough, and more than enough.

satis verborum. [L.] Enough of words; no more need be said.

sauve qui peut. [F.] Let him save himself who can.

savoir-faire. [F.] The knowing how to act; tact.

savoir-vivre. [F.] Good breeding; refined manners.

scripsit. [L.] Wrote (it).

sculpsit. [L.] Engraved (it).

secundum artem. [L.] According to art (*or* rule).

semper idem. [L.] Always the same.

semplice. [It.] Simple; plain.

seriatim. [L.] In a series; one by one.

sic itur ad astra. [L.] Such is the way to the stars, or to immortality.

sic passim. [L.] So here and there throughout; so everywhere.

sic transit gloria mundi. [L.] Thus passes away the glory of this world.

sicut ante. [L.] As before.

similia similibus curantur. [L.] Like things are cured by like.

simplex munditiis. [L.] Elegant in simplicity.

sine cura. [L.] Without charge or care.

sine die. [L.] Without a day being appointed.

sine qua non. [L.] Without which, not; something indispensable.

siste, viator. [L.] Stop, traveler.

sit tibi terra levis. [L.] Light lie the earth upon thee.

soi-disant. [F.] Self-styled.

sotto voce. [It.] In an undertone.

spero meliora. [L.] I hope for better things.

splendide mendax. [L.] Nobly untruthful; untrue for a good object.

sponte sua. [L.] Of one's (*or* its) own accord.

status quo. [L.] The state in which; the existing condition.

stet. [L.] Let it stand; do not delete.

suaviter in modo, fortiter in re. [L.] Gentle in manner, resolute in execution.

sub judice. [L.] Under consideration.

sub rosa. [L.] Under the rose; confidentially.

succès d'estime. [F.] A partial success, or one based on certain merits.

sui generis. [L.] Of its own peculiar kind; in a class by itself.

summum bonum. [L.] The chief good.

sunt lacrimæ rerum. [L.] There are tears for things; misfortunes call for tears.

suppressio veri. [L.] A suppression of the truth.

sursum corda. [L.] Lift up your hearts.

suum cuique. [L.] Let every one have his own.

tableau vivant. [F.] A living picture; the representation of some scene by a group of persons.

table d'hôte. [F.] A public dinner at an inn or hotel.

tabula rasa. [L.] A smooth or blank tablet.

tant mieux. [F.] So much the better.

tant pis. [F.] So much the worse.

te Deum laudamus. [L.] We praise Thee, O God (*or rather*, as God).

te judice. [L.] You being the judge.

tempus fugit. [L.] Time flies.

terminus ad quem. [L.] The term (or limit) to which.

terminus a quo. [L.] The term (or limit) from which.

terra firma. [L.] Solid earth; a secure foothold.

terra incognita. [L.] An unknown country.

tertium quid. [L.] A third something; a nondescript.

tiers état. [F.] The third estate; the commons.

timeo Danaos et dona ferentes. [L.] I fear the Greeks, even when they bring gifts.

tot homines, quot sententiæ. [L.] So many men, so many minds.

toto cælo. [L.] By the whole heavens; diametrically opposite.

tour de force. [F.] A notable feat of strength or skill.

tout à fait. [F.] Wholly; entirely.

tout à l'heure. [F.] Instantly.

tout au contraire. [F.] On the contrary.

tout de suite. [F.] Immediately.

tout ensemble. [F.] The whole taken together.

tu quoque. [L.] You also.

ubi supra. [L.] Where above mentioned.

ultima Thule. [L.] Most distant Thule; utmost limit.

una voce. [L.] With one voice; unanimously.

und so weiter. [G.] And so forth.

urbi et orbi. [L.] To the city and to the world.

utile dulci. [L.] The useful with the agreeable.

ut infra. [L.] As below.

ut supra. As above.

væ victis. [L.] Woe to the vanquished.

vale. [L.] Farewell.

valet de chambre. [F.] A personal attendant; a body servant.

varium et mutabile semper femina. [L.] Woman is ever a changeful and capricious thing.

veni, vidi, vici. [L.] I came, I saw, I conquered. (Cæsar's message to the senate when he conquered Pharnaces, king of Pontus.)

verbatim et literatim. [L.] Word for word and letter for letter.

verbum sat sapienti. [L.] A word is enough for a wise man.

via, veritas, vita. [L.] The way, the truth, the life.

vice versa. [L.] The terms of the case being interchanged or reversed; conversely.

videlicet. [L.] Namely (lit., one may see).

vide ut supra. [L.] See what is stated above.

vi et armis. [L.] By force and arms; by main force.

vincit qui se vincit. [L.] He conquers who conquers himself.

virginibus puerisque. [L.] For maidens and boys.

vis a tergo. [L.] A force from behind.

vis-à-vis. [F.] Opposite; face to face.

vis inertiæ. [L.] The power of

inertia; resistance to force applied.

vis medicatrix naturæ. [L.] The healing power of nature.

vis vitæ. [L.] Living force; energy.

vivat regina (rex)! [L.] Long live the queen (king)!

viva voce. [L.] By the living voice; orally.

vive la bagatelle! [F.] Long live trifles (or frivolity)!

vive le roi! [F.] Long live the king!

vogue la galère! [F.] Row the galley; come what may!

voilà. [F.] Behold; there is; there are.

voilà tout. [F.] That's all.

vox et præterea nihil. [L.] A voice and nothing more; sound but no sense.

vox populi, vox Dei. [L.] The voice of the people is the voice of God.

vraisemblance. [F.] Probability; apparent truth.

vulgo. [L.] Commonly.

Wanderjahr. [G.] Year of wandering.

Wanderlust. [G.] Passion for traveling (or wandering).

Weltanschauung. [G.] World view; theory or conception of life or of the world in all its aspects.

Weltschmerz. [G.] World sorrow; sentimental pessimism.

Zeitgeist. [G.] Time-spirit; spirit of the age.

zum Beispiel. [G.] For example.

ABBREVIATIONS USED
IN WRITING AND PRINTING

A

a. About; acre; adjective; after-noon; answer; are (metric system); at.

A. Academician; Academy; America; American; artillery.

A. A. A. Amateur Athletic Association.

A. A. A. S. American Association for the Advancement of Science.

A. A. of A. Automobile Association of America.

A. A. U. Amateur Athletic Union.

ab. About.

A. B. Artium Baccalaureus (L., Bachelor of Arts); (also l. c.) able-bodied (seaman).

abbr., or abbrev. Abbreviated; abbreviation.

abd. Abdicated.

A. B. F. M. American Board of Foreign Missions.

abl. Ablative.

Abp. Archbishop.

abr. Abridged; abridgment.

abs. Absolutely; abstract.

A. B. S. American Bible Society.

A. C. Alpine Club; ambulance corps; ante Christum (L., before Christ); Army Corps.

Acad. Academy.

acc. Acceptance; account; accusative.

acct. Account.

ad. (*pl.* ads.) Advertisement.

a. d. After date; ante diem (L., before the day).

A. D. Anno Domini (L., in the year of our Lord).

A. D. C. Aid-de-camp; aide-de-camp.

ad fin. Ad finem (L., at the end).

ad inf. Ad infinitum (L., to infinity).

ad int. Ad interim (L., in the meantime).

adj. Adjective.

Adj., or Adjt. Adjutant.

Adj. Gen. Adjutant General.

ad. lib. Ad libitum (L., at pleasure).

Adm. Admiral; Admiralty.

admix. Administratrix.

admr. Administrator.

admx. Administratrix.

adv. Ad valorem; adverb; advocate.

Adv. Advent.

Adv. Gd. Advance guard.

advt. Advertisement.

æ., æt., ætat. Ætatis (L., of age, aged).

A. E. F. American Expeditionary Forces.

AF. or A.-F. Anglo-French.

457

aff. Affectionate; affirmative; affirming.

afft. Affidavit.

Afr. Africa; African.

A. G. Adjutant General; Advance guard; Attorney-general.

agr., *or* **agric.** Agriculture; agricultural.

agt. Agent.

A. H. Anno Hegiræ (L., in the year of the Hegira).

A. H. C. Army Hospital Corps.

A. I. American Institute.

Ala. Alabama.

A. L. A. American Library Association; Automobile Legal Association.

ald., *or* **aldm.** Alderman.

Alex. Alexander.

alg. Algebra.

alt. Alternate; altitude; alto.

Alta. Alberta (Canada).

Am. America; American; ammunition.

a. m. Ante meridiem (L., before noon).

A. M. Anno mundi (L., in the year of the world); Annus Mirabilis (L., the Wonderful Year, i.e., 1666); Artium Magister (L., Master of Arts).

A. M. D. Army Medical Department.

Amer. America; American.

A. M. S. Army Medical Staff.

amt. Amount.

anal. Analogous; analogy; analysis; analytic.

anat. Anatomy.

anc. Ancient; anciently.

anon. Anonymous.

ans. Answer.

ant. Antonym; antiquarian.

Ant. Anthony; Antigua.

anthrop. Anthropology; anthropological.

antiq. Antiquities; antiquarian.

A. N. Z. A. C., *or* **Anzac.** Australian and New Zealand Army Corps.

A. O. Army order.

A. O. C. Army Ordnance Corps.

A. O. D. Army Ordnance Department.

A. O. F. Ancient Order of Foresters.

A. O. H. Ancient Order of Hibernians.

aor. Aorist.

A. P. C. Army Pay Corps.

A. P. D. Army Pay Department.

Apoc. Apocalypse; Apocrypha; Apocryphal.

app. Appendix; appointed.

App. Apostles.

approx. Approximately.

Apr. April.

aq., **Aq.** Aqua (L., water).

Ar. Arabian; Arabic.

A. R. Anno regni (L., in the year of the reign); Army Regulations.

A. R. A. Associate of the Royal Academy (of Arts, London).

Arab. Arabian; Arabic.

arch. Archaic; archaism; archery; archipelago; architect; architecture.

Arch. Archibald.

archaeol. Archæology.

Archd. Archdeacon; Archduke.

arith. Arithmetic.

Ariz. Arizona.

Ark. Arkansas.

Arm. Armenian.

arr. Arranged; arrived; arrivals.

art. Article; artificial; artillery; artist.

Art. *or* **A.** Artillery.

AS., *or* **A.-S.** Anglo-Saxon.

A. S. C. Army Service Corps; Army Staff Corps (British Army).

A. S. C. E. American Society of Civil Engineers.

A. S. M. E. American Society of Mechanical Engineers.

assd. Assigned.

assn. Association.

assoc. Associate; association.

asst. Assistant.

A. S. S. U. American Sunday School Union.

astr., astron. Astronomer; astronomy.

astrol. Astrologer; astrology.

Atl. Atlantic.

att., atty. Attorney.

at. wt. Atomic weight.

A. U. C. Ab urbe condita (L., from the founding of the city; i.e., Rome, about 753 B. C.).

Aug. August.

Aus., Aust. Austria; Austrian.

Austral. Australasia; Australia.

Auth. Ver. Authorized Version.

auxil. Auxiliary.

av. Avenue; average.

A. V. Artillery Volunteers; Authorized Version.

A. V. C. Army Veterinary Corps.

A. V. D. Army Veterinary Department.

ave. Avenue.

A. W. L. Absent with Leave.

A. W. O. L. Absent without Leave.

ax. Axiom.

az. Azure.

B

b. Base; bass; battery; bay; book; born; brother.

B. A. Bachelor of Arts; British Academy; British America.

B. Agr. Bachelor of Agriculture.

bal. Balance.

bap. Baptized.

Bapt. Baptist.

bar. Barometer; barometric; barrel.

Barb. Barbados.

barr. Barrister.

Bart. Baronet.

bat., batt., *or* **bn.** Battalion.

batt. *or* **b.** Battery.

bbl. (*pl.* **bbls.**) Barrel.

B. C. Before Christ; British Columbia.

B. C. L. Bachelor of Civil Law.

bd. Board; bond; bound.

B. D. Bachelor of Divinity.

bdl. (*pl* **bdls.**) Bundle.

b. e. Bill of exchange.

B. E. F. British Expeditionary Forces.

Belg. Belgian; Belgium.

Benj. Benjamin.

B. ès L. Bachelier ès Lettres (F. Bachelor of Letters).

bg. (*pl.* **bgs.**) Bag.

b. h. p. Brake horse power.

B. I. British India.

Bib. Bible; Biblical.

biog. Biographer; biography.

biol. Biologist; biology.

bk. Bank; book.

bkg. Banking.

bkt. (*pl.* **bkts.**) Basket.

b. l. Bill of lading; breech-loading.

B. L. Bachelor of Laws.

bldg. (*pl.* **bldgs.**) Building.

ABBREVIATIONS

B. Litt. Bachelor of Literature, *or* of Letters.

B. L. R. Breech-loading rifle.

b. m. Board measure.

B. M. Bachelor of Medicine; Brigade Major.

B. Mus. Bachelor of Music.

b. o. Branch office; buyer's option.

Boh. Bohemia; Bohemian.

Bol. Bolivia.

bor. Borough.

bot. Botanical; botanist; botany.

Bp. Bishop.

b. p. Below proof; bill of parcels; bills payable.

B. P. O. E. Benevolent and Protective Order of Elks.

br. Brig; brother; brown.

Br. British.

Br. Am. British America.

b. rec. Bills receivable.

brig. Brigade; brigadier.

Brit. Britain; British.

bro. (*pl.* bros.) Brother.

b. s. Balance sheet; bill of sale.

B. S. Bachelor of Surgery.

B. Sc. Bachelor of Science.

bu., bus. Bushel; bushels.

bul. Bulletin.

Bulg. Bulgaria; Bulgarian.

B. V. M. Beata Virgo Maria (L., Blessed Virgin Mary).

Bvt. Brevet; breveted.

Brig. Gen. Brigadier General.

C

c. Carton; cathode; cent; centime; centimeter; century; chapter, child; circa (L., about); cost; cubic; current.

C. Cape; Catholic; centigrade (thermometer); Chancellor; Congress; Conservative; Consul; Corps; Court.

C. A. Chartered Accountant; Chief Accountant; Confederate Army; Controller of Accounts; Court of Appeal.

cal. Calendar; calends; calorie.

Calif. California.

Cam., Camb. Cambridge.

Can. Canada; Canadian.

Cant. Canterbury, Canticles.

Cantab. Cantabrigiensis (L., of Cambridge).

Cantuar. Cantuaria (LL., Canterbury); Cantuariensis (LL., of Canterbury).

cap. Capital; capitalize; capitulum (L., chapter); captain.

Capt. Captain.

car. Carat; carpentry.

Card. Cardinal.

cash. Cashier.

cat. Catalogue; catechism.

cath. Cathedral.

Cath. Catherine; Catholic.

cav. Cavalry.

C. B. Cape Breton; Cavalry Brigade; Chief Baron; Common Bench; Companion of the Bath; Confined to Barracks.

cc. Cubic centimeter, *or* centimeters.

c. c. Compte courant (F., account current); cubic centimeter, *or* centimeters.

C. C. Caius College (Cambridge, Eng.); Circuit Court; Civil Court; County Clerk.

C. C. D. Commander of Coast Defenses.

C. C. P. Court of Common Pleas.

c. d. v. Carte de visite.
C. E. Church of England; Civil Engineer; Corps of Engineers.
cel. Celebrated.
Celt. Celtic.
cen. Central; century.
cent. Centigrade; central; century; centum.
cert. Certificate; certify.
certif. Certificate; certificated.
cf. Confer (i.e., compare).
C. F. A. Chief of Field Artillery.
c. f. & i. *or* **c. f. i.** Cost, freight, and insurance.
cg. Centigram.
C. G. Captain General; Captain of the Guard; Coast Guard; Commanding General; Consul General.
C. G. H. Cape of Good Hope.
C. G. S. *or* **c. g. s.** Centimeter-gram-second (system of units); Chief of General Staff in the field.
ch. Chapter; chief; child; church.
Ch. Chancery; Charles; China; Church.
C. H. Captain of the Horse; Courthouse; Customhouse.
chanc. Chancellor; chancery.
chap. Chaplain; chapter.
Chas. Charles.
chem. Chemical; chemist; chemistry.
Chin. China; Chinese.
Ch. J. Chief Justice.
Chr. Christ; Christian; Christopher.
chron. Chronological; chronology.
Chron. Chronicles.
chs. Chapters.

c. i. f. Cost, insurance, and freight.
circ. Circa. circiter, circum (L., about).
cit. Citation, cited; citizen.
civ. Civil; civilian.
C. J. Chief Justice.
cl. Centiliter; class; clause; clergyman; cloth.
class. Classic; classical; classification.
cld. Cleared; colored.
clk. Clerk.
cm. Centimeter.
cml. Commercial.
C. M. Certificated Master; common meter; Corresponding Member; court-martial.
C. M. G. Companion of St. Michael and St. George.
cml. Commercial.
Co. Company; county.
c. o. Care of; carried over.
C. O. Colonial Office; Commanding Officer; Crown Office.
coad. Coadjutor.
C. O. D. Cash, or collect, on delivery.
C. of S. Chief of Staff.
cog. Cognate.
col. College; collegiate; colonial; colony; colored; column.
Col. Colonel; Colossians.
coll. Colleague; collection; collector; college.
collat. Collateral; collaterally.
colloq. Colloquial; colloquially.
Colo. Colorado.
Col. Sergt. Color Sergeant.
com. Comedy; commentary; commerce; common; commonly; communication.
Com. Commander; Commis-

sion; Commissioner; Committee; Commodore.

comdg. Commanding.

Comdr. Commander.

Comdt. Commandant.

comp. Compare; comparative; composer; compositor; compound; comprising.

Com. Ver. Common Version.

con. Contra (L., against).

Cong. Congregational; Congress; Congressional.

conj. Conjunction.

Conn. Connecticut.

const. Constable; constitution.

cont. Containing; contents; continent; continue; continued.

contemp. Contemporary.

contr. Contracted; contraction; contrary.

cor. Corner; cornet; corrected; correction; correlative; correspondent; corresponding.

Cor. Corinthians.

Corp. Corporal.

cos. Cosine.

cosec. Cosecant.

cot. Cotangent.

cp. Compare.

c. p. Candle power; chemically pure.

C. P. Common Pleas; Common Prayer; Court of Probate.

C. P. A. Certified public accountant.

cps. Coupons.

C. P. S. Clerk of Petty Sessions.

cr. Created; credit; creditor; crown.

cresc. Crescendo.

C. S. Christian Science; Civil Service.

C. S. A. Confederate States Army; Confederate States of America.

C. S. C. Conspicuous Service Cross.

C. S. I. Companion of the Star of India (Brit. order).

C. S. N. Confederate States Navy.

C. S. O. Chief Signal Officer.

ct. Cent; county

cts. Cents; centimes.

cu., cub. Cubic.

cur. Currency; current.

C. V. Common Version.

c. w. o. Cash with order.

cwt. Hundredweight *or* hundredweights.

cyc., *or* **cyclo.** Cyclopedia; cyclopedic.

C. in C. Commander in Chief.

D

d. Date; daughter; day; dead; degree; denarius, *or* denarii (L., penny *or* pence); deputy; died; dime; dollar; dose.

D. Democrat; department; Deus (L., God); Duke; Dutch.

Dan. Danish, Daniel.

D. A. R. Daughters of the American Revolution.

dat. Dative.

dau. Daughter.

D. C. Da capo (It., from the beginning); Dental Corps; District Court; District of Columbia.

D. C. L. Doctor of Civil Law.

d. d. Days after date.

D. D. Divinitatis Doctor (L., Doctor of Divinity).

D. D. S. Doctor of Dental Surgery.

Dea. Deacon.

deb. Debenture.

dec. Declension; declination; decorative.

Dec. December.

def. Defendant; definition.

deft. Defendant.

deg. Degree.

del. Delegate; delineavit (L., he, *or* she, drew it).

Del. Delaware.

Dem. Democrat; Democratic.

Den. Denmark.

dep. Department; departs; deponent; deputy.

dept. Department; deponent.

der., *or* **deriv.** Derivation; derivative; derived.

Deut. Deuteronomy.

D. F. Dean of the Faculty; Defensor Fidei (L., Defender of the Faith).

dft. Defendant; draft.

dg. Decigram.

D. G. Dei gratia (L., by the grace of God); Deo gratias (L., thanks to God); Director General; Dragoon Guards.

diam. Diameter.

dict. Dictator; dictionary.

dim., *or* **dimin.** Diminuendo; diminutive.

dis. Discipline; discount.

disc. Discount; discovered.

disct. Discount.

disp. Dispensatory.

dist. Distant; distinguished; district.

div. Divide; divided; dividend; divine; division; divisor.

dl. Deciliter.

D. Lit. Doctor of Literature.

D. L. O. Dead Letter Office.

dm. Decimeter.

do. Ditto.

dol. (*pl.* dols.) Dollar; dollars.

dom. Domestic; dominion.

D. O. M. Deo Optimo Maximo (L., to God, the Best, the Greatest).

D. O. R. C. Dental Officers' Reserve Corps.

dow. Dowager.

doz. Dozen; dozens.

dpt. Department; deponent.

dr. Dram; drawer.

Dr. Debtor; doctor.

dram. pers. Dramatis personæ.

d. s. Dal segno (It., from the sign: — *musical direction*); day's sight; days after sight.

D. S. Director of Supplies.

D. Sc. Doctor of Science.

D. S. C. Distinquished Service Cross.

D. S. O. Distinquished Service Order (British, Army and Navy).

D T Double Time; "rush." (Signal)

D. T.'s. Delirium tremens. *Colloq.*

Du. Dutch.

D. V. Deo volente (L., God willing).

D. V. M. Doctor of Veterinary Medicine.

D. V. S. Director of Veterinary Services.

dwt. Pennyweight *or* pennyweights.

E

E. Earl; Earth; East; Eastern; Engineer; English.

ea. Each.

Ebor. Eboracum (L., York); Eboracensis (L., of York).

E. C. Eastern Central (Postal District, London); Established Church.

eccl., *or* eccles. Ecclesiastical.

Eccl., *or* Eccles. Ecclesiastes.

Ecclus. Ecclesiasticus.

Ecua. Ecuador.

ed. Edition; editor.

E. D. Eastern Department; Extra Duty.

Edin. Edinburgh.

edit. Edition.

Edw. Edward.

E. E. Early English; Electrical Engineer; errors expected.

E. E. & M. P. Envoy Extraordinary and Minister Plenipotentiary.

Eg. Egypt; Egyptian.

e. g. Exempli gratia (L., for example).

E. I. East India; East Indies.

elec. Electrical; electrician; electricity.

Eliz. Elizabeth; Elizabethan.

Em. Emmanuel; Emily; Emma.

E. M. F. Electromotive force.

Emp. Emperor; Empress.

ency., *or* encyc. Encyclopedia.

ENE. East-northeast.

eng. Engineer; engraving.

Eng. England; English.

engin. Engineer; engineering.

entom. Entomology.

E. O. Engineer Officer.

E. O. R. C. Engineer Officers' Reserve Corps.

Eph. Ephesians; Ephraim.

Epiph. Epiphany.

Epis., *or* Episc. Episcopal.

eq. Equal; equivalent.

ESE. East-southeast.

esp., *or* espec. Especially.

Esq. Esquire.

est., *or* estab. Established.

Esth. Esther.

et al. Et alibi (L., and elsewhere); et alii (L., and others).

etc. Et cetera (L., and others, and so forth).

et seq. Et sequens (L., and the following).

et sqq. Et sequentes (L., and the following), *masc. & fem. pl.*, or sequentia, *neut. pl.*

etym., *or* etymol. Etymology.

ex. Examined; example; excursion; executed; executive; export; extract.

ex div. Without dividend.

Exod. Exodus.

exp. Export; express.

Expl. Explosives.

exr. Executor.

exrx. Executrix.

ext. External; extinct; extra; extract.

Ezek. Ezekiel.

F

f. Farthing; fathom; feminine; fine; flower; folio; foot; forte; franc.

F. Fahrenheit; French.

F. A. Field Artillery.

fac. Facsimile.

Fahr. Fahrenheit.

F. A. I. A. Fellow of the American Institute of Architects.

fam. Familiar; family.

F. A. M. Free and Accepted Masons.

far. Farriery; farthing.

F. A. R. C. Field Artillery Reserve Corps.

F. B. A. Fellow of the British Academy (scientific society).

F. C. Free Church (of Scotland).

fcap. Foolscap.

fcp. Foolscap.

F. D. Fidei Defensor (L., Defender of the Faith).

Feb. February.

fem. Feminine.

ff. Folios; following (pages); fortissimo.

F. F. V. First Families of Virginia.

f. i. For instance.

fict. Fiction.

fig. Figurative; figuratively; figure.

Fin. Finland; Finnish.

fir. Firkin; firkins.

fl. Florin; flourished; fluid.

Fl. Flanders; Flemish.

Fla. Florida.

Flem. Flemish.

fm. Fathom.

F. M. Field Marshal; Foreign Mission.

fo. Folio.

F. O. Field Officer; Field Order.

f. o. b. Free on board.

fol. Folio; following.

for. Foreign.

fort. Fortification.

fr. Fragment; franc; from.

Fr. Father; France; Frau; French; Friar.

Fred. Frederick.

freq. Frequent; frequentative.

F. R. G. S. Fellow of the Royal Geographical Society (London).

Fri. Friday.

F. R. S. Fellow of the Royal Society (London).

frs. Francs.

F. S. Field Service.

ft. Feet; foot; fort; fortified.

fur. Furlong; further.

fut. Future.

G

g. Gauge; genitive; gram; guide; guinea or guineas; gulf.

G. German.

Ga. Georgia.

G. A. General Assembly.

gal. (*pl.* gals.) Gallon.

Gal. Galatians.

G. A. R. Grand Army of the Republic.

gaz. Gazette; gazetteer.

G. B. Great Britain.

G. B. & I. Great Britain and Ireland.

G. C. Grand Chancellor (*or* Chaplain, Chapter, Council, Conclave, etc.).

g. c. d. Greatest common divisor.

g. c. m. Greatest common measure.

G. C. M. General Court Martial.

Gd. Guard.

gen. Gender; general; generic; genitive; genus.

Gen. General; Genesis.

gent. Gentleman.

Geo. George.

geog. Geographer; geographic; geographical; geography.

geol. Geologic; geological; geologist; geology.

geom. Geometry.

ger. Gerund.

Ger. German; Germany.

G. H. Q. General Headquarters.

gi. Gill; gills.

G. L. Grand Lodge.

gm. Gram.

G. M. Grand Master.

G. O. General order.

G. O. C. General Officer Commanding.

gov. Government; governor.

Gov. Gen. Governor General.

govt. Government.

G. P. Gloria Patri (L., Glory to the Father); Graduate in Pharmacy.

G. P. O. General Post Office.

gr. Grain; grand; great; gross.

Gr. Greece; Greek; Grecian.

gram. Grammar.

Gr. Br., Gr. Brit. Great Britain.

G. S. General Secretary; General Service; General Staff; Grand Scribe; Grand Secretary.

gt. Gilt; great; gutta (L., drop).

gtt. Guttæ (L., drops).

gun. Gunnery.

H

h. Harbor; hard; hardness; height; high; hour; husband.

H., HQ., or Hqrs. Headquarters.

ha. Hectare.

H. A. Horse Artillery.

Hab. Habakkuk.

Hag. Haggai.

H. B. C. Hudson's Bay Company.

H. B. M. His (or Her) Britannic Majesty.

H. C. Heralds' College, House of Commons.

h. c. f. Highest common factor.

H. E. High explosive; His Eminence; His Excellency.

Heb. Hebrew; Hebrews.

hectol. Hectoliter.

hectom. Hectometer.

H. E. I. C. Honorable East India Company.

her. Heraldry.

hg. Hectogram; heliogram.

H. G. His (or Her) Grace; Horse Guards, High German.

H. H. His (or Her) Highness; His Holiness (the Pope).

hhd. Hogshead; hogsheads.

H. I. H. His (or Her) Imperial Highness.

H. I. M. His (or Her) Imperial Majesty.

Hind. Hindustan; Hindustani.

hist. Historian; historical; history.

H. J. Hic jacet (L., here lies).

hl. Hectoliter.

H. L. House of Lords.

hm. Hectometer.

H. M. His (or Her) Majesty.

H. M. S. His (or Her) Majesty's Service; or Ship.

ho. House.

Hon. Honorable; honorary.

hort. Horticulture.

Hos. Hosea.

Hosp. Hospital.

H. P., or h. p. Half pay; high pressure; horse power.

hr. (pl. hrs.) Hour.

H. R. House of Representatives.

H. R. E. Holy Roman Emperor, or Empire.

H. R. H. His (or Her) Royal Highness.

H. S. H. His (or Her) Serene Highness.

ht. Height.

Hun., Hung. Hungarian; Hungary.

H. W. M. High-water mark.
Hy. Henry.
hyd. Hydrostatics.
hyp. Hypothesis; hypothetical.

I

I. Imperator (L., Emperor); island.
I. A. Indian Army.
ib., *or* **ibid.** Ibidem (L., in the same place).
Ice., Icel. Iceland; Icelandic.
id. Idem (L., the same).
I. D. R. Infantry Drill Regulations.
i. e. Id est. (L., that is).
i. h. p. Indicated horse power.
IHS. A symbol representing Greek IH (ΣΟΤ) Σ Jesus.
ill., illus., illust. Illustrated; illustration.
Ill. Illinois.
imp. Imparted; imperative; imperfect; imperial; impersonal; imported; importer.
in. (*pl.* **ins.**) Inch.
inc. Including; inclusive; incorporated; increase.
incl. Including; inclusive.
incog. Incognito.
incor. Incorporated.
ind. Independent; indicative; indigo.
Ind. India; Indian; Indiana.
inf. Infantry; infinitive.
I. N. R. I. Iesus Nazarenus, Rex Iudæorum (L., Jesus of Nazareth, King of the Jews).
ins. Inches; inscribed; inspector; insurance.
insp. Inspector.
inst. Instant; institute; institution.

int. Interest; interior; interjection; internal; international; interpreter; intransitive.
interj. Interjection.
intrans. Intransitive.
in trans. In transitu (L., on the way).
introd. Introduction; introductory.
I. O. O. F. Independent Order of Odd Fellows.
I. O. U. I owe you.
I R. Inland Revenue; Internal Revenue.
I. R. C Infantry Reserve Corps.
Ire. Ireland.
is. Island; isle.
Isa. Isaiah.
isl. Island; isle.
It. Italian; Italy.
ital. Italic, italics.
Ital. Italian; Italy.
I. W. Isle of Wight.

J

J. Judge: Justice.
J. A. Judge Advocate.
Jam. Jamaica.
Jan. January.
Jap. Japan; Japanese.
Jas. James.
Jav. Javanese.
J. C. Jesus Christ; Julius Cæsar; jurisconsult.
J. C. D. Juris Civilis Doctor (L., Doctor of Civil Law).
Jer. Jeremiah.
JJ. Justices.
Jno. John.
Jon., Jona. Jonathan.
Jos. Joseph.
Josh. Joshua.
Jour. Journal; journeyman

J. P. Justice of the Peace.
Jr. Junior.
Judg. Judges.
Jun., or jun. Junior.
Junc. Junction.
jus., just. Justice.

K

K. King; Kings; Knight.
Kans. Kansas
K. B. King's Bench.
K. C. Knights of Columbus.
K. C. B. Knight Commander of the Bath (Brit. order).
kg. Kilogram.
K. G. Knight of the Garter.
Ki. Kings.
kilom. Kilometer.
K. K. K. Ku-Klux Klan.
kl. Kiloliter.
km. Kilometer; kingdom.
K. M. Knight of Malta (European religious order).
knt. Knight.
K. O. Commanding Officer.
K. P. Kitchen Police; Knight or Knights of Pythias.
K. T. Knight Templar.
Ky. Kentucky.

L

l. Lake; land; latitude; leaf; league; left; length; libra (L., a pound); line; link; liter.
L. Lady; Latin; Law; Liber (L., book); Liberal; Low.
La. Louisana.
Lab. Labrador.
Lam. Lamentations.
lat. Latitude.
Lat. Latin.
lb. (pl. lbs.) Libra or libræ (L., pound or pounds).

l.c. Loco citato (L., in the place cited); lower case.
L. C. Lord Chamberlain; Lord Chancellor.
L/C Letter of Credit.
L. C. J. Lord Chief Justice.
l. c. m. Least common multiple.
Ld., ld. Lord.
L. D. Lady Day; (or LD.) Low Dutch.
Ldp. Lordship.
lea. League.
leg. Legal; legate; legato; legislative; legislature.
Lev. Leviticus.
LG., or L. G. Low German.
LGr., or L. Gr. Low Greek.
l. h. Left hand.
L. H. A. Lord High Admiral.
L. I. Light Infantry; Long Island.
lib. Liber (L., book); librarian; library.
Lieut. or Lt. Lieutenant.
lin. Lineal; linear.
liq. Liquid; liquor.
lit. Liter; literal; literally; literary; literature.
Lit. D. Literarum Doctor (L., Doctor of Letters).
Lith. Lithuanian.
Litt. D. Litterarum Doctor (L., Doctor of Letters).
LL., or L. L. Late Latin; Low Latin.
L. L. Lord Lieutenant.
LL. B. Legum Baccalaureus (L., Bachelor of Laws).
LL. D. Legum Doctor (L., Doctor of Laws).
log. Logarithm.
lon., or long. Longitude.
L. S. Licentiate in Surgery.
L. S. D., or £. s. d., or l. s. d.

ABBREVIATIONS

Libræ, solidi, denarii (L., pounds, shillings, pence).

Lt. *or* **Lieut.** Lieutenant.

l. t. Long ton.

M

m. Male; manual; married; masculine; measure; medicine; medium; meridian; meter; middle; mile; mill; minute; month; moon; morning; mountain.

M. Majesty; Manitoba; Marshal; Marquis; Monsieur.

M. A. Magister Artium (L., Master of Arts); Military Academy.

Mac., Macc. Maccabees.

mach. Machinery.

Mad. Madam.

mag. Magazine; magnitude.

Maj. Major.

Mal. Malachi.

man. Manège; manual.

Manit. Manitoba.

manuf. Manufactory; manufacture.

mar. Maritime.

Mar. March.

March. Marchioness.

Marq. Marquis.

mas., *or* **masc.** Masculine.

Mass. Massachusetts.

math. Mathematician; mathematics.

Matt. Matthew.

max. Maximum.

M. C. Medical Corps; Member of Congress.

Md. Maryland.

M. D. Medicinæ Doctor (L., Doctor of Medicine).

mdse. Merchandise.

Me. Maine.

ME., *or* **M. E.** Middle English.

M. E. Mechanical, Military, *or* Mining Engineer; Methodist Episcopal; Most Excellent.

meas. Measure.

mech. Mechanics; mechanical.

med. Medical; medicine; medieval; medium.

Medit. Mediterranean.

mem. Memento; memoir; memorandum; memorial.

mer. Meridian; meridional.

Messrs. Messieurs.

metal. Metallurgy.

meteor. Meteorology.

Meth. Methodist.

Mex. Mexican; Mexico.

Mf., *or* **mf.** Mezzo forte (It., moderately loud).

mfg. Manufacturing.

mfr. (*pl.* **mfrs.**) Manufacturer.

mg. Milligram.

Mgr. Monseigneur; Monsignore.

M. H. G., *or* **MHG.** Middle High German.

M. H. R. Member of the House of Representatives.

M. I. Mounted Infantry.

Mic. Micah.

Mich. Michaelmas; Michigan.

mid. Middle; midshipman.

mil. Military; militia.

min. Minim; minimum; mining; minister; minor; minute.

Minn. Minnesota.

Min. Plen. Minister Plenipotentiary.

misc. Miscellaneous.

Miss. Mississippi.

ml. Mail; milliliter.

M. L. A. Modern Language Association.

M. L. G., or **MLG.** Middle Low German.

Mlle. Mademoiselle.

mm. Millimeter.

MM. Their Majesties; Messieurs.

Mme. (*pl.* Mmes.) Madame (*pl.* Mesdames).

mo. (*pl.* mos.) Month.

Mo. Missouri.

M. O. Medical officer; money order.

mod. Moderate; moderato (It., moderately); modern.

Moham. Mohammedan.

mol. wt. Molecular weight.

Mon. Monastery; Monday.

Monsig. Monseigneur; Monsignor.

Mont. Montana.

Mor. Morocco.

M. O. R. C. Medical Officers' Reserve Corps.

M. P. Member of Parliament.

M. P. C. Member of Parliament, Canada.

m. p. h. Miles per hour.

Mr. Mister.

M. R. C. Medical Reserve Corps.

Mrs. Mistress.

MS., or **ms.** Manuscript.

M. S. Master of Science; Master of Surgery.

m. s. l. Mean sea level.

MSS. or **mss.** Manuscripts.

mt. (*pl.* mts.) Mount; mountain.

mun. Municipal.

mus. Museum; music; musician.

Mus. B. Musicæ Baccalaureus (L., Bachelor of Music).

Mus. D. or **Musc. Doc.** Musicæ Doctor(L., Doctor of Music).

M. W. Most Worshipful; Most Worthy.

myg. Myriagram.

myl. Myrialiter.

mym. Myriameter.

myth. Mythology.

N

n. Natus (L., born); nephew; neuter; new; nominative; note; noun; number.

N. Navy; Noon; Norse; North; Northern.

N. A. National Academy; National Army; North America; North American.

N. A. A. National Automobile Association.

Nah. Nahum.

nat. National; native; natural.

Nath. Nathanael; Nathaniel.

naut. Nautical.

nav. Naval; navigable; navigation.

N. B. New Brunswick; North Britain; North British; nota bene (L., note well, or take notice).

N. C. New Church; Nurses' Corps; North Carolina.

N. C. O. Noncommissioned Officer.

n. d. No date.

N. Dak. North Dakota.

N. E. New England.

N. E. A. National Education Association.

Nebr. Nebraska.

N. E. D. New English Dictionary;—better, O. E. D. (which see).

neg. Negative.

Neh. Nehemiah.

471 ABBREVIATIONS

Neth. Netherlands.

neut. Neuter.

Nev. Nevada.

N. F. Newfoundland; (or NF.) Norman French.

Ng. Norwegian.

N. G. National Guard; New Granada; (Slang) no good.

N. Gr., or NGr. New Greek.

N. H. New Hampshire.

Nicar. Nicaragua.

N. J. New Jersey.

N. L., or NL. New Latin.

N. Lat. North latitude.

N. Mex. New Mexico.

NNE. North-northeast.

NNW. North-northwest.

N. O. Natural order (Bot.); New Orleans.

No., or no. (pl. Nos., nos.) Numero (L., [by] number).

nol. pros. Nolle prosequi (L., to be unwilling to prosecute).

nom. Nominative.

non seq. Non sequitur (L., it does not follow).

Nor. Norman; North.

Norw., or Nor. Norway; Norwegian.

Nov. November.

N. P. New Providence; Notary Public.

nr. Near.

N. R. North Riding; North River.

N. S. National Society; New Series; New Style (since 1752); Novia Scotia.

N. S. W. New South Wales.

N. T. New Testament; Northern Territory.

Num. Numbers.

NW. Northwest; Northwestern.

N. W. T. Northwest Territories.

N. Y. New York.

N. Z. New Zealand.

O

O. Old; Ontario; Order.

o/a. On account (of).

ob. Obiit (L., he, or she, died).

Obad. Obadiah.

obdt. Obedient.

obj. Object; objection; objective.

obl. Oblique; oblong.

obs. Observation; observatory; obsolete.

obt. Obedient.

oc. Ocean.

Oct. October.

O. D., or OD. Old Dutch.

O. E., or OE. Old English.

O. E. Omissions excepted.

O. E. D. Oxford English Dictionary.

O. F., or OF. Old French.

off. Offered; officer; official; officinal.

O. H. G., or OHG. Old High German.

O. H. M. S. On His (or Her) Majesty's Service.

O. K., or OK. Correct; all right. Cant.

Okla. Oklahoma.

ol. Oleum (L., oil).

O. M. Old measurement; Order of Merit.

Ont. Ontario.

O. O. R. C. Ordnance Officer ' Reserve Corps.

op. Opera; opposite; opus.

opp. Opposed; opposite.

opt. Optative; optics.

Or. Oriental.

O. R. C. Order of the Red Cross; Officers' Reserve Corps.

ord. Ordained; order; ordinance; ordinary; ordnance.

Oreg. Oregon.

orig. Original; originally.

O. S. Old School; Old Series; Old Style; ordinary seaman.

O. T. Old Testament.

O. T. C. Officers' Training Camp.

Oxon. Oxonia (L., Oxford); Oxoniensis (L., Oxonian).

oz. Ounce; ounces.

P

p. Page; part; participle; past; penny; piano (It., softly); pint; pipe; pole; population; professional.

P. Pastor; pater (L., father); père (F., father); post; president; priest; prince.

Pa. Pennsylvania.

p. a. Participial adjective; per annum (L., by the year).

P/A. Power of attorney; private account.

Pac. Pacific.

pam. Pamphlet.

Pan. Panama.

par. Paragraph; parallel; parenthesis; parish.

Para. Paraguay.

parl. Parliament; parliamentary.

part. Participle.

pass. Passive.

P. B. Prayer Book.

p. c. Per cent; postal card; post card.

pd. Paid.

P. E. Presiding Elder; Protestant Episcopal.

P. E. I. Prince Edward Island.

pen. Peninsula.

Pent. Pentecost.

per an. Per annum (L., by the year).

per ct. Per cent.

perf. Perfect.

perh. Perhaps.

pers. Person; personal.

Pers. Persia; Persian.

pert. Pertaining.

Pet. Peter.

pf. Preferred.

Pg. Portugal; Portuguese.

P. G. M. Past Grand Master.

Phar. Pharmacy; Pharmacopœia.

Ph. B. Philosophiæ Baccalaureus (L., Bachelor of Philosophy).

Ph. D. Philosophiæ Doctor (L., Doctor of Philosophy).

Ph. G. Graduate in Pharmacy.

Phil. Philemon; Philip; Philippians; Philippine.

Phila. Philadelphia.

philol. Philology; philologist.

philos. Philosopher; philosophical; philosophy.

physiol. Physiologist; physiology.

P. I. Philippine Islands.

pinx. Pinxit (L., he, *or* she, painted it).

pk. (*pl.* pks.) Peck.

pkg. (*pl.* pkgs.) Package.

pl. Place; plural.

plf., *or* **plff.** Plaintiff.

plup., *or* **plupf.** Pluperfect.

plur. Plural.

pm. Premium.

P. M., *or* **p. m.** Post meridiem.

(L., afternoon); post mortem.

P. M. G. Postmaster-General.

P. O. Post office; Province of Ontario.

P. O. B. Post-office box.

P. O. D. Pay on delivery; Post Office Department.

Pol. Poland; Polish.

pol., polit. Political.

pol. econ. Political economy.

pop. Popular; population.

Port. Portugal; Portuguese.

pos. Positive; possessive.

poss. Possession; possessive.

pp. Pages; past participle; pianissimo.

p. p. Past participle; postpaid.

P. P. C. *or* **p. p. c.** Pour prendre congé (F., to take leave).

pph. Pamphlet.

p. pr. Present participle.

P. Q. Previous question; Province of Quebec.

pr. Pair; present; price; priest; prince.

Pr. Preferred stock.

P. R. Puerto Rico.

prep. Preparatory; preposition.

pres. President; presidency.

Presb. Presbyterian.

pret. Preterit.

prin. Principal.

priv. Privative.

prob. Probably; problem.

Prof. Professor.

pron. Pronominal; pronoun; pronounced; pronunciation.

propr. Proprietor.

pros. Prosody.

Prot. Protestant.

pro tem. Pro tempore (L., temporarily).

prov. Provident; province; provisional.

Prov. Provençal; Proverbs; Provost.

prox. Proximo (L., next, of the next month).

prs. Pairs.

Prus. Prussia; Prussian.

Ps. Psalm; Psalms.

P. S. Postscriptum (L., postscript); Privy Seal.

pseud. Pseudonym.

psychol. Psychologist; psychology.

pt. (*pl.* pts.) Part; payment; pint; point; port.

P. T., *or* **p. t.** Post town.

p. v. Post village.

pwt. Pennyweight; pennyweights.

pxt. See *pinx.*

Q

q. Quart; queen; query; question; quintal; quire.

Q. Quebec (province)

Q. E. D. Quod erat demonstrandum (L., which was to be demonstrated).

Q. F. Quick-Fire, *or* quick-firing.

ql. Quintal.

Q. M. Quartermaster.

Q. M. G. Quartermaster-General.

Q. M. O. R. C. Quartermaster Officers' Reserve Corps.

Q. M. S. Quartermaster-Sergeant.

qr. (*pl.* qrs.) Quadrans (L., a farthing); quarter; quire.

qt. Quantity; (*pl.* qts.) quart.

qu. Quart; quarterly; queen; query; question.

ques. Question.

ABBREVIATIONS

qy. Query.

R

r. Railroad; railway; rare; received; rector; resides; retired; right; river; rises; road; rod; rood; royal.

R. Rabbi; Radical; Réaumur; Republican; response.

R. A. Rear Admiral; Regular Army; Royal Academy; Royal Artillery.

rad. Radical; radix.

R. C. Red Cross; Roman Catholic.

R. C. A. Reformed Church in America.

Re. Rupee.

R. E. Reformed Episcopal; Right Excellent; Royal Engineers.

Réaum. Réaumur.

rec. Receipt; recipe; record; recorded; recorder.

recd. Received.

rec. sec. Recording secretary.

rect. Receipt; rector; rectory.

ref. Referee; reference; referred; reformation; reformed.

Ref. Ch. Reformed Church.

reg. Regent; region; register; registered; registry; regular.

Reg. Regina (L., queen).

regt. Regiment.

rel. Relating; relative (-ly); religion; religious.

rep. Repeat; report; reporter; representative; republic.

Rep. Republican.

Repub. Republic; Republican.

retd. Returned.

rev. Revenue; reverse; review; revise; revised; revision; revolution.

Rev. Revelation; Reverend.

Rev. Ver. Revised Version.

R. F., *or* **r. f.** Rapid-fire.

R. F. D. Rural Free Delivery.

R. G. S. Royal Geographical Society (London).

r. h. Right hand.

R. H. Royal Highness.

rhet. Rhetoric; rhetorical.

R. I. Rhode Island.

R. I. P. Requiescat in pace (L., may he, *or* she, rest in peace).

riv. River.

rm. Ream.

R. M. Resident Magistrate; Royal Marines.

R. M. S. Royal Mail Steamer.

R. N. Royal Navy.

R. N. R. Royal Naval Reserve.

ro. Rood.

Robt. Robert.

Rom. Roman; Romance; Romans.

Rom. Cath. Roman Catholic.

R. O. T. C. Reserve Officers' Training Corps (*or* Camp).

R. P. O. Railroad Post Office.

rpt. Report.

R. R. Railroad.

Rs. Rupees.

R. S. Recording Secretary; Revised Statutes.

R. S. V. P. Répondez, s'il vous plaît (F., reply, if you please).

Rt. Hon. Right Honorable.

Rt. Rev. Right Reverend.

Rum. Rumania; Rumanian.

Rus., *or* **Russ.** Russia; Russian.

R. V. Revised Version; Rifle Volunteers.

R. W. Right Worshipful; Right Worthy.

Ry. Railway.

R. Y. S. Royal Yacht Squadron.

S

s., *or* S. Section; see; series; shilling; signed; singular; son; stem; sun; surplus.

S. Sabbath; Saint; Saxon; school; senate; Socialist; Society; Socius (L., Fellow); soprano; South; Southern.

S. A. Salvation Army; Small-arms; South Africa; South America; South Australia.

sa. Sable.

Sab. Sabbath.

S. Afr. South Africa; South African.

Salv. Salvador.

Sam. Samaritan; Samuel.

S. Amer., *or* S. Am. South America; South American.

S. & T. Supply and Transport.

Sans. Sanskrit.

S. A. R. South African Republic.

Sar. Sardinia; Sardinian.

Sask. Saskatchewan.

Sat. Saturday.

Sax. Saxon; Saxony.

sb. Substantive.

S. B. Bachelor of Science; South Britain.

sc. Scene; and see sci., scil., scr., sculp.

Sc. Scotch; Scottish.

s. c. Small capitals.

S. C. Signal Corps; South Carolina; Staff Corps; Supreme Court.

Scand. Scandinavia; Scandinavian.

S. caps. Small capitals.

sch. Scholium; schooner.

sci. Science; scientific.

scil. Scilicet (L., namely).

Scot. Scotch; Scotland; Scottish.

scr. Scruple.

Script. Scripture.

sculp. Sculpsit (L., he, *or* she, carved it).

s. d. Sine die (L., without [appointing] a day).

S. Dak. South Dakota.

SE. Southeast.

sec. Secant; second; secretary; section; secundum (L., according to).

Sec. Leg. Secretary of Legation.

sect. Section.

Sem. Seminary; Semitic.

Sen. Senate; Senator; Senior.

Sep., *or* Sept. September; Septuagint.

ser. Series; sermon.

serg., sergt., *or* Sgt. Sergeant.

Serv. Servian.

s. g. Specific gravity.

S. G. Solicitor-general; Surgeon-General.

Sgt. Maj. Sergeant-Major.

Sh., *or* sh. Share; shilling; shillings.

Shak. Shakespeare.

S. I. Sandwich Islands; Staten Island.

Sib. Siberia; Siberian.

Sic. Sicilian; Sicily.

sing. Singular.

S. J. Society of Jesus.

S. J. C. Supreme Judicial Court.

Skr., *or* Skt. Sanskrit.

S. L. Solicitor at Law.

S. Lat. South latitude.

Slav. Slavic; Slavonic.

sld. Sailed.

S. M. Sa Majesté (F., His, *or* Her, Majesty); Sergeant-Major; Society of Mary

sm. c., *or* **sm. caps.** Small capitals.

S. O., *or* **s. o.** Seller's option.

S. O. Staff Officer; Signal Officer; Special Order.

soc. Society.

S. of Sol. Song of Solomon.

sol. Solution.

sop. Soprano.

S. O. R. C. Signal Officers' Reserve Corps.

sov. Sovereign.

sp. Species; specimen; spelling; spirit.

Sp. Spain; Spaniard; Spanish.

s. p. Sine prole (L., without issue).

S. P. C. A. Society for Prevention of Cruelty to Animals.

S. P. C. C. Society for Prevention of Cruelty to Children.

specif. Specifically.

sp. gr. Specific gravity.

S. P. Q. R. Senatus Populusque Romanus (L., the Senate and People of Rome); small profits, quick returns.

spt. Seaport.

sq. Squadron.

sq. Sequens (L., the following [one]); square.

sqq. Sequentes (L., the following [ones]).

Sr. Sir; Senior.

S. R. S. Fellow (L., Socius) of the Royal Society.

ss. Scilicet (L., namely); semis (L., half).

S. S. Steamship; Supply Sergeant.

SSE. South-southeast.

SSW. South-southwest.

st. Stanza; stone; stet (L., let it stand).

St. Saint; Strait; Street.

stat. Statuary; statue; statutes.

S. T. D. Sacræ Theologiæ Doctor (L., Doctor of Sacred Theology).

str. Steamer.

Sub. Subaltern.

subj. Subject; subjunctive.

subst. Substantive; substitute.

suff. Suffix.

Sun. Sunday.

sup. Superior; superlative; supine; supplement; supra (L., above).

Sup. C. Superior Court; Supreme Court.

superl. Superlative.

Sup. O. Supply Officer.

supp. Supplement.

Supt. Superintendant.

surg. Surgeon; surgery.

surv. Surveying; surveyor.

s. v. Sub verbo (L., under the word); sub voce (L., under the title).

S. V. Sancta Virgo (L., Holy Virgin); Sanctitas Vestra (L., Your Holiness).

SW. Southwest.

Sw., *or* **Swed.** Sweden; Swedish.

Switz. Switzerland.

syn. Synonym; synonymous.

Syr. Syria; Syriac.

T

t. Temperature; tenor; time; tome; ton; town; township; transitive.

T. Territory; Testament; trains; Turkish.

tan. Tangent.

tel. Telegram; telegraph; telephone.

Tenn. Tennessee.

ter. Terrace; territory.

Test. Testament.

Teut. Teuton; Teutonic.

Tex. Texas.

Th. Thomas.

Theo. Theodore; Theodosia.

Theoph. Theophilus.

Thess. Thessalonians.

Tho., *or* **Thos.** Thomas.

Thurs. Thursday.

Tim. Timothy.

T. M. True mean.

T. N. T. Trinitrotoluene *or* Trinitrotoluol.

t. o. Telegraph office; turn over.

topog. Topographical; topography.

tp. Township.

tr. Translated; translation; translator; transpose; treasurer; trustee.

trav. Travel; traveler.

treas. Treasurer; treasury.

trig. Trigonometric; trigonometrical; trigonometry.

Trin. Trinity.

trop. Tropic; tropical.

T. S. Transport and Supply.

T. T. Telegraphic transfer; Trinity term.

T. U. Trade Union.

Tues. Tuesday.

Turk. Turkey; Turkish.

typ. Typographer; typographic (-ical); typography.

U

U. Uncle; Unionist; upper.

U. K. United Kingdom.

ult. Ultimately; ultimo.

Unit. Unitarian.

univ. Universally; university.

Univ. Universalist.

U. of S. Afr. Union of South Africa.

U. P. C. United Presbyterian Church.

Uru. Uruguay.

U. S. Uncle Sam; United States.

U. S. A. United States Army; United States of America.

U. S. C. United States of Colombia.

U. S. M. United States Mail; United States Marine.

U. S. M. A. United States Military Academy.

U. S. N. United States Navy.

U. S. N. A. United States Naval Academy.

U. S. N. G. United States National Guard.

U. S. S. United States Senate; United States Ship *or* Steamer.

usu. Usual; usually.

u. s. w. Und so weiter (G., and so forth).

V

v. Verb; verse; version; versus; very; vicar; vice-; vide (L., see); village; vocative; volume; von (G., of).

V. Venerable; Victoria; Viscount, Volunteers.

Va. Virginia.

v. a. Verb active.

V. A. Vicar Apostolic; Vice Admiral.

var. Variant; variation; variety; various.

Vat. Vatican.

vb. n. Verbal noun.

V. C. Veterinary Corps; Vice Chancellor; Victoria Cross.

Ven. Venerable; Venice.
Venez. Venezuela.
ver. Verse; verses.
Vet. Veterinary.
V. G. Vicar-general.
v. i. Verb intransitive.
Vic. Victoria.
vid. Vide (L., see).
vil. Village.
Vis., *or* **Visc.** Viscount.
viz. Videlicet (L., namely).
V. M. D. Veterinariæ Medicinæ Doctor (L., Doctor of Veterinary Medicine).
v. n. Verb neuter.
voc. Vocative.
vocab. Vocabulary.
vol. (*pl.* vols.) Volume; volunteer.
vol. Volcano; volcanic.
V. P. Vice-President.
v. r. Verb reflexive.
V. R. Victoria Regina (L., Queen Victoria).
V. Rev. Very Reverend.
vs. Versus.
v. s. Vide supra (L., see above).
V. S. Veterinary Surgeon.
Vt. Vermont.
v. t. Verb transitive.
Vul. Vulgate.
vv. Verses; violins.

W

w. Wanting; week; wide; wife; with.
W. Wales; Washington; Welsh; West; Western.
W. A. West Africa; Western Australia.
Wash. Washington.
W. C. Wesleyan Chapel; Western Central (Postal District, London).

W. C. T. U. Woman's Christian Temperance Union.
W. D., *or* **War D.** War Department.
Wed. Wednesday.
w. f. Wrong font.
w. g. Wire gauge.
W. G. C. Worthy Grand Chaplain.
W. G. M. Worthy Grand Master.
whf. Wharf.
W. I., *or* **W. Ind.** West Indies; West Indian.
Wis. Wisconsin.
Wisd. of Sol. Wisdom of Solomon.
wk. Week.
W. long. West longitude.
Wm. William.
W. M. Worshipful Master.
WNW. West-northwest.
W. O. War Office.
wp. Worship.
W. R. Water reserve; West Riding.
WSW. West-southwest.
wt. Weight.
W. Va. West Virginia.
Wyo. Wyoming.

X

X. Χριστος (Gr., Christ).
X-c., *or* **X-cp.** Ex coupon.
Xmas [no period] Christmas.
Xn. Christian.
Xnty., *or* **Xty.** Christianity.
Xper., *or* **Xr.** Christopher.
Xt. Christ.

Y

y. Yard; year.

yd. (*pl.* yds.) Yard.

Y. M. C. A. Young Men's Christian Association.

Y. M. Cath. A. Young Men's Catholic Association.

Y. M. C. U. Young Men's Christian Union.

Y. P. S. C. E. Young People's Society of Christian Endeavor.

yr. (*pl.* yrs.) Year; younger; your.

Y. W. C. A. Young Women's Christian Association.

Z

Zach. Zacharias; Zachary.

Zeb. Zebadiah; Zebedee.

zoogeog. Zoogeography.

zool. Zoological; zoologist; zoology.

Z. S. Zoological Society.

Zech. Zechariah.

Zeph. Zephaniah.

physiology, and other scientific problems of his time. But today he is best known for his *Thesaurus,* a book which, ironically enough, he always considered a mere side line.

The basic principle of Roget's *Thesaurus,* which has been scrupulously observed in *Roget's Pocket Thesaurus* and in *Roget's INTERNATIONAL Thesaurus,* is the *grouping of words according to their ideas* rather than the listing of words, as the dictionaries do, according to the alphabet. This is the secret of a genuine thesaurus and is the basis for its remarkable usefulness.

Good writing depends on using the exact word; but how often do you have to grope—usually without success—for the exact word to fit the idea you have in mind? A thesaurus solves just that problem. With a thesaurus you start with an idea and find the word or phrase that suits it. A dictionary, on the other hand, is just the reverse: you start with a word and find its definition. It is impossible, because of the very nature of these two basic reference books, to compile a thesaurus in dictionary form, and it was the genius of Roget which saw this first and the wisdom of subsequent editors which has warned them not to tamper with a proved success.

Roget's Pocket Thesaurus and the more complete *Roget's INTERNATIONAL Thesaurus* are arranged in two basic sections. The first, or main text, consists of hundreds of lists of related words and phrases. These lists cover all areas of knowledge. Originally devised by Peter Roget, they represent a famous breakdown of knowledge which, in its own right, was a feat of human intelligence. Within these lists are placed words and phrases of related meanings; the words themselves are clustered into tiny groups of almost synonymous meanings. But these groups grow and spread like animal cells into a network of related meanings so that if, for example, you want to find a word similar in meaning, though not completely synonymous, to "gay," a thesaurus can help you where a dictionary of synonyms cannot. No dictionary of synonyms has been so useful or enjoyed such success as Roget's *Thesaurus.*

The second section is the all-important index. Here are listed in alphabetical order all the words of the first section and the exact places where they appear. "Gay," for example, appears several places in the text: it is listed in its senses of bright, cheerful, and showy. The index tells you this, and shows you where to turn to find the lists of related words and phrases for every one of these basic meanings of "gay." Without this index a thesaurus is useless. It is the quick and efficient key that unlocks the hundreds of lists of related words and phrases—it is the essential key that is lacking in so-called "dictionary thesauruses."

The extraordinary usefulness of *Roget's Pocket Thesaurus* and *Roget's INTERNATIONAL Thesaurus* is attested to by many famous writers. Kenneth Roberts has written: "I can't possibly remember how many copies of this book I've owned and worn to tatters; but ever since the days when I was writing verse for the old *Life*, I have regarded it as the most valuable reference book that an author could have." Mary Roberts Rinehart said that she has "used at least four of these books since I first commenced to write, and even the fourth one is now in poor shape." And Philip Van Doren Stern wrote that "with the exception of the dictionary, it is the reference book I most often use and find indispensable for that elusive word that slips the mind when you want it most. To the professional writer whose everyday job has to do with words the book is an absolute necessity."

Roget's Pocket Thesaurus, then, and *Roget's INTERNATIONAL Thesaurus* derive their extraordinary usefulness from the fidelity with which they adhere to Peter Mark Roget's original concept. Naturally both volumes have been expanded. For example, many new listings have had to be added to Roget's original divisions of knowledge to provide room for the advances in science and technology which even this amazing doctor did not dream of. Altogether, in the larger edition, there are more than 200,000 words and phrases, and in both editions appear contemporary American colloquialisms and slang.